Communications in Computer and Information Science 2343

Series Editors

Gang Li, *School of Information Technology, Deakin University, Burwood, VIC, Australia*
Joaquim Filipe , *Polytechnic Institute of Setúbal, Setúbal, Portugal*
Zhiwei Xu, *Chinese Academy of Sciences, Beijing, China*

AF172774

Rationale

The CCIS series is devoted to the publication of proceedings of computer science conferences. Its aim is to efficiently disseminate original research results in informatics in printed and electronic form. While the focus is on publication of peer-reviewed full papers presenting mature work, inclusion of reviewed short papers reporting on work in progress is welcome, too. Besides globally relevant meetings with internationally representative program committees guaranteeing a strict peer-reviewing and paper selection process, conferences run by societies or of high regional or national relevance are also considered for publication.

Topics

The topical scope of CCIS spans the entire spectrum of informatics ranging from foundational topics in the theory of computing to information and communications science and technology and a broad variety of interdisciplinary application fields.

Information for Volume Editors and Authors

Publication in CCIS is free of charge. No royalties are paid, however, we offer registered conference participants temporary free access to the online version of the conference proceedings on SpringerLink (http://link.springer.com) by means of an http referrer from the conference website and/or a number of complimentary printed copies, as specified in the official acceptance email of the event.

CCIS proceedings can be published in time for distribution at conferences or as post-proceedings, and delivered in the form of printed books and/or electronically as USBs and/or e-content licenses for accessing proceedings at SpringerLink. Furthermore, CCIS proceedings are included in the CCIS electronic book series hosted in the SpringerLink digital library at http://link.springer.com/bookseries/7899. Conferences publishing in CCIS are allowed to use Online Conference Service (OCS) for managing the whole proceedings lifecycle (from submission and reviewing to preparing for publication) free of charge.

Publication process

The language of publication is exclusively English. Authors publishing in CCIS have to sign the Springer CCIS copyright transfer form, however, they are free to use their material published in CCIS for substantially changed, more elaborate subsequent publications elsewhere. For the preparation of the camera-ready papers/files, authors have to strictly adhere to the Springer CCIS Authors' Instructions and are strongly encouraged to use the CCIS LaTeX style files or templates.

Abstracting/Indexing

CCIS is abstracted/indexed in DBLP, Google Scholar, EI-Compendex, Mathematical Reviews, SCImago, Scopus. CCIS volumes are also submitted for the inclusion in ISI Proceedings.

How to start

To start the evaluation of your proposal for inclusion in the CCIS series, please send an e-mail to ccis@springer.com.

Hailong Sun · Hongfei Fan · Yongqiang Gao ·
Xiaokang Wang · Dongning Liu · Bowen Du ·
Tun Lu
Editors

Computer Supported Cooperative Work and Social Computing

19th CCF Conference, ChineseCSCW 2024
Hohhot, China, July 12–14, 2024
Revised Selected Papers, Part I

 Springer

Editors
Hailong Sun
Beihang University
Beijing, China

Hongfei Fan
Tongji University
Shanghai, China

Yongqiang Gao
Inner Mongolia University
Hohhot, China

Xiaokang Wang
Hainan University
Haikou, China

Dongning Liu
Guangdong University of Technology
Guangzhou, China

Bowen Du
Tongji University
Shanghai, China

Tun Lu
Fudan University
Shanghai, China

ISSN 1865-0929   ISSN 1865-0937 (electronic)
Communications in Computer and Information Science
ISBN 978-981-96-2372-3   ISBN 978-981-96-2373-0 (eBook)
https://doi.org/10.1007/978-981-96-2373-0

This Springer imprint is published by the registered company Springer Nature Singapore Pte Ltd.
The registered company address is: 152 Beach Road, #21-01/04 Gateway East, Singapore 189721, Singapore

If disposing of this product, please recycle the paper.

Preface

Welcome to ChineseCSCW 2024, the 19th CCF Conference on Computer Supported Cooperative Work and Social Computing.

ChineseCSCW 2024 was organized by the China Computer Federation (CCF), and co-hosted by the CCF Technical Committee on Cooperative Computing (CCF TCCC) and Inner Mongolia University, in Hohhot, Inner Mongolia, China, during 12–14 July 2024. The conference was also supported by Guangdong Hengdian Information Technology Co., Ltd. and SCHOLAT. The theme of the conference was *Human-Centered Collaborative Intelligence*, which reflects the emerging trend of the combination of artificial intelligence, human-system collaboration, and AI-empowered applications.

ChineseCSCW (initially recognized as CCSCW) is a highly reputable conference series on computer-supported cooperative work (CSCW) and social computing in China with a long history. It aims to bring together Chinese and overseas CSCW researchers, practitioners and educators, with a particular focus on innovative models, theories, techniques, algorithms and methods, as well as domain-specific applications and systems, from both technical and social aspects in CSCW and social computing. The conference was initially held biennially since 1998, and has been held annually since 2014.

This year, the conference received 200 submissions, and after a rigorous double-blind peer review process, only 52 of them were eventually accepted as full papers, resulting in an acceptance rate of 26%. The program also included 18 short papers. Both full papers and short papers were orally presented. In addition, the conference featured 6 keynote speeches, 7 high-level technical seminars, the 5th ChineseCSCW Cup Big Data Competition (Final Round), the Forum for Outstanding Young Scholars, the Forum for Presentations of Top-Venue Papers, and an awards ceremony. We are grateful to the distinguished keynote speakers, *Yunhao Liu* from *Tsinghua University*, *Yiqiang Chen* from *Institute of Computing Technology, Chinese Academy of Sciences*, *Lei Ren* from *Beihang University*, *Yongdong Zhang* from *University of Science and Technology of China*, *Yaochu Jin* from *Westlake University*, and *Minghui Zhou* from *Peking University*.

We hope that you enjoyed ChineseCSCW 2024.

November 2024
                                                      Tianruo Yang
                                                      Guanglai Gao

Organization

Steering Committee

Bin Hu	Beijing Institute of Technology, China
Weiqing Tang	China Computer Federation, China
Ning Gu	Fudan University, China
Xiaoping Liu	Hefei University of Technology, China
Yong Tang	South China Normal University, China
Yuqing Sun	Shandong University, China
Zhiwen Yu	Harbin Engineering University, China
Shaozi Li	Xiamen University, China
Xiangwei Zheng	Shandong Normal University, China
Tun Lu	Fudan University, China

General Chairs

Tianruo Yang	Zhengzhou University, China
Guanglai Gao	Inner Mongolia University, China

Vice Chairs

Jiantao Zhou	Inner Mongolia University, China
Lizhen Cui	Shandong University, China

Program Committee Chairs

Hailong Sun	Beihang University, China
Tun Lu	Fudan University, China
Hongfei Fan	Tongji University, China
Baoqi Huang	Inner Mongolia University, China

Organization Committee Chairs

Xiaoping Li	Guangdong University of Technology, China
Yongqiang Gao	Inner Mongolia University, China
Xiaokang Wang	Hainan University, China
Dongning Liu	Guangdong University of Technology, China

Publication Chairs

Hongfei Fan	Tongji University, China
Dongning Liu	Guangdong University of Technology, China

Paper Award Chairs

Bin Guo	Northwestern Polytechnical University, China
Yichuan Jiang	Southeast University, China
Weineng Chen	South China University of Technology, China
Xiaochun Yang	Northeastern University, China

Paper Recommendation Chairs

Yiming Tang	Hefei University of Technology, China
Honghao Gao	Shanghai University, China
Lianyong Qi	China University of Petroleum (East China), China
Yang Chen	Fudan University, China

CSCW Cup Competition Chairs

Jian Cao	Shanghai Jiao Tong University, China
Ying Gao	South China University of Technology, China
Chaobo He	South China Normal University, China
Junfeng Zhao	Inner Mongolia University, China

Major Program Forum Chairs

Yong Tang	South China Normal University, China
Yuqing Sun	Shandong University, China

Outstanding Young Scholars Forum Chairs

Tong Wang	Harbin Engineering University, China
Weineng Chen	South China University of Technology, China

Top-Venue Paper Presentation Forum Chairs

Peng Zhang	Fudan University, China
Tengfei Liu	Hangzhou Institute of Technology, Xidian University, China

Publicity Chairs

Xiangwei Zheng	Shandong Normal University, China
Tao Sun	Inner Mongolia University, China
Yinzhang Guo	Taiyuan University of Science and Technology, China
Bo Jiang	Zhejiang Gongshang University, China

Sponsorship Chairs

Xiaoping Li	Guangdong University of Technology, China
Min Jiang	Xiamen University, China
Weihui Dai	Fudan University, China
Jing Gao	Guangdong Hengdian Information Technology Co., Ltd., China

Finance Chairs

Yan Wang	Inner Mongolia University, China
Meiju Yu	Inner Mongolia University, China

Website Chairs

Jianguo Li	South China Normal University, China
Ronghua Lin	South China Normal University, China

Program Committee

Tie Bao	Jilin University, China
Ying Bi	Zhengzhou University, China
Zhan Bu	Nanjing Audit University, China
Hongming Cai	Shanghai Jiao Tong University, China
Yongming Cai	Guangdong Pharmaceutical University, China
Yuanzheng Cai	Minjiang University, China
Zhicheng Cai	Nanjing University of Science and Technology, China
Buqing Cao	Hunan University of Science and Technology, China
Donglin Cao	Xiamen University, China
Jian Cao	Shanghai Jiao Tong University, China
Jingjing Cao	Wuhan University of Technology, China
Chao Chen	Chongqing University, China
Jianhui Chen	Beijing University of Technology, China
Liangyin Chen	Sichuan University, China
Long Chen	Southeast University, China
Longbiao Chen	Xiamen University, China
Ningjiang Chen	Guangxi University, China
Qingkui Chen	University of Shanghai for Science and Technology, China
Wang Chen	China North Vehicle Research Institute, China
Weineng Chen	South China University of Technology, China
Xin Chen	Taiyuan University of Science and Technology, China
Yang Chen	Fudan University, China
Yanru Chen	Sichuan University, China
Yaxi Chen	Southwest Minzu University, China
Zhen Chen	Yanshan University, China
Zonggan Chen	South China Normal University, China
Shiwei Cheng	Zhejiang University of Technology, China
Xiaohui Cheng	Guilin University of Technology, China
Yuan Cheng	Wuhan University, China

Jinhua Cui	Huazhong University of Science and Technology, China
Lizhen Cui	Shandong University, China
Zongmin Cui	Jiujiang University, China
Weihui Dai	Fudan University, China
Wei Dao	Tisson Regaltec Communications Tech. Co., Ltd., China
Xianghua Ding	Fudan University, China
Xinyi Ding	Zhejiang Gongshang University, China
Wanchun Dou	Nanjing University, China
Bowen Du	Tongji University, China
Guodong Du	Yanshan University, China
Changjie Fan	NetEase (Hangzhou) Network Co., Ltd., China
Hongfei Fan	Tongji University, China
Yili Fang	Zhejiang Gongshang University, China
Lunke Fei	Guangdong University of Technology, China
Liang Feng	Chongqing University, China
Shanshan Feng	Shandong Normal University, China
Jiaojiao Fu	East China University of Science and Technology, China
Honghao Gao	Shanghai University, China
Jing Gao	Guangdong Hengdian Information Technology Co., Ltd., China
Liping Gao	University of Shanghai for Science and Technology, China
Shan Gao	Harbin Engineering University, China
Ying Gao	South China University of Technology, China
Yuan Gao	Hunan University, China
Yunjun Gao	Zhejiang University, China
Qingyuan Gong	Fudan University, China
Ning Gu	Fudan University, China
Bin Guo	Northwestern Polytechnical University, China
Kun Guo	Fuzhou University, China
Wei Guo	Shandong University, China
Yinzhang Guo	Taiyuan University of Science and Technology, China
Tao Han	Zhejiang Gongshang University, China
Fei Hao	Shaanxi Normal University, China
Chaobo He	South China Normal University, China
Fazhi He	Wuhan University, China
Bin Hu	Lanzhou University, China
Daning Hu	Southern University of Science and Technology, China

Liang Hu	Tongji University, China
Wenting Hu	Jiangsu Open University, China
Yanmei Hu	Chengdu University of Technology, China
Changqin Huang	South China Normal University, China
Lu Jia	China Agricultural University, China
Tao Jia	Southwest University, China
Bin Jiang	Hunan University, China
Bo Jiang	Zhejiang Gongshang University, China
Jiuchuan Jiang	Nanjing University of Finance and Economics, China
Min Jiang	Xiamen University, China
Weijin Jiang	Hunan University of Technology and Business, China
Wenchao Jiang	Guangdong University of Technology, China
Yali Jiang	Shandong University, China
Yichuan Jiang	Southeast University, China
Lanju Kong	Shandong University, China
Liqian Lai	Jiaying University, China
Chunying Li	Guangdong Polytechnic Normal University, China
Diankui Li	Jiamusi University, China
Dongsheng Li	IBM Research China, China
Guoliang Li	Tsinghua University, China
Hengjie Li	Lanzhou University of Arts and Science, China
Jianguo Li	South China Normal University, China
Jingjing Li	South China Normal University, China
Junli Li	Jinzhong University, China
Li Li	Southwest Univeresity, China
Pu Li	Zhengzhou University of Light Industry, China
Renfa Li	Hunan University, China
Shaozi Li	Xiamen University, China
Taoshen Li	Guangxi University, China
Weimin Li	Shanghai University, China
Xiaoping Li	Guangdong University of Technology, China
Yong Li	Tsinghua University, China
Lu Liang	Guangdong University of Technology, China
Yunji Liang	Northwestern Polytechnical University, China
Hao Liao	Shenzhen University, China
Bing Lin	Fujian Normal University, China
Dazhen Lin	Xiamen University, China
Jinjiao Lin	Shandong University of Finance and Economics, China
Ronghua Lin	South China Normal University, China

Yongguo Ling	Guangxi University, China
Chanjuan Liu	Dalian University of Technology, China
Cong Liu	Shandong University of Science and Technology, China
Dongning Liu	Guangdong University of Technology, China
Hong Liu	Shandong Normal University, China
Huazhong Liu	Hainan University, China
Jing Liu	Xidian University, China
Li Liu	Chongqing University, China
Ning Liu	Shandong University, China
Shijun Liu	Shandong University, China
Shufen Liu	Jilin University, China
Tengfei Liu	Hangzhou Institute of Technology, Xidian University, China
Xiaoping Liu	Hefei University of Technology, China
Yuechang Liu	Jiaying University, China
Yupeng Liu	Harbin University of Science and Technology, China
Zhaowei Liu	Yantai University, China
Zhihan Liu	Central South University, China
Zitao Liu	Jinan University, China
Dianjie Lu	Shandong Normal University, China
Hong Lu	Shanghai Polytechnic University, China
Huijuan Lu	China Jiliang University, China
Qiang Lu	Hefei University of Technology, China
Tun Lu	Fudan University, China
Haoyu Luo	South China Normal University, China
Zhiming Luo	Xiamen University, China
Chen Lv	Shandong Normal University, China
Jun Lv	Yantai University, China
Mingjie Lv	Zhejiang Lab, China
Peng Lv	Central South University, China
Pin Lv	Guangxi University, China
Xiao Lv	Naval University of Engineering, China
Hui Ma	Zhongshan Institute, University of Electronic Science and Technology of China, China
Keji Mao	Zhejiang University of Technology, China
Chao Min	Nanjing University, China
Li Ni	Anhui University, China
Haiwei Pan	Harbin Engineering University, China
Li Pan	Shandong University, China
Yinghui Pan	Shenzhen University, China

Yijie Peng	Peking University, China
Lianyong Qi	China University of Petroleum (East China), China
Sihang Qiu	National University of Defense Technology, China
Jiaxing Shang	Chongqing University, China
Yanjun Shi	Dalian University of Technology, China
Yuliang Shi	Shanda Dareway Company Limited, China
Xiaoxia Song	Shanxi Datong University, China
Songzhi Su	Xiamen University, China
Hailong Sun	Beihang University, China
Ruizhi Sun	China Agricultural University, China
Yuling Sun	East China Normal University, China
Yuqing Sun	Shandong University, China
Wenan Tan	Nanjing University of Aeronautics and Astronautics, China
Shan Tang	Shanghai Polytechnic University, China
Weiqing Tang	China Computer Federation, China
Xiaoyong Tang	Changsha University of Technology, China
Yan Tang	Hohai University, China
Yiming Tang	Hefei University of Technology, China
Yong Tang	South China Normal University, China
Yizheng Tao	China Academy of Engineering Physics, China
Shaohua Teng	Guangdong University of Technology, China
Fengshi Tian	China People's Police University, China
Zhuo Tian	Institute of Software, Chinese Academy of Sciences, China
Binhui Wang	Nankai University, China
Chengji Wang	Central China Normal University, China
Dakuo Wang	IBM Research, USA
Hongbin Wang	Kunming University of Science and Technology, China
Hongjun Wang	Southwest Jiaotong University, China
Hongpo Wang	Beijing University of Science and Technology, China
Jia Wang	Xinjiang University, China
Jingbin Wang	Fuzhou University, China
Lei Wang	Dalian University of Technology, China
Li Wang	Taiyuan University of Technology, China
Lu Wang	Harbin Engineering University, China
Shuang Wang	Southeast University, China
Tao Wang	Minjiang University, China

Tianbo Wang	Beihang University, China
Tong Wang	Harbin Engineering University, China
Wanyuan Wang	Southeast University, China
Wei Wang	Huazhong University of Science and Technology, China
Xiaogang Wang	Shanghai Dianji University, China
Xiaokang Wang	Hainan University, China
Yijie Wang	National University of Defense Technology, China
Yingjie Wang	Yantai University, China
Zhenxing Wang	Shanghai Polytechnic University, China
Zhiwen Wang	Guangxi University of Science and Technology, China
Zijia Wang	Guangzhou University, China
Zongyue Wang	Jimei University, China
Yiping Wen	Hunan University of Science and Technology, China
Ling Wu	Fuzhou University, China
Quanwang Wu	Chongqing University, China
Xiaokun Wu	South China University of Technology, China
Zhengyang Wu	South China Normal University, China
Chunhe Xia	Beihang University, China
Daoxun Xia	Guizhou Normal University, China
Fangxiong Xiao	Jinling Institute of Technology, China
Jing Xiao	South China Normal University, China
Xiaolan Xie	Guilin University of Technology, China
Yi Xie	National University of Defense Technology, China
Zhiqiang Xie	Harbin University of Science and Technology, China
Yu Xin	Harbin University of Science and Technology, China
Huanliang Xiong	Jiangxi Agricultural University, China
Guandong Xu	Education University of Hong Kong, China
Heyang Xu	Henan University of Technology, China
Hongfeng Xu	Guizhou Normal University, China
Jiuyun Xu	China University of Petroleum, China
Yonghui Xu	Shandong University, China
Xiao Xue	Tianjin University, China
Yaling Xun	Taiyuan University of Science and Technology, China
Jiaqi Yan	Nanjing University, China
Xiaohu Yan	Shenzhen Polytechnic University, China

Bo Yang	University of Electronic Science and Technology, China
Chao Yang	Hunan University, China
Dingyu Yang	Alibaba Group, China
Gang Yang	Northwestern Polytechnical University, China
Jing Yang	Hainan University, China
Jing Yang	Harbin Engineering University, China
Lin Yang	Shanghai Computer Software Technology Development Center, China
Tianruo Yang	Zhengzhou University, China
Xiaochun Yang	Northeastern University, China
Ziyi Yang	Beijing Institute of Technology, China
Yan Yao	Qufu Normal University, China
Xiaoyan Yin	Northwestern University, China
Jianyong Yu	Hunan University of Science and Technology, China
Shanping Yu	Beijing Institute of Technology, China
Xianchuan Yu	Beijing Normal University, China
Xu Yu	Qingdao University of Science and Technology, China
Yang Yu	Sun Yat-sen University, China
Zhengtao Yu	Kunming University of Science and Technology, China
Zhiwen Yu	Harbin Engineering University, China
Zhiyong Yu	Fuzhou University, China
Chengzhe Yuan	Guangdong Polytechnic Normal University, China
Junying Yuan	Guangzhou Southern College, China
An Zeng	Guangdong University of Technology, China
Dajun Zeng	Institute of Automation, Chinese Academy of Sciences, China
Liang Zeng	Beijing Institute of Technology, China
Zhihui Zhan	South China University of Technology, China
Changyou Zhang	Institute of Software, Chinese Academy of Sciences, China
Chaowei Zhang	Yangzhou University, China
Hongbo Zhang	Huaqiao University, China
Jia Zhang	Jinan University, China
Jifu Zhang	Taiyuan University of Science and Technology, China
Jing Zhang	Southeast University, China
Liang Zhang	Fudan University, China
Libo Zhang	Southwest University, China
Miaohui Zhang	Jiangxi Academy of Sciences, China

Peng Zhang	Fudan University, China
Senyue Zhang	Shenyang Aerospace University, China
Shaohua Zhang	Shanghai Business School, China
Wei Zhang	Guangdong University of Technology, China
Xiaowei Zhang	Lanzhou University, China
Xin Zhang	Jiangnan University, China
Ying Zhang	Northwestern Polytechnical University, China
Yong Zhang	Shenzhen Institute of Advanced Technology, Chinese Academy of Sciences, China
Zhiqiang Zhang	Zhejiang University of Finance and Economics, China
Zili Zhang	Southwest University, China
Hong Zhao	Guangzhou Institute of Technology, Xidian University, China
Tianfang Zhao	Jinan University, China
Jiaoling Zheng	Chengdu University of Information Technology, China
Xiangwei Zheng	Shandong Normal University, China
Jinghui Zhong	South China University of Technology, China
Ning Zhong	Beijing University of Technology, China
Jiantao Zhou	Inner Mongolia University, China
Yifeng Zhou	Southeast University, China
Yu Zhou	Shenzhen University, China
Huiling Zhu	Jinan University, China
Jia Zhu	South China Normal University, China
Jianhua Zhu	City University of Hong Kong, China
Jie Zhu	Nanjing University of Posts and Telecommunications, China
Nengjun Zhu	Shanghai University, China
Tingshao Zhu	Institute of Psychology, Chinese Academy of Sciences, China
Xia Zhu	Southeast University, China
Xianjun Zhu	Jinling Institute of Technology, China
Yanhua Zhu	First Affiliated Hospital of Guangdong Pharmaceutical University, China
Qiaohong Zu	Wuhan University of Technology, China

Contents – Part I

**Human-Machine-Things Fusion and Human-AI Collaborative
Computing**

Contents – Part II

Collaborative Data, Software and Services

Trend

AISCW: Artificial Intelligence Supported Cooperative Work The New Frontier of CSCW

Meilin Shi[1], Guiling Wang[2,3], Shaohua Zhang[4], Jinlei Jiang[1], and Yong Xiang[1](✉)

[1] Computer Science Department, Tsinghua University, Beijing 100084, China
{shiml,jjlei,xyong}@tsinghua.edu.cn
[2] Beijing Key Laboratory on Integration and Analysis of Large-scale Stream Data, Beijing, China
wangguiling@ncut.edu.cn
[3] School of Information Science and Technology, North China University of Technology, Beijing 100144, China
[4] Camford Royal School, Beijing 102211, China
hillfree@126.com

Abstract. Under today's natural environmental, social and technological conditions, the global and large-scale challenges faced by humanity are becoming increasingly significant, making collaborative work increasingly important. Computer-Supported Cooperative Work (CSCW) is anticipated to assume a more pivotal role in modern society and within the fabric of production and daily life. In recent years, Artificial Intelligence has witnessed remarkable advancements, and the "cooperative intelligence" of AI systems has been enhanced. The role of computers in supporting human collaboration is no longer limited to an auxiliary role but also serves as a cooperative role, bringing new challenges to the study of CSCW, ranging from basic collaborative theories to key technologies. This paper proposes a new frontier in CSCW, AI Supported Cooperative Work (AISCW) and its system research. The objective is to take use of AI technologies to enhance and optimize human collaborative activities. By delving into the interplay between CSCW and AI, this paper outlines the foundational concepts, key issues and potential research focal points of AISCW.

Keywords: CSCW · AISCW · Cooperative AI

1 Introduction

Human society is a closely collaborative group, Computer Supported Cooperative Work (CSCW) is an inevitable outcome of humanity's progression into the information age. It is committed to exploring the essence and characteristics of collaborative work and to designing systems that support this collaboration through computer technology. In the context of today's natural environment, societal structures, and technological advancements, human groups are confronted with an increasing array of global and large-scale challenges, which underscores the growing importance of collaborative work. It is anticipated that CSCW will play an increasingly vital role in contemporary society and in various aspects of production and daily life.

In recent years, AI (Artificial Intelligence) has made groundbreaking advancements, with AI outperforming general human capabilities in various specific domains. The "collaborative" abilities of AI have been strengthened, granting it the capacity to "cooperate" with humans on certain tasks, or what is termed "Cooperative Intelligence." This has shifted the role of computers from being mere assistants to becoming cooperative partners in human collaboration. AI endowed with "Cooperative Intelligence" has infused new energy into the research of CSCW, presenting new challenges that span from foundational theories of collaborative mechanisms to critical technical issues. For instance, what are the essential characteristics of the collaborative mechanisms among humans and AI agents, among multiple AI agents, and between humans and multiple AI agents? How do these mechanisms differ from those of human-to-human collaboration? How can we design AI agents or systems of multiple AI agents that more significantly enhance human collaborative efficiency? And so forth.

In light of this context, the CSCW field must increase its attention to such issues, which we collectively label as issues of AI Supported Cooperative Work (AI Supported Cooperative Work, AISCW). The objective of studying these issues is to leverage AI technologies to amplify and refine human collaborative activities, marking it as a new frontier in CSCW research.

The subsequent sections of this paper will review and forecast the research on CSCW and AI in Sect. 2, delve into the relationship between CSCW and AI in Sect. 3, and endeavor to define the concept, connotation, and extension of AISCW in Sect. 4. Sections 5 and 6 will propose theoretical issues and potential research starting points within the AISCW research domain. Lastly, Sect. 7 concludes the paper.

2   Background Overview

2.1   CSCW Revisited: Thoughts and Considerations

Computer-Supported Cooperative Work (CSCW) is defined as a group of individuals dispersed across different locations using computers and network technology to collaboratively coordinate and work together on a task. It includes the development of collaborative work systems, research into group working methodologies, investigation into technologies that support group efforts, and the creation of application systems. By establishing an environment conducive to collaborative work, it aims to improve the methods of information exchange, overcome or minimize the barriers of time and space, conserve the time and energy of workers, and enhance the quality and efficiency of group work. This, in turn, increases the overall benefits for enterprises, institutions, organizations, and society at large, as well as the quality of life for humanity [13]. In a word, CSCW is an inevitable outcome of the convergence of communication technology with computer and network technologies, growing alongside the progression of the information age.

Since the concept of CSCW was formally introduced in 1984, it has evolved over nearly four decades. Research in the CSCW domain in China commenced in the mid-1990s, leading to the establishment of research goals, theoretical frameworks, clusters of research questions, key technological systems, typical application cases, academic journals, scholarly societies or organizations, and academic conferences, all of which have gained an impressive impact [8, 12].

Different from conventional computer science domains like computer networks and databases, CSCW stands out as a unique interdisciplinary field. It intersects with various disciplines, including computer science, social sciences, psychology, management, law, and ethics, focusing on both the development of collaborative computing tools and the analysis of human social collaboration through computer technology. CSCW researchers have recognized that CSCW technologies are not exclusive and are not strictly tied to CSCW domain, whether established or emerging. The coherence of CSCW as an academic field originates not from specific technologies but from a collective interest in the essence and requirements of collaborative work and the objective of engineering computer technology to facilitate it [12]. The genesis of CSCW was the realization by researchers from diverse technical and academic backgrounds that their research issues were interconnected.

Therefore, in CSCW research, it is essential for researchers from different directions and disciplines to engage in broader and more interdisciplinary exchanges. The scope and focus of CSCW research are continuously discussed and developed through such interactions, which is the norm in the field.

CSCW researchers have noted that the collaborative tools and technologies they develop, such as collaborative writing systems, video conferencing, workflow management, and virtual environments, frequently evolve into key tools in other domains. Some may find this puzzling, but it underscores that CSCW is not tightly bound to any specific technologies. The hallmark achievements of CSCW include not only concrete technological products but also theoretical contributions such as an understanding of human collaborative behavior.

We should emphasize and highlight the essence of CSCW, which is its focus on the essence and requirements of collaborative work, the comprehension of collaborative behaviors and mechanisms, and the research into the principles and methodologies for computer-supported collaboration. These theoretical contributions are distinctive to CSCW. The dissemination of CSCW's tools and technologies, like groupware, into other fields as representative technologies, demonstrates the extensive influence of CSCW on the advancement of other disciplines and technologies, highlighting its indispensable role.

2.2   AI and Foundational Models: Current Research Landscape

The term Artificial Intelligence (AI) was officially introduced in 1956 and is considered one of the three major scientific and technological achievements of the

20th century, alongside space technology and atomic energy. AI refers to the artificial simulation of human intelligence on machines (computers), or the process of endowing machines with intelligence similar to that of humans. Consequently, the discipline of AI studies how to construct intelligent machines (intelligent computers) or intelligent systems that can simulate, extend, and amplify human intelligence.

The evolution of AI is broadly categorized into three eras based on the prevailing interests of the AI community. The "reasoning era" from 1956 to the mid-1960s emphasized logic-based automated reasoning. The "knowledge era," marked by knowledge engineering, lasted from the 1970s to the mid-1980s. The "learning era," from the 1990s to the 2020s, has been defined by machine learning and deep learning.

In the 2020s, OpenAI introduced the "Scaling Law," which shows that large language model (LLM) performance scales linearly with exponential growth in parameters, data volume, and training time, with minimal dependency on model structure and hyperparameter tuning [9]. Guided by this law, researchers have shifted their focus towards the study of large language model foundations, conducting extensive related research with a more effective use of computational resources and data.

Foundational models, including large language model and the multi-modal foundational models like the embodied intelligence model PaLM-E [5], have shown the ability to generalize within certain domains. While some members of the public and computer scientists may believe that certain large language models, like GPT-4, have passed the Turing test, a rigorous examination reveals that current large language models cannot be said to have fully passed the test [2]. For instance, their performance on logic puzzles is significantly different from that of humans; when questions that large language models can answer correctly are rephrased, humans can still provide the correct response, but models like ChatGPT often cannot. As a result, researchers argue that the abilities exhibited by large language models are "fluent in speech but without true comprehension of what is being said." This may be because large language models learn solely from language, in a manner different from human learning. They are not embodied in the physical world and thus cannot experience the connection between language and objects, attributes, and sensations as humans do. Consequently, for humans, we can infer that someone has mastered certain abstract concepts and can complete other cognitive tests based on their performance in exams like the GRE or the bar exam. However, we cannot make the same inference about large language models [2].

Furthermore, training large language models comes at the cost of consuming vast computational resources. They also have many limitations and unresolved issues in areas such as understanding human emotions and intentions, social intelligence, multimodal understanding, autonomous learning, and creativity, and are not yet capable of replacing human abilities across all cognitive and perceptual tasks [18]. Upholding the 3H principles-Helpfulness, Honesty, and

Harmlessness-in the outputs of large language models is a formidable challenge in this research field [19].

In summary, the research progress of foundational models has demonstrated their strong generalization abilities. Some researchers consider certain foundational models, like GPT-4, as early versions of Artificial General Intelligence (AGI) systems [2]. However, the study of foundational models and AGI is still in its infancy, with many pressing issues yet to be addressed.

3 Integrating AI with CSCW: A Chapter on Synergy

In recent years, CSCW researchers have found that they can leverage the advancements in LLM and AI research to better understand and address issues in human collaboration. In fact, natural language processing (NLP) technologies were integrated into CSCW systems even before the advent of LLM to support and enhance human-computer interaction, and machine learning algorithms are often used to analyze and comprehend the collaborative behaviors and patterns of team members.

AI has approached or even surpassed human performance on certain specific tasks, endowing it with the capability to "cooperate" with humans in those tasks. Some researchers have introduced concepts such as the Embodied Turing Test [17] and Embodied Intelligence [11, 14] to advance the development of AI systems that more closely emulate human capabilities. These systems should have the capabilities to sense, move and interact in the physical world. The focus of the Embodied Intelligence test is no longer on specific abilities as in the traditional Turing Test, such as language or games, but on the abilities shared by all animals through millions of years of evolution. In other words, in the physical world, the behavior of an Embodied Intelligence system should be indistinguishable from that of a real biological entity in the same environment.

The introduction of Embodied Turing Test and Embodied Intelligence holds significant implications for CSCW research. This means that within the realm of CSCW studies, the collaborative subjects are no longer solely human but must also include AI agents and AI systems. In fact, in some digital games, collaboration between humans and AI agents is already a common occurrence. Moreover, in the "Metaverse", a digital construct that reflects or surpasses the real world and interacts with it, the entities of human collaboration have also exceeded the conventional understanding of human participants.

At the same time, AI researchers have also found it necessary to consider collaborative intelligence as a distinct research direction within artificial intelligence. AI systems need to understand human society and possess the intelligence to collaborate with humans in order to integrate into it. Psychological research has found that the brains of young children develop fully only through social interaction. Similarly, AI systems also require collaborative capabilities, and CSCW's understanding of collaborative behavior and how computer technology can support human collaboration has laid a certain foundation for the study of collaborative intelligence [3].

3.1 AI's Support for CSCW

CSCW focuses on how people use technology to collaborate and achieve a common goal. As a technological asset, AI is incorporated within CSCW. How to better integrate AI with CSCW to realize efficient human-computer collaboration has attracted attention, and many exploratory works have emerged. Based on the role of AI in collaborative systems, AI's support for CSCW can be roughly divided into three categories, detailed as follows.

(1) "Assistant": AI's Supportive Role in CSCW

Typical CSCW collaborative environments, or "groupware," include email systems, virtual meeting platforms, discussion forums, social media messaging platforms, workflow and business process management systems, collaborative writing, design, and educational systems. AI's support and enhancement of various collaborative environments or tools have been evident for a long time. AI algorithms can train a model based on collaborative historical data that characterizes and models the relationships between variables. The models it provides, such as statistical analysis, prediction, and generation, can be used to enhance the original functions of collaborative environments. For instance, machine learning classification algorithms have long been applied to email systems; in virtual meeting systems and social media platforms, proactive schedule reminders, content, or friend recommendations based on predictive and recommendation algorithms can improve collaboration efficiency.

Current foundational models, such as large language and multimodal models, are trained on vast unannotated text or multimodal samples. Constructed with deep neural networks comprising billions of parameters, they are fine-tuned with a generative framework for supervised tasks, significantly improving performance and showcasing robust generalization across a range of tasks. The abilities of large models in question answering, document drafting, code generation, and mathematical problem-solving can be incorporated into various collaborative tools, including email and collaborative writing.

Take workflow systems and business process management systems as another example. During system operation, a large amount of process data is generated, including modeling data, event log data, and external historical data related to the process. These data can be considered high-quality domain data specific to business process management. They can be used for further fine-tuning on the basis of a well-trained large model, enabling the model to perform tasks specific to business process management systems, such as interpreting the execution process and results, generating process descriptions, assisting in decision-making based on user input and process context, automating repetitive tasks, and assisting process business personnel in analysis and decision-making. Many researchers and companies have started attempts in this area, such as SAX4BPM [6], ProcessGPT [1], etc.

(2) "Collaborator": AI as a Partner in Enhancing CSCW

With the advancement of AI capabilities, especially the emergence and rapid development of LLM, AI's performance on specific tasks has approached or even surpassed that of humans. For instance, in the ImageNet competition, AI's recognition error rate is lower than humans; AI's translation quality in certain language pairs has exceeded human levels; the AlphaGo program defeated the world champion; and AI's diagnostic accuracy in some diseases (such as skin cancer, breast cancer) has surpassed professional doctors. The perception of AI in the CSCW field is also changing, no longer seeing it merely as a supportive tool for collaborative environments and tools, but as a key factor in problem-solving, an equal "collaborator" with humans. Under this trend, new concepts continue to emerge, including human-machine collaboration, human-AI collaboration, and human-machine teaming.

Cai et al. [16] explored the potential of human-AI collaboration in ensuring sustainable security. The authors believe that by collaborating with AI, human capabilities can be enhanced, and a more resilient and sustainable security ecosystem can be established; at various stages such as secure development, secure interaction, and incident response, AI as a collaborator can amplify the efforts of stakeholders such as software developers, security experts, and end-users, guiding them to implement sustainable security practices.

Wang et al. [15] discussed the impact of automated AI (AutoAI) technology on the work practices of data scientists. They found that AutoAI can become a new partner for data science teams, providing assistance in education, collaboration, and data science practices: as a collaborator, AutoAI can help improve work efficiency, especially in labor-intensive tasks such as data cleaning, feature engineering, and model building; as a teacher, AutoAI can help educate data scientists and those aspiring to enter the field by demonstrating how to build models and select features to impart best practices.

Fan et al. [7] affirmed the potential of AI in user experience (UX) evaluation, analyzing usability test video tasks, and further explored how AI can effectively collaborate with human evaluators in terms of explanations and synchronization. Their study found that AI providing explanations can better support the analytical work of UX evaluators and received more positive evaluations, regardless of synchronous or asynchronous presentation; without explanations, synchronous AI compared to asynchronous AI can more improve the performance and engagement of UX evaluators.

It should be noted that although AI has surpassed humans in many specific tasks, it has not yet universally surpassed humans in broad, general tasks. Although the generalization performance of large models has been broken through, the era of "Artificial General Intelligence" (AGI) has not truly begun or has just been unveiled. In fact, there is still much debate over how to define and achieve AGI. The arrival of the AGI era or the emergence of AI that passes the Embodied Intelligence Turing Test will be a symbolic breakthrough event for AI in the future. Human intelligence is not centered on optimizing fixed goals, and the ability to collaborate with and learn from others is equally important for AI [10]. It can be anticipated that AI in the AGI era and AI that passes the Embodied Intelligence Turing Test will have higher collaboration capabilities and efficiency in collaboration with humans. This is one of the positive implications of future AI development for CSCW that is worth paying attention to.

(3) "Innovator": AI Pioneers Novel Collaborative Approaches

AI algorithms might negatively influence human collaboration, as seen in social media platforms where improper recommendations could lead to group polarization. Yet, researchers are exploring whether AI can stimulate collaboration, questioning if AI systems can offer solutions to enhance human cooperation.

Researchers constructed a reinforcement learning neural network based on a trial-and-error mechanism and conducted both simulation experiments and real-world experiments with over 1000 human participants. The results were striking: in a system without AI support, participants initially joined the game with altruistic intentions, but over time, independent and selfish behaviors gradually dominated. In contrast, the AI-supported system prevented this pattern; members who received AI recommendations were more collaborative throughout the game [3].

Further research revealed that the AI system's support for collaboration was significantly more effective than some traditional social science methods (such as punishing selfish behavior). Unlike conventional strategies, the reinforcement learning-based AI system did not exhibit punishment or isolation of selfish behaviors but instead gently encouraged cooperation with generous members and avoidance of collaboration with those who did not participate.

This indicates that well-designed AI algorithms can fully promote human collaboration and that human collaboration mechanisms may observe or explore new possibilities for further optimization from AI algorithms.

3.2   CSCW's Contributions to AI

(1) CSCW: Establishing Foundations for Collaborative Intelligence Research through the Study of Human Collaboration

As previously discussed, AI researchers have recognized that current AI models are typically constructed based on "optimization" of targets or reward functions. However, human intelligence is not centered on optimizing fixed goals. To endow AI systems with human-like intelligence, they must also acquire the ability to collaborate with and learn from others. Achieving this requires a foundational understanding of human collaborative intelligence.

Take autonomous driving systems as an example, their effective operation is inseparable from collaborative intelligence. For instance, correctly understanding the goals and intentions of other drivers (or driving agents) can further predict the movements of other vehicles and proactively respond accordingly. If it can coordinate routes and speeds with other vehicles, it can reduce traffic congestion and accidents. It also needs to understand and respond to traffic police gestures or signal necessary information to other driving vehicles. This illustrates the significant role of collaborative intelligence in scenarios requiring multi-agent collaboration to achieve a common goal [4].

CSCW has accumulated a series of theoretical, tool, and methodological research findings on how to use computer technology to analyze and understand human collaborative behavior, establish collaborative work environments, and eliminate or reduce collaboration barriers. These can serve as the foundation for research in collaborative intelligence.

(2) **CSCW: Enabling AI System R&D through Collaborative Environments, Tools, and Infrastructure**

Initially, AI system R&D is frequently a collaborative effort, occasionally necessitating extensive cooperation. CSCW's developed communication protocols, environments, tools, and infrastructure facilitate large-scale, multi-participant collaboration, improve efficiency, and promote knowledge sharing, offering essential environmental and tool support for those developing AI systems.

Moreover, in the experimental phase of collaborative intelligence, there is a requirement to build realistic and simulated collaborative settings, compile and develop collaborative datasets, and analyze and assess collaboration logs and outcomes. The environments, tools, and infrastructure provided by CSCW research offer the necessary technical backing for these tasks.

Additionally, CSCW research aids AI development teams in gaining a deeper understanding of the nuances of human collaboration, ensuring that AI system development positively contributes to human collaborative efforts.

(3) **CSCW: Addressing AI's Validation Gaps in the Physical World**

AI systems are commonly tested and verified within controlled experimental settings. However, their effectiveness in the authentic, complex, and open-ended physical world cannot be self-validated, where CSCW can offer significant assistance.

CSCW's support for human collaboration enables the physical-world testing and validation of AI systems through cooperative human interaction. With CSCW tools, users can participate more actively in AI decision-making, offering critical validation and feedback.

4   The Concept, Connotation, and Extension of AISCW

Our previous discussions have outlined the mutually reinforcing relationship between AI and CSCW. Distinguished from traditional computing technologies that support human collaboration in an auxiliary role, AI's role in enhancing CSCW has evolved from supportive to collaborative. AI algorithms now offer innovative solutions for refining collaborative mechanisms within human society.

Conversely, CSCW research underpins and complements the study of collaborative intelligence, with AI systems or agents endowed with such intelligence further amplifying human collaborative capabilities. While traditional CSCW has concentrated on the auxiliary aspects of constructing environments and systems to support collaborative activities, the collaborative role of AI systems introduces a spectrum of extended issues. These include the mechanisms of collaboration, collaborative systems, and their assessment, which warrant further investigation. From this perspective, we introduce the concept of "AI Supported Cooperative Work (AISCW)," which involves leveraging AI technologies to augment and optimize human collaborative endeavors.

AISCW is related to research in Human-Machine Interaction, AI Alignment, and Cooperative AI, but it is not equivalent to these concepts. Human-Machine Interaction and AI Alignment emphasize the existence of a clear principal, such as a human user (the principal) issuing instructions to the machine (the agent), which is responsible for executing these instructions. Cooperative AI involves multiple agents with their own preferences, and when solving problems, it is necessary to consider the preferences of these different agents, focusing on the collaboration between multiple AI agents, people, and AI agents and people. AISCW also involves multiple agents with their own preferences and focuses on the collaboration between multiple AI agents, people, and AI agents and people. However, different from Cooperative AI, AISCW studies how AI agents as an intelligent node participate in human collaboration. In AISCW research, the ultimate goal of studying the collaboration between multiple AI agents is not to promote collaboration between multiple AI agents (which is the goal of Cooperative AI), but to better enable them to participate in human collaboration as a node. Human-Machine Interaction researchers emphasize how humans as principals interact with machines or AI, while AISCW emphasizes the interaction and collaboration mechanisms between the two, such as communication, interaction, and negotiation mechanisms. AI Alignment researchers are concerned with all issues of how AI agents align with human values, while AISCW is concerned with how AI agents, as collaborative nodes, align with human values.

AISCW, with the goal of enhancing and optimizing human collaboration, includes research into various forms of cooperative endeavors. It encompasses not only the study of AI's role in supporting traditional human collaboration but also the study of collaboration between AI agents and humans, as well as collaboration among AI agents themselves. This is because, while AISCW is primarily concerned with human group collaboration, the trajectory of AI development aims for a more extensive and profound integration into human society. As intelligent nodes in collective collaborations, AI agents will amplify the collaborative capacity of human groups through effective cooperation with both humans and other AI agents. Thus, collaboration between AI agents and with humans is pivotal to realizing the goals of AISCW.

Currently, a variety of AISCW systems already exist. We classify AISCW systems based on three dimensions: temporality, spatiality, and the density of collaboration. To elaborate, the temporal dimension distinguishes between synchronous and asynchronous collaboration methods; the spatial dimension differentiates between remote and local collaborations; and the collaboration dimension measures the frequency of collaborative interactions. Using this classification, a three-dimensional model of various AISCW systems can be constructed, as illustrated in Fig. 1. A brief overview of several primary AISCW systems is as follows:

(1) LLM supported BPM systems. They facilitate remote, asynchronous collaboration among individuals. These systems, underpinned by LLMs, offer interpretation and Q&A regarding the execution and outcomes of collaborative processes, enabling the automated generation of collaborative workflows suitable for scenarios with high collaboration density and intensive knowledge.

(2) Autonomous driving systems and search and rescue robots. They support synchronous collaboration between AI agents and humans, catering to scenarios with high collaboration density.

(3) AI-supported remote education systems. They support synchronous teaching activities, whether remote or local, with collaboration intensity varying from sparse lecture-style interactions to more intense team project-based teaching.

(4) AI agent-supported metaverse collaborative spaces and online intelligent collaboration platforms. These platforms can support remote collaboration and

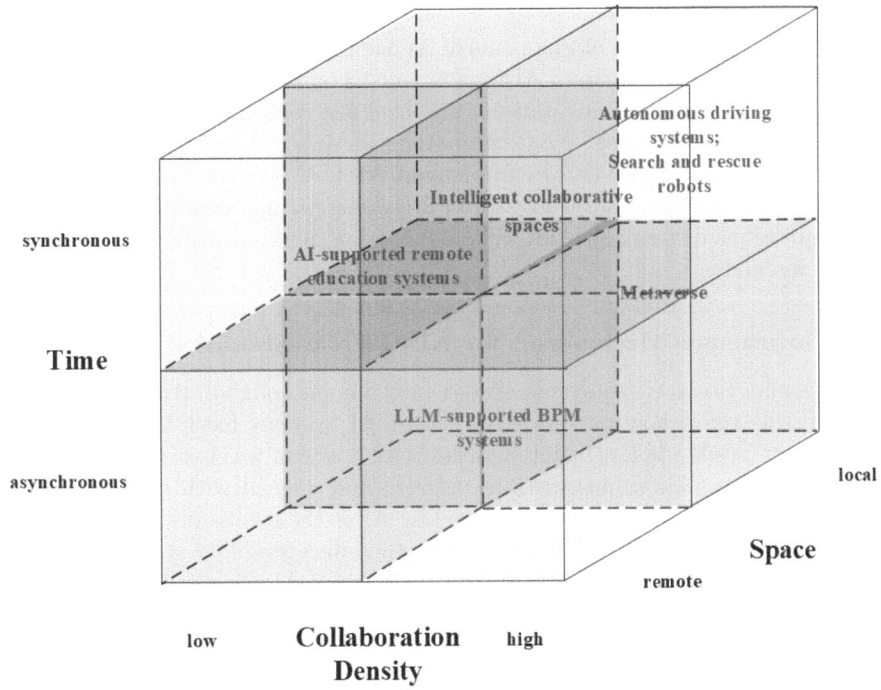

Fig. 1. A Taxonomy of AI Supported Cooperative Work (AISCW) Systems

provide local support for co-located users. They can facilitate both synchronous collaboration needed for virtual meetings or real-time gaming and asynchronous collaboration when immediate interaction with AI agents is not required. The intelligent collaboration platforms offer both synchronous and asynchronous collaboration capabilities, as well as supporting remote and local interactions with varying degrees of collaborative intensity.

5 Exploring Theoretical Concerns of AISCW

5.1 AISCW's System Architecture

The selection of theoretical models for AISCW research encompasses understanding the unique collaborative intents and behaviors among AI agents, multiple AI agents, and humans within AISCW. It also includes models for communication, interaction, negotiation, and complementary collaboration among these entities, as well as the system architecture models for AISCW.

Building the theoretical framework for AISCW research is a fundamental theoretical issue in AISCW studies. It involves researching how to construct various aspects of AISCW theoretical research, proposing, and planning corresponding research questions and directions.

5.2 Collaboration Mechanisms with AI Agents and Humans as Collaborative Entities

How do the collaboration mechanisms of AI agents and multiple AI agents differ from those between humans? AI agents must comprehend human objectives and intentions, engage in negotiation, and leverage complementary strengths in collaboration with humans. What characteristics define the synergy between AI agents and humans? How can we implement AISCW collaboration mechanisms that capitalize on the complementarity between AI and human interactions? These questions distinguish AISCW collaboration mechanisms from traditional CSCW research.

5.3 Governance Mechanisms for AISCW Collaboration

As AI agents become deeply integrated into human collaborative activities as collaborative roles, how can we ensure that AI systems meet human privacy and security needs when utilizing information? How can we ensure that AI algorithms' decision-making processes are ethical and aligned with human values? How can we ensure that the facts utilized by AI or the results obtained are verified by the real world? How can we improve the interpretability of AI algorithms so that human collaborative entities can understand AI decision logic, establish trust in AI systems, and build complementary collaborative relationships, etc.? In summary, how to govern AISCW systems and the complex collaborative networks between AI agents, multi-AI agents, and humans supported by AISCW? These are inescapable issues for AISCW, collectively referred to as "Collaborative Governance Mechanisms for AISCW."

5.4   Evaluation Metrics and Measurement Methods for AISCW

How can we measure the collaborative capabilities of AI systems or AI agents? We say that when the collaborative capabilities of AI systems or agents approach or exceed the general level of human collaborative capabilities, it signifies AI's leap from an assistant role to a collaborative role in human collaboration. So, how can we correctly evaluate and measure AI's collaborative capabilities?

5.5   Interdisciplinary Research Methods for AISCW

AISCW research extends beyond computer science to include fields like sociology, law, ethics, and psychology, necessitating collaborative interdisciplinary studies.

AISCW calls for a redefinition of legal entities and statuses for humans and AI agents and must confront potential human aversion to AI agents, among other challenges.

6   Potential Research Starting Points

Below are some potential research topics, technologies, and starting points for AISCW.

- Collaborative mechanisms, Key technologies, and System Construction between AI Agents and Humans
  - Defining roles and methods of AI intervention across various collaboration domains.
  - Investigating collaborative tools and key technologies within AISCW, such as intelligent interpretation and Q&A for workflow execution in process management systems, natural language-based generation of collaborative process documentation, and data-driven auxiliary analysis and decision-making for collaborative processes.
  - Exploring multi-sensory human-computer interactions for embodied intelligence, including tactile, visual, and auditory modalities.
  - Integrating affective computing into AISCW to facilitate more natural interactions and collaborative experience.
  - Examining synchronization mechanisms in AISCW, focusing on continuous, multi-party asynchronous cooperation between AI agents and humans.
- Concrete Manifestations of AI in AISCW
  - Investigating wearable devices as intelligent nodes within collaborative environments.
  - Endowing embodied intelligence with social and collaborative capabilities.
- Security and Ethical Considerations for AISCW Systems
  - Addressing alignment with human moral values and ethical decision-making in AISCW.
  - Ensuring data security and privacy protection within AISCW frameworks.
- Demonstrative Applications of AISCW in Specific Domains

- Applying AISCW in targeted areas such as autonomous vehicles, industrial settings, medical care, education, and domestic services.
- The Psychological Impact of AI as a Collaborator
  - Studying the effects of AI collaboration on the mental health of different age groups, including adolescents and the elderly.
  - Analyzing both the positive and negative influences of AI collaboration on human cooperative behaviors.

7 Conclusion

With the breakthrough development of AI in recent years, the role of AI systems in promoting CSCW has evolved from being supportive to collaborative. AI is now even capable of providing new solutions for improving collaborative mechanisms within human society.

Traditional CSCW research has primarily focused on the supportive role of computer technology in constructing environments and systems to support collaborative activities. In contrast, AI systems, as collaborative partners in human activities, introduce a range of theoretical and key technological issues that require further research.

It is hoped that this paper will inspire domestic CSCW scholars to take an interest in and prioritize the research and application development of AI Supported Cooperative Work (AISCW).

References

1. Beheshti, A., et al.: ProcessGPT: transforming business process management with generative artificial intelligence. In: 2023 IEEE International Conference on Web Services (ICWS), pp. 731–739. IEEE (2023)
2. Biever, C.: The easy intelligence tests that AI chatbots fail. Nature **619**, 686–689 (2023)
3. Dafoe, A., Bachrach, Y., Hadfield, G., Horvitz, E., Larson, K., Graepel, T.: Cooperative AI: machines must learn to find common ground. Nature **593**(7857), 33–36 (2021)
4. Dafoe, A., et al.: Open problems in cooperative AI. arXiv preprint arXiv:2012.08630 (2020)
5. Driess, D., et al.: Palm-e: an embodied multimodal language model. arXiv preprint arXiv:2303.03378 (2023)
6. Fahland, D., Fournier, F., Limonad, L., Skarbovsky, I., Swevels, A.J.E.: How well can large language models explain business processes? arXiv preprint arXiv:2401.12846 (2024)
7. Fan, M., Yang, X., Yu, T., Liao, Q.V., Zhao, J.: Human-AI collaboration for UX evaluation: effects of explanation and synchronization. Proc. ACM Hum. Comput. Interact. **6**(CSCW1), 1–32 (2022). https://doi.org/10.1145/3512943
8. Gu, N.: My experience and reflections on CCF academic services (2023). https://www.ccf.org.cn/Membership/Individual_member/Stories/2023-06-14/792664.shtml. Accessed 25 Apr 2024

9. Kaplan, J., et al.: Scaling laws for neural language models. arXiv preprint arXiv:2001.08361 (2020)
10. Mitchell, M.: Debates on the nature of artificial general intelligence. Science **383**(6689), eado7069 (2024)
11. Savva, M., et al.: Habitat: a platform for embodied AI research. In: Proceedings of the IEEE/CVF International Conference on Computer Vision, pp. 9339–9347 (2019)
12. Schmidt, K., Bannon, L.: Constructing CSCW: the first quarter century. Comput. Support. Cooper. Work (CSCW) **22**, 345–372 (2013)
13. Shi, M., Xiang, Y., Yang, G.: Computer-Supported Cooperative Work: Theory and Application. Publishing House of Electronics Industry (2000)
14. Smith, L., Gasser, M.: The development of embodied cognition: six lessons from babies. Artif. Life **11**(1–2), 13–29 (2005)
15. Wang, D., et al.: Human-AI collaboration in data science: exploring data scientists' perceptions of automated AI. Proc. ACM Hum.-Comput. Interact. **3**(CSCW), 1–24 (2019). https://doi.org/10.1145/3359313
16. Wanling, C., Liliana, P., Kushal, R., John, M., Bashar, N., Gavin, D.: Human-AI collaboration for sustainable security: opportunities and challenges. In: USENIX Symposium on Usable Privacy and Security (SOUPS), pp. 1–5 (2023)
17. Zador, A., et al.: Catalyzing next-generation artificial intelligence through NeuroAI. Nat. Commun. **14**(1), 1597 (2023)
18. Zhang, Q., Gui, T., Zheng, R., Huang, X.: Large Language Model: From Theory to Practice. Shanghai (2023). https://intro-llm.github.io/
19. Zhao, W.X., et al.: A survey of large language models. arXiv preprint arXiv:2303.18223 (2023)

CSCW and Social Computing

A Centrality-Guided Modularity Optimization Algorithm for Overlapping and Nested Community Detection in Opportunistic Networks

Shoucheng Wang[1], Xulong Guo[2], and Gang Xu[1(✉)]

[1] Inner Mongolia University, Hohhot 010021, China
csxugang@imu.edu.cn
[2] Inner Mongolia Branch of National Computer Network Emergency Response Technical Team/Coordination Center of China, Hohhot 010021, China

Abstract. This paper introduces a centrality-guided modularity optimization algorithm for overlapping and nested community detection (CG-MONCD), aimed at addressing community structure identification in opportunistic networks. Characterized by data transmission through sporadic encounters between nodes without the need for stable communication links, the CG-MONCD algorithm constructs a weighted graph model by quantifying the frequency and duration of encounters, as well as energy consumption. Incorporating a centrality-based initial community construction strategy and a method for identifying overlapping nodes, it effectively detects overlapping and nested communities within the network. Experimental results demonstrate that this algorithm outperforms existing methods in community detection, modularity optimization, and intra-community edge density, accurately revealing the network's nested communities and hierarchical features, thereby enhancing communication efficiency and network stability.

Keywords: Opportunistic Networks · Overlapping and Nested Communities · Community Detection · Central Nodes

1 Introduction

Opportunistic networks [1] are self-organizing systems that do not rely on a complete path between source and destination nodes. Instead, they utilize node mobility and chances for encounters to achieve network communication, following a "store-carry-forward" paradigm.

In practical applications, nodes in opportunistic networks are often carried by individuals, reflecting human social attributes and behavior patterns, which makes the accurate detection of community structures essential for analyzing network characteristics and structures. Community detection [2] is a crucial aspect of studying opportunistic networks, aiming to partition nodes into groups with tight internal connections but relative isolation from other communities.

This paper introduces a Centrality-Guided Modularity Optimization algorithm for Overlapping and Nested Community Detection (CG-MONCD). It begins by designing a method to quantify social relationships in opportunistic networks based on metrics such as the number of encounters between nodes, total encounter duration, and energy consumption, thereby constructing a weighted graph model. Furthermore, the study introduces an initial community construction strategy based on node centrality and a method for identifying overlapping nodes that may belong to multiple communities. Experimental results demonstrate that the CG-MONCD algorithm outperforms others in community detection, modularity optimization, and maintaining intra-community edge density. Nested modularity analysis further highlights the significant effectiveness of the CG-MONCD algorithm in revealing nested communities within the network structure.

2 Related Work

Community detection in opportunistic networks faces significant challenges primarily due to the mobility of nodes causing spatiotemporal variations in community membership and the unresolved issue of effectively integrating the social attributes of nodes [3–5]. Innovative methods have been proposed to address the challenges posed by network dynamics. For instance, Li et al. [6] utilized Bayesian inference and backpropagation algorithms to dynamically construct communities, enhancing data transmission efficiency. Ma et al. [7] explored an overlapping community detection algorithm using short-term interactions and local information. Zhang et al. [8] enhanced the accuracy of community structure detection using the Maximum Connection Probability (MCP) method, while Xu et al. [9] addressed the issue of non-reusability of community division results with a hierarchical mapping method, reducing the time required for community division.

Innovations and methodological developments in community detection have addressed challenges such as network dynamics, complexity, and the integration of social attributes, advancing the field's boundaries and application impacts. For example, Yazdanparast et al. [10] proposed the Fast Fuzzy Modularity Maximization method and its multi-cycle variant, effectively identifying network communities. Yuan et al. [11] transformed the modularity maximization problem into a continuous non-convex optimization problem with an efficient method based on modularity. Liu et al. [12] proposed an overlapping community detection algorithm that refines communities after network coarsening based on local overlapping modularity. Further, Guo et al. [13] introduced a new algorithm based on Local Modularity Density, optimizing community quality through a two-stage process of core region detection and local community expansion. Moradi et al. [14] proposed the multi-objective optimization method MOGGA+, combining multi-objective genetic algorithms and local search strategies to adaptively identify community structures in the network. Zhuo et al. [15] obtained core communities through non-negative matrix factorization and adjusted the degree of community overlap through expansion and contraction processes. Shang et al. [16] proposed the FCCNI algorithm, which effectively enhances the accuracy of overlapping community detection by integrating internal and external connections, label correction based on node intimacy, and a comprehensive consideration of structure and attributes.

3 Algorithm Design

3.1 Methodology for the Quantification of Social Relations

In the exploration of opportunistic networks, analyzing the social relationships between nodes is crucial. This paper quantifies these relationships using three primary metrics: the number of encounters between nodes, the total duration of encounters, and the energy consumed during message transmission using the Prophet routing algorithm. The frequency and duration of encounters assess the intensity of social interactions, reflecting the strength of social ties. Energy consumption serves as an indicator of communication costs, encompassing not just the depletion of physical resources but also the social costs of information transmission. For instance, nodes with high energy consumption might indicate their role as key information relays or bridges within communities.

Given the original dataset X_i (where i represents different metrics), which includes indicators such as the number of encounters between nodes, total encounter duration, and energy consumption. The normalized value $x_i \in X_i$ for each metric $x_{norm,i}$ can be calculated using the following formula:

$$x_{norm,i} = \frac{x_i - min(X_i)}{max(X_i) - min(X_i)} \tag{1}$$

where $min(X_i)$ and $max(X_i)$ represent the minimum and maximum values in the dataset, respectively. Formula (1) converts the original data into a range between 0 and 1, making different metrics comparable. This allows us to quantify each metric within a unified framework, ensuring fairness and accuracy in the analysis.

The construction of the weighted graph is based on the normalized social interaction metrics, including the number of encounters, total encounter duration, and energy consumption, to intuitively represent the interaction characteristics between nodes. The weight of an edge can be calculated using the following formula:

$$w = w_1 x_{norm,1} + w_2 x_{norm,2} + w_3 x_{norm,3} \tag{2}$$

In this weighted graph, each node represents an individual in the network, and the weight of the edges directly reflects the interaction intensity between these individuals.

3.2 Initial Community Construction

The analysis of the preprocessed weighted graph aims to identify central nodes using two key metrics: degree centrality and closeness centrality. Degree centrality measures a node's direct connections with other nodes, while closeness centrality reflects the average distance between a node and all other nodes in the graph. By combining these two metrics, the algorithm can accurately locate central nodes within communities.

The initial community construction strategy employs a method based on node centrality metrics. This method selects the top $a\%$ nodes as central nodes by setting a threshold a, ranking all nodes based on their degree centrality and closeness centrality. Subsequently, for each central node, a step is performed where the node is combined with its neighboring node with the highest connection weight to form an initial small-scale community. Other nodes that are not selected as central nodes each form an independent community. This process constructs the initial community structure by merging central nodes with their strongest connected neighboring nodes and treating unselected nodes as independent communities.

3.3 Identification of Overlapping Nodes

Overlapping nodes, which may belong to multiple communities, are identified by calculating the weighted community affiliation and betweenness centrality. This calculation step is crucial for accurately identifying overlapping community structures, allowing nodes to simultaneously exist in multiple communities, reflecting the more subtle phenomenon of community overlap in complex networks.

For each node n in the network, its weighted community affiliation CA(n) can be represented as:

$$CA(n) = \{C_i : A_i\} \tag{3}$$

where C_i represents the community, and A_i is the affiliation degree of node n to community C_i. The calculation method is as follows:

$$A_i = \sum_{v \in N(n) \cap C_i} w(n, v) + \alpha \times \sum_{u \in NN(n) \cap C_i} w(n, u) \tag{4}$$

Here, $N(n)$ and $NN(n)$ represent the direct neighbors and second-order neighbors of node n, respectively. $w(n, v)$ and $w(n, u)$ denote the connection weights between node n and its direct neighbor v as well as its second-order neighbor u, respectively. α represents the weight ratio used when considering second-order neighbors. Finally, the community affiliation degree of each node is normalized as follows:

$$A_i^{norm} = \frac{A_i}{\sum_{C_k} A_k} \tag{5}$$

Where C_k represents all communities in the network, ensuring that the comparison of affiliation degrees is based on a unified standard.

Combining the weighted community affiliation with betweenness centrality allows for an in-depth analysis and identification of overlapping nodes. This approach considers both the strength of the association between nodes and communities and the strategic position of nodes within the network structure. A node identified as an overlapping node must meet two criteria: firstly, its weighted community affiliation must exceed a preset threshold, indicating significant links to multiple communities; secondly, its betweenness centrality must rank in the top 20% of all nodes, highlighting its critical role in connecting different communities within the network. This strategy ensures that only nodes with strong associations to multiple communities and key positions in the network structure are accurately identified as overlapping nodes. These nodes play a crucial bridging role, facilitating information flow between communities and maintaining the overall connectivity and stability of the network.

3.4 CG-MONCD Algorithm

The algorithm presented in this paper is specifically designed to identify and analyze overlapping and nested community structures in opportunistic networks. The CG-MONCD algorithm is implemented through the following steps:

Step 1: Construct a weighted graph using three quantified metrics: the number of encounters between nodes, the total encounter duration, and the energy consumption under the Prophet routing algorithm. Central nodes are selected based on the top a% rankings of degree centrality and closeness centrality. These nodes are then combined with their most strongly connected neighboring nodes to form communities, while unselected nodes form individual communities. Calculate the modularity of the initial community structure to provide a baseline for community optimization.

Step 2: Calculate each node's community modularity. If moving a node to a neighboring community increases modularity, execute the move. Continue until no further improvements are possible.

Step 3: Treat communities as super-nodes, creating a new network with weighted edges based on the original inter-community edges. Assess modularity to evaluate community merging.

Step 4: Continuously optimize community division and merging until modularity does not improve, aiming to form larger community structures.

Step 5: Identify nodes that belong to multiple communities by calculating weighted community affiliation and betweenness centrality. Directly select nodes with weighted community affiliation exceeding a predetermined threshold and high betweenness centrality, identifying them as important overlapping nodes. Perform further internal community division for each community, excluding divisions with low modularity.

The CG-MONCD algorithm employs hierarchical clustering to effectively uncover complex social structures within networks (Fig. 1).

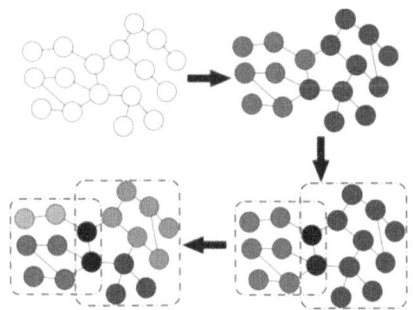

Fig. 1. Community Detection Process Illustration.

4 Experimental Results and Analysis

4.1 Simulation Environment Configuration

The experiments in this paper were conducted using the open-source simulation tool ONE (Opportunistic Network Environment), developed by the Nokia Research Center in Finland. The simulation data include node information, the number of encounters, the average duration of encounters, and the energy consumption of nodes. These data were set and collected in the ONE 1.6.0 opportunistic network simulation environment. The main simulation parameters are set as follows (Table 1):

Table 1. Simulation Experiment Parameters.

Simulation Parameters	Value
Scenario.endTime	432000
Group.workDayLength	36000
Group.router	ProphetRouter
Group.speed	0.5, 1.5
Group1.nrofHosts	6
Group2.nrofHosts	94
Events1.interval	50,70
Group.movementModel	WorkingDayMovement

Simulation ran for a total of 6 days, divided into 12-h time slices, each containing 100 nodes. The encounters and communications between node pairs within each time slice were considered as social relationship edges between the node pairs, named after the node pairs. The node mobility model used was WorkingDayMovement. For each time slice, the number of encounters, encounter duration, and energy consumption of node pairs were recorded, assigning probability values to the social relationship edges between nodes and forming a weighted graph for social relationships in each time slice.

4.2 Parameter Setting Experiments

Experiments calculate the weighted degree and closeness centrality of all nodes to determine their importance, selecting central nodes based on top 5%, 10%, 15%, and 20% thresholds. Within the SIR model, the influence of these nodes on disease spread is tested with an infection probability of 0.1, 30 simulation steps, and central nodes as the initial infection source. Each simulation is repeated 100 times to calculate the average infections, with control experiments using randomly selected nodes for comparison.

Figure 2 shows that nodes selected based on centrality metrics result in higher average infection numbers in disease spread simulations compared to randomly selected nodes. This finding underscores the significant role of central nodes in network propagation processes.

To explore the impact of different weighted community affiliation thresholds on network community structures and modularity optimization, we systematically adjusted the thresholds and evaluated their effects. The results, shown in Fig. 3, indicate that a threshold of 0.5 consistently improved modularity, achieving a score of 0.62 in the 36-h dataset. Therefore, the 0.5 threshold is considered a balanced choice, effectively enhancing internal community cohesiveness and external distinction.

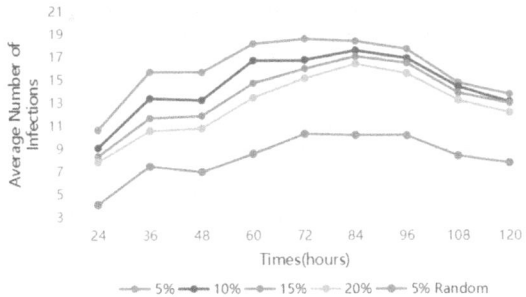

Fig. 2. Simulation of the Impact of Different Proportions of Central Nodes in Disease Spread.

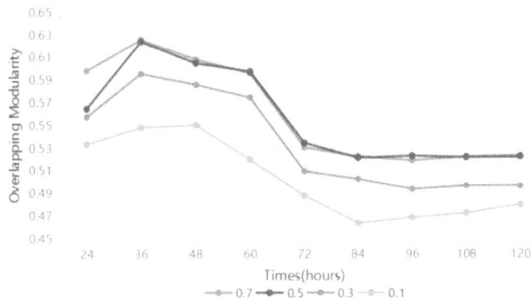

Fig. 3. The Impact of Weighted Community Affiliation Threshold on Overlapping Modularity Optimization.

4.3 Algorithm Comparison and Analysis

To compare the ability of different algorithms in identifying changes in network community structure over time slices, we evaluated the performance of the algorithms using two metrics: overlapping modularity and intra-community edge density. The CPM (Clique Percolation Method) algorithm is a community detection method based on the gradual diffusion of cliques. The LFM (Local Fitness Method) algorithm is based on locally optimizing the community "fitness" function.

Figure 4 shows the variation in overlapping modularity of the CG-MONCD, CPM, and LFM algorithms over time slices. The CG-MONCD algorithm generally exhibits higher modularity, indicating its strong community detection capability. In contrast, the performance of CPM and LFM is unstable, with their overlapping modularity significantly decreasing at certain time points.

Overall, the CG-MONCD algorithm demonstrates robust performance, particularly showing significant advantages in specific time slices. This reflects the CG-MONCD algorithm's ability to adapt to the dynamic changes of the network and more accurately partition communities.

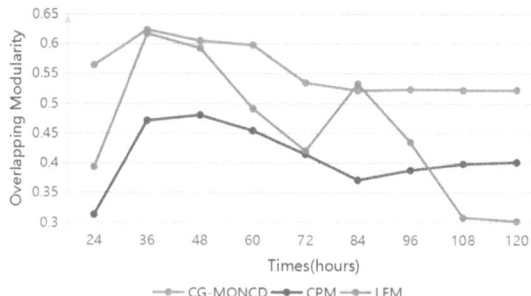

Fig. 4. Comparative Analysis of Overlapping Modularity.

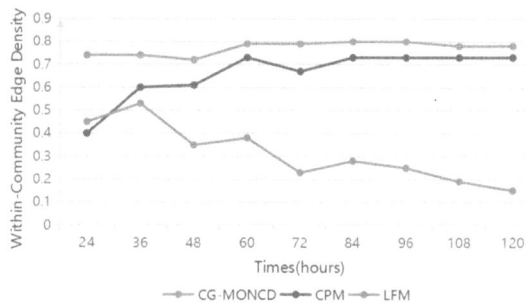

Fig. 5. Comparative Analysis of Intra-Community Edge Density.

Figure 5 shows the trend of intra-community edge density over time slices, measuring the proportion of connections within the same community. The CG-MONCD algorithm maintains a stable community structure with an intra-community edge density around 0.7, while the CPM and LFM algorithms show a decline over time.

4.4 Nested Modularity Analysis

Nested Modularity is a metric used to measure the nestedness of community structures in a network, specifically designed for analyzing complex networks with hierarchical community structures. This metric evaluates whether there are further subdivided sub-communities within communities in the network and calculates the modularity of the sub-community structures within each primary community. This quantifies the hierarchical organizational complexity of the network.

As shown in Fig. 6, the CG-MONCD algorithm detects a high percentage of nested communities in most time slices, peaking at 48 and 72 slices. This indicates strong community structure characteristics during these periods. Figure 7 shows the variation of nested modularity over time, remaining high except for a decline between the 60 and 84 time slices. This means the community structure is evident in most time slices, and the algorithm stably detects it. The analysis demonstrates the algorithm's effectiveness in identifying nested communities within the network.

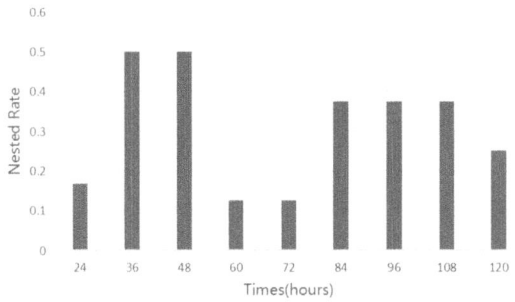

Fig. 6. Nested Community Detection Rate Across Different Time Slices.

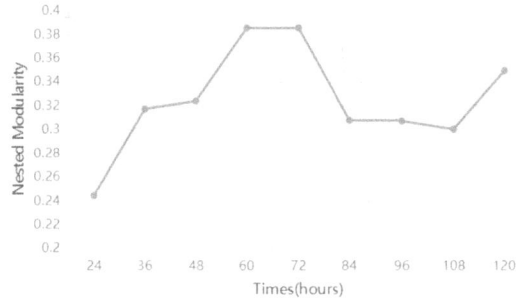

Fig. 7. Nested Modularity Across Different Time Slices.

5 Conclusion

This paper introduces a Centrality-Guided Modularity Optimization algorithm for Overlapping and Nested Community Detection (CG-MONCD), designed to identify overlapping and nested community structures in opportunistic networks. By constructing a weighted graph model based on the number of encounters, total encounter duration, and energy consumption, this algorithm accurately describes and effectively identifies community structures within the network. Experimental results show that CG-MONCD surpasses existing algorithms in community detection, modularity optimization, and intra-community edge density maintenance; future work will focus on optimizing computational efficiency and exploring applications in dynamic networks.

Acknowledgments. This work was supported by the National Natural Science Foundation of China under Grants 62061036; the University Youth Science and Technology Talent Development Project (Innovation Group Development Plan) of Inner Mongolia A. R. of China under Grants NMGIRT2318; the Self-Open Project of Engineering Research Center of Ecological Big Data, Ministry of Education; the China Scholarship Council.

Disclosure of Interests. The authors declare that they have no known competing financial interests or personal relationships that could have appeared to influence the work reported in this paper.

References

1. Xiong, Y., Sun, L., Niu, J., et al.: 机会网络 [Opportunistic networks]. 软件学报 [J. Softw.] **20**(01), 124–137 (2009). (in Chinese)
2. Fortunato, S., Newman, M.E.J.: 20 years of network community detection. Nat. Phys. **18**(8), 848–850 (2022)
3. Malik, A.: A social relationship-based energy efficient routing scheme for opportunistic internet of things. ICT Express **9**(4), 697–705 (2023)
4. Cui, Y., Li, P., Liu, H., et al.: 基于校园机会网络的协作小组缓存调度策略 [Cooperative group caching scheduling strategy based on campus opportunistic networks]. 电子学报 [J. Electron.] **49**(12), 2399–2406 (2021). (in Chinese)
5. Gou, F., Wu, J.: Novel data transmission technology based on complex IoT system in opportunistic social networks. Peer-to-Peer Netw. Appl. **16**(2), 571–588 (2023)
6. Li, L., Gou, F., Wu, J.: Modified data delivery strategy based on stochastic block model and community detection in opportunistic social networks. Wirel. Commun. Mob. Comput. **2022**, 1–16 (2022)
7. Ma, X., Ouyang, Z., Bai, L., et al.: An overlapping community detection algorithm for opportunistic networks. In: 2014 IEEE Computers, Communications and IT Applications Conference, pp. 110–115. IEEE (2014)
8. Zhang, Y., Han, Y., Li, J., et al.: Community detection using maximum connection probability in opportunistic network. In: 2013 4th International Conference on Intelligent Systems, Modelling and Simulation, pp. 475–480. IEEE (2013)
9. Xu, G., Wang, X., Shi, Y., et al.: Community detection in opportunistic networks based on hierarchical mapping. In: 2019 IEEE 23rd International Conference on Computer Supported Cooperative Work in Design (CSCWD), pp. 243–248. IEEE (2019)
10. Yazdanparast, S., Havens, T.C., Jamalabdollahi, M.: Soft overlapping community detection in large-scale networks via fast fuzzy modularity maximization. IEEE Trans. Fuzzy Syst. **29**(6), 1533–1543 (2020)
11. Yuan, Q., Liu, B.: Community detection via an efficient nonconvex optimization approach based on modularity. Comput. Stat. Data Anal. **157**, 107163 (2021)
12. Liu, Z., Xiang, B., Guo, W., et al.: Overlapping community detection algorithm based on coarsening and local overlapping modularity. IEEE Access **7**, 57943–57955 (2019)
13. Guo, K., Huang, X., Wu, L., et al.: Local community detection algorithm based on local modularity density. Appl. Intell. **52**(2), 1238–1253 (2022)
14. Moradi, M., Mohammadi, K., Moradi, P.: A multi-objective optimization method for community detection using a novel heuristic search (2024)

15. Zhuo, Z., Chen, B., Yu, S., et al.: Overlapping community detection using expansion with contraction. Neurocomputing **565**, 126989 (2024)
16. Shang, R., Wang, S., Zhang, W., et al.: Evolutionary multi-objective overlapping community detection based on fusion of internal and external connectivity and correction of node intimacy. Appl. Soft Comput. **154**, 111414 (2024)

Weakly Supervised Video Anomaly Detection Method Based on Multi-scale Feature Fusion and Contrastive Loss

Kun Yang, Zhiming Luo$^{(\boxtimes)}$, and Shaozi Li

Xiamen University, Xiamen 361005, China
zhiming.luo@xmu.edu.cn

Abstract. Weakly supervised video anomaly detection plays a pivotal role in widely deployed surveillance systems. Most existing methods are based on the multi-instance learning paradigm, determining the predicted label of a video based on segments with higher prediction scores. During training, the model predominantly focuses on the segment with the highest anomaly score or the top-k highest-scored segments, neglecting the other segments. This bias towards certain segment features during training results in missed and false detections of anomaly segments, subsequently impacting the performance of video anomaly detection. In this paper, we introduce a contrastive loss strategy to uncover easily overlooked normal and abnormal segments, enhancing the distinction between normal and abnormal segments through contrastive loss. Additionally, we propose a multi-scale feature fusion approach to learn features from different scales of videos and integrate them into a more comprehensive feature representation to accommodate the diversity of anomaly events. Experimental results on the UCF-Crime and XD-Violence datasets validate the efficacy of our proposed method.

Keywords: Video anomaly detection · Weakly supervised · Contrastive loss · Multi-scale feature fusion

1 Introduction

Video anomaly detection (VAD) [11,14] is a critical task in surveillance video analysis, which can be used to detect abnormal events that may endanger public safety. With the rapid development of informatization, the application of surveillance systems has become increasingly widespread, and video anomaly detection technology has become a hot topic in the field of computer vision.

Video anomaly detection currently mainly consists of two approaches: unsupervised and weakly supervised. Unsupervised video anomaly detection trains models using only normal data and considers data deviating from the normal pattern as anomalies [12]. However, these methods often lead to overfitting due to the lack of anomaly information during training. Weakly supervised methods, with significant detection performance at low annotation costs, have gained

H. Sun et al. (Eds.): ChineseCSCW 2024, CCIS 2343, pp. 32–46, 2025.
https://doi.org/10.1007/978-981-96-2373-0_3

increasing attention. Most existing weakly supervised methods are based on the multiple-instance learning paradigm. Sultani et al. [15] modeled video anomaly detection as a multiple instance learning task and used the highest score of each video bag as the video's anomaly score. Wan et al. [18] further selected the average of the top scores after sorting the scores in each video bag as the video's anomaly score. Tian et al. [16] proposed a ranking loss based on the magnitude of video features and selected the top-k segment features for ranking. However, these methods have limitations: anomalies in videos are rare and may be masked by a large number of normal video frames; the number of anomalies in videos is not fixed, and the ranking loss tends to select some segments with the highest anomaly scores, leading to the model favoring specific anomaly segments and ignoring others. This results in insufficient learning of the differences between anomalous and normal segments, causing missed detections and false alarms, thereby limiting overall anomaly detection performance.

To overcome these issues, we propose a contrastive loss strategy, which encourages the model to identify abnormal segments that are easily overlooked and normal segments that are easily misclassified in videos. By increasing the distinctiveness between abnormal and normal segments through contrastive loss, the model learns more discriminative feature representations. Additionally, we introduce a class activation module to differentiate between normal and abnormal videos using different activation weights. Furthermore, recognizing the importance of temporal information in video anomaly detection, we design a multi-scale feature fusion module to comprehensively learn temporal feature representations, thereby enhancing the accuracy and robustness of anomaly detection.

In summary, our main contributions are as follows:

(1) We propose a Multi-scale Feature Fusion Module, which can learn the temporal information in the video by fusing the video features of different scales, so as to capture the feature representation of the video in more detail.
(2) To enhance the distinction between normal and abnormal video segments, we propose a Contrastive Loss Strategy, which mines segments that are easily overlooked or misdirected, prompting the model to learn more discriminative feature representations.
(3) To validate our method, we conducted experiments on two benchmark datasets, UCF-Crime and XD-Violence, and extensive experimental results showed the effectiveness of our method.

2   Related Work

2.1   Unsupervised Video Anomaly Detection

Unsupervised video anomaly detection refers to training the model solely on normal samples. It captures patterns of normal behavior and identifies deviations from these patterns as anomalies [1,10]. Wang et al. [19] used Variational Autoencoders (VAE) to model normal videos, proposing a stacked fully connected Variational Autoencoder and skip-connection Convolutional VAE to detect anomalies in video data. Liu et al. [8] designed an object-centric scene inference network to learn both global scene regularities and object-specific normal patterns, using a scene memory network for video frame reconstruction. Cheng et al. [5] introduced an unsupervised spatiotemporal graph convolutional network-enhanced frame prediction model.

2.2   Weakly Supervised Video Anomaly Detection

Weakly supervised video anomaly detection methods solely utilize readily available video-level labels to enhance the detection performance of anomaly events [6,12,15,16,22]. Zhang et al. [26] defined an internal loss for multi-instance learning to constrain the function space of weakly supervised problems, which considers the lowest and highest anomaly instance scores within each bag. Zhong et al. [27] regarded the anomaly behavior detection task under weakly supervised conditions as a supervised learning task under noisy labels and designed a graph convolutional network to correct noisy labels. Lv et al. [9] introduced unbiased multi-instance learning aimed at learning ambiguous segments to obtain unbiased anomaly features, thereby improving the method of multi-instance learning.

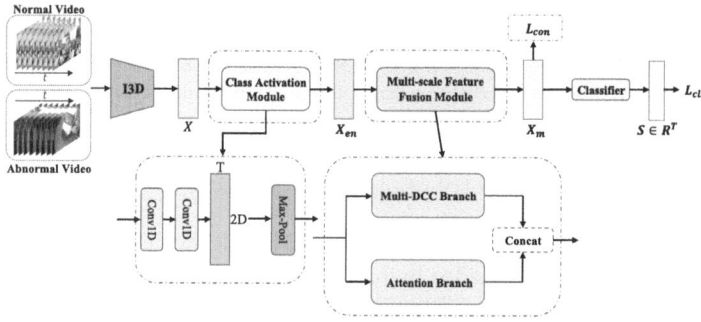

Fig. 1. The overall architecture of the proposed method.

3   Method

3.1   Overall Architecture

As illustrated in Fig. 1, our method consists of the Class Activation Module, Multi-Scale Feature Fusion Module, and Contrastive Loss. We employ a weakly supervised approach based on multiple instance learning, training the model using both normal videos and videos containing anomalies. Initially, video segment features X are extracted using the I3D network model. Subsequently, the Class Activation Module produces class activation features X_{en} based on varying activation weights. Following this, the Multi-Scale Feature Fusion Module generates features X_m that capture multi-scale temporal information. Finally, the classifier produces video segment scores S.

3.2   Class Activation Module

In weakly supervised video anomaly detection, it's crucial to learn discriminative features between normal and abnormal classes using video-level labels. Typically, we first extract video segment features using an I3D model pre-trained on the Kinetics-400 dataset [3]. However, since the dataset mainly focuses on temporal and spatial features of actions, it performs poorly in capturing representative normal and abnormal information, which is different from the objectives of video anomaly detection tasks. To address this, we introduce a class activation module to extract different video features based on activation weights from different domains. Specifically, as illustrated in Fig. 1, the class activation module consists of two convolutional layers and a max-pooling layer. For the extracted video features $X \in R^{T \times d}$, they are first mapped to the same feature space through convolutional layers,

$$X' = Conv\text{-}1(X), \tag{1}$$

then, the feature dimension is doubled using convolutional layers to obtain $X'' \in R^{T \times 2D}$,

$$X'' = Conv\text{-}2(X'), \tag{2}$$

finally, the class activation features are obtained through a max-pooling layer. Specifically, for the obtained 2D-dimensional features, max-pooling is performed over the ranges $0 : D$ and $D : 2D$ to yield the class activation module output feature X_{en},

$$X_{en} = max[X''_{0:D}, X''_{D:2D}]. \tag{3}$$

3.3   Multi-Scale Feature Fusion Module

Given the uncertainty in the locations, duration, and quantity of abnormal events in abnormal videos, as well as their correlation with scenes, we introduce a multi-scale feature fusion module. This module learns features at different scales and leverages the relationships between different segments to obtain more representative feature representations. As shown in Fig. 1, the module primarily consists of a Multi-Scale Dilated Causal Convolution Branch(Multi-DCC Branch), designed to extract time features at various scales, and an Attention Branch, aimed at capturing the relationships between video segments and the overall video duration to model scene information.

As shown in Fig. 3, the multi-scale dilated causal convolution branch consists of three dilated causal convolutions with different dilation rates. Figure 2a illustrates the causal convolution [17] with a kernel size of 2. In this convolution, the feature at a given time step in the next layer depends only on the current time step and previous time steps of the upper layer, effectively capturing the temporal dependencies in videos without introducing future noise information. Dilated convolution [23] introduces a dilation rate parameter based on traditional convolution operations. This allows for the expansion of the convolutional kernel's

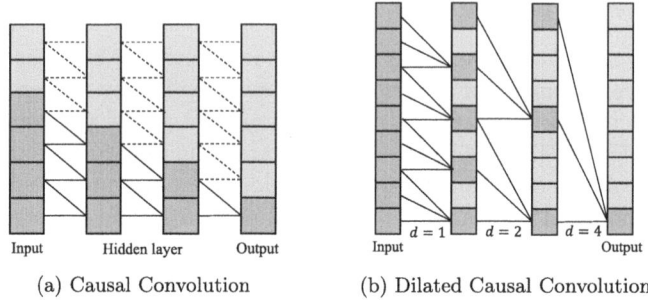

(a) Causal Convolution   (b) Dilated Causal Convolution

Fig. 2. Causal Convolution and Dilated Causal Convolution Diagrams

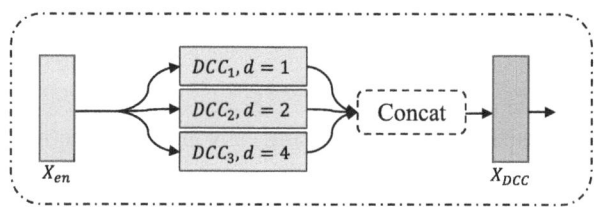

Fig. 3. Diagram of the Multi-Scale Dilated Causal Convolution branch

receptive field without increasing its size, enabling the network to capture features at different scales. Figure 2b shows the dilated causal convolution with a kernel size of 3, where the dilation factors d are 1, 2, and 4. The computation process of the multi-scale dilated causal branch is as follows:

$$X_{DCC} = \text{Concat}(DCC_1(X), DCC_2(X), DCC_3(X)), \qquad (4)$$

where $DCC_i, i \in 1, 2, 3$ represents the three layers of Dilated Causal Convolution, and Concat denotes concatenation along the feature dimension.

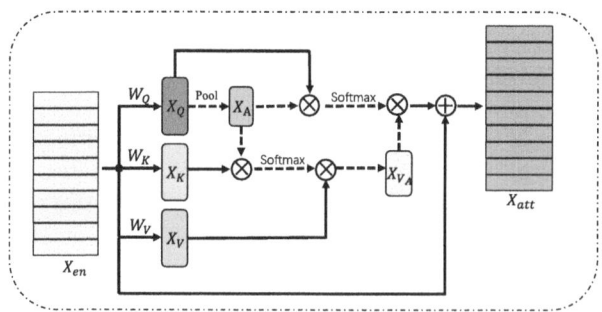

Fig. 4. Attention Branch Diagram

To capture the global temporal relationships between video segments, our method employs an attention branch, as illustrated in Fig. 4. For the input features X, we first obtain the query vector X_Q, the key vector X_K, and the value vector X_V,

$$X_Q = W_Q X, X_K = W_K X, X_V = W_V X, \tag{5}$$

then, the query X_Q is pooled to obtain X_A,

$$X_A = Pool(X_Q). \tag{6}$$

Then, X_A is used as the query to compute attention with X_K and X_V,

$$X_{V_A} = Softmax(\frac{X_A X_K^T}{\sqrt{d}})V, \tag{7}$$

where d represents the scaling factor, then X_Q serves as the query, X_A as the key vector, and X_{V_A} as the value vector to compute attention,

$$Attention(X_Q, X_A, X_{V_A}) = Softmax(\frac{X_Q X_A^T}{\sqrt{d}})X_{V_A}. \tag{8}$$

The overall computation process for this branch is represented as:

$$X_{att} = X + Softmax(\frac{X_Q X_A^T}{\sqrt{d}})Softmax(\frac{X_A X_K^T}{\sqrt{d}})V. \tag{9}$$

Through the multi-scale feature fusion module, we obtain the video feature representation X_m that learns time information at different scales,

$$X_m = Concat(X_{DCC}, X_{att}). \tag{10}$$

3.4   Contrastive Loss Strategy

To enhance the distinction between normal and abnormal video segments, we propose a contrastive loss strategy. Initially, we identify the normal and abnormal segments within the video, as illustrated in Fig. 5, let V^n denote the normal video with its prediction score as S^n, and V^a represent the abnormal video with its score as S^a. Initially, based on the anomaly scores, we select the top k highest scoring segments from S^n as hard-to-distinguish normal segments, denoted as V_{HN}^n, and the bottom k lowest scoring segments from S^n as easy-to-distinguish normal segments, denoted as V_{EN}^n. Additionally, we choose the top k highest scoring segments from S^a as easy-to-distinguish abnormal segments, denoted as V_{EA}^a.

When selecting hard-to-distinguish abnormal segments, as illustrated in Fig. 5, we first binarize the anomaly scores S^a of the abnormal video. We then filter out missed abnormal segments using a sliding window. Based on the continuity of abnormal events, if most segments within the window are abnormal, we label the segments marked as normal as potential missed abnormal segments.

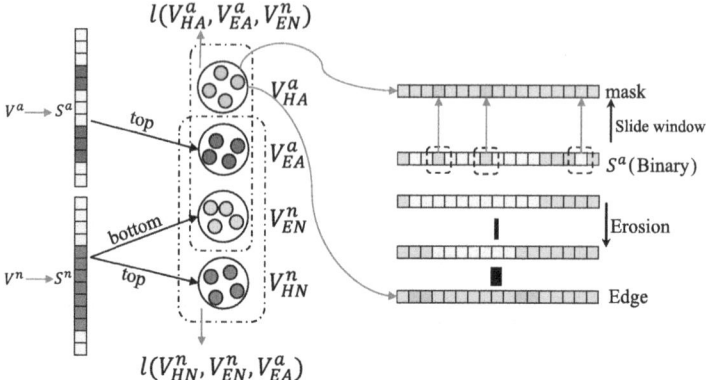

Fig. 5. Contrastive Loss Segment Selection Schematic

As the sliding window traverses the entire video, we obtain a mask where the recorded segments represent the missed abnormal segments. For segments at the boundaries, we apply morphological erosion operations. Using various erosion factors, we identify the difference between the eroded sequence and the original sequence as boundary segments. These boundary segments, along with the segments recorded from the sliding window operation, are considered hard-to-separate abnormal segments and denoted as V_{HA}^a.

The contrastive loss is applied to two combinations, as depicted within the dashed box in Fig. 5. In the first combination, the contrastive loss aims to increase the dissimilarity between easy-to-distinguish normal segments and hard-to-distinguish abnormal segments, as well as easy-to-distinguish abnormal segments. In the second combination, the contrastive loss is utilized to widen the dissimilarity between easy-to-distinguish abnormal segments and hard-to-distinguish normal segments, along with easy-to-distinguish normal segments. The contrastive loss defined between V_{HA}^a, V_{EA}^a, and V_{EN}^n is:

$$l(V_{HA}^a, V_{EA}^a, V_{EN}^n) = \sum_{x_i \in V_{HA}^a, x_j \in V_{EA}^a} log \frac{exp(x_i^T \cdot x_j/\tau)}{exp(x_i^T \cdot x_j/\tau) + \sum_{x \in V_{EN}^n} exp(x_i^T \cdot x/\tau)},$$
(11)

where τ is the temperature coefficient. Similarly, the contrastive loss between V_{HN}^n, V_{EN}^n, and V_{EA}^a is:

$$l(V_{HN}^n, V_{EN}^n, V_{EA}^a) = \sum_{x_i \in V_{HN}^n, x_j \in V_{EN}^n} log \frac{exp(x_i^T \cdot x_j/\tau)}{exp(x_i^T \cdot x_j/\tau) + \sum_{x \in V_{EA}^a} exp(x_i^T \cdot x/\tau)}.$$
(12)

The overall contrastive loss is defined as:

$$L_{con} = l(V_{HA}^a, V_{EA}^a, V_{EN}^n) + l(V_{HN}^n, V_{EN}^n, V_{EA}^a).$$
(13)

3.5   Loss Functions

At the video level, our method employs binary cross-entropy loss using video-level labels for supervision. For a video V with predicted scores $S = s_1, ...s_T$, we define its anomaly score $\hat{y}$ as the average score of the top N segments. The true label is denoted by y, where 0 represents normal and 1 represents an anomaly. The video classification loss is defined as:

$$L_{cls} = -\frac{1}{B} \sum_{i=1}^{B} (y_i log(\hat{y}_i) + (1 - y_i)log(1 - \hat{y}_i)), \qquad (14)$$

where B represents the batch size. Additionally, due to the scarcity of abnormal events in videos and considering the sparsity of abnormal segments, we add sparse regularization loss to the scores of abnormal videos. For the scores of segments in the abnormal video, denoted as $S^a = s_1^a, s_2^a, ...s_T^a$, the sparse loss $L_{sparsity}$ is defined as:

$$L_{sparsity} = \sum_{i}^{T} s_i^a. \qquad (15)$$

Moreover, we introduce a smooth loss [15] to enhance the temporal smoothness of anomaly scores between adjacent video segments. The smooth loss L_{smooth} is defined as:

$$L_{smooth} = \sum_{i}^{T-1} (s_i^a - s_{i+1}^a)^2. \qquad (16)$$

Overall, combining the contrastive loss, the loss function for our proposed method is as follows:

$$L = L_{cls} + L_{con} + \lambda_1 L_{sparsity} + \lambda_2 L_{smooth}. \qquad (17)$$

4   Experiments

4.1   Datasets and Evaluation Metrics

Datasets. Similar to previous work [16, 20], we used two weakly supervised anomaly detection benchmark datasets, XD-Violence [21] and UCF-Crime [15], for experiments and analysis. **UCF-Crime** is a large-scale real-world video anomaly detection dataset, comprising 128 h of video data collected from 1900 long untrimmed real-world surveillance videos. The training set consists of 800 normal videos and 810 anomaly videos, while the test set includes 150 normal videos and 140 anomaly videos, covering 13 types of anomalies. **XD-Violence** is a video dataset designed for violence detection, collected from various sources including movies and TV shows. It contains 4754 untrimmed videos totaling 217 h, covering six types of violence. The training set comprises 3954 videos, while the test set consists of 500 violent videos and 300 non-violent videos.

Evaluation Metrics. Following previous methods [16, 20], we use the area under the receiver operating characteristic curve (AUC) to evaluate the effectiveness of our method on the UCF-Crime dataset. Meanwhile, we adapt Average Precision (AP) to assess the performance of our method on the XD-Violence.

4.2   Implementation Details

Our method is implemented based on the PyTorch framework and trained on a single NVIDIA RTX A4000 GPU. For fair comparison in experiments, our method utilizes an I3D network model pre-trained on the Kinetics-400 dataset to extract video segment features, with each segment consisting of 16 frames. During the training phase, each video is divided into 200 segments with a batch size set to 128. We use the Adam optimizer [7] for optimization with an initial learning rate of 0.0001 and weight decay of 0.00005; the number of epochs is set to 3000. In the loss function, the weights λ_1 and λ_2 are set to $8e-5$ each. For the dilated causal convolution, dilation factors are set to 1, 2, and 4 respectively; the number of selected video segments k is 14; the sliding window size is 10 with a scaling factor of 0.8. The classifier employs a Multi-Layer Perceptron (MLP) structure with units of 512 and 128 respectively, followed by ReLU activation functions and Dropout regularization after each layer, and a Sigmoid function is used in the last layer to obtain the anomaly scores for video clips.

Table 1. Comparison of different methods on the UCF-Crime dataset.

Methods	Feature	AUC(%)
MIST [6]	I3D(RGB)	82.30
RTFM [16]	I3D(RGB)	84.30
Wu *et al.* [20]	I3D(RGB)	84.89
WSTR [25]	I3D(RGB)	83.17
BN-SVP [13]	I3D(RGB)	83.39
WAGCN [2]	I3D(RGB)	84.67
Pu *et al.* [12]	I3D(RGB)	85.12
BE-WSVAD [22]	I3D(RGB)	84.05
TEVAD [4]	I3D(RGB)	84.90
ours	I3D(RGB)	**85.28**

Table 2. Comparison of different methods on the XD-Violence dataset.

Methods	Feature	AP(%)
Sultani *et al.* [15]	I3D(RGB)	73.20
HL-Net [21]	I3D(RGB)	73.67
Wu *et al.* [20]	I3D(RGB)	75.90
RTFM [16]	I3D(RGB)	77.81
Pu *et al.* [12]	I3D(RGB)	80.72
Zhang *et al.* [24]	I3D(RGB)	78.74
BE-WSVAD [22]	I3D(RGB)	78.08
TEVAD [4]	I3D(RGB)	79.80
ours	I3D(RGB)	**83.65**

4.3   Comparison with Other Methods

In this section, we present the experimental results of our method on two widely used benchmark datasets compared with other methods. For a fair comparison, all compared methods are based on weakly supervised learning for video anomaly detection and utilize a pre-trained I3D model as the feature extraction network.

Results on UCF-Crime. Table 1 shows the AUC score of the method in this chapter and other methods on the UCF-Crime dataset, as shown in the table, our method achieves the highest AUC score of 85.28%, which is better than the methods of other models, which indicates the effectiveness of our proposed method. Compared with WAGCN [2], which is a graph convolution-based approach, we achieve a 0.61% improvement; Our method improves by 0.98% when compared to the RTFM [16] method, which uses only a small number of video segments features for comparison.

Results on XD-Violence. Table 2 shows the results of the average precision (AP) of our method compared to other methods on the XD-Violence dataset, and it can be seen from the results in the table that our method achieves the highest AP score of 83.65% compared to the weakly supervised-based video anomaly detection method, which is better than all other comparison methods, indicating the effectiveness of our method for detection performance improvement. Compared to RTFM [16], our method improves AP by 5.84%. Compared with MIL based method by Pu et al. [12], we achieve a 2.93% improvement.

Table 3. Ablation studies on Class Activation Module(CAM) and Multi-scale Feature Fusion Module(MFM) components.

CAM	MFM		XD-Violence(AP%)	UCF-Crime(AUC%)
	Multi-DCC	Attention		
-	-	-	73.32	80.55
✓	-	-	76.48	80.91
-	✓	✓	80.98	83.28
✓	✓	-	80.94	82.45
✓	-	✓	81.58	83.21
✓	✓	✓	**83.65**	**85.28**

4.4 Ablation Studies

Effectiveness of Different Components. Table 3 presents the results of ablation experiments on different components of our method. The results indicate that the model performance is improved by incorporating different components. When only the Class Activation Module is added, the AP of XD-Violence and the AUC of UCF-Crime increase by 3.16% and 0.36%, respectively, demonstrating the effectiveness of the class activation module in improving detection accuracy. When only the multi-scale feature fusion module is added, the AP of XD-Violence increases by 7.66% and the AUC of UCF-Crime increases by 2.73%, indicating the effectiveness of feature fusion at different scales. By adding both the class activation module and the multi-scale feature fusion module simultaneously, the best results are achieved on XD-Violence and UCF-Crime, with improvements in AP and AUC by 10.33% and 5.53%, respectively. This highlights that the combination of these two modules brings the greatest performance enhancement to the model.

Meanwhile, we conduct ablation experiments on the multi-scale feature fusion module and observe that using either the multi-scale causal convolution branch or the attention branch alone resulted in performance improvements. This indicates the effectiveness of learning local multi-scale temporal features to capture local variations within video segments and modeling global temporal features of video scenes. Furthermore, when both branches were used simultaneously, the model's performance was further enhanced, suggesting that the information learned from the two branches can complement each other, thereby improving the model's ability to detect anomalous events. Ablation experiments on different modules demonstrate the effectiveness of our proposed method.

Table 4. Ablation studies on Losses.

L_{cls}	L_{con}	$L_{sparsity}$	L_{smooth}	XD-Violence(AP%)	UCF-Crime(AUC%)
✓	-	-	-	80.76	81.17
✓	✓	-	-	82.43	84.12
✓	-	✓	✓	81.33	82.30
✓	✓	✓	✓	**83.65**	**85.28**

Effectiveness of Different Loss. To further analyze the impact of the loss function, we conducted an ablation study on different combinations of loss functions to evaluate the detection performance. As shown in Table 4, when using only the video classification loss, the model achieved an AP of 80.76% on the XD-Violence dataset and an AUC of 81.17% on the UCF-Crime dataset. Using this as a baseline, the improvement in detection performance by adding sparse loss and smooth loss demonstrates the effectiveness of these two losses in constraining the model's prediction scores. Further addition of the contrastive loss resulted in an additional improvement in detection performance, with the AP of XD-Violence and the AUC of UCF-Crime increasing by 1.48% and 2.78%, respectively. This confirms the effectiveness of the contrastive loss strategy in enhancing the model's discriminative ability at the clip level and underscores the efficacy of the proposed contrastive loss strategy.

Effectiveness of the Contrastive Loss. To further investigate the impact of the contrastive loss, we visualized the features of video segments with and without utilizing the contrastive loss using t-SNE on both datasets. From Fig. 6 and Fig. 7, it is evident that without employing the contrastive loss, the boundary between normal and abnormal segments in the videos appears relatively ambiguous, with a higher number of prediction errors. Conversely, when the model incorporates the contrastive loss, the boundary between normal and abnormal segments becomes clearer, leading to a reduction in misclassified data. This effect is particularly pronounced on the XD-Violence dataset, possibly due to its dataset's diversity and an increased number of abnormal segments, making it more susceptible to false negatives and false positives. The visualization results of features also validate the effectiveness of the contrastive loss strategy proposed in our method.

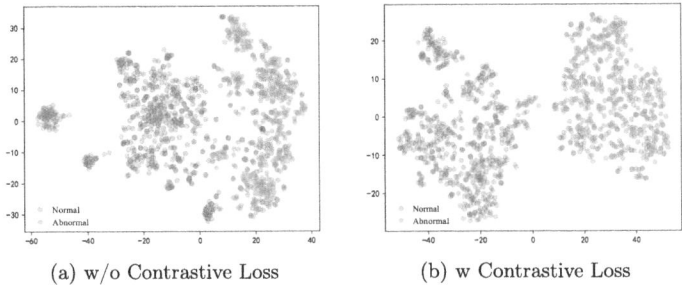

(a) w/o Contrastive Loss   (b) w Contrastive Loss

Fig. 6. Visualization of features with and without Contrastive Loss on XD-Violence

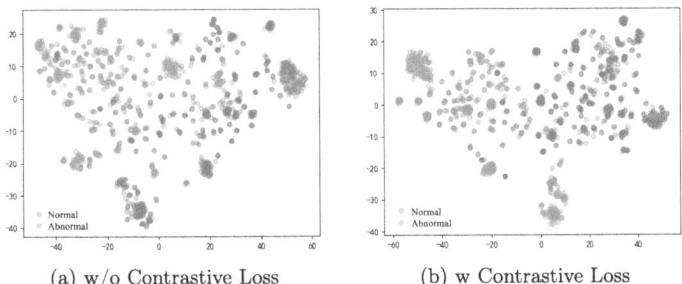

(a) w/o Contrastive Loss   (b) w Contrastive Loss

Fig. 7. Visualization of features with and without Contrastive Loss on UCF-Crime

4.5 Qualitative Results

We present qualitative results on two datasets in Figs. 8 and 9. As shown in Fig. 8, the qualitative results of our method on the UCF-Crime dataset are given, and Fig. 9 gives the qualitative results on the XD-Violence dataset, and the shaded areas indicate the parts containing the anomaly occurrence. Among them, the anomaly in Fig. 8a is the burglary of two people, including two time periods of breaking in and leaving, the anomaly in Fig. 8b is two people stealing in the supermarket, Fig. 9a is a continuous fight scene, and Fig. 9b is a fight scene with different people changing multiple perspectives and different time periods. Small anomalous events and a large number of anomalous events can be detected, and the boundary detection of abnormal events is also clear, which indicates that our method has good robustness and demonstrates the effectiveness of our proposed method in improving detection performance.

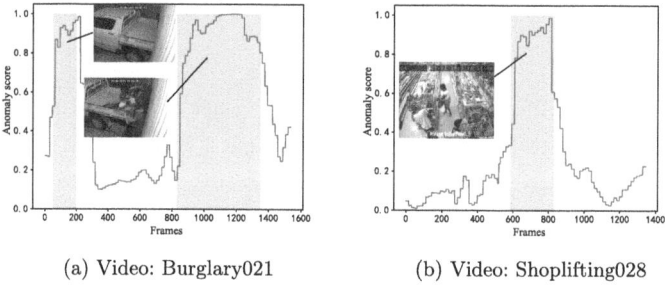

(a) Video: Burglary021   (b) Video: Shoplifting028

Fig. 8. Qualitative results of anomaly detection performances on UCF-Crime, the shaded area indicates the time period where anomalies occur.

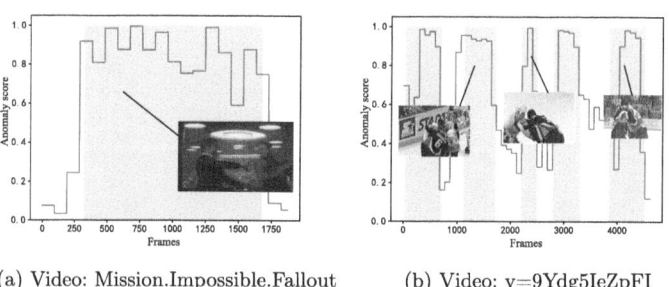

(a) Video: Mission.Impossible.Fallout   (b) Video: v=9Ydg5IeZpFI

Fig. 9. Qualitative results of anomaly detection performances on XD-Violence, the shaded area indicates the time period where anomalies occur.

5   Conclusion

In this paper, we propose a weakly supervised video anomaly detection method based on multi-scale feature fusion and contrastive loss. Our approach considers the diversity of anomalies in videos and obtains a more comprehensive and detailed representation through multi-scale feature fusion. To enhance the model's anomaly detection performance, we introduce a contrastive loss strategy to improve the model's discrimination between abnormal and normal segments. Experiments on the UCF-Crime and XD-Violence datasets validate the effectiveness of our method.

References

1. Aslam, N., Kolekar, M.H.: A-vae: attention based variational autoencoder for traffic video anomaly detection. In: 2023 IEEE 8th International Conference for Convergence in Technology (I2CT), pp. 1–7. IEEE (2023)
2. Cao, C., Zhang, X., Zhang, S., Wang, P., Zhang, Y.: Adaptive graph convolutional networks for weakly supervised anomaly detection in videos. IEEE Signal Process. Lett. **29**, 2497–2501 (2022)
3. Carreira, J., Zisserman, A.: Quo vadis, action recognition? A new model and the kinetics dataset. In: Proceedings of the IEEE/CVF Conference on Computer Vision and Pattern Recognition, pp. 6299–6308 (2017)
4. Chen, W., Ma, K.T., Yew, Z.J., Hur, M., Khoo, D.A.A.: TEVAD: improved video anomaly detection with captions. In: Proceedings of the IEEE/CVF Conference on Computer Vision and Pattern Recognition, pp. 5548–5558 (2023)
5. Cheng, K., Zeng, X., Liu, Y., Zhao, M., Pang, C., Hu, X.: Spatial-temporal graph convolutional network boosted flow-frame prediction for video anomaly detection. In: ICASSP 2023-2023 IEEE International Conference on Acoustics, Speech and Signal Processing (ICASSP), pp. 1–5. IEEE (2023)
6. Feng, J.C., Hong, F.T., Zheng, W.S.: Mist: multiple instance self-training framework for video anomaly detection. In: Proceedings of the IEEE/CVF Conference on Computer Vision and Pattern Recognition, pp. 14009–14018 (2021)
7. Kingma, D.P., Ba, J.: Adam: a method for stochastic optimization. arXiv preprint arXiv:1412.6980 (2014)
8. Liu, Y., Guo, Z., Liu, J., Li, C., Song, L.: Osin: object-centric scene inference network for unsupervised video anomaly detection. IEEE Signal Process. Lett. **30**, 359–363 (2023)
9. Lv, H., Yue, Z., Sun, Q., Luo, B., Cui, Z., Zhang, H.: Unbiased multiple instance learning for weakly supervised video anomaly detection. In: Proceedings of the IEEE/CVF Conference on Computer Vision and Pattern Recognition, pp. 8022–8031 (2023)
10. Meher, C.K., Nayak, R., Pati, U.C.: Dual stream variational autoencoder for video anomaly detection in single scene videos. In: 2022 2nd Odisha International Conference on Electrical Power Engineering, Communication and Computing Technology (ODICON), pp. 1–6. IEEE (2022)
11. Pang, G., Shen, C., Cao, L., Hengel, A.V.D.: Deep learning for anomaly detection: a review. ACM Comput. Surv. (CSUR) **54**(2), 1–38 (2021)
12. Pu, Y., Wu, X.: Locality-aware attention network with discriminative dynamics learning for weakly supervised anomaly detection. In: 2022 IEEE International Conference on Multimedia and Expo (ICME), pp. 1–6. IEEE (2022)
13. Sapkota, H., Yu, Q.: Bayesian nonparametric submodular video partition for robust anomaly detection. In: Proceedings of the IEEE/CVF Conference on Computer Vision and Pattern Recognition, pp. 3212–3221 (2022)
14. Şengönül, E., Samet, R., Abu Al-Haija, Q., Alqahtani, A., Alturki, B., Alsulami, A.A.: An analysis of artificial intelligence techniques in surveillance video anomaly detection: a comprehensive survey. Appl. Sci. **13**(8), 4956 (2023)

15. Sultani, W., Chen, C., Shah, M.: Real-world anomaly detection in surveillance videos. In: Proceedings of the IEEE/CVF Conference on Computer Vision and Pattern Recognition, pp. 6479–6488 (2018)
16. Tian, Y., Pang, G., Chen, Y., Singh, R., Verjans, J.W., Carneiro, G.: Weakly-supervised video anomaly detection with robust temporal feature magnitude learning. In: Proceedings of the IEEE/CVF International Conference on Computer Vision, pp. 4975–4986 (2021)
17. Van Den Oord, A., et al.: WaveNet: a generative model for raw audio. arXiv preprint arXiv:1609.03499 (2016)
18. Wan, B., Fang, Y., Xia, X., Mei, J.: Weakly supervised video anomaly detection via center-guided discriminative learning. In: 2020 IEEE International Conference on Multimedia and Expo (ICME), pp. 1–6. IEEE (2020)
19. Wang, T., et al.: Generative neural networks for anomaly detection in crowded scenes. IEEE Trans. Inf. Forensics Secur. 14(5), 1390–1399 (2018)
20. Wu, P., Liu, J.: Learning causal temporal relation and feature discrimination for anomaly detection. IEEE Trans. Image Process. 30, 3513–3527 (2021)
21. Wu, P., et al.: Not only look, but also listen: learning multimodal violence detection under weak supervision. In: Vedaldi, A., Bischof, H., Brox, T., Frahm, J.-M. (eds.) ECCV 2020. LNCS, vol. 12375, pp. 322–339. Springer, Cham (2020). https://doi.org/10.1007/978-3-030-58577-8_20
22. Yang, Z., Guo, Y., Wang, J., Huang, D., Bao, X., Wang, Y.: Towards video anomaly detection in the real world: a binarization embedded weakly-supervised network. IEEE Trans. Circuits Syst. Video Technol. 34, 4135–4140 (2023)
23. Yu, F., Koltun, V.: Multi-scale context aggregation by dilated convolutions. arXiv preprint arXiv:1511.07122 (2015)
24. Zhang, C., et al.: Exploiting completeness and uncertainty of pseudo labels for weakly supervised video anomaly detection. In: Proceedings of the IEEE/CVF Conference on Computer Vision and Pattern Recognition, pp. 16271–16280 (2023)
25. Zhang, D., Huang, C., Liu, C., Xu, Y.: Weakly supervised video anomaly detection via transformer-enabled temporal relation learning. IEEE Signal Process. Lett. 29, 1197–1201 (2022)
26. Zhang, J., Qing, L., Miao, J.: Temporal convolutional network with complementary inner bag loss for weakly supervised anomaly detection. In: 2019 IEEE International Conference on Image Processing (ICIP), pp. 4030–4034. IEEE (2019)
27. Zhong, J.X., Li, N., Kong, W., Liu, S., Li, T.H., Li, G.: Graph convolutional label noise cleaner: Train a plug-and-play action classifier for anomaly detection. In: Proceedings of the IEEE/CVF Conference on Computer Vision and Pattern Recognition, pp. 1237–1246 (2019)

Heterogeneous Information Network Embedding Based on Adaptive Meta-Schema Considering Relation Distinction and Semantic Preservation

Ling Wu[1,2,3], Pingping Gao[1,2,3], Jinlu Lu[1,2,3]($\boxtimes$), Kun Guo[1,2,3], and Qishan Zhang[4]

[1] College of Computer and Data Science, Fuzhou University, Fuzhou 350108, China
wuling1985@fzu.edu.cn, 3098387609@qq.com, 1063060962@qq.com
[2] Engineering Research Center of Big Data Intelligence, Ministry of Education, Fuzhou 350108, China
[3] Fujian Key Laboratory of Network Computing and Intelligent Information Processing (Fuzhou University), Fuzhou 350108, China
[4] Xianda College of Economics and Humanities, Shanghai International Studies University, Shanghai, China

Abstract. Many real-world networks can be treated as heterogeneous information networks (HINs) that consist of various types of nodes, like different proteins and molecules in biological networks and different authors and papers in citation networks. Multiple network data mining tasks can be conducted on HINs to capture the complex relationships between multi-type nodes. In recent years, random walk based HIN embedding has drawn increasing attention. Furthermore, the meta-path or meta-graph guided random walk is one of the most widely used techniques in HIN embedding methods. However, existing HIN embedding methods still face several difficulties. Firstly, the meta-paths or meta-graphs often need to be predefined, which relies heavily on domain knowledge and incomplete information coverage. Secondly, these methods treat all relations without distinction, which inevitably limits the capability of HIN embedding. Thirdly, they do not focus on preserving finer-grained meta-graph semantics. In this paper, a HIN embedding algorithm based on adaptive meta-schema considering relation distinction and semantic preservation (HINEAS) is proposed. In order to avoid the selection of meta-paths or meta-graphs, an adaptive meta-schema extraction is designed. In heterogeneous node sequence generation, a biased random walk strategy based on the adaptive meta-schema is presented to embed the different relationships' influence. Finally, an enhanced embedding strategy based on semantic preservation of the adaptive meta-schema is proposed to effectively extract topology and preserve the meta-graph's fine-grained semantics. Experiments on real-world datasets show that HINEAS significantly outperforms state-of-the-art methods.

Keywords: Heterogeneous information network · meta-schema · random walk · relation distinction · semantic preservation.

H. Sun et al. (Eds.): ChineseCSCW 2024, CCIS 2343, pp. 47–63, 2025.
https://doi.org/10.1007/978-981-96-2373-0_4

1   Introduction

The real-life information networks containing multi-type nodes and edges are called heterogeneous information networks (HINs). For example, in a citation network that contains author, paper, and journal nodes, the relations between nodes could be the writing between authors and papers, the submitting between authors and journals, and the publishing between papers and journals. In recent years, HIN has been applied to capture the complex relations between nodes in real-life networks to improve the performance of many downstream tasks such as node classification [7], community detection [12], and link prediction [9].

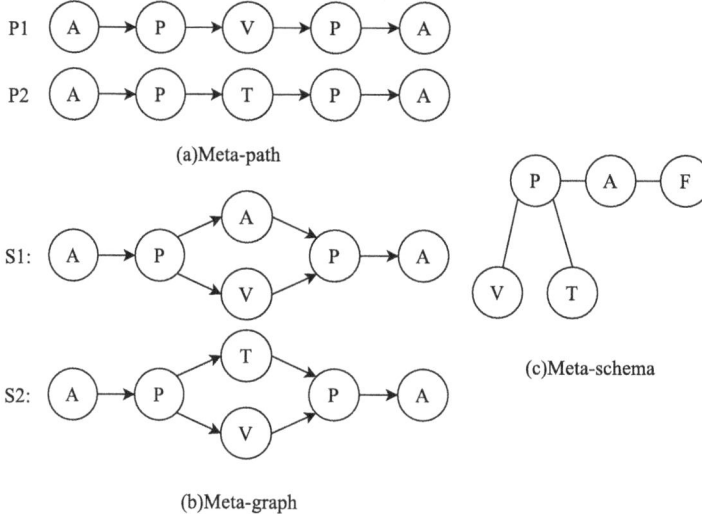

Fig. 1. Meta-path, Meta-graph and Meta-schema in the DBLP network. P, A, F, V and T denote paper, author, institution, conference and term, respectively.

To capture the rich semantics in HINs, meta-paths [17] (such as P1 and P2 in Fig. 1 (a)), which are sequences composed of multi-type nodes, have emerged as a practical semantic mining tool for HINs. More recently, meta-graphs (such as S1 and S2 in Fig. 1 (b)) have been proposed to capture more precise semantics in HINs with its more expressive capability [4,6,20] than meta-path. Although meta-path and meta-graph guided HIN embedding methods sustain rapid development, they still face several challenges. First, most existing HIN embedding methods need to predefine meta-paths or meta-graphs, which may be significantly rely on domain knowledge. Additionally, these commonly used meta-path or meta-graph may cause information loss due to incomplete coverage of the sampling node type, as shown in Fig. 1 (a), (b), there are A, P, T, and V types without F type. Second, most existing random walk based HIN embedding methods do not distinguish the relations between different types of nodes, and they ignore the impact of the semantics of different relations on the embedding vectors. For example, if a paper can be written by multiple authors and published in only one conference, then the conference and the authors have different impacts on the paper and require different amounts of sampling. It is a challenging problem to distinguish different semantics without relying on domain knowledge. Finally, meta-graph is only used to guide the walk and the deeper semantics they can express are not retained. But existing random walk methods based on meta-graph [4,20] are unable to preserve the fine-grained semantics hidden in the meta-graphs.

In this paper, we propose a Heterogeneous Information Network Embedding algorithm based on Adaptive meta-Schema considering relation distinction and semantic preservation (HINEAS) to address the above issues. First, a simple and fast automatic relation-distinguishable meta-schema extraction strategy is designed to distinguishes relationships that have commonalities simply and quickly. Second, a biased random walk strategy based on the new meta-schema is developed to consider the influence of different relations in random walks. Finally, we propose an enhanced embedding strategy based on the semantic preservation of a meta-schema to make the nodes with close semantic relations also close in the embedding space. The main contributions of this paper are summarized as follows.

- The automatic relation-distinguishable meta-schema extraction strategy reduces HINEAS' dependence on domain knowledge and avoids incomplete information coverage brought by the manual selection of simple meta-paths or meta-graphs, which improves the quality of embedding.
- The biased random walk strategy based on relation distinction can automatically embed the influence of different relations in heterogeneous node sequence generation, which increases the embedding vectors' discernibility of the heterogeneous relations between nodes.
- The enhanced embedding strategy can retain fine-grained semantic information in the embedding, that is, make the nodes with close semantic relations also close in the embedding space, thus improving the downstream tasks' accuracy.

2   Related Work

Existing HIN embedding methods are mainly guided by meta-paths or meta-graphs and can be divided into message-passing, relation-learning, and random walk based [18].

The message-passing methods aim to learn node embedding by aggregating the information from nodes' neighbors. R-GCN [15] uses graph convolutional networks to model relational data and takes into account the heterogeneity of relations by learning multiple convolutional matrices. HetGNN [19] is developed based on random sampling of heterogeneous neighbors of a fixed size and encoding them into groups according to node types. Node embedding are obtained by the fusion of information between groups.

The relation-learning methods start with different types of relations and their characteristics in HINs to model network heterogeneity. RHINE [16] classifies the relations in heterogeneous networks into two categories: affiliation and interaction relations, and models them differently. CMG2vec [21] designed a scalable semantic structure called Composite Meta-graph(CMG), and utilized an autoencoder to learn the relationships between different orders of nodes. CoNR [1] considers the influence of relationship representations and proposes a relationship encoder that encodes node information into relationship representations.

The random-walk-based approaches obtain the co-occurrence relation between nodes by sampling their neighbors to generate node embedding. Meta-path2vec [3] samples random walks controlled by meta-paths and learns embedding using the Skip-Gram model [10]. Metagraph2Vec [20] extends metapath2vec by setting up a meta-graph to guide random walks to capture more contextual semantic information. SILK [5] uses a dynamically updated guidance matrix to guide random walks and considers the balance of node types. SchemaWalk [14] designed a random walk to uniformly sample all edge types within the network schema.

3   Preliminaries

Definition 1 (Heterogeneous Information Network). A heterogeneous information network is defined as a graph $G = (V, E, A)$, where V and E are the node and edge sets, respectively. $A = a_k$ is a set of node types where a mapping function $\phi : V \rightarrow A$ maps any node $v_i \in V$ to a node type $a_k \in A$. For a HIN, $|A| > 1$, where $|\cdot|$ returns the number of elements in a set. Each edge $e \in E$ connects two different node types, that is, for any edge $e(v_i, v_j)$, we have $\phi(v_i) \neq \phi(v_j)$.

Definition 2 (Meta-path). A meta-path $P(G)$ is a sequence of node types defined on HIN G in the form of $P = a_1 \rightarrow a_2 \rightarrow \cdots a_{L-1} \rightarrow a_L$, where L is the length of path P, $a_i \in A(i = 1, ..., L) \wedge a_{i-1} \neq a_i$.

Definition 3 (Meta-graph). A meta-graph is a directed acyclic graph $M(G) = (V_M, P_M, a_s, a_t)$ defined on HIN G, where $V_M \subset A$ and each meta-path $P \in$ path set P_M is a path from the source node type a_s to the target node type a_t.

Definition 4 (Meta-schema). A meta-schema is a graph $T(G) = (V_T, E_T)$ defined on HIN G where $V_T = A$ and an edge $e(a_i, a_j) \in E_T$ exists if there is at least one edge connecting a node of type a_i to another node of type $a_j(i \neq j)$.

4   Proposed Method

HINEAS is composed of three steps, as shown in Fig. 2.
Step 1: Relation-distinguishable meta-schema extraction. The conception of relation here is borrowed from the three types of relations (1:1, 1:N, and N:M) between entities in an entity-relation (ER) diagram in the relational database.

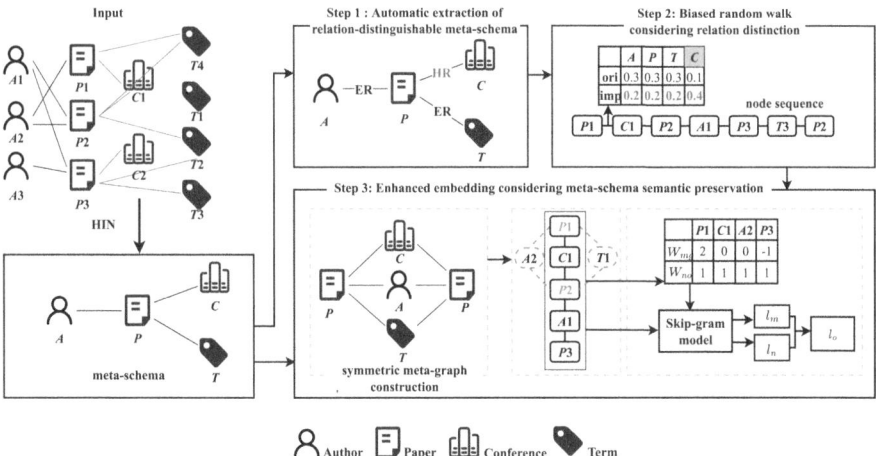

Fig. 2. Framework of HINEAS. A1, A2 and A3 denote three nodes of type A indexed with 1, 2, and 3, respectively. The same notation applies to node types P, C and T.

Step 2: Biased random walk considering relation distinction. Random walk is conducted on the network to emphasize the 1:N relation between nodes that better portrays the close relationship between two node types than other relations.

Step 3: Enhanced embedding considering meta-schema semantic preservation. First, generate symmetric meta-graphs (where the source and target node types are identical, that is, $a_s = a_t$) based on the meta-schema automatically extracted in step 1. Second, enhance the objective function of the Skip-Gram model by emphasizing the close relations between the node types recognized in the symmetric meta-graphs in sliding windows.

The detailed implementation is introduced in the following subsections.

4.1   Automatic Extraction of Relation-Distinguishable Meta-Schema

In this section, we design a strategy to automatically extract relation-distinguishable meta-schema without domain knowledge to completely cover all types of nodes. Inspired by the ability of ER diagram to distinguish relations, we can divide the relations into equality and hierarchy relations based on the meta-schema defined in the HIN. The definitions of equality and hierarchy relations are given as follows.

Definition 5 (Equality Relation). Given any two node types a_i and a_j in node type set A in HIN G, if each node of type a_i has more than one neighbor of node type a_j and vice versa, the edge $e(a_i, a_j)$ in the meta-schema $T(G)$ is said to express an equality relation $N:M$ (borrowed from the many-to-many relation of two entities in the field of ER diagram). We define an indicator $ER(e)$, the value of which is 1 if edge e expresses an equaltiy relation between two node types and 0, otherwise.

Definition 6 (Hierarchy Relation). Given any two node types a_i and a_j in node type set A in HIN G, if each node of type a_i has more than one neighbor of node type a_j while each node of type a_j has at most one neighbor of type a_i, the edge $e(a_i, a_j)$ in the meta-schema $T(G)$ is said to express a hierarchy relation 1:N (borrowed from the one-to-many relation of two entities in the field of ER diagram). We define an indicator $HR(e)$, the value of which is 1 if edge e expresses a hierarchy relation between two node types and 0, otherwise.

We use the DBLP[1] network to illustrate these two types of relationships. In DBLP, a "paper" contains multiple "term"s and a "term" exists in multiple "paper". Therefore, the relation between "paper" and "term" is an equality relation. So is the relation between "author" and "paper". In contrast, a "paper" can only be published in one "conference" while a "conference" generally includes multiple "paper"s. Therefore, the relation between "conference" and "paper" is a hierarchy relation. Figure 3 shows an example of the extraction of meta-schema corresponding to node type P in DBLP. In HINs, the equality relation is more often observed than the hierarchy relation because it represents a loose relationship between nodes. The hierarchy relation represents a more specific relation between nodes and is usually more valuable than the equality relation. Therefore, we focus on the relation distinction and the extraction of the hierarchy relation in this work.

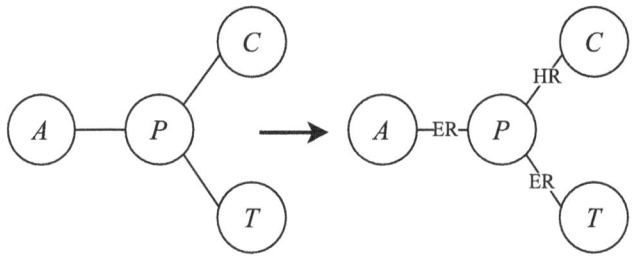

Fig. 3. Automatic relation-distinguishable meta-schema extraction

The automatic extraction of a relation-distinguishable meta-schema is composed of two substeps: (1) Extract all node types from a network to construct a meta-schema. An edge is created to connect two node types in the meta-schema if there is an edge in the original network connecting two nodes of the two types. (2) Label ER or HR for the relations between two node types according to Definition 5 and Definition 6.

4.2   Biased Random Walk Considering Relation Distinction

In this section, we design a random walk strategy that distinguishes the different importance of equality and hierarchy relations and is biased towards the latter

---

[1] https://github.com/zechengz/hin-dataset.

to generate node sequences for the Skip-Gram model. Traditional random walk strategies treat a node's neighbors equally, which neglects the different influences of each on the decision of the next hop from the node. In this work, we distinguish such influence based on the extracted meta-schema in the previous step to make a biased random walk. Specifically, given a node v, the number of edges starting from v that follow the equality relation is calculated as follows:

$$n_v^{ER} = \sum \{1| \text{ if } e \in N_e(v) \wedge ER(e) = 1\} \tag{1}$$

where $N_e(v)$ denotes the neighboring edge set of v. Similarly, the number of edges starting from v that follow the hierarchy relation can be calculated as follows:

$$n_v^{HR} = \sum \{1 \mid \text{ if } e \in N_e(v) \wedge HR(e) = 1\} \tag{2}$$

We set a parameter C to control the influence of the hierarchy relation. Specifically, if the ratio of the number of edges in the hierarchy to the total number of edges is greater than C, we use a parameter α to calculate the transitional probability from node"v" to its neighbor "u". Otherwise, a parameter β is used to calculate the transitional probability, as shown in the equation (3).

$$P(u|v) = \begin{cases} \frac{n_v^t \times \alpha}{n_v^{ER} + n_v^{HR} \times \alpha} & \text{if } \frac{n_{HR}}{|E|} \geq C \\ \frac{n_v^t + n_v^{ER} \times \beta}{n_v^{ER}(1 + \beta \times k_{HR}) + n_v^{HR}} & \text{if } \frac{n_{HR}}{|E|} < C \end{cases} \tag{3}$$

where k_{HR} denotes the number of types of v's neighbors that have hierarchy relations with it. n_v^t is the number of v's neighbors whose type is t, $t = \phi(u)$. n_{HR} is the number of edges of hierarchy relations in the whole network. $|E|$ denotes the number of edges. $\alpha > 1$, $\beta < 1$, $C > 0$. The setting of the values of α, β, and C are studied in the parameter experiment.

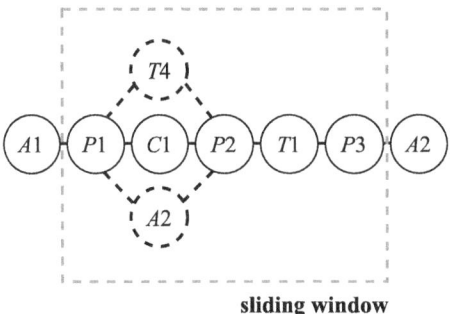

sliding window

Fig. 4. Node pairs in a sliding window

4.3   Enhanced Embedding Considering Meta-Schema Semantic Preservation

After obtaining node sequences, we can use the Skip-Gram model to learn node embedding, which requires generating node pairs surrounding the center node of each sliding window. The traditional manners for node pair generation treat each node pair equally. However, we think the nodes in a node pair sharing more similar relations than others have closer relations and should be given higher weight. Figure 4 gives an example to illustrate the rationality of our idea, where papers $P1$ and $P2$ have the same term $T4$ and author $A2$ and are published at the same conference $C1$. Therefore, node pair $(P1, P2)$ should receive more attention than other pairs, such as $(P3, P2)$. In conclusion, we should consider the difference between node pairs in the node sequences generated based on the aforementioned relation-distinguishable meta-schema to preserve fine-grained semantics hidden in the meta-schema. We divide the enhanced embedding process into three substeps as follows:

Substep1: Construct the objective node type's symmetric meta-graph based on a network's relation-distinguishable meta-schema. We start with a HIN G and extract its meta-schema T_G, then build a symmetry meta-graph based on the objective node type. Figure 5 shows an example of constructing a symmetry meta-graph based on the objective node type P in DBLP. For all meta-paths, the source and target node types in the meta-graph are P. The node types in the paths are all called intermediate node types.

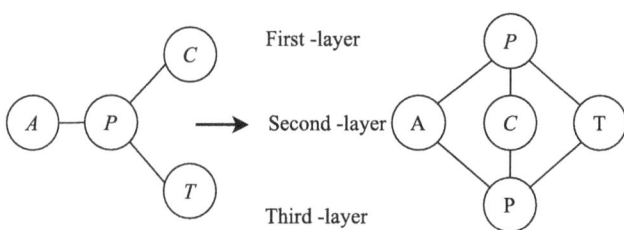

Fig. 5. Symmetric meta-graph construction based on the relation-distinguishable meta-schema of DBLP.

Substep 2: Calculate each node pair's weight according to the symmetric meta-graph. For a sliding window, we calculate the weight $W_{mg}(v_c, v_j)$ for each node pair (v_c, v_j) in it, where v_c is the center node and v_j is the context node, as follows:

$$W_{mg}(v_c, v_j) = \begin{cases} I(v_c, v_j) & \text{if } \phi(v_c) = \phi(v_j) \wedge I(v_c, v_j) > 0 \\ 0 & \text{if } \phi(v_c) \neq \phi(v_j) \\ -1 & \text{if } \phi(v_c) = \phi(v_j) \wedge I(v_c, v_j) = 0 \end{cases} \tag{4}$$

where $I(v_c, v_j)$ returns the number of types which common neighbors of v_c and v_j belong to. ϕ means the node type. By setting the weight of node pair (v_c, v_j)

to $I(v_c, v_j)$, we emphasize the importance of the node pair where v_c and v_j share similar heterogeneous neighbors.

Substep 3: Construct and optimize the loss function of the Skip-Gram model. For each pair (v_c, v_j), we define the following objective function:

$$L_{mg} = -\log \sigma \left(W_{mg} \left(v_c, v_j \right) \times Z_c Z_j \right) \tag{5}$$

where σ is the sigmoid function, and Z_c and Z_j are the embedding of node v_c and v_j, respectively.

Besides considering the preservation of the meta-graph fine-grained semantic in loss L_{mg}, it is also necessary to consider the preservation of the traditional general contextual semantic similarity loss. Therefore, we construct an overall loss function as follows:

$$L_{ov} = -\log \sigma \left(Z_c Z_j \right) + \sum_{ne.g.} E_{v_l \sim P_D} \left[\log \sigma \left(-Z_c Z_l \right) \right] + \gamma L_{mg} \tag{6}$$

where neg is the number of negative samples and v_l is the negative samples from the unigram distribution. γ is a non-negative balance coefficient. If $\gamma = 0$, the loss function is consistent with the Skip-Gram model. If $\gamma > 0$, both the fine-grained information of the contextual meta-graph and the general contextual information are considered.

Table 1. Dataset details

Network	#Nodes	#Edges	#Classes	$\frac{n_{HR}}{|E|}$	Description
DBLP	37791	170794	4	0.0842	The network contains four types of nodes: 14475 authors, 14376 papers, 20 conferences, and 8920 terms.
Yelp	3913	38680	3	0.2003	The network contains five types of nodes: 1286 users, 2614 businesses, 9 star ratings, 2 service types, and 2 booking types.
AMiner	82212	53084	3	0.1254	The network contains four types of nodes: 18174 authors, 9208 papers, 54800 terms, and 30 conferences.
MovieLens	2672	103834	8	0.0091	The network contains four types of nodes: 943 users, 8 age groups, 21 occupations, 1682 movies, and 18 movie titles.

5   Experiments

5.1   Dataset

We conducted experiments on five heterogeneous network datasets, including the citation networks DBLP[2], Aminer[3], the merchant review network Yelp [8]

---

[2] https://github.com/zechengz/hin-dataset.
[3] https://github.com/librahu/HIN-Datasets-for-Recommendation-and-Network-Embedding.

and the movie network MovieLens[4]. The summary statistics of the datasets are presented in Table 1, where the $\frac{n_{HH}}{|E|}$ of each network is calculated for the experiment on parameter C of HINEAS. A low value of $\frac{n_{HH}}{|E|}$ indicates that the hierarchy relation gains more advantage than other relations in the network.

5.2   Baseline Algorithms

We chose NMI [2] and F-score(including Macro-F1 and Micro-F1) [11] which are the most commonly used metrics in graph analysis tasks to evaluate HINEAS with the following baselines:

1. **DeepWalk** [13] is the earliest homogeneous network embedding algorithm that captures node context through uniform random walks to learn node embedding.
2. **Metapath2vec** [3] formalizes meta-path-based random walks to generate heterogeneous neighborhoods and then leverages a heterogeneous skipgram model to perform node embedding.
3. **Metagraph2vec** [20] uses meta-graphs to guide random walk and learn latent embedding for multiple types of nodes in HINs.
4. **R-GCN** [15] is a message-passing algorithm that uses graph convolutional networks to model relational data. It takes into account the heterogeneity of relations by learning multiple convolutional matrices.
5. **SILK** [5] uses the guidance matrix to guide the walk, the model can learn the importance of node types autonomously, and the guidance matrix can be corrected after multiple iterations.
6. **CMG2vec** [21] designed a scalable semantic structure called Composite Meta-graph(CMG), and utilized an autoencoder to learn the relationships between different orders of nodes.
7. **SchemaWalk** [14] designed a random walk to uniformly sample all edge types within the network schema.

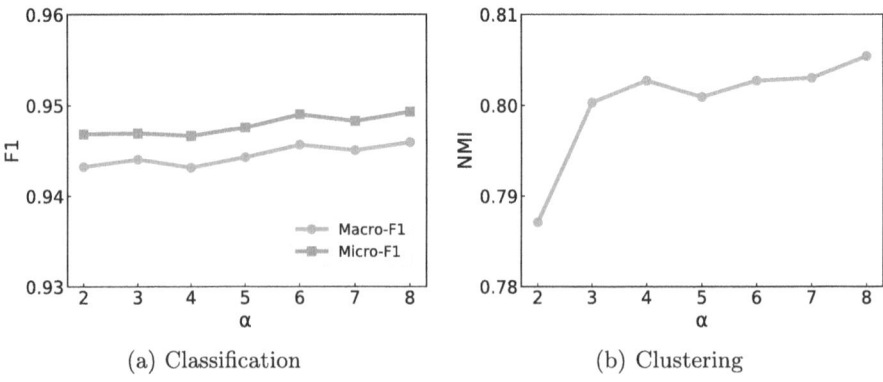

(a) Classification   (b) Clustering

Fig. 6. Result of the parameter experiment of α on DBLP

---

[4] https://grouplens.org/datasets/movielens.

5.3   Experimental Settings

For the methods that require inputting meta-paths or meta-graphs, such as Metapath2vec and Metagrapth2vec, we selected popular metapaths used in existing works and select the ones achieving the best results. Moreover, we investigate the influence of parameters α, β, γ and C on HINEAS's node classification and clustering accuracy on DBLP and MovieLens.

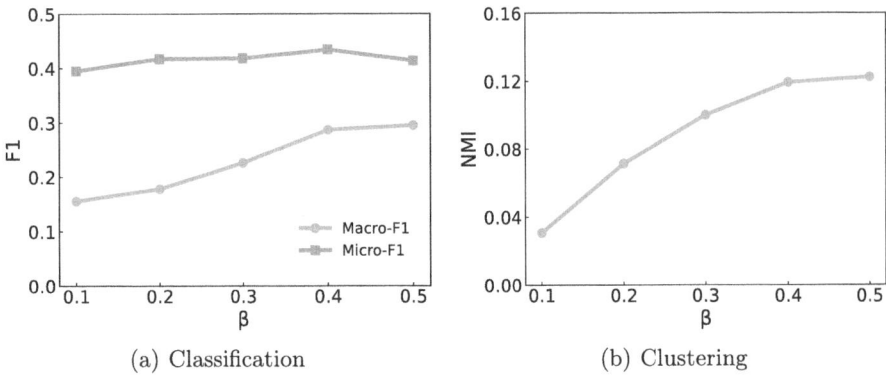

(a) Classification   (b) Clustering

Fig. 7. Result of the parameter experiment of β on MovieLens

Parameter α. As described in Subsect. 4.2, parameter α is used to control the calculation of the transitional probability from nodes v to u when $n_{HR}/|E| \geq C$. As shown in Fig. 6, the classification accuracy of HINEAS increases gradually as the value of α increases. In contrast, the clustering accuracy of HINEAS goes up violently at first and stabilizes quickly, which reflects the importance of considering the hierarchy relation in node clustering. Therefore, we set $\alpha \geq 8$ in the remaining experiments.

Parameter β. As described in Subsect. 4.2, parameter β is used to control the calculation of the transitional probability from nodes v to u when $n_{HR}/|E| < C$. As shown in Fig. 7, with the increase of the value of β, both the classification and clustering accuracy of HINEAS increase, which means that considering the hierarchy relation has a positive influence on the HINEAS. Therefore, we set $\beta \geq 0.4$ in the remaining experiments.

Parameter γ. As described in Subsect. 4.3, parameter γ is used to control the contribution of the loss L_{mg} considering meta-schema semantic preservation. As shown in Fig. 8, with the increase of the value of γ, the classification accuracy of HINEAS is almost unchanged. In contrast, the clustering accuracy of HINEAS increases rapidly at first and becomes stable quickly, just like the result in Fig. 6(b), which reflects the importance of considering meta-schema semantic preservation in node clustering. Therefore, we set $\gamma \geq 0.4$ in the remaining experiments.

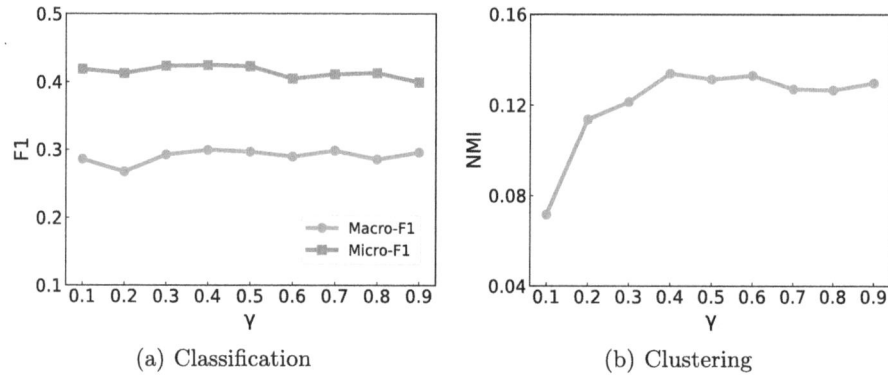

Fig. 8. Result of the parameter experiment of γ on MovieLens

Parameter C. As described in Subsect. 4.2, parameter C is used to look at the differences between the number of HR and ER relations using different random walk strategies. As shown in Fig. 9, when the value of C is increased from 0.025 to 0.05 on MovieLens, the classification and clustering accuracy of HINEAS increases quickly to around 0.3 and then stabilizes. On DBLP, HINEAS' accuracy practically remains unchanged, with the exception of a little drop in its NMI value at $C = 0.075$. According to the experimental results, we set C to 0.05 in the remaining experiments.

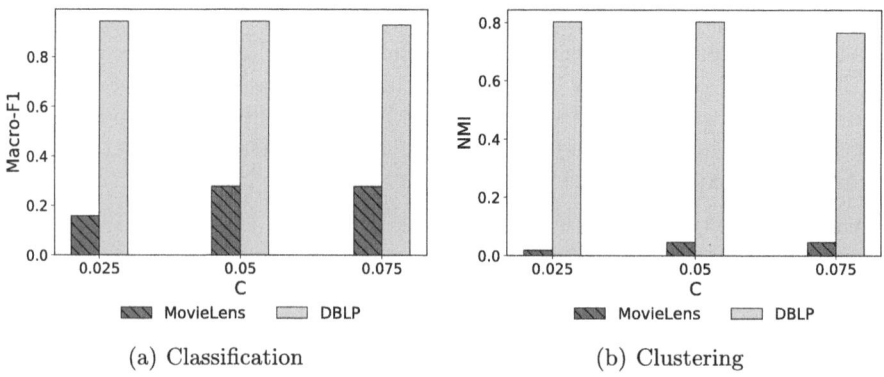

Fig. 9. Result of the parameter experiment of C on MovieLens and DBLP

Table 2. Result of the accuracy experiment on node classification

dataset	metric	Deepwalk	Metapath2vec	Metagraph2vec	R-GCN	SILK	CMG2vec	SchemaWalk	HINEAS
DBLP	NMI	0.7640	0.8216	0.7890	0.7186	0.8179	**0.8258**	0.8001	**0.8309**
	Micro-F1	0.9273	0.9384	0.9372	0.9101	**0.9413**	0.9165	0.9254	**0.9495**
	Macro-F1	0.9236	0.9347	0.9342	0.9067	**0.9374**	0.9012	0.9205	**0.9456**
YELP	NMI	0.4386	0.3824	0.3167	0.3162	0.3604	0.4228	**0.4528**	**0.4805**
	Micro-F1	0.7699	0.7553	0.7304	0.7036	0.7361	**0.7782**	0.7623	**0.7927**
	Macro-F1	0.7320	0.6857	0.6638	0.6407	0.6862	0.7235	**0.7292**	**0.7495**
AMiner	NMI	0.9211	0.9909	0.9822	0.6917	**0.9910**	0.9723	0.9890	**0.9955**
	Micro-F1	0.9834	0.9885	0.9978	0.9189	**0.9984**	0.9826	0.9925	**0.9997**
	Macro-F1	0.9838	0.9886	0.9979	0.9178	**0.9986**	0.9864	0.9956	**0.9997**
MovieLens	NMI	0.0540	0.0892	0.0822	0.1395	0.1549	**0.1677**	0.1601	**0.1727**
	Micro-F1	0.3756	0.3703	0.3756	0.3439	**0.4144**	0.3965	0.4058	**0.4392**
	Macro-F1	0.1567	0.2024	0.1512	0.2318	**0.3455**	0.3453	0.3396	**0.3856**

5.4   Performance Comparison

For the node classification task, we trained a logistic classifier by radomly sampling 80% of the labeled nodes and testing it using the remaining 20%. For the node clustering task, we use K-means to cluster the node embedding. Experimental results averaged over 10 runs are reported. Tables 2 and 3 show the experimental results. The numbers underlined and in bold font are the highest accuracy values of all algorithms run on a network. The numbers only in bold font are the second-highest accuracy values.

Table 3. Result of the accuracy experiment on node clustering

dataset	metric	Deepwalk	Metapath2vec	Metagraph2vec	R-GCN	SILK	CMG2vec	SchemaWalk	HINEAS
DBLP	NMI	0.7364	0.7845	0.7835	0.7853	0.7698	**0.7907**	0.7887	**0.8054**
	Micro-F1	0.9129	0.9315	0.9319	0.9051	0.9203	**0.9326**	0.8825	**0.9378**
	Macro-F1	0.9078	0.9266	0.9271	0.9006	0.9172	**0.9306**	0.8801	**0.9337**
Yelp	NMI	0.0107	0.3631	0.0103	0.1904	**0.3830**	0.3056	0.2889	**0.3935**
	Micro-F1	0.3779	**0.6667**	0.3779	0.5784	0.6517	0.5558	0.6287	**0.6928**
	Macro-F1	0.3485	**0.6185**	0.3474	0.5396	0.5667	0.4885	0.6012	**0.6246**
AMiner	NMI	0.4566	0.5169	**0.5576**	0.4938	0.4817	0.5336	0.5430	**0.6521**
	Micro-F1	0.7260	0.7445	**0.7527**	0.7224	0.7233	0.6165	0.6527	**0.7482**
	Macro-F1	0.7112	0.7371	**0.7373**	0.7190	0.7273	0.5856	0.6403	**0.7434**
MovieLens	NMI	0.0482	0.0390	0.0481	0.0038	0.1083	**0.1185**	0.0468	**0.1280**
	Micro-F1	0.1972	0.2173	0.1951	0.2110	**0.2657**	0.2512	0.2223	**0.2746**
	Macro-F1	0.1481	0.1470	0.1474	0.1523	**0.1575**	0.1355	0.1403	**0.1640**

As shown in Table 2, HINEAS achieves the highest accuracy in all networks when compared to the baselines in node classification, which demonstrates the significant effect of distinguishing different relations between nodes in random walks and considering meta-schema semantic preservation in embedding vector generation. Additionally, compared to the methods using meta-paths or meta-graphs, HINEAS does not need to depend on domain knowledge. The results are shown in Table 3 prove the superiority of HINEAS to other algorithms in all networks in node clustering again. The accuracy experiment verifies that the strategies employed in HINEAS are pervasively effective in multiple network data mining tasks.

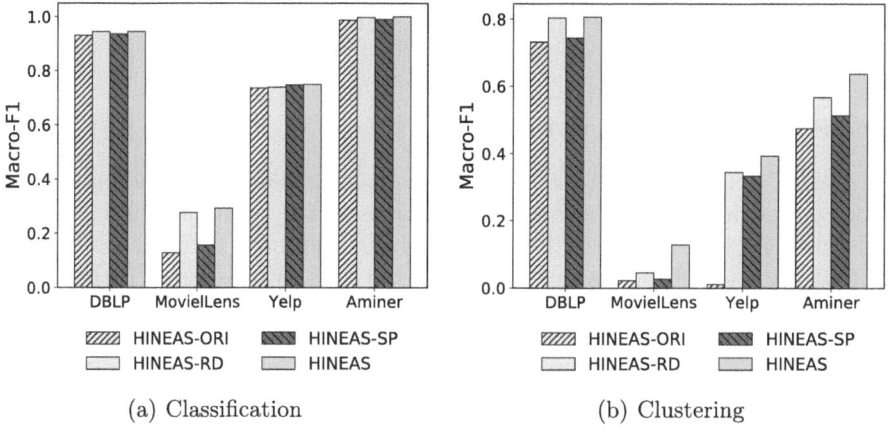

(a) Classification   (b) Clustering

Fig. 10. Result of the ablation study

5.5   Ablation Study

In this section, we abbreviate HINEAS without any strategy as HINEAS-ORI, that is, HINEAS-ORI uses the traditional random walk and does not consider semantic preservation. HINEAS-RD considering only the biased random walk based on relation-distinguishable meta-schema. HINEAS-SP considering only enhanced embedding for fine-grained semantic information preservation. As shown in Fig. 10, first, the NMI and Macro-F1 values of HINEAS-RD and HINEAS-SP are consistently higher than that of HINEAS-ORI, which proves the effectiveness of considering different relations between nodes in random walks and retaining fine-grained semantic information in embedding. Second, HINEAS-

RD achieves higher accuracy than HINEAS-SP in all networks except Yelp, which reveals that the biased random walk strategy is generally more effective than the enhanced embedding strategy. Finally, the NMI and Macro-F1 values of HINEAS outperform HINEAS-ORI, HINEAS-RD and HINEAS-SP, demonstrating that the combination of all strategies really brings the largest benefit to embedding and the subsequent network.

6 Conclusion

In this paper, we propose a heterogeneous information network embedding algorithm HINEAS based on the automatic relation-distinguishable meta-schema extraction, the biased random walk considering relation distinction and the enhanced network embedding retaining fine-grained semantic information preservation. The meta-scheme extraction strategy helps distinguish the different influences of the relations between nodes to deduce the meta-schema of a network automatically. The biased random walk strategy helps put different emphasis on different relations in node sequence generation. The enhanced network embedding strategy helps consider the influence of different node types in embedding to retain the fine-grained semantic information of the meta-graphs generated by a network's meta-schema. Comprehensive experiments, including node classification and clustering tasks, demonstrate the effectiveness of the strategies in HINEAS.

Acknowledgements. This work was supported in part by the National Natural Science Foundation of China under Grant 62002063, in part by the Fujian Natural Science Funds under Grant 2020J05112, the National Key Research and Development Plan of China under Grant No. 2021YFB3600503, the Major Science and Technology Project of Fujian Province under Grant No. 2021HZ022007.

References

1. Li, W., Ni, L., Wang, J., Wang, C.: Collaborative representation learning for nodes and relations via heterogeneous graph neural network. Knowl. Based Syst. **255**, 109673 (2022)
2. Danon, L., Diaz-Guilera, A., Duch, J., Arenas, A.: Comparing community structure identification. J. Stat. Mech: Theory Exp. **2005**(09), P09008 (2005)
3. Dong, Yuxiao, C.N.V., Swami, A.: metapath2vec: scalable representation learning for heterogeneous networks. In: Proceedings of the 23rd ACM SIGKDD International Conference on Knowledge Discovery and Data Mining, pp. 135–144 (2017)
4. Fang, Y., et al.: Metagraph-based learning on heterogeneous graphs. IEEE Trans. Knowl. Data Eng. **33**(1), 154–168 (2019)
5. Hao, Y., Wang, X., Wang, X., Wang, X., Chen, C., Song, M.: Walking with attention: self-guided walking for heterogeneous graph embedding. IEEE Trans. Knowl. Data Eng. **34**, 6047–6060 (2021)

6. Huang, Z., Zheng, Y., Cheng, R., Sun, Y., Mamoulis, N., Li, X.: Meta structure: Computing relevance in large heterogeneous information networks. In: Proceedings of the 22nd ACM SIGKDD International Conference on Knowledge Discovery and Data Mining, pp. 1595–1604 (2016)
7. Ji, M., Han, J., Danilevsky, M.: Ranking-based classification of heterogeneous information networks. In: Proceedings of the 17th ACM SIGKDD International Conference on Knowledge Discovery and Data Mining, pp. 1298–1306 (2011)
8. Jiang, H., Song, Y., Wang, C., Zhang, M., Sun, Y.: Semi-supervised learning over heterogeneous information networks by ensemble of meta-graph guided random walks. In: Proceedings of the Twenty-Sixth International Joint Conference on Artificial Intelligence, pp. 1944–1950 (2017)
9. Liben-Nowell, D., Kleinberg, J.: The link prediction problem for social networks. In: Proceedings of the Twelfth International Conference on Information and Knowledge Management, pp. 556–559 (2003)
10. Mikolov, T., Chen, K., Corrado, G., Dean, J.: Efficient estimation of word representations in vector space. arXiv preprint arXiv:1301.3781 (2013)
11. Opitz, J., Burst, S.: Macro f1 and macro f1. arXiv preprint arXiv:1911.03347 (2019)
12. Opsahl, T., Panzarasa, P.: Clustering in weighted networks. Soc. Netw. **31**(2), 155–163 (2009)
13. Perozzi, B., Al-Rfou, R., Skiena, S.: Deepwalk: online learning of social representations. In: Proceedings of the 20th ACM SIGKDD International Conference on Knowledge Discovery and Data Mining, pp. 701–710 (2014)
14. Samy, A.E., Giaretta, L., Kefato, Z.T., Girdzijauskas, V.: Schemawalk: schema aware random walks for heterogeneous graph embedding. In: Companion Proceedings of the Web Conference 2022, pp. 1157–1166. WWW 2022, Association for Computing Machinery (2022)
15. Schlichtkrull, M., Kipf, T.N., Bloem, P., van den Berg, R., Titov, I., Welling, M.: Modeling relational data with graph convolutional networks. In: Gangemi, A., et al. (eds.) ESWC 2018. LNCS, vol. 10843, pp. 593–607. Springer, Cham (2018). https://doi.org/10.1007/978-3-319-93417-4_38
16. Shi, C., Lu, Y., Hu, L., Liu, Z., Ma, H.: Rhine: relation structure-aware heterogeneous information network embedding. IEEE Trans. Knowl. Data Eng. **34**(01), 433–447 (2022)
17. Sun, Y., Han, J., Yan, X., Yu, P.S., Wu, T.: Pathsim: meta path-based top-k similarity search in heterogeneous information networks. Proc. VLDB Endow. **4**(11), 992–1003 (2011)
18. Yang, C., Xiao, Y., Zhang, Y., Sun, Y., Han, J.: Heterogeneous network representation learning: a unified framework with survey and benchmark. IEEE Trans. Knowl. Data Eng. **01**, 1–1 (2020)
19. Zhang, C., Song, D., Huang, C., Swami, A., Chawla, N.V.: Heterogeneous graph neural network. In: Proceedings of the 25th ACM SIGKDD International Conference on Knowledge Discovery & Data Mining, pp. 793–803 (2019)

20. Zhang, D., Yin, J., Zhu, X., Zhang, C.: MetaGraph2Vec: complex semantic path augmented heterogeneous network embedding. In: Phung, D., et al. (eds.) PAKDD 2018. LNCS (LNAI), vol. 10938, pp. 196–208. Springer, Cham (2018). https://doi.org/10.1007/978-3-319-93037-4_16
21. Zhang, Z., Huang, J., Tan, Q., Sun, H., Zhou, Y.: Cmg2vec: a composite meta-graph based heterogeneous information network embedding approach. Knowl. Based Syst. **216**, 106661 (2021)

RoleScan: Enhancing Social Bot Detection Using Social Role Vector

Wen Wen[1], Min Gao[1], Qingyuan Gong[2], Xin Wang[1], and Yang Chen[1(✉)]

[1] Shanghai Key Lab of Intelligent Information Processing, School of Computer Science, Fudan University, Shanghai, China
{wwen24,mgao21}@m.fudan.edu.cn, {xinw,chenyang}@fudan.edu.cn
[2] Research Institute of Intelligent Complex Systems, Fudan University, Shanghai, China
gongqingyuan@fudan.edu.cn

Abstract. The increase in social media users has led to the rise of social bots, which can disrupt online environments and threaten user privacy. This study presents RoleScan, a novel framework that integrates Social Role Vector (SRV) and Graph Attention Network v2 (GATv2) to detect social bots more accurately. We are the first to formulate the social bot detection problem by considering users' properties and social influence. RoleScan extracts user features and text features from user profiles and tweets, and uses SRV to capture the social features. SRV is based on node centrality measurement, structural hole theory, and social capital theory, offering a comprehensive view of the influence of a user within the network. By leveraging an attention mechanism, RoleScan focuses on pivotal features and connections, enhancing its ability to differentiate between bots and humans. The experimental results show that RoleScan outperforms existing models, achieving an AUC of 0.887. An ablation study further highlights the critical role of incorporating social features into the detection process. Our study not only enhances the social bot detection performance, but also offers new insights into the users' diverse roles within social networks.

Keywords: Social bot detection · Social role vector · Graph attention network · Structural hole theory

1 Introduction

With the popularization of mobile devices and the advancement of network technology, the number of social media users is increasing rapidly. For instance, the newly launched social app, Threads, exceeded 100 million users in just five days of its launch on July 5, 2023 [48]. By March 2024, the daily active users on the X/Twitter platform reached 250 million [45]. This vast user base has led to the widespread use of online social networks in daily communication, news dissemination, public relations, and marketing [23]. However, there is a notable presence of social bots, i.e., automated accounts controlled by programs. Varol et al. [42]

© The Author(s), under exclusive license to Springer Nature Singapore Pte Ltd. 2025
H. Sun et al. (Eds.): ChineseCSCW 2024, CCIS 2343, pp. 64–79, 2025.
https://doi.org/10.1007/978-981-96-2373-0_5

indicated that 9%-15% of active Twitter accounts were bots in 2017. Moreover, the traces of the continuous evolution of bots can be found from [9,14]. The rise of malicious social bots has polluted the network environment and harmed users' privacy by spreading political misinformation and stealing personal information [42]. Therefore, detecting bots on social networks is crucial for information security [16], public opinion guidance [40], and user privacy protection [44].

Many researchers are focused on detecting social bots. Traditional feature-based classifiers aim to capture informative features from user profiles and tweets to identify social bots from human users [4,11,13,26]. In addition to these methods, graph-based approaches consider the natural graph structure of users and utilize graph representation learning methods to detect social bots [14,32,35,37]. However, these approaches do not consider the different roles that users play within the social network.

In this study, we introduce the concept of *Social Role Vector (SRV)*, which incorporates node centrality [18] and structural hole-related metrics [6,31] to capture the social features of users from different perspectives. SRV can comprehensively reflect the influence of a node within the network. By integrating SRV with GATv2 [5], an attention mechanism to selectively focus on important features and neighbors, we can more effectively distinguish between social bots and humans, thereby significantly improving the accuracy of detection. Our main contributions are summarized as follows:

- We define a set of graph structural metrics to form SRV, based on node centrality measurement, social structural hole and social capital theories. SRV could be further utilized to distinguish between bots and human users.
- We propose RoleScan, a novel framework based on graph representation learning for social bot detection. RoleScan considers comprehensive features from users' social networks, tweets, and profiles. Based on these features, RoleScan integrates GATv2 to learn informative user representations and classifies social bots from human users.
- Extensive results demonstrate that our method outperforms existing representative methods with an AUC of 0.887. Additionally, an ablation study highlights the significance of social features.

2   Related Work

Two kinds of methods are mainly used to detect bots in social networks: traditional machine learning-based methods and graph-based methods. We will discuss them as follows.

Traditional Machine Learning-Based Methods. Traditional bot detection classifiers combine feature engineering with classic machine learning methods. The features include metadata, descriptions, and dynamic features such as tweet frequency and sentiment. Kudugunta et al. [26] utilized features including the number of statuses and account verification status. Lee et al. [28] focused on redirection of URLs in tweets. Yang et al. [46] explored classification methods based on websites mentioned in tweets. Traditional machine learning classifiers used for Twitter bot detection include logistic regression [4], support vector machines [11], random forests [3,10] and long short-term memory neural networks [26]. However, as bots have evolved to mimic human behavior by altering their metadata and replicating humans' tweets, the effectiveness of these methods has been decreasing. This trend has led to a shift towards more advanced, graph-based detection techniques [9].

Graph-Based Methods. These methods leverage graph representation learning techniques to learn social relationships between users. These methods employ various graph embedding approaches, such as node2vec [22], as well as graph neural networks (GNNs) like graph convolutional network (GCN) [24], to better capture the complex interconnections among users. For example, Bot2Vec [37] employs node2vec to detect bots based on community interactions. BotFinder [30] also uses node2vec to transform nodes into vectors to input into the LightGBM classification model. Moreover, BotMoE [34] utilizes relational graph convolutional networks (RGCN) to derive representations of the network structure, integrating them with an expert classification system. DCGNN [35] employs a dual-channel GNN to effectively distinguish between human users and social bot accounts. Although these methods perform well in bot detection tasks, they have not fully considered the social roles of nodes when dealing with complicated social network graphs, which poses certain limitations.

3   Social Role Vector for Social Influence Evaluation

In this section, we propose SRV to evaluate a node's influence. In Sect. 3.1, we discuss how relying on a single metric is insufficient to assess a user's social influence and the need for a more comprehensive approach. In Sect. 3.2, we provide an overview of SRV, explaining its theoretical foundations. In Sect. 3.3, we present the formulas for the various centrality and structural hole-related metrics that constitute the SRV. In Sect. 3.4, we calculate the SRV metrics and compare their cumulative distribution between human and bot accounts to show the usefulness of SRV.

3.1   Background

In the analysis of social networks, commonly used metrics like centrality and structural hole-related metrics have their advantages in revealing network characteristics. For example, degree centrality identifies the most connected nodes, betweenness centrality pinpoints nodes that act as critical bridges within the network, and closeness centrality determines nodes with the shortest paths to all other nodes. However, when assessing a user's social influence, relying on a single metric has limitations. Although each metric excels at detecting specific phenomena, it may not capture other important structural characteristics of the network comprehensively.

As illustrated in Fig. 1, although nodes g and h are not prominent in degree centrality, they each occupy the highest ranks in closeness and betweenness centrality and act as structural hole spanners, connecting different social communities. Analyzing the node with the most connections in the social network to infer influence could lead to misunderstandings. Each metric attempts to capture some distinct characteristic within the network, but their applicability is limited when dealing with scientific problems that require different types of insights. Just as text features are extracted through models like TF-IDF [39], which uses vectors to represent word meanings, vectors can represent more complicated information, with each dimension representing a feature or attribute. In this section, we adopt a multidimensional approach to introduce a comprehensive metric for measuring a node's influence within the network.

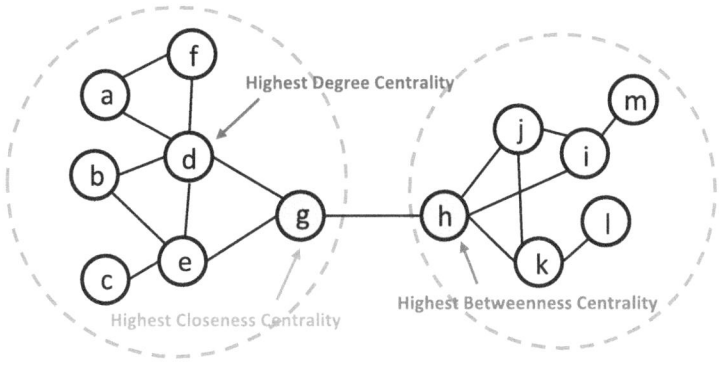

Fig. 1. A social graph with highlighted centrality metrics and structural hole spanners. Node d has the highest degree centrality (normalized) at **0.417**. Node g has the highest closeness centrality (normalized) at **0.522**. Node h displays the highest betweenness centrality (normalized) at **0.561**. Nodes g and h act as structural hole spanners, bridging disconnected parts of the network. No single metric could capture the full extent of the importance of a node.

3.2 Overview of SRV

According to Friedkin's theory [18], centrality metric serve as indicators of an individual's social influence. Many studies [12,27] have explored node centrality metrics to measure the influence of a node.

According to structural hole theory [7], structural hole spanners, like nodes g and h in Fig. 1, bridge structural holes and occupy advantageous positions within the network. A recent study by Gong et al. [21] applies structural hole theory to analyze graphs and detect malicious accounts, showcasing the effectiveness of structural hole-related metrics.

In social capital theory, when analyzing social capital from a structural dimension, network centrality and structural holes are often utilized [8]. For example, as a significant concept within this theory, bridging social capital represents associations that bridge between communities, groups, or organizations, just like the role of structural hole spanners [29]. This type of social capital can provide valuable new information and yield numerous benefits, including enhanced information acquisition and greater social influence [1]. In summary, centrality-related metrics help identify nodes that are well-connected and potentially influential due to their positions, and structural hole-related metrics highlight nodes that facilitate critical connections between network clusters. By combining these two perspectives, we propose SRV, which combines several centrality metrics and four structural hole-related metrics, as shown in Table 1. SRV represents the social roles and importance of nodes within the network.

Table 1. Metrics in SRV

	Features	Metrics
Social Role Vector's Composition	Centrality-Related	Betweenness Centrality
		Closeness Centrality
		Degree Centrality
		In-Degree Centrality (Directed Graph)
		Out-Degree Centrality (Directed Graph)
		PageRank Centrality
		Laplacian Centrality
	Structural Hole Theory-Related	Effective Size
		Efficiency
		Constraint
		Hierarchy

3.3 Metrics in SRV

First, we will introduce the centrality-related metrics used in SRV. We assume that there is a graph $G = (V, E)$ consisting of a set of nodes V and a set of edges E, and the number of nodes in the graph is $|V| = n$.

Betweenness Centrality. The betweenness centrality of a node v, proposed by Freeman [17], counts the fraction of shortest paths going through v as:

$$\alpha = BC(v) = \sum_{s \neq v \neq t} \frac{\sigma_{st}(v)}{\sigma_{st}}, \tag{1}$$

where σ_{st} represents the total number of shortest paths from node s to node t, and $\sigma_{st}(v)$ represents the number of those shortest paths passing through v.

Closeness Centrality. The closeness centrality of a node v, proposed by Bavelas [2], is measured as the inverse of the average distance from it:

$$\beta = CC(v) = \frac{n-1}{\sum_{u \neq v} d(v, u)}, \tag{2}$$

where $d(v, u)$ is the shortest-path distance between node v and u in G. For disconnected graphs, where distances between some node pairs are infinite, we treat the closeness centrality of such pairs as 0 to ensure calculability.

Degree Centrality. The degree centrality [41] of a node v counts how many neighbors it has:

$$\delta = DC(v) = \deg(v), \tag{3}$$

where $\deg(v)$ is the degree of v. Since $\deg_{in}(v)$ gives the in-degree and $\deg_{out}(v)$ gives the out-degree of node v, in a directed graph there are

$$\delta_{in} = DC_{in}(v) = \deg_{in}(v), \tag{4}$$

$$\delta_{out} = DC_{out}(v) = \deg_{out}(v). \tag{5}$$

Laplacian Centrality. The Laplacian centrality [38] of a node v is measured by the drop in the Laplacian energy after deleting node v from the graph. The Laplacian energy is the sum of the squared eigenvalues of a graph's Laplacian matrix:

$$E_L(G) = \sum_{i=0}^{n} \lambda_i^2, \tag{6}$$

where λ_i are the eigenvalues of G's Laplacian matrix. The Laplacian centrality is defined as:

$$\zeta = LC(v, G) = \frac{E_L(G) - E_L(G_v)}{E_L(G)}, \tag{7}$$

where $E_L(G_v)$ is the Laplacian energy of graph G after deleting node v.

PageRank Centrality. The PageRank algorithm captures the intuition that connections to a webpage contribute to its importance, which is influenced by the importance of the pages that link to it [36]. The PageRank centrality for a node v is given by

$$\rho = PR(v) = \frac{1-d}{n} + d \sum_{u \in M(v)} \frac{PR(u)}{\deg_{out}(v)}, \tag{8}$$

where d is the damping factor, $M(v)$ represents nodes linking to v, and $\deg_{out}(v)$ is the number of links outgoing from node u. If the out-degree of u is zero, we let $\deg_{out}(v) = 1$.

Structural hole theory encompasses the ego network, which comprises one node as the ego and the surrounding nodes to whom the ego is directly connected, known as the alters. The edge set consists of all the edges between these nodes.

Effective Size. Effective size [6] measures the number of non-redundant connections a node v has, indicative of its access to structural holes:

$$\epsilon = ES(v) = \sum_{u \in N(v)} \left(1 - \sum_q p_{vq} m_{uq} \right), \quad q \neq v, u \tag{9}$$

where $N(v)$ is the set of neighbors of v, each q is a node different from v and u in the ego network, p_{vq} is the mutual weight of the edge linking v and q and m_{uq} is the mutual weight of u and q divided by the largest weight between u and any of u's neighbors.

Efficiency. Efficiency [6] is the ratio of the benefits a node derives from its ties relative to their maintenance costs, indicating how effectively a node utilizes its connections. Given the node v and its alters N, the efficiency of a node v is defined as:

$$\phi = EF(v) = \frac{ES(v)}{N}. \tag{10}$$

Constraint. Constraint [6] measures the degree of dependency a node v has on other nodes, calculated based on the concentration of a node's ties among those connected to its neighbors. The constraint for a node v is computed as the sum of local constraints l_{vu} [7]:

$$\gamma = C(v) = \sum_{u \in N(v)} l_{vu}, \tag{11}$$

$$l_{vu} = \left(p_{vu} + \sum_q p_{vq} p_{qu} \right)^2, \quad q \neq v, u \tag{12}$$

where the definitions of $N(v)$ and p_{vu} is the same as Eq. 9.

Hierarchy. Hierarchy [6] quantifies the focus of constraints within a node's neighborhood, reflecting aspects of structural hole positions. The hierarchy for a node v is given by

$$\eta = HI(v) = \frac{\sum_{u \in N(v)} \left(\frac{l_{vu}}{C(v)} \right) \ln \left(\frac{l_{vu}}{C(v)} \right)}{\ln(N)}, \tag{13}$$

where the definitions of N, $N(v)$, $C(v)$ and l_{vu} is the same as Eq. 10 and Eq. 11.

3.4 Comparison Between Bots and Human Users

We utilize EasyGraph (https://easy-graph.github.io/), an open-source library designed to analyze and manipulate graph data efficiently [19], to build a graph based on following relationship between users and calculate metrics mentioned above. We make comparisons between bots and human users, as shown in Fig. 2. The dataset used here is introduced in Sect. 5.1. Figure 2a reveals that humans have higher closeness centrality, indicating they can reach other nodes in the network more quickly, which implies better accessibility to information. Figure 2b shows that humans have higher Laplacian centrality, suggesting they contribute more to the overall connectivity and robustness of the network. Figure 2c shows that bots have higher constraint values, indicating stronger dependencies on immediate neighbors and restricted behaviors. Figure 2d shows that humans have a larger effective size, indicating more diverse connections within the network, while bots are more peripheral.

According to the analysis of centrality and structural hole-related metrics (including metrics not shown above, which have distributions similar to those displayed), we can observe significant differences between human and bot accounts on these metrics. SRV combines these metrics to comprehensively reflect the influence of each account within the network, and can serve as social features to differentiate between bot and human accounts. According to Eqs. 1–13, the SRV for a node v in a directed graph G is defined as follows

$$SRV(v) = \left[\alpha, \beta, \delta_{in}, \delta_{out}, \zeta, \rho, \epsilon, \phi, \gamma, \eta \right]^T. \tag{14}$$

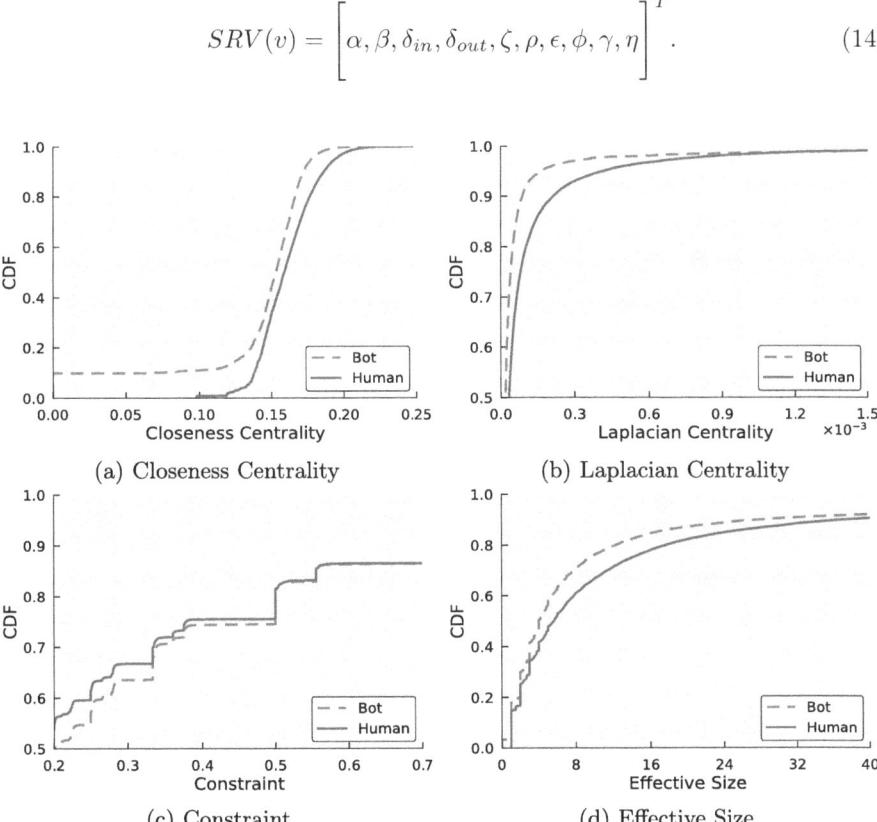

(a) Closeness Centrality

(b) Laplacian Centrality

(c) Constraint

(d) Effective Size

Fig. 2. Cumulative Distribution Functions (CDFs) of Metrics in SRV for Human and Bot Accounts.

4   System Design of RoleScan

Figure 3 presents an overview of our proposed RoleScan framework with SRV and dynamic graph attention network. Firstly, we extract user information and textual information from the dataset and calculate centrality and structural hole-related metrics. Subsequently, we encode the information and build SRV to obtain three features. These features are then input into a 2-layer GATv2 model [5] to learn informative user representations. After that, we classify social bots from human users with the MLP and softmax layer.

4.1   Problem Formulation

The goal of the bot detection task is to develop a classifier function f, which discriminates between human users and bots. For each Twitter user $\mathcal{V}$, the classifier considers its profile $\mathcal{P}$, textual content $\mathcal{T}$, and social network $\mathcal{S}$. The function f aggregates these inputs to predict a binary label $\hat{y}$. Here, $\hat{y} = 1$ denotes a bot, and $\hat{y} = 0$ denotes a human. The function can be expressed as $f(\mathcal{V}(\mathcal{P}, \mathcal{T}, \mathcal{S})) \rightarrow \hat{y}$.

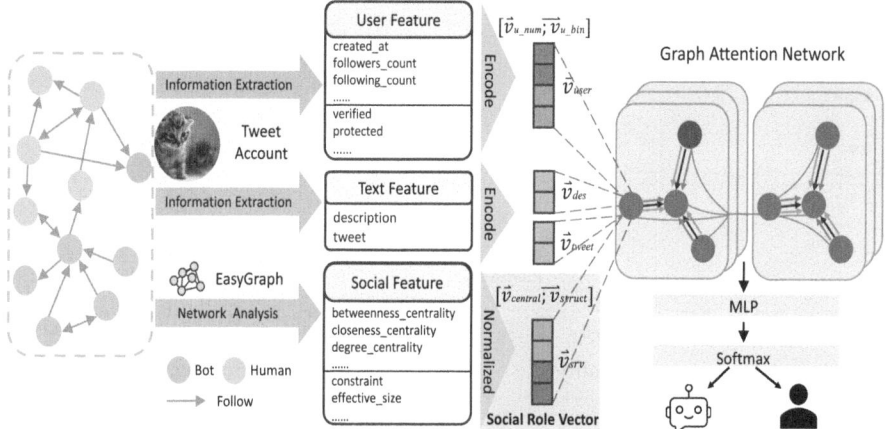

Fig. 3. Overview of our proposed framework RoleScan.

4.2   Feature Extraction

User Features. We extract user profile information from the data obtained via the Twitter API. User features are classified into numerical and binary properties, as detailed in Table 2. We apply Z-score normalization to the numerical properties and transform them using a fully connected layer. For binary properties, we implement one-hot encoding. The numerical and binary vectors, denoted as v_{u_num} and v_{u_bin}, respectively, are then concatenated to form a complete user feature vector v_{user} with dimensions 14×1.

Table 2. User attributes.

Category	Feature Name	Description
Numerical user attributes	followers_count	number of followers
	followings_count	number of followings
	tweet_count	number of tweets
	listed_count	number of lists
	active days	number of active days
	user name length	user name character count
	screen name length	screen name character count
Binary user attributes	entities	has entities or not
	location	has location or not
	protected	protected or not
	verified	verified or not
	url	has URL or not
	profile_image_url	has profile image or not
	pinned_tweet_id	has pinned tweet or not

Text Features. We employ the pre-trained RoBERTa model [33] to encode user descriptions and tweets, transforming them into vector representations. The vectors for user descriptions and tweets are denoted as v_{des} and v_{tweet}, respectively, each with dimensions 768×1. The encoding process can be formalized as

$$v_{des} = \text{RoBERTa(user description)}, \tag{15}$$

$$v_{tweet} = \text{RoBERTa(tweets)}. \tag{16}$$

Social Features. According to Eq. 14, we can use a 10×1-dimension vector to represent user's social features as

$$v_{srv} = \left[\alpha, \beta, \delta_{in}, \delta_{out}, \zeta, \rho, \epsilon, \phi, \gamma, \eta \right]^{T}. \tag{17}$$

Combined Feature Vector. The combined feature vector for a node can be represented as:

$$h = [\boldsymbol{v}_{\text{user}}, \boldsymbol{v}_{\text{des}}, \boldsymbol{v}_{\text{tweet}}, \boldsymbol{v}_{\text{srv}}]^T. \tag{18}$$

4.3 Attentive Social Relations Learning

In the RoleScan framework, GATv2 [5] is utilized to dynamically weigh the contributions of different features extracted from user tweets, social role vectors, and account characteristics, effectively incorporating complicated interactions within the network. In the standard GAT [43], the learned layers $\mathbf{W}$ and $\mathbf{a}$ are applied consecutively, and thus can be collapsed into a single linear layer. To address this limitation, GATv2 simply applies the layer $\mathbf{a}$ after the nonlinearity and applies the layer $\mathbf{W}$ after the concatenation operation. This simple modification makes a significant difference in the expressiveness of the attention function. Furthermore, GATv2 achieves better performance on classification problems.

The attention coefficients are computed as

$$\alpha_{ij} = \frac{\exp(\mathbf{a}^T \text{LeakyReLU}(\mathbf{W}[h_i \| h_j]))}{\sum_{k \in \mathcal{N}_i} \exp(\mathbf{a}^T \text{LeakyReLU}(\mathbf{W}[h_i \| h_k]))}, \tag{19}$$

where $\mathbf{W}$ is a weight matrix applied to every node, $\mathbf{a}$ is a learnable parameter vector of the attention mechanism, h_i is the feature vector of node i, $\|$ denotes concatenation, $\mathcal{N}_i$ is the set of neighbors of node i in the graph, LeakyReLU is the activation function.

Once the attention coefficients are computed, the new node features h_i' are updated using the weighted sum of the features of its neighbors:

$$h_i' = \text{LeakyReLU}\left(\sum_{j \in \mathcal{N}_i} \alpha_{ij} \mathbf{W} h_j\right). \tag{20}$$

Multi-Head Attention. The RoleScan employs a multi-head attention mechanism [5] to stabilize the learning process and to capture various aspects of the information from the neighbors more effectively. The node representation is obtained by concatenating the outputs of all the heads:

$$h_i = \Big\|_{k=1}^{K} h_i^{(k)}, \tag{21}$$

where K is the total number of attention heads. Specifically, we use 8-head attention mechanism in the experiment.

4.4 Learning and Optimization

In the RoleScan framework, the node representation h_i obtained from the GATv2 layers is further processed by a MLP and then used in a softmax layer to classify Twitter bots:

$$\hat{y}_i = \text{softmax}(W_o \cdot \phi(W_1 \cdot h_i + b_1) + b_o), \tag{22}$$

where W_1, b_1, W_o, and b_o are learnable parameters. ϕ is a non-linear activation function, and $\hat{y}_i$ is the predicted output for the i-th user. We use the cross-entropy loss with an L_2 regularization, helps the model learn accurately while avoiding overfitting:

$$L = -\sum_{i \in Y} [y_i \log(\hat{y}_i) + (1 - y_i) \log(1 - \hat{y}_i)] + \lambda \sum_{w \in \theta} w^2, \quad (23)$$

where Y represents the set of annotated users within the training dataset, y_i is the ground truth label, and θ includes all the parameters the model can adjust.

5 Experiments and Analysis

This section presents the experimental evaluation of RoleScan. We first describe our dataset, and then compare RoleScan with various baselines. We also conduct an ablation study to understand the contribution of different components of RoleScan. Throughout our analysis, we use the Area Under the Curve (AUC) as our evaluation metric. AUC is widely used in bot detection research [30,32,47]. It is insensitive to the distribution of positive and negative samples. The calculation formula is as follows:

$$\text{AUC} = \int_0^1 \text{TPR}(\text{FPR}) \, d(\text{FPR}), \quad (24)$$

where TPR and FPR represent the true positive rate and false positive rate of the classification model at different thresholds, respectively.

5.1 Dataset

Many existing datasets do not have the following relationships and graph structures, making them unsuitable for our analysis [20,47]. To address this issue, we select a representative recent dataset, Twibot-22 [15], for our study. In Twibot-22, the large number of nodes makes computing metrics such as structural holes very time-consuming. Additionally, the dataset has a class imbalance problem, with bots accounting for only 11.74% of the nodes. To address these challenges, we employ a Breadth-First Search (BFS) approach on Twibot-22 to sample 30,000 nodes and 382,379 edges based on the following relationships between nodes. In this sampled subset, the proportion of bot nodes is 20.98%.

5.2 Baselines

We compare RoleScan with the following representative baselines:

- SGBot [47] mainly obtains the user features from metadata on the profiles and utilizes the random forest classifiers for social bot identification.

- LOBO [10] introduces an innovative testing approach by training all bot categories except the target class, with the aim of evaluating the generalizability of bot classification from known to unknown bot types.
- Bot-Detective [25] extracts 36 features from each user's metadata and the latest 20 tweets and classifies users with random forest model.
- DCGNN [35] features two distinct channels: a burst-aware channel that uses an adaptive-pass filter to capture bot activities, and a static-aware channel that employs a low-pass filter to analyze user characteristics. Given that our dataset only contains information on following relationships, we only employ the static-aware channel.

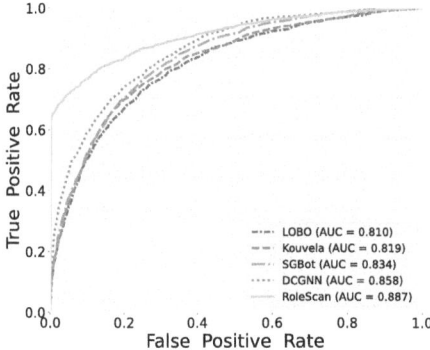

Table 3. Comparison of RoleScan with baselines.

Model	AUC
LOBO	0.810
Bot-Detective	0.819
SGBot	0.834
DCGNN	0.858
RoleScan	**0.887**

Fig. 4. Comparison of ROC curves for different models.

5.3 Detection Performance

Table 3 and Fig. 4 demonstrate RoleScan's superior performance. Graph-based deep learning models like DCGNN and RoleScan outperform traditional machine learning approaches, with RoleScan achieving the highest AUC of 0.887. Compared with traditional models such as LOBO (AUC = 0.810) and Bot-Detective (AUC = 0.819), RoleScan's advanced techniques are more effective. While SGBot (AUC = 0.834) and DCGNN (AUC = 0.858) perform well, RoleScan slightly surpasses them, especially at lower false positive rates.

5.4 Ablation Study

To assess the contributions of the SRV and the attention mechanism to the detection performance of our bot detection model, we conduct an ablation study. We remove each component from our full model and evaluate the impact on the AUC. We create three variations, i.e. (1) RoleScan without SRV, (2) RoleScan

Table 4. Ablation study.

Model	AUC
RoleScan w/o SRV	0.867
RoleScan w/o Attention	0.865
RoleScan w/o Dynamic Attention	0.872
RoleScan	**0.887**

without attention mechanism (simple GCN [24]), (3) RoleScan without dynamic attention mechanism (standard GAT).

Table 4 presents the results of our ablation study. We obtain the following findings. 1) All components contribute to the detection performance of RoleScan. 2) Two variants (RoleScan w/o SRV and RoleScan w/o Attention) of RoleScan exhibited a decline in performance. This could be attributed to the fact that both the attention mechanism and the SRV can learn more knowledge from users' social structures.

6   Conclusion

Our study introduces RoleScan, a novel model that integrates SRV and GATv2 for social bot detection task. We define a set of representative graph metrics as SRV. Specifically, SRV is composed of centrality-related and structural hole-related metrics, providing a multi-dimensional representation of a user's influence within the network. By combining SRV with GATv2, RoleScan effectively captures pivotal structural features and considers the importance of neighbors, leading to an improved differentiation between bots and human users. Our experimental results show that RoleScan achieves state-of-the-art performance, with an AUC of 0.887, surpassing existing methods. The ablation study highlights the significant contributions of SRV and GATv2 to the detection performance, highlighting the importance of considering social features. The proposal of SRV offers insights into the diverse roles users play within social networks, which can inspire future research and applications.

Acknowledgements. This work has been sponsored by National Natural Science Foundation of China (No. 62072115, No. 62102094), Shanghai Science and Technology Innovation Action Plan Project (No. 22510713600).

References

1. Adler, P.S., Kwon, S.W.: Social capital: prospects for a new concept. Acad. Manag. Rev. **27**(1), 17–40 (2002)
2. Bavelas, A.: Communication patterns in task-oriented groups. J. Acoust. Soc. Am. **22**, 725–730 (1950)

3. Beskow, D.M., Carley, K.M.: Bot-hunter: a tiered approach to detecting and characterizing automated activity on Twitter. In: SBP-BRiMS (2018)
4. Beskow, D.M., Carley, K.M.: Its all in a name: detecting and labeling bots by their name. Comput. Math. Organ. Theory **25**, 24–35 (2019)
5. Brody, S., Alon, U., Yahav, E.: How attentive are graph attention networks? In: ICLR (2022)
6. Burt, R.S.: Structural Holes: the Social Structure of Competition. Harvard University Press, Cambridge (1992)
7. Burt, R.S.: Structural holes and good ideas. Am. J. Sociol. **110**, 349–399 (2004)
8. Claridge, T.: Introduction to social capital theory. Social Capital Research. (2018)
9. Cresci, S.: A decade of social bot detection. Commun. ACM **63**, 72–83 (2020)
10. Echeverría, J., et al.: LOBO: evaluation of generalization deficiencies in Twitter bot classifiers. In: ACSAC (2018)
11. Efthimion, P.G., Payne, S., Proferes, N.: Supervised machine learning bot detection techniques to identify social Twitter bots. SMU Data Sci. Rev. **1**, 5 (2018)
12. Farooq, A., et al.: Detection of influential nodes using social networks analysis based on network metrics. In: iCoMET, pp. 1–6 (2018)
13. Fazil, M., Sah, A.K., Abulaish, M.: DeepSBD: a deep neural network model with attention mechanism for socialbot detection. IEEE Trans. Inf. Forensics Secur. **16**, 4211–4223 (2021)
14. Feng, S., et al.: BotRGCN: Twitter bot detection with relational graph convolutional networks. In: ASONAM (2021)
15. Feng, S., et al.: Twibot-22: towards graph-based Twitter bot detection. In: NeurIPS (2024)
16. Ferrara, E., et al.: The rise of social bots. Commun. ACM **59**, 96–104 (2016)
17. Freeman, L.: A set of measures of centrality based on betweenness. Sociometry **40**, 35–41 (1977)
18. Friedkin, N.E.: Theoretical foundations for centrality measures. Am. J. Sociol. **96**, 1478–1504 (1991)
19. Gao, M., et al.: EasyGraph: a multifunctional, cross-platform, and effective library for interdisciplinary network analysis. Patterns **4**, 100839 (2023)
20. Gilani, Z., et al.: Of bots and humans (on Twitter). In: Proceedings of IEEE ACM International Conference on Advances in Social Network Analysis and Mining (2017)
21. Gong, Q., et al.: Detecting malicious accounts in online developer communities using deep learning. IEEE Trans. Knowl. Data Eng. **35**, 10633–10649 (2023)
22. Grover, A., Leskovec, J.: node2vec: scalable feature learning for networks. In: ACM SIGKDD (2016)
23. Jin, L., et al.: Understanding user behavior in online social networks: a survey. IEEE Commun. Mag. **51**, 144–150 (2013)
24. Kipf, T.N., Welling, M.: Semi-supervised classification with graph convolutional networks. In: ICLR (2017)
25. Kouvela, M., Dimitriadis, I., Vakali, A.: Bot-detective: an explainable Twitter bot detection service with crowdsourcing functionalities. In: MEDES, pp. 55–63 (2020)
26. Kudugunta, S., Ferrara, E.: Deep neural networks for bot detection. Inf. Sci. **467**, 312–322 (2018)
27. Lawyer, G.: Understanding the influence of all nodes in a network. Sci. Rep. **5**, 8665 (2015)
28. Lee, S., Kim, J.: WarningBird: a near real-time detection system for suspicious urls in Twitter stream. IEEE Trans. Dependable Secure Comput. **10**, 183–195 (2013)

29. Leonard, M.: Bonding and bridging social capital: reflections from belfast. Sociology **38**, 927–944 (2004)
30. Li, S., et al.: BotFinder: a novel framework for social bots detection in online social networks based on graph embedding and community detection. World Wide Web **26**, 1793–1809 (2023)
31. Lin, Z., et al.: Structural hole theory in social network analysis: a review. IEEE Trans. Comput. Social Syst. **9**, 724–739 (2022)
32. Liu, F., et al.: Accou2vec: a social bot detection model based on community walk. IEEE Trans, Dependable Secure Comput (2023)
33. Liu, Y., et al.: Roberta: a robustly optimized Bert pretraining approach. arXiv preprint arXiv:1907.11692 (2019)
34. Liu, Y., et al.: BotMoE: Twitter bot detection with community-aware mixtures of modal-specific experts. In: ACM SIGIR (2023)
35. Lyu, N., et al.: DCGNN: dual-channel graph neural network for social bot detection. In: CIKM (2023)
36. Page, L., et al.: The PageRank citation ranking: bringing order to the web. In: The Web Conference (1999)
37. Pham, P., et al.: Bot2Vec: a general approach of intra-community oriented representation learning for bot detection in different types of social networks. Inf. Syst. **103**, 101771 (2021)
38. Qi, X., et al.: Laplacian centrality: a new centrality measure for weighted networks. Inf. Sci. **194**, 240–253 (2012)
39. Ramos, J., et al.: Using TF-IDF to determine word relevance in document queries. In: ICML (2003)
40. Rossi, S., et al.: Detecting political bots on Twitter during the 2019 Finnish parliamentary election. In: HICSS (2020)
41. Shaw, M.E.: Group structure and the behavior of individuals in small groups. J. Psychol. **38**, 139–149 (1954)
42. Varol, O., et al.: Online human-bot interactions: detection, estimation, and characterization. In: ICWSM (2017)
43. Velickovic, P., et al.: Graph attention networks. In: ICLR (2018)
44. Volkova, S., et al.: Inferring latent user properties from texts published in social media. In: AAAI (2015)
45. XData: Data(@xdata)/x. https://x.com/XData. Accessed 4 May 2024
46. Yang, C., Harkreader, R., Gu, G.: Empirical evaluation and new design for fighting evolving Twitter spammers. IEEE Trans. Inf. Forensics Secur. **8**, 1280–1293 (2013)
47. Yang, K.C., et al.: Scalable and generalizable social bot detection through data selection. In: AAAI (2020)
48. Zuckerberg, M.: Mark zuckerberg (@zuck) on Threads. https://www.threads.net/@zuck. Accessed 4 May 2024

Blockchain-Based Traffic Accident Evidence Management Scheme

Qi An, Yi Zhao, Meiju Yu$^{(\boxtimes)}$, Rula Sa, Qiaomei Gao, and Jin Zhang

College of Computer Science-College of Software Inner Mongolia University, Hohhot,
China
csymj@imu.edu.cn

Abstract. The management of evidence for traffic accidents under
surveillance video faces numerous challenges. Currently, traffic accidents
evidence heavily relies on manual video review, and manually stored in
third-party databases. This method of evidence storage cannot ensure the
reliable source and trustworthy storage of evidence. Therefore, we propose a framework that combines deep learning with blockchain technology for traffic accident evidence management. It focuses on securely storing accident evidence and efficiently extracting accident information, providing a practical solution for traffic accident evidence management. In
this framework, blockchain is combined with IPFS to overcome the drawbacks of centralized evidence storage, ensuring the security of evidence
while alleviating the problem of limited blockchain storage capacity. Furthermore, a traffic accident evidence forensic model (YOLO-MBC) is
constructed, which uses artificial intelligence to replace manual evidence
collection. This not only ensures the reliability of evidence sources but
also enhances the efficiency of evidence collection. Finally, experimental
results demonstrate that the framework achieves secure evidence storage
and the accuracy of the accident evidence forensic model (YOLO-MBC)
reaches 92.4%, meeting the practical requirements of traffic accident evidence management.

Keywords: Deep learning · YOLOv5 · Blockchain · Forensics ·
Accident detection

1 Introduction

In the past decade, the number of traffic accidents has sharply increased, with
1.35 million people dying in road traffic accidents each year [17]. Obtaining
evidence for some particular cases has become extremely challenging, such as
accidents that occur without any eyewitnesses. Due to their ability to record
long-term scenes in specific areas, surveillance footage has become one of the
most crucial pieces of evidence in accident assessment. When significant traffic
accidents occur, traffic police should promptly collect, forensic, and archive traces
and physical evidence related to the case, to be used by subsequent judicial

H. Sun et al. (Eds.): ChineseCSCW 2024, CCIS 2343, pp. 80–94, 2025.
https://doi.org/10.1007/978-981-96-2373-0_6

authorities [23]. However, in judicial practice, there are still many pain points in various aspects such as evidence collection, forensic, archiving, and retrieval for traffic accidents.

It is essential to promptly extract relevant information and segments related to the accidents. These serve as the basis for understanding the accident process and determining liability. The forensic analysis of road surveillance videos often relies on manual review methods. These methods typically require significant time to pinpoint the precise moment of the accident from the video footage. Moreover, subjective cognitive differences or visual fatigue may lead to the omission of critical information during manual video review, thereby affecting the accuracy of accident forensics.

Judicial, traffic management, and other departments typically store accident evidence through localized certification or notarization methods. However, this approach may lead to data tampering or loss, making it difficult to ensure the reliability and security of the evidence. Furthermore, evidence needs to be shared among multiple parties in judicial procedures. To prevent malicious transmission or exploitation, it is necessary to implement traceable control and public constraints on physical actions. Therefore, the manner in which accident evidence is stored, shared, and preserved greatly influences its admissibility and probative value [19].

Blockchain, as a distributed shared database, possesses characteristics such as decentralization, immutability, and traceability [11]. This provides new insights for evidence storage. Utilizing blockchain for storing judicial evidence not only ensures the objectivity and authenticity of data results but also regulates related behaviors to be fair, transparent, and legal [24]. However, existing solutions that use blockchain technology to address the issue of evidence storage suffer from two main problems. Firstly, the majority of current judicial evidence storage models uploading electronic evidence to the chain after collection, which fails to guarantee the authenticity of the evidence. Blockchain technology cannot ensure the objectivity and truthfulness of data "before being recorded on the chain". Secondly, the storage mechanism of existing evidence chains is unsuitable for storing large data files such as videos and images. Storing all collected data on the chain results in increasing access costs.

The main contributions of this study can be summarized as follows:

(1) We propose a blockchain-based deep learning evidence storage framework, covering the entire process of evidence collection, extraction, storage, and retrieval. The application of blockchain-driven secure storage in the field of judicial evidence ensures the security of evidence data.

(2) In the evidence extraction process, we develop a new forensic model called YOLO-MBC. YOLO-MBC automatically identifies and extracts evidence from surveillance videos. It transforms the traditional "passive" forensic process into "automatic" forensic, ensuring both the reliability of evidence sources and enhancing the efficiency of evidence extraction.

(3) We conduct a security analysis of the framework and collect a dataset of traffic accidents and non-accidents from surveillance videos to evaluate the

YOLO-MBC model. Experimental results demonstrate that our approach can achieve secure storage of evidence and enable rapid and effective forensics.

2   Related Work

2.1   Evidence Frame Extraction Technology

The extraction of evidence in traffic accidents typically begins with accident detection, followed by the extraction of frames relevant to the accident as evidence. In [22], Yao proposed an unsupervised method for detecting traffic accidents using onboard cameras. By calculating bounding boxes to identify participants in traffic scenes, it is possible to infer whether collisions occurred between participants. Gao [6] analysed the width variation characteristics of the rectangular boxes of moving objects during normal driving and accident processes, detection of rear-end collisions and accidents at road intersections was achieved. However, these methods still face challenges in complex features and diverse accident environments.

In recent years, deep learning, as a branch of machine learning, has been widely applied in video processing. Mohammed [4] proposed a traffic accident detection and alarm system consisting of three models. Initially, it utilizes the YOLOv5 and DeepSORT models for real-time monitoring and tracking of vehicles. Subsequently, the YOLOv5 model is used to detect and classify the severity of accidents. Finally, a transfer learning algorithm based on ResNet152 is employed to detect fire ignition situations after accidents. In [18], to enhance the adaptability of accident detection methods in different traffic scenarios, D Tian established a new image dataset CAD-CVIS, consisting of various types of accidents, weather conditions, and accident locations. The deep neural network algorithm YOLO-CA is used to detect accidents and their locations. However, the aforementioned algorithms have complex network structures and their detection accuracy falls short of practical application requirements.

In this study, to strike a balance between speed and accuracy in the accident detection task, we modify the network architecture of YOLOv5 to achieve traffic accident detection in surveillance videos. This lays a solid foundation for the subsequent evidence storage stage.

2.2   Blockchain Evidence Storage

Electronic evidence has been widely applied in various aspects of judicial practice. Governments of various countries have made numerous attempts to integrate blockchain technology with judicial practice. The Supreme People's Court of China issued the "Provisions of the Supreme People's Court on Several Issues Concerning the Trial of Cases by Internet Courts" , which explicitly affirmed the validity of using blockchain for evidence [24]. In Europe, 22 EU member states collaborated to develop the European Blockchain Services Infrastructure [7] and referred to evidence stored on the chain as "electronic evidence". This indicates that blockchain-based evidence can rely on legal protection and be used in a broader range of fields.

In the academic field, scholars have already applied blockchain technology in conjunction with judicial evidence. G. Maciá-Fernández et al. have recognized the risks associated with current online behavior and proposed the idea of using blockchain platforms to preserve evidence of online behavior, thus ensuring its tamper-proof nature [12]. However, they don't consider the storage mode of electronic evidence. Liza Ahmad et al. [2] propose a blockchain-based electronic evidence supervision framework. It utilizes blockchain technology to store evidence metadata while also storing evidence in reliable storage media. Additionally, smart locks are added between judicial institutions, lawyers, and other professionals to ensure data integrity. Ding et al. [5] address the data security and trust issues in traditional electronic evidence storage by designing an electronic evidence storage system based on Hyperledger Fabric [3], and they use the InterPlanetary File System (IPFS) to store electronic evidence to solve the blockchain capacity problem. However, these solutions all involve placing evidence on the chain after it has been collected. This means that the authenticity of the evidence before being placed on the chain cannot be guaranteed.

Therefore, in this study, accident evidence originates from the evidence extraction stage of the previous section and is stored in a consortium blockchain that supports image evidence. This not only ensures the secure storage of evidence but also ensures its reliable source.

3 Blockchain-Based Traffic Accident Evidence Storage Scheme

3.1 Blockchain Deep Learning Evidence Storage Framework

We proposes a traffic accident evidence management framework under road monitoring. The system framework is illustrated in Fig. 1. This framework adopts a consortium blockchain network, composed of five entities: Data Centers, Stakeholders (public security bureaus, courts, insurance companies, other institutions, etc.), InterPlanetary File System (IPFS), Blockchain, and Authorization Center. The functions of each entity are as follows:

(1) Data Centers: Each data center is responsible for collecting surveillance videos within its region and using the evidence forensic model YOLO-MBC to identify evidence frames, which are then uploaded to the blockchain as accident evidence.
(2) Stakeholders: Each stakeholders possesses a pair of keys for identity verification. Authenticated entities have the authority to retrieve evidence relevant to specific cases. Each retrieval is recorded as a transaction on the blockchain, facilitating subsequent accountability.
(3) IPFS: Used for storing evidence of traffic accidents. Storing all evidence directly on the blockchain could lead to significant strain on the network. Therefore, the IPFS is employed to address this need.

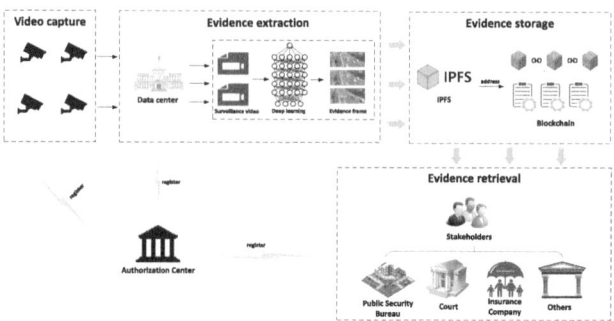

Fig. 1. Traffic accident evidence management framework.

(4) Blockchain: Blockchain be used for transactional data during the judicial evidence management process (entity registration information, evidence storage addresses, evidence retrieval records). The blockchain provides a secure means of storing information in an untrusted environment without the need for intermediaries.

(5) Authorization Center: Responsible for managing nodes in the consortium blockchain. The authorization center generates system-wide parameters and handles registration and identity verification for various entities. When a user initiates a registration request with the authorization center, the corresponding keys are generated for the requesting user.

The workflow of this framework includes entity registration, evidence encryption and storage stages, and evidence retrieval stages.

Entity Registration. When establishing a blockchain network system, initialization settings are required. A large prime number q is selected, and a generator g for the group $\mathbb{Z}_q^*$ is determined, with both q and g publicly disclosed as system parameters. A random number s is generated as the master private key SUK, where $s \in \mathbb{Z}_q^*$. The system public key PUK is g^s. The system may update the public parameters at certain time intervals according to actual needs to ensure long-term security.

(1) When a Data Center or stakeholder P applies to join the blockchain, they select a random number sk_P as their private key and compute their public key pk_P, as shown in Equation (1) and (2). Subsequently, P broadcasts their identity information and pk_P to the blockchain for verification. Due to the discrete logarithm problem, it is difficult for others to derive the private key sk_P from pk_P.

$$sk_P \in (1, q - 1) \tag{1}$$

$$pk_P = g^{sk_P} \mod q \tag{2}$$

(2) When other node P_i in the network receives a request message from node P, it verifies P identity proof and checks whether the same public key pk_P exists

in the blockchain to ensure the uniqueness of node P. If the identity verification is correct and the local blockchain does not store the public key pk_P, P_i approves P join request. According to the system rules, P_i generates an identity identifier ID_P for node P and broadcasts it. When other nodes successfully verify P identity and generate the same ID_P, node P joins the network successfully, and the sk_P, pk_P, ID_P become effective.

Evidence Storage. It covers the entire process of evidence from generation to on-chain.

a. The original evidence is uploaded to IPFS. The Data Center (DC) uses YOLO-MBC to extract traffic accident evidence (Evidence) and generates an encryption key K_i using the local cryptographic system. Using K_i to generate $E_{Eve} = (Evidence \| K_i)$, which is uploaded to IPFS. IPFS returns the storage address of the original $Evidence$, CID_{Eve} to the data center. Subsequently, K_i is encrypted using the system's public key PUK to generate $E_{K_i} = ENCRYPT(K_i \| PUK)$, which is then sent to the authorization center (AC) for storage.

b. Evidence summary is uploaded to IPFS. The DC calculates the hash value of the accident evidence $H_{Eve} = HASH(Evedence)$, and the hash value of the storage address $HCID_{Eve} = HASH(CID_{Eve})$. The DC signs $HCID_{Eve}$ and H_{Eve} using the private key sk_{DC}. Signature is to prevent tampering during the transmission process. After assembling the summary file into DATA, it is sent to any IPFS node, as shown in Eqs. (3) and (4).

$$Sign1 = SIGN((HCID_{Eve}, H_{Eve}) \| sk_{DC}) \tag{3}$$

$$DATA = \{pk_{DC}, E_{K_i}, Time, ID_{DC}, CID_{Eve}, HE_{Eve}, Sign1\} \tag{4}$$

c. IPFS returns address of the evidence summary. The IPFS node verifies the signature using the public key pk_{DC} from the $DATA$. Then, the IPFS node saves $DATA$, obtaining the hash label CID_{DATA}.

d. DC assembles the transaction. The data center obtains CID_{DATA} and constructs the on-chain transaction structure Tx to send to the blockchain node, as shown in Equation (5) and (6).

$$Sign2 = SIGN(HASH(CID_{DATA}) \| sk_{DC}) \tag{5}$$

$$Tx = \{pk_{DC}, Time, ID_{DC}, CID_{DATA}, Sign2\} \tag{6}$$

e. Blockchain validates and adds Tx to Blockchain. Blockchain node verifies the $Sign2$ to ensure the authenticity of Tx. Simultaneously, Tx obtains CID_{DATA} and sends a query request to the IPFS. By comparing the public key pk_{DC} in $DATA$ and in Tx, we verify whether the off-chain and on-chain data originate from the same DC. Finally, Blockchain node broadcasts Tx to other nodes in the blockchain network. And after reaching consensus, the transaction is packaged into blocks and appended to the consortium chain.

Request Evidence. The complete process by which Stakeholder Q requests evidence based on the evidence generation time ($Time$) and the ID of the respective data center (ID_{DC}), and obtains the original evidence.

a. Sending a query request to the blockchain node. Q signs and sends a query request REQ to the blockchain node, as shown in Eqs. (7) and (8).

$$Sign3 = SIGN(HASH(CID_{DC}, Time)\|sk_Q) \tag{7}$$

$$REQ = \{pk_Q, Time, ID_{DC}, Sign3\} \tag{8}$$

b. Returning the query results. The blockchain node verifies the $Sign3$ using pkQ from REQ. If the signature is verified, it retrieves the corresponding $TxHash$ from the chain based on $Time$ and ID_{DC} in REQ. The query results RES are returned to the Q. And generates evidence retrieval record transaction Tx' for future accountability purposes.

$$RES = \{Time, ID_{DC}, TxHash\} \tag{9}$$

$$Tx' = \{pk_Q, RES\} \tag{10}$$

c. Sending a query request to the IPFS. Q receives TxHash, and based on the properties of the Merkle tree, locates the evidence transaction Tx corresponding to TxHash. Q extracts the CID_{DATA} from Tx and sends it to the IPFS node to request download.

d. Obtaining the $Evidence$. IPFS returns $DATA$ based on the CID_{DATA} provided by Q. Q obtains E_{K_i} and CID_{Eve} from the $DATA$. Q sends E_{K_i} to the AC for decryption. AC decrypts E_{K_i} using the private key SUK to obtain Ki and returns it to Q. Q uses K_i to find E_{Eve} based on CID_{Eve}, decrypts the ciphertext CID_{Eve}, and obtains the $Evedence$.

3.2   Accident Forensics Model YOLO-MBC

The identification and extraction of traffic accident evidence are centralized in the data center. Therefore, in the actual deployment of detection models, while ensuring detection efficiency, it is essential to choose detection models that are small in size, low in computational cost, and highly scalable. Hence, we propose YOLO-MBC for accident forensics.

We improve YOLOv5 from two aspects: backbone network and feature fusion, with specific structures as shown in Fig. 2. MobileNetV3 serves as the backbone, achieving a lighter design. The neck network utilizes the improved feature extraction network BNet, which integrates semantic information from deep networks into shallow networks. Additionally, the C3_B module is designed to replace each C3 in the neck, capturing additional feature information. These improvements aim to enhance spatial and semantic information, improve detection accuracy, while maintaining operational speed.

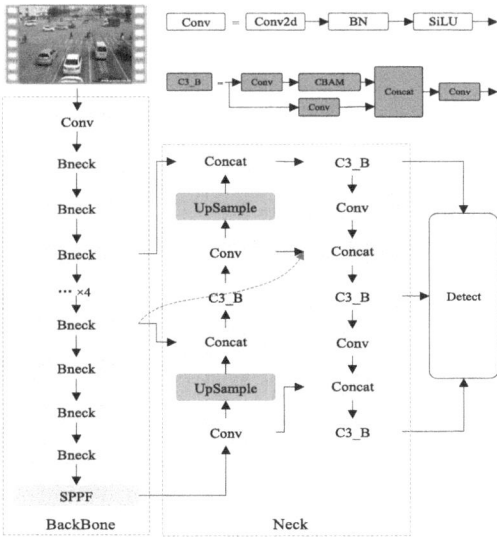

Fig. 2. Network structure of YOLO-MBC.

Improve Backbone. In YOLOv5, CSPDarknet53 or ResNet backbone networks are used, but these two network models have relatively large parameter sizes. We are looking for a relatively lightweight network model to ensure high detection accuracy while minimizing computational overhead and memory usage as much as possible.

MobileNetV3 [8] is a lightweight convolutional neural network architecture that preserves depth-wise separable convolution (DSC) from MobileNetV1 [9] and inherits the inverted residual structure from MobileNetV2 [16]. Additionally, it introduces the squeeze-and-excite (SE) attention mechanism [10], which allows the network to recalibrate channel feature responses by explicitly modeling interdependencies between channels, enabling it to focus on features with more informative content. MobileNetV3 achieves a good balance between model performance and size, with lower computational complexity and memory consumption. Therefore, in this paper, MobileNetV3-small is used to replace the original feature extraction network in YOLOv5s.

Improve Neck. Detecting traffic accidents in surveillance videos differs from standard object detection because surveillance cameras are typically positioned at higher angles. This results in objects of different sizes within frames. To address the limitations of the aforementioned, we design an improved PANet structure called BNet, as shown in Fig. 3. We introduce cross-layer connections between the backbone and the neck at the P4 layer. During aggregation, this enables the model to more effectively utilize semantic and shallow positional information. This enhances the model's accuracy in accident detection without increasing computational complexity.

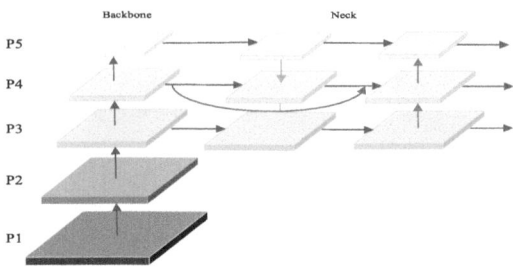

Fig. 3. BNet network structure.

Additionally, due to the similarity between vehicle shapes and background environments, some collision features are easily overlooked. We have designed a new module called C3_B to replace each C3 in the Neck, enhancing the network's focus on detecting targets, as shown in Fig. 4. We introduced CBAM into C3. CBAM [21] consists of a Channel Attention Module (CAM) and a Spatial Attention Module (SAM). The dual-channel attention mechanism can enhance the model's ability to extract feature information at different levels and select key information relevant to the current task objectives.

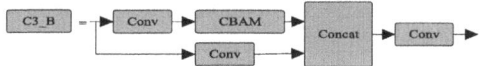

Fig. 4. C3_B network structure.

Extracting Evidence. If no new accident frames are detected within 30 s after the accident occurs, we bundle the previous accident frames as evidence. We stipulate that the timestamp extracted from the first accident frame in a group of evidence serves as the evidence generation time.

4   Security Analysis

Integrity of Evidence. Evidence information extracted by the data center is stored as transactions on the blockchain. Tx contains the storage address CID_{DATA} of the evidence summary *Data*. *Data* includes the storage address CID_{Eve} of the original evidence *Evidence*. Any changes to *Data* and *evidence* will result in changes to the storage addresses CID. Furthermore, due to the consensus mechanism on the blockchain, it is nearly impossible to modify transactions on the blockchain. The core features of blockchain and IPFS ensure the integrity of accident evidence stored on IPFS. Therefore, once evidence is stored on IPFS and the blockchain, attackers cannot tamper with it.

Confidentiality of Evidence. The data center encrypts Evidence with the symmetric key K_i using AES and then stores it in IPFS. Subsequently, K_i is encrypted with the system's public key PUK. Any Q wishing to access the evidence must undergo authentication by the authorization center. Only after authentication can they obtain K_i. Under this premise, attackers cannot access the ciphertext or obtain the symmetric key K_i. Therefore, the confidentiality of the data is ensured.

5 Results and Discussion

5.1 Experimental Environment

The blockchain experiments are based on the Hyperledger Fabric, with the Ubuntu 20.04.3 operating system and 8GB of RAM. The off-chain storage location is IPFS 0.30.1. The deep learning experimental environment is Python 3.9 with Torch 2.0. The processor is an Intel(R) Xeon(R) CPU E5-2666 v3 @ 2.90GHz, and the graphics card is an NVIDIA RTX 3060 Ti 32GB. The image sizes are uniformly resized to 640×640. The experiments utilize the Adam optimizer with an initial learning rate of 0.01, a weight decay coefficient of 0.001, momentum of 0.937, and a maximum of 300 iterations. The images are uniformly resized to 640×640, and the total number of training iterations is 300.

5.2 Dataset

We search for videos and images containing vehicle accidents on websites such as Kaggle and YouTube. To improve the applicability in practical detection, we specifically select videos and images captured from traffic surveillance cameras. We use labeling to annotate the data samples and complete the dataset creation work. To enhance the robustness of the dataset, we apply image augmentation techniques to process frames of traffic accident footage, as shown in Fig. 5. The final dataset consists of 2200 frames of accident footage and 1000 frames of non-accident footage. These images will be randomly allocated into an 80% training dataset and a 20% validation dataset.

Fig. 5. Display of Vehicle Accident Part Dataset. (a) is Original image. (b) is Grayscale image. (c) is Gaussian noise and Cutout image. (d) is Flip image.

5.3 Ablation Experiment

The experiment evaluate the validation set based on precision, recall, mAP@0.5, parameters, and model size.

The results of the ablation experiments are shown in Table 1. Using Bneck as the backbone network of YOLOv5, the model achieved a precision increase of 0.6% while reducing the parameter count. Incorporating the improved Feature Pyramid Network BNet into YOLOv5 resulted in a 2.1% increase in precision and a 3.9% increase in mAP@0.5, with a significant increase in recall to 85.2%. This improvement compensates for the feature loss caused by downsampling, thus enhancing the performance of the accident detection model. After using the improved C3 module C3_B in the Neck, the precision increased by 1.1%, mAP@0.5 increased by 1%, and recall reached 82.1%. Furthermore, the combination of BNet and C3_B significantly enhances the performance of the Neck network. Not only does it optimize the fusion effect of different feature layers, but it also highlights the features of traffic accidents. It results in a 3.9% increase in precision, a 5% increase in mAP@0.5, and a recall rate of 88.5%. However, this led to a larger model computational load. Therefore, the model achieved maximum performance after improving both the Backbone and Neck (using Bneck, BNet, and C3_B). Compared to the baseline model, the precision of traffic accident detection reached 92.4%, mAP@0.5 reached 90.4%, and the recall rate reached 88%, while the model's computational load decreased by nearly half.

Table 1. Ablation experimental results

Model	P (%)	R (%)	mAP@0.5 (%)	Params (10^6)	Size (MB)
YOLOv5s	88.0	78.5	84.0	7.012	14.4
YOLOv5s + Bneck	88.6	76.7	84.9	3.524	7.5
YOLOv5s + BNet	90.1	85.2	87.9	7.078	14.4
YOLOv5s + C3_B	89.1	82.1	85.0	7.012	14.4
YOLOv5s + Bneck + BNet	90.3	85.9	88.5	3.531	7.5
YOLOv5s + Bneck + C3_B	88.7	86.1	89.5	3.524	7.5
YOLOv5s + BNet + C3_B	91.9	88.5	89.0	7.078	14.4
YOLOv5-MBC	92.4	88.0	90.4	3.524	7.5

5.4 Comparative Experiments

To further validate the effectiveness and superiority of the proposed algorithm, we compare YOLOv5-MBC with YOLOv3 [14], YOLOv3-tiny [1], YOLOv5, YOLOv7 [20], and YOLOv8 [15], as shown in Table 2. Among them, YOLOv3-tiny has the lowest parameter and computational cost, but its accuracy is only

87.1%, the lowest among all models. Although YOLOv7 achieves an accuracy of 93.2%, its parameter count reaches 36.479. YOLOv3 and YOLOv8 have higher accuracies compared to YOLOv5, reaching 91.3% and 89.9% respectively, but overall performance is still inferior to YOLOv5-MBC. Additionally, we compare YOLOv5-MBC with iS-YOLOv5. YOLOv5-MBC's Precision, Recall, and mAP@0.5 are 0.8%, 1%, and 0.1% higher than iS-YOLOv5 [13], respectively. In summary, YOLO-MBC has high detection accuracy, as well as fewer parameters and computations, making it suitable for traffic accident detect and forensic in daily life.

Table 2. Comparison results between YOLOv5-MBC and other algorithms

Model	P (%)	R (%)	mAP@0.5 (%)	Params (10^6)
YOLOv3	91.3	79.9	88.9	9.301
YOLOv3-tiny	87.1	77.2	83.5	2.171
YOLOv5s	88.0	78.5	84.0	7.012
YOLOv7	93.2	87.1	90.5	36.479
YOLOv8	89.9	85.4	89.3	3.006
iS-YOLOv5	91.6	87.0	90.3	7.078
YOLOv5-MBC	92.4	88.0	90.4	3.524

5.5 Efficiency Analysis of Encryption and Decryption

Our evidence data consists of images, which are very large files. To further validate the advantages of the encryption algorithm selected by this model, we compare it with the RSA (Rivest-Shamir-Adleman) algorithm. AES encryption and decryption, RSA encryption and decryption are performed on files of sizes 1MB, 2MB, 3MB, 4MB, and 5MB, respectively, and the average time is calculated over 5 tests. The results, as shown in Fig. 6, indicate that the encryption and decryption time based on AES is much shorter than that based on RSA. When the evidence file is less than 3MB, the encryption time of the method used in this paper is within 10ms, indicating that in the encryption and decryption scenarios of evidence, the proposed solution can reduce the encryption and decryption time to the millisecond level.

5.6 Storage Performance Analysis

To better simulate real-world scenarios, we directly compares the upload and download efficiency of IPFS on the public network. Experiments are conducted using evidence documents of sizes 1 MB, 2 MB, 3MB, 4MB, and 5MB. Upload and download experiments are repeated 5 times, and their average times are calculated, with results shown in Fig. 7. IPFS adopts a distributed storage mechanism with file fragmentation operations at its core. Consequently, compared

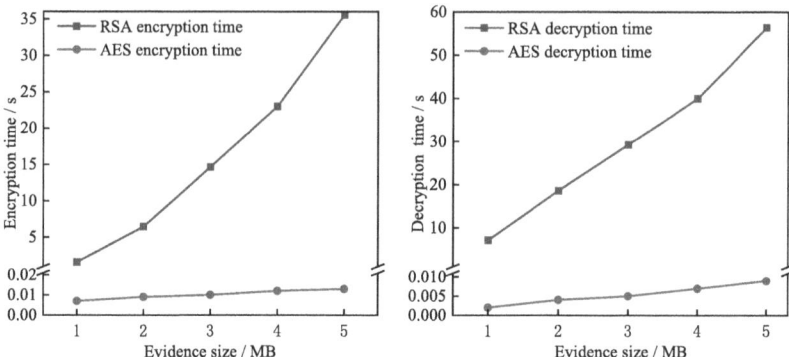

Fig. 6. Encryption and Decryption Time Comparison.

to cloud storage, IPFS may require additional time. The IPFS storage mechanism demonstrates excellent performance and can meet practical storage and retrieval needs. Additionally, IPFS provides immutability and decentralization for evidence, which are crucial for evidence storage.

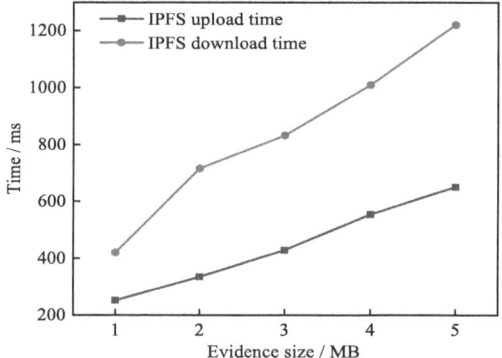

Fig. 7. Off chain Storage Performance.

6   Conclusions

In this study, we innovatively propose a framework that combines blockchain and deep learning to forensic, store, and retrieve traffic accident evidence. To meet practical needs, the framework integrates IPFS, alleviating the pressure of large-scale evidence data on the blockchain. Additionally, the framework includes a novel model, YOLO-MBC, for traffic accident forensics. Specifically, we enhance the Backbone and Neck parts of YOLOv5, designing a new feature pyramid network, BNet, and C3_B. Moreover, to make the model more suitable for forensic analysis in surveillance videos, we collect a dataset consisting exclusively of frames captured from surveillance angles showing accidents or non-accidents. Finally, to evaluate the proposed framework, we first analyze the security of blockchain certification. Then, we assess the performance of the YOLO-MBC model in terms of Precision, Recall, and mAP@0.5, comparing it with other mainstream algorithms. Experimental results demonstrate that the framework is secure and reliable, with YOLO-MBC achieving Precision, Recall, and mAP@0.5 of 92.4%, 88.0%, and 90.4%, respectively. The combination of blockchain and deep learning effectively addresses issues such as unclear evidence sources and insecure evidence storage, providing new insights for future traffic accident certification.

Acknowledgements. This research is supported by the Inner Mongolia Nature Fund project number No. 2023MS06020, Self-funding Project of Engineering Research Center of Ecological Big Data, Ministery of Education.

References

1. Adarsh, P., Rathi, P., Kumar, M.: Yolo v3-tiny: object detection and recognition using one stage improved model. In: 2020 6th International Conference on Advanced Computing and Communication Systems (ICACCS), pp. 687–694. IEEE (2020)
2. Ahmad, L., Khanji, S., Iqbal, F., Kamoun, F.: Blockchain-based chain of custody: towards real-time tamper-proof evidence management. In: Proceedings of the 15th International Conference on Availability, Reliability and Security, pp. 1–8 (2020)
3. Androulaki, E., et al.: Hyperledger fabric: a distributed operating system for permissioned blockchains. In: Proceedings of the Thirteenth EuroSys Conference, pp. 1–15 (2018)
4. Basheer Ahmed, M.I., et al.: A real-time computer vision based approach to detection and classification of traffic incidents. Big Data Cogn. Comput. **7**(1), 22 (2023)
5. Ding, Y., Xiang, H., Luo, D., Zou, X., Liang, H.: Scheme for electronic certificate storage by combining fabric technology. J. Xidian Univ. **47**(05), 113–121 (2020)
6. Gao, S., Li, W., Hao, D., Wang, H., Zhou, J.: Traffic incident detection based on the width characteristic of the moving object marker. Int. J. Inf. Commun. Technol. **16**(4), 285–296 (2020)
7. Holotescu, C.: Understanding blockchain technology and how to get involved. In: The 14thInternational Scientific Conference eLearning and Software for Education-Bucharest, April **19**, 20 (2018)
8. Howard, A., et al.: Searching for mobilenetv3. In: Proceedings of the IEEE/CVF International Conference on Computer Vision, pp. 1314–1324 (2019)
9. Howard, A.G., et al.: Mobilenets: efficient convolutional neural networks for mobile vision applications. arXiv preprint arXiv:1704.04861 (2017)
10. Hu, J., Shen, L., Sun, G.: Squeeze-and-excitation networks. In: 2018 IEEE/CVF Conference on Computer Vision and Pattern Recognition, pp. 7132–7141 (2018). https://doi.org/10.1109/CVPR.2018.00745

11. Huynh-The, T., et al.: Blockchain for the metaverse: a review. Futur. Gener. Comput. Syst. **143**, 401–419 (2023)
12. Maciá-Fernández, G., Gómez-Hernández, J.A., Robles, M., García-Teodoro, P.: Blockchain-based forensic system for collection and preservation of network service evidences (2019)
13. Mahaur, B., Mishra, K.: Small-object detection based on YOLOV5 in autonomous driving systems. Pattern Recogn. Lett. **168**, 115–122 (2023)
14. Redmon, J., Farhadi, A.: Yolov3: an incremental improvement. arXiv preprint arXiv:1804.02767 (2018)
15. Reis, D., Kupec, J., Hong, J., Daoudi, A.: Real-time flying object detection with yolov8. arXiv preprint arXiv:2305.09972 (2023)
16. Sandler, M., Howard, A., Zhu, M., Zhmoginov, A., Chen, L.C.: Mobilenetv2: inverted residuals and linear bottlenecks. In: Proceedings of the IEEE Conference on Computer Vision and Pattern Recognition, pp. 4510–4520 (2018)
17. Sulistyono, S., Fikria, L., Maliq, T., Hasanuddin, A., Ishak, S.: Road safety improving in blackspot of mount Bromo tourist road access, east java. In: IOP Conference Series: Earth and Environmental Science, vol. 1294, p. 012015. IOP Publishing (2024)
18. Tian, D., Zhang, C., Duan, X., Wang, X.: An automatic car accident detection method based on cooperative vehicle infrastructure systems. IEEE Access **7**, 127453–127463 (2019)
19. Vangala, A., Bera, B., Saha, S., Das, A.K., Kumar, N., Park, Y.: Blockchain-enabled certificate-based authentication for vehicle accident detection and notification in intelligent transportation systems. IEEE Sens. J. **21**(14), 15824–15838 (2020)
20. Wang, C.Y., Bochkovskiy, A., Liao, H.Y.M.: Yolov7: Trainable bag-of-freebies sets new state-of-the-art for real-time object detectors. In: 2023 IEEE/CVF Conference on Computer Vision and Pattern Recognition (CVPR), pp. 7464–7475 (2023). https://doi.org/10.1109/CVPR52729.2023.00721
21. Woo, S., Park, J., Lee, J.-Y., Kweon, I.S.: CBAM: convolutional block attention module. In: Ferrari, V., Hebert, M., Sminchisescu, C., Weiss, Y. (eds.) ECCV 2018. LNCS, vol. 11211, pp. 3–19. Springer, Cham (2018). https://doi.org/10.1007/978-3-030-01234-2_1
22. Yao, Y., Xu, M., Wang, Y., Crandall, D.J., Atkins, E.M.: Unsupervised traffic accident detection in first-person videos. In: 2019 IEEE/RSJ International Conference on Intelligent Robots and Systems (IROS), pp. 273–280. IEEE (2019)
23. Yuan, Q., Peng, Y., Xu, X., Wang, X.: Key points of investigation and analysis on traffic accidents involving intelligent vehicles. Transp. Safety Environ. **3**(4), tdab020 (2021)
24. Zhang, H., Wang, R., Cai, K.: Research on the application and examination of electronic evidence preserved on the blockchain in Chinese copyright judicial practice. Comput. Law Secur. Rev. **52**, 105891 (2024)

Statistical Analysis of Human Mobility in Online Communities

Yao Wang[1], Zhiwen Yu[1,2(✉)], Ying Zhang[1], Shuming Hu[1], and Bin Guo[1]

[1] School of Computer Science, Northwestern Polytechnical University, Xi'an 710129, Shaanxi, China
{wyao,hushuming}@mail.nwpu.edu.cn, {zhiwenyu,izhangying,guob}@nwpu.edu.cn
[2] Harbin Engineering University, Harbin 150001, Heilongjiang, China

Abstract. In recent years, the study of human mobility in physical space has been a prominent topic in human behavior studies. With the advent of the digital age, human social and behavioral patterns have undergone significant changes, particularly with regard to human behavior in cyberspace, which has garnered widespread attention. This study focuses on online communities. Firstly, based on a real dataset of human mobility in online communities, we carefully explore the relevant statistical features, especially concerning differences in human mobility and webpage browsing behavior between online communities, and conduct a detailed analysis. Given the macroscopic differences between online and physical spaces, this paper then deeply compares the statistical aspects of human mobility between online communities and physical spaces, finding differences on a smaller temporal scale. This study investigates the factors influencing human online mobility decisions, exploring how community activity levels affect mobility decisions from the perspective of community attributes. This lays the groundwork for future analyses of the potential mechanisms driving human mobility decisions.

Keywords: Human Mobility · Online Communities · Statistical Analysis

1 Introduction

In recent years, with the continuous development of communication and positioning technologies, a wealth of high-precision datasets containing individual mobility trajectories has emerged. This has fueled the quantitative study of human mobility patterns, leading to the development of many models that explain and simulate human mobility decisions accurately [1]. As smartphones become more common, increasingly more people worldwide are spending significant time in virtual spaces, moving activities such as shopping, socializing, and entertainment online. In this context, research on human mobility patterns has embraced a new dimension: human mobility in cyberspace.

Existing research has demonstrated that certain online activities are driven by mechanisms analogous to those influencing physical behaviors [2,3]. However, a fundamental distinction between online mobility and human mobility in physical spaces lies in the absence of a metric for physical distance in the virtual realm. It is well known that human mobility in physical space is constrained by various factors, such as transportation, economic resources, and policy frameworks. When mobility transitions online, these limitations ostensibly vanish, creating the illusion that one can navigate cyberspace freely with just a few clicks. In reality, however, people are limited by sources of information and personal interests, preventing them from easily accessing certain areas of the web.

Given this analysis, it is evident that the factors influencing decision-making in online mobility differ distinctly from those in physical movement. To address this issue, it is essential to first identify the characteristic patterns of online mobility and further investigate the underlying mechanisms. Thanks to the multi-community structure of popular online platforms, we can examine cross-regional mobility patterns within the same platform. These studies, in turn, could promote the development of design [4], regulatory [5], and governance strategies for multi-community platforms.

In this paper, we explore human online activities by treating communities as locations in cyberspace and movements across these communities as spatial movements. The main contributions of this paper are summarized as follows: Firstly, we conducted a systematic study of human mobility within cyberspace, especially focusing on online communities. We analyzed the unique aspects of human mobility within these communities, noting the intuitive differences from other online platforms and emphasizing the distinct statistical features of mobility compared to webpage browsing behaviors. Secondly, we conducted a systematic analysis of human mobility in both physical spaces and online communities, comparing their statistical differences with a focus on temporal aspects. The absence of physical and economic constraints in virtual spaces results in distinct impacts on human mobility compared to physical movements. Finally, we investigated the factors influencing decision-making in online mobility, including the level of community activity. This study sets the groundwork for quantifying the 'cost' of human mobility between online communities and analyzing the mechanisms that influence decision-making in human mobility.

2   Related Work

Many efforts have been devoted to studying human mobility in physical spaces, with a key focus on establishing models to simulate human movement and replicate the statistical properties of empirical data. One of the most well-known models proposed in 2010 is the Exploration and Preferential Return (EPR) model [6], which divides human mobility into exploration and return mechanisms and quantifies the decision-making of human movement through the probabilities of these mechanisms. Furthermore, a plethora of models has emerged subsequently, considering factors such as memory effects and location attractiveness.

These include the container model [7], the d-EPR model [8], the PEPR model [9], the CMM model [10], and others. These modeling studies of human mobility have played a crucial role in advancing applied research areas such as traffic prediction [11], urban planning [12], and epidemic prevention [13].

Although there is extensive research on human mobility in physical spaces, studies exploring human mobility across multiple online communities are scarce, largely due to the lack of a metric to quantify transfer costs in cyberspace. Existing research includes aspects such as inter-community information dissemination [14], community evolution [15], and inter-community differences [16]. However, these studies are primarily descriptive or only consider coarse-grained user group levels, without delving into the statistical characteristics and underlying mechanisms of online mobility. In 2019, researchers extended the EPR model to the cross-community mobility in cyberspace [17]. This choice is undoubtedly ingenious, as the EPR model is one of the few dynamic models that only require raw data support and do not consider spatial distances between locations. Furthermore, some researchers have identified three patterns of participant mobility in multi-community platforms [18]. Some researchers have focused on studying the similarities and differences between web browsing and location-based social network check-in behaviors [19].

3   Dataset

In this paper, our data is primarily sourced from Reddit, a globally recognized online community platform. Due to its vast user base and rich data resources, the platform's dataset is frequently utilized in social network and computational sociology research. We chose this dataset for several key reasons: First, Reddit comprises numerous subreddits focused on various topics. Users can browse, post, and comment across these subreddits, enabling us to analyze user mobility within the same platform. Second, the dataset contains comprehensive user activity trajectories, allowing us to study the activities of each active user who hasn't deleted their account during a specified period. This ensures analytical accuracy and minimizes statistical biases from data loss.

We selected a three-month data slice from January 1 to March 31, 2015. After removing deactivated accounts and bots, this slice contained over 140 million historical records from more than 3.9 million active users across 70,000 subreddits. To ensure the validity and generalizability of our results, we excluded users with fewer than 100 activity records, leaving over 36 million records from 13,000 users. By treating each subreddit as a distinct location, we consider users moving and leaving traces across different subreddits as moving between these locations.

4   Human Mobility in the Cyberspace

In this section, we use several statistical metrics commonly applied in physical space mobility studies to analyze their applicability on online community platforms. To identify the unique characteristics of human mobility between online communities, we compare statistical features of web browsing behavior with those of mobility across online communities. This analysis aims to show that human mobility in cyberspace varies significantly across different online scenarios, a distinction not found in physical space mobility.

4.1   Patterns of Online Mobility

Existing research categorizes human mobility in physical spaces into exploratory and return behaviors [8]. Similarly, these patterns are observed in the digital realm [17]. Therefore, this section explores online mobility by analyzing the statistical characteristics of exploratory and return behaviors.

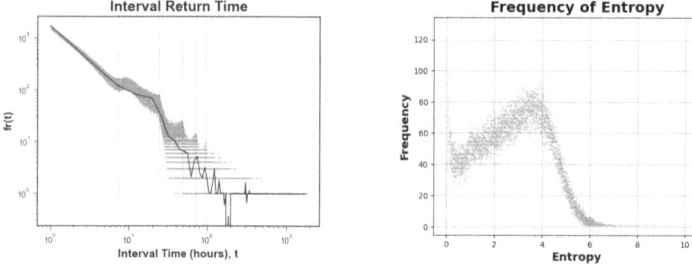

Fig. 1. (a) The interval return time of online mobility, with gray dashed lines at 7.5, 24, 48, 72, and 96 h (Color figure online). (b) The frequency distribution of user trajectory entropy.

Return Behavior Analysis. In human mobility studies, return behavior, characterized by the consistent revisiting of previously explored locations, is evident in both physical and digital spaces. This regularity highlights the significant role of memory in mobility decision-making. Specifically, the memory effect closely aligns with individuals' daily routines, satisfaction of needs, and environmental interactions, thereby influencing their behavioral patterns. Analyzing the time intervals between revisits within online communities deepens our understanding of how memory shapes online behavior. These statistical insights offer empirical evidence for memory mechanisms in human behavior and provide a framework for exploring various factors influencing user behavior in virtual environments.

In our experimental study, we obtained the distribution illustrated in Fig. 1a. The return interval distribution displays a distinct power-law characteristic, a statistical property commonly observed across various natural and social phenomena. Additionally, the data exhibit significant long-tail behavior. The graph's time interval distribution shows several inflection points at 7.5 h, 24 h, 48 h, 72 h, and 96 h, as marked by dashed lines. Peaks in the distribution occur every 24 h, highlighting clear periodic features. It is well-known that human mobility in physical spaces follows cyclical patterns dictated by daily activities such as work, returning home, shopping, and exercise. Despite the lack of similar constraints for online community visits, a 24-hour periodicity remains evident. Notably, there is an observable increase between 7.5 and 9 h, consistent with the typical human sleep duration of around 8 h.

Exploratory Behavior Analysis. In addition to return behaviors, exploratory behavior represents a significant facet of human mobility, characterized by visits to previously unexplored locations. In physical space, exploratory behavior often reflects an individual's activity space. In the context of online mobility, it indicates the breadth of a person's interests, given that each community encompasses a variety of topics. Typically, the size of an individual's activity space in physical space is quantified using the metric of the radius of gyration. However, this measure is not applicable in cyberspace, where movement between communities does not entail the same explicit costs associated with physical distance. To quantify a user's exploratory range online, we employ two metrics: the number of communities explored and the entropy of trajectory. The entropy of a user's trajectory, H_u, is calculated using Shannon entropy,

$$H_u = -\sum_{i=1}^{n} p_i \log_2 p_i, \tag{1}$$

where p_i denotes the frequency with which the user visits subreddit i. The first metric directly reflects the extent of a user's diverse interests, while the second measures the randomness of a user's activity trajectory, indirectly revealing the breadth of their interests. Higher entropy values indicate more unpredictable visitation patterns, suggesting a greater extent of exploration across new communities.

We first calculated each user's trajectory entropy and found that the frequency of entropy values equal to zero far exceeds that of other values. After excluding cases with zero entropy, we plotted the distribution of user trajectory entropy, as shown in Fig. 1b. The figure reveals a peak near an entropy value of 4, in addition to the zero-entropy peak, suggesting the presence of two distinct user groups with different mobility patterns. To verify this hypothesis, we used k-means clustering, an unsupervised learning method, with the user's trajectory entropy and the number of explored communities as coordinates. The elbow method was used to determine the optimal number of clusters. In Fig. 2a, the elbow plot and the first-order difference of inertia decline identify two clusters as optimal. The clustering results are shown in Fig. 2b, revealing that one group of users has high entropy and has explored more communities, suggesting a preference for exploration. In contrast, the other group demonstrates the opposite pattern.

Although existing studies have highlighted the differences between human mobility in physical spaces and browsing behavior across web pages [19], there

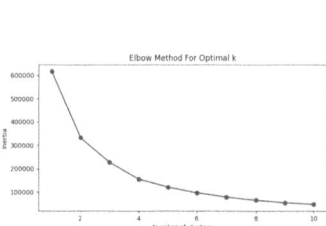 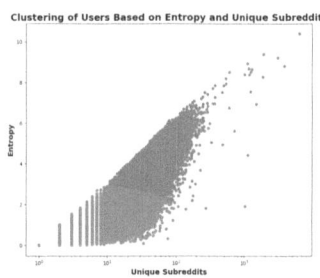

Fig. 2. (a). Elbow graph illustrating the inertia values across different cluster counts to determine the optimal k for k-means clustering. The inertia shows a significant decrease up to 2 clusters, then levels off, suggesting that the best number of clusters is 2. (b). Scatter plot illustrating user clustering based on entropy and the number of unique subreddits visited. The color distinction identifies two main user groups: orange for users with lower entropy and fewer subreddit interactions, and blue for users with higher entropy and extensive subreddit interactions. (Color figure online)

remains a gap in the in-depth research on mobility patterns within online communities. This gap exists because browsing behaviors differ from the mobility patterns found in online communities. First, individuals browse web pages more randomly and non-linearly, guided by personal interests, needs, and preferences. In contrast, mobility within network communities is often constrained by community structures and rules, such as user group affiliation and social network connections. Second, during browsing, individuals prioritize the quality, accuracy, and credibility of webpage content to gain knowledge and value. On the other hand, mobility within network communities is more influenced by emotional factors and social needs, such as seeking social support and enjoying social prestige.

4.2   Particularity of Mobility Between in Communities

This subsection aims to identify the statistical differences between mobility in online communities and browsing behavior. Based on these findings, we propose that studying mobility patterns in online spaces requires more tailored research methods than those used for studying human mobility in physical spaces, given the unique characteristics of specific online platforms. Our web browsing dataset consists of approximately 5 million anonymous web browsing records from 521 users between September 2010 and May 2014.

We first computed the frequency distribution of time intervals between two successive actions for two distinct behaviors, as shown in Fig. 3. Differences between these behaviors are most pronounced over short time scales, ranging from 0 to 100 s. Web browsing behavior shows a higher frequency of short time intervals than online community mobility, with the latter presenting a more uniform distribution. Additionally, web browsing behavior exhibits a pronounced heavy-tailed effect, possibly indicating faster browsing speeds. This can

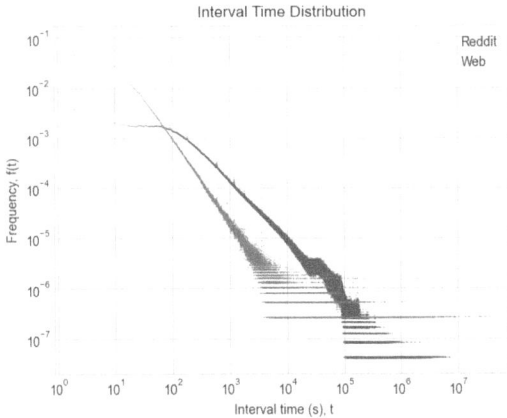

Fig. 3. Distribution of interval times between activities, comparing web browsing with mobility in online communities.

be attributed to the nature of web browsing, which is typically focused on one-way information processing with limited interactions, leading to shorter time intervals. In contrast, online community users tend to engage in more interaction and communication, such as posting or replying, resulting in longer time intervals. Furthermore, online community platforms may limit speech frequency, further extending these intervals.

This section provides experimental evidence indicating that mobility within online communities is influenced by social and other factors, causing significant deviations in statistical properties compared to other online behaviors. Due to the more intricate network architecture of cyberspace compared to physical space, cross-platform mobility research requires tailored approaches that reflect the unique characteristics of different online platforms.

5 Analogy Between Physical Space and Cyberspace

Intuitively, significant differences likely exist between human mobility in physical space and cyberspace. This is primarily because traveling long distances in the physical world is constrained by various factors, such as traffic conditions and economic considerations, which are absent in cyberspace. As a result, mobility within cyberspace appears to be less restricted. Whether statistical differences in human mobility exist between these two spaces will be analyzed and compared in depth in this section.

For our comparative study, we selected the publicly available Brightkite dataset as the offline data source. This location-based social network (LBSN) check-in dataset contains approximately 51,400 users and 4.7 million location check-ins over a 54-month period.

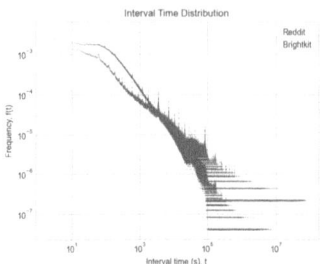 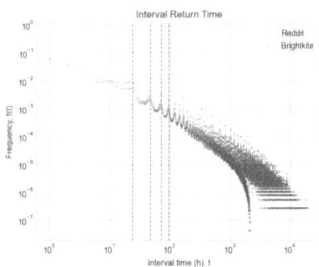

Fig. 4. (a). The distribution of interval time of mobility in two spaces. (b). The distribution of interval return times for mobility in two spaces. Each grey dash line represents 24 h (Color figure online).

5.1   Interval Time

Similar to the previous section, our analysis begins with the distribution of time intervals between two consecutive actions for users in both datasets, as illustrated in Fig. 4a. Both types of mobility show no significant differences in their time interval distributions when the time intervals are shorter than 10 s or longer than 100 s, where they exhibit remarkable consistency. Contrary to our expectations, movement across online communities does not involve rapid switching between different communities with negligible transfer costs. The primary difference is observed in the 10 to 100-second range, likely because the switching cost in online movement is much lower than in physical movement. Furthermore, a significant peak at 28,800 s (8 h) aligns with the known human daily routine.

These findings indicate that while virtual and physical mobility differ mainly in activity rates at shorter time horizons due to the influence of physical space-related costs, these differences diminish over longer periods, suggesting that various human activities are influenced by some common factors, leading to convergence.

5.2   Interval Return Time

As previously mentioned, exploration and return are crucial aspects of human mobility, whether in virtual or physical spaces. Next, we will analyze return intervals and exploration rates to uncover the similarities and differences between mobility in these two realms.

We present the distributions of interval return times in Fig. 4b, employing hours as the unit of measurement, and observe a notably consistent periodic behavior across both datasets. The observed peaks suggest the presence of circadian rhythms, aligning with specific behavioral patterns, including daily commutes to home or work, and weekly visits to retail locations. Such trends in physical mobility are anticipated, given the routine physical limitations imposed by daily activities. Remarkably, despite the lack of these physical constraints in virtual mobility, similar patterns continue to manifest.

5.3   Time-Related Exploratory

Exploration is another characteristic behavior of human mobility. We now analyze the differences in exploration patterns between these two forms of mobility.
In physical space, the radius of gyration is commonly used to measure a person's
typical exploration distance, which is known to increase logarithmically up to
saturation limits [20]. However, as noted earlier, physical distance is not applicable in virtual space, and no metrics are available to gauge transfer costs between
online communities. Thus, it is not possible to quantify users' exploration ranges
using the radius of gyration.

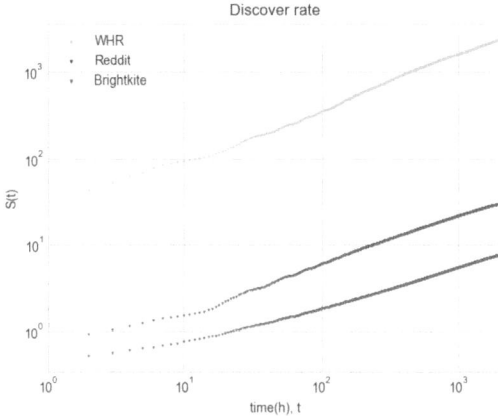

Fig. 5. The temporal discovery rate of mobility in physical space, online communities
and web browser.

Instead, we use the real-time count of visited communities to measure the
expansion of user exploration across online communities. Let $S_u(t)$ denote the
number of communities user u has explored at time t. By averaging across the
total number of users $N(t)$ at time t, we obtain the average number of communities visited by all users at time t, denoted as $S(t)$, which is given by

$$S(t) = \frac{\sum_u S_u(t)}{N(u)}. \tag{2}$$

In Fig. 5, the exploration metric $S(t)$ is depicted for all three datasets, encompassing the web browsing dataset, which demonstrates a sublinear scaling characterized by the relationship $S(t) \sim t^\mu$ in each dataset. Our analysis indicates
that the exploration rate associated with webpage browsing behavior exceeds
that observed in moving between online communities or physical locations by
two orders of magnitude. This discrepancy arises from the almost limitless number of webpages compared to online communities and physical locations. Additionally, browsing webpages lacks physical or social constraints, enabling easier
access to information and facilitating the discovery of new locations.

Through experimental fitting, we calculated the values of μ for the three datasets: $\mu_{Web} \approx 0.497$, $\mu_R \approx 0.488$, and $\mu_{BK} \approx 0.532$. Although the exploration rate for mobility between online communities is of a similar magnitude to that of physical space mobility, its trend more closely resembles that of web browsing behavior. This finding suggests that there are certain differences in the underlying mechanisms influencing online and physical mobility patterns.

6   Human Dynamics of Mobility in Cyberspace

Previous empirical studies have shown striking similarities between the statistical feature of physical and virtual mobility. However, differences remain, especially over shorter timescales. These similarities and differences imply the existence of shared decision mechanisms underlying human mobility behavior in both spaces, while fundamental distinctions persist. While decision mechanisms influencing human mobility in physical space have been extensively studied, our understanding of the decision mechanisms driving human mobility between online communities is still limited. Therefore, in this section, we explore the factors impacting human mobility in cyberspace, focusing on community attributes.

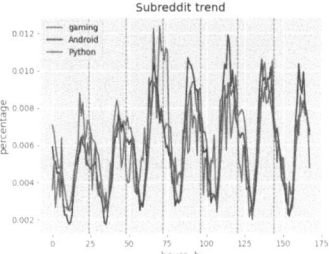 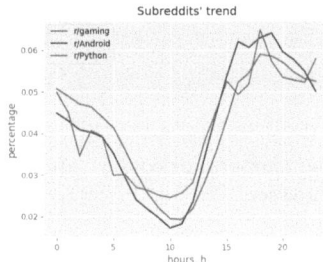

Fig. 6. (a). Average hourly trend of new comments throughout a week. (b). Average hourly trend of new comments over a 24-hour period.

It is well known that locations in the physical world serve specific functions, such as working in an office, relaxing at home, or dining in a restaurant. The activity levels of these places rarely impact people's decisions to choose them as destinations. However, people visit online communities with specific intentions, like chatting and discussing, and are less inclined to visit communities with low communication compared to highly active ones. Thus, the activity level of an online community directly affects users' willingness to participate in discussions.

To test this hypothesis, we devised an approach that assesses the activity levels of online communities. By measuring the frequency of new comments per hour, we gauge the degree of community engagement. For generalizability, we selected three distinct subreddits (/r/gaming, /r/Android, and /r/Python) of varying sizes (91,434, 11,580, and 1,926 members, respectively) and comment counts (669,411, 96,954, and 7,511, respectively). The activity levels of each subreddit were analyzed hourly and are presented in Fig. 6a. Despite their differences in size, all three subreddits exhibit similar trends, suggesting the universality of our conclusions. We chose subreddits with broad subjects to maximize global participation, though Reddit only provides UTC timestamps for comments. Nevertheless, Fig. 6b reveals convergence in average daily trends, indicating that users post comments according to subreddit activity levels, even if the timing is suboptimal due to time differences.

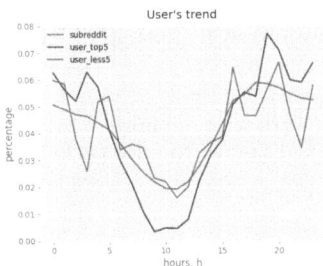

Fig. 7. Hourly trends in comments for both user types, compared to the trend of new comments in the subreddit /r/gaming.

To further validate our findings, we analyzed specific user types within the /r/gaming subreddit. We categorized all users into three groups: loyal, average, and rare users. Users who contribute more than 500 comments are considered loyal users, those who contribute fewer than 500 but more than 30 comments are referred to as average users, and those contributing fewer than 30 comments are termed rare users. We selected the five most active users who contributed 9,104 comments in total, as well as five average users who each had around 300 comments in /r/gaming subreddit and this group have a total of 8,900 comments in whole Reddit. Analysis shows that both groups were similarly active on Reddit, though the first group was more active in /r/gaming, while the second group was more active in other subreddits.

We further investigated how activity levels in /r/gaming affected both groups' engagement, comparing their activity to the subreddit's overall trends. As depicted in Fig. 7, both groups' activity levels changed consistently with /r/gaming's trends. This implies that even if users are not particularly active in a subreddit, their likelihood of visiting it increases when the subreddit's activity level is high.

7   Conclusion and Future Work

This research focuses on human mobility within online community platforms. Using a real dataset, this study has systematically examined the statistical features of mobility, especially highlighting the differences between human mobility and page browsing behaviors across online communities. Furthermore, acknowledging the significant differences between online and physical environments, this paper provides a thorough comparison of human mobility statistics between these realms, identifying variations at finer temporal scales. Moreover, by considering the unique attributes of online communities, this study has explored factors influencing decision-making in online mobility, uncovering key influences such as community activity level. These findings lay the groundwork for future investigations into the decision-making mechanisms of human mobility.

Looking ahead, we aim to quantify the 'cost' of user mobility between communities, or the 'distance' in cyberspace. This metric will allow us to adapt more established frameworks from physical space to better simulate mobility in online environments.

Acknowledgements. This work was supported by the National Natural Science Foundation of China (No. 61960206008, No. 62032020, No. 62272390).

References

1. Barbosa, H., et al.: Human mobility: models and applications. Phys. Rep. **734**, 1–74 (2018)
2. Wang, X., et al.: Foraging patterns in online searches. Phys. Rev. E **95**(3), 032145 (2017)
3. Hantula, D.A., et al.: Online shopping as foraging: the effects of increasing delays on purchasing and patch residence. IEEE Trans. Prof. Commun. **51**(2), 147–154 (2008)
4. Li, W., et al.: Users' subsequent innovation after organizational adoption: evidence from an online game user innovation community. Internet Res. **33**(4), 1446–1472 (2023)
5. Weld, G., et al.: Perceptions of Moderators as a Large-Scale Measure of Online Community Governance. arXiv preprint. arXiv:2401.16610 (2024)
6. Song, C., et al.: Modelling the scaling properties of human mobility. Nat. Phys. **6**(10), 818–823 (2010)
7. Alessandretti, L., et al.: The scales of human mobility. Nature **587**(7834), 402–407 (2020)
8. Pappalardo, L., et al.: Returners and explorers dichotomy in human mobility. Nat. Commun. **6**(1), 8166 (2015)
9. Schläpfer, M., et al.: The universal visitation law of human mobility. Nature **593**(7860), 522–527 (2021)
10. Xu, F., et al.: Emergence of urban growth patterns from human mobility behavior. Nat. Comput. Sci. **1**(12), 791–800 (2021)
11. Uherek, E., et al.: Transport impacts on atmosphere and climate: land transport. Atmos. Environ. **44**(37), 4772–4816 (2010)
12. Lee, M., et al.: Morphology of travel routes and the organization of cities. Nat. Commun. **8**(1), 2229 (2017)
13. Eubank, S., et al.: Modelling disease outbreaks in realistic urban social networks. Nature **429**(6988), 180–184 (2004)
14. Kumar, S., et al.: Community interaction and conflict on the web. In: Proceedings of the 2018 World Wide Web Conference, pp. 933–943 (2018)

15. Lin, Z., et al.: Better when it was smaller? Community content and behavior after massive growth. In: Proceedings of the International AAAI Conference on Web and Social Media, pp. 132-141 (2017)
16. Hessel, J., et al.: Science, askscience, and badscience: on the coexistence of highly related communities. In: Proceedings of the International AAAI Conference on Web and Social Media, pp. 171–180 (2016)
17. Hu, T., et al.: To return or to explore: Modelling human mobility and dynamics in cyberspace. In: Proceedings of the 2019 World Wide Web Conference, pp. 705–716 (2019)
18. Hu, T., et al.: Life in the "Matrix": human mobility patterns in the cyber space. In: Proceedings of the International AAAI Conference on Web and Social Media, pp. 121–130 (2018)
19. Hazarie, S., et al.: Uncovering the differences and similarities between physical and virtual mobility. J. R. Soc. Interface **17**(168), 20200250 (2020)
20. Gonzalez, M.C., et al.: Understanding individual human mobility patterns. Nature **453**(7196), 779–782 (2008)

SFSGNN: Soft Feature Selection Graph Neural Network for Alleviating Data Sparsity in Click-Through Rate Prediction

Junming Zhou[1], Chao Chang[2,3]([✉]), Weisheng Li[1,2], Ronghua Lin[1,2], Zhengyang Wu[1,2], and Yong Tang[1,2]

[1] South China Normal University, Guangzhou, China
[2] Pazhou Lab, Guangzhou, China
changchao@m.scnu.edu.cn
[3] Guangzhou Panyu Polytechnic, Guangzhou, China

Abstract. Click-Through Rate (CTR) prediction, which estimates the probability of a user clicking on a particular item, plays an important role in online advertising and recommender systems. However, data sparsity remains a significant challenge in achieving accurate CTR prediction results. Fortunately, semi-supervised node classification techniques offer a potential solution to this problem. To this end, this paper proposes a semi-supervised node classification model named Soft Feature Selection Graph Neural Network (SFSGNN), which is designed for alleviating data sparsity in CTR prediction. Firstly, the integration of key modules, including node generation, graph construction, and soft feature selection networks, enables SFSGNN to effectively leverage the limited known user-item interaction data to predict the unknown user-item interactions. Furthermore, the SFSGNN can effectively address the data sparsity issue by utilizing the prediction results as augmented data for training the CTR prediction models. Extensive experiments conducted on three real-world datasets demonstrate the effectiveness of SFSGNN in alleviating data sparsity in CTR prediction.

Keywords: Click-through rate prediction · Data sparsity · Semi-supervised node classification · Graph neural networks

1 Introduction

In many applications such as online advertising and recommender systems, click-through rate (CTR) is a key indicator in business valuation, which estimates the probability of a user clicking or interacting with a particular item [11]. For applications with a large user base, even a small improvement on CTR can potentially contribute to a large increase in the overall revenue [1]. Therefore, accurate CTR prediction results is crucial for enhancing user experience, optimizing advertising effectiveness, and achieving personalized recommendations.

H. Sun et al. (Eds.): ChineseCSCW 2024, CCIS 2343, pp. 108–123, 2025.
https://doi.org/10.1007/978-981-96-2373-0_8

However, challenges related to data sparsity remain unresolved. Data sparsity refers to the extremely limited interactions between users and items. Typically, the input dataset for CTR prediction is large scale and highly sparse. In the case of data sparsity, it is difficult for CTR prediction models to capture users' preferences and items' characteristics accurately. Therefore, how to alleviate the data sparsity is a top priority in current research. Existing methods for alleviating data sparsity can be broadly classified into two categories: rating imputation and utilizing side information [4]. Despite the success of these methods, there are still some limitations. Rating imputation methods alleviate the data sparsity by filling in missing ratings, but they may introduce inaccuracies in the ratings. In contrast, using side information is often an effective way to learn user preferences and mitigate data sparsity [3]. However, noise may arise when the correlation between the side information and the target task is weak.

Fortunately, semi-supervised node classification techniques provide a potential solution to overcome data sparsity. This is because the semi-supervised node classification has two standout benefits. Firstly, it can leverage limited labeled nodes to predict the labels of all unknown nodes. Secondly, it can accurately capture user preferences and item characteristics [16]. Therefore, in this paper, we propose a semi-supervised node classification model named Soft Feature Selection Graph Neural Network (SFSGNN), which generalizes the previous state-of-the-art node classification algorithm Feature Selection Graph Neural Network [12]. Specifically, SFSGNN takes both labeled and unlabeled user-item interactions as input. Firstly, the node generation module models the input data as nodes and constructs corresponding feature vectors. Then, the KNN graph construction module leverages cosine similarity to construct a graph from these nodes. Finally, the adjacency matrix and the nodes feature matrices are fed into the soft feature selection network, which predicts the labels of the unlabelled nodes. Furthermore, to alleviate the data sparsity, the prediction results of SFSGNN can be used as augmented data to train the CTR prediction models. Extensive experiments conducted on three real-world datasets demonstrate the effectiveness of SFSGNN in alleviating data sparsity in CTR prediction.

The rest of the paper is organized as follows. Section 2 presents the related work of this paper. Section 3 describes the main architecture of our proposed model. The experimental results and the analysis are shown in Sect. 4. Section 5 finally concludes this paper.

2   Related Work

In this section, we introduce the related work in three aspects: graph neural networks, semi-supervised node classification, and CTR prediction.

2.1   Graph Neural Networks

Graph Neural Networks have become an indispensable tool in graph data mining in recent years. The core idea of GNNs is graph message propagation [25]. Based on graph neighborhood aggregation, Liu et al. proposed Graph Convolutional Network (GCN) [8] for label prediction, which provides a new idea for graph spectral information propagation. By adopting a self-attention layer, Velickovic et al. proposed Graph Attention Networks (GATs) [15] to perform attention neighborhood aggregation. Hamilton et al. proposed GraphSAGE [7], which efficiently generates embeddings for unseen nodes by aggregating node feature information. In order to solve the problem of the limitation of the number of GAT heads, Sarıgün et al. proposed a method called Multi-Masked Aggregator (MMA) [13], which combines trainable auxiliary models with different or the same aggregators and lifts the limitation on the number of GAT heads. In order to avoid the problem of over-smoothing in GCN models, Maurya et al. proposed a simple two-layer GNN model FSGNN [12] that employs a soft selection mechanism to learn the importance of features during model training. Since GNN can consider both node features and graph structure, it can be applied to graph-related tasks such as graph-level classification, node-level classification, and link prediction.

2.2   Semi-supervised Node Classification

Semi-Supervised Node Classification is one of the most important tasks in graph learning, where the goal is to predict labels for all nodes given only a fraction of labeled ones. Label Propagation Algorithm (LPA) [2] is a traditional method for semi-supervised node classification. LPA assumes that connected nodes may share the same labels, so it can iteratively propagate the labels of labeled nodes to unlabeled nodes along the edges. With the rapid development of deep learning in recent years, GNNs have achieved excellent performance in semi-supervised node classification. The semi-supervised classification based on GCN proposed by Kipf et al. [8] is one of the most representative works in applying GNNs to semi-supervised node classification. In addition, several researchers have demonstrated that unifying different semi-supervised node classification methods can effectively improve the classification performance of models. Wang et al. proposed an end-to-end model GCN-LPA [17] that unifies GCN and LPA for improving the performance of semi-supervised node classification.

2.3   CTR Prediction

Click-Through Rate (CTR) prediction, which estimates the probability of a user clicking on a particular item, plays an important role in online advertising and recommender systems [11]. With the continuous expansion of deep learning research, a variety of excellent CTR prediction models have emerged. DeepFM [6] replaces the Wide component of the Wide&Deep with a FM to improve the cross-interaction capability of the model. xDeepFM [9] enhances the Wide&Deep by introducing a compressed interaction network layer to explicitly generate final-level feature combinations. MaskNe [24]t uses the MaskBlock structure as the basic unit, which significantly improves the ability to capture complex interactions. DCN v2 [23] improves the network structure of DCN [22] feature crossover the crossover network has stronger expressive ability and more effective feature crossover learning ability. FinalMLP [10] integrates feature selection layers and interaction aggregation layers on two MLP networks, enabling complementary feature interaction learning between the two streams. Apart from learning embedding and interaction on handcrafted features, many works attempts to leverage knowledge graphs as side information to enhance the performance of CTR prediction models. RippleNet [18] is an end-to-end framework for knowledge graph-aware recommendation, aiming at CTR prediction. KGCN [21] is a knowledge graph-based model that utilizes rich semantic information to improve the accuracy of CTR prediction. MKR [20] is a multi-task learning method for enhanced CTR prediction using knowledge graph. Despite the great success of these CTR prediction models, the problem of data sparsity still needs to be addressed urgently.

3   Proposed Model

To alleviate the issue of data sparsity in CTR prediction, this paper proposes a semi-supervised node classification model named Soft Feature Selection Graph Neural Network (SFSGNN). In the following, we will first introduce the preliminaries of our work, followed by a detailed description of our model.

3.1   Preliminary

In this section, we formulate our task with necessary notations. There a set of M users $\mathcal{U} = \{u_1, u_2, \cdots, u_M\}$, a sets of N items $\mathcal{I} = \{i_1, i_2, \cdots, i_N\}$. The user-item interactions dataset are denoted as $D = \{(u_t, i_t, r_{u_t i_t})\}_{t=1}^{M \times N}$, where u_t represents the user, i_t represents the item, and $r_{u_t i_t}$ represents the interaction feedback between user u_t and the item i_t. Particularly, $r_{u_t i_t} = 1$ means that user u clicked on item i before, while $r_{u_t i_t} = 0$ means the opposite. In this paper, we use $r_{u_t i_t} \in \phi$ to indicate that there is no record of whether the user u clicked on the item i before. Based on whether $r_{u_t i_t} \in \phi$, the user-item interactions D can be divided into labeled dataset $L = \{(u_t, i_t, r_{u_t i_t}) | r_{u_t i_t} \in \{0, 1\}\}_{t=1}^{l}$ and unlabeled dataset $U = \{(u_t, i_t, r_{u_t i_t}) | r_{u_t i_t} \in \phi\}_{t=l+1}^{M \times N}$.

3.2   Model Overview

Different to the FSGNN [12], the proposed SFSGNN model has two distinctive features. Firstly, it exploits the idea of semi-supervised node classification to mine the unknown user-item interactions. Secondly, it is a plug-and-play module that can be easily applied to any CTR prediction model. Figure 1 shows the main architecture of the SFSGNN model, which consists of three main modules: node generation, KNN graph construction, and soft feature selection network. Specifically, SFSGNN takes both labeled and unlabeled user-item interactions as input. Firstly, the node generation module models the input data as nodes and constructs corresponding feature vectors. Then, the KNN graph construction module leverages cosine similarity to construct a graph from these nodes. Finally, the adjacency matrix and the nodes feature matrices are fed into the soft feature selection network, which predicts the labels of the unlabelled nodes. Furthermore, to alleviate the data sparsity, the prediction results of SFSGNN can be used as augmented data to train the CTR prediction models. In the following sections, we delve deeper into the details of each module.

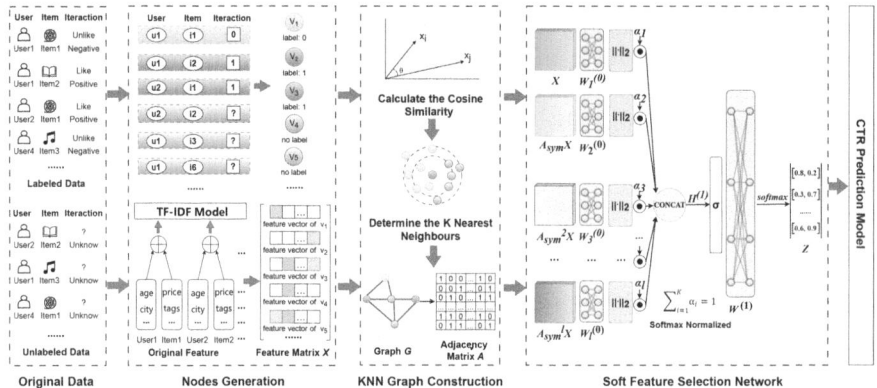

Fig. 1. The main architecture of the proposed SFSGNN.

3.3   Nodes Generation

In this module, each element (u, i, r_{ui}) of the labeled dataset L is treated as a labeled node, and r_{ui}, which serves as the interaction feedback between user u and the item i, is considered as the label of that labeled node. Due to the missing value of r_{ui}, each element of the unlabeled dataset U is considered as a unlabeled node. After obtaining all the nodes and their corresponding labels according to the above operation, it is also necessary to construct feature vectors for each node. Firstly, we traverse all the nodes and fuse the basic information of users (e.g., age, gender, etc.) and items (e.g., price, brand, etc.) corresponding to the nodes to form multiple long texts containing key attribute information. Subsequently, we split and filter these long texts to obtain multiple document representations containing n key words. By calculating and combining the weights of each word in these document representations using the TF-IDF algorithm, the feature vector of each node is obtained. The formula of the TF-IDF algorithm can be expressed as

$$TF - IDF_{i,j} = \frac{n_{i,j}}{\sum_k n_{k,j}} \times \log \frac{|D|}{|\{j : t_i \in d_j\}|}, \qquad (1)$$

where $n_{i,j}$ denotes the number of occurrences of word i in document j. $\sum_k n_{k,j}$ denotes the total number of occurrences of all words in document j. $|D|$ denotes the total number of documents. And $|\{j : t_i \in d_j\}|$ denotes the number of documents containing the word t_i. Finally, the feature vectors of each node are combined to construct a node feature matrix X. Each row of X represents a feature vector of a node, while each column represents a specific feature or attribute.

3.4   KNN Graph Construction

After obtaining all nodes and their feature vectors, we need to establish the connectivity between these nodes to construct a complete graph structure. Based on the obtained node feature vectors, the cosine similarity between each node can be calculated as follows:

$$S(v_i, v_j) = \frac{\sum_{i=1}^{n} (x_i \times x_j)}{\sqrt{\sum_{i=1}^{n} (x_i)^2} \times \sqrt{\sum_{i=1}^{n} (x_j)^2}}, \tag{2}$$

where v_i and v_j are two different nodes. x_i and x_j are the n-dimensional feature vectors of nodes v_i and v_j. Once all inter-node similarities have been identified, the similarity list of each node can be sorted to determine the K most similar neighbours of each node. By connecting each node to its K most similar neighbours, the KNN graph G with its adjacency matrix A is obtained.

3.5   Soft Feature Selection Network

As the core component of SFSGNN, the soft feature selection network is a simple two-layer graph neural network. The module employs parallel input and soft selection mechanism, which can efficiently identify and learn the key features of nodes and their neighbors. The module receives the feature matrices of the nodes as well as the adjacency matrix of the graph as inputs, aiming to predict the labels (i.e., potential user interactions) of unlabelled nodes. In addition, the predictive results can be used as augmentation data to further train the CTR prediction models, thus effectively mitigating the challenges posed by data sparsity. In the following, we will detail the main design strategy of this module.

Feature Aggregation. Given the adjacency matrix A and the feature matrix X, the feature aggregation process can be defined as a function:

$$g(X, A, P) \rightarrow \{X, \hat{A}_{sym}X, \hat{A}_{sym}^2 X, \cdots, \hat{A}_{sym}^P X\}. \tag{3}$$

Specifically, the function takes the node feature matrix X, the adjacency matrix A, and the number of hops for propagating features P as inputs. Firstly, self-loops are added to the input adjacency matrix A to ensure that the features of the nodes themselves are taken into account in the feature aggregation process, as follows:

$$\hat{A} = A + I, \tag{4}$$

where I is the identity matrix. Subsequently, $\hat{A}$ is symmetrically normalised to balance the contribution of different nodes to the feature aggregation, as follows:

$$\hat{A}_{sym} = \hat{D}^{-\frac{1}{2}}\hat{A}\hat{D}^{-\frac{1}{2}}, \tag{5}$$

where $\hat{D}$ is the diagonal degree matrix of $\hat{A}$. Finally, we multiply the obtained $\hat{A}_{sym}$ with the feature matrix X to aggregate the features from the P-hop neighbours of each node. By considering the features of the node itself and its neighbours within a range of at most P hops, we obtain $P+1$ different node features, including the node's own features.

Feature Selection. As features are aggregated over many hops, some features are useful and correlate with the label distribution, while others are not very useful for learning and act more like noise to the model. Therefore, we need to perform feature selection on the input features. In the process of feature selection, all features are input in parallel. Firstly, each input feature undergoes a linear transformation through a unique linear layer, followed by L2 normalization to maintain the size of each feature vector within a consistent range. Then, the magnitude of these features is scaled by the scalar values constrained by the softmax function. During the training process, the scalar values of relevant features corresponding to the labels increase towards 1 while others decrease towards 0. By adjusting the scalar values of each feature dynamically, the model can learn which features are relevant to the task and which are redundant or irrelevant. Since we are not using a binary selection of features, we term this selection procedure as "soft-selection" of features. Finally, after performing feature selection in parallel channels, we concatenate the resulting outputs and use them as input features for the next layer. Suppose there are L input feature matrices, the above operation can be formulated as

$$H^{(1)} = \mathop{\|}_{l=1}^{L} \alpha_l(\hat{X}_l W_l^{(0)})_{norm}. \tag{6}$$

Here $\|$ is the concatenation operation. $\hat{X}_l$ is the l-th input feature matrix. α_l is the scalar of X_l, where $\sum_{l=1}^{L} \alpha_l = 1$. $W_l^{(0)}$ is the unique weight matrix of $\hat{X}_l$. $(\cdot)_{norm}$ is the L2-normalization operation.

Classification and Model Optimization. After feature selection from the previous layer, we obtain the input feature $H^{(1)}$. Firstly, we apply the ReLU activation function to the input feature $H^{(1)}$ to introduce nonlinear properties. Subsequently, the output from the ReLU activation is mapped to the second linear layer for further feature transformation. Finally, to obtain the probability distribution of each node belonging to different categories, we apply the softmax function to the output of the second linear layer. The above operation can be formulated as:

$$Z = \text{softmax}(\text{ReLU}(H^{(1)})W^{(1)}), \tag{7}$$

where Z is the probability distribution of the input data over the different categories. $W^{(1)}$ is the weight matrix, which is a learnable parameter. The softmax activation function, which is defined as

$$\text{softmax}(x_i) = \frac{exp(x_i)}{\sum_i exp(x_i)}, \tag{8}$$

is applied row-wise. And the cross-entropy loss is calculated by:

$$\mathcal{L} = -\sum_{l \in L} \sum_{f=1}^{F} \mathcal{Y}_{lf} \ln Z_{lf}, \tag{9}$$

where $\mathcal{Y}_{lf}$ represents the true label of the l-th labeled node. Z_{lf} represents the predicted probability of the l-th node belonging to the f-th category. By backpropagating the loss gradient, the model can update the weights $W^{(0)}$ and $W^{(1)}$ of neural network as well as the value of the scalar α_l. Once trained, the model can be used for the prediction of labels of unlabeled nodes. As mentioned in Sect. 3.1, each element of the unlabeled dataset U represents a user-item interaction triplet $(u_t, i_t, r_{u_t i_t})$. Therefore, the predicted label of the unlabeled node $r_{u_t i_t}$ is equivalent to potential user-item interactions. As a result, to alleviate the data sparsity, these potential user-item interactions can be used as augmented data for the training of CTR prediction models.

4   Experiments

In this section, we conduct extensive experiments on three real-world datasets to show the effectiveness of our proposed model.

4.1   Datasets

The following three commonly used sparse datasets are adopted for our experiments: **Book-Crossing (Book)**[1], **Last.FM (Music)**[2], **MovieLens-Latest-samll (Movie)**[3]. Since the datasets mentioned above are explicit feedback, we adopt the methodology proposed by [21] to transform them into implicit feedbacks and subsequently construct the knowledge graph. Finally, we adhere to the partitioning scheme introduced by [14] to split the instances into three distinct sets: labeled data comprising 20%, unlabeled data also accounting for 20%, and the remaining 60% serving as the test data. The basic statistics of the three datasets after processing are reported in Table 1.

---

[1] http://www2.informatik.uni-freiburg.de/~cziegler/BX/.
[2] https://grouplens.org/datasets/hetrec-2011/.
[3] https://github.com/rexrex9/kb4recMovielensDataProcess.

4.2   Baselines and Evaluation Metrics

We compare the proposed SFSGNN with the state-of-the-art node classification methods, including LPA [2], GCN [8], GAT [15], LPA-GCN [17], MMA [13] and FSGNN [12]. The brief description of the above baseline methods is presented in Sect. 2. All the compared baseline models are publicly accessible. Furthermore, we adopt three widely used evaluation metrics: ACC (Accuracy), AUC (Area Under Curve), and Loss (Cross entropy), to evaluate the offline performance. Note that higher ACC, AUC and lower Loss values indicate better performance.

Table 1. The basic statistics of the three datasets.

Dataset	Book	Music	Movie
# users	17860	1872	610
# items	17496	3846	8639
# interactions	139746	42346	97930
# density	0.0041%	0.28%	0.52%
# KG entities	150369	9393	102569
# KG relation	25	60	32
# KG triples	151500	15518	499474
# labeled data	27950	8470	19586
# unlabeled data	27949	8469	19586
# test data	83847	25407	58758

4.3   Implementation Details

We conduct a grid search for parameter selection. We tune the learning rate from $\{10^{-4}, 2 \times 10^{-4}, 5 \times 10^{-4}, 2 \times 10^{-2}\}$, the size of the hidden dimensions from $\{8, 16, 32, 64, 128, 256\}$, the hops of feature aggregation from $\{1, 2, 3, 4\}$, and the neighbor sampling sizes from $\{20, 50, 100\}$. The Adam optimization is utilized with a batch size of 1024 to optimize all trainable parameters. All experiments are conducted on a NVIDIA Tesla v100 GPU.

4.4   Comparison with Baselines

Table 2 shows the comparison results of different models on three benchmark datasets. The results show that the proposed SFSGNN achieves similar or superior performance compared with the baselines when only a few labeled samples are provided. This validates the significant advantage of SFSGNN in overcoming data sparsity. Compared with the other baseline methods, the performance of LPA was average. The main reason for this is that LPA only utilizes node labels rather than node features, which limits its capability in node classification. GAT and MMA performed the worst among all the baseline models. This is because they cannot handle very sparse or high-dimensional graph data well. GCN performs well in benchmarks but not on the Movie dataset. The reason for this phenomenon may be that shallow GCN networks are unable to propagate labeling information over a large area, while deep GCN networks may lead to over-smoothing problems. Notably, LPA-GCN performs well in all baselines. This proves that combining different node classification methods is helpful in improving the classification accuracy of the model.

4.5 Ablation Study

To investigate the contribution of each design strategies of our proposed SFS-GNN model, we conduct an ablation study and report the results in Fig. 2. We notice that adjusting each design strategies of our proposed model leads to a decrease in accuracy. When a random method is adopted to replace the KNN Graph Construction (KGC) module, the model will not be able to construct the graph based on the similarities between the data. Removing the soft selection (Soft) mechanism, the model will not be able to reduce its dependence on noise or irrelevant features. Setting a unique weight matrix $W^{(0)}$ for each input feature is designed to capture the importance and relevance of different features. If the same weight matrix is used for all input features, the model will not be able to distinguish the importance between different features. L2-normalization keeps the size of each feature vector within the same range. Without L2-normalization, the weights of certain features in the model may become too large or too small. Therefore, all the proposed design strategies are necessary for our model.

Table 2. The experimental results on three datasets.

Model	Book		Music		Movie	
	Loss	ACC	Loss	ACC	Loss	ACC
LPA	0.7581	0.5296	0.6061	0.6239	0.7390	0.5414
GCN	0.6134	0.6831	0.6703	0.6681	0.7730	0.4395
GAT	0.7301	0.4057	0.7910	0.3660	0.7139	0.4380
LPA-GCN	**0.5630**	**0.7220**	0.5384	0.7694	0.6880	0.5620
MMA	0.8259	0.4135	0.9225	0.6446	0.8713	0.4440
FSGNN	0.5733	0.7008	0.5484	0.7659	0.6990	0.6248
SFSGNN (Ours)	0.5701	0.7044	**0.4749**	**0.7719**	**0.5707**	**0.7043**
Improve.(%)	−1.26%	−2.43%	+18.42%	+0.32%	+17.04%	+25.32%

Note: Best results are in bold. Suboptimal results are underlined.

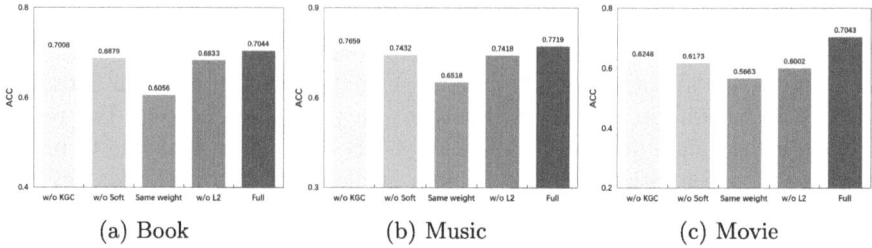

(a) Book   (b) Music   (c) Movie

Fig. 2. The ablation result of SFSGNN.

4.6   Parameter Analysis

In this section, we will analyse how the parameters affects the performance of our proposed SFSGNN model.

- **The number of hops of feature aggregation.** As shown in Fig. 3, the proposed model is able to reach its own best performance when the number of hops of feature aggregation is properly set (from 2 to 3). This phenomena can be explained by the fact that a small number of hops makes it difficult for the model to aggregate neighborhood information, while a large number of hops causes problems with over-smoothing.
- **The value of K.** The value of K represents the number of neighbors of each node in the KNN graph construction module. As evident from Fig. 4, the value of K for achieving the best model performance varies across different datasets. This phenomenon is easy to explain. A smaller value of K limits the model's ability to capture information from adjacent regions, while a larger value of K makes the model more susceptible to noise interference.
- **Hidden dimensions.** From the Fig. 5, we can see that for the Book and Music datasets, the best model performance is achieved when 8 or 16 hidden dimensions are used. However, for the Movie dataset, 64 hidden dimensions are necessary to achieve a comparable level of performance. These variations highlight that a single set of design choices may not apply to all datasets and some level of exploration is required.

4.7   Case Study on Alleviating Data Sparsity

To further validate the effectiveness of the proposed SFSGNN model in alleviating data sparsity in CTR prediction, a case study is conducted by using the aforementioned three sparse datasets. In this case study, we apply the proposed SFSGNN method to CTR prediction models and compare the experimental results before and after its application. The baseline for this case study can be categorized into two types: deep learning-based CTR prediction models (including: DeepFM [6], xDeepFM [9], DCN-V2 [23], MaskNet [24], FinalMLP [10]) and knowledge graph-based CTR prediction models (including: Ripplenet

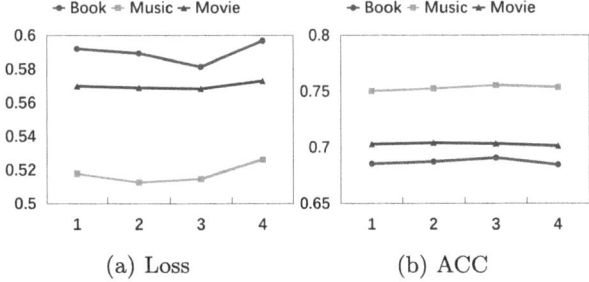

Fig. 3. The result of Loss and ACC w.r.t. different hops in feature aggregation.

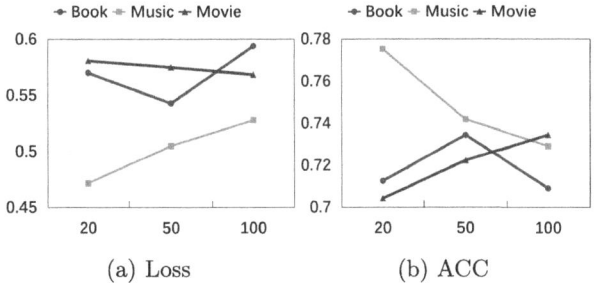

Fig. 4. The result of Loss and ACC w.r.t. different values of K.

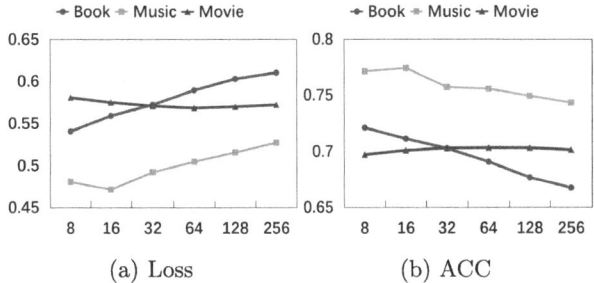

Fig. 5. The result of Loss and ACC w.r.t. different hidden dimensions.

[18], KGCN [21], MKR [20], KGNN-LS [19], KGFER [5]). All models selected for experiments have been trained to ensure the reliability of the experiments.

Table 3 shows the experimental results before and after applying the proposed SFSGNN to the CTR prediction models. The results show that the performance of almost all baseline models is improved through the application of our proposed strategy. Only a few knowledge graph-based baselines show performance degradation after applying our proposed strategy. This can be attributed to the introduction of noise unrelated to the task during the application of our strat-

Table 3. The experimental results before and after applying the proposed SFSGNN to the CTR prediction models.

Model	Book			Music			Movie		
	Loss	AUC	ACC	Loss	AUC	ACC	Loss	AUC	ACC
DeepFM	0.633	0.612	0.609	0.683	0.667	0.668	0.707	0.625	0.627
DeepFM+Ours	0.647	0.684	0.685	0.680	0.700	0.700	0.662	0.637	0.637
Improve.(%)	−2.21	**11.76**	**12.47**	**0.43**	**4.94**	**4.79**	**6.36**	**1.92**	**1.59**
xDeepFM	0.630	0.614	0.612	0.685	0.520	0.520	0.666	0.623	0.627
xDeepFM+Ours	0.615	0.684	0.684	0.564	0.743	0.744	0.659	0.636	0.637
Improve.(%)	**2.38**	**11.40**	**11.76**	**17.66**	**42.88**	**43.07**	**1.05**	**2.08**	**1.59**
DCNv2	0.684	0.670	0.671	0.580	0.719	0.719	0.676	0.625	0.625
DCNv2+Ours	0.625	0.693	0.694	0.576	0.735	0.735	0.645	0.628	0.637
Improve.(%)	**8.62**	**3.43**	**3.42**	**0.68**	**2.22**	**2.22**	**4.58**	**0.48**	**1.92**
MaskNet	1.242	0.670	0.670	0.705	0.704	0.704	0.665	0.599	0.580
MaskNet+Ours	0.601	0.675	0.676	0.582	0.731	0.731	0.665	0.632	0.637
Improve.(%)	**51.61**	**0.74**	**0.89**	**17.44**	**3.83**	**3.83**	0.00	**5.50**	**9.82**
FinalMLP	0.691	0.582	0.588	0.611	0.708	0.708	0.670	0.621	0.615
FinalMLP+Ours	0.609	0.677	0.677	0.602	0.723	0.723	0.643	0.637	0.641
Improve.(%)	**11.86**	**16.32**	**15.13**	**1.47**	**2.11**	**2.11**	**4.02**	**2.57**	**4.22**
Ripplenet	0.663	0.675	0.639	0.732	0.775	0.712	0.6966	0.744	0.680
Ripplenet+Ours	0.583	0.705	0.614	0.710	0.803	0.735	0.682	0.774	0.706
Improve.(%)	**12.06**	**4.44**	<u>−3.91</u>	**3.00**	**3.61**	**3.23**	**2.09**	**4.03**	**3.82**
KGCN	0.627	0.521	0.509	0.718	0.721	0.656	0.685	0.725	0.665
KGCN+Ours	0.544	0.651	0.601	0.651	0.798	0.724	0.662	0.747	0.685
Improve.(%)	**13.23**	**24.95**	**18.07**	**9.33**	**10.67**	**10.36**	**3.35**	**3.03**	**3.00**
MKR	0.653	0.698	0.658	0.729	0.779	0.730	0.688	0.701	0.648
MKR+Ours	0.602	0.723	0.685	0.701	0.792	0.736	0.671	0.767	0.701
Improve.(%)	**7.81**	**3.58**	**4.10**	**3.84**	**1.66**	**0.82**	**2.47**	**9.41**	**8.17**
KGNN-LS	0.611	0.502	0.490	0.647	0.705	0.642	0.678	0.722	0.662
KGNN-LS+Ours	0.539	0.617	0.578	0.646	0.680	0.614	0.659	0.759	0.690
Improve.(%)	**11.78**	**22.90**	**17.95**	**0.15**	<u>−3.54</u>	<u>−4.36</u>	**2.80**	**5.12**	**4.22**
KGFER	0.492	0.705	0.645	0.548	0.775	0.658	0.540	0.799	0.679
KGFER+Ours	0.465	0.728	0.664	0.524	0.785	0.699	0.570	0.778	0.660
Improve.(%)	**5.48**	**3.26**	**2.94**	**4.37**	**1.29**	**6.23**	<u>−5.55</u>	<u>−2.62</u>	<u>−2.79</u>

Note: Improved percentages are in bold. Decreasing percentages are underlined.

egy. It is worth noting that the more sparse the dataset (sparsity: Book >Music >Movie), the more significant the benefits of applying our model to the CTR prediction models. For systems with a large user base, even a minor improvement in CTR may potentially lead to a significant increase in overall revenue [1]. Therefore, the results of this case study fully demonstrates the effectiveness of our proposed SFSGNN model in alleviating data sparsity in CTR prediction.

5   Conclusion

To alleviate the data sparsity in CTR prediction, this paper proposes a semi-supervised node classification model named Soft Feature Selection Graph Neural Network (SFSGNN). Firstly, the integration of key modules, including node generation, graph construction, and soft feature selection networks, enables SFS-GNN to effectively leverage the limited known user-item interaction data to predict the unknown user-item interactions. Furthermore, the SFSGNN can effectively address the data sparsity issue by utilizing the prediction results as augmented data for training the CTR prediction models. Extensive experiments on three real-world sparse datasets demonstrate the effectiveness of SFSGNN in alleviating the data sparsity in CTR prediction. While the proposed model exhibits promising results, it still has some limitations. Firstly, the proposed model has a large memory requirement. Secondly, the proposed model does not support directed edges and edge features. In future research, we will focus on addressing these limitations and further improve our model.

Acknowledgements. This work is supported in part by the National Natural Science Foundation of China under Grant 62377015, the Research Cultivation Fund for The Youth Teachers of South China Normal University under Grant 23KJ29, and the Scientific Research Innovation Project of Graduate School of South China Normal University under grant 2024KYLX068.

References

1. Cheng, W., Shen, Y., Huang, L.. Adaptive factorization network: learning adaptive-order feature interactions. In: Proceedings of the AAAI Conference on Artificial Intelligence, pp. 3609–3616 (2020)
2. Cheng, Y., Shan, C., Shen, Y., Li, X., Luo, S., Li, D.: Label propagation for graph label noise. CoRR **abs/2310.16560** (2023)
3. Dong, X., Yu, L., Wu, Z., Sun, Y., Yuan, L., Zhang, F.: A hybrid collaborative filtering model with deep structure for recommender systems. In: Proceedings of the AAAI Conference on Artificial Intelligence, vol. 31, no. 1, June 2022
4. Duan, R., Jiang, C., Jain, H.K.: Combining review-based collaborative filtering and matrix factorization: a solution to rating's sparsity problem. Decis. Support Syst. **156**, 113748 (2022)
5. Fan, H., Zhong, Y., Zeng, G., Ge, C.: Improving recommender system via knowledge graph based exploring user preference. Appl. Intell. **52**(9), 10032–10044 (2022)
6. Guo, H., TANG, R., Ye, Y., Li, Z., He, X.: DeepFM: a factorization-machine based neural network for CTR prediction. In: Proceedings of the Twenty-Sixth International Joint Conference on Artificial Intelligence (2017)

7. Hamilton, W., Ying, Z., Leskovec, J.: Inductive representation learning on large graphs. In: Neural Information Processing Systems (2017)
8. Kipf, T.N., Welling, M.: Semi-supervised classification with graph convolutional networks. In: 5th International Conference on Learning Representations, ICLR 2017, Toulon, France, 24–26 April 2017, Conference Track Proceedings. OpenReview.net (2017)
9. Lian, J., Zhou, X., Zhang, F., Chen, Z., Xie, X., Sun, G.: xDeepFM: combining explicit and implicit feature interactions for recommender systems. In: Proceedings of the 24th ACM SIGKDD International Conference on Knowledge Discovery & Data Mining, KDD 2018, London, UK, 19–23 August 2018, pp. 1754–1763. ACM (2018)
10. Mao, K., Zhu, J., Su, L., Cai, G., Li, Y., Dong, Z.: FinalMLP: an enhanced two-stream MLP model for CTR prediction. In: Williams, B., Chen, Y., Neville, J. (eds.) Thirty-Seventh AAAI Conference on Artificial Intelligence, AAAI 2023, Thirty-Fifth Conference on Innovative Applications of Artificial Intelligence, IAAI 2023, Thirteenth Symposium on Educational Advances in Artificial Intelligence, EAAI 2023, Washington, DC, USA, 7–14 February 2023, pp. 4552–4560. AAAI Press (2023)
11. Mauro, N., Ardissono, L., Cena, F.: Supporting people with autism spectrum disorders in the exploration of PoIs. Commun. ACM **65**(2), 101–109 (2022)
12. Maurya, S.K., Liu, X., Murata, T.: Simplifying approach to node classification in graph neural networks. J. Comput. Sci. **62**, 101695 (2022)
13. Sarıgün, A., Rifaioglu, A.S.: Multi-mask aggregators for graph neural networks. In: The First Learning on Graphs Conference (2022)
14. Sharma, D., Jones, M.: Efficiently learning the graph for semi-supervised learning. In: Evans, R.J., Shpitser, I. (eds.) Uncertainty in Artificial Intelligence, UAI 2023, Pittsburgh, PA, USA, July 31–4 August 2023. Proceedings of Machine Learning Research, vol. 216, pp. 1900–1910. PMLR (2023)
15. Velickovic, P., Cucurull, G., Casanova, A., Romero, A., Liò, P., Bengio, Y.: Graph attention networks. In: 6th International Conference on Learning Representations, ICLR 2018, Vancouver, BC, Canada, April 30–May 3 2018, Conference Track Proceedings. OpenReview.net (2018)
16. Wang, B., Li, A., Li, H., Chen, Y.: GraphFL: a federated learning framework for semi-supervised node classification on graphs. Cornell University - arXiv (2020)
17. Wang, H., Leskovec, J.: Unifying graph convolutional neural networks and label propagation. CoRR **abs/2002.06755** (2020)
18. Wang, H., et al.: RippleNet: propagating user preferences on the knowledge graph for recommender systems. In: Proceedings of the 27th ACM International Conference on Information and Knowledge Management (2018)
19. Wang, H., et al.: Knowledge-aware graph neural networks with label smoothness regularization for recommender systems. In: Proceedings of the 25th ACM SIGKDD International Conference on Knowledge Discovery & Data Mining, KDD 2019, Anchorage, AK, USA, 4–8 August 2019, pp. 968–977. ACM (2019)
20. Wang, H., Zhang, F., Zhao, M., Li, W., Xie, X., Guo, M.: Multi-task feature learning for knowledge graph enhanced recommendation. In: The World Wide Web Conference (2019)
21. Wang, H., Zhao, M., Xie, X., Li, W., Guo, M.: Knowledge graph convolutional networks for recommender systems. In: The World Wide Web Conference (2019)
22. Wang, R., Fu, B., Fu, G., Wang, M.: Deep & cross network for ad click predictions. In: Proceedings of the ADKDD 2017 (2017)

23. Wang, R., et al.: DCN V2: improved deep & cross network and practical lessons for web-scale learning to rank systems. In: Proceedings of the Web Conference 2021 (2021)
24. Wang, Z., She, Q., Zhang, J.: MaskNet: introducing feature-wise multiplication to ctr ranking models by instance-guided mask (2021)
25. Wu, Z., Pan, S., Chen, F., Long, G., Zhang, C., Yu, P.S.: A comprehensive survey on graph neural networks. IEEE Trans. Neural Netw. Learn. Syst. **10**, 4–24 (2021)

How Effective is the Shorts Transformation of Traditional Media? An Analysis from the Perspective of User-Generated Content

Pu Zhang and Corey Kewei Xu[✉]

The Hong Kong University of Science and Technology (Guangzhou), Guangzhou 511453, China
coreyxu@hkust-gz.edu.cn

Abstract. The digital transformation of traditional media outlets has become a critical imperative in the evolving media landscape. As traditional media grapple with the challenges of adapting to the rise of digital and social media platforms, understanding the factors that shape their performance and user engagement on these emerging channels is of paramount importance. This study examines the comparative performance of a traditional media account with a government background (Hubei Daily) and a specialized new media account (Cover News) on Douyin platform, with a focus on the distribution of emotional sentiment and thematic diversity in user-generated content. We collected 19,343 comments from "Hubei Daily," with 18,792 valid (97.15%), and 36,737 comments from "Cover News," with 28,910 valid (78.69%). Our research used a BERT fine-tuned model for sentiment analysis, TF-IDF for keyword extraction, keyword co-occurrence analysis, and a large language model for topic modeling. This approach allowed us to capture a wide range of discussion topics and understand the thematic focus. Findings show that the new media account covered broader topics, whereas the traditional media account had a more concentrated thematic focus. Typically, such events should generate negative emotions and discussions around accountability. However, the study indicates that users are more cautious in their comments on official media, suggesting ineffective digital transformation by traditional media. This underscores the need for traditional media to better understand and adapt to content preferences and engagement patterns of shorts platform users, highlighting the complexities of transitioning to emerging platforms and the importance of effective content strategies and meaningful user engagement.

Keywords: Online Public Opinion · Media Transformation · Social Media Analytics

1 Introduction

The rapid growth of shorts platforms, such as TikTok and Instagram Reels, has presented both opportunities and challenges for traditional print media outlets seeking to transform and adapt to the digital age. Many established media organizations have launched operations on these platforms to attract a wider, often younger, audience [1, 2]. However, the effectiveness of this transformation remains a subject of ongoing debate.

© The Author(s), under exclusive license to Springer Nature Singapore Pte Ltd. 2025
H. Sun et al. (Eds.): ChineseCSCW 2024, CCIS 2343, pp. 124–137, 2025.
https://doi.org/10.1007/978-981-96-2373-0_9

On one side of the debate, scholars argue that traditional media's transition to shorts platforms is a necessary and promising strategy. They contend that by leveraging the unique features and user behaviors of these platforms, traditional media can expand their reach, enhance audience engagement, and ultimately secure their long-term viability in the digital landscape [3]. The ability to create compelling, platform-tailored content and foster meaningful user interactions is seen as crucial for traditional media's successful transformation.

On the other hand, critics argue that the transition to shorts platforms may not be a panacea for traditional media's woes. They suggest that the distinct content preferences and engagement patterns of these platforms pose significant challenges for traditional media, which are often accustomed to longer-form, text-based reporting [4, 5]. The ability to effectively manage and leverage user-generated content, such as comments and shares, is also cited as a key determinant of success in this new media environment [6].

Ultimately, the question of whether traditional media's transformation efforts on shorts platforms have been successful remains unresolved. Addressing this gap is crucial, as the outcome of this transition can have far-reaching implications for the future of traditional media and the broader media ecosystem. By conducting a comparative analysis of user-generated content on traditional media and new media accounts, this study aims to assess the effectiveness of traditional media in the process of digital transformation.

This study specifically examines the differences in the sentiment and thematic content of over 48,000 user comments on short video posts about the same event, published by two distinct media accounts "Cover News" and "Hubei Daily" on the Douyin platform. By conducting a comparative analysis of user comments on matched content from traditional print media and new media accounts, this study aims to evaluate the effectiveness of traditional media's transformation efforts on shorts platforms.

2 Related Work

2.1 Media Transformation

The digital age has presented traditional media outlets with the imperative to transform and adapt. Küng explored the transformation strategies of traditional media in the digital era, emphasizing the need to reshape organizational culture and business models [7]. The author argued that successful transformation requires traditional media to fundamentally rethink their value propositions, organizational structures, and operational processes to align with the demands of the digital landscape.

Similarly, Goyanes and Dürrenberg investigated the transformation practices of Spanish newspapers on digital platforms [8]. The study examined the factors that influenced the newspapers' efforts to establish an online presence, including organizational resources, technological capabilities, and market conditions. The findings suggested that the effectiveness of traditional media's digital transformation was contingent on their ability to develop appropriate content strategies and business models for the new media environment.

Collectively, these studies underscore the significant challenges and complexities involved in the digital transformation of traditional media. Successful transformation requires traditional media to not only develop new technical and operational capabilities but also fundamentally rethink their organizational structures, value propositions, and business models to align with the demands of the digital age.

2.2 User-Generated Content on Social Media Platforms

User-generated content (UGC) has become an integral part of social media platforms, with significant implications for media organizations. Kaplan and Haenlein proposed a classification of UGC and its applications on social media, highlighting the diverse forms of user-created content, such as blogs, wikis, and social networking posts [9]. The authors emphasized the importance of understanding the characteristics and motivations of UGC for media organizations seeking to leverage these platforms effectively.

Diakopoulos and Naaman explored the role of user comments in news reporting, examining their impact on the quality and credibility of news coverage [10]. The study found that user comments can provide valuable feedback and insights, but they can also introduce biases and misinformation that can undermine the integrity of news reports. This underscores the need for traditional media to carefully manage and moderate user-generated content on their digital platforms.

Ziegele et al. further investigated the mechanisms by which user comments influence the dissemination of news reports [11]. The researchers found that the volume, sentiment, and interactivity of user comments can significantly affect the reach and engagement of news content on social media. This suggests that traditional media's ability to foster meaningful user engagement and manage the narrative around their content can be crucial for the success of their digital transformation efforts.

The research on UGC in the social media context highlights the importance for traditional media to understand and effectively leverage user-generated content on their digital platforms. Navigating the complexities of user engagement, content moderation, and narrative control can be critical factors in determining the success of traditional media's transition to the new media landscape.

2.3 Shorts Social Media Platforms

The rise of shorts platforms has been a significant development in the media landscape, presenting both opportunities and challenges for traditional media outlets. Cheng et al. studied the user behavior characteristics and dissemination mechanisms of platforms such as Vine [12]. The researchers found that shorts content on these platforms tends to have high engagement rates and rapid diffusion, driven by factors like video length, content type, and user interactions.

Bakhshi et al. explored the content dissemination features of image-sharing platforms like Instagram, which have also become a popular medium for shorts content [13]. The study highlighted the role of visual cues, emotional appeal, and social context in driving the virality of content on these platforms. These findings suggest that the success of traditional media's transformation efforts on shorts platforms may depend on their ability to create content that resonates with the unique characteristics and user behaviors of these platforms.

Hu et al. conducted a comparative analysis of user behavior across various social media platforms, including shorts platforms [14]. The researchers found significant differences in the types of content, user engagement, and social interactions on these platforms, underscoring the need for traditional media to tailor their strategies and content to the specific dynamics of each platform.

The research on shorts social media platforms emphasizes the distinct user behaviors, content preferences, and dissemination mechanisms that characterize these emerging media environments. For traditional media seeking to transition to these platforms, understanding and adapting to these platform-specific dynamics can be crucial for achieving effective and sustainable transformation.

3 Methodology

To examine the effectiveness of traditional media's transformation efforts on shorts platforms, this study employs a multi-pronged methodological approach. First, a data collection process is implemented to gather user-generated content from matched content posted by traditional media and new media accounts on the Douyin (TikTok's Chinese version) platform. Next, sentiment analysis techniques are leveraged to evaluate the polarity of the collected user comments, with a focus on those expressing negative sentiment. Finally, topic modeling methods are utilized to uncover the dominant themes and discussions emerging from the negatively-valenced comments. By comparing the UGC patterns across the traditional and new media accounts, we were able to conduct a comprehensive analysis of the sentiment and thematic content within the user comments, enabling them to compare the differences between the two media accounts' portrayals of the Changsha building collapse event. The technical approach and logical framework of this study is shown in the Fig. 1 below.

3.1 Data Preparation

On May 12, 2022, a 17-story commercial building in Changsha, Hunan province, collapsed, resulting in significant loss of life and property. This incident sparked widespread public attention and discussion on social media platforms like Douyin. The comments on video posts about the collapse provide a unique opportunity to examine public reaction and media framing of the event.

We analyzed the most liked video content related to the incident. The most popular video was published by Cover News, receiving 755,000 likes and 375,000 forwards. Cover News, a new media account, has 32.449 million followers and 2.16 billion total likes. Hubei Daily, a traditional media account, received 218,000 likes and 44,000 forwards for its most popular video. It has 47.823 million followers and 2.78 billion total likes.

Using a Python crawler, we collected comments from the videos with IDs "7322022728809188649" (Hubei Daily) and "7321936745338096931" (Cover News). After data collection, we cleaned the data by converting and removing emojis and other

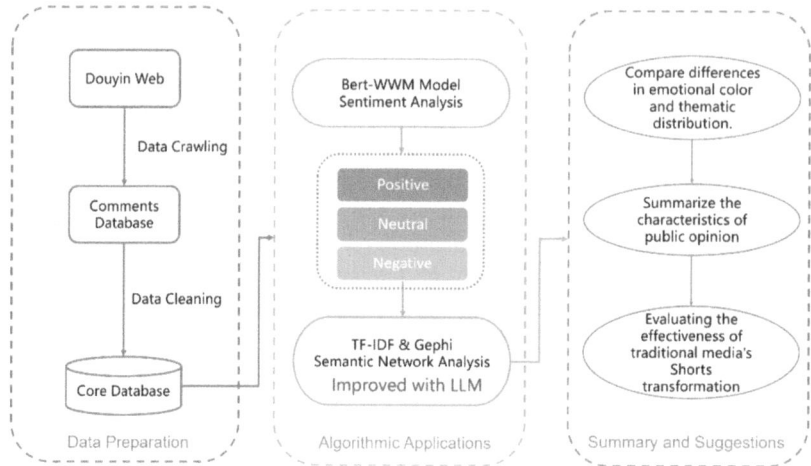

Fig. 1. Research Logical Framework Diagram

meaningless characters, eliminating irrelevant comments, handling missing data, and normalizing the text for further analysis.

3.2 Sentiment Analysis

To evaluate the distribution of emotional sentiment in the user comments, we used a pre-training BERT model [15].The Chinese BERT-wwm is a state-of-the-art natural language processing model that has demonstrated strong performance in various text classification tasks, including sentiment analysis [16]. The model achieves 95% accuracy for the general task of sentiment analysis of short texts and can be used for this task [16]. The model then processed each comment and output a sentiment score from 0 to 1, indicating the likelihood of the comment being positive, negative, or neutral. Here we make 0.2 as a small interval, and the specific correspondence is shown in Table 1 below [17].

By applying the Bert-wwm model to the entire dataset of user comments, the researchers were able to obtain a detailed distribution of the emotional sentiment expressed across the comments. This sentiment analysis provided a quantitative measure of the overall sentiment tendencies within the comments, which was then used to inform the subsequent thematic analysis. The researchers paid particular attention to the comments that exhibited negative sentiment, as these were the focus of the thematic analysis and comparison between the two media accounts' portrayals of the Changsha building collapse event.

3.3 Thematic Analysis

After conducting sentiment analysis, researchers focused on comments with negative sentiment. To uncover key themes within these comments, they used a keyword co-occurrence semantic network technique based on the TF-IDF (Term Frequency-Inverse Document Frequency) algorithm [18].

Table 1. Corresponding Table of Emotional Intensity Relationships

Typical corpus	Emotional intensity score	Emotional tendency
It's tragic!	0–0.2	Strongly negative
That's unfortunate!	0.2–0.4	Negative
Hopefully, there will be no new casualties tomorrow	0.4–0.6	Neutral
Go for it! Peace and safety!	0.6–0.8	Positive
Trust in the government! It's going to be okay!	0.8–1.0	Strongly positive

They constructed a co-occurrence network where high TF-IDF score keywords were represented as nodes, connected based on their co-occurrence within comments [19]. This helped identify key themes associated with negative sentiment [20].

To enhance the analysis, researchers used ChatGPT 4.0 to cluster and refine these themes. This AI system's semantic understanding and contextual reasoning abilities grouped the themes into coherent categories, providing a deeper understanding of the topics and concerns in the negative comments.

Combining TF-IDF-based keyword analysis with ChatGPT 4.0's clustering capabilities allowed researchers to uncover key themes linked to negative sentiment in user comments about the Changsha building collapse across the two media accounts.

4   Results

4.1   Distribution of Comments Data

The total number of comments collected from "Cover News" is 36,737, and the valid data after processing is 28,910, the data validity rate is 78.69%. We uniquely attribute the comments posted in an hour to this hour, and the result of this collation is shown in Fig. 2 below. We can clearly find that the topic hotness shows a periodic change, which is related to the time period when people use the software. Meanwhile, the time heat shows a gradual decline overall.

The total number of comments collected from "Hubei Daily" is 19,343, and the valid data after processing is 18,792, the data validity rate is 97.15%. After conducting the same organizing steps, the results obtained are shown in Fig. 3 below. We can clearly notice that the number of replies to the content posted by the media account peaks higher (on an hourly scale), but the heat declines more quickly.

4.2   Sentiment Analysis Results

Sentiment analysis for "Cover News"
The sentiment analysis algorithm was used to assign scores to the 28,910 comments

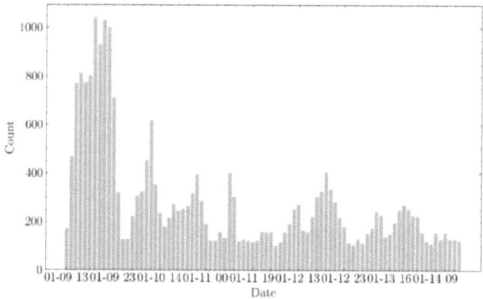

Fig. 2. Distribution of Comments Data from Cover News

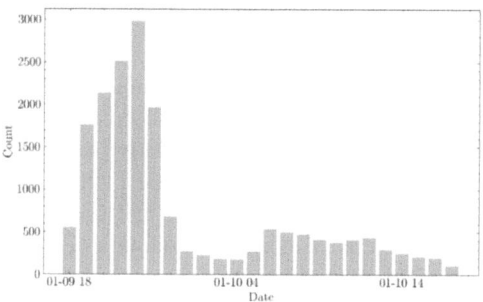

Fig. 3. Distribution of Comments Data from Hubei Daily

from "Cover News", and the results are shown in Fig. 4 below. It can be found that the number of texts with negative emotional coloring significantly exceeds the number of texts with positive emotional coloring, and the distribution of the number of texts with each emotional score shows an overall trend of gradually decreasing from negative to positive.

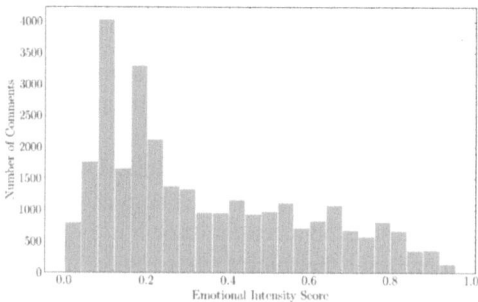

Fig. 4. Distribution of Sentiment Scores of Comments from Cover News

Sentiment analysis for "Hubei Daily"

The sentiment analysis algorithm was used to assign scores to the 18,792 comments from

"Hubei Daily", and the results are shown in Fig. 5 below. It is noticeable that a large number of comments with neutral emotional overtones appear, not unlike the results of the previous sections.

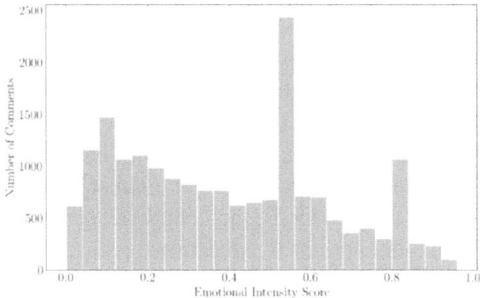

Fig. 5. Distribution of Sentiment Scores of Comments from Hubei Daily

Comparative Analysis

The analysis of comment engagement showed that the "Cover News" video content generated a higher volume and intensity of user comments compared to the "Hubei Daily" posts, indicating that the former's coverage was more effective in capturing public attention and eliciting active discussion. The sentiment analysis further highlighted the differences in the distribution of positive, negative, and neutral sentiment expressed by users, with the "Cover News" comments exhibiting a higher proportion of negative sentiment (Table 2).

Table 2. Comparison of the percentage of the emotional color

Emotional Tendency	Cover News	Hubei Daily
Strongly Negative	40.00%	28.90%
Negative	23.50%	22.50%
Neutral	17.10%	27.30%
Positive	13.90%	12.10%
Strongly Positive	5.6%	9.2%

4.3   Thematic Analysis Results

To further investigate the differences in the user comments, the researchers conducted a thematic analysis focusing on the comments that exhibited negative sentiment tendencies. Using a keyword co-occurrence semantic network approach based on TF-IDF, combined with theme clustering powered by ChatGPT 4.0, the researchers identified the following key themes:

Thematic Analysis of Cover News

Emotional and Human Impact: Dominated by keywords such as "tears", "heartache", "deceased", and "family members". This cluster emphasizes immediate emotional responses, personal losses, and the deep impact on the families and friends of the victims. It highlights discussions on the need for psychological support and community solidarity.

Educational and Professional Impact: Featuring terms like "college students", "medical students", "study medicine", and "achievement". This cluster focuses on the educational and career aspirations affected by the incident. It addresses the impact on the academic community, potential disruptions to educational paths, and the truncated dreams of young professionals.

Structural and Safety Concerns: With keywords such as "tofu-dreg project", "dangerous buildings", and "earthquake". This cluster addresses concerns about building integrity. It highlights issues related to construction standards, material quality, regulatory compliance, and the enforcement of safety protocols.

Social Critique and Responsibility: Integrating keywords like "black heart", "landlord", "rent a house", and "condemned." This cluster explores societal reactions and responsibilities. It examines the roles of property owners, builders, and potential corrupt practices, focusing on accountability and moral obligations in housing and student accommodations.

Each cluster represents a distinct yet interconnected aspect of the overall discussion, forming a comprehensive picture of the incident's multifaceted impact. This holistic approach aids in understanding the tragedy's effects, supporting structured responses to prevent future occurrences, and aiding those affected (Fig. 6).

Fig. 6. Semantic Network Co-occurrence of Cover News Comments

Thematic Analysis of Hubei Daily

After visualization, the keyword co-occurrence map, shown in Fig. 7, reveals an intricate network of themes and relationships grouped into three distinct clusters:

Construction and Infrastructure Integrity: This cluster includes keywords such as "construction", "design", "material", "foundation", "cement", and "building". It focuses on the structural aspects of the collapsed dormitory, examining construction material quality and architectural integrity. Discussions may involve building regulations, material adequacy, and proper construction practices to ensure safety.

Human Impact and Emotional Response: Centered around keywords like "tears", "heartache", "deceased", "family", and "sad", this theme highlights the emotional and human impact of the tragedy. It encompasses personal stories, expressions of grief and solidarity, and societal responses to the event.

Responsibility and Legal Implications: Featuring keywords such as "responsibility", "landlord", "violation", "legal", and "developer", this cluster addresses accountability for the tragedy, including potential negligence and legal repercussions. It explores the roles of various stakeholders, such as university administration, building developers, and local government officials, in maintaining safety standards.

These interconnected themes create a comprehensive discussion covering technical, emotional, and administrative responses to the tragedy. Such a map helps navigate complex issues, ensuring all aspects are addressed to prevent future incidents and provide justice and closure for the victims.

These themes interconnect, with each impacting and influencing the others, creating a comprehensive discussion that covers the technical, emotional, and administrative responses to the tragedy. The community might use such a map to navigate through complex issues, ensuring all aspects are addressed to prevent future incidents and to provide justice and closure for the victims.

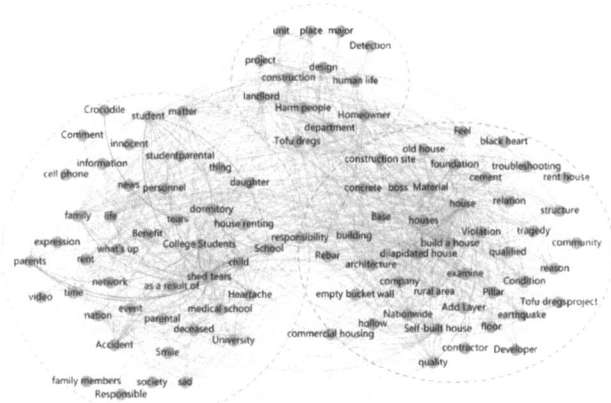

Fig. 7. Semantic Network Co-occurrence of Hubei Daily Comments

The thematic analysis of the negatively-valenced comments provided additional insights into the contrasting ways in which the two media accounts' coverage was perceived and discussed by the public. The "Cover News" comments tended to emphasize themes related to building safety, government responsibility, and the need for accountability, while the "Hubei Daily" comments focused more on expressions of grief and discussions around the potential causes of the collapse.

5 Discussion

5.1 Time Series Characteristics

The comparative analysis of user-generated content revealed notable inconsistencies in the volume of comments across the traditional media and new media accounts. Contrary to expectations, the specialized new media account (Cover News) exhibited a significantly higher number of user comments compared to the traditional media account (Lakeland Daily News). This suggests that the new media outlet may have been more effective in fostering user engagement and interactivity on the shorts platform [21].

The disparity in comment volume highlights challenges in traditional media's digital transformation efforts. While traditional media organizations possess established brand recognition and journalistic expertise, they struggle to match the user engagement levels seen on newer digital platforms. This finding aligns with previous research indicating that the content preferences and engagement patterns of shorts platform users often diverge from traditional media's established strategies [22].

The stark contrast in comment volume between traditional and new media accounts underscores the need for traditional media to adapt to the unique dynamics of shorts platforms. Leveraging user-generated content, such as comments, could be crucial for the success of their transformation efforts in this evolving media landscape. Investigating the factors driving these engagement disparities can provide valuable insights for strategic decision-making [23].

Future research could explore the underlying factors contributing to these patterns, such as the editorial practices of media outlets, audience demographics, preferences, and the broader social and political context. Expanding the analysis to include a wider range of media sources and platforms could yield a more comprehensive understanding of the interplay between media reporting and online public sentiment [24].

5.2 Sentiment Characteristics

The sentiment analysis revealed further disparities between traditional and new media accounts. Contrary to expectations, the traditional media account (Hubei Daily) exhibited a more positive emotional tone in user comments compared to the new media account (Cover News). This suggests that traditional media might be more successful in fostering positive sentiment among its audience on shorts platforms.

However, a closer examination shows that despite the traditional media account's relatively positive sentiment, user comments across both accounts generally exhibited a negative tone. Typically, user comments on disaster-related events are highly negative, focusing on blame and criticism. This trend was less pronounced on the traditional media account, likely because users are more cautious about commenting on official accounts [25].

This discrepancy highlights challenges in traditional media's digital transformation. While they can generate positive content, they struggle to resonate with the audience and shift overall sentiment positively [21]. The prevalence of negative sentiment suggests a disconnect between traditional media's efforts and user preferences on shorts platforms [26].

Understanding the factors driving sentiment patterns on shorts platforms is crucial. Analyzing audience emotional responses and the drivers of negative sentiment can refine content strategies and digital transformation efforts. Bridging the gap between traditional media's positive messaging and the audience's negative sentiment is vital for their successful transition to emerging platforms [27].

5.3 Thematic Characteristics

Topic modeling analysis revealed significant disparities in the breadth and diversity of user-generated discussions between traditional and new media accounts. Contrary to expectations, the new media account (Cover News) had a wider range of discussion topics, reflecting more diverse content. In contrast, discussions on the traditional media account (Hubei Daily) were more concentrated within narrower themes [5].

This suggests that while traditional media outlets have made efforts to create more appealing content as part of their digital transformation, they still face challenges in meeting the diverse content preferences of shorts platform users. The new media account's ability to capture and reflect a broader range of user interests has led to more extensive engagement [6].

The concentrated discussion topics on the traditional media account indicate limitations in its content strategies, constrained by conventional frameworks and agenda-setting practices. This limitation could hinder traditional media's ability to resonate with the content preferences and discussion habits of shorts platform users, affecting user engagement and loyalty [28].

6   Limitations and Future Work

While this study offers valuable insights into user engagement, sentiment, and thematic content differences across short video posts about the Changsha building collapse by "Cover News" and "Hubei Daily," several limitations should be acknowledged for future research.

First, the analysis is limited to user comments on a single social media platform, Douyin. These findings may not be generalizable to other platforms or forms of online discourse, as user behavior varies across digital environments. Additionally, the study focuses only on user comments, not on the content and framing of the media accounts' video posts. A deeper comparative analysis of the video content and journalistic practices could further clarify the factors behind the observed variations in public response. Lastly, the reliance on automated sentiment analysis and thematic clustering techniques may not fully capture the nuanced and contextual nature of human expression and opinion.

7 Conclusion

This study examined the differences in user engagement, sentiment, and thematic content across the short video posts about the Changsha building collapse event by the "Cover News" and "Hubei Daily" media accounts on the Douyin platform. The findings reveal notable disparities in the patterns of public response, suggesting that the two media outlets may have framed and reported on the event in divergent ways, leading to distinct perceptions and reactions among their respective audiences.

The transformation of traditional media has not been as successful as one might have hoped. While traditional media outlets have become more reflective and nuanced in their coverage, they have struggled to match the effectiveness of specialized new media accounts when it comes to user-generated content. New media platforms have empowered individuals to share their own perspectives and experiences, creating a more diverse and dynamic information landscape. In contrast, the shift in traditional media has been more incremental, with legacy outlets still grappling with the challenges of adapting to the digital age.

Despite the increased sophistication of traditional media, their content still tends to lack the immediacy, interactivity, and sense of community that characterizes successful new media initiatives. Audiences today expect to not just consume information, but to actively participate in its creation and dissemination. Ultimately, the transformation of media is an ongoing process, and the relative success of traditional and new media outlets will depend on their ability to adapt to the changing needs and expectations of their audiences. The future of media will likely be defined by a hybrid approach that leverages the strengths of both traditional and new media formats.

References

1. Bossetta, M.: The digital architectures of social media: comparing political campaigning on Facebook, Twitter, Instagram, and Snapchat in the 2016 U.S. election. J. Mass Commun. Q. **95**(2), 471–496 (2018)
2. Weimann, G., Masri, N.: Research note: spreading hate on TikTok. Stud. Confl. Terr. **46**(5), 752–765 (2023)
3. Zhang, X., Wu, Y., Liu, S.: Exploring shorts application addiction: socio-technical and attachment perspectives. Telematics Inform. **42**, 101243 (2019)
4. Ksiazek, T.B., Peer, L., Zivic, A.: Discussing the news. Digit. Journal. **3**(6), 850–870 (2015)
5. Ziegele, M., Weber, M., Quiring, O., et al.: The dynamics of online news discussions: effects of news articles and reader comments on users' involvement, willingness to participate, and the civility of their contributions*. Inf. Commun. Soc. **21**(10), 1419–1435 (2018)
6. Kümpel, A.S.: The Matthew effect in social media news use: assessing inequalities in news exposure and news engagement on social network sites (SNS). Journalism **21**(8), 1083–1098 (2020)
7. Küng, L.: Going digital: a roadmap for organisational transformation. Reuters Institute for the Study of Journalism (2017)
8. Goyanes, M., Dürrenberg, C.: A taxonomy of newspapers based on multi-platform and paid content strategies: evidences from Spain. Int. J. Media Manag. **16**(1), 27–45 (2014)
9. Kaplan, A.M., Haenlein, M.: Users of the world, unite! The challenges and opportunities of social media. Bus. Horiz. **53**(1), 59–68 (2010)

10. Diakopoulos, N., Naaman, M.: Towards quality discourse in online news comments. Association for Computing Machinery, Hangzhou, China (2011)
11. Ziegele, M., Breiner, T., Quiring, O.: What creates interactivity in online news discussions? An exploratory analysis of discussion factors in user comments on news items. J. Commun. **64**(6), 1111–1138 (2014)
12. Cheng, J., Adamic, L., Dow, P.A., et al.: Can cascades be predicted? Association for Computing Machinery, Seoul, Korea (2014)
13. Bakhshi, S., Shamma, D., Kennedy, L., et al.: Why we filter our photos and how it impacts engagement. In: Proceedings of the International AAAI Conference on Web and Social Media, vol. 9, no. 1, pp. 12–21 (2021)
14. Hu, Y., Manikonda, L., Kambhampati, S.: What we Instagram: a first analysis of instagram photo content and user types. In: Proceedings of the International AAAI Conference on Web and Social Media, vol. 8, no. 1, pp. 595–598 (2014)
15. Devlin, J., Chang, M.-W., Lee, K., et al.: Bert: pre-training of deep bidirectional transformers for language understanding. arXiv preprint arXiv:1810.04805 (2018)
16. Cui, Y., Che, W., Liu, T., et al.: Pre-training with whole word masking for Chinese Bert. IEEE/ACM Trans. Audio Speech Lang. Process. **29**, 3504–3514 (2021)
17. Zhang, P., Zhang, H., Kong, F.: Research on online public opinion in the investigation of the "7–20" extraordinary rainstorm and flooding disaster in Zhengzhou, China. Int. J. Disaster Risk Reduct. **105**, 104422 (2024)
18. Zhu, Z., Jie, L., Li, D., et al.: Hot topic detection based on a refined TF-IDF algorithm. IEEE Access **7**, 26996–27007 (2019)
19. Montemurro, M.A., Zanette, D.H.: Keywords and co-occurrence patterns in the Voynich manuscript: an information-theoretic analysis. PLoS ONE **8**(6), e66344 (2013)
20. Wang, Q., Chen, Z., Guo, J., et al.: Project keyword lexicon and keyword semantic network based on word co-occurrence matrix. J. Comput. Appl. **35**(6), 1649 (2015)
21. Krstic, A.: Digital transformation of journalism and media in Serbia: what has gone wrong? Journalism **25**(5), 1014–1030 (2024)
22. Lowenstein-Barkai, H.: 'Why should we turn to fascists in their own language?' Affordances and constraints of networked counterpublics as experienced by the group members. Inf. Commun. Soc. (2023)
23. Parks, P.: "Find the Joy": a war correspondent's tweets and the rise of an affective age in news. Digit. Journal. (2023)
24. Trillo-Dominguez, M., Salaverria, R., Codina L., et al.: SCImago Media Rankings (SMR): situation and evolution of the digital reputation of the media worldwide. Profesional De La Informacion **32**(5) (2023)
25. Marques, F.P.J., Vos, T.P.: Advancing comparative studies in political communication research: what factors explain the transformation of media systems?. Int. Commun. Gaz. **86**(7), 521–540 (2024)
26. Huang, L.K., Liu, F., Huang, M.X.: Accelerating bainite transformation by concurrent pearlite formation in a medium Mn steel: experiments and modelling. J. Mater. Sci. Technol. **176**, 211–223 (2024)
27. Taher, A.: Stakeholders' opinions support the people-process-technology framework for implementing digital transformation in higher education. Technol. Pedagog. Educ. **32**(5), 555–567 (2023)
28. Ksiazek, T.B., Peer, L., Lessard, K.: User engagement with online news: conceptualizing interactivity and exploring the relationship between online news videos and user comments. New Media Soc. **18**(3), 502–520 (2016)

On the Prediction of Open Source Software Ecosystem Health Based on Time Series Analysis

Ziwen Liu[1], Yijun Shen[1(✉)], Zuozhou Zhang[1], Yu Guo[1], and Hailong Sun[1,2]

[1] State Key Laboratory of Complex and Critical Software Environment (CCSE),
Beihang University, Beijing, China
`{ziwen_liu,shenyijun,zzzhang,zy2321314,sunhl}@buaa.edu.cn`
[2] Hangzhou Innovation Institute, Beihang University, Beijing, China

Abstract. Open Source Software (OSS) is a cornerstone of the computing field and a staple in our daily lives, with its health and sustainability being crucial for the global software infrastructure. In the field of OSS ecosystem health assessment, most existing platforms cannot predict the future health of the project, which limits the community's grasp of the potential risks and development trends of the project. In addition, existing OSS ecosystem health prediction research faces problems such as limited data set size, low prediction accuracy, and poor model generalization ability. To address the limitations above, we first collect extensive weekly indicator data from a multitude of open source projects and achieve multi-source data integration. Then this paper proposes an OSS ecosystem health prediction method based on frequency domain convolution to fuse adjacent frequency features. Experimental results indicate that the proposed method not only improves the performance but also provides consistent prediction accuracy and stability in multiple open source projects. Finally we implement an OSS ecosystem health prediction system, which showcase the effectiveness of our proposed method in providing a reliable assessment tool for the OSS community.

Keywords: OSS ecosystem · Health prediction · Time series prediction

1 Introduction

In the realm of computer science, the significance of OSS cannot be overstated, as it underpins both the digital infrastructure and the daily operations of our modern society. Leveraging platforms such as GitHub, the proliferation and impact of OSS projects have experienced exponential growth, surging from an estimated 44 million projects in 2019 to a staggering 89 million by 2023 [1]. This expansive community, comprising millions of individuals, corporations, and institutions, actively engages in the open source movement, aspiring to harness collective intelligence and foster the incubation of pioneering technological advancements.

H. Sun et al. (Eds.): ChineseCSCW 2024, CCIS 2343, pp. 138–149, 2025.
https://doi.org/10.1007/978-981-96-2373-0_10

The health of the OSS ecosystem is inherently linked to the innovation and sustainability of the broader software industry.

However, the burgeoning scale and intricacy of OSS projects have rendered the task of prognostication regarding their health and longevity increasingly arduous. A substantial number of GitHub projects terminate within their first year [2]. A cursory search for the query "Is this dead" on GitHub yields over 360,000 pertinent issues [3]. This phenomenon underscores the immense challenges faced by project initiators, incubators, newcomers, and end-users, who must navigate a sea of projects with a high rate of attrition.

Existing health prediction methodologies mostly rely on traditional machine learning, whose prediction accuracy is not high enough. Furthermore, evaluation prediction models are usually verified in a decentralized manner, that is, they are verified separately on different project datasets, which cannot fully reflect the generalization ability of the model. In addition, existing research is often based on smaller data sets, which in turn hampers its broader applicability.

In response to these limitations, this paper proposes a novel framework for predicting the health of the OSS ecosystem. The proposed framework is designed to select pertinent indicators, harness historical data from OSS projects, and employ sophisticated time series forecasting algorithms to predict the health status and development trends of open source software projects. The overall contributions are as follows:

- Collect weekly indicator data from a wide range of open source projects, and achieve an integrated synthesis of multi-source data across various projects;
- Propose and verify a method FreNTS for predicting the ecological health of OSS based on a frequency domain convolution time series prediction model;
- Design an OSS ecological health prediction system that is integrated with the above health prediction model.

2   Related Work

Predicting the Health of the OSS Ecosystem. Recent studies have harnessed machine learning and statistical methods to forecast and dissect software health indicators. Notable works include Weber and Luo's application of random forests to gauge Python project popularity [5], Borges et al.'s multivariate regression predicting GitHub stars [6], and Wang et al.'s [7] regression model identifying long-term contributors in "Ruby on Rails." Bao et al.'s comparative study highlighted the superiority of random forest in predicting contributors across projects [8]. Kikas et al.'s random forest model [9] and Jarczyk et al.'s generalized linear models have respectively forecasted issue closure times and analyzed factors affecting closure rates [10]. Qi et al. utilized commit counts to measure human input in workload estimation [11], while Chen et al.'s linear regression aimed to predict project forks for GitHub recommendations [12]. Xia et al. [13] and Lustosa et al. [14] advanced prediction accuracy and efficiency through machine learning optimizations and hyper-parameter configuration techniques, respectively. Overall, the existing research provides valuable insights into the prediction of open source software health. Future research is expected to improve the prediction accuracy and model robustness by introducing deep learning techniques, expanding datasets, and developing comprehensive prediction models.

Time Series Forecasting Technology. The research field of time series forecasting has undergone a transformation from traditional statistical models to deep learning, integrating a variety of technologies and greatly enriching forecasting methods and practical applications. TAMP-S2GCNets [15] and AGCRN [16], GNN-based models, have performed well in time series prediction, simulating complex serial dependencies between variables in the time domain. In addition, Transformer-based prediction models such as Reformer [17] and Informer [18] have effectively captured long-term dependencies in time series through attention mechanisms. Multilayer Perceptron (MLP) performs well in processing complex data. Models such as N-BEATS [19] and DEPTS [20] demonstrate the high efficiency of MLP in time series forecasting. In general, the field of time series prediction has evolved from traditional statistical methods to deep learning, and then to the integration of diverse technologies such as GNN, Transformer, frequency domain analysis, and MLP, providing more accurate and efficient solutions for prediction tasks in practical applications.

3   OSS Ecosystem Health Prediction Method

3.1   Data Collection

This paper will use the latest data (as of December 2023) to predict the health indicators of open source projects. Based on previous work [13,14], this study re-collects the latest multi-indicator datasets of thousands of OSS projects and expands the time dimension of data collection from monthly to weekly.

The health prediction indicators of OSS projects are shown in Table 1. These indicators reflect the technical activity and community participation of the project, and weekly data is easy to collect. This study did not attempt to develop a comprehensive OSS project health indicator system, but based on the aforementioned indicators, the prediction method in this paper can work well on thousands of projects, and it is prudent to infer that this method will continue to be effective when new indicators emerge.

This paper extracts features of about 330,000 weeks of time series data from 1,162 open source repositories for analysis. Due to the rate limit of the GitHub API, the GHAchive data archive is used to obtain the latest and accurate health prediction indicators of the selected repositories. This study built a ClickHouse database to store and process GHAchive data. For each project, activity data from July 29, 2018 to December 31, 2023 was screened, and all features were collected and calculated on a weekly basis.

Table 1. Health Predictors.

Feature	Description
dates	End date for weekly data collection
weekly commits	Total number of commits created in the last week
weekly contributors	Total number of contributors who made at least one commit in the last week
weekly open PRs	Total number of pull requests opened in the last week
weekly closed PRs	Total pull requests closed in the last week
weekly merged PRs	Total pull requests merged in the last week
weekly open issues	Total number of issues opened in the last week
weekly closed issues	Total number of issues closed last week
weekly issue comments	Total number of question comments created in the last week
weekly stargazers	Total number of new stars received in the past week
weekly forks	Total number of forks that occurred last week

3.2 Cross-Project Data Integration

Traditional OSS project health prediction models cannot fully reflect the generalization ability of the model. To address this challenge, this study used a cross-project data integration strategy to deal with issues such as data consistency, time alignment, and feature standardization to ensure that the integrated dataset can effectively support model training. These steps are critical to improving the generalization ability of the model. Specifically, this study integrated 1,162 CSV files collected from GHAchive, each as an independent data subset. Data preprocessing includes missing value and outlier processing to ensure the integrity and accuracy of the data. Subsequently, each data subset was divided into training set, validation set, and test set at a ratio of 8:1:1.

To deal with the time alignment problem, the following measures were taken: 1) Consistency of time series within files: Allocate data in chronological order to ensure data continuity and integrity; 2) Independence of time series between files: Ensure that the time series between subsets are independent of each other, without overlap or intersection; 3) Time continuity between training and validation sets: Set sequence length, label, and prediction length parameters to ensure that the time series of the validation set is a continuation of the time series of the training set; 4) Timestamp feature extraction: Convert timestamp data into features such as season, month, date, and hour to enhance the model's understanding of the periodicity and trend of time series data.

Through the above processing, the preprocessed and feature-extracted data are compiled into a unified dataset for model training, verification, and testing. This dataset integrates multi-source data and is normalized.

3.3 Time Series Prediction Method Based on Frequency Domain Convolution

Problem Definition: Let $[X_1, X_2 \ldots X_T] \in \mathbb{R}^{N \times T}$ represent a multivariate time series dataset with N sequences and T timestamps, where $X_t \in \mathbb{R}^N$ represents the multivariate value of the N sequences at timestamp t. Take the time series window $\mathbf{X}_t = [X_{t-L+1}, X_{t-L+2}, \ldots, X_t] \in \mathbb{R}^{N \times L}$ of length L at timestamp t as the model input; define the prediction target window with a length of τ at timestamp t as $\mathbf{Y}_t = [X_{t+1}, X_{t+2}, \ldots, X_{t+\tau}] \in \mathbb{R}^{N \times \tau}$. The task of time series prediction is to use the historical observations $\mathbf{X}_t$ to predict the future value $\hat{\mathbf{Y}}_t$.

In order to integrate the features of adjacent frequencies, this study improved the FreTS model architecture [4] and proposed a time series prediction method FreNTS (Frequency-aware Neighborhood Time Series) based on frequency domain convolution. Adjacent frequency components in the frequency domain are associated with the short time series structure of the signal. By extracting the features of these adjacent frequencies, the model can learn local frequency domain information and improve robustness and accuracy, even in the presence of noise and interference.

The architecture of FreNTS is shown in Fig. 1, which includes the domain conversion/reversal stage, the frequency domain FCB (Frequency Convolution Block), and the corresponding two learners, namely the frequency channel learner and the frequency time learner. In addition, the dimension expansion block is applied before the data input to enhance the processing capability of the model. Specifically, the input $\mathbf{X}_t \in \mathbb{R}^{N \times L}$ is multiplied by the weight vector $\phi_d \in \mathbb{R}^{1 \times d}$ to obtain a more expressive hidden representation $\mathbf{H}_t \in \mathbb{R}^{N \times L \times d}$.

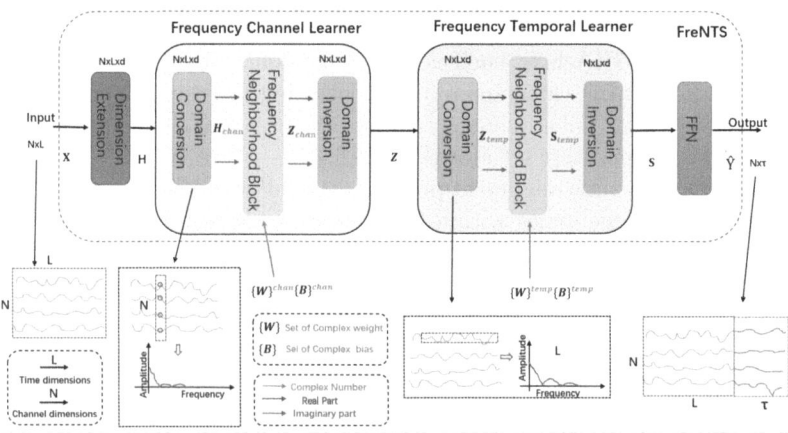

Fig. 1. FreNTS Architecture Diagram.

Domain Conversion/Inversion. Using Fourier transform to decompose the time series signal into different frequency components, the input $\mathbf{H}$ is converted to the frequency domain $\mathcal{H}$, which is achieved by the following formula:

$$\mathcal{H}(f) = \int_{-\infty}^{\infty} \mathbf{H}(v)e^{-j2\pi fv}\,dv$$

$$= \int_{-\infty}^{\infty} \mathbf{H}(v)\cos(2\pi fv)\,dv + j\int_{-\infty}^{\infty} \mathbf{H}(v)\sin(2\pi fv)\,dv \tag{1}$$

Among them, f is the frequency variable, v is the integral variable, j represents the imaginary unit.

FreNTS performs domain conversion on the channel dimension and time dimension respectively. After the frequency domain learning is completed, $\mathcal{H}$ can be converted back to the time domain through the following inverse conversion formula:

$$\mathbf{H}(v) = \int_{-\infty}^{\infty} \mathcal{H}(f)\,e^{j2\pi fv}df = \int_{-\infty}^{\infty} (\mathcal{R}e(\mathcal{H}(f)) + jIm(\mathcal{H}(f)))e^{j2\pi fv}df \tag{2}$$

The spectrum represents the combination of cosine and sine waves with different frequencies and amplitudes in $\mathcal{H}$, revealing the periodic properties of the time series signal. Analyzing the spectrum can better identify the prominent frequencies and periodic patterns in the time series.

Frequency Channel Learner. FreNTS convolves the frequency channels of all timestamps together, rather than slicing and reconnecting the channels. The model can more comprehensively capture the dependencies between adjacent frequencies in time series data. The frequency channel learner takes $\mathbf{H}_t \in \mathbb{R}^{N \times L \times d}$ as input and performs frequency channel learning in the following way:

$$\mathcal{H}_{chan} = DomainConversion_{(chan)}(\mathbf{H}_t)$$
$$\mathcal{Z}_{chan} = FCB\left(\mathcal{H}_{chan},\ \{\mathcal{W}\}^{chan},\ \{\mathcal{B}\}^{chan}\right) \tag{3}$$
$$\mathbf{Z}_t = DomainInversion_{(chan)}(\mathcal{Z}_{chan})$$

where hem, $DomainGonversion_{(chan)}$ and $DomainInversion_{(chan)}$ indicate that these operations are performed along the channel dimension. $\mathcal{Z}^{chan}$ is the output of the FCB module, which is then converted from the frequency domain back to the time domain $\mathbf{Z}_t$.

Frequency Temporal Learner. The frequency-time learner aims to learn temporal patterns in the frequency domain. FreNTS convolves the timestamps of all frequency channels together, which increases the resolution of the model in extracting frequency domain information. It takes the output $\mathbf{Z}_t \in \mathbb{R}^{N \times L \times d}$ of the frequency channel learner as input and applies the frequency-domain time learner in the following way:

$$\mathcal{Z}_{temp} = DomainConversion_{(temp)}(\mathbf{Z}_t)$$
$$\mathcal{S}_{temp} = FCB\left(\mathcal{Z}_{temp}, \{\mathcal{W}\}^{temp}, \{\mathcal{B}\}^{temp}\right) \tag{4}$$
$$\mathbf{S}_t = DomainInversion_{(temp)}\left(\mathcal{S}_{temp}\right)$$

The FCB module acts on the complex weight set $\{\mathcal{W}\}^{temp}$ and the bias set $\{\mathcal{B}\}^{temp}$. $\mathcal{S}_{temp}$ is the output of the FCB module and is converted back to the time domain S_t.

Projection. The learned channel and time dependencies are used to predict the next τ timestamps, and the prediction result is $\hat{Y}_t \in \mathbb{R}^{N \times \tau}$. This process is implemented through a two-layer feedforward network (FFN), which only contains one step of forward propagation to avoid error accumulation. The prediction formula can be expressed as:

$$\tilde{Y}_t = \sigma(\mathbf{S}_t \phi_1 + \mathbf{b_1})\phi_2 + \mathbf{b_2} \tag{5}$$

Among them, $\mathbf{S}_t \in \mathbb{R}^{N \times L \times d}$ is the output of the frequency-time learner, σ is the activation function, $\phi_1 \in \mathbb{R}^{(L^* d) \times d_h}$ and $\phi_2 \in \mathbb{R}^{d_h \times \tau}$ are weights, $\mathbf{b}_1 \in \mathbb{R}^{d_h}$ and $\mathbf{b}_2 \in \mathbb{R}^{d\tau}$ are bias terms, and d_h is the inner dimension size.

Complex Convolution. As shown in Fig. 2(b), assuming that the input is a complex number $V = V_r + jV_i$, the convolution kernel is $K = K_r + jK_i$, and the bias is $B = B_r + jB_i$, the calculation formula is as follows:

$$\begin{aligned} K * V + B &= (K_r + jK_i) * (V_r + jV_i) + B_r + jB_i \\ &= (K_r * V_r - K_i * V_i + B_r) + j(K_r * V_i + K_i * V_r + B_i) \end{aligned} \tag{6}$$

In the implementation process, two normal convolutions $Conv_1$ and $Conv_2$ are used instead, and their weights and biases are K_1, K_2 and B_1, B_2 respectively, so that they can be equivalently replaced when the following formula is satisfied.

$$K_r = K_1, \quad K_i = K_2, \quad B_r = B_1 - B_2, \quad B_i = B_1 + B_2 \tag{7}$$

At this time, the original complex convolution becomes:

$$\begin{aligned} K * V + B &= ((K_1 * V_r + B_1) - (K_2 * V_i + B_2)) \\ &\quad + j((K_1 * V_i + B_1) + (K_2 * V_r + B_2)) \\ &= (\mathcal{C}onv_1(V_r) - \mathcal{C}onv_2(V_i)) \\ &\quad + j(\mathcal{C}onv_1(V_i) + \mathcal{C}onv_2(V_r)) \end{aligned} \tag{8}$$

Frequency Convolution Block (FCB). As shown in Fig. 2(a), it includes 2 permute operations and 3 complex convolution operations: the first permute operation transforms the dimension of the input frequency domain features so that the last dimension is the frequency domain dimension of current concern, which is convenient for subsequent 1×3 convolution to extract features; the first 1×1 convolution performs a linear transformation on each channel to capture the linear combination of features between channels, and at the same time expands the embedded feature dimension to twice the original, thereby improving the model representation capability; the 1×3 convolution focuses on adjacent frequency components, captures the local characteristics between frequency domain features, and improves the frequency domain resolution; the second 1×1 convolution performs further feature fusion and linear transformation on the output of the previous convolution step to enhance the representation capability and restore it to the original number of channels; the last permute operation restores the dimensional relationship of the original frequency domain features.

4 Experiments

4.1 Experimental Setup

Experimental Objectives:

RQ1: If you want to build a snowflake based infrastructure, FreTS based on the OSS based storage system?

RQ2: Does integrating datasets across projects have an impact on model performance?

RQ3: Does the improved FreNTS model improve on the integrated dataset compared to FreTS?

Baseline: In order to evaluate FreTS and traditional health prediction methods, this paper selects the following representative traditional health prediction methods and the most advanced time series prediction methods for comparison, namely: LTSF-linear [40], Sneaker [14], GS [44], RS [44], DE [45] and SWAY [46]. The benchmark methods are selected based on two factors. First, LTSF-linear has shown good performance on many time series datasets. Second, random forest models adjusted using Sneaker, GS, RS, DE, and SWAY have all been used for health prediction tasks.

Evaluation Metrics: To evaluate RQ1, the performance metric margin of error (MRE) used by Xia [13] is used to measure the prediction results of the experiment.

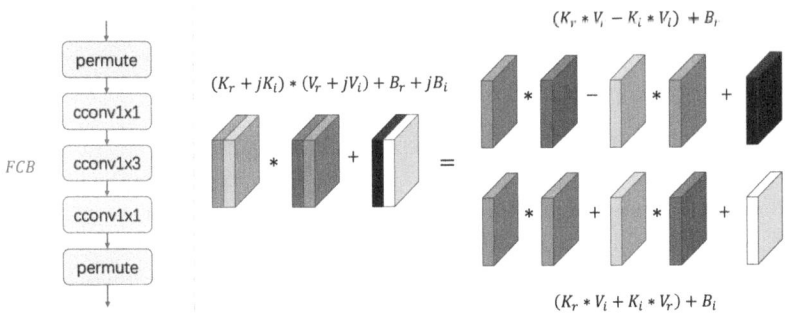

(a) FCB module   (b) Frequency domain convolution CConv

Fig. 2. Frequency Neighborhood Block.

$$MRE = \frac{|PREDICT - ACTUAL|}{ACTUAL} \quad (9)$$

To answer RQ2 and RQ3, this paper uses MSE as the loss function, MAE and RMSE as evaluation metrics.

Implementation Details: For RQ1: According to Table 1, select the three most important prediction indicators: 1) C = weekly commits; 2) I = weekly closed issues; 3) R = weekly closed PRs. The experiment is conducted around these three indicators, and each indicator is predicted separately. Finally, the median MRE and IQR of the experimental results of all projects are counted.

4.2   Experimental Results Analysis

RQ1. The experimental results of RQ1 are shown in Table 2. The values in bold indicate the best prediction results. FreTS and LTSF-Linear methods show excellent performance in most cases. The experimental results show the potential of FreTS model in OSS health prediction.

Table 2. RQ1 Experimental Results.

approaches	Commits		Closed PRs		Closed Issues	
	MRE Median	MRE IQR	MRE Median	MRE IQR	MRE Median	MRE IQR
FreTS	**1.43**	**1.02**	**0.89**	**0.54**	**1.17**	**1.71**
LTSF-linear	3.34	2.08	3.34	2.08	3.34	2.08
Sneaker	4.28	4.50	1.98	3.54	3.07	13.82
GS	4.34	6.71	3.34	4.66	8.75	10.75
RS	6.98	5.96	5.68	8.93	9.30	15.48
DE	7.14	7.89	10.27	9.60	10.63	11.08
SWAY	6.86	6.45	2.42	5.44	10.57	5.64

RQ2. As shown in Table 3, we first use a common training set (train-all dataset) to train a FreTS model, and then use this model to predict the test set of 1162 different data subsets. Finally, we count the median and mean of MAE and RMSE of all experimental results. Then, we use 1162 data subsets to train 1162 FreTS models, train and test each subset separately, and also count the median and mean of MAE and RMSE of all experimental results for comparison. The experimental results show that the model trained with the integrated dataset is more stable in performance and usually outperforms the model trained separately. The integration of datasets can effectively improve the stability and generalization ability of the model, and has more advantages in dealing with health prediction tasks.

Table 3. RQ2 Experimental Results.

Datasets	MAE Median	MAE Mean	RMSE Median	RMSE Mean
train-all	**0.0741**	**0.0766**	**0.111**	**0.111**
Individual Subsets	0.0757	0.0774	0.113	0.113

RQ3. Table 4 shows a comparison of the performance of the improved algorithm FreNTS with the benchmark algorithms FreTS and LTSF-linear on the integrated data set. The experimental results show that FreNTS has improved both MAE and RMSE performance indicators compared to the FreTS model and LTSF-linear. By introducing new improvement measures, the prediction performance was successfully improved, and the generalization ability of the model was focused on, thus providing strong support for the actual scenario application of the health prediction model.

Table 4. RQ3 Experimental results.

Approaches	MAE	RMSE
FreTS	0.0752	0.120
LTSF-linear	0.0769	0.121
FreNTS	**0.0735**	**0.119**

5   System Implementation

This system relies on Github and Gitee as data sources. Clickhouse and Elastic Search databases are used in the data layer for data storage and management.

The business layer of the system includes health rankings, evaluation and prediction backend implementation. Specifically, it consists of three modules: basic data collection, evaluation model calculation, and real-time status prediction. The basic data collection module uses Grimoirlab to collect multi-source data from Github and Gitee platforms; the evaluation model calculation module refers to the evaluation system of OSS Compass to score the health of open source projects; the real-time status prediction module obtains historical data through Clickhouse and predicts future trends.

6   Conclusion

This paper proposes a method for predicting the ecological health of open source software based on a frequency domain convolution time series prediction model.

In order to solve the problems of small time series data size and poor generalization ability of the prediction model, we focus on collecting weekly indicator data of a large number of open source projects and realize the integration of multi-source data across projects. Furthermore, by improving the time series prediction model based on frequency domain multilayer perceptrons (MLPs), the frequency domain convolution operation is used to fuse adjacent frequency features, which effectively improves the accuracy of the prediction. Experimental results show that the proposed method not only improves the performance but also supports cross-project application. Finally, an open source software ecological health prediction system is implemented based on the proposed method.

Future research should focus on developing more accurate open source software ecosystem health prediction models, especially by introducing new deep learning algorithms and more fine-grained project data to improve the accuracy and real-time nature of predictions. This includes in-depth analysis of indicators such as developer activity, code submission frequency, and problem resolution speed.

Acknowledgements. This work was supported by National Natural Science Foundation of China under Grant No. 62141209.

References

1. Github Octoverse. https://octoverse.github.com. Accessed 30 Nov 2023
2. Ait, A., Izquierdo, J.L.C., Cabot, J.: An empirical study on the survival rate of GitHub projects. In: Proceedings of the 19th International Conference on Mining Software Repositories (MSR), pp. 365–375 (2022)
3. Github.Search.   https://github.com/search?q=is+this+dead&type=issues. Accessed 30 June 2024
4. Yi, K., et al.: Frequency-domain MLPs are more effective learners in time series forecasting. In: Proceedings of the 37th International Conference on Neural Information Processing Systems (NIPS), pp. 76656–76679 (2024)
5. Weber, S., Luo, J.: What makes an open source code popular on git hub? In: 2014 IEEE International Conference on Data Mining Workshop, pp. 851–855 (2014)
6. Borges, H., Hora, A., Valente, M. T.: Predicting the popularity of github repositories. In: Proceedings of the The 12th International Conference on Predictive Models and Data Analytics in Software Engineering, pp. 1–10 (2016)
7. Wang, T., Zhang, Y., Yin, G., Yu, Y., Wang, H.: Who will become a long-term contributor? A prediction model based on the early phase behaviors. In: Proceedings of the 10th Asia-Pacific Symposium on Internetware, pp. 1–10 (2018)
8. Bao, L., Xia, X., Lo, D., Murphy, G.C.: A large scale study of long-time contributor prediction for github projects. IEEE Trans. Software Eng. **47**(6), 1277–1298 (2019)
9. Kikas, R., Dumas, M., Pfahl, D.: Using dynamic and contextual features to predict issue lifetime in github projects. In: Proceedings of the 13th International Conference on Mining Software Repositories (MSR), pp. 291–302 (2016)
10. Jarczyk, O., Jaroszewicz, S., Wierzbicki, A., Pawlak, K., Jankowski-Lorek, M.: Surgical teams on GitHub: modeling performance of GitHub project development processes. Inf. Softw. Technol. **100**, 32–46 (2018)

11. Qi, F., Jing, X.Y., Zhu, X., Xiaoyuan, X., Baowen, X., Shi, Y.: Software effort estimation based on open source projects: case study of Github. Inf. Softw. Technol. **92**, 145–157 (2017)
12. Chen, F., Li, L., Jiang, J., Zhang, l.: Predicting the number of forks for open source software project. In: Proceedings of the 2014 3rd International Workshop on Evidential Assessment of Software Technologies, pp. 40–47 (2014)
13. Xia, T., Fu, W., Shu, R., Agrawal, R., Menzies, T.: Predicting health indicators for open source projects (using hyperparameter optimization). Empir. Softw. Eng. **27**, 122 (2022)
14. Lustosa, A., Menzies, T.: Learning from very little data: on the value of landscape analysis for predicting software project health. ACM Trans. Softw. Eng. Methodol. **33**, 1–22 (2023)
15. Chen, Y., Segovia-Dominguez, I., Coskunuzer, B., Gel, Y.: TAMP-S2GCNets: coupling time-aware multipersistence knowledge representation with spatio-supra graph convolutional networks for time-series forecasting. In: International Conference on Learning Representations. openreview.net (2021)
16. Bai, L., Yao, L., Li, C., Wang, X., Wang, C.: Adaptive graph convolutional recurrent network for traffic fore-casting. Adv. Neural. Inf. Process. Syst. **33**, 17804–17815 (2020)
17. Kitaev, N., Kaiser, Ł., Levskaya, A.: Reformer: the efficient transformer. In: International Conference on Learning Representations. openreview.net (2020)
18. Zhou, H., et al.: Informer: beyond efficient transformer for long sequence time-series forecasting. In: Proceedings of the AAAI Conference on Artificial Intelligence, vol. 35, no. 12, pp. 11106–11115 (2021)
19. Oreshkin, B. N., Carpov, D., Chapados, N., Bengio, Y.: N-BEATS: neural basis expansion analysis for interpretable time series forecasting. In: International Conference on Learning Representations. openreview.net (2020)
20. Fan, W., et al.: DEPTS: deep expansion learning for periodic time series forecasting. In: International Conference on Learning Representations. openreview.net (2022)

Knowledge Graph-Enhanced Session-Based Recommendation with Two-Stage Feature Filtering

Chang Liu, Ruolin Li, Ronghua Lin$^{(\boxtimes)}$, Dingding Li, Jiemin Chen, and Yong Tang

School of Computer Science, South China Normal University, Guangzhou, China
{liuchang6780,liruolin,rhlin,dingly,chenjiemin,ytang}@m.scnu.edu.cn

Abstract. Session-based recommendation has demonstrated notable advantages, since it dynamically adjusts recommendations based on user's behavior and context within the current session. Recently, researchers have extensively investigated the integration of knowledge graphs (KGs) into recommendation systems, with Graph Neural Network (GNN) achieving impressive results in deeply exploring and learning the relationships between users. However, despite these encouraging results, previous studies have overlooked the semantic information of items within sessions and the contextual environment outside sessions, making it challenging to mine the complex associations between items. Simultaneously, traditional algorithms encounter issues with high computational costs and excessive memory usage. To address the above challenges, in this paper, we propose a KG-enhanced session-based recommendation with two-stage feature filtering, named KGFF-SR. We introduce KG as an external knowledge base and utilize the link information between entities in the graph to enrich the session graph. Furthermore, we propose a two-stage item feature filtering mechanism to capture potential relationships between users and items while reducing computational and storage costs effectively. We conduct extensive experiments on three real-world public sub-datasets, and the results show that our proposed method significantly outperforms powerful baseline models in performance.

Keywords: Session-based Recommendation · Knowledge Graph · Gate Graph Neural Networks · Feature Filtering

1 Introduction

Personalized recommendation, aimed at predicting users' future interactive behaviors, has emerged as a core demand for enhancing the online experience. However, existing methods may face challenges in promptly adapting to real-time changes in user interests. For instance, collaborative filtering (CF) often yields unsatisfactory recommendation results when user behavioral interaction

H. Sun et al. (Eds.): ChineseCSCW 2024, CCIS 2343, pp. 150–165, 2025.
https://doi.org/10.1007/978-981-96-2373-0_11

data is sparse [17]. Both for users and items, traditional recommendation systems face challenges in making accurate recommendations due to the insufficient availability of behavioral data, resulting in the cold-start problem [16].

To address users' need for personalized recommendations, session-based recommendation has emerged as a promising approach. In contrast to traditional CF methods that rely on historical interactions [14], the session-based recommendation provides real-time recommendations based on a user's current session information [18]. Currently, deep learning technology has made significant strides in session-based recommendation systems [2]. Among them, GNN has demonstrated remarkable capabilities in modeling user relationships for recommendation purposes [6] and has been widely adopted across various recommendation scenarios. However, existing GNN-based session recommendation methods often rely on pre-defined social networks [9], which may introduce discrepancies between the social graph and users' shared interests. Consequently, utilizing static social networks to learn user information may limit the effectiveness of recommendation algorithms, particularly in scenarios where users' interests evolve rapidly.

In this paper, we propose a KG-enhanced session-based recommendation KGFF-SR which contains a two-stage item feature filtering. Firstly, we introduce KG as the external knowledge base, incorporating the first-order neighbors of entities as the external context of items. Through transformation operations, we map contextual entity embeddings from entity space to context space, ensuring the preservation of the original semantic information. Secondly, we design a two-stage item feature filtering mechanism. In the first stage, we introduce a learnable lightweight function to extract the k_1 most relevant items to the user from all potential neighbors. Given the vast number of items in recommendation systems, our method reduces unnecessary computational overhead while exploring all potential connections in the graph. Furthermore, to determine the weight of each item and construct the user's interest representation, we utilize the Gated Graph Neural Network (GGNN) with a multi-head attention mechanism to capture user's global interests. Building upon the first-stage filtering, we define a fine-grained filtering process for the second stage. The second-stage filtering adaptively selects k_2 neighbors that are most intriguing to the user based on the coarse-grained results of the first stage. By incorporating the interactions between users and items, including user's recent interaction behaviors, our two-stage filtering mechanism can accurately predict user's immediate interests and generate personalized recommendations for target users.

The contributions of this paper are summarized as follows.

– We integrate KG as an external knowledge base into the session-based recommendation system. Specifically, we utilize the link information within the KG to augment the directed relationship graph of the session sequence.
– We employ GGNN to propagate neighbor information to item nodes. To further capture the user's global preferences, we introduce a multi-head attention mechanism to generate a more accurate representation of user preferences.

– Through the two-stage item feature filtering, we effectively explore potential links between users and items, which can reduce computational costs while maintaining satisfactory recommendation performance.

2   Related Work

2.1   Session-Based Recommendation System

Session-based recommendation has recently emerged as a vibrant area of research. Diverging from traditional single-query approaches, session-based recommendation systems deeply consider the user's historical behavior and current context [18], committed to providing users with personalized recommendation results based on the user's current session [19].

Significant strides have been achieved in session-based recommendation systems [13]. Simultaneously, researchers are actively exploring and applying deep learning technology to optimize session recommendation systems. Sequential methods based on Recurrent Neural Network (RNN) have been proposed, aiming to predict users' next behaviors based on their previous ones. For instance, GRU4Rec [8] utilizes GRU to model users' session behavior, enhancing the performance over basic GRU models. Hidasi et al. [6] have notably improved system performance by introducing a novel ranking loss function, enabling the direct learning of session representations from previous clicks and subsequently generating recommendations. Li et al. [10] proposed a hybrid encoder (NARM) combined with the attention mechanism, using the attention mechanism on RNN to capture the user's sequential behavioral characteristics to more accurately grasp the user's core needs.

Nowadays, GNN has gained considerable attention in research as a tool for generating representations for graph-structured data [27]. GNN offers a means to convert user behavior data into a graph structure, enabling the deep mining of complex relationships between user behaviors to enhance recommendation effectiveness. SR-GNN [23] is the first GNN-based method that uses the attention mechanism to generate session representation while learning item representation. HGNN [1] is based on hybrid-order propagation, which avoids insignificant patterns and captures complex dependencies in propagations. The target attention GNN [26] successfully captures the user's interest changes by activating diverse target items.

2.2   KG-Enhanced Recommendation

Knowledge Graph has found extensive application in recommendation systems as both representation and storage structures. Organized in the form of (entity, relationship, entity) tuples, KG provides structured information that has been demonstrated to be pivotal in improving the performance and interpretability of recommendation systems [25].

Generally, KG embedding techniques are effective methods used to map entities and relationships to low-dimensional vector spaces [7]. In recommendation systems, these embeddings can capture relation information between entities, thereby improving recommendation performance. For example, Zhang et al. [20] proposed KGAT, which employs an attention-based neighborhood aggregator to model relationships between different entities. CD-KGE [12] utilized cross-domain knowledge from KG and embedded the cross-domain KG into the rec-ommendation system using an end-to-end learning mode. On the other hand, path-based recommendation is another approach that leverages KG to enhance recommendation systems [15], which utilizes the meta-paths in KG to discover potential user interests. For example, HGAN [3] uses embedding information in KG to identify hidden attributes of items, thus improving recommendation per-formance. KPRN [21] adopts LSTM networks to model the extracted meta-paths and aggregate user preferences along each path by fully connected layers.

3   Problem Formulation

Table 1. Notations.

Symbols	Description
U	the set of users
V	the set of items
$A_s^{(out)}$	out-degree matrix
$A_s^{(in)}$	in-degree matrix
$S_T^u = \{v_{s,1}, v_{s,2}, ..., v_{s,n}\}$	items in user's s session
m	the number of users
n	the number of items
d	embedding dimensions
e	the external context of entity
$\overline{e}$	the context vector of entity e
M_{r_n}	the projection transformation matrix
$H, b, W_z, W_r, W_o, U_z, U_O, U_r$	the trainable learning bias
S	the probability matrix of the influence of the source node s on the target node t
$\overline{S}[u, t]$	the inferred asymmetric similarity from user u to his/her neighbor t
$\widehat{z_{v_{s,i}}}$	the rating of item $v_{s,i}$
$\hat{y}$	the click probability score of each candidate item $v_{s,i}$

Firstly, given the user set $U = u_1, u_2, \ldots, u_m$ and item set $V = v_1, v_2, \ldots, v_n$ where m is the number of users and n is the number of items, we denote the rating matrix of user-item as $R^{m \times n}$. We then construct session graph as $G_S = <V_s, E_s>$, where each node $v_{s,i} \in V_s$ represents the clicked item, and the directed edge $(v_{s,i-1} \rightarrow v_{s,i}) \in E_s$ represents user clicks the item $v_{s,i-1}$ and then clicks the item $v_{s,i}$ in the s-th session. In KG, $\overline{e}$ is represented as the context vector of each entity e. For item $v_{s,i}$, we select the top-k_1 vertices with the highest probabilities in V_s as coarse filtering neighbor items, which are denoted as N_{v_1}. N_{v_2} denotes the neighbor items selected from N_{v_1} after the second-stage item feature filtering. The task of this work is to explore potential links between items through two-stage item feature filtering, and predict the clicked probability $\hat{y}$ of each candidate item according to the current session.

Table 1 summarizes the notions and key concepts used in this paper.

4   The Proposed Method

In this section, we detail our proposed method KGFF-SR. The architecture of KGFF-SR is illustrated in Fig. 1.

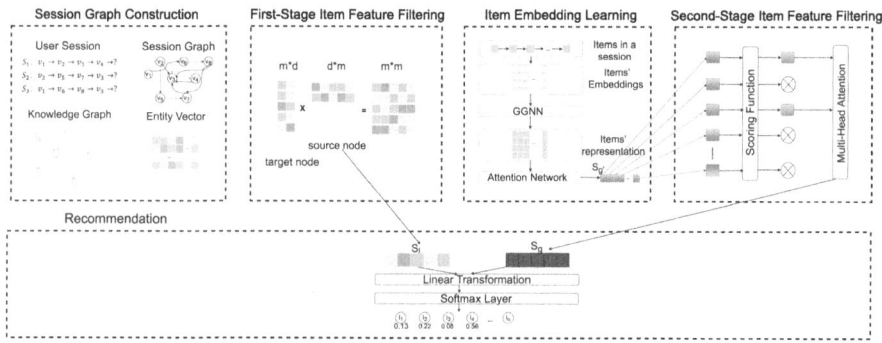

Fig. 1. The overview of the model structure of KGFF-SR.

4.1   Session Graph Construction

For a given session, we construct the clicking sequence as a directed graph $G_S = <V_s, E_s>$. Since several items may appear in the session repeatedly, we define two adjacency matrices which are the out-degree matrix $A_s^{(out)} \in \mathbb{R}^{m \times m}$ and in-degree matrix $A_s^{(in)} \in \mathbb{R}^{m \times m}$. The row vectors of $A_s^{(in)}$ and $A_s^{(out)}$ respectively encode the incoming and outgoing edges of the corresponding item. To be applied to GGNN, here, by taking the one-hot vector of the items as input, each item is embedded into a d-dimensional vector.

4.2   Knowledge Graph Introduction

In this section, we introduce KG as an external knowledge base. We leverage the entity relationships within KG triples to enhance the association links between items and extend the session graphs.

In KG, entities with shared adjacent entities are typically regarded as having a strong semantic similarity. Hence, we propose to construct the external context using KG. Our approach involves employing knowledge representation learning to represent both the context of the knowledge graph and the context of the session as an external context representation. The primary goal is to evaluate the semantic relevance between two entities.

For a given KG, KG embedding mainly focuses on learning the representations of graph entities and relations. In our proposed method, we first associate each item with entities in KG and extract the first-order neighbors of these entities as the item's external context. Secondly, we leverage the triplets in KG and utilize KG embedding techniques such as TransE, TransH, and TransR to learn the representations of these entities. Finally, we employ the item matrix to uniformly project entity embeddings from various entity spaces into a context vector space. In KG, the external context of entity e is represented as the set of its first-order neighbors. The entity context set is formulated as:

$$\text{context}(e) = \{e_n \mid (e, r, e_n) \in G \cup (e_n, r, e) \in G\}, \tag{1}$$

where G represents the knowledge graph, and r is he relationship between entities.

However, considering the vast number of entities in KG, performing such computational operations becomes challenging. To generate a simplified representation of item's external context, we fuse the entity vectors within the entity context set. Specifically, for each entity e, we obtain the context $\bar{e}$ of each entity as shown in Eq. (2).

$$\bar{e} = \tanh\left(M_{r_1} e_1 + M_{r_2} e_2 + ... + M_{r_n} e_n + b\right), \tag{2}$$

where $\bar{e}$ represents the context vector of entity e. $M_{r_n} \in \mathbb{R}^{d \times d}$ is the projection transformation matrix, $b \in \mathbb{R}^{d \times 1}$ is the trainable learning bias.

4.3   First-Stage Item Feature Filtering

In the first-stage item feature filtering, KGFF-SR can discover and quantify the similarity dependencies between numerous items at a coarse-grained level. We first propose a linear transformation of the entity context vector $\bar{e}$ after KG embedding. This transformation yields the parameter matrix $A_{tar}, A_{src}^T \in \mathbb{R}^{n \times n}$, which represents the embedding of target node t and source node s respectively. The first-stage filtering can obtain the asymmetric similarity matrix as:

$$S = \text{ReLU}\left(\tanh\left(A_{tar}, A_{src}^T\right)\right), \tag{3}$$

In Eq. (3), two parameter matrices A_{tar}, A_{src}^T are multiplied, followed by a non-linear gradient mapping using the ReLU(tanh($\cdot$)) function, aiming to prevent the problem of gradient disappearance. Each entry $S_{t,s}$ in the matrix S represents the probability that the source node s influences the target node t. For user u, we select the top-k_1 items with the highest probability of influence shown in Eq. (4), as the results of the first coarse-grained filtering.

$$N_{v_1} = \text{argtop}_{k_1}\left(S_t\right). \tag{4}$$

4.4 Item Embedding Learning

In this section, we elaborate on the process of deriving latent vectors of nodes through GGNN. Specifically, we propose an interest representation generation method based on multi-head attention with GGNN, which consists of two steps. Firstly, we learn the item representation based on the previously constructed session graph in Sect. 4.1 by using GGNN. We utilize the graph adjacency matrix to transfer neighborhood item information and update the item representation [1]. Secondly, after extracting the item representation, we use the multi-head attention mechanism to integrate the vector representations of all items, thereby obtaining the user's global interest vector.

In the first step, for each item $v_{s,i} \in V_s$, $v_{s,i}^t \in \mathbb{R}^{d \times 1}$ represents the vector representation of $v(s,i)$ after t update steps and it is initialized as the item embedding vector, as shown in Eq. (2). $v_{s,i}^t$ is updated as follows based on GGNN:

$$a_{s,i}^{(out),t} = \left[V_{s,1}^{t-1}, V_{s,2}^{t-1}, ..., V_{s,n}^{t-1} \right] \left(A_{s,i}^{(out)} \right)^{\top}, \tag{5}$$

$$a_{s,i}^{(in),t} = \left[V_{s,1}^{t-1}, V_{s,2}^{t-1}, ..., V_{s,n}^{t-1} \right] \left(A_{s,i}^{(in)} \right)^{\top}, \tag{6}$$

$$a_{s,i}^t = H \left[a_{s,i}^{(out),t}; a_{s,i}^{(in),t} \right] + b, \tag{7}$$

$$z_{s,i}^t = \sigma \left(W_z a_{s,i}^t + U_z V_{s,i}^{t-1} \right), \tag{8}$$

$$r_{s,i}^t = \sigma \left(W_r a_{s,i}^t + U_r V_{s,i}^{t-1} \right), \tag{9}$$

$$\widetilde{v}_{s,i}^t = tanh \left(W_o a_{s,i}^t + U_o \left(r_{s,i}^t \odot V_{s,i}^{t-1} \right) \right), \tag{10}$$

$$v_{s,i}^t = \left(1 - z_{s,i}^t \right) \odot V_{s,i}^{t-1} + z_{s,i}^t \odot \widetilde{V}_{s,i}^t, \tag{11}$$

where $v_{s,i}^{t-1}$ is the item representation of $v_{s,i}$ in the $(t-1)$-th update step. $\left[v_{s,1}^{t-1}, v_{s,2}^{t-1}, ..., v_{s,n}^{t-1} \right]$ is item representation list in the session graph. $z_{s,i}^t, r_{s,i}^t \in \mathbb{R}^{d \times 1}$ are the reset gate and update gate respectively. $\sigma(\cdot)$ denotes the sigmoid function. $A_{s,i}^{out}, A_{s,i}^{in} \in \mathbb{R}^{1 \times m}$ are the i-th row vectors in A_s^{out}, A_s^{in}, which corresponding to item $v_{s,i}$, are the keys to determine how the items propagate the features. The symbol $\odot$ performs point-wise product. $a_{s,i}^{(out),t}, a_{s,i}^{(in),t}$ represent the embeddings of the output and input edges, respectively. $H \in \mathbb{R}^{d \times 2d}$, $b \in \mathbb{R}^{d \times 1}$, $W_z \in \mathbb{R}^{d \times d}$, $W_r \in \mathbb{R}^{d \times d}$, $W_o \in \mathbb{R}^{d \times d}$, $U_z \in \mathbb{R}^{d \times d}$, $U_r \in \mathbb{R}^{d \times d}$, $U_o \in \mathbb{R}^{d \times d}$ are learnable parameters.

4.5 Fine-Grained Item Feature Filtering

In this section, building upon the first coarse-grained item feature filtering, we employ a two-layer adaptive GNN to conduct fine-grained filtering of user interests, aiming to delve deeper into potential connections and dependencies within item attributes.

Previous research has highlighted that in real-world recommendation systems, certain key attributes significantly influence recommendation scenarios [24], leading to the asymmetry of the adjacency matrix. To this end, we propose to utilize a two-layer adaptive GNN to extract the nonlinear and asymmetric relationships between item attributes as shown in Eq. (12):

$$\widetilde{S}\left[u,t\right] = \mathrm{ReLU}\left(h^T \mathrm{ReLU}\left(W_2 \mathrm{concat}\left(\left[s_{T+1}^t, s_T^t\right] + b_2\right)\right)\right), \tag{12}$$

where $\widetilde{S}\left[u,t\right] \in \mathbb{R}^{n \times n}$ is the similarity matrix in the second-stage filtering. This process will be performed only when t is in the result of the first-stage feature filtering and otherwise, the result is assigned 0 directly. $W_2 \in \mathbb{R}^{d \times 2d}, h \in \mathbb{R}^d, b_2 \in \mathbb{R}^d$ are the learnable parameters to form the adjacency matrix $\widetilde{A}$, which is defined as follows:

$$\widetilde{N}_{v_2} = \mathrm{argtop}_{k_2}\left(\widetilde{S}\left[u,:\right]\right), \tag{13}$$

$$\widetilde{A}\left[s,t'\right] = \begin{cases} \mathrm{softmax}\left(\widetilde{S}\left[s,t'\right]\right), & t' \in N_{v_2} \\ 0 & t' \notin N_{v_2} \end{cases}. \tag{14}$$

where $\widetilde{N}_{v_2}$ is the top-k_2 most relevant neighbor items of u selected from $\widetilde{S}\left[u,t\right]$ through the second-stage self-learning.

After the second fine-grained neighbor filtering, the final global interest vector representation is defined as follows:

$$s_g = \widetilde{A}\left[s,t'\right]\left[u,:\right]), \tag{15}$$

$$head_k = \sum_{i=1}^{n-1} \mathrm{Attention}\left(Q^k v_i^k, K^k v_i^k, V^k v_i^k\right), \tag{16}$$

$$\mathrm{Attention}\left(q,k,v\right) = \mathrm{softmax}\left(\frac{qk^T}{\sqrt{d_k}}\right)v, \tag{17}$$

where $Q^k, K^k, V^k \in \mathbb{R}^{d \times d}$ represent linear transformation parameters. The subvector is divided into d_k dimension and the shrinkage dot product of all items will be conducted. Finally, the attention weight is normalized through the softmax function.

Based on literature research, it's commonly assumed that the user's local interest remains unchanged over a period of time. Thus, in GGNN, each output vector of the session sequences signifies the user's local interest, where the final-clicked item in the session serves as the user's current local interest s_l.

By utilizing s_g and s_l of user u that we have previously obtained, the global and local interest vectors are merged as shown in Eq. (18) to obtain the user's hybrid mixed interest vector representation.

$$s_m = W\left[s_g, s_l\right], \tag{18}$$

where $W \in \mathbb{R}^{d \times 2d}$ is the projection mapping matrix.

4.6   Recommendation

To mitigate the issue of vanishing gradients and to incorporate the influence of the user's recent behavior and neighbor context, we conduct a dot product operation based on the user's mixed interest vector representation s_m. Subsequently, we utilize the softmax function to generate the click probability $\hat{y}$ for each candidate item as follows:

$$\widehat{z_m} = s_m^T V_s, \tag{19}$$

$$\hat{y} = \text{softmax}\left(\widehat{z_m}\right), \tag{20}$$

where $\widehat{z_m}$ is the recommendation scores of items, and $\hat{y}$ represents the click probability of each item.

During the learning of model parameters, each session data is split through data enhancement processing, and the BPTT algorithm is used for training. The loss function is defined as cross-entropy loss as follows:

$$L\left(\hat{y}\right) = -\sum_{i=1}^{m} y_i log\left(\hat{y}\right) + \left(1 - y_i\right) log\left(1 - \hat{y}\right), \tag{21}$$

where y represents the one-hot encoding of the target recommended item.

5   Experiment Setup

5.1   Datasets

To comprehensively evaluate our proposed KGFF-SR, we conduct experiments on different volumes of the real-world dataset MovieLens-20M [5], which is a widely used benchmark dataset for movie recommendations. This dataset comprises 20,000,263 movie ratings (pointing from 1 to 5) for 27,278 movies by 138,493 users, with a total of 465,564 movie tags. It's worth noting that GGNN necessitates pre-construction of adjacency matrices during training, which consumes significant memory and computational resources. Therefore, we conducted experiments on subsets of the MovieLens-20M. Descriptive statistics of the data are presented in Table 2.

Table 2. Dataset information.

Dataset	Number of movies	Number of ratings	Number of sessions	Average length
MovieLens-20M 1/64	1,932	312,508	12,648	48.069
MovieLens-20M 1/16	5,586	1,237,016	53,594	45.710
MovieLens-20M 1/4	20,650	5,000,066	82,117	40.625

To generate sessions, we partition the user behavior time series into session sequences using a time interval of 30 min, and we limit the session length to a maximum of 40. Following [6], we filter out the sessions with a length of 1 and the items that occur less than 5 times.

For the knowledge graph, we use an open-source KG of MovieLens datasets with 652,025 triples and 213,099 entities. We follow OpenKE [4] and use different KG embedding methods to obtain entity embeddings.

5.2   Baselines

We compare our proposed method KGFF-SR with the following baselines.

- **Item-KNN** [11] is an item-based collaborative filtering algorithm that uses historical interaction data between users and items to generate recommendations.
- **NARM** [10] utilizes RNN enhanced with an attention mechanism to effectively discern the user's primary intent and sequential patterns.
- **GRU4Rec** [6] leverages GRU to model user sequences for generating recommendation outcomes. It adopts a session-parallel mini-batch process and employs ranking-based loss functions to effectively train the model.
- **SR-GNN** [23] employs the original GGNN for session-based recommendation. It captures intricate item transitions that traditional session-based recommendation systems struggle to reveal using the session graph
- **SR-HGNN** [1] proposes a hybrid-order propagation based on GGNN and assigns weight to representations of different orders by attention mechanism.
- **SR-CAAN** [22] integrates external knowledge bases and Knowledge Graphs (KGs), leveraging attention mechanisms to acquire the external context of sessions. Each session is depicted as a fusion of external contexts.

5.3   Evaluation Metrics

The following evaluation metrics are adopted.

- **Recall@k** measures the number of items in the recommendation list that align with the user's actual interests and are successfully recommended, which is calculated as shown in Eq. (22).

$$\text{Recall@}k = \frac{1}{|u|} \sum_{u \in U} \frac{|T(u) \cap R(u, K)|}{|T(u)|} \tag{22}$$

- **MRR@k** (Mean Reciprocal Rank) represents the average sum of the reciprocals of the first correct result in the recommendation list, which is calculated as shown in Eq. (23).

$$\text{MRR@}k = \frac{1}{Q} \sum_{i=1}^{|Q|} \frac{1}{rank_i} \tag{23}$$

5.4   Parameter Settings

All the parameters are initialized using a Gaussian distribution with a mean of 0 and a standard deviation of 0.1. In fairness, the dimensions of item embedding are all fixed to 800. We employ the mini-batch Adam optimizer to optimize these parameters, starting with an initial learning rate set to 0.001, which decays by a factor of 0.1 after every 4 epochs. The batch size and $L2$ penalty are set as 50 and 10^{-4}, respectively. For the first-stage item feature filtering, we choose SGD as the optimizer to expedite the convergence, as it operates and learns only once per epoch.

6   Experimental Results and Analysis

6.1   Comparison with Baseline Methods

To demonstrate the overall performance of KGFF-SR, we compare it with other baseline methods. The overall performance in terms of Recall@20 and MRR@20 is shown in Table 3. The best results are highlighted in boldface.

Table 3. Comparison between different models on Movielens-20M 1/64, Movielens-20M 1/16 and Movielens-20M 1/4, in terms of Recall@k and MRR@k(k = 20).

Method	MovieLens-20M 1/64		MovieLens-20M 1/16		MovieLens-20M 1/4	
	Recall@20	MRR@20	Recall@20	MRR@20	Recall@20	MRR@20
Item-KNN	44.371	33.653	46.367	37.062	11.053	2.770
NARM	46.874	39.025	49.136	39.725	12.573	2.937
GRU4Rec	44.218	35.412	46.504	37.021	11.037	1.993
SR-GNN	49.877	41.268	50.937	41.135	13.032	2.981
SR-HGNN	50.637	40.908	51.257	40.870	13.124	3.087
SR-CAAN	50.980	**41.736**	52.923	42.073	13.071	3.032
KGFF-SR	**51.735**	41.603	**53.033**	**42.718**	**13.151**	**3.075**

In KGFF-SR, we integrate the KG into session-based recommendation system. By leveraging a multi-head attention mechanism, we explore potential connections among all users via a two-stage filtering, ensuring computational tractability and scalable scalability. The experimental results demonstrate that our proposed method KGFF-SR outperforms other baselines on all three datasets.

In Table 3, it is easy to see that KG-enhanced methods, including SR-CAAN and our method KGFF-SR, outperform the GNN-based method SR-GNN. This highlights the importance of incorporating users' dynamic interests to enrich user representations. Experimental results reveal that Item-KNN achieves superior performance compared to GRU4Rec on some metrics. This can be attributed to GRU4Rec's strict sequential modeling of sessions, whereas Item-KNN leverages item similarities rather than merely relying on session order. In addition, it underscores that the movie scenario does not establish an evenly weighted sequence of items strictly within session sequences. Another RNN-based method NARM is inferior to our proposed method since it only uses a single attention mechanism to capture user global interests. This is reflected in KGFF-SR which uses a multi-head attention mechanism to delve deeper into session considerations. It extracts item-item relationships by constructing a complex relationship graph encompassing user behavior and item semantics.

6.2 Performance of Varying Embedding Sizes

In this section, we explore the impact of various item embedding sizes on the recommendation performance. To this end, we conduct pre-training on the knowledge graph and utilize the TransE method for evaluation. As shown in Fig. 2, the experimental results clearly demonstrate that as the embedding size increases, the model's recommendation performance significantly improves before the dimension reaches 800.

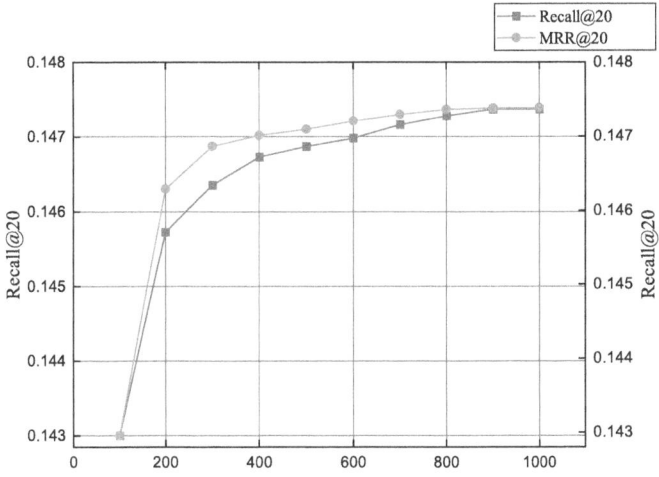

Fig. 2. Performance by varying the embedding sizes of TransE.

6.3 Ablation Studies

We conduct ablation experiments on MovieLens-20M 1/16 and MovieLens-20M 1/4 respectively to verify the effectiveness of our proposed two-stage feature filtering. To validate our method, we name the different ablation models of KGFF-SR as follows.

- **W/O first-filtering**. In this model, we remove the first-stage item feature filtering. Instead, we substitute the outcomes of the initial first-stage filtering with the item context neighbors from the original session graph.
- **W/O second-filtering**. In this model, we remove the second-stage item feature filtering. We leverage results from the first coarse-grained filtering to directly carry out subsequent recommendation work.

Table 4. Effect of two-stage item feature filtering.

Variation	MovieLens-20M 1/16		MovieLens-20M 1/4	
	Recall@20	MRR@20	Recall@20	MRR@20
W/O first-filtering	12.611	2.872	**12.051**	2.736
W/O second-filtering	11.937	2.802	11.503	2.377
KGFF-SR	**13.152**	**3.075**	10.073	**3.192**

The findings from our ablation experiments are summarized in Table 4. The results indicate that removing any filtering component leads to a certain reduction in the model's recommendation performance. Upon comparison between the two filtering methods, we observe that our approach incorporating the second-stage filtering yields superior performance. This is because the recommendation accuracy relies on the user's global interests. Since the first-stage filtering solely captures the user's local interests while the second-stage filtering expands the recommendation scope, it leads to clearer recommendation objectives.

6.4 Computational Cost

In this section, we evaluate the computational cost of KGFF-RS by constructing different sub-datasets which consist of 5,000, 15,000, 30,000, and 60,000 users, respectively, and their interaction records according to MovieLens-20M. The training time and memory usage of KGFF-SR on GPU RTX4090 24G are shown in Table 5.

Table 5. The computation cost on different user scales based on MovieLens-20M.

User Scale	Training Time (s/epoch)				Memory Occupation (MiB)			
	SR-GNN	w/o 1-st Filtering	w/o 2-nd Filtering	KGFF-SR	SR-GNN	w/o 1-st Filtering	w/o 2-nd Filtering	KGFF-SR
5k	6.5	4.3	3.6	4.7	21437	16714	3563	3491
15k	207	171	153	157	–	–	5061	4871
30k	–	–	1142	1247	–	–	7446	7083
60k	–	–	2798	2803	–	–	20376	18625

In Table 5 that KGFF-SR exhibits substantial improvements compared to SR-GNN regarding training time and memory usage. Filtering item features can enhance system efficiency by reducing unnecessary data transmission and processing, thereby reducing server and bandwidth requirements. This optimization enables the system to better accommodate real-time user interactions and handle high-load requests effectively.

Simultaneously, the experimental results demonstrate that the memory consumption of KGFF-SR and KGFF-SR without second-stage filtering is similar because the number of user inputs after the first-stage filtering closely mirrors the original number of inputs without any processing. The majority of computations stem from the first-stage filtering process. In contrast, KGFF-RS without the first-stage filtering directly conducts second-stage adaptive graph structure learning for all users. Despite a small number of users, the capacity of the second-stage filtering to learn graph structures is restricted, leading to a limited filter on neighbor nodes and substantial memory usage.

7   Conclusion

In this paper, we propose a KG-enhanced session-based recommendation with two-stage feature filtering. In summary, our method integrates KG into the session-based recommendation system and leverages GGNN and a multi-head attention mechanism to augment user global interest representation. Besides, we conduct effective feature learning alongside feature filtering to reduce computational costs. We evaluate our method on three sub-datasets of MovieLens-20M. The experimental results demonstrate the superiority of KGFF-SR over other baselines.

Acknowledgements. This work is partly supported by the National Key Research and Development Program of China (Research and Demonstration Application of Key Technologies for Personalized Learning Driven by Educational Big Data) under Grant 2023YFC3341200 and the Research Cultivation Fund for The Youth Teachers of South China Normal University under Grant 23KJ29.

References

1. Chen, Y.H., Huang, L., Wang, C.D., Lai, J.H.: Hybrid-order gated graph neural network for session-based recommendation. IEEE Trans. Industr. Inf. **18**(3), 1458–1467 (2021)
2. Da'u, A., Salim, N.: Recommendation system based on deep learning methods: a systematic review and new directions. Artif. Intell. Rev. **53**(4), 2709–2748 (2020)
3. Guo, J., et al.: HGAN: hierarchical graph alignment network for image-text retrieval. IEEE Trans. Multimedia **25**, 9189–9202 (2023)
4. Han, X., et al.: OpenKE: an open toolkit for knowledge embedding. In: Proceedings of the 2018 Conference on Empirical Methods in Natural Language Processing: System Demonstrations, pp. 139–144 (2018)
5. Harper, F.M., Konstan, J.A.: The movieLens datasets: history and context. ACM Trans. Interact. Intell. Syst. (TIIS) **5**(4), 1–19 (2015)
6. Hidasi, B., Karatzoglou, A., Baltrunas, L., Tikk, D.: Session-based recommendations with recurrent neural networks. arXiv preprint arXiv:1511.06939 (2015)
7. Huang, Y., Zhao, F., Gui, X., Jin, H.: Path-enhanced explainable recommendation with knowledge graphs. World Wide Web **24**(5), 1769–1789 (2021)
8. Jannach, D., Ludewig, M.: When recurrent neural networks meet the neighborhood for session-based recommendation. In: Proceedings of the Eleventh ACM Conference on Recommender Systems, pp. 306–310 (2017)

9. Kumar, C., Abuzar, M., Kumar, M.: MGU-GNN: minimal gated unit based graph neural network for session-based recommendation. Appl. Intell. **53**(20), 23147–23165 (2023)
10. Li, J., Ren, P., Chen, Z., Ren, Z., Lian, T., Ma, J.: Neural attentive session-based recommendation. In: Proceedings of the 2017 ACM on Conference on Information and Knowledge Management, pp. 1419–1428 (2017)
11. Linden, G., Smith, B., York, J.: Amazon.com recommendations: item-to-item collaborative filtering. IEEE Internet Comput. **7**(1), 76–80 (2003)
12. Liu, J., Huang, W., Li, T., Ji, S., Zhang, J.: Cross-domain knowledge graph chiasmal embedding for multi-domain item-item recommendation. IEEE Trans. Knowl. Data Eng. **35**(5), 4621–4633 (2022)
13. Pang, Y., et al.: Heterogeneous global graph neural networks for personalized session-based recommendation. In: Proceedings of the Fifteenth ACM International Conference on Web Search and Data Mining, pp. 775–783 (2022)
14. Ranjbar Kermany, N., Yang, J., Wu, J., Pizzato, L.: Fair-SRS: a fair session-based recommendation system. In: Proceedings of the Fifteenth ACM International Conference on Web Search and Data Mining, pp. 1601–1604 (2022)
15. Shi, D., Wang, T., Xing, H., Xu, H.: A learning path recommendation model based on a multidimensional knowledge graph framework for e-learning. Knowl.-Based Syst. **195**, 105618 (2020)
16. Tahmasebi, F., Meghdadi, M., Ahmadian, S., Valiallahi, K.: A hybrid recommendation system based on profile expansion technique to alleviate cold start problem. Multimedia Tools Appl. **80**, 2339–2354 (2021)
17. Tai, W., Lan, T., Wu, Z., Wang, P., Wang, Y., Zhou, F.: Improving session-based recommendation with contrastive learning. User Model. User-Adap. Inter. **33**(1), 1–42 (2023)
18. Wang, S., Cao, L., Wang, Y., Sheng, Q.Z., Orgun, M.A., Lian, D.: A survey on session-based recommender systems. ACM Comput. Surv. (CSUR) **54**(7), 1–38 (2021)
19. Wang, S., Zhang, Q., Hu, L., Zhang, X., Wang, Y., Aggarwal, C.: Sequential/session-based recommendations: challenges, approaches, applications and opportunities. In: Proceedings of the 45th International ACM SIGIR Conference on Research and Development in Information Retrieval, pp. 3425–3428 (2022)
20. Wang, X., He, X., Cao, Y., Liu, M., Chua, T.S.: KGAT: knowledge graph attention network for recommendation. In: Proceedings of the 25th ACM SIGKDD International Conference on Knowledge Discovery & Data Mining, pp. 950–958 (2019)
21. Wang, X., Wang, D., Xu, C., He, X., Cao, Y., Chua, T.S.: Explainable reasoning over knowledge graphs for recommendation. In: Proceedings of the AAAI Conference on Artificial Intelligence, vol. 33, pp. 5329–5336 (2019)
22. Wu, J., Ou, Z., Song, M.: Session-based recommendation with context-aware attention network. In: Proceedings of the 2019 7th International Conference on Information Technology: IoT and Smart City (2019)
23. Wu, S., Tang, Y., Zhu, Y., Wang, L., Xie, X., Tan, T.: Session-based recommendation with graph neural networks. In: Proceedings of the AAAI Conference on Artificial Intelligence, vol. 33, pp. 346–353 (2019)
24. Yang, Y., Huang, C., Xia, L., Huang, C.: Knowledge graph self-supervised rationalization for recommendation. In: Proceedings of the 29th ACM SIGKDD Conference on Knowledge Discovery and Data Mining, pp. 3046–3056 (2023)

25. Yang, Y., Huang, C., Xia, L., Li, C.: Knowledge graph contrastive learning for recommendation. In: Proceedings of the 45th International ACM SIGIR Conference on Research and Development in Information Retrieval, pp. 1434–1443 (2022)
26. Yu, F., Zhu, Y., Liu, Q., Wu, S., Wang, L., Tan, T.: TAGNN: target attentive graph neural networks for session-based recommendation. In: Proceedings of the 43rd International ACM SIGIR Conference on Research and Development in Information Retrieval, pp. 1921–1924 (2020)
27. Zhang, C., Zheng, W., Liu, Q., Nie, J., Zhang, H.: SEDGN: sequence enhanced denoising graph neural network for session-based recommendation. Expert Syst. Appl. **203**, 117391 (2022)

Interactive Programming Knowledge Tracing with Adversarial Training

Ruolin Li, Ronghua Lin$^{(\boxtimes)}$, Dingding Li, Jiemin Chen, and Yong Tang

South China Normal University, Guangzhou 510631, Guangdong, China
{liruolin,rhlin,dingly,chenjiemin,ytang}@m.scnu.edu.cn

Abstract. The task of Programming Knowledge Tracing (PKT) is to predict student next programming performance using their history interactions with questions. Though rich features have been utilized in PKT such as code text, most existing methods only consider temporal features in student answer sequences. However, actual student programming process are more complex. In this work, we propose Interactive Programming Knowledge Tracing (IPKT), which uses an Interactive Memory Network (IMN) combined with Adversarial Training (AT) to simulate the learning process of reviewing question. Firstly, we design the IMN which learns the relation between knowledge state with answer information as the PKT backbone. Meanwhile, we predict the performance of the next question by fully connected network and use AT to enhance model's generalization of the question recognition. Extensive experiments are conducted on two real-world datasets and the experimental results demonstrate the effectiveness of our proposed model.

Keywords: Knowledge Tracing · LSTM network · Programming Learning · Adversarial Training

1 Introduction

Modeling student knowledge to predict future performance on the next questions, called Knowledge Tracing (KT), is a fundamental feature of an intelligent tutoring system [1]. With the rapid development of the Internet, online programming learning is becoming more and more popular, showing a trend of "programming for all". Thus, it's of significance to analyze the student knowledge state and guide them for better learning strategies using programming knowledge tracing (PKT).

KT models use student past interaction (question, response, skill required by question) as the training input to predict their answer performance when faced with the next question. With the rapid development of deep neural networks, a large number of knowledge tracing networks based on deep learning (DKT) have emerged [6–10]. Typical DKT apply Recurrent Neural Networks (RNNs) [30] to capture temporal dynamics in a sequence of interactions between questions and answers by a student, and based on that, to predict the student's answer for a new question [31]. However, student response to open-ended programming questions with unlimited solution space contains rich learning information. PKT can utilize feature in datasets from exclusive programming areas to

© The Author(s), under exclusive license to Springer Nature Singapore Pte Ltd. 2025
H. Sun et al. (Eds.): ChineseCSCW 2024, CCIS 2343, pp. 166–178, 2025.
https://doi.org/10.1007/978-981-96-2373-0_12

innovate. Recent work add the joint embedding of code features and answer correctness to represent individualized programming submissions, which effectively achieve better performance [2, 4, 13, 17].

The above methods only consider the time features in the set of student interactions. In the real world, student psychological behaviors are more complex. According to [18, 29], it has been proven that student skills improve through repeated review. In programming learning, student will submit code several times until the response is correct. Thus, when answering programming questions, student answer changes will be more susceptible to reviewing question. We suggest that this behavior can be learned using non-linear interactions in PKT.

To better model the student programming learning process in real-life human learning psychology and behavior, we propose an approach named Interactive Programming Knowledge Tracing (IPKT), which combines the Interactive Memory Network (IMN) with Adversarial Training (AT). Firstly, for simulating the student reviewing behavior, we design the IMN which contains an Interactive Layer and a Dual-LSTM network and the student knowledge state will be updated by it. Besides, to improve the model's ability to recognize the features of programming questions, we add the question embeddings as the perturbed adversarial perturbations (AEs) in adversarial training. The AEs in AT are based on the gradient of the question embedding. To summarize, the main contributions of this work are:

- We design IMN to simulate the review behaviors in modelling for programming learning. In the Interactive Layer of IMN, we use a more appropriate method to prevent the problem that the vector will converge to 0.
- AT is introduced into our model training to enhance the generalization of our model. We jointly train the original clean inputs and the corresponding perturbed AEs.
- We conduct a set of experimental studies using two real-world data collected from online programming platforms to fully evaluate the performance of the proposed model. We synthetically demonstrate the effectiveness of the proposed model compared with a series of baselines and ablation studies.

2 Related Work

2.1 Online Programming Learning Prediction

Students' interaction to open-ended programming questions with unlimited solution space contains rich learning information. Based on available research, programming learning prediction can be divided into two parts: traditional performance-based prediction methods and answer-generation prediction methods.

On the one hand, traditional performance-based predictions generate the score of the next question to predicting student state. Early methods use a combination of logistic models [11] and probabilistic models [15]. Emerson et al. [14] evaluate the accuracy of a logistic regression model based on multiple blocks using four categories of student characteristics in their self-developed programming system. [12] first applies DKT for programming knowledge tracking, they use Abstract Syntax Tree (AST) to extract code embeddings and feed into RNNs to model the learning process of multiple code submissions from student. Wang et al. [13] argue that replacing the DKT-based RNNs model with an LSTM can better capture the student learning state over time. In their model, fewer than two code submissions are excluded, which aims to learn the recursive relationship of multiple submissions. On the other hand, answer generation prediction methods generate predicted text to match real student answers. Jiang et al. [16] and Liu et al. [17] use code-generative approach to simulate student submitted answers that contain incorrect information. They perform model accuracy assessment by generating sequences of abstract syntax tree editing distances between generated answers and the standard answers. However, these above approaches presuppose that each practice question must have an existing corresponding standard answer or a set of rich features.

In the end, our model meticulously divides the input information without sufficient data features, interacts the knowledge state with their answer information and utilizes a two-layer LSTM network to separate the student programming skills and debugging skills.

2.2 Adversarial Training

Adversarial training (AT) improves model robustness by introducing noise into the training process and normalizing the model parameters, which is originally applied to image classification with continuous input data [20]. Miyato et al. [22] apply RNN rather than origin input to incorporated perturbations at each training step to minimize the loss function for text classification tasks. Similarly, in another work, Yasunaga et al. [23] employ character-level embeddings with Bi-LSTM models by AT, which adds perturbations to the input at the character level embeddings to maximize the classifier loss function during training. Meanwhile, several methods are proposed to explore the use of AT to model other tasks. Wu et al. [23] improve the precision of relation extraction in multi-instance multi-label learning frameworks by applying AT. Yang et al. [25] argue that AT enhances the model's ability to learn examples characterized by low-frequency words, while have limit in in defending against artificial adversarial examples. Using adversarial noise into the output embedding layer, Wang et al. [31] optimize the running speed of the model. In KT task, Conti et al. [26] have proposed the use of AT improve the lack of robustness of KT models in the face of small datasets, but cannot solve the problem of data sparsity. Though AT reveals promising results on these tasks above, it has not yet been applied in the field of PDK, which will be the main focus of this paper.

3 Problem Definition

Given a set of questions Q, submitted code C and corresponding answer score R, the traditional history interaction $\widehat{X}_h$ between student and questions can be demonstrated as $\widehat{X}_h = \{(q_i, r_i, c_i)|i = 1, \ldots, n\}$, where n is the length of interactions. Considering that programming questions can be answered multiple times, there isn't always a direct correspondence between questions and submissions. For the question q_i, there will exist several submissions $s_i = \{(r_{ij}, c_{ij})|j = 1, \ldots, k\}$, where r_{ij} and c_{ij} are the j-th answer result and submitted code on the same question q_i. Hence, we can redefine the history interaction as $X_h = \{\{(q_i, r_i, c_i)|i = 1, \ldots, t\}$, where $t = \sum_n^i |s_i|$ and $X_i = (q_i, r_i, c_i)$ is the i-th interaction. Additionally, in PKT, the answer results $r \in \{0,1\} = 1$ means the submitted codes pass all the test points of the programming question, otherwise r equals the percentage decimals of number of test points passed. Based on the sequences of history interactions X_h, our goal is to predict the possible score of the answers r_{t+1}, as well as the next programming question process performance r_p_{t+1} in the next question q_{t+1}, as shown in Eq. (1).

$$r_{t+1}, r\_p_{t+1} = P(1|X_h, q_{t+1}) \tag{1}$$

4   Model Architecture

As shown in Fig. 1, our entire IPKT framework consists of five components, including Embedding layer, IMN, Performance Prediction, Model Optimization and Adversarial Training. We will introduce our model in the i-th time step as an example in the following.

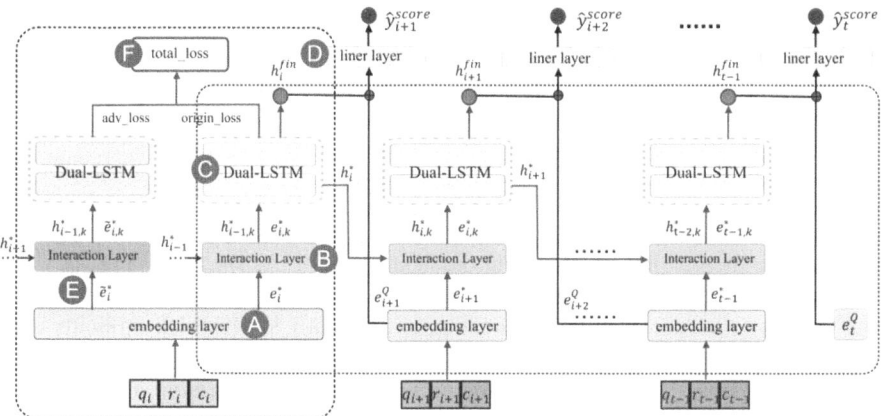

Fig. 1. The architecture of the IPKT model. For the sake of simplicity, we utilize the symbol $*$ to abbreviate the annotations CK and CA.

4.1   Embedding Layer

We create a question embedding matrix $Q \in \mathbb{R}^d$ and an answer result embedding matrix $R \in \mathbb{R}^d$ as the embeddings layer (Fig. 1A), where d denotes the dimension of the embedding. These two embedding matrices transform the origin input q_i and r_i from X_i into one-hot coding vectors e_i^Q and e_i^R. According to [3, 4], we construct a graph called Code Knowledge Graph (CKG) to learn the features from submitted code c_i such as the structure of variables, functions, and control flow. Based on the CKG representation, we create a Code Ability Graph (CAG) to capture changes in the student submitted code iterations between c_{i-1} and c_i. Subsequently, we use GGNN [5] to learn the e_i^{CKG} and e_i^{CAG}. Specifically, the GGNN uses its message passing and node updating mechanisms to aggregate information from neighboring nodes over multiple iterations. This allows the GGNN to effectively capture the structural features from the CKG, as well as the iterative changes in the student's code submissions as represented in the CAG. Notably, when X_i is the initial submission in the same question, $e_i^{CAG} = 0$. Finally, we use e_i^{CK} and e_i^{CA} to represent the student's Code Knowledge (CK) and Code Ability (CA) for solving the question q_i. The questions and answers result embeddings e_i^Q and e_i^R will be added. For the i-th time step, the student CK and CA can be represented as:

$$e_i^{CK} = W_1\left(e_i^Q \oplus e_i^R \oplus e_i^{CKG}\right) \tag{2}$$

$$e_i^{CA} = W_2\left(e_i^Q \oplus e_i^R \oplus \hat{e}_i^{CK} \oplus e_i^{CAG}\right) \tag{3}$$

Where $e_i^{CK}, e_i^{CK} \in \mathbb{R}^d$ and $W_1 \in \mathbb{R}^{3d \times d}$, $W_2 \in \mathbb{R}^{4d \times d}$ is the learnable parameters. The symbol $\oplus$ denotes the concatenation operation, while i denotes the i-th time step.

4.2 Interactive Memory Network (IMN)

We propose a new memory network IMN as the PKT backbone for learning the student programming knowledge status. IMN contains two parts: the Dual-LSTM and the Interactive Layer.

Dual-LSTM. To compartmentalize student states of knowledge more logically, we divide it into programming skills h_i^{CK} and debugging skill h_i^{CA}, which h_i^{CK} are generated by e_i^{CK} in Eq. (2) and h_i^{CA} are generated by e_i^{CA} in Eq. (3). Both of these will work together on predicting the possibility of solving the next question. As shown in (Fig. 1C), the Dual-LSTM are modelled to learn separately student two skills above.

Firstly, we incorporated positional gating g_i for Dual-LSTM, which explicitly captures the sequential dependencies in same question. Positional gating g_i is set as the all-one vector if X_i is not the initial submission in the same question. h_{i-1}^{CK} and h_{i-1}^{CA} are reserved only in the same question and reset in the next question. The process of updating h_{i-1}^{CK} is shown in Eq. (4), which h_{i-1}^{CA} can be calculated similarly to h_{i-1}^{CK}.

$$h_{i-1}^{CK} = g_i \odot h_{i-1}^{CK} + (1 - g_i) \odot h_{i-1}^{CK} \tag{4}$$

Where the symbol $\odot$ denotes the Hadamard product operation. Then Dual-LSTM can be formulated as follows. In Dual-LSTM, we use two LSTM layers [20] to learn h_i^{CK} and h_i^{CA} separately as shown in Eqs. (5) and (6).

$$h_i^{CK} = Dual_{LSTM}\left(h_{i-1}^{CK}, e_i^{CK}\right) \tag{5}$$

$$h_i^{CA} = Dual_{LSTM}\left(h_{i-1}^{CA}, e_i^{CA}\right) \tag{6}$$

Interactive Layer. We design the Interactive Layer (Fig. 1B) to simulate the student process of reviewing the question for enhancing contextual modelling. The specific details are as shown in (Fig. 2). In this module, we set the code knowledge e_i^{CK} and code ability e_i^{CA} in Eq. (2) and (3) as the information reviewed, which contains the question and the

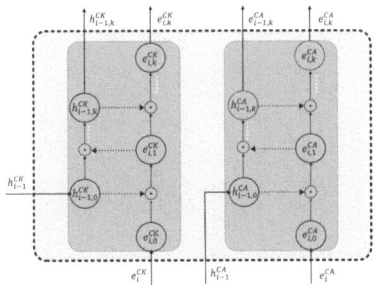

Fig. 2. The structure of the Interactive Layer.

corresponding answer. Before entering Dual-LSTM, e_i^{CK} and e_i^{CA} interacted with student programming skills h_{i-1}^{CK} and debugging skills h_{i-1}^{CA} from the previous Dual-LSTM cell. This module can be viewed as enriching the additive dynamics of the recursive transformation, fusing additional information while maintaining consistency with the original input range. The previous states $e_{i,0}^{CK} = e_i^{CK}$, $h_{i-1,0}^{CK} = h_{i-1}^{CK}$ are transformed linearly, fed through a sigmoid. After k repetitions of this mutual gating cycle, the set of last values $h_{i-1,k}^{CK}, e_{i,k}^{CK}, h_{i-1,k}^{CA}, e_{i,k}^{CA}$ are fed to the next Dual-LSTM cell.

It is worth that the interaction only makes sense when the student last ability is retained, so we will only interact when positional gating $g_i = 1$ (in Eq. (4)). To preventing output from getting smaller and converging to 0, we add the learning parameters W_a, W_b into each round interaction. The process of $h_{i-1,r}^{CK}$ interact with $e_{i,k-1}^{CK}$ is shown in Eqs. (7) and (8), which $h_{i-1,r}^{CA}$ interacts with $e_{i,k-1}^{CK}$ can be calculated similarly to above.

$$h_{i-1,r}^{CK} = W_a \sigma \left(e_{i,k-1}^{CK} \right) \odot h_{i-1,k-2}^{CK} \tag{7}$$

$$e_{i,r}^{CK} = W_b \sigma \left(h_{i,k-1}^{CK} \right) \odot e_{i,k-2}^{CK} \tag{8}$$

Where the number of $k \in \mathbb{N}$ is a hyperparameter, which denotes the round of interactions. The operation σ denotes the sigmoid activation function.

4.3 Performance Prediction

We combine the student programming skills h_i^{CK} and debugging skills h_i^{CA} together working on forming his final knowledge state h_i^{fin}. The final knowledge state h_i^{fin} can be represented by the following:

$$h_i^{fin} = relu \left(W_{fin} \left(e_{i+1}^q \oplus h_i^{CK} \oplus h_i^{CA} \right) + b_{fin} \right) \tag{9}$$

Where $relu$ is an activation function defined as the positive part of its argument. With the final knowledge state h_i^{fin}, as we expressed in Eq. (1), we combine h_i^{fin} with the question embedding e_{i+1}^q (Fig. 1D). Finally, the next programming question process score $\hat{y}_{i+1}^{score}$

and question performance $\hat{y}_{i+1}^{r\_p}$ predicted in the next question q_{i+1} are shown as Eqs. (10) and (11).

$$\hat{y}_{i+1}^{score} = \sigma\left(W_{score}h_i^{fin} + b_{score}\right) \tag{10}$$

$$\hat{y}_{i+1}^{rp} = \sigma\left(W_{rp}h_i^{fin} + b_{rp}\right) \tag{11}$$

The operation σ denotes the sigmoid activation function. All above of that is a complete prediction process for question q_{i+1}.

4.4   Model Optimization and Adversarial Training

To learn the parameters in the IMN, for the binary criterion, we choose the cross-entropy logarithmic loss between the predicted value $\hat{y}_{i+1}^{score}$ and the actual answer r_{i+1}^{score} in r_{i+1}. For the continuous criterion, we choose the MSE loss between the predicted value $\hat{y}_{i+1}^{r\_p}$ and the actual score $r_{i+1}^{r\_p}$ in r_{i+1} as the objective function. Based on the Eqs. (1–3, 9–11), the loss function $F(x)$ can be represented as shown in Eqs. (12–14).

$$Loss_{origin} = F\left(e_i^{CK}, e_i^{CA}, q_{i+1}, r_{i+1}^{score}, r_{i+1}^{rp}\right) = \alpha loss_\alpha + \beta loss_\beta \tag{12}$$

$$loss_\alpha = \sum_{i=1}^{T}\left(r_{i+1}^{score}\log\hat{y}_{i+1}^{score} + \left(1 - r_{i+1}^{score}\right)\log\left(1 - \hat{y}_{i+1}^{score}\right)\right) \tag{13}$$

$$loss_\beta = \sum_{j=1}^{T}\left|y_{i+1}^{rp} - r_{i+1}^{rp}\right| \tag{14}$$

Where the symbol α, β is the hyperparameter. Then we use Adversarial Training to enhance the generalization of our KT model by jointly training the original clean inputs and the corresponding perturbed AEs (Fig. 1E). To achieve this goal, following [24], we add perturbations on the origin question embedding e_i^Q. Specifically, after model learning and loss calculating, the grad $grad$ concerning the question embeddings e_i^Q is used to generate the perturbations ε corresponding. The adversarial question embedding $\tilde{e}_i^Q$ contained the perturbations ε can be formulated as:

$$\tilde{e}_i^Q = e_i^Q + \varepsilon \tag{15}$$

$$\varepsilon = \epsilon\frac{grad}{\|grad\|_2}, where grad = \nabla_{e^Q}F \tag{16}$$

Where the ϵ is an efficient and fast gradient approximation method [26] to provide a non-iterative solution for computing with $L2$ norm constraint. The symbol ∇_{e^Q} denotes the gradient of F to question embedding e_i^Q. Based on the above, the adversarial loss $loss_{adv}$ can be constructed by the new current embedding $\tilde{e}_i^{CK}$, $\tilde{e}_i^{CA}$ integrated with the adversarial question embedding $\tilde{e}_h^Q$. The construction methods of $\tilde{e}_i^{CK}$ and $\tilde{e}_i^{CA}$ are similar to Eqs. (2) and (3) respectively, with the only difference being the replacement of e_i^Q by $\tilde{e}_i^Q$. Finally, shown in (Fig. 1F), we jointly use both the original loss $loss_{origin}$ and adversarial loss $loss_{adv}$ to update by minimizing the total loss $loss_{total}$, as shown in Eqs. (17) and (18).

$$loss_{total} = loss_{origin} + \gamma\, loss_{adv} \tag{17}$$

$$loss_{adv} = F\left(\tilde{e}_i^{CK}, \tilde{e}_i^{CA}, q_{i+1}, r_{i+1}^{score}, r_{i+1}^{rate}\right) \tag{18}$$

Where the symbol γ is the hyperparameter.

5   Experiment

In this section, we compare the proposed IPKT model with other knowledge tracing approaches in our dataset. Besides, we conduct ablation studies to justify the effectiveness of two major components in IPKT.

5.1   Experimental Setting

Dataset. We use two real world datasets AIZU_Cpp and Atcoder_C from two online programming platforms. AIZU_Cpp is provided by the Project_CodeNet [19] released by IBM, including student interaction codes for multiple programming languages. We select the benchmark composed of users who use C to conduct questions in AIZU.org. The corresponding dataset contains 5268 students with 271189 submissions from 2206 exercises. Atcoder_C is provided by the online programming competition website Atcoder.org[1], composed of exercise practice with C language. The resulting dataset contains 6282 students with 425238 submissions from 1670 questions. We partition both datasets, allocating 60% for training, 20% for performance evaluation, and the remaining 20% for testing.

Parameter Setting and Performance Metric. As to the implementation parameters of the neural layers, we use uniform random initialization for faster convergence. We set the learning rate as 0.0001, mini batches as 128 and use dropout with p $= 0.4$ to alleviate overfitting. Hyper-parameter α and β in Eq. (12) are both set to 0.5, while γ in Eq. (17) is set to 0.3. Besides, the round k is set to 5 in Interactive Layer. We repeat the experiments three times on each model.

Following the KT methods [26], we use the Accuracy (ACC) and Area Under Curve (AUC) metrics to measure the prediction performance of each method. Both of them fall within the range of 0 to 1, with higher values indicating better performance. Besides, student first submission scores, last submission scores, and average answer scores in the same question are considered as indicators for tracing the coding ability of model, we used the root-mean-square error (RMSE) to quantify the gap between predicted and actual scores (Table 1).

Baseline Models. To evaluate the effectiveness of our proposed model, we use the following models as our baselines:

---

[1] Https://atcoder.jp

- codeBERT [3] is a bimodal pre-trained model for programming language. Leveraging the capabilities of codeBERT, we encode source code and utilize one of the typical LSTM [20] to capture the complete learning trajectory of students to accomplish the prediction task of PKT.
- DKT [6] This method represents the initial effort to apply DNNs to KT, which uses RNNs/LSTM to model student history learning sequences.
- PDKT [7] This method uses both question information and code information as features to train model. Due to we didn't find publicly available PLcodeBERT in this method, we used codeBERT [3] instead.
- EERNNA/M [28] As the one of most recent KT models which utilize exercise content embedding for tracing knowledge mastery, we choose both EERNNA and EERNNM applied to the task of PKT.
- PST [4] is a recent PKT method that uses a more efficient method of utilizing code embedding.

5.2　Prediction

Table 2 reports the performance comparison between these baselines and our proposed IPKT on two real-world datasets. There are some specific details of which our observations and analysis are as follows:

　　Code-learning based methods: codeBERT is based on the Code-learning method. It does not use a specific programming language in pretraining and is generalizable, thus student code submission in our two C datasets can be represented well, especially for the ACC metrics of the AIZU_Cpp dataset. However, the simple DKT backbone still limits his performance.

　　DNN-based method: DKT and EERNNA/M all belong to the DNN-based methods. As a classical deep knowledge tracking method, DKT still has a high performance to predicting exercises in the programming domain, which is higher than Code-based methods in terms of the metrics suggesting that the use of RNNs for outcome prediction is effective. However, it directly applies RNN/LSTM in KT without considering the subject characteristics. The rise in its performance without using additional features is limited. Thus, EERNNA/M show better performance because of the addition of question context embedding.

　　Program-task-based methods: PDKT and PST belong to the Program-task-based methods. Compared to the PDKT and DNN-based methods, PST shows better performance in all the metrics of our two datasets, which indicates that PST's use of the code features is effective. Besides PST model performance in all the metrics of both datasets except for the AUC metrics of the AIZU_Cpp dataset, which is lower than that of codeBERT probably because PST receives some kind of hindrance in learning code features in this dataset.

　　Our method: In general, IPKT is higher than our baseline in all metrics on both datasets, except for the last submission scores metrics of the Atcoder_C dataset. In our model, we use the Interactive Layer to learn more information from input, thus there are additional information support in predicting the first submission scores, but probably weak predicting the last submission scores metrics. Since we perform adversarial learning for code embeddings, our proposed method is instrumental in delivering more robust code embeddings, for solving the problem of poor PST performance on the AIZU_Cpp dataset in AUC.

Table 1. Statistics of the datasets.

Dataset	AIZU_Cpp	Atcoder_C
of students	5268	6282
of questions	2206	1670
of submissions	271189	425238
Avg. Submission of students	51.48	67.69
Avg. Score of students	0.77	0.62
AC rate of final submission	74.30%	97.17%

Table 2. Overall student performance prediction results.

Dataset	AIZU_Cpp					Atcoder_C				
Methods	AUC	ACC	RMSE	RMSE	RMSE	AUC	ACC	RMSE	RMSE	RMSE
codeBERT	0.5054	0.9600	0.2309	0.3165	0.1765	0.6679	0.8001	0.3017	0.3592	0.3005
PDKT	0.5078	0.9184	0.3054	0.3773	0.2662	0.6066	0.7556	0.3494	0.3970	0.3569
DKT	0.5119	0.9588	0.2714	0.3689	0.1918	0.6966	0.8100	0.2962	0.3576	0.2954
EERNNA	0.5022	0.9598	0.2535	0.3519	0.1765	0.7106	0.8040	0.2998	0.3597	0.2954
EERNNM	0.5258	0.9592	0.2501	0.3475	0.1746	0.7138	0.8085	0.2952	0.3556	0.2908
PST	0.5281	0.9596	0.2239	0.3073	0.1731	0.7159	0.8107	0.2875	**0.3453**	0.2862
IPKT	**0.5402**	**0.9630**	**0.2218**	**0.3012**	**0.1689**	**0.7231**	**0.8168**	**0.2762**	0.3530	**0.2813**

5.3 Ablation Studies

In this section, we conduct thorough ablation studies to justify the effectiveness of the key components of our IPKT, including the implementation of AT and the proposed Interactive Layer for PKT.

Effective of the Interactive Layer. In our work, the PKT backbone is the proposed IMN module, where the key is a customized Interactive Layer (IL) that adaptively learns information between from previous student state and current answer content which simulates the situation of reviewing behaviors in programming process to make a more accurate prediction. To verify the effectiveness of this module, we train an IPKT model with the Interactive Layer and a corresponding degraded one (a sole Dual-LSTM model) without the Interactive Layer to accomplish KT (namely w/o IL), respectively. The quantitative results are shown in Table 3. We can observe that equipped with the Interactive

Layer, the IMN module efficiently improves the average five indicators across all the datasets, demonstrating its superiority in boosting the performance of PKT.

Effective of the implementation of AT. To enhance the robustness of IPKT and. we apply AT to construct adversarial perturbations of question and add them on the original interaction embeddings as adversarial examples. The original and adversarial examples are further used to jointly train the KT model. Then we apply another strategy which only trains model by original examples. Based on the results in Table 4, we can observe that the implementation of AT outperforms the alternative. This suggests that AT can improve the generalization of the model over clean inputs.

Table 3. Effective of the Interactive Layer.

Dataset	AIZU_Cpp					Atcoder_C				
Methods	AUC	ACC	RMSE	RMSE	RMSE	AUC	ACC	RMSE	RMSE	RMSE
w/o IL	0.5399	0.9616	0.2209	0.3020	0.1701	0.7103	0.8034	0.2750	0.2855	0.2769
IPKT	0.5402	0.9630	0.2268	0.3012	0.1689	0.7231	0.8168	0.2862	0.3395	0.2813

Table 4. Effective of the implementation of AT

Dataset	AIZU_Cpp					Atcoder_C				
Methods	AUC	ACC	RMSE	RMSE	RMSE	AUC	ACC	RMSE	RMSE	RMSE
W/o AT	0.5399	0.9621	0.2245	0.2961	0.1741	0.7052	0.8077	0.2948	0.3355	0.2800
IPKT	0.5402	0.9630	0.2268	0.3012	0.1689	0.7231	0.8168	0.2862	0.3395	0.2813

6   Conclusion and Future Work

Programming skills have been the essential literacy in the digital age. The PKT is an entirely new application for KT that combines knowledge tracking and programming education while lacking relevant studies. This paper proposes a novel PKT model, known as IPKT, which includes the IMN and AT in model. Firstly, we interact the previous student knowledge state in model with the current question information This approach helps capture the behavior of reviewing questions, which is inherent in most real-world programming scenarios but often ignores in previous studies on predicting student performance in PKT. Additionally, we introduce the AT in our model to enhance the generalization ability of model. In AT, we train both the original clean inputs and the corresponding perturbed adversarial examples simultaneously. Experiments comparing different baselines and ablation studies exhibit its effectiveness and superiority.

In the future, we plan to challenge datasets that contain more various attribute information to predict student status more accurate. Furthermore, we plan to incorporate regularization terms into our loss function to improve consistency in programming predictions.

Acknowledgments. This work is supported in part by the National Key Research and Development Program of China (Research and Demonstration Application of Key Technologies for Personalized Learning Driven by Educational Big Data) under Grant 2023YFC3341200.

References

1. VanLehn, K.: The behavior of tutoring systems. Int. J. Artif. Intell. Educ. **16**(3), 227–265 (2006)
2. Mao, Y., et al.: "Knowing" When" and" Where": temporal-ASTNN for student learning progression in novice programming Tasks. Int. Educ. Data Min. Soc. (2021)
3. Feng, Z., et al.: Codebert: a pre-trained model for programming and natural languages. arXiv preprint arXiv:2002.08155 (2020)
4. Li, R., et al.: PST: measuring skill proficiency in programming exercise process via programming skill tracing. In: Proceedings of the 45th International ACM SIGIR Conference on Research and Development in Information Retrieval (2022)
5. Li, Y., et al.: Gated graph sequences neural networks. arXiv preprint arXiv:1511.05493 (2015)
6. Piech, C., et al.: Deep knowledge tracing. Adv. Neural Information Proces. Syst. **28** (2015)
7. Zhu, R., et al.: Programming knowledge tracing: a comprehensive dataset and a new model. In: 2022 IEEE International Conference on Data Mining Workshops (ICDMW). IEEE (2022)
8. Corbett, A.T., Anderson, J.R.: Knowledge tracing: modeling the acquisition of procedural knowledge. User Model. User-Adap. Inter. **4**, 253–278 (1994)
9. Zhang, J., et al.: Dynamic key-value memory networks for knowledge tracing. In: Proceedings of the 26th international conference on World Wide Web (2017)
10. Mao, Y.: One minute is enough: early prediction of student success and event-level difficulty during novice programming tasks. In: Proceedings of the 12th International Conference on Educational Data Mining (EDM 2019) (2019)
11. Wang, L., et al.: Learning to represent student knowledge on programming exercises using deep learning. Int. Educ. Data Min. Soc. (2017)
12. Wang, L., et al.: Deep knowledge tracing on programming exercises. In: Proceedings of the Fourth (2017) ACM Conference on Learning@ Scale (2017)
13. Emerson, A., et al.: Predicting early and often: predictive student modeling for block-based programming environments. Int. Educ. Data Min. Soc. (2019)
14. Kasurinen, J., Nikula, U.: Estimating programming knowledge with Bayesian knowledge tracing. ACM SIGCSE Bull. **41**(3), 313–317 (2009)
15. Jiang, B., et al.: Knowledge tracing within single programming practice using problem-solving process data. IEEE Trans. Learn. Technol. **13.4**, 822–832 (2020)
16. Liu, N., et al.: Open-ended knowledge tracing for computer science education. In: Proceedings of the 2022 Conference on Empirical Methods in Natural Language Processing (2022)
17. Hagger, M.S., et al.: The strength model of self-regulation failure and health-related behaviour. Health Psychol. Rev. **3.2**, 208–238 (2009)
18. Puri, R., et al.: Codenet: a large-scale ai for code dataset for learning a diversity of coding tasks. arXiv preprint arXiv:2105.12655 (2021)
19. Hochreiter, S., Schmidhuber, J.: Long short-term memory. Neural Comput. **9**(8), 1735–1780 (1997)

20. Ian, J., Shlens, J., Szegedy, C.: Explaining and harnessing adversarial examples. arXiv preprint arXiv:1412.6572 (2014)
21. Miyato, T., Dai, A.M., Goodfellow, I.: Adversarial training methods for semi-supervised text classification. arXiv preprint arXiv:1605.07725 (2016)
22. Yasunaga, M., Kasai, J., Radev, D.: Robust multilingual part-of-speech tagging via adversarial training. arXiv preprint arXiv:1711.04903 (2017)
23. Wu, Y., Bamman, D., Russell, S.: Adversarial training for relation extraction. In: Proceedings of the 2017 Conference on Empirical Methods in Natural Language Processing (2017)
24. Yang, Z., et al.: Improving machine reading comprehension via adversarial training. arXiv preprint arXiv:1911.03614 (2019)
25. Conti, M., et al.: Distributed data source verification in wireless sensor networks. Inform. Fus. **10.4**, 342–353 (2009)
26. Xiaopeng, et al.: Enhancing knowledge tracing via adversarial training. In: Proceedings of the 29th ACM International Conference on Multimedia (2021)
27. Liu, Q., et al.: Ekt: Exercise-aware knowledge tracing for student performance prediction. IEEE Trans. Knowl. Data Eng. **33.1**, 100–115 (2019)
28. Dignath, C., Büttner, G.: Components of fostering self-regulated learning among students. A meta-analysis on intervention studies at primary and secondary school level. Metacogn. Learn. **3**, 231–264 (2008)
29. Lipton, Z.C., Berkowitz, J., Elkan, C.: A critical review of recurrent neural networks for sequence learning. arXiv preprint arXiv:1506.00019 (2015)
30. Abdelrahman, G., Wang, Q., Nunes, B.: Knowledge tracing: a survey. ACM Comput. Surv. **55**(11), 1–37 (2023)
31. Wang, D., Gong, C., Liu, Q.: Improving neural language modeling via adversarial training. In: International Conference on Machine Learning. PMLR (2019)

An Energy-Aware IoT Functions Offloading Strategy in Solar-Powered Edge Environment for Smart Agriculture

Han Cao, Long Chen$^{(\boxtimes)}$, Jinquan Zhang, Shuang Wang, and Xia Zhu

School of Computer Science and Engineering, Southeast University, Nanjing, China
{220222036,chen_long,zhangjq,shuangwang,zhuxia}@seu.edu.cn

Abstract. Edge intelligence is a new trend for monitoring and management in remote animal husbandry. However, the deployment of IoT applications in remote Edge Servers (ESs) faces significant challenges, such as limited computing and battery resources of servers and the mobility of sensors. In this paper, we consider the problem of IoT functions offloading in solar-powered edge environments. The computational, communication, and energy consumption models were established first. A novel approach Energy and Container State aware Offloading Algorithm (ECSOA) was proposed to schedule functions among ESs. ECSOA uses the NSGA-II algorithm to determine optimal parameters, ensuring efficient energy usage and service delivery. Our real-time simulation experiments demonstrate that ECSOA significantly reduces system energy consumption and the number of function rejections, presenting a promising solution for sustainable and reliable serverless edge computing in IoT-enabled animal husbandry.

Keywords: edge computing · serverless computing · computation offloading · smart agriculture · NSGA-II

1 Introduction

The advent of IoT spurred new and enhanced applications across domains, including animal husbandry. Ranchers can utilize sensors to achieve real-time livestock monitoring, encompassing parameters such as feed intake, weight gain, and health status. Simultaneously, they can monitor various natural environments, including soil moisture, air temperature, wind speed, and solar radiation intensity [2]. With these data, ranchers can gain a better understanding of patterns and trends within the husbandry process through artificial intelligence techniques, thus enabling them to make more informed decisions and achieve more sustainable production [13,20].

As shown in Fig. 1, we focus on the scenario of remote pastures, which has the following characteristics: Firstly, because ranchers often require migration based on climate and soil conditions, utilizing solar-powered batteries for numerous

© The Author(s), under exclusive license to Springer Nature Singapore Pte Ltd. 2025
H. Sun et al. (Eds.): ChineseCSCW 2024, CCIS 2343, pp. 179–196, 2025.
https://doi.org/10.1007/978-981-96-2373-0_13

dispersed sensors and ESs can help ranchers avoid the hassle of connecting to the power grid every time they migrate, making it a portable and feasible solution [1,23]. Secondly, due to the considerable distance between pastures and mobile base stations, the communication quality between pasture equipment and the internet is often unreliable. Hence, employing wireless self-organizing network communication [2,6] and substituting cloud computing with edge computing represent suitable solutions [21,30]. Thirdly, there are numerous cases where serverless computing is employed at the edge [7,17]. Leveraging serverless edge computing can facilitate effortless deployment of optimized machine learning model functions to ESs, eliminating numerous complexities such as coding, code optimization, environment deployment, and more [24]. This brings significant convenience to non-technical individuals operating devices. Fourthly, in the pasture, sensors typically upload data to the nearest ES at regular intervals, and an ES can also offload function data to other ESs for computation.

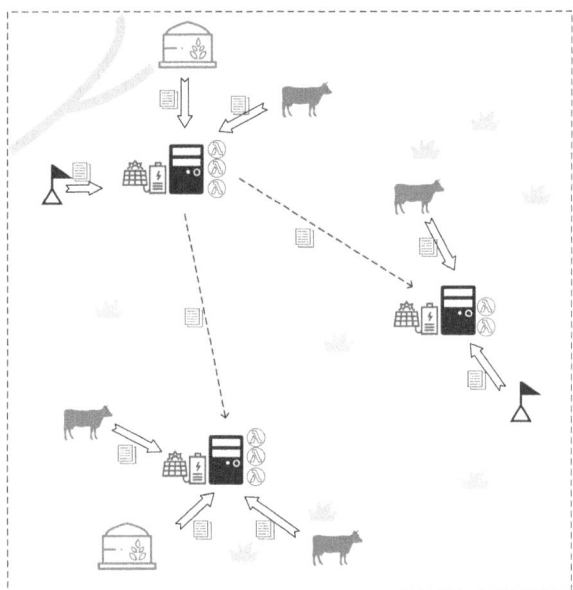

Fig. 1. Edge computing system model

Based on the aforementioned scenario, the problem characteristics we consider are as follows. Firstly, the batteries of the ESs are simultaneously charged and discharged. The charging power is determined by the illumination intensity, while the discharge power is mainly determined by the computation and transmission power of the ES. Therefore, the battery level of each ES dynamically changes over time. Secondly, the system includes sensors worn by livestock. Consequently, the positions of these sensors change with the movement of the livestock, leading to changes in their designated ES for data uploading. Thirdly, resources are deployed at the granularity of functions, and functions are executed within containers. Furthermore, we consider the different states in the lifecycle of containers, as well as features such as container reuse and container cold start.

The above characteristics all contribute to the complexity of function data offloading scheduling. Firstly, the use of solar-powered devices introduces the issue of battery depletion. Low battery levels can result in an ES losing its ability to compute and offload functions. Therefore it's necessary to consider the battery constraints to prevent any ES from depleting its battery when offloading. Secondly, due to the mobility of sensors, the workload on different ESs varies over time. To prevent energy or resource depletion, the challenge lies in offloading functions from heavily loaded ESs to more suitable ones. Thirdly, for the same ES, cold starting a container consumes more energy and resources compared to reusing idle containers, and thus should be avoided as much as possible. However, when an ES has no idle container available for reuse, the decision between local cold starting and offloading functions to other ESs needs to be made.

In this paper, we focus on how function data can be offloaded between ESs to minimize energy consumption and the number of rejections as much as possible. This article mainly makes the following contributions:

- Using mathematical formulas, we propose the computation, communication, and energy consumption models for this scenario. These models are also applicable to other serverless edge computing scenarios.
- We propose an *Energy and Container State aware Offloading Algorithm (ECSOA)*. This is the first approach to optimize energy consumption by considering container states in the serverless edge computing scenario. Regarding the scarcity of battery capacity, *ECSOA* estimates the energy consumption generated by different actions, allowing it to choose the offloading decision with lower energy consumption, thus avoiding premature depletion of the battery.
- For the issue of load unbalanced among ESs caused by sensor mobility, *ECSOA* considers offloading functions to more suitable ESs when resources are insufficient or local computing energy consumption is high, thereby avoiding resource and energy depletion. Furthermore, for the three threshold values used in *ECSOA*, we use the NSGA-II algorithm to search optimal values, ensuring better offloading decisions.
- For the cold start issue, due to its awareness of container states, *ECSOA* fully leverages the reuse of idle containers to reduce the occurrence of cold starts, thereby increasing resource utilization.

The paper is structured as follows. Section 2 reviews the related work. Section 3 introduces the system model. Section 4 proposes the computation offloading strategies. Section 5 presents the experimental methodology, comparative algorithms, and experimental results. Section 6 concludes this paper and discusses the future work.

2   Related Work

Recently, there have been numerous articles focusing on the technology, applications, and challenges of edge computing in smart agriculture or livestock farming [12,21,30]. In these edge environments, the task offloading scheduling is worthy of our attention [11]. Furthermore, some studies have specifically addressed the energy consumption issues during offloading [8]. Zhang et al. [29] considered scenarios where unmanned aerial vehicles (UAVs) equipped with ESs provide services to Internet of Things (IoT) devices, considering three modes of task offloading. Through optimizing bit allocation, slot scheduling, power allocation, and UAV trajectory design, this paper aimed to reduce the overall energy consumption of the system. Long et al. [19] proposed a semi-online fault-tolerant offloading method (UDQF) to optimize service offloading efficiency, energy consumption, and system reliability. They also employed semi-online learning-based offloading strategies to address edge node failures. Bozorgchenani et al. [5] aimed to reduce energy consumption and latency by formulating a constrained multi-objective optimization problem (CMOP). They treated the number of sub-tasks offloaded between computing nodes as a solution and employed a genetic algorithm to obtain an approximate optimal solution. Wang et al. [27] proposed an effective multi-objective evolutionary algorithm, namely $MOEAD\_MEC$ algorithm, to address the minimization of response time, energy consumption, and cost simultaneously. However, the above works neither consider resource allocation at the function granularity nor take into account the influence of different states of containers on energy consumption.

The energy consumption and service quality issues of serverless edge computing are also worthy of attention [3]. Aslanpour et al. [4] considered the scenario of agricultural IoT, where sensor nodes powered by solar panels utilize a zone-oriented and priority-based function offloading algorithm. This aimed to save energy and increase the number of available nodes. Ko et al. [18] considered the scenario of splitting tasks into sub-tasks and offloading them as functions to serverless providers. To balance the cost and time of parallel execution of functions, they formulated the problem as a constrained Markov decision process and transformed it into a linear programming problem for resolution. Pan et al. [22] transformed the Container Caching jointly with Request Distribution (C2RD) problem into an integer linear programming problem, balancing startup delay costs and container retention costs in the objective function. The paper also indicates that in the multi-node scenario, it can be transformed into a multi-store ski-rental problem. Zheng et al. [31] considered function workflows in edge environments by designing a packet caching strategy and proposed a two-tier dynamic programming algorithm to minimize cold start delays to the maximum extent possible. However, the aforementioned works failed to simultaneously consider both energy consumption and service quality, which are crucial for the serverless edge computing system.

3   System Models

3.1   System Model

The overall system model of the pasture is illustrated in Fig. 1. In a certain area of the pasture, there are n_s homogeneous ESs powered by solar panels. In addition, there are three different types of IoT devices, namely *animal collars*, *barn devices*, and *agro-meteo stations*, each equipped with varying numbers and types of sensors. Among them, *animal collars* are used for locating livestock and measuring their vital signs, *barn devices* are utilized to measure the living environment of livestock, and *agro-meteo stations* are employed to measure the soil and air environmental indicators of the crops used to feed livestock. The positions of *barn devices* and *agro-meteo stations* are fixed, while the location of *animal collars* changes with the movement of livestock. The IoT devices do not possess function computing capabilities but can upload the collected data to the nearest ES. Upon receiving the data, the ES may consider local computation or offloading the data to other ESs for processing.

3.2   Computation Model

Our work is based on a three-tier structure consisting of *ES-container-function*. In our work, both the ESs and containers are homogeneous. The ESs have identical computational capabilities and memory space. Additionally, following [5], we utilize Floating Point Operations per Second (FLOPS) to characterize the computational resources of the ESs. On an ES, multiple containers can be run using its limited resources. And each container has four states: cold start, running, idle, and killed. After a cold start, the container enters the running state, and upon completion of running the function, it transitions to the idle state. If the container does not receive any new tasks within a certain time frame, it is killed, otherwise, it continues to run and transitions back to the idle state after execution. We assume the system employs the same artificial intelligence application, hence each container will occupy the same computational resources $flops_c$ and storage resources mem_c on the ES after cold start. And they require the same cold start time $t^{cs'}$ and maximum idle time $t^{idle'}$. Functions can be computed either after a container cold start or by selecting an idle container through container reuse. Additionally, according to [22], a container can only execute one function at a time.

In addition to the aforementioned computing resources, there are three types of IoT nodes in the pasture, and each node uploads a specific number of task data to the ES at regular intervals, according to [2]. Each task k has a data size s_k, and due to varying computational requirements per unit of data, according to [5], we introduce the concept of Floating Point Operations per task data size, denoted as op_k. Consequently, the computational load of task k is given by $flop_k = s_k \times op_k$, and the computation time is

$$t^k = flop_k / flops_c. \tag{1}$$

3.3   Communication Model

According to the Rayleigh fading channel model [25], the rate of ES_i to transmit data to ES_j can be obtained from

$$R_{i,j} = W_{i,j} \log_2(1 + \frac{p_i h}{D_{i,j}^\omega N}) \tag{2}$$

where $W_{i,j}$ is the transmission channel bandwidth. p_i is the transmission power of ES_i. N and h are the channel white Gaussian noise and the channel fading coefficient, respectively. $D_{i,j}$ is the distance between ES_i and ES_j, and ω is the channel path loss exponent. Therefore, the transmission time of task k from ES_i to ES_j can be obtained as

$$t_{i,j}^k = s_k/R_{i,j}. \tag{3}$$

3.4   Energy Model

Energy Consumption Model. Energy consumption includes non-communication energy consumption and communication energy consumption.

For non-communication energy consumption, Kansal et al. [16] and Khan et al. [14] assumed that the power of ES is a linear function of CPU usage rate, considering a rough fit without taking into account resources such as memory and disk space. Thus for the ith homogeneous server ES_i, its initial battery capacity is b, its computational resource is $flops_{es}$, and we assume that its idle power when not running any containers is P^{idle}, while its maximum power when running containers is P^{max}. Additionally, to illustrate the impact of different states of containers on energy consumption, we introduce the symbol P^{mid}, specifically, when certain containers utilize all computational resources of ES_i and these containers are in the idle state, the power consumption of ES_i is denoted as P^{mid}. ES_i's total lifespan is t_i^{total}. For any container $C_j \in ES_i$, its cold start time is $t^{cs'}$ and execution time is $t_j^{run'}$, while its total lifespan is $t_j^{total'}$. λ represents the cold start energy consumption factor. The total non-communication energy consumption of ES_i can be calculated using the following equation, and the corresponding power breakdown diagram is shown in Fig. 2:

$$
\begin{aligned}
E_i' = {} & P^{idle} t_i^{total} \\
& + (P^{max} - P^{mid}) \sum_{C_j \in ES_i} \frac{flops_c}{flops_{es}} t_j^{run'} \\
& + \lambda(P^{max} - P^{mid}) \sum_{C_j \in ES_i} \frac{flops_c}{flops_{es}} t^{cs'} \\
& + (P^{mid} - P^{idle}) \sum_{C_j \in ES_i} \frac{flops_c}{flops_{es}} t_j^{total'}
\end{aligned}
\tag{4}
$$

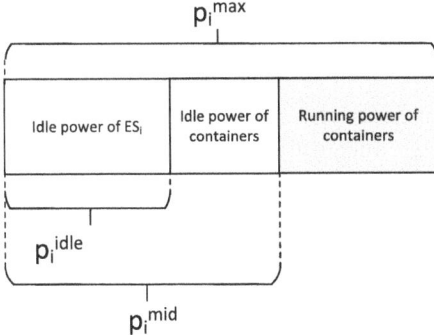

Fig. 2. Power Breakdown Diagram

For communication energy consumption, according to Eq. 3, the energy consumption value for offloading data of task k from ES_i to ES_j can be obtained as $e_{i,j}^k = p_i t_{i,j}^k$. In conclusion, if the offloading set of ES_i is off_i, then the total energy consumption of ES_i is given by

$$E_i^{cons} = E_i^{'} + \sum_{off_i} e_{i,j}^k. \tag{5}$$

Energy Harvesting Model. Since the power of solar panels is proportional to the irradiance [15], we assume that the irradiance at a certain moment t is irr_t. By multiplying with coefficient γ, we can obtain the energy harvesting power $p_t^{harv} = \gamma irr_t$. Then, the energy harvested by ES_i from time t_1 to t_2 is

$$E_i^{harv} = \int_{t_1}^{t_2} p_t^{harv} \, dt \tag{6}$$

3.5   Optimization Objectives

In this paper, we primarily optimize two objectives: energy consumption and service quality. Specifically, since idle power remains constant and does not change with scheduling strategies, we focus on optimizing the dynamic energy consumption of ES, denoted as

$$E_i^{dyna} = E_i^{cons} - P^{idle} t_i^{total}. \tag{7}$$

For service quality, we primarily consider the number of rejected tasks. In our work, tasks will be rejected under two conditions: one is when the energy level of the ES to which the task is uploaded is too low to handle the task; the other is when the ES that needs to compute the task does not have idle containers available, and the remaining computational or memory resources are too small to generate new containers.

4   Energy and Container State Aware Offloading Algorithm

In this section, we propose the *Energy and Container State aware Offloading Algorithm (ECSOA)* and utilize the *NSGA-II* algorithm to obtain optimal parameters, thereby jointly optimizing energy consumption and rejection count.

4.1   ECSOA

As shown in Algorithm 4-1, when ES ES_{rec} receives a function computation request f_k, the *ECSOA* can make offloading decisions for the function, determining whether the function should be offloaded and which ES's container will compute the function. It mainly consists of the following steps:

Algorithm 4-1: Energy and Container State aware Offloading Algorithm (ECSOA)

Data: ES_{rec} that receives function request f_k, list of ESs l_{es}, threshold th_e, th_b, th_r.
Result: The returned result is a triplet $Result(Bool_{loc}, ES_{tgt}, Con_{des})$, where $Bool_{loc}$ indicates whether the f_k is computed locally. And f_k needs to be computed by the container Con_{des} of ES ES_{tgt}.

1 $cands_{es} \leftarrow check(l_{es}, ES_{rec}, th_b, th_r)$;
2 **if** $cands_{es}$ *is not null and* ES_{rec} *has no idle container* **then**
3      $ES_{tgt} \leftarrow select(ES_{rec}, f_k, l_{es}, cands_{es}, th_e)$;
4   **if** ES_{tgt} *is* ES_{rec} **then**
5          $Bool_{loc} \leftarrow true$;
6   **else**
7          $Bool_{loc} \leftarrow false$;
8   **end**
9 **else**
10     $Bool_{loc} \leftarrow true$;
11     $ES_{tgt} \leftarrow ES_{rec}$;
12 **end**
13 **if** ES_{tgt} *has an idle container* **then**
14   Find the last killed container Con_{last} among the idle containers of ES_{tgt} ;
    // warm start
15   Return $Result(Bool_{loc}, ES_{tgt}, Con_{last})$;
16 **else**
    // cold start
17   Return $Result(Bool_{loc}, ES_{tgt}, null)$;
18 **end**

---

1. *ECSOA* checks each ES and obtains a list of candidate ESs that can be offloaded and used for computation, referred to as $cands_{es}$.

2. If the list $cands_{es}$ is empty, it indicates that there is no ES available for offloading, so the function can only be computed locally. Additionally, if ES_{rec} has idle containers, container reuse (warm start) ensures that the function is not rejected while consuming less energy. Therefore, the function will also be computed locally. Hence, only when neither of these two conditions are established, do we consider invoking *select* to determine where the function should be offloaded.

3. The *select* will choose the suitable target ES ES_{tgt} in $cands_{es}$ while ensuring that the energy consumption for offloading to other ES is not excessively high.

4. After obtaining the ES_{tgt}, if it has idle containers, we choose the container that was killed last for reuse, this strategy ensures that the remaining idle containers are killed earlier, thus guaranteeing lower energy consumption. If ES_{tgt} does not have idle containers, then we initiate a cold start to create a new container.

4.2   Check Offloadable ESs

We define the conditions under which an ES cannot accept function offloading requests from other ESs. For *check* in Algorithm 4-1, it iterates over each ES, and if ES_i satisfies all of the following conditions, it is considered eligible for being offloaded and computing:

1. The ratio of remaining battery capacity to battery capacity for ES_i is greater than the battery threshold th_b. This condition ensures that ES_i has sufficient battery capacity for computation.

2. The utilization rates of both computation and storage resources are less than th_r, or ES_i currently has idle containers. This is because when the resource utilization of an ES is too high and the ES has no idle containers, upon receiving an offloading request, the ES cannot reuse containers and lacks the resources required for cold start, thus it cannot handle the function.

Algorithm 4-2: Check Offloadable ESs

Data: $l_{es}, ES_{rec}, th_b, th_r$.

Result: List of ESs $cands_{es}$ that can be offloaded.

1 $cands_{es} \leftarrow null$;

2 **foreach** ES_i in l_{es} **do**

3   **if** ES_i *satisfies item 1 and item 2* **then**

4 | Add ES_i to the list $cands_{es}$;

5   **end**

6 **end**

7 Return $cands_{es}$;

4.3 Select Target ES

As shown in Algorithm 4-3 (*select* in Algorithm 4-1), this algorithm will choose the target ES ES_{tgt} in $cands_{es}$ with the minimum energy consumption e, while ensuring that the energy consumption for offloading to ES_{tgt} is not excessively high. e includes computation energy, transmission energy $e_{rec,i}^k$, and cold-start energy e_{cs}. Since homogeneous machines have the same computational power and time, the computation energy can be omitted in the comparison.

It is worth noting that in the scenario where the candidate is ES_{rec} and it has no available resources, we aim to offload the function to another ES, thus, we set e of ES_{rec} to positive infinity. However, this may lead the algorithm to prioritize offloading the function to other ESs, even if it incurs significant energy consumption. Therefore, we introduce the threshold th_e to address this issue. That is, if $e > th_e$, the function f_k will not be offloaded to that ES. Moreover, the algorithm will reject this function if there is no ES with $e \leq th_e$.

Algorithm 4-3: Select Target ES

Data: $ES_{rec}, f_k, l_{es}, cands_{es}, th_e$.
Result: ES_{tgt}.

1 **foreach** ES_i in $cands_{es}$ **do**
2   **if** ES_i is ES_{rec} **then**
3   **if** *The resources of ES_i are fully utilized* **then**
4             $e \leftarrow +\infty$;
5   **else**
6             $e \leftarrow e_{cs}$;
7   **end**
8   **else**
9   **if** ES_i has an idle container **then**
10             $e \leftarrow e_{rec,i}^k$;
11   **else**
12             $e \leftarrow e_{cs} + e_{rec,i}^k$;
13   **end**
14   **if** $e > th_e$ **then**
15   continue;
16   **end**
17   **end**
18   Select the ES_{tgt} with the minimum e;
19 **end**
20 Return ES_{tgt};

4.4 NSGA-II

We use the *NSGA-II* algorithm to search for better solutions, and the solution is denoted as $\phi = \{th_e, th_b, th_r\}$. We utilize tournament selection as the selection operator, randomly choosing two individuals from the population and conducting a binary tournament. The crossover probability is p_c, and it is performed using a two-point crossover method, where two crossover points are randomly selected in the solution vector, and partial gene exchange is then conducted. Subsequently, we perform polynomial mutation [9] with a probability p_m. The update formula for the mutation operator is as follows,

$$v_k' = v_k + \delta(u_k - l_k)$$
$$\delta = \begin{cases} [2u + (1 - 2u)(1 - \delta_1)^{\eta_m+1}]^{\frac{1}{\eta_m+1}} - 1 & u \leqslant 0.5 \\ 1 - [2(1 - u) + 2(u - 0.5)(1 - \delta_2)^{\eta_m+1}]^{\frac{1}{\eta_m+1}} & u > 0.5 \end{cases}$$

where v_k' and v_k are the mutated and original element values, respectively, u_k and l_k are the upper and lower bounds, u is a random number from the interval $[0, 1]$, η_m is the mutation distribution parameter, and $\delta_1 = (v_k - l_k)/(u_k - l_k)$, $\delta_2 = (u_k - v_k)/(u_k - l_k)$. We set the population size to $|\Phi|$ and iterate the algorithm for ε rounds to obtain the Pareto optimal solutions.

5 Experiment

5.1 Experiment Setting

Our experiments use real-time simulation, which relies on a time-based minimum heap. Its principle involves popping the action that occurs at the minimum time from the heap each time, such as function offloading, container cold start, etc., then executing that action, and adding the next action to the heap based on logic. The update of energy consumption occurs before executing the action to ensure that the battery levels of each ES are correct at each decision point.

We assume that the pasture is a square with a side length of 1000 m. And we select the *Sandy Bridge (Xeon 2670)* as the physical host model for ES. The energy consumption and computational performance parameters of this host are referenced from [10,16] respectively. We utilize data from the XIHE Energy Meteorological Big Data Platform [28] and select the irradiance data for 24 h in Nanjing on January 3, 2023, for our experiment. Specific parameters related to tasks, resources and *NSGA-II* are listed separately in Table 1, Table 2 and Table 3. For the application of the *NSGA-II* algorithm, we divide the dataset into a training set and a testing set. Firstly, we use the training set to train superior solutions, then we evaluate the performance of these solutions using the testing set.

Table 1. Task parameters

IoT Node	Nodes Number	Tasks per node	Interval	Task Data Size	Operations
Animal Collar	80	4	5 (min)	5–35 (MB)	1G (FLOP/MB)
Barn Device	3	6	10 (min)	20–45 (MB)	5G (FLOP/MB)
Agro-meteo Station	3	7	15 (min)	20–50 (MB)	7G (FLOP/MB)

Table 2. Resource parameters

Parameter	Value
n_s	6
$flops_{es}$, $flops_c$(G FLOPS)	251.7, 10
mem_{es}, mem_c(GB)	384, 15
$t^{cs'}$, $t^{idle'}$ (s)	10, 300
P^{idle}, P^{mid}, P^{max}(W)	55, 57, 105
b(J)	50000
$W_{i,j}$(MHz)	10^7
p_i(W)	1
ω, h, N	2, 10^{-3}, 10^{-9}

5.2   Comparison Algorithms

- **LOCAL**: All tasks received by the ES will be computed locally. If the ES cannot process the task due to insufficient battery power or resources, the task will be rejected.
- **LOWRES**: Upon receiving a task, if the ES can compute it locally, it will do so; otherwise, the task will be offloaded to the ES with the lowest resource utilization rate that can compute the task. If no other ES can handle the task, it will be rejected.
- **EAFS**: Implemented based on the *Energy-Aware Function Scheduling* algorithm described in [4].

Table 3. NSGA-II parameters

Parameter	Value
η_m	1
$|\Phi|$	30
ε	50
p_c, p_m	0.8, 0.4
$l_k^{th_c}$, $u_k^{th_c}$ (J)	0, 20
$l_k^{th_b}$, $u_k^{th_b}$	0, 0.4
$l_k^{th_r}$, $u_k^{th_r}$	0, 0.4

– **SCORE**: In [26], the algorithm selects the ES with the highest score for offloading each time. This score is determined by the utilization rates of computational resources, memory resources, and offloading transmission time.

5.3   Performance Analysis

The experimental results on energy consumption and rejection for the five algorithms are shown in Fig. 3. A group of points with the same color in the bottom left corner of the graph corresponds to the solutions generated by *ECSOA* combined with the *NSGA-II* algorithm. The objective function values of these solutions and the solution generated by the *LOWRES* algorithm, collectively form the Pareto optimal frontier.

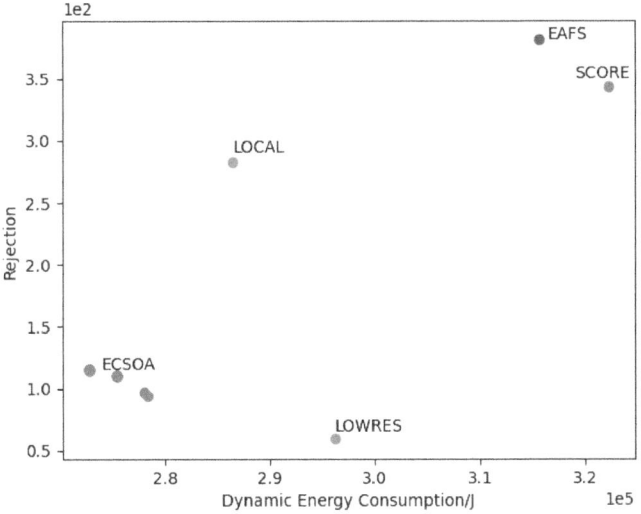

Fig. 3. Solutions to the bi-objective problem

Next, we analyze the kernel density curves of the Pareto optimal solution sets obtained through *NSGA-II* for three different thresholds, as depicted in Fig. 4. The results indicate that the values of th_e are concentrated around 12, which is greater than the cold start energy consumption, and the excess energy compared to the cold start energy can be utilized for function data offloading. The values of th_b are primarily distributed between 0 and 0.15. This indicates that the threshold for battery capacity should not be set too high, as it may accelerate the depletion of energy in ES with low battery levels, consequently increasing the rejection counts. The values of th_r are distributed across the entire parameter range we specified, indicating that energy consumption and rejection are not highly sensitive to the resource threshold. To identify the cause of this

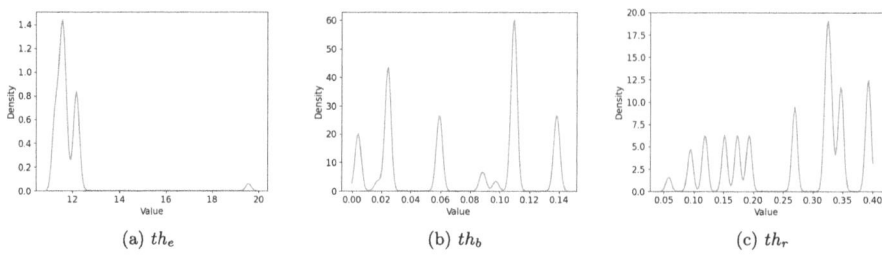

Fig. 4. The kernel density curves of the three thresholds

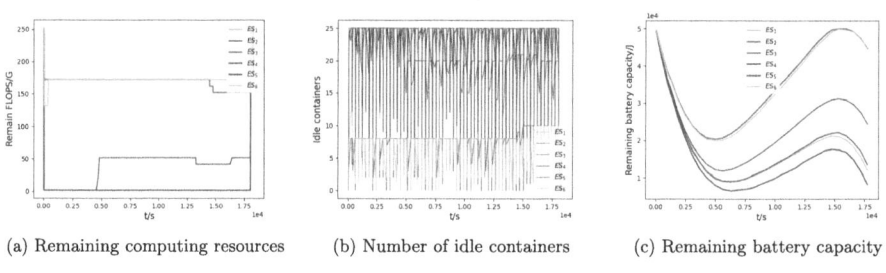

(a) Remaining computing resources   (b) Number of idle containers   (c) Remaining battery capacity

Fig. 5. Information of each ES in *ECSOA*

phenomenon, we select one solution $\phi = \{11.700, 0.054, 0.052\}$ from the Pareto optimal solution set, and we characterize the information of all ESs in the system when using the *ECSOA*, as shown in Fig. 5. Although Fig. 5a indicates that the remaining computing resources of most ESs are relatively scarce, Fig. 5b shows that most of the time, ESs have idle containers. Therefore, a large number of container reuses reduce the sensitivity of the algorithm to th_r.

To better interpret the algorithm results, we have compiled statistics on the number of cold starts and offloading for different algorithms, as shown in Fig. 6. In theory, the algorithm that rejects fewer functions tends to require more energy for computation. However, the *ECSOA* algorithm achieves the lowest energy consumption while rejecting fewer functions, indicating its significant effectiveness in reducing dynamic energy consumption. On the one hand, the algorithm minimizes cold starts to the lowest among the five algorithms by reusing containers as much as possible. On the other hand, it effectively offloads lots of functions to more suitable ESs, resulting in better performance. For the *LOWRES* algorithm, since it offloads function data to the ES with the lowest resource utilization whenever local resources are full, it can minimize the number of function rejections by offloading and cold starts. However, it does not consider whether the transmission energy consumption is excessive or whether container reuse is available, thus leading to more energy consumption. The *LOCAL* algorithm, due to its restriction on offloading, inevitably results in more function rejections. However, it also implies no transmission energy consumption, leading to lower energy consumption. The essence of the *EAFS* algorithm is to decide function offloading based on the remaining battery levels of each ES. For instance, when the local battery level is high, priority is given to local computation, while insufficient battery levels prompt consideration of offloading tasks to ESs with higher battery levels. However, a high remaining battery level does not necessarily imply that the ES has sufficient computational resources. Moreover, the energy consumption resulting from frequent data transmission when battery levels are low may not be lower than that of local computation. Therefore, *EAFS* overlooks the utilization rate of computational resources and the energy consumption associated with transmission, resulting in relatively high rejection counts and energy consumption. The *SCORE* algorithm prioritizes function computation on the ES with ample remaining computational and storage resources and minimal transmission time. However, this algorithm has the highest number of cold starts and offloading, indicating that many functions are offloaded to ESs without idle containers, resulting in additional energy consumption due to cold starts and offloads compared to local computation.

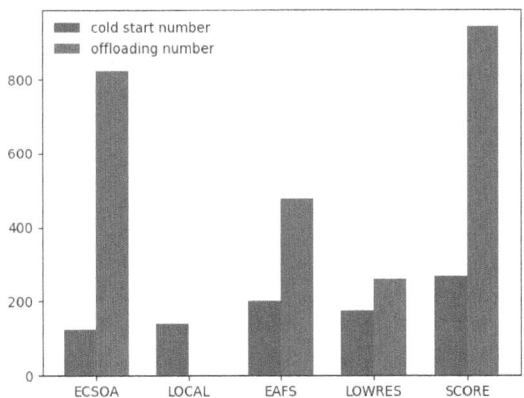

Fig. 6. The number of cold starts and offloading

Figure 7a and Fig. 7b respectively display the overall remaining battery levels and the total dynamic energy consumption of all ESs over time. In Fig. 7a, the curve variations are determined by the combined effects of charging power and power consumption. The solar charging power initially increases and then decreases over time. When the charging power exceeds the power consumption, the curve rises; conversely, it declines. In Fig. 7b, the dynamic energy consumption shows roughly linear growth, and its slope is slightly higher than $P_{mid} - P_{idle}$. This is because the sensors send data at intervals, and the computation time for functions is not long, resulting in containers being idle for most of the time. The decrease in slope towards the end of the straight line is due to no new request arriving, so the containers change into the idle state, thus gradually reducing the system's dynamic energy consumption rate to 0. The results from both graphs indicate that the *ECSOA* algorithm consistently outperforms in terms of energy consumption.

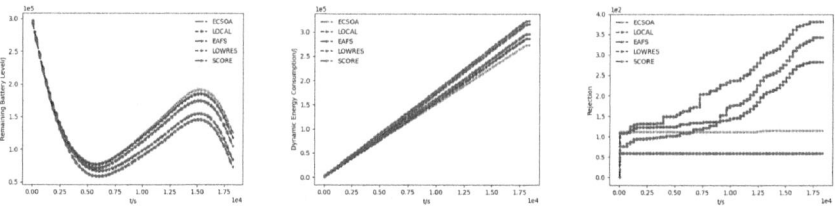

(a) The remaining battery level over time (b) The dynamic energy consumption over time (c) The function rejection count over time

Fig. 7. Metrics over time

Figure 7c illustrates the curve of the total rejection count of all ESs over time. It can be observed that the *ECSOA* algorithm rejects a certain number of functions at the beginning of the system startup, but similar to the results of the *LOWRES* algorithm, there is no significant increase in rejection count thereafter. This indicates that the *ECSOA* algorithm effectively reduces the number of function rejections through offloading.

6   Conclusion

In this paper, we focus on the scenario of remote pastures with multiple fixed and mobile sensors, along with multiple solar-powered serverless edge servers. We propose the system model, computation model, transmission model, and energy model. We believe that these models are not only applicable to this paper but also have generality for other serverless edge computing scenarios. Addressing the issues of insufficient battery power and computational resources, we take into account the different states of containers and the energy consumption resulting from various scenarios. So we propose the *ECSOA* and then optimize its parameters using genetic algorithms. The experimental results show that our proposed algorithm exhibits significant advantages in reducing the system's dynamic energy consumption and minimizing the number of function rejections. Finally, we analyze the results and reasons for different algorithms. In addition to the above work, we believe that in this scenario, considering the joint request offloading and container caching problem, as well as the offloading problem under heterogeneous servers or heterogeneous containers, are all worthy of further research in the future.

Acknowledgements. This work is supported by the National Key Research and Development Program of China (No. 2022YFB3305500), the National Natural Science Foundation of China (Nos. 62102080), Natural Science Foundation of Jiangsu Province (No. BK20210204).

References

1. Abas, K., Obraczka, K., Miller, L.: Solar-powered, wireless smart camera network: an IoT solution for outdoor video monitoring. Comput. Commun. **118**, 217–233 (2018)
2. Alonso, R.S., Sittón-Candanedo, I., Óscar García, Prieto, J., Rodríguez-González, S.: An intelligent edge-IoT platform for monitoring livestock and crops in a dairy farming scenario. Ad Hoc Netw. **98**, 102047 (2020)
3. Aslanpour, M.S., et al.: Serverless edge computing: vision and challenges. In: Proceedings of the 2021 Australasian Computer Science Week Multiconference, ACSW 2021. Association for Computing Machinery, New York (2021)
4. Aslanpour, M.S., Toosi, A.N., Cheema, M.A., Gaire, R.: Energy-aware resource scheduling for serverless edge computing. In: 2022 22nd IEEE International Symposium on Cluster, Cloud and Internet Computing (CCGrid), pp. 190–199 (2022)
5. Bozorgchenani, A., Mashhadi, F., Tarchi, D., Salinas Monroy, S.A.: Multi-objective computation sharing in energy and delay constrained mobile edge computing environments. IEEE Trans. Mob. Comput. **20**(10), 2992–3005 (2021)
6. Cambra, C., Díaz, J.R., Lloret, J.: Deployment and performance study of an ad hoc network protocol for intelligent video sensing in precision agriculture. In: Garcia Pineda, M., Lloret, J., Papavassiliou, S., Ruehrup, S., Westphall, C.B. (eds.) ADHOC-NOW 2014. LNCS, vol. 8629, pp. 165–175. Springer, Heidelberg (2015). https://doi.org/10.1007/978-3-662-46338-3_14
7. Cassel, G.A.S., Rodrigues, V.F., da Rosa Righi, R., Bez, M.R., Nepomuceno, A.C., André da Costa, C.: Serverless computing for internet of things: a systematic literature review. Future Gener. Comput. Syst. **128**, 299–316 (2022)
8. Cong, P., Zhou, J., Li, L., Cao, K., Wei, T., Li, K.: A survey of hierarchical energy optimization for mobile edge computing: a perspective from end devices to the cloud. ACM Comput. Surv. **53**(2) (2020)
9. Deb, K., Goyal, M., et al.: A combined genetic adaptive search (geneAS) for engineering design. Comput. Sci. Inform. **26**, 30–45 (1996)
10. GadgetVersus: Intel sandy bridge GFLOPS performance (2024). https://gadgetversus.com/processor/intel-sandy-bridge-gflops-performance/
11. Islam, A., Debnath, A., Ghose, M., Chakraborty, S.: A survey on task offloading in multi-access edge computing. J. Syst. Architect. **118**, 102225 (2021)
12. Kalyani, Y., Collier, R.: A systematic survey on the role of cloud, fog, and edge computing combination in smart agriculture. Sensors **21**(17), 5922 (2021)
13. Kamilaris, A., Kartakoullis, A., Prenafeta-Boldú, F.X.: A review on the practice of big data analysis in agriculture. Comput. Electron. Agric. **143**, 23–37 (2017)
14. Kansal, A., Zhao, F., Liu, J., Kothari, N., Bhattacharya, A.A.: Virtual machine power metering and provisioning. In: Proceedings of the 1st ACM Symposium on Cloud Computing, SoCC 2010, pp. 39–50. Association for Computing Machinery, New York (2010)
15. Karimiafshar, A., Hashemi, M.R., Heidarpour, M.R., Toosi, A.N.: Effective utilization of renewable energy sources in fog computing environment via frequency and modulation level scaling. IEEE Internet Things J. **7**(11), 10912–10921 (2020)
16. Khan, A.A., Zakarya, M., Buyya, R., Khan, R., Khan, M., Rana, O.: An energy and performance aware consolidation technique for containerized datacenters. IEEE Trans. Cloud Comput. **9**(4), 1305–1322 (2021)
17. Kjorveziroski, V., Filiposka, S., Trajkovik, V.: IoT serverless computing at the edge: a systematic mapping review. Computers **10**(10), 130 (2021)

18. Ko, H., Pack, S., Leung, V.C.M.: Performance optimization of serverless computing for latency-guaranteed and energy-efficient task offloading in energy-harvesting industrial IoT. IEEE Internet Things J. **10**(3), 1897–1907 (2023)
19. Long, T., Ma, Y., Xia, Y., Xiao, X., Peng, Q., Zhao, J.: A mobility-aware and fault-tolerant service offloading method in mobile edge computing. In: 2022 IEEE International Conference on Web Services (ICWS), pp. 67–72 (2022)
20. Muangprathub, J., Boonnam, N., Kajornkasirat, S., Lekbangpong, N., Wanich-sombat, A., Nillaor, P.: IoT and agriculture data analysis for smart farm. Comput. Electron. Agric. **156**, 467–474 (2019)
21. O'Grady, M., Langton, D., O'Hare, G.: Edge computing: a tractable model for smart agriculture? Artif. Intell. Agric. **3**, 42–51 (2019)
22. Pan, L., Wang, L., Chen, S., Liu, F.: Retention-aware container caching for serverless edge computing. In: IEEE INFOCOM 2022 - IEEE Conference on Computer Communications, pp. 1069–1078. IEEE Press (2022)
23. Sadowski, S., Spachos, P.: Solar-powered smart agricultural monitoring system using internet of things devices. In: 2018 IEEE 9th Annual Information Technology, Electronics and Mobile Communication Conference (IEMCON), pp. 18–23 (2018)
24. Services, A.W.: Aws IoT greengrass ML inference (2024). https://aws.amazon.com/greengrass/ml/?nc1=h_ls
25. Sklar, B.: Rayleigh fading channels in mobile digital communication systems. I. characterization. IEEE Commun. Mag. **35**(9), 136–146 (1997)
26. Wang, J., Chen, H., Zhou, F., Sun, M., Huang, Z., Zhang, Z.: A-DECS: enhanced collaborative edge-edge data storage service for edge computing with adaptive prediction. Comput. Netw. **193**, 108087 (2021)
27. Wang, P., Li, K., Xiao, B., Li, K.: Multiobjective optimization for joint task offloading, power assignment, and resource allocation in mobile edge computing. IEEE Internet Things J. **9**(14), 11737–11748 (2022)
28. XIHE: XIHE-energy (2023). https://xihe-energy.com/
29. Zhang, T., Xu, Y., Loo, J., Yang, D., Xiao, L.: Joint computation and communication design for UAV-assisted mobile edge computing in IoT. IEEE Trans. Industr. Inf. **16**(8), 5505–5516 (2020)
30. Zhang, X., Cao, Z., Dong, W.: Overview of edge computing in the agricultural internet of things: key technologies, applications, challenges. IEEE Access **8**, 141748–141761 (2020)
31. Zheng, S., Liu, B., Lin, W., Ye, X., Li, K.: A package-aware scheduling strategy for edge serverless functions based on multi-stage optimization. Futur. Gener. Comput. Syst. **144**, 105–116 (2023)

Understanding the Use of Collaboration Tables in Crisis Response

Yubo Shu[1], Peng Zhang[1(✉)], Hansu Gu[2], Wenjia Liu[1], Xinyue Yu[1], Tun Lu[1], and Ning Gu[1]

[1] Fudan University, Shanghai, China
{ybshu20,zhangpeng_,lutun,ninggu}@fudan.edu.cn,
{liuwj21,yuxy22}@m.fudan.edu.cn
[2] Seattle, USA
hansug@acm.org

Abstract. Social applications like social media and collaboration platforms have been essential mediums for crisis response. Recently, we have observed that the online collaborative table, originally designed for online office collaboration, have been transformed into a new platform for crisis response. However, since these online tables were not specifically designed for crisis management, the patterns of how they are utilized in crisis responding context remain unclear. For this problem, we collected online tables used in four crisis events and made a quantitative analysis to explore the characteristics of interaction-pattern, usage-pattern, and role-pattern in the new crisis response applications. The results suggest that the online collaboration table plays an important role in seeking and providing support, verifying the authenticity of the information, and tracking the latest events. Diverse user roles were also uncovered in the collaborative table-based crisis response scenario, such as help seekers, leaders and moderators. Based on these results, we propose insights into the design of crisis-oriented collaboration tables to improve the ability to urgent respond in a crisis.

Keywords: crisis informatics · collaboration platforms · online tables

1 Introduction

Researchers have noted an increasing trend of using social applications for crisis response. For example, after the 2017 Mexico earthquake, 792,665 users turned to Twitter for disaster updates [5]. During COVID-19 outbreak from December 2019 to May 2020, 134,337 Wikipedia users made 973,940 edits to 4,238 virus-related articles to share updates and advice [9]. Despite not being originally designed for crisis response, the large user base and real-time information sharing capabilities of these platforms make them valuable for crisis management [21].

Analyzing how people use social applications for crisis response has become a key research focus, divided into two categories: social media and online collaboration platforms. Yan Qu [16] analyzes microblog content from the Sichuan earthquake, and Reuter [18] examines Twitter user roles after the 2011 "Super Outbreak." Sophia B. Liu [11] studies the use of the iCoast annotation tool for hurricane impacts, and Brian C. Keegan [8] investigates Wikipedia revisions after the 2011 earthquake and Fukushima meltdown. Both categories research three patterns: 1) Interaction-pattern, analyzing user-platform interactions; 2) Usage-pattern [20], examining platform functions during crises; 3) Role-pattern [3], understanding user engagement and roles on the platforms.

Recently, online collaboration tables have begun to be used for crisis response. For instance, during the severe rainstorm and flooding in Henan Province, China, on 20 July 2021, a Tencent Docs collaboration table[1] was created. It received 53,428 edits from 4,084 people and over 660 million views, playing a significant role in disseminating information about trapped people, relief goods, rescue teams, and emotional support. Despite its importance, the crisis response modes-including interaction, usage, and role patterns-of this emerging platform remain unknown. Specifically: (1) How do people organize and operate collaboration tables during a crisis? (2) What content is generated in these tables? (3) What roles exist in this new crisis response application?

Researching crisis response patterns in collaboration tables presents several challenges. First, extracting user operation details is complex due to varied operations like inserting text, copying, pasting, and version rollback, especially in platforms like Tencent Docs where operations are intermixed. Second, analyzing semi-structured user-generated content requires considering both text and table structure, but existing methods primarily focus on text features. Third, analyzing user roles is difficult due to user anonymity in collaboration tables, unlike social media where profiles provide user characteristics. To address these challenges, we collected tables used in different crises (flood, typhoon, and epidemic) with varying scales (less or more than 1,000 collaborators) and performed a quantitative analysis to study interaction, usage, and role patterns.

Our analysis revealed three phases of collaboration table use in crisis response: initial, development, and fading. Collaboration tables are crucial for seeking and providing support, verifying information, and tracking events. We identified 11 user roles, including help seekers, leaders, and moderators. These findings suggest the need for group functionality to accelerate the initial phase, manage user permissions, and integrate with social media during crises. Our contributions include:

1. Collect and process records data on a new scenario where online collaboration tables are used for crisis response.
2. Investigating the crisis response modes of collaboration tables, we identified characteristics of interaction, usage, and role patterns.
3. Based on our findings, we propose insights for designing crisis response-oriented collaborative tables.

---

[1] The link of the collaboration table for disaster response in Henan: https://docs.qq.com/sheet/DUG9pRWRsSlRyeHVn?tab=m3zysg (In the table, people's privacy information has been removed by volunteers after the crisis.).

2   Related Work

Crisis Response in Social Applications. Crisis informatics examines how information and communication technologies (ICT) can respond to crises [15,19,22]. With ICT development, various social applications, especially social media and online collaboration platforms, are used in crises [2,5]. Reuter et al. [20] reviewed 30 crisis response cases on social media over 15 years, identifying six types of information: sympathy and emotional support, donations and volunteering, caution and advice, infrastructure and utilities, and other useful information. Kaufhold et al. [6,18] identified six roles in social media-based crisis response: helper, reporter, retweeter, repeater, reader, and moderator. Research on crisis response in online collaboration platforms mainly focuses on Wikipedia. Keegan et al. [7] found that many people used Wikipedia to search for and share information after a crisis. Another study [8] examined user activity on Wikipedia following the Fukushima nuclear disaster. Recent research analyzed article dynamics, revisions, and user activity during different stages of COVID-19 [9], revealing how external events drove edits and how revisions spread. In summary, previous studies mainly focused on interaction, usage, and role patterns in crisis response.

Online Collaboration. Exploring how people collaborate has long been a focus for researchers. Since the 1990s, many systems supporting collaborative editing have been developed and tested [1]. With advancements in collaborative editing and cloud computing technologies, platforms like Google Docs and Tencent Docs have become popular for online collaboration. Wang et al. [24] developed a tool to visualize collaborative edits in Google Docs by tracking edit positions and times. Olson et al. [13] analyzed how students used Google Docs for school assignments, finding that leadership and balanced co-editing improved collaboration quality. Le et al. [10] studied the temporal and spatial characteristics of collaborative editing in online documents, noting higher efficiency when users collaborated. These studies primarily investigate user roles and editing patterns, typically involving fewer than ten collaborators [10,23]. In contrast, our work involves a larger number of users (e.g., 4084 editors on a collaboration table), presenting greater challenges in modeling and analyzing user behavior.

3   Methodology

3.1   Data Corpus

Data Collection. Tencent Docs is an online platform similar to Google Docs and Sheets, allowing users to edit documents and tables synchronously on PC and mobile devices. Recently, it has become essential for managing crisis-related activities and information exchange about distressed persons, material assistance, and damage warnings. We collected data from four crisis response collaboration tables during the following events, listed in ascending order of operation count:

1. COVID-19 Lockdown of Fudan University (Fudan): Lockdown at Fudan University, Shanghai, on November 25, 2021, due to the epidemic.
2. Yuyao Typhoon (Yuyao): Typhoon struck Yuyao City, China, on July 27, 2021.
3. COVID-19 Lockdown of Zhejiang University (Zhejiang): Lockdown at Zhejiang University on November 25, 2021, due to reported cases.
4. Henan Rainstorm (Henan): Severe rainstorm in Henan, China, on July 20, 2021.

The four crises differ in location, urgency level, duration, time range, and total operations. These characteristics enhance the representativeness of our study. The basic attributes of these collaboration tables are summarized in Table 1.

Table 1. The basic attributes of collaboration tables under the crises.

	CrisisType	UsersCount	OperationsCount
Fudan	Epidemic	532	3032
Yuyao	Typhoon	449	4298
Zhejiang	Epidemic	2530	7690
Henan	Storm Flood	4084	53428

Build Data Corpus. To perform a quantitative analysis of the data, we need to know the detailed information in each operation, such as the time of editing and the operation type. We identified the primary operation types in the table and extracted the detailed attributes for each type. Finally, we constructed our dataset, consisting mainly of the following features:

1) User id: Unique identifier of each user in the table.
2) Operation id: Unique identifier of an operation.
3) Operation time: The time when the operation occurred.
4) Edited sheet: The sheet where the operation occurred.
5) Operation version: The version of the table where the operation occurred.
6) Operation categories: There are 50+ categories in tables, such as adding cells, copying rows.
7) The starting row: For operations on an area, it indicates the coordinates of the first row.
8) The starting column: For operations on an area, it indicates the coordinates of the first column.
9) The ending row: For operations on an area, it indicates the coordinates of the last row.
10) The ending column: For operations on an area, it indicates the coordinates of the last column.
11) Content: The text, links, images, and other information brought by the operation.

3.2 Operation Analysis Method

To get a deeper insight into the complex operations, we categorized the operations into several groups by content characteristics. First, operations are initially classified into content-oriented and non-content-oriented. Content-oriented operations: Inserting, deleting, or modifying the content of collaboration tables. Non-content-oriented operations: All the other operations that do not belong to content-oriented operations are defined as non-content-oriented, including formatting-related and table structure-related revisions. We further categorized content-oriented and non-content-oriented operations into five fine-grained levels according to the involved elements. **Cell-level:** The operation is to edit only one cell, e.g., inserting text into a cell. **Row-level:** The operation is to edit one or more rows, e.g., adding a new row. **Column-level:** The operation is to edit one or more columns, adding a new column. **Area-level:** The operation is to edit a rectangular area (rows and columns) in the table. **Table-level:** The operation is to edit the whole table, e.g., changing the table's name.

Besides operations, we also extracted the proximity relationships among different operations. We define the proximity relationships of operations according to edit positions and edit time [12]. Two operations have a proximity relationship if they meet the following three conditions: 1) The two operations are conducted by different users; 2) The two operations occur in the same sheet and have overlapping cells; 3) The time gap between the two operations does not exceed one version interval (6 min). For example, after user A enters a line of a distress message, user B then helps to modify the format and highlight the status of the trapped person. These two operations thus form a proximity relationship.

3.3   Content Analysis Method

To understand the characteristics of user-generated content in the crisis response collaboration tables, we have analyzed the content of each cell by considering the structural characteristics of the tables. The following gives our detailed content analysis procedures. **Table Head Extraction:** A column's name indicates its content, and the combination of column names reflects the sheet's functional design. Therefore, we extract the column names of each sheet. **Content Complement:** After extracting column names, we concatenate each cell's content with the corresponding column name to understand the user's message. For example, users might enter "Yes" or "No" under columns like "Urgent or not" or "Verified or not." This helps us infer whether a situation is urgent or if the information is verified. Additionally, since each row typically represents a record, we organize user-generated content by row. **Annotation Definition:** We identified a specific column for user annotations. These annotations fall into three categories: information verification, urgency, and rescue status. For example, in the "Unrescued People's Information" table from the Henan rainstorm, users marked whether a rescue message was "Verified or not," indicating its authenticity.

4   Results

4.1   Operation Perspective

To understand user operation patterns in the collaboration table, we first examine the overall distribution of operations over time. Figure 1 shows an initial spike in edits, followed by a decrease, a general rise, and then a gradual decline, with low and fluctuating activity in the later stages.

Cell, Row, Column, Area, Table Level. Figure 2 depicts the accumulative distribution of operations at the cell-level, row-level, column-level, area-level and

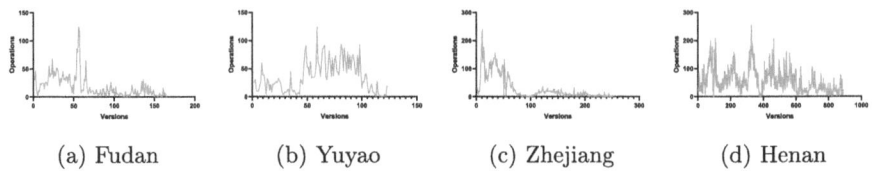

(a) Fudan   (b) Yuyao   (c) Zhejiang   (d) Henan

Fig. 1. The overall distributions of operations over versions in four crises.

table-level. The results show that, in all cases, there are more cell-level operations in the collaboration tables than operations at other levels. Figure 3 shows the process of creating, editing, and deleting sheets during crises. Initially, users organize sheets for different scenarios, with the first sheets focused on helping affected individuals. For example, the first sheets are "Rescue Needs" for the Henan rainstorm and "Seek for Help Information" for the Yuyao typhoon. During the lockdowns at Fudan and Zhejiang Universities, the first sheets are "11.25 Material Needs and Sharing" and "Campus Supply and Demand." These initial sheets attract numerous operations.

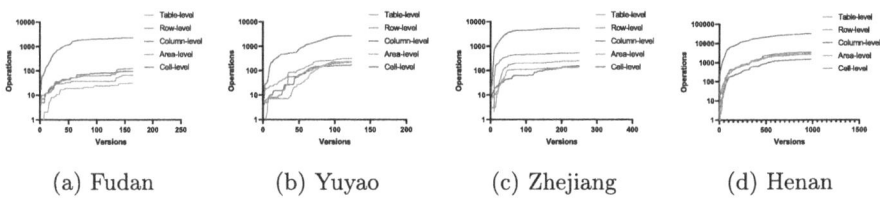

(a) Fudan   (b) Yuyao   (c) Zhejiang   (d) Henan

Fig. 2. The accumulative distribution of operations at different levels.

Content and Format. Figure 4 shows that both content-oriented and non-content-oriented operations in the four crisis response tables follow similar trends, with content-oriented operations generally being more numerous. Figure 5 indicates that non-content-oriented operations dominate at the table, row, column, and area levels, while content-oriented operations are more at the cell level.

4.2   Content Perspective

We analyzed user-generated content in the tables using topic modeling and examined the three types of content annotations in the crisis response tables.

Topic Analysis. Using the Latent Dirichlet Allocation (LDA) model, we extracted content topics based on the highest coherence value: four for Zhejiang and Yuyao, five for Fudan, and eighteen for Henan. We interpreted these topics using corresponding keywords and sentences. Detailed results are in Appendix:

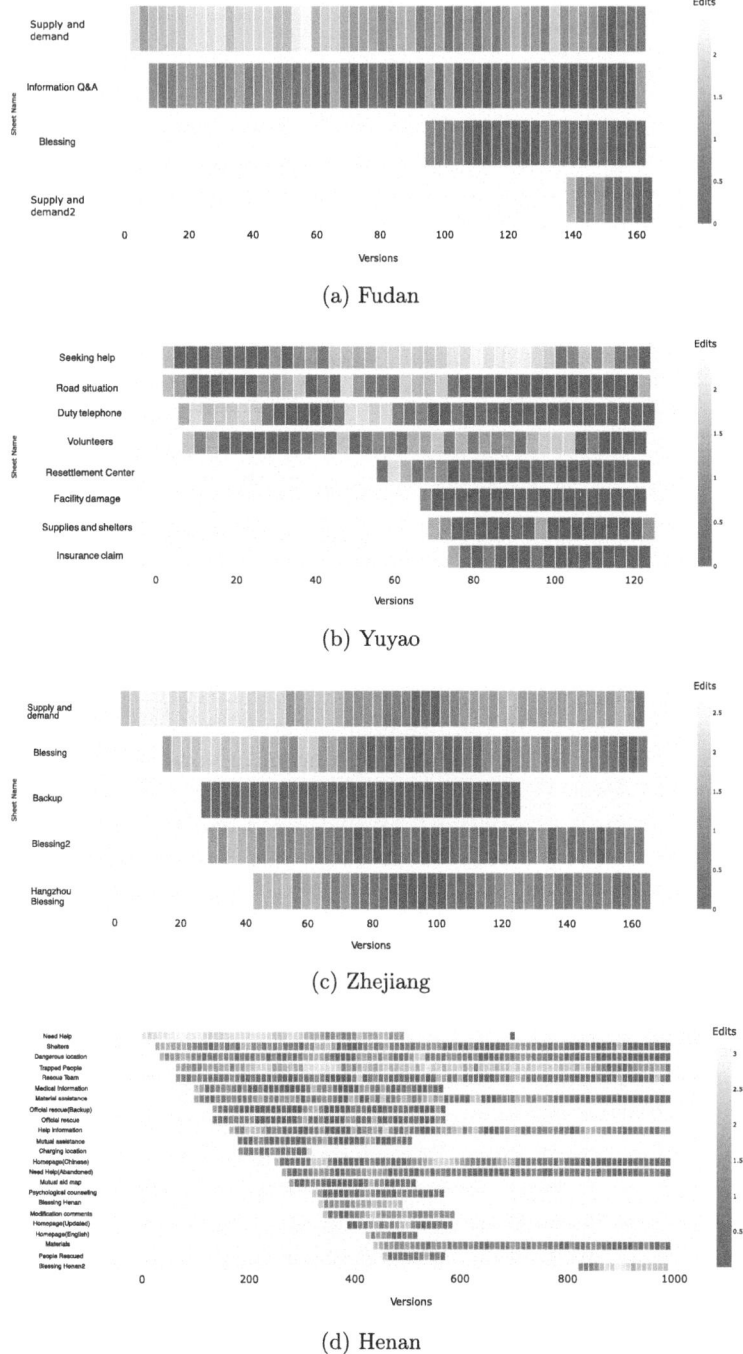

(a) Fudan

(b) Yuyao

(c) Zhejiang

(d) Henan

Fig. 3. The figures show the process of users' organizing and editing tables. Each bar shows the life of a sheet and high brightness means experiencing more operations. We sort sheets from top to bottom by their creation order.

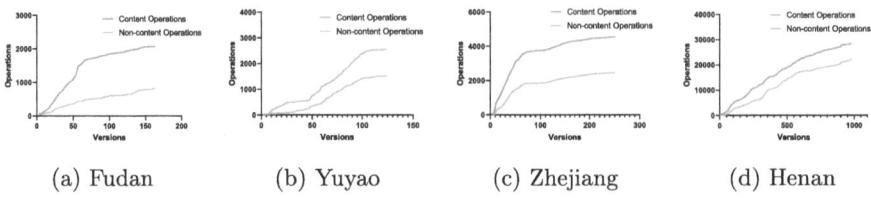

(a) Fudan   (b) Yuyao   (c) Zhejiang   (d) Henan

Fig. 4. The accumulative distribution of content and non-content operations.

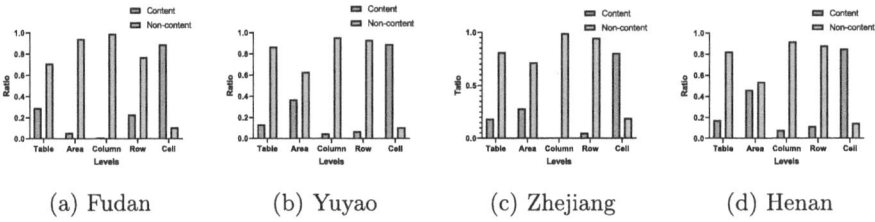

(a) Fudan   (b) Yuyao   (c) Zhejiang   (d) Henan

Fig. 5. The proportion of content and non-content operations in the five levels

Tables 7, 6, 4, and 5. The analysis shows distinct topics for each crisis: "provide materials" (Fudan), "obstructed roads" (Yuyao), "emotional support" (Zhejiang), and "seek help" (Henan). To highlight content characteristics, we compared collaboration table topics with the taxonomy of crisis response content in previous research, which classified social media crisis response into six categories: Affected Individuals (AI), Infrastructure & Utilities (IU), Donations & Volunteers (DV), Caution & Advice (CA), Sympathy & Emotion Support (SES), and Other Useful Information (O.) [14]. Figure 6 shows that two categories commonly occur: Affected Individuals and Donations & Volunteers. For Affected Individuals, Fudan and Zhejiang cases involve requesting supplies, Yuyao involves requesting rescue, and Henan involves requesting rescue, materials, and information about trapped and missing people. For Donations & Volunteers, Fudan and Zhejiang involve material assistance, Yuyao involves rescue team information, and Henan involves both rescue team and volunteer information. This indicates that the primary functions of collaboration tables are coordinating help seekers and providers during crises.

Content Annotation Analysis. As mentioned in the methodology section, we further extracted content annotation in tables based on particular columns. The three types of content annotation are verification annotation, urgency annotation, and rescue situation annotation. Figure 7 shows the time difference between content and its annotation, with annotating speed decreasing from verification to urgency and rescue status. After a help request is posted, editors first verify authenticity, then assess urgency, and finally confirm the safety status. Rescue situation annotations include "waiting rescue," "rescuing," and "rescued," indicating real-time tracking by users.

	Fudan	Yuyao	Zhejiang	Henan
AI	A2	B3	C3	D{1,11,13,16}
IU		B1,B2	C4	D2,D8
DV	A1	B4	C2	D7,D15
CA				D5,D9
SES	A3		C1	D18
O.	A4,A5			D{3,4,6,10,12,14,17}

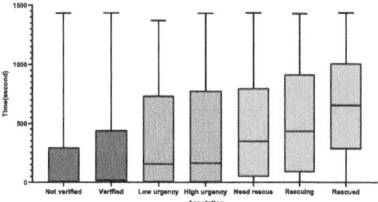

Fig. 6. The relation between tables' topics and crisis response. The specific topic of a particular table is annotated like "A1", "B1", "C1" or "D1", which is detailed demonstrated in Appendix.

Fig. 7. The time difference between the appearance of the annotation and the annotated content

4.3 User Perspective

We conducted re-engagement, cohort, and role analysis to obtain more insights into users' participation in collaboration tables.

Re-engagement Analysis. We consider a user who has edited tables not only in the current version but also in a previous version as a re-engagement user. Figure 8 shows an accumulative number of re-engagement users in the four collaboration tables. Initially, the total number of users is small, but the percentage of re-engagement users is high. Figure 9 shows the proportion of re-engagement users: 38% in the 10th version of the Fudan table, 66% in the Yuyao table, 53% in the Zhejiang table, and 60% in the 20th version of the Henan table. As the total number of users increases, the proportion of re-engagement users drops. The re-engagement ratio stabilizes at 32% for Fudan, 29% for Yuyao, 15% for Zhejiang, and 25% for Henan. In version 320 of the Henan table, user numbers explode, but re-engagement does not increase, causing the re-engagement rate to fall from 27% to 21% within 24 h of the table's creation.

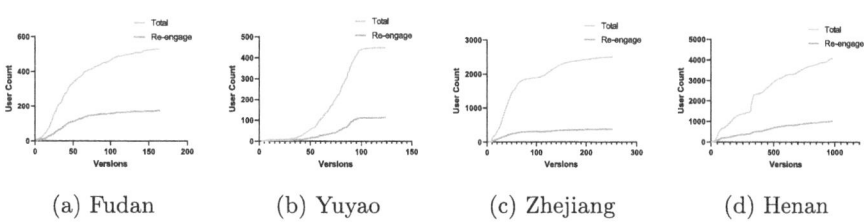

(a) Fudan   (b) Yuyao   (c) Zhejiang   (d) Henan

Fig. 8. Changes of re-engagement users and total users with increase of versions.

Cohort Analysis. To understand which users become re-engagement editors, we conducted a cohort analysis. Users who first engage within the same hour form a cohort. Figure 10 shows that early-stage users (red and orange) tend

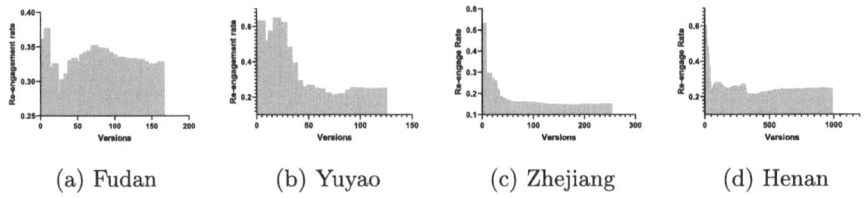

(a) Fudan   (b) Yuyao   (c) Zhejiang   (d) Henan

Fig. 9. Proportions of re-engagement users and total users with increase versions.

Table 2. The roles distribution in the Fudan, Yuyao, Zhejiang, and Henan crises

Crisis	HS	HP	IS	IP	ESP	OP	I.	CM	FM	L.	O.
Fudan	11.19%	46.86%	9.87%	9.24%	5.85%	–	–	3.82%	5.02%	1.88%	4.24%
Yuyao	52.63%	15.53%	–	9.41%	–	–	–	5.67%	7.11%	3.02%	6.63%
Zhejiang	8.50%	18.90%	–	–	49.07%	–	–	11.53%	6.38%	2.96%	2.46%
Henan	32.45%	4.23%	-	8.30%	7.19%	2.87%	3.25%	19.13%	18.3%	2.16%	2.10%

to continue editing, while most mid-stage users contribute only briefly. In the Henan table, many newcomers joined between 23:00 on the 21st and 1:00 on the 22nd due to social media spread, but most quit quickly.

Role Analysis. We combined each user's edit history into a document and used LDA modeling, similar to topic clustering in our mentioned content analysis, to identify 11 roles in the four crisis response collaboration tables.

1) **Helper seeker (HS):** people who ask for help at the collaboration table.
2) **Helper provider (HP):** people who provide help at the collaboration table.
3) **Emotion support provider (ESP):** users who provide emotional support.
4) **Opinion provider (OP):** users who provide opinions, e.g. how to manage tables
5) **Information seeker (IS):** users who ask for useful information related to crises
6) **Information provider (IP):** users who provide useful information related to crises
7) **Leader (L.):** users who manage the crisis response collaboration table, e.g., design tables.
8) **Format moderator (FM):** users who make non-content-oriented operations.
9) **Content moderator (CM):** users who maintain and manage the content at the table
10) **Instructor (I.):** users who provide instruction information at the collaboration table
11) **Other (O.):** users who do not belong to the above ten categories. We find two representative groups of other roles in our cases. The first group of users is similar to "Flitter" proposed in the research of Wikipedia [4]. These users make a simple operation (e.g., creating an empty sheet) and leave the table. The second group are vandalisms who insert expletives into the collaboration table or repeatedly delete imperative sheets.

Table 2 shows the distribution of roles in four cases. In the Fudan crisis, helper providers are the majority, while emotional support providers dominate in the Zhejiang crisis. Help seekers are the largest group in the Henan and Yuyao crises. Five roles are common across all cases: helper seeker, helper provider, content moderator, format moderator, and leader. This highlights the main functions of crisis response tables: matching help seekers with providers and ensuring management and leadership. Our role analysis aligns with previous research on crisis response and collaborative writing. The helper provider and emotional support provider roles correspond to the Helper role in social media scenarios [18], while content moderators and format moderators correspond to the Moderator role [6].

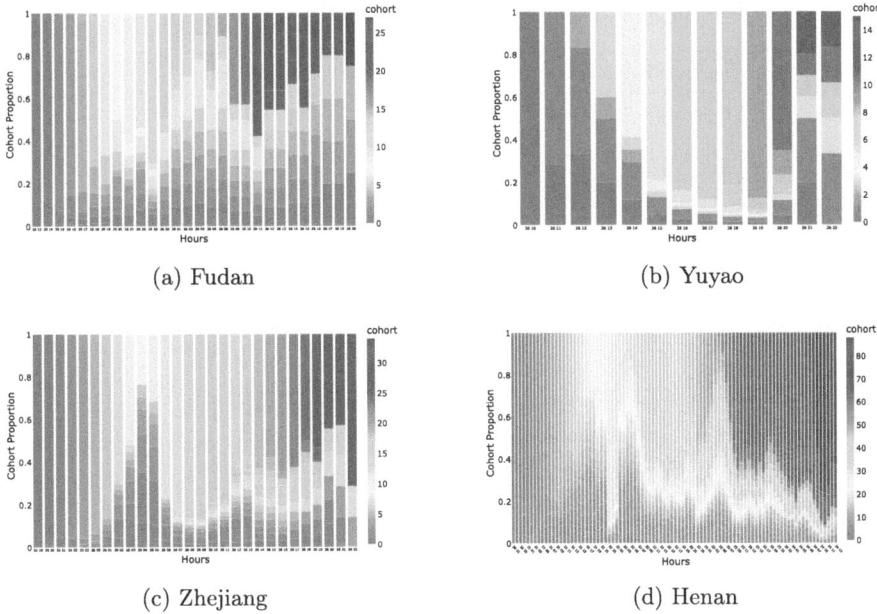

(a) Fudan   (b) Yuyao

(c) Zhejiang   (d) Henan

Fig. 10. The proportion of cohorts in each hour of collaboration. The same color means the same cohort and the length of a particular color bar shows proportion of the corresponding cohort users. (Color figure online)

5 Discussion

These results reveal operation, content, and user roles in these table-based crisis responses, providing evidence for broader themes summarized in Table 3.

Theme 1: The Crisis Response Modes of Collaboration Tables. Our analysis of operations, content, and users offers insights into crisis response modes in collaboration tables. Fine-grained operations (cell-level) are more frequent than coarse-grained ones (row, column, area, table levels), likely helping to avoid conflicts and maintain format. Despite differing crises, common topics include help-seeking and help-providing. Content annotations enable users to verify authenticity, prioritize content, and update statuses, potentially mitigating issues of fake information and duplication [17]. Common roles across tables include help providers, help seekers, leaders, content moderators, and format moderators, suggesting a well-organized and coordinated response.

Theme 2: The Crisis Response Phases of the Collaboration Tables. The crisis response process of collaboration tables can be divided into three phases: initial, development, and end. The initial phase involves rapid edits focused on help requests like material assistance and rescue actions, with engaged users. In the development phase, newcomers join, creating new sheets and expanding functions to include information on dangerous buildings, shelter locations,

Table 3. Mapping between findings and discussion themes.

Perspective	Analysis	Theme1	Theme2	Theme3	Theme4
Operation	Figure 1		✓		
	Figure 2	✓	✓		✓
	Figure 3	✓	✓		✓
	Figure 4	✓	✓	✓	✓
	Figure 5	✓			✓
Content	Tables 4, 5, 6, 7	✓			✓
	Figure 6	✓			✓
User	Figure 8		✓	✓	
	Figure 8		✓	✓	
	Figure 10		✓	✓	
	Table 2	✓			✓

opinions, and blessings, though some unrelated tables are short-lived. In the end phase, as the crisis subsides, the number of editors decreases, table functions stabilize, and non-content-oriented operations increase.

Theme 3: The Impact of Wide Spread of Collaboration Tables. Spreading crisis response tables can potentially impact user experience and table maintenance. In the Henan crisis, a Tencent report titled "24 h for a collaboration table" spread widely on social media, drawing many users to edit the table. This led to several observations: numerous synchronous edits appeared to affect operational fluency, with some users commenting on the table's slowness. Re-engagement and cohort analysis suggested that many new users contributed briefly before leaving. Compared to other crisis tables, the Henan tables showed a higher number of non-content-oriented operations during the spread, indicating possible challenges in managing the table's format.

Theme 4: Collaboration Table vs. Social Media Crisis Responses. Several studies have focused on social media-based crisis response, prompting a comparison with our findings. Collaboration table-based responses can be slower due to the lack of a Pre-Crisis stage and fewer social connections. Both approaches share common content topics, like Affected Individuals and Donations & Volunteers, indicating primary intentions of seeking and providing help. However, collaboration tables excel in information validation. Role analysis reveals that content and format moderators manage content and format efficiently, whereas social media moderators often struggle with outdated, false, or duplicate content.

6   Implications

Our research offers insights for improving collaboration table-based crisis response. **First, we suggest adding authority management to crisis**

response collaboration tables. We identified 11 roles with unique editing patterns, such as cell-level content edits by information providers and area-level edits by format moderators. Currently, most users have broad editing permissions, which can lead to table overload and vandalism. For instance, in the Henan crisis table, some users repeatedly deleted useful content. Assigning specific editing permissions to different roles, such as limiting operation levels or access to certain tables, could mitigate these issues. **Second, we recommend providing sheet templates for different crisis types.** Creating and defining worksheets requires time and effort, potentially delaying important information processing. Some user-created sheets are often inappropriate and quickly deleted. Suitable templates would enable quick initialization of crisis response tables, streamlining the response process. **Third, we recommend integrating collaboration table content with social media.** An automated tool could collect and transport crisis-related information from social media to the table, ensuring timely updates. For instance, help requests on social media could be recorded in a "Need Help" sheet, with comments added as annotations. Conversely, updates in the table, such as marking a request as "Rescued," could be reflected on social media posts, keeping more people informed of changes.

7 Limitation

The main limitation of this study is the inability to access final operation records due to table closures. For privacy and security reasons, table owners may restrict public editing but allow a few volunteers to continue. While we can observe ongoing changes, we cannot access the operation records for these changes. However, as these changes are limited, we believe this has a minor impact on our findings.

8 Conclusion

In this research, we analyzed crisis response mechanisms in online collaboration tables, focusing on operations, content, and user interactions. By collecting and processing data from various crisis events, we identified patterns in interaction, usage, and roles. Our findings reveal the nuances of collaboration table dynamics and lead to actionable design recommendations to enhance crisis response effectiveness. We also explored the interplay between collaboration table-based and social media-based crisis responses, offering additional insights into digital crisis management. Future work will expand to include a more diverse range of collaboration tables from different crises, aiming to strengthen the generalizability and reliability of our findings and improve digital platforms for crisis management.

Acknowledgements. This work is supported by the National Key Research and Development Program of China under Grant No. 2021YFC3300201 and the National Natural Science Foundation of China (NSFC) under the Grant No.61932007. Peng Zhang and Tun Lu are faculty members of School of Computer Science, Fudan University. Tun Lu is also a faculty of Shanghai Key Laboratory of Data Science, Fudan Institute on Aging, MOE Laboratory for National Development and Intelligent Governance, and Shanghai Institute of Intelligent Electronics & Systems, Fudan University.

A   Appendix

Table 4. Topic analysis in tables' content of Fudan crisis.

Index	Topic	Top Words	Rate
A1	Provide materials	provide, location, phone, mask, toothpaste	36.33%
A2	Require materials	phone, demand, mask, emergency, contact lens	27.48%
A3	Emotional support	come on, brother, warm, friends, classmates	16.35%
A4	Ask situation	question, satisfaction, new, not, wechat	10.46%
A5	Answer situation	campus, lockdown, answer, prevention, personnel	9.38%

Table 5. Topic analysis in tables' content of Yuyao crisis.

Index	Topic	Top Words	Rate
B1	Obstructed roads	road condition, closure, impact, date, intersection	56.53%
B2	Refuge	street, community, Yuyao, disaster avoidance	20.24%
B3	Seek help	situation, location, phone, urgent, transfer	16.53%
B4	Rescue team	team, phone, maintenance, volunteer, Yuyao	6.70%

Table 6. Topic analysis in tables' content of Zhejiang crisis.

Index	Topic	Top Words	Rate
C1	Emotional Support	come on, Zhejiang, peace, blessing, Hangzhou	56.44%
C2	Provide materials	category, available, phone, location, blankets	21.53%
C3	Require materials	materials, location, phone, need, urgency	15.41%
C4	Refuge	Zhejiang, phone, provision, hotel, stay	6.61%

Table 7. Topic analysis in tables' content of Henan crisis.

Index	Topic	Top Words	Rate
D1	Seek help	the old, trapped, phone, already, unable	14.69%
D2	Refuge	phone, location, contact, source, community	11.60%
D3	Verification	verified, situation, verifying, not yet, microblog	10.46%
D4	Fine-grained loc.	road, intersection, nearby, meter, street	8.79%
D5	Warnings	water cut-off, transfer, safety, direct, rise	8.66%
D6	Status: not rescued	waiting, rescue status, update time, not, unable	5.86%
D7	Rescue team	phone, telephone, rescue team, rescue, emergency	4.97%
D8	Damaged facilities	region, collapse, electric leakage, rainstorm, source	4.78%
D9	Advice	information, name, please, delete, person, sheet	4.03%
D10	Status: rescued	rescue, success, date, obtained, already	3.91%
D11	Missing people	contact, signal, no access, no connection, phone	3.89%
D12	Coarse-grained loc.	district, city, Zhengzhou, nationality, center	3.85%
D13	Material shortage	materials, urgent, fast, need, phone	2.88%
D14	Urgency degree	urgent, phone, baby, mother, hospital	2.46%
D15	Volunteer	location, phone, vehicle, team, Zhengzhou	2.45%
D16	Trapped persons	trapped, town, villagers, roof, time	2.40%
D17	Instructions	provide, click, Tencent, situation, news	2.22%
D18	Emotional support	come on, Henan, beg, Zhengzhou, consider	2.07%

References

1. Beck, E.E.: A survey of experiences of collaborative writing. In: Sharples, M. (ed.) Computer Supported Collaborative Writing. Computer Supported Cooperative Work, pp. 87–112. Springer, London (1993). https://doi.org/10.1007/978-1-4471-2007-0_6
2. Bubendorff, S., Rizza, C., Prieur, C.: Construction and dissemination of information veracity on French social media during crises: comparison of twitter and wikipedia. J. Contingencies Crisis Manag. **29**(2), 204–216 (2021)
3. Eismann, K., Posegga, O., Fischbach, K.: Collective behaviour, social media, and disasters: a systematic literature review (2016)
4. Faraj, S., Jarvenpaa, S.L., Majchrzak, A.: Knowledge collaboration in online communities. Organ. Sci. **22**(5), 1224–1239 (2011)
5. Flores-Saviaga, C., Savage, S.: Fighting disaster misinformation in Latin America: the# 19s Mexican earthquake case study. Pers. Ubiquit. Comput. **25**(2), 353–373 (2021)
6. Kaufhold, M.A., Reuter, C.: Vernetzte selbsthilfe in sozialen medien am beispiel des hochwassers 2013/linked self-help in social media using the example of the floods 2013 in Germany. i-com **13**(1), 20–28 (2014)
7. Keegan, B., Gergle, D., Contractor, N.: Hot off the wiki: structures and dynamics of Wikipedia's coverage of breaking news events. Am. Behav. Sci. **57**(5), 595–622 (2013)
8. Keegan, B.C.: Emergent social roles in Wikipedia's breaking news collaborations. In: Bertino, E., Matei, S.A. (eds.) Roles, Trust, and Reputation in Social Media Knowledge Markets. CSS, pp. 57–79. Springer, Cham (2015). https://doi.org/10.1007/978-3-319-05467-4_4
9. Keegan, B.C., Tan, C.: A quantitative portrait of Wikipedia's high-tempo collaborations during the 2020 coronavirus pandemic. arXiv preprint arXiv:2006.08899 (2020)
10. Nguyen, H.L., Ignat, C.-L.: Time-position characterization of conflicts: a case study of collaborative editing. In: Nolte, A., Alvarez, C., Hishiyama, R., Chounta, I.-A., Rodríguez-Triana, M.J., Inoue, T. (eds.) CollabTech 2020. LNCS, vol. 12324, pp. 65–80. Springer, Cham (2020). https://doi.org/10.1007/978-3-030-58157-2_5
11. Liu, S.B.: Crisis crowdsourcing framework: designing strategic configurations of crowdsourcing for the emergency management domain. Comput. Support. Coop. Work. (CSCW) **23**(4–6), 389–443 (2014)
12. Lowry, P.B., Curtis, A., Lowry, M.R.: Building a taxonomy and nomenclature of collaborative writing to improve interdisciplinary research and practice. J. Bus. Commun. (1973) **41**(1), 66–99 (2004)
13. Olson, J.S., Wang, D., Olson, G.M., Zhang, J.: How people write together now: beginning the investigation with advanced undergraduates in a project course. ACM Trans. Comput.-Hum. Interact. (TOCHI) **24**(1), 1–40 (2017)
14. Olteanu, A., Vieweg, S., Castillo, C.: What to expect when the unexpected happens: social media communications across crises. In: Proceedings of the 18th ACM Conference on Computer Supported Cooperative Work & Social Computing, pp. 994–1009 (2015)
15. Palen, L., Anderson, K.M.: Crisis informatics-new data for extraordinary times. Science **353**(6296), 224–225 (2016)
16. Qu, Y., Huang, C., Zhang, P., Zhang, J.: Microblogging after a major disaster in china: a case study of the 2010 Yushu earthquake. In: Proceedings of the ACM 2011 Conference on Computer Supported Cooperative Work, pp. 25–34 (2011)

17. Reuter, C., Hartwig, K., Kirchner, J., Schlegel, N.: Fake news perception in Germany: a representative study of people's attitudes and approaches to counteract disinformation (2019)
18. Reuter, C., Heger, O., Pipek, V.: Combining real and virtual volunteers through social media. In: ISCRAM (2013)
19. Reuter, C., Hughes, A.L., Kaufhold, M.A.: Social media in crisis management: an evaluation and analysis of crisis informatics research. Int. J. Hum.-Comput. Interact. **34**(4), 280–294 (2018)
20. Reuter, C., Kaufhold, M.A.: Fifteen years of social media in emergencies: a retrospective review and future directions for crisis informatics. J. Contingencies Crisis Manag. **26**(1), 41–57 (2018)
21. Reuter, C., Kaufhold, M.A., Spielhofer, T., Hahne, A.S.: Social media in emergencies: a representative study on citizens' perception in Germany. In: Proceedings of the ACM on Human-Computer Interaction, vol. 1(CSCW), pp. 1–19 (2017)
22. Soden, R., Palen, L.: Informating crisis: expanding critical perspectives in crisis informatics. In: Proceedings of the ACM on Human-Computer Interaction, vol. 2(CSCW), pp. 1–22 (2018)
23. Sundgren, M., Jaldemark, J.: Visualizing online collaborative writing strategies in higher education group assignments. Int. J. Inf. Learn. Technol. **37**(5), 351–373 (2020). https://doi.org/10.1108/IJILT-02-2020-0018
24. Wang, D., Olson, J.S., Zhang, J., Nguyen, T., Olson, G.M.: DocuViz: visualizing collaborative writing. In: Proceedings of the 33rd Annual ACM Conference on Human Factors in Computing Systems, pp. 1865–1874 (2015)

An Inference Method for Professional Texts with Computational Expressions Under Few-Shot Scenarios

Leiwen Yang[1($\boxtimes$)], Wei Zheng[1], Feng Yuan[2], and Yuqing Sun[1]

[1] School of Software, Shandong University, Jinan, China
leoiwan@foxmail.com , sun_yuqing@sdu.edu.cn
[2] Shandong Shanda Oumasoft Co. Ltd., Jinan, China
sdyuanf@sina.com

Abstract. We propose an inference method for complex professional texts with computational expressions. We use the expert rules to locate and rewrite the expressions. We adopt the pre-trained language model as the initial model and select the high quality samples from historical dataset for pre-training the model. The positive samples in the prompt are retrieved from the high-quality data that are similar to the inferred instance and the negative ones are generated by expert rules. For the target task, we fine-tune the model with the given few samples. Experimental results show that the performance of this method outperforms baselines and is applicable to low-resource scenarios.

Keywords: Short Text Inference · Computational Expression · Few-shot Scenario

1 Introduction

Short text review is the practical application of text inference, which evaluates students' texts based on the given reference. In many specialty exams, there often exist computational expressions in text, such as the example in Fig. 1, where the numbers and symbols contain the special meanings, that exceed the understanding capabilities of the traditional language models. Thus it is a challenge to infer this kind of professional texts with computational expressions.

Previous research has focused on inferring texts based on the human-labelled datasets by using the pre-trained language models [1,2]. For example, Gao et al. compute the similarities between text features and manually set a similarity threshold for text inference [3]. Herasymovych et al. use reinforcement learning to learn the similarity threshold [4]. Sarkar et al. concatenate, align, or apply the mutual attention on features for inference and classification [5]. Compared to the above neural networks, tree-based classifiers offer better interpretability [6].

With the emergence of large language models (LLM for short), there is an increasing trend of applying these models to text inference tasks. Users can

H. Sun et al. (Eds.): ChineseCSCW 2024, CCIS 2343, pp. 213–219, 2025.
https://doi.org/10.1007/978-981-96-2373-0_15

Reference texts	Students' texts	Review results
借：使用权资产1560.34、租赁负债——未确认融资费用439.66；贷：租赁负债——租赁付款额1800、银行存款200。	借：投资性房地产200万元。贷：银行存款200万元。借：财务费用15万元。贷：银行存款15万元……。	语义表述一致
差错更正对甲公司2x21年度营业利润的影响金额=-(3100-2960)-445=-585(万元)。	材料一：营业收入=100－2000=－1900；营业利润不变。材料二：营业收入不变；营业利润=－165……	语义表述不一致

Fig. 1. Examples of Professional Texts with Computational Expressions.

directly infer texts without any task-specific model training [7]. But this kind of approaches do not work well on the professional texts with computational expressions [8].

To solve the computational expression problem, some approaches adopt the chain of thought [9] to assist the model step-by-step reasoning. For example, Kojima et al. incorporate the prompt with prefix "let's think step by step" for LLMs [10]. Wang et al. [11] generate multiple computational paths to derive the results and aggregate them through voting, which improves the model accuracy. Lightman et al. [12] propose an automatic verification method for correcting the reasoning results. Sanh et al. also demonstrate that the quality of prompts significantly influences the model performance [13]. The computational expression and text inference are often studied independently, the above methods focus on the reasoning of computational expressions, and do not pay attention to text inference.

In this paper, we propose a method for inferring complex professional texts with computational expressions. We adopt the pre-trained language model as the initial model and select the high quality samples from historical dataset for pre-training the initial model. The positive samples in the prompt are retrieved from the high-quality data that are similar to the inferred instance and the negative ones are generated by expert rules. For the target task, we fine-tune the pre-trained model with the given few samples.

Experimental results on the real educational examination review data show that our method outperforms other methods in terms of performance. Even under low-resource scenarios, it achieves satisfactory results, meeting the requirements of practical applications.

2 Method

The proposed method consists of three main parts: rule guided data augmentation Sect. 2.1, pre-training Sect. 2.2 and fine-tuning Sect. 2.3 the inference model, as shown in Fig. 2. Details are given below.

2.1 Rules Guided Data Augmentation

Recognize Expressions from Text. Computational expressions consist of numbers and arithmetic operators, which have special meanings that are distinct from

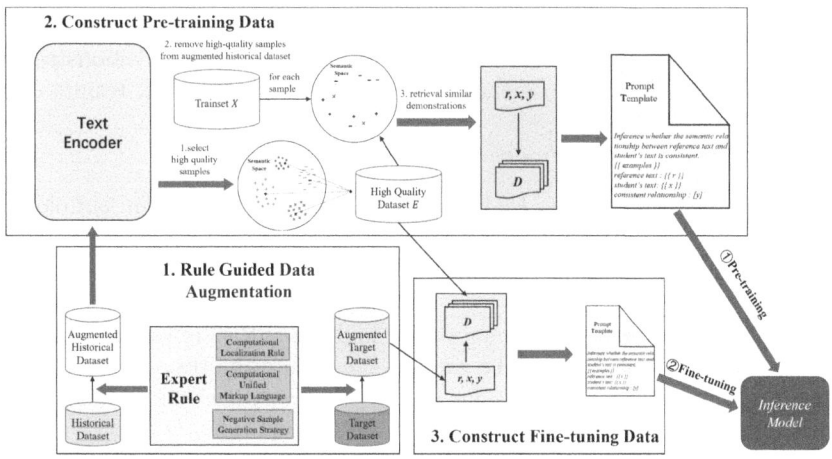

Fig. 2. The Proposed Method

usual texts and have significant impacts on the text semantics. So we adopt the expert rules to recognize these computational expressions in texts. For example, the rule $(? : d * .? d + [+ - /]) + d .? d+$ locates the expressions containing numbers, decimal points, and basic arithmetic operators.

Rewrite the Expressions with the Unified Markup Language. We design the unified computation markup language (UML for short) to rewrite the recognized texts. For example, the special tokens [s_i_t] and [e_i_t] are added to both sides of an expression to emphasize the integer arithmetics, while the special tokens [s_f_t] and [e_f_t] are used to emphasize float the arithmetics.

Since in the student's texts, the same calculation process may be expressed by different forms, another function of the unified computational markup language is to align them with each others. For example, these expressions $600 * 0.01 = 6$, $600 * 1\% = 6$ and $600/100 = 6$ are with the same meanings. The unified expression can reduce the difficulty for inferring the meaning of expressions.

Construct the Negative Samples for a Given Correct Expression. Computational expressions have a decisive impact on the semantics of the text. To make the model understand the meaning of different calculation processes, we design negative sample strategy to generate multiple negative samples for each correct computational expressions. For each positive samples, we rewrite the calculation process of an expression by changing some values and symbols. For example, $600 * 0.01 = 6$ can be rewritten as $600 * 0.01 = 7$ and $600 + 0.01 = 6$. By this, the diversity of computing process is enriched.

2.2 Pre-training the Text Inference Model with Historical Data

We adopt the historical data for data augmentation, as discussed in Sect. 2.1. Then we construct the prompts with these data.

Prompt Construction. We design the prompt template $\mathcal{T}(x, D, r, y)$ to construction the model inputs, where x means a student's text, D means demonstrations that are similar to x. r and y mean the reference text and review results corresponding to x, respectively.

The construction steps are given as follows:

1. The high quality samples E: for the augmented dataset, the samples are grouped by labels. After encoding texts, we use $k - means$ to cluster sample in each group. We select the center sample as the high quality sample and add it to E.
2. The training samples X: we remove the high quality samples from the augmented samples. The rest of the samples constitute the training samples X.
3. The similar demonstrations D: for each $x \in X$, we select the closest sample in each group from E to form the similar demonstrations D [14].

Pre-training Model. We use the above constructed data to pre-train the text inference model. Our objective is to maximize the conditional probability $p(y|x, r)$, where p is the result probability predicted by the model. The loss function is the cross entropy loss.

$$\mathcal{L} = -y \log p + (1 - y) \log (1 - p) \tag{1}$$

2.3 Fine-tuning the Text Inference Model with a Few Samples in Target Task

For the target task, we also adopt a few labeled samples in target task for data augmentation, as discussed in Sect. 2.1 For each sample in the augmented dataset, relevant demonstrations are retrieved from the high quality samples from the pre-training phase, as discussed in Sect. 2.2, to construct context inputs. During the fine-tuning process, the loss function is similar to that of the pre-training process.

3 Experiments

3.1 Dataset and Implementation Details

We use the data of the 2022 accountant examination (AR21 for short) for experiments, which includes 21 questions. Each question contains 1 to 5 knowledge points, with the reference texts for the knowledge points. The first 14 questions are used as the historical data, while the remaining 7 questions are used as the target dataset under the low-resource scenarios. The statistics of the dataset are shown in Table 1.

The initial model's weights are sourced from the transformers library by Huggingface[1]. This study uses the Qwen-1_8B as the initial model for our method,

---

[1] https://huggingface.co.

Table 1. The Statistics of Dataset.

dataset	question	number/question	total
train	14	8897	124549
test	7	8243	57707

with the hyper-parameters set to the default from finetune.py[2]. For retrieving the similar demonstrations, the bge-large-zh-v1.5 is used as the embedding model. During k-means clustering, k is set to 50.

We use accuracy and macro-f1 as the evaluation metric. The metric value is the average of three experiments on multiple problems.

As the comparison methods, we select the traditional text inference methods, categorizing BERT's CLS output, referred to here as **Supervised**. Additionally, **NLIPT** [15] is used as a comparative method with hyper-parameters following the original paper's settings. Furthermore, **COT** [10] is used as another comparative method. Since the COT does not require fine-tuning the model, it cannot be directly applied under low-resource settings. The experiments with the COT involve using 1, 3, and 5 demonstrations per input.

3.2   Results and Analysis

The experimental results on AE21 is shown in Table 2. The low-resource scenarios are each question random select 20,50,100 samples, respectively.

As the amount of training data increases, the performance of all methods generally improves. In the 20 samples/question low-resource scenario, our method outperforms the NLIPT, indicating its effectiveness in the low-resource settings. In the 100samples/question scenario, our method approaches the performance of supervised training with all training data. Notably, the simple COT method shows the much lower performance compared to other methods. This method may cause the LLM to focus only on the calculation process and ignore other texts. For such tasks, LLM should focus on both the expressions and the texts.

According to the results of the ablation experiments, each component of our method proves the positive effect to performance. In particular, historical data has an important impact on method performance.

Based on the experimental results in the 0 samples/question column of Table 2, our method demonstrates the zero-shot capability although it shows a considerable gap compared to the fine-tuned results. On the one hand, there is no labelled sample to indicate the target task domain and the label spaces. On the other hand, the training corpus of the large language models does not include the task domain.

---

[2] https://github.com/QwenLM/Qwen.

Table 2. Experimental Results on AE21.

samples/question	-		0		20		50		100	
	acc	f1	acc	f1	acc	f1	acc	f1	acc	f1
Supervised	99.26	99.26	44.08	30.87	77.57	77.38	88.05	88.05	94.90	94.90
NLIPT	-	-	-	-	94.02	94.01	94.26	94.26	96.65	96.65
Ours	-	-	55.36	43.31	**96.94**	**96.94**	**97.29**	**97.29**	**98.19**	**98.19**
w/o UML	-	-	-	-	95.94	95.94	97.27	97.27	97.37	97.37
w/o PT	-	-	-	-	80.77	80.69	88.57	88.57	94.46	94.46
w/o PT+UML	-	-	57.33	41.29	80.77	80.69	89.72	89.72	94.83	94.83
COT demonstration		-		1		3		5		
	-	-	-	-	51.90	34.17	49.30	33.17	49.25	33.01

4 Conclusion

This paper presents a specialty text inference method tailored for mixed computational expressions. We adopt the pre-trained language model as the initial model and select the high quality samples from historical dataset for pre-training the model. The positive samples in the prompt are retrieved from the high-quality data that are similar to the inferred instance and the negative ones are generated by expert rules. For the target task, we fine-tune the pre-trained model with the given few samples. Experimental results demonstrate that this method performs well in the low-resource scenarios and outperforms baselines. For the future work, we are planning to conduct the interpretability analyses on evaluation results.

References

1. Devlin, J., Chang, M.-W., Lee, K., Toutanova, K.:. BERT: pre-training of deep bidirectional transformers for language understanding. In: NAACL (2019)
2. Liu, Y., Ott, M., Goyal, N., et al.: RoBERTa: a robustly optimized BERT pre-training approach. arXiv:1907.11692 (2019)
3. Gao, T., Yao, X., Chen, D.: Simple contrastive learning of sentence embeddings. In: EMNLP, Simcse (2021)
4. Herasymovych, M., Märka, K., Lukason, O.: Using reinforcement learning to optimize the acceptance threshold of a credit scoring model. ASC **84**, 105697 (2019)
5. Sarkar, S.: Effectiveness of deep networks in NLP using BiDAF as an example architecture. arXiv:2109.00074 (2021)
6. Lundberg, S.M., Erion, G.G., Lee, S.-I.: Consistent individualized feature attribution for tree ensembles. Methods **5**(13), 25 (2018)
7. Zhang, N., Li, L., Chen, X., et al.: Differentiable prompt makes pre-trained language models better few-shot learners. In: ICLR (2021)
8. Sun, X., Li, X., Li, J., et al.: Text classification via large language models. In: EMNLP (2023)

9. Wei, J., Wang, X., Schuurmans, D., et al.: Chain-of-thought prompting elicits reasoning in large language models. In: NeurIPS (2022)

10. Kojima, T., Gu, S., Reid, M., Matsuo, Y., Iwasawa, Y.: Large language models are zero-shot reasoners. In: NeurIPS (2022)

11. Wang, X., Wei, J., Schuurmans, D., et al.: Self-consistency improves chain of thought reasoning in language models. In: ICLR (2022)

12. Lightman, H., Kosaraju, V., Burda, Y., et al.: Let's verify step by step. In: ICLR (2023)

13. Sanh, V., Webson, A., Raffel, C., et al.: Multitask prompted training enables zero-shot task generalization. In: ICLR (2021)

14. Johnson, J., Douze, M., Jégou, H.: Billion-scale similarity search with GPUs. IEEE Trans. Big Data **7**(3), 535–547 (2019)

15. Yang, L., Yang, T., Yuan, F., et al.: Professional text review under limited sampling constraints. In: ChineseCSCW (2023)

Who Are the Blockchain Pioneers?
A Framework for Measuring Scholars' Influence

Li Zhu⊙, Sichao Yuan, Ya Liu⊙, and Jiaqi Yan(✉)⊙

Nanjing University, Nanjing 210023, China
jiaqiyan@nju.edu.cn

Abstract. Scholars play a crucial role in driving scientific innovation and progress. However, existing methods for evaluating scholars' academic influence have limitations in capturing their innovation contributions, especially in emerging interdisciplinary fields characterized by rapid development. Therefore, we propose a method for evaluating scholars' influence based on their scientific innovation roles. Taking the blockchain field as an example, we first define four innovation roles for academic papers based on their citation relationships within the field. We then map these roles onto individual scholars using a paper-author correspondence. A sliding time window analysis captures the dynamic evolution of scholars' roles over different periods. The results reveal insightful role transitions of scholars over time and their diverse influences across topics, providing a more comprehensive perspective on their research contributions. Through case analysis and comparative analysis with traditional metrics, we validate the effectiveness of our method in identifying influential scholars, emerging innovators, and interdisciplinary contributors.

Keywords: Academic influence · Diffusion of innovations · Citation network · Scholar ranking

1 Introduction

In the process of technological globalization, new scientific and technological innovations are continually emerging. Taking blockchain as an example, since Satoshi Nakamoto [1] first introduced Bitcoin in 2008, a plethora of new concepts such as Ethereum, consortium blockchains, NFTs, and Metaverse have developed. Scholars play a crucial role within the innovation ecosystem [2]. They not only propel the advancement of fundamental theories and the development of new technologies but also lead in exploring the practical applications and potential impacts of these technologies. Analyzing the influence of scholars helps us understand how contributors from diverse backgrounds and disciplines drive technological progress and further facilitate interdisciplinary collaboration.

Evaluation systems need to account for the varying nature of research across fields and career stages [3]. Emerging interdisciplinary fields like blockchain are

H. Sun et al. (Eds.): ChineseCSCW 2024, CCIS 2343, pp. 220–234, 2025.
https://doi.org/10.1007/978-981-96-2373-0_16

characterized by rapid development, strong innovation, and interdisciplinary overlap, making traditional evaluation methods [4–6] inadequate. In these fields, many promising young scholars may not yet have accumulated a large number of citations and collaborations, but their work may have significant innovation and future impact. Identifying these emerging innovators is crucial for optimizing the allocation of research resources and promoting the healthy development of the entire field [3].

Moreover, in the context of interdisciplinary research, the contributions of scholars from different fields are often difficult to fully reflect using traditional metrics. We need more nuanced methods to capture the unique value brought by researchers working across disciplinary boundaries [7]. By evaluating scholars based on their innovative roles, we can better recognize those who are bridging different areas of knowledge and driving the field forward in different ways. Therefore, we propose a method for evaluating scholars' influence based on scientific innovation roles. By clearly defining scholars' innovation roles, this method aims to better evaluate their impact in advancing new theories, methods, or technologies. Initially, the method involves multi-stage role segmentation of academic papers through citation relationship analysis, and then mapping these roles to authors using document-author correspondence to accurately identify each scholar's role. Additionally, a sliding time window analysis is employed to flexibly capture the evolution of scholars' roles over time, more accurately depicting changes in their influence within the field. Through this approach, we can provide a more comprehensive evaluation of an author's influence within their domain, thereby facilitating the identification of key influencers and guiding academic policy and funding distribution, further promoting the development of scientific research.

2   Related Work

Two types of methods are commonly used in evaluating scholars' academic influence: bibliometric methods and network analysis methods.

Bibliometric methods utilize indicators such as the number of publications, citation frequency, and average citations per article to evaluate academic influence. The h-index, proposed by Hirsch [8] in 2005, is a well-established and widely adopted method that considers both the number of publications and citation frequency, making it useful for evaluating a scholar's academic achievements. Guide2Research, for instance, uses the h-index as a key metric for identifying top scientists. To address the limitations of the h-index, such as its inability to reflect declines in academic influence and its lack of consideration for disciplinary differences, various h-index variants have been developed, including the g-quotient [9], the p-index [10], and the v-index [11].

Network analysis methods for evaluating scholars' influence involves ranking the importance of nodes based on network structure indicators. Commonly used indicators include degree centrality, betweenness centrality, closeness centrality, and the PageRank method. Degree centrality assesses a node's influence by the number of directly connected nodes. Betweenness centrality identifies a node as important if it lies on many paths between other nodes, reflecting the node's control over resources. Closeness centrality measures a node's independence, indicating higher centrality for nodes that are closer to others within the network. Erjia Yan et al. [12] applied network centrality indicators to measure scholars' influence and analyzed their correlation with bibliometric indicators such as citation counts, demonstrating the applicability of centrality indicators as measures of scholars' influence. Subsequently, Erjia Yan et al. [13] applied the PageRank method to co-authorship networks and compared it with h-index results, proving the effectiveness of PageRank in evaluating scholars' academic influence.

Existing methods for quantifying scholars' influence have some limitations. Traditional methods rely on scholars' historical accumulation, making it difficult to reflect research innovation and identify promising young scholars. Additionally, traditional influence evaluation methods struggle to capture rapidly changing emerging trends in a timely manner. This is especially true in the context of multidisciplinary intersections, where the contributions of scholars from different fields are not adequately reflected. Moreover, these methods do not consider the dynamic changes in academic influence.

3   Scholars' Influence Evaluation Model Based on Scientific Innovation Roles

The framework of the scholars' influence evaluation model based on scientific innovation roles proposed in this paper is illustrated in Fig. 1. It comprises the following three steps: (1) Taking the field of blockchain as an example, the collected scientific paper dataset is divided into distinct datasets for various topics. (2) The roles of paper nodes within the citation networks are identified based on the scientific innovation role recognition method defined in this paper, where the roles of papers may evolve over time or across the topics. (3) Based on the relationship between scholars and papers, the Scientific Innovation Role Index of scholars is calculated, and scholars are ranked by each role. This allows for the analysis of role changes among scholars across different periods and different topics, evaluating the influence and positioning of scholars in innovation of their research fields.

3.1   Data Sources and Processing

We take the blockchain field as an example. Blockchain represents a typical emerging and interdisciplinary field that has rapidly evolved since its inception in 2008, integrating concepts and methods from diverse disciplines such as computer science, cryptography, economics, and law. The field is characterized by rapid innovation and technological breakthroughs, with new concepts and applications emerging in quick succession. Besides, as an emerging field, blockchain

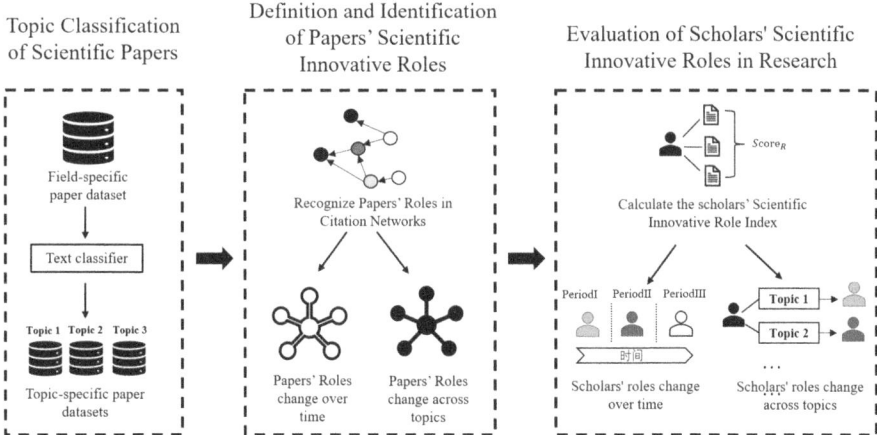

Fig. 1. Scholars' influence evaluation model based on scientific innovation roles.

research presents unique challenges in evaluating scholarly influence, where traditional bibliometric methods may not fully capture the contributions of early innovators or interdisciplinary researchers. This rapid pace of innovation and interdisciplinary nature make blockchain an ideal case study for examining how scholars from various backgrounds contribute to and influence an emerging field.

We collected bibliographic data from the Science Citation Index (SCI) and Social Sciences Citation Index (SSCI) databases for articles published from 2012 to 2022 on the topics of blockchain and cryptocurrency. After excluding records with missing titles or abstracts, we obtained 12,265 valid bibliographic records. Based on expert opinions in this field, blockchain research papers are divided into three primary topics: blockchain technology, blockchain application, and blockchain governance. Each primary topic is further subdivided into secondary topics. For example, blockchain application research encompasses applications in real economy and virtual economy.

The multi-label classification of scientific papers was performed using the TextRCNN model from NeuralClassifier [14], acknowledging that individual papers may pertain to multiple topics. Table 1 presents the distribution of papers across topics following the classification process.

3.2 Defining and Identifying the Scientific Innovation Roles of Papers

After completing the processing of scientific paper data, these data are applied to the construction of citation networks to further explore the roles played by scientific papers in the process of knowledge innovation and dissemination. In diffusion of innovations theory [15], Everett Rogers divides the people who adopt innovation into five categories in chronological order: innovators, early adopters, early majority, late majority, and laggards. Specifically, innovators are willing

Table 1. Statistics of scientific papers on various topics of blockchain research.

Primary topic	Secondary topic	Number of papers
Blockchain Technology	Core Technology	1792
	Collaborative Technology	2663
	Platforms and Projects	61
Blockchain Application	Real Economy	7021
	Virtual Economy	502
Blockchain Governance	Market Governance	2587
	Technical Governance	258
	Legal Governance	62

to try new technologies and play a key role in the early stages of innovation; early adopters are usually opinion leaders with relatively high social status; the early majority is more cautious, not actively leading the trend but playing a bridging role in the diffusion of innovations; the late majority is skeptical about innovations and often requires more social proof or pressure to accept innovation; while laggards are conservative and traditional, only accepting innovation when it becomes mainstream.

We analogize this concept to the citation diffusion of scientific papers, where the citation relationship can be viewed as the adoption and absorption of knowledge among scientific papers, which is also a manifestation of innovation diffusion. In existing research, Min Chao et al. [16] divided the citing scientific papers that directly cite a given scientific paper into similar five roles based on the time order for the innovation diffusion of a single scientific paper. However, for an entire research field, it is not enough to distinguish roles solely based on time order. A later innovation may be rapidly and widely recognized and applied due to its groundbreaking nature, and its influence may surpass that of earlier research.

We redefine the roles in scientific innovation according to the actual functions and positions of scientific papers in the knowledge network, in order to accurately describe the contributions of various types of research to the academic field. Within a specific academic field, the number of citations made by a scientific paper is fixed, while the number of citations it received will increase over time and as the number of papers in the field increases. Therefore, we construct a citation network with citing papers as source nodes and cited papers as target nodes. From this perspective, the act of being cited is viewed as the process of creating and disseminating new knowledge, while the act of citing is viewed as the process of absorbing and adopting new knowledge. Based on these behaviors of creating and absorbing new knowledge, we divide scientific papers into five different roles in scientific innovation, as shown in Table 2. Since laggards have not yet appeared in this academic field, this role will not be considered in this paper.

Table 2. Definition and characteristics of scientific innovation roles of papers.

Innovation Role	Citation Relationship	Position in Field	Knowledge Diffusion Behavior
Pioneer	Citing=0&Cited>0	Innovation pioneer	Only create knowledge
Leader	Cited> Citing>0	Opinion leaders	Create knowledge more than absorb knowledge
Early Follower	Citing≥Cited>0	Have had some accumulation	Create knowledge less than absorb knowledge
Late Follower	Citing>0&Cited=0	Newly joined or not yet been recognized	Only absorb knowledge
Laggard	Cited=0&Citing=0	Outside the field	/

Changes in the Roles of Paper Over Time. The citation count of a paper is fixed, while the number of citations it receives may increase over time. This changing relationship between the number of citations received and given can affect the paper's role in its field. If a newly published paper cites existing papers in the field, it initially plays the role of a late follower in that field. Over time, as the paper's citations increase, it can evolve from a late follower to an early follower, and from an early follower to a leader. Conversely, if a paper does not cite other works, it may be considered a potential pioneer in the field. If it later becomes cited by other publications in the field, its role may shift to that of a pioneer. The evolution of the roles in scientific innovation is depicted in Fig. 2.

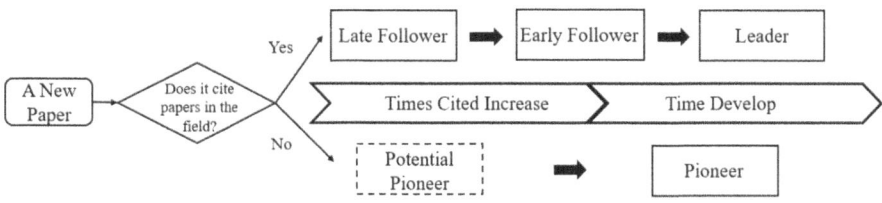

Fig. 2. Scholars' influence evaluation model based on scientific innovation roles.

Taking Fig. 3 as an example, the changes in the scientific innovation roles of nodes are explained in detail. The evolution process is divided into five periods (I, II, III, IV, V) in chronological order. The color of the nodes, from dark to light, represents pioneers, leaders, early followers, and late followers respectively. In Period I, node A creates a brand-new field, awaiting discovery and recognition.

In Period II, node C joins the field by citing A. As a result, Node A's role shifts to that of a pioneer, and Node C becomes a late follower in the field. In Period III, node B acknowledges and cites both A and C. While A's role remains unchanged, C becomes an early follower due to being cited, and B is marked as a late follower because it cites but is not cited. At this time, an independent node H appears outside the field. Since H does not cite any articles within the field, it is marked as a potential pioneer. In Period IV, nodes E and F join the field by citing B and C respectively. B transitions to an early follower, and C becomes a leader as its number of citations received exceeds the number of citations it made. Concurrently, Node H connects to the network through F and becomes another pioneer. In Period V, nodes D and G join the network. D cites B, becoming a late follower in the field; similarly, G cites F, making G a late follower as well. At this time, B's citations received surpass its citations made, making it another leader in the field. E and F, due to being cited, transition from late followers to early followers.

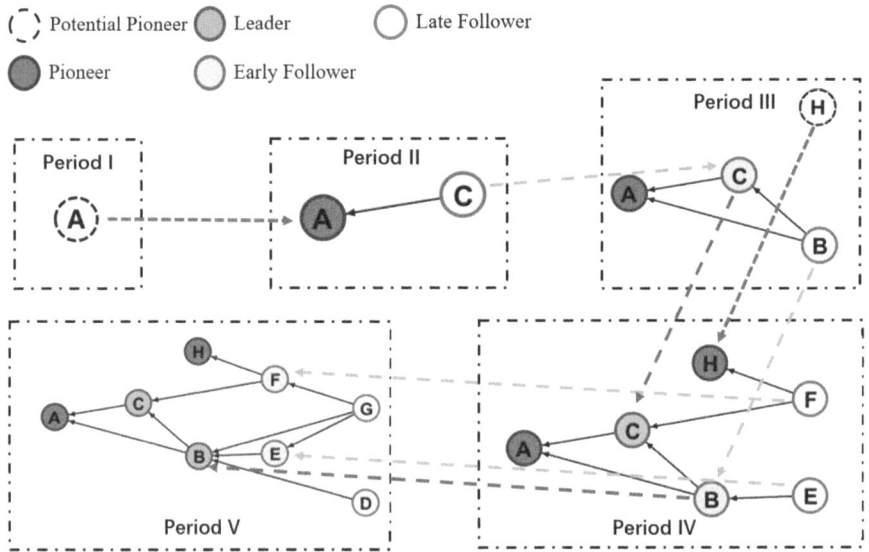

Fig. 3. An example of changes in scientific innovation roles of paper nodes over time.

Changes in the Roles of Paper Across Topics. A large research field can often be divided into multiple research topics such as theory and application. A single research paper can also encompass research content from multiple topics. The citation networks in different topics often varies, changing the relationship between the number of citations received and given. Therefore, the same paper can play different roles in scientific innovation in different topics. As shown in

Fig. 4, in the citation network of Topic 1, Node B has given 2 citations and received none, thus it is classified as a late follower. However, in the citation network of Topic 2, Node B is a pioneer in this field, as it has been cited by 3 nodes and does not give any citations.

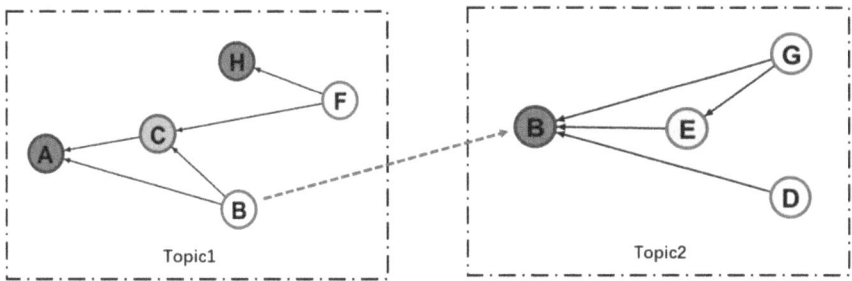

Fig. 4. An example of changes in scientific innovation roles of paper nodes across topics.

3.3   Mapping Scholars' Roles in Scientific Innovation

We further extend the concept of scientific innovation roles from individual papers to scholars. By analyzing the positions and roles of all papers authored by a scholar within the citation diffusion network, we can depict the scholar's role in the academic community, gaining insights into the scholar's actual contributions and influence in the processes of scientific innovation and knowledge dissemination.

The contribution of a paper to the field is represented by the scientific innovation role value of the paper node. Since the contributions of different scientific innovation roles vary, and the contributions of different nodes within the same role also differ, it is necessary to assign a value to each paper node to quantify the differences. For this purpose, we use the PageRank of paper nodes in the citation network as the measure of node contribution. The innovation role value D_{v_i} of a paper node v_i is defined as:

$$D_{v_i} = PR\left(v_i\right) \tag{1}$$

where $PR\left(v_i\right)$ represents the PageRank value of the paper node in the citation network.

Since a paper is usually co-authored by multiple collaborators, with each author contributing differently, it is necessary to assign different collaborator weights to the different authors of each paper. We adopt the collaborator research contribution weights in Table 3.

Table 3. Collaborator research contribution weights.

Number of Authors	First Author	Second Author	Third Author	Fourth Author	Fifth Author	Sixth Author
1	1					
2	0.6	0.4				
3	0.6	0.25	0.15			
4	0.6	0.2	0.1	0.1		
5	0.6	0.1	0.1	0.1	0.1	
6	0.6	0.1	0.1	0.1	0.05	0.05

The author position weights are represented as a 6×6 contribution matrix W; a_{mn} represents the element in the $m-th$ row and $n-th$ column.

$$W = \begin{vmatrix} 1 & 0 & 0 & 0 & 0 & 0 \\ 0.6 & 0.4 & 0 & 0 & 0 & 0 \\ 0.6 & 0.25 & 0.15 & 0 & 0 & 0 \\ 0.6 & 0.2 & 0.2 & 0.1 & 0 & 0 \\ 0.6 & 0.1 & 0.1 & 0.1 & 0.1 & 0 \\ 0.6 & 0.1 & 0.1 & 0.1 & 0.05 & 0.05 \end{vmatrix} \tag{2}$$

For a scholar S who participated in writing the literature v_i as the $n-th$ author, the scholar's contribution is $a_{mn}(m \leq 6)$, with m indicating that the article v_i has m authors in total. If $m \geq 6$, we only consider the contributions of the first six authors.

Finally, by combining the scientific innovation role value of the papers with the author contribution weights, the four types of scientific innovation role indices corresponding to each scholar are calculated to reflect the role of the authors in knowledge innovation and dissemination within their research fields. Specifically, if the paper v_i in the given field paper set V is classified into the innovation role R, then the role index R for scholar S who is an author of this paper is calculated as:

$$\text{Score}_{v_i,R} = D_{v_i} \times a_{mn} \tag{3}$$

Combining formulas (1) and (3), the role index R for scholar S in the entire field paper set V is obtained by summing the product of the innovation role value D_{v_i} of each R role paper v_i in which the scholar participated and the scholar's contribution a_{mn} to each paper, calculated as:

$$\text{Score}_{V,R} = \sum_i PR(v_i) \times a_{mn} \tag{4}$$

Through this method, it is possible to comprehensively evaluate a scholar's scientific impact within their field, providing a quantitative perspective for academic assessment and better understanding the scholar's contributions to the process of scientific innovation.

4   Results

4.1   Within-Topic Analysis

The scientific innovation roles of papers may change over time, and accordingly, the scientific innovation indices of the authors are updated. Therefore, we divide the development period into four time periods: 2012 to 2019, 2020, 2021, and 2022. Taking the research topic 'core technology' in blockchain field as an example, for each period, we calculated the four types of scientific innovation role indices for all scholars in this topic and classified and ranked the scholars accordingly. Tables 4, 5, 6 and 7 respectively show the top ten scholars for each role across all time segments.

Table 4. Scholar innovation role rankings in "core technology" research of blockchain from 2012–2019.

Pioneer	Authors	Leader	Authors	Early Follower	Authors	Late Follower	Authors
1	Christidis, K (0.0521)	1	Casamatta, C (0.0055)	1	Frankenreiter, J (0.0206)	1	Kim, S (0.0031)
1	Devetsikiotis, M (0.0521)	1	Biais, B (0.0055)	1	Hermstruewer, Y (0.0206)	1	Guadamuz, A (0.0031)
3	Kraft, D (0.01301)	1	Bisiere, C (0.0055)	3	He, ZG (0.0108)	1	Cho, H (0.0031)
4	Patel, V (0.0084)	1	Bouvard, M (0.0055)	3	Koeppl, TV (0.0108)	4	Yuan, Y (0.0027)
5	Taylor, PG (0.0082)	5	Kumar, ES (0.0050)	3	Cong, LW (0.0108)	4	Wang, FY (0.0027)
5	Krzesinski, AE (0.0082)	5	Conti, M (0.0050)	3	Chiu, J (0.0108)	6	Wang, SP (0.0018)
5	Goebel, J (0.0082)	5	Lal, C (0.0050)	7	Abou Jaoude, J (0.0029)	6	Zhang, YL (0.0018)
5	Keeler, HP (0.0082)	5	Ruj, S (0.0050)	7	Saade, RG (0.0029)	8	Liu, XM (0.0016)
9	Lee, JH (0.0073)	9	Kim, HW (0.0041)	9	Niyato, D (0.0026)	9	Lee, JH (0.0016)
10	O'Hara, K (0.0061)	9	Jeong, YS (0.0041)	10	Salah, K (0.0022)	10	Yang, Z (0.0016)

Table 5. Scholar innovation role rankings in "core technology" research of blockchain from 2012–2020.

Pioneer	Authors	Leader	Authors	Early Follower	Authors	Late Follower	Authors
1	Christidis, K (0.0438)	1	He, ZG (0.0086)	1	Koeppl, TV (0.0074)	1	Lee, JH (0.0012)
1	Devetsikiotis, M (0.0438)	1	Cong, LW (0.0086)	1	Chiu, J (0.0074)	1	Pournaras, E (0.0012)
3	Kraft, D (0.0093)	3	Conti, M (0.0042)	3	Hermstruewer, Y (0.0034)	1	Culha, D (0.0012)
4	Krzesinski, AE (0.0071)	3	Ruj, S (0.0042)	4	Frankenreiter, J (0.0026)	1	Mihaljevic, MJ (0.0012)
4	Keeler, HP (0.0071)	3	Kumar, ES (0.0042)	5	Saade, RG (0.0015)	1	Kim, S (0.0012)
4	Goebel, J (0.0071)	3	Lal, C (0.0042)	5	Abou Jaoude, J (0.0015)	1	Zhang, JBN (0.0012)
4	Taylor, PG (0.0071)	7	Salah, K (0.0040)	7	Guadamuz, A (0.0013)	1	Boukis, A (0.0012)
8	Gramoli, V (0.0068)	8	Hasan, HR (0.0037)	8	Rezaeibagha, F (0.0011)	1	Frattolillo, F (0.0012)
9	Lee, JH (0.0042)	9	Casamatta, C (0.0037)	8	Mu, Yi (0.0011)	1	Pang, Y (0.0012)
10	Jiang, P (0.0032)	10	Bouvard, M (0.0034)	7	Bozic, N (0.009)	3	Zuo, YJ (0.0006)

The results reveal that Christidis, K., and Devetsikiotis, M., consistently rank as pioneers in all phases, demonstrating their research's sustained high innovativeness. Kraft, D., although always a pioneer, has seen a decline in his ranking. Gramoli, V. entered the forefront of pioneers starting in 2020, potentially driving some significant innovations in the field. He, ZG, and Cong, LW transitioned from early followers to leaders starting in 2019, indicating that their research has gradually gained recognition and made increasing contributions to

Table 6. Scholar innovation role rankings in "core technology" research of blockchain from 2012–2021.

Pioneer	Authors	Leader	Authors	Early Follower	Authors	Late Follower	Authors
1	Devetsikiotis, M (0.0340)	1	He, ZG (0.0074)	1	Hermstruewer, Y (0.0019)	1	Das, D (0.0009)
1	Christidis, K (0.0340)	1	Cong, LW (0.0074)	2	Frankenreiter, J (0.0014)	2	Choo, KKR (0.0006)
3	Kraft, D (0.0075)	3	Chiu, J (0.0066)	3	Saleh, F (0.0014)	3	Lee, NY (0.0006)
4	Krzesinski, AE (0.0066)	3	Koeppl, TV (0.0066)	4	Bouraga, S (0.0011)	3	Wang, FY (0.0006)
4	Taylor, PG (0.0066)	5	Kumar, ES (0.0043)	5	Saade, RG (0.0009)	3	Zhou, W (0.0006)
4	Goebel, J (0.0066)	5	Lal, C (0.0043)	5	Abou Jaoude, J (0.0009)	3	Kim, S (0.0006)
4	Keeler, HP (0.0066)	5	Ruj, S (0.0043)	7	Secci, S (0.0009)	3	Mihaljevic, MJ (0.0006)
8	Gramoli, V (0.0041)	5	Conti, M (0.0043)	7	Pujolle, G (0.0009)	3	Lu, Y (0.0006)
9	Lee, JH (0.0034)	9	Niyato, D (0.0039)	7	Belotti, M (0.0009)	3	Zhang, JBN (0.0006)
10	Jiang, P (0.0032)	10	Bouvard, M (0.0034)	7	Bozic, N (0.009)	3	Zuo, YJ (0.0006)

Table 7. Scholar innovation role rankings in "core technology" research of blockchain from 2012–2022.

Pioneer	Authors	Leader	Authors	Early Follower	Authors	Late Follower	Authors
1	Christidis, K (0.0277)	1	Cong, LW (0.0067)	1	Hermstruewer, Y (0.0010)	1	Tian, JF (0.0005)
1	Devetsikiotis, M (0.0277)	1	He, ZG (0.0067)	2	Frankenreiter, J (0.0008)	2	Das, D (0.0005)
3	Kraft, D (0.0063)	3	Koeppl, TV (0.0057)	3	Ferrer-Gomila, JL (0.0005)	3	Wang, Y (0.0004)
4	Goebel, J (0.0056)	3	Chiu, J (0.0057)	3	Kushch, S (0.0005)	4	Zhou, W (0.0004)
4	Krzesinski, AE (0.0056)	5	Niyato, D (0.0038)	5	Lu, Y (0.0004)	5	Javaid, N (0.0004)
4	Keeler, HP (0.0056)	6	Conti, M (0.0037)	6	Yan, Z (0.0004)	6	Guo, B (0.0003)
4	Taylor, PG (0.0056)	6	Lal, C (0.0037)	7	Robinson, P (0.0004)	7	Lee, NY (0.0003)
8	Gramoli, V (0.0033)	6	Ruj, S (0.0037)	8	Guadamuz, A (0.0004)	7	Drusinsky, D (0.0003)
9	Jiang, P (0.0030)	6	Kumar, ES (0.0037)	9	Chang, XL (0.0004)	7	Qiu, J (0.0003)
9	Wen, QY (0.0030)	10	Xiong, ZH (0.0031)	10	Liyanage, M (0.0004)	7	Tariq, U (0.0003)

the field. Kumar, ES, Conti, M, Ruj, S, and Lal, C consistently rank as leaders, showing their enduring influence in the blockchain field. Hermstruewer, Y, and Frankenreiter, J have been early followers in all stages, continually focusing on this research topic. Lee, JH was both a pioneer and a leader until 2020, reflecting his early significant contributions to blockchain core technology. These changes in scientific innovation roles reflect the dynamic evolution of scholars' innovative roles and influence over time. Such changes are likely influenced by shifts in scholars' research interests, technological trends, and the community's acceptance levels.

4.2   Cross-Topic Analysis

Scholars may choose multiple topics to conduct their research, and their roles as scientific innovators may vary across these topics. Scholars with interdisciplinary research capabilities can facilitate the integration of knowledge between different fields, promoting the development of interdisciplinary studies. Deep engagement in a specific topic indicates that a scholar has established a substantial knowledge base and expertise in that area, while engagement in multiple topics demonstrates the breadth of their research. This section analyzes the changes in scientific innovation roles of scholars across different topics such as collaborative technology, market governance, real-economy application, and core technology from 2012 to 2022. The role rankings of scholars are shown in Tables 8, 9 and 10.

Table 8. Scholar innovation role rankings in "collaborative technology" research of blockchain from 2012–2022.

Pioneer	Authors	Leader	Authors	Early Follower	Authors	Late Follower	Authors
1	Herbaut, N (0.0114)	1	Novo, O (0.0174)	1	Kisi, N (0.0009)	1	Zhu, LH (0.0004)
1	Negru, D (0.0114)	2	Niyato, D (0.0075)	2	Kumar, N (0.0007)	2	Yi, HB (0.0003)
3	Ouahman, AA (0.0111)	3	Zhang, Y (0.0073)	3	Park, JH (0.0007)	2	Jeong, YS (0.0003)
3	Abou Elkalam, A (0.0111)	4	Xiong, ZH (0.0062)	4	Tanwar, S (0.0005)	4	Park, JH (0.0003)
3	Ouaddah, A (0.0111)	5	Wang, P (0.0061)	5	Yi, HB (0.0005)	5	Guizani, M (0.0003)
6	Park, JH (0.0100)	6	Han, Z (0.0053)	6	Yu, FR (0.0004)	6	Yu, FR (0.0002)
7	Sharma, PK (0.0089)	7	Zhang, Y (0.0050)	7	Niyato, D (0.0004)	7	Tanwar, S (0.0002)
8	Wen, JT (0.0047)	8	Yu, FR (0.0043)	8	Javaid, N (0.0004)	8	Jiao, TY (0.0002)
8	Zhang, Y (0.0047)	9	Maharjan, S (0.0033)	9	Choo, KKR (0.0004)	9	Yassine, A (0.0002)
9	Jeong, YS (0.0045)	10	Liu, H (0.0033)	10	Wu, YL (0.0004)	9	Bhattacharjya, A (0.0002)

Table 9. Scholar innovation role rankings in "market governance" research of blockchain from 2012–2022.

Pioneer	Authors	Leader	Authors	Early Follower	Authors	Late Follower	Authors
1	Dwyer, GP (0.0137)	1	Urquhart, A (0.0272)	1	Bouri, E (0.0013)	1	Cohen, G (0.0005)
2	Dyhrberg, AH (0.0125)	2	Dyhrberg, AH (0.0165)	2	Grobys, K (0.0011)	2	Bouri, E (0.0004)
3	Edelman, B (0.0093)	3	Kristoufek, L (0.0158)	3	Kristoufek, L (0.0009)	3	Kristoufek, L (0.0004)
3	Boehme, R (0.0093)	4	Bouri, E (0.0131)	4	Corbet, S (0.0009)	4	Urquhart, A (0.0004)
3	Moore, T (0.0093)	5	Katsiampa, P (0.0123)	5	Yarovaya, L (0.0008)	5	Ahmed, WMA (0.0003)
3	Christin, N (0.0093)	6	Fry, J (0.0118)	6	Bekiros, S (0.0008)	5	Xie, P (0.0003)
7	Selgin, G (0.0075)	7	Roubaud, D (0.0113)	7	Lahmiri, S (0.0007)	5	Treiblmaier, H (0.0003)
8	Swartz, L (0.0065)	8	Cheah, ET (0.0113)	8	Naeem, MA (0.0007)	8	Mohamad, A (0.0003)
8	Nelms, TC (0.0065)	9	Bariviera, AF (0.0086)	9	Shahzad, SJH (0.0007)	9	Cossu, A (0.0003)
8	Maurer, B (0.0065)	10	Yermack, D (0.0065)	10	Yousaf, I (0.0007)	10	Yousaf, I (0.0003)

As is shown in the results, Niyato, D primarily plays a leadership role in the core technology topic, while in collaborative technology, he is both a leader and an early follower, showing significant contributions in these two critical areas and reflecting the breadth of his research. Kumar, N is mainly an early follower in collaborative technology and both a leader and an early follower in real-economy application, indicating his early research and significant contributions in these fields. Tanwar, S is an early follower in both blockchain collaborative technology and real-economy application, suggesting a broad research interest in the blockchain field. Xiong, ZH holds a leadership position in both core technology and collaborative technology research, demonstrating profound expertise and influence in these areas. Yu, FR is a leader in collaborative technology and an early follower in real-economy application, showing diverse research interests and varying influence across different topics.

Table 10. Scholar innovation role rankings in "real-economy application" research of blockchain from 2012–2022.

Pioneer	Authors	Leader	Authors	Early Follower	Authors	Late Follower	Authors
1	Kshetri, N (0.0107)	1	Zhang, Y (0.0032)	1	Choi, TM (0.0006)	1	Varzaru, AA (0.0003)
2	Svetinovic, D (0.0079)	2	Choi, TM (0.0030)	2	Tanwar, S (0.0005)	2	Tanwar, S (0.0002)
3	Aitzhan, NZ (0.0079)	3	Sarkis, J (0.0026)	3	Kumar, N (0.0005)	3	Kim, SK (0.0002)
4	Zheng, ZB (0.0043)	4	Choo, KKR (0.0024)	4	Byun, YC (0.0004)	4	Salah, K (0.0001)
5	Chen, XP (0.0043)	5	Kouhizadeh, M (0.0023)	5	Javaid, N (0.0003)	5	Jayaraman, R (0.0001)
6	Dai, HN (0.0043)	6	Kang, JW (0.0023)	6	Shahbazi, Z (0.0003)	6	Lian, GH (0.0001)
6	Wang, HM (0.0043)	7	Cong, LW (0.0023)	7	Yi, HB (0.0003)	6	Jeong, YS (0.0001)
6	Xie, SA (0.0043)	7	He, ZG (0.0023)	8	Yu, FR (0.0003)	8	Choo, KKR (0.0001)
9	Sikorski, JJ (0.0036)	9	Yu, R (0.0022)	9	Park, JH (0.0003)	9	Gupta, R (0.0001)
9	Haughton, J (0.0036)	10	Kumar, N (0.0021)	10	Garg, L (0.0002)	10	Zhu, LH (0.0001)

Also, we find that scholars in market governance and those engaged in blockchain technology and application research rarely overlap, which may reflect significant differences in research objectives and methods across disciplines, leading to the scarcity of interdisciplinary research. This phenomenon suggests that although interdisciplinary research faces challenges, it also contains critical opportunities to drive disciplinary advancements.

4.3   Case Study

To validate the effectiveness and scientific validity of the scholars' influence evaluation method based on scientific innovation roles proposed in this paper, this section will select typical author cases for case analysis.

In the core technology topic of blockchain, scholar Cong, LW followed Chiu, J and others into this research area in 2019. He referenced two papers including 'The Blockchain Folk Theorem' and published 'Blockchain Disruption and Smart Contracts.' Initially, this article only received two citations in 2019. According to our method, Cong, LW's early-follower-index is calculated to be 0.0108, which places him high in the ranking of early followers. With this score, Cong, LW can be considered a quintessential early follower, demonstrating the ability to identify and engage with potentially influential research at an early stage, before it gained widespread attention in the field. By the end of 2020, the cited number of this paper had increased to 8. At this point, Cong, LW's leader-index is calculated to be 0.0086, placing them among the top-ranked leaders in the field, indicating that Cong, LW gradually established reputation and influence in the field and transitioned from an early follower to a leader. Cong, LW continued to delve into this area and published another relevant paper 'Decentralized Mining in Centralized Pools' in 2021. By 2022, these two papers had garnered a total of 26 citations in the core technology area, significantly boosting his leadership status in the field.

To compare our method with traditional metrics, let's consider the h-index. At the end of 2019, Cong, LW's h-index in the blockchain core technology field would have been 1, as he had only one paper with at least one citation. This low h-index would not have captured his potential as an emerging scholar in the field. Even by 2020, with 8 citations for his paper, his h-index would still be 1, failing to reflect his growing influence and transition to a leadership role.

In contrast, our method, based on the innovation roles, effectively revealed Cong, LW's transition from an early follower to a leader. It captured the rapid increase in his growing influence (citations from 2 to 8 to 26) over a short period. Moreover, our method considered the context of his publications, recognizing his role as an early follower who quickly established leadership in a new, rapidly evolving field. By 2022, while Cong, LW's h-index in blockchain core technology field would have increased to 2, it still wouldn't fully capture the significant impact of his papers or his leadership status in the field. Our method, however, provides a more nuanced picture of his influence trajectory, highlighting not just the quantity of citations but also the timing and context of his contributions.

These quantitative data demonstrate the efficacy of the scholars' influence evaluation method based on the segmentation of the times cited of this paper innovation roles, effectively revealing the transition process from early followers to leaders. Unlike the h-index, which may lag in reflecting rapid changes in influence, especially in fast-moving fields like blockchain, our method provides a more dynamic and contextual evaluation of a scholar's influence and role in the field.

5   Conclusion

Scholars, as an essential component of the innovation ecosystem, play a crucial role in advancing technological progress. By analyzing their influence, we can understand how individual contributions drive knowledge and innovation across various fields. Addressing the shortcomings of existing scholars' influence models in evaluating emerging fields, we propose a scholars' influence evaluation framework based on the scientific innovation roles, taking blockchain field as an example.

We define paper scientific innovation roles into pioneer, leader, early follower, and late follower based on the theory of innovation diffusion, and further map the research roles of the papers to the scholar level, thereby assessing the role positioning and its changes for scholars within the field. The proposed method provides a more detailed perspective by analyzing the research roles assumed by scholars, more comprehensively demonstrating their actual innovation contributions and value in various domains.

While this method has shown promising results in the emerging and interdisciplinary field of blockchain, its universal applicability requires further validation. This would contribute to the development of a more versatile and flexible system for evaluating scholarly influence, ultimately providing more comprehensive tools for academic assessment across various fields.

References

1. Haislup, B.D., Trent, S., Sequeira, S., Murthi, A.M., Wright, M.A.: The relationship between academic influence, NIH funding, and industry payments among academic shoulder and elbow surgeons. J. Shoulder Elbow Surg. **31**(11), 2431–2436 (2022)
2. Nakamoto, S.: Bitcoin: a peer-to-peer electronic cash system (2008)
3. Hicks, D., Wouters, P., Waltman, L., De Rijcke, S., Rafols, I.: Bibliometrics: the Leiden Manifesto for research metrics. Nature **520**(7548), 429–431 (2015)
4. Garfield, E.: Citation indexes for science: a new dimension in documentation through association of ideas. Science **122**(3159), 108–111 (1955)
5. Schubert, A.: Using the h-index for assessing single publications. Scientometrics **78**(3), 559–565 (2009)
6. Zhang, J., Luo, Y.: Degree centrality, betweenness centrality, and closeness centrality in social network. In: 2017 2nd International Conference on Modelling. Simulation and Applied Mathematics (MSAM2017), pp. 300–303. Atlantis Press, Bangkok (2017)
7. Wang, J., Li, Y., Jia, Y., Zhang, P.: A method for scholars' influence evaluation based on representative papers. In: 2022 4th International Conference on Machine Learning. Big Data and Business Intelligence (MLBDBI), pp. 71–77. IEEE, Shanghai (2022)
8. Hirsch, J.E.: An index to quantify an individual's scientific research output. Proc. Natl. Acad. Sci. **102**(46), 16569–16572 (2005)
9. Egghe, L.: An improvement of the h-index: the g-index. ISSI Newslett. **2**(1), 8–9 (2006)
10. Prathap, G.: Is there a place for a mock h-index? Scientometrics **84**(1), 153–165 (2010)
11. Li, H.Y., Xu, Q., Li, N.K.: A new improved indicator for the influence evaluation of the field-v-index. J. Inf. **34**(12), 38–43 (2015)
12. Yan, E., Ding, Y.: Applying centrality measures to impact analysis: a coauthorship network analysis. J. Am. Soc. Inform. Sci. Technol. **60**(10), 2107–2118 (2009)
13. Yan, E., Ding, Y.: Discovering author impact: a PageRank perspective. Inf. Process. Manag. **47**(1), 125–134 (2011)
14. NeuralClassifier. https://github.com/Tencent/NeuralNLP-NeuralClassifier. Accessed 1 July 2024
15. Rogers, E.M.: Diffusion of Innovations, 5th edn. Free Press, New York (2003)
16. Min, C., Ding, Y., Li, J., Sun, J.J.: The diffusion of citations for individual publications. J. China Soc. Sci. Tech. Inf. **37**(4), 341–350 (2018)

Adaptive DeepWalk and Prior-Enhanced Graph Neural Network for Scholar Influence Maximization in Social Networks

Yijia Wang[1], Junjie Lin[1], Yong Tang[1,3], Chengzhe Yuan[2,3(✉)], and Luming Zhang[1]

[1] School of Computer Science, South China Normal University, Guangzhou, China
{wangyj,jjlin,ytang,lmzhang}@m.scnu.edu.cn
[2] School of Electronic and Information, Guangdong Polytechnic Normal University, Guangzhou, China
[3] Pazhou Lab, Guangzhou, China
ycz@gpnu.edu.cn

Abstract. With the rapid development of academic social media, the problem of node influence diffusion in scholar social networks has increasingly received extensive attention from the field of influence maximization (IM). Existing learning-based methods for solving the IM problem usually rely solely on network topology or individual node activities, lacking comprehensive consideration of both network topology and important information of nodes, leading to poor model performance. By comprehensively considering the network topology as well as the global information and importance of nodes, we propose a deep reinforcement learning (DRL) framework, named APGD-IM, which is based on an adaptive DeepWalk algorithm and a prior-enhanced graph neural network (GNN), aiming to optimize the performance degradation caused by the above issue. Specifically, we propose an adaptive DeepWalk algorithm DRA based on attention mechanism and node importance information, along with a prior-enhanced GNN module PGNN, for generating node embeddings. These embeddings are then used to learn parameters by combining double deep Q-network to address scholar influence maximization problem in social networks. Experimental results on four real-world social networks demonstrate that our proposed model outperforms other baseline methods and maintains stable performance advantages across different diffusion models.

Keywords: Influence maximization · Attention mechanism · Graph neural networks · Social networks

1 Introduction

Social networks have become integral components of contemporary society, playing a crucial role in facilitating the dissemination of information and sharing knowledge. In the academic field, social networks are also of great importance. Academic social networks provide scholars with a platform to share

H. Sun et al. (Eds.): ChineseCSCW 2024, CCIS 2343, pp. 235–250, 2025.
https://doi.org/10.1007/978-981-96-2373-0_17

research findings, exchange academic perspectives, and seek collaborators, such as SCHOLAT.com and ResearchGate.net. However, with the rapid development of academic social media, scholars are facing challenges of information cocoons and disciplinary barriers. Therefore, it is critical to accurately identify and utilize influential spreaders to maximize the spread of important information. Influence maximization (IM) is an important research topic in the field of social network analysis, which has received widespread attention from scholars in recent years. The IM problem aims to find a set of seed nodes that maximizes the spread of influence in a social network [20].

In the past few decades, researchers have proposed various types of IM algorithms. Kempe et al. [13] first formulated IM as a combinatorial optimization (CO) problem and provided a greedy algorithm. However, the greedy algorithm is inefficient due to the fact that it needs to invoke Monte Carlo simulation at each iteration, which inspired the emergence of numerous improved algorithms [7,18]. Subsequently, a series of IM algorithms have been proposed, including heuristic algorithms [5,9,11], approximation algorithms [28–30], etc. Although these algorithms enhance the efficiency of solving the IM problem, they suffer from low accuracy and poor scalability respectively, resulting in suboptimal performance. Furthermore, with the rapid development of deep learning and reinforcement learning (RL) in recent years, a growing trend has emerged towards addressing the IM problem through learning-based approaches due to their adaptive capabilities. Some methods employ RL to solve the IM problem and achieve impressive results [4,14,19]. However, these approaches rely solely on network topology, neglecting the important information of nodes, which leads to poor model performance. Conversely, some works rely solely on individual node activities to select seed nodes, such as IMINFECTOR [24]. By ignoring the network topology, these methods lack adaptability to different networks.

To address the above problems, inspired by [4], we propose a deep reinforcement learning (DRL) framework, named APGD-IM (Adaptive DeepWalk and Prior-enhanced Graph neural network with double Deep Q-networks for Influence Maximization), to optimize the performance by comprehensively considering the network topology as well as the global information and importance features of nodes. In this paper, we use RL to address the IM problem, framing it as a task of finding the optimal strategy for selecting k seed nodes to maximize influence spread. Since deep Q-network [23] (DQN) has the problem of over-optimism, we employ its improved version, Double DQN [31] (DDQN), for parameters learning. To comprehensively consider both the network topology and important node information, we propose an adaptive DeepWalk method, DRA (DeepWalk with Random walk with restart and Attention), to learn the initial node embeddings, holistically capturing the global and local structures of the network. Additionally, by introducing an attention mechanism into random walk with restart (RWR) and dynamically adjusting the walking strategy based on node importance features, we enhance the focus on important information and improve the adaptability of model to different network topologies. Furthermore, we propose a prior-enhanced graph neural network (GNN) module, PGNN, for generating node embeddings. These embeddings are subsequently utilized in the following DDQN. Specifically, we introduce heuristic embeddings containing global information and importance features of nodes as additional inputs and guidance information for GNN, which makes the node embeddings more reliable. The main contributions of this paper can be summarized as follows:

- We propose a learning-based framework, APGD-IM, to optimize the performance degradation caused by relying solely on single information.
- We propose an adaptive DeepWalk method, DRA, which introduces an attention mechanism and dynamically adjusts the walking strategy, enabling the model to focus on more important information and comprehensively capture the network topology.
- We propose a prior-enhanced GNN module, PGNN, to improve the quality of node embeddings which are inputs to the following DDQN by introducing global information and importance features of nodes as additional inputs and guidance information.
- Extensive experiments are conducted to demonstrate the performance of our proposed model, indicating that in academic social networks and other application scenarios, APGD-IM outperforms other methods in identifying seed nodes to maximize influence.

2 Related Work

2.1 Learning-Based Influence Maximization

Kempe et al. [13] first formulated IM as a CO problem, proving that the IM problem is NP-hard, which has inspired widespread research in the field of IM. In recent years, with the development of deep learning and reinforcement learning, an increasing number of studies have employed learning-based approaches to address the IM problem. Kumar et al. [15] interpreted the IM problem as a pseudo-regression task, combining the graph embedding method with GNN-based regressor to predict node influence scores and select seed nodes. Panagopoulos et al. [24] proposed a model-independent influence maximization method, IMINFECTOR, which learns node representations from diffusion cascades rather than relying on network topology to choose seed nodes. Khalil et al. [14] first designed a DRL framework S2V-DQN for the CO problem, which utilizes the IM problem to test the performance and selects the seed nodes by combining the graph embedding and DRL method. Similarly, Li et al. [19] proposed the DRL model PIANO by modifying S2V-DQN to solve the IM problem. Chen et al. [4] introduced a DRL framework ToupleGDD to address the IM problem, which combines GNN and DRL to select seed nodes. However, these methods either rely on network topology or node activities, without comprehensively considering both the network topology and the important information of nodes. This limitation resulted in insufficient representational capability of the generated node embeddings, thereby resulting in poor model performance.

2.2 User Influence Metrics for Prior Enhancement

Many methods select the top k nodes with the highest influence score as seed nodes to maximize the spread of influence [15,34]. Therefore, node influence metrics are crucial for solving the IM problem in social networks. Researchers usually use node importance ranking metrics to measure the influence of nodes in social networks, including degree centrality [10], clustering coefficient [2], betweenness centrality [22], eigenvector centrality [3], closeness centrality [35], etc. These metrics can effectively describe the global information of nodes and reflect their influence. To better adapt to the need of IM problem in social networks, we regard representative node influence metrics as user importance features, and use them as the walking guidance and additional input information for generating node embeddings, thereby enhancing the representation capability of node embeddings and improving the effectiveness of influence maximization.

3 The Proposed Framework

In this section, we propose the APGD-IM framework, which is illustrated in Fig. 1. Specifically, we introduce the adaptive DeepWalk method DRA to generate initial node embeddings. These embeddings are then fed into the prior-enhanced GNN module PGNN to generate the final node embeddings. Subsequently, we construct a parameterized function $\hat{Q}(v, S; \Theta)$ and learn parameter Θ using DDQN, allowing the function to approximate the gain $\sigma(v; S)$ obtained after selecting a seed node each time. Then we utilize the ε-greedy policy to choose the next seed node. The details of the APGD-IM framework are described in the following subsections.

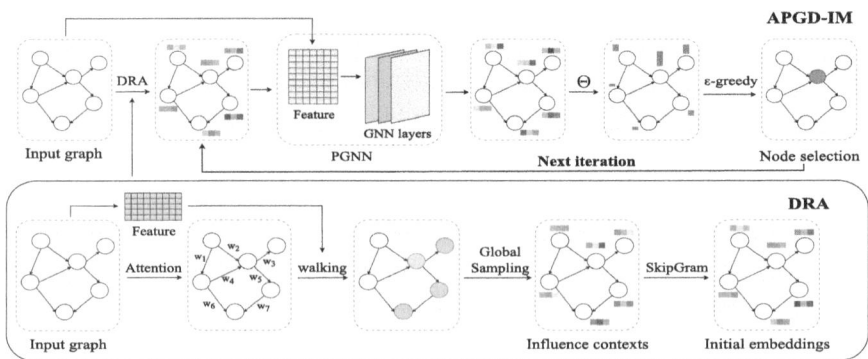

Fig. 1. The framework of APGD-IM.

3.1   Obtaining Initial Embeddings via DRA

In the IM problem, the social network is usually represented by a directed graph, whether a node will be activated is essentially determined by the state of its in-neighbors, the influence ability of these in-neighbors, and the tendency to be influenced by them [4]. Therefore, for node v, its embedding contains three components: S_v, T_v, and A_v, where $S_v \in \mathbb{R}^l$ represents the ability of node v to influence other nodes, $T_v \in \mathbb{R}^l$ represents the tendency of being activated by other nodes, and $A_v \in \mathbb{R}$ represents the activation state of node v. Compared to randomly generating initial embeddings, generating initial node embeddings using DeepWalk method can be more effective in stabilizing the training of Geometric-DQN [12]. Therefore, we propose an adaptive DeepWalk method DRA to generate initial node embeddings. The complete process of DRA is illustrated in Algorithm 1. The details are as follows.

Generating Influence Context. Inspired by Inf2vec [8], for node v, influence context I_v consists of two parts in our method: local influence context and global influence context. We use the improved RWR method to generate local influence context L_v, while the global influence context G_v is sampled randomly from the r-hop out-neighbors of v.

Most studies using the RWR strategy choose to use a fixed restart probability for all nodes, ignoring the differences in node importance. Using the same restart probability leads to insufficient exploration of important nodes and excessive exploration of less important ones, thus reducing the quality of influence context. Therefore, in DRA, we dynamically adjust the restart probability of nodes based on their importance feature. Degree centrality is one of the quantitative metrics that reveals the importance of nodes in a network [6]. Nodes with higher degree centrality are often key nodes in the social network, requiring more extensive exploration of their neighbors. For this reason, we assign a higher restart probability to nodes with a high degree centrality. Specifically, we introduce a node feature weight Φ, to dynamically adjust the restart probability. After computing Φ for all nodes, we normalize them to the range of $[0.1, 0.3]$ as the restart probability α of each node. For node $u \in V$, $\Phi(u)$ can be calculated as follows:

$$\Phi(u) = \lambda \cdot C_{in}(u) + (1 - \lambda) \cdot C_{out}(u) \tag{1}$$

where $C_{in}(u)$ and $C_{out}(u)$ represent the in-degree centrality and out-degree centrality of u respectively. Parameter $\lambda \in [0, 1]$ is used to control the weight of $C_{in}(u)$ and $C_{out}(u)$.

Given that each node in reality has a different contribution to the social network, it is crucial to consider the relative importance between nodes when selecting nodes during the walking process. Since the relative importance between nodes is proportional to their similarity [36], we introduce an attention mechanism into RWR to assign appropriate importance weight w to each edge based on the similarity between nodes. During the walking process, node is selected based on w of the edges among the current node and its out-neighbors. Specifically, for

$(u, v) \in E$, w_{uv} is defined as follows:

$$w_{uv} = \frac{\text{simi}\,(u, v) * val_{uv}}{\sum_{v'}^{(D)} \text{simi}\,(u, v') * val_{uv'}} \qquad (2)$$

where val_{uv} indicates whether there is an edge from node u to node v. If such an edge exists, $val_{uv} = 1$; otherwise, $val_{uv} = 0$. D is the set of out-neighbors of node u, and simi(u, v) represents the similarity between nodes u and v. In a network with N nodes, simi(u, v) is defined as follows:

$$\text{simi}\,(u, v) = \beta \cdot (|\Gamma(u) \bigcap \Gamma(v)|) + (1 - \beta) \cdot \frac{N}{d_{uv}} \qquad (3)$$

Inspired by CN [1], we calculate the similarity between nodes based on their centrality and the number of common neighbors, where $\frac{N}{d_{uv}}$ represents the closeness centrality between two nodes, d_{uv} is the shortest distance between nodes u and v, $\Gamma(v)$ denotes the neighbors of node v, and the parameter $\beta \in [0, 1]$ is used to control the importance of common neighbors and centrality.

By introducing an attention mechanism into RWR, we can allocate more attention to important information during the walking process, thereby enhancing the authenticity and effectiveness of the influence context.

Learning Parameters. We use SkipGram to learn parameters, maximizing the probability of nodes in I_u being influenced by node u, and then converting the influence context into initial node embeddings. In this process, we employ negative sampling to train the SkipGram model. Specifically, for node $u \in V$, we randomly generate a set of nodes as negative samples, which avoids overfitting while improving training efficiency.

3.2   Prior-Enhanced GNN

Most learning-based IM methods rely solely on network topology to generate node embeddings, reducing the quality of node embeddings. Therefore, we propose a prior-enhanced GNN module, PGNN, which introduces heuristic embeddings containing both node global information and importance features of nodes as additional inputs and guiding information for GNN, to enhance the quality and reliability of node embeddings.

Heuristic Embeddings. We comprehensively integrate multiple representative influence metrics to describe global information and the importance of nodes. And consolidate the features as additional heuristic embeddings for GNN, enhancing the reliability of node embeddings. Specifically, we incorporate degree centrality (DC) [10], betweenness centrality (BC) [22], eigenvector centrality (EC) [3], closeness centrality (CC) [35], and clustering coefficients (C) [2] to

Algorithm 1 DRA

Input: Network $(\mathcal{G})$, length of local and global influence context (l, g)
Output: Initial node embeddings(E)
1: $\alpha \leftarrow$ Normalize $\Phi(u)$ for each u;
2: **for** node $u \in \mathcal{G}$ **do**
3:     $L_u \leftarrow$ Sample l nodes starting from u based on the α_u and importance weights
        w between nodes;
4:     $G_u \leftarrow$ Uniformly sample g nodes from $N_{out}^r(u)$;
5:     $I_u = L_u \cup G_u$;
6: **end for**
7: $E \leftarrow$ SkipGram(I);
8: **return** E;

---

describe global information and importance of nodes. After computing the above metrics, we aggregate the information to obtain H as the features of nodes:

$$H = [DC^T, BC^T, EC^T, CC^T, C^T] \tag{4}$$

Subsequently, we utilize H as heuristic embeddings and subsequent guiding information, which are combined with the initial node embeddings to serve as inputs for GNN.

Combined Graph Neural Networks. Inspired by [4], We employ three combined GNNs to effectively capture the interactions among node state, node influence capacity, and the tendency of the node to be influenced by others, namely: (1) Status Network: model the activation state of nodes; (2) Source Network: model the influence capacity of nodes; (3) Target Network: model the tendency of nodes to be influenced by others. Given the currently selected seed set S_t, we update node representations through GNNs.

Similar to DRA, we introduce an attention mechanism to dynamically capture the relative importance between nodes in each of GNNs, and assign appropriate importance weights to the edges with normalization using LeakyReLU [21]. Considering the diverse factors affecting each part of node embedding, in the Status Network and Target Network, we aggregate the influence of the in-neighbors of the current node u to obtain $a_u^{(k)}, t_u^{(k)}$, while in the Source Network, we aggregate the influence of the out-neighbors of the current node u to obtain $s_u^{(k)}$. For the activation state $A_u^{(k+1)}$ at the $(k+1)$-th layer, if node u is selected into the current seed set S_t, $A_u^{(k+1)} = 1$, otherwise, $A_u^{(k+1)}$ is updated by $a_u^{(k)}$ at the k-th layer. Subsequently, for the source representation $S_u^{(k+1)}$ at the $(k+1)$-th layer, we update it by combining the source representation $S_u^{(k)}$ of node u, $s_u^{(k)}$, and its activation state $A_u^{(k)}$ at the k-th layer. Similarly, for the target representation $T_u^{(k+1)}$ of node u at the $(k+1)$-th layer, we update it by combining the target representation $T_u^{(k)}$ of node u, $t_u^{(k)}$, and its activation state $A_u^{(k)}$ at the k-th layer.

After K iterations, the embedding of node u can be obtained by concatenating these three parts: $[A_u^{(K)}, S_u^{(K)}, T_u^{(K)}]$. The reward function obtained by adding node u to the current seed set is defined as:

$$\hat{Q}(u, S_t; \Theta) = \theta_1^\top \text{ReLU}\left(\left[\theta_2 S_u^{(K)}, \theta_3 \sum_{v \in S_t} S_v^{(K)}, \theta_4 \sum_{w \in V \setminus (S_t \cup \{u\})} T_w^{(K)}\right]\right) \quad (5)$$

where $\theta_1 \in \mathbb{R}^{3l}, \theta_2, \theta_3, \theta_4 \in \mathbb{R}^{l \times l}$ are parameters. Since $\hat{Q}(u, S_t; \Theta)$ uses the embeddings calculated from PGNN, $\hat{Q}(u, S_t; \Theta)$ depends on $\{\theta_i\}_{i=1}^4$ and PGNN. We train these parameters (denoted by Θ) by RL.

3.3 Approximate Rewards

The IM problem can be naturally formulated as RL problem: (1) Action: Selecting a node into the current seed set; (2) State: Indicating whether a node is a seed node; (3) Transition: When a node is selected as a seed node, the state changes from 0 to 1; (4) Reward: The cumulative reward change when node u is selected as a seed node; (5) Policy: Guiding the selection of the next seed node.

We adopt DDQN [31] to learn the parameters in $\hat{Q}(u_t, S_t; \Theta)$ to approximate the optimal Q-function for the above RL problem. Specifically, we employ two networks: the primary network and the auxiliary network, parameterized by Θ and Θ' respectively. The auxiliary network assists in estimating the Q-values for future states during the training process of the primary network, with parameters Θ' updated based on Θ every k cycles. We define a *cycle* as the sequence of adding nodes from an empty seed set to its completion, and we define a *move* as adding a node to the seed set. To enhance the accuracy of future reward estimation, we utilize l-move Q-learning [27] for parameter updates, with parameters updated after waiting for l moves. Additionally, we employ fitted Q-iteration [25] and experience replay to accelerate learning convergence. The update process involves minimizing the following squared loss Lo:

$$Lo = (y - \hat{Q}(u_t, S_t; \Theta))^2 \quad (6)$$

where $y = \sum_{i=0}^{n-1} \gamma^i r(S_{t+i}, u_{t+i}) + \gamma^n \max_v \hat{Q}(v, S_{t+n}; \Theta')$, and $\gamma \in [0, 1]$ is the discount rate, determining the importance of future rewards.

4 Experiments

4.1 Datasets

We evaluate our model using four real-world social network datasets, whose statistical attributes are shown in Table 1. The brief of the social networks is as follows: (1) wiki-Vote [26]: A social network includes Wikipedia voting data from its inception until January 2008. Edge from node i to node j represents that user i voted on user j; (2) Email [26]: A directed social network of emails in an email leak in 2016. A directed edge in the dataset denotes that a person has

Table 1. Statistical attributes of the datasets.

Dataset	Nodes	Edges	Average degree	Type
wiki-Vote	889	2914	6.56	directed
Email	1891	39264	5.92	directed
Bitcoin	5881	35592	12.1	directed
SCHOLAT	16007	202248	25.27	undirected

sent an email to another person; (3) Bitcoin [16,17]: A who-trusts-whom social network of people who trade using Bitcoin on a platform called Bitcoin OTC; (4) SCHOLAT [33]: An academic social network contains friendships, collaborative relationships, and co-learning relationships between users of SCHOLAT.com.

We use 15 random Erdos-Renyi (ER) graphs with node sizes varying from 15 to 50 for training and four real-world social networks for testing. Our model is applicable to both directed and undirected graphs. For undirected graphs, we replace each edge with two reversed directed edges. In all datasets, we determine edge weight using the in-degree setting.

4.2 Baselines

We compare our APGD-IM with the following learning-based methods to evaluate the superiority of our approach:

- S2V-DQN [14]: A classic model that first applied DRL to the CO problem. Notably, we use a modified version of S2V-DQN, as mentioned in [4], to address the IM problem.
- IMINFECTOR [24]: An IM method that learns node representations from diffusion cascades to select seed nodes.
- ToupleGDD [4]: A state-of-the-art solution that uses DRL to solve the IM problem.

4.3 Evaluation Metrics

Influence Scale $N(k)$: Since our model can be easily adapted to different diffusion patterns, we choose two representative models that are commonly used in the IM problem, IC and LT models, to evaluate the performance of our model. We use a weighted cascade version of the IC model, where the propagation probability of edge (u, v) is set to $1/C_{in}(v)$ ($C_{in}(v)$ denotes the in-degree of node v). For the LT model, the threshold θ is set to be uniformly sampled from [0.3, 0.6] for each node v. The final results are obtained from the average of 10 runs of the experiments. $N(k)$ represents the total number of final infected nodes when the seed set size is k. $k \in \{10, 20, 30, 40, 50\}$.

Average Distance Between Seed Nodes. D_{avg}: D_{avg} represents the average distance between seed nodes. Since seeds should be sufficiently dispersed to avoid the redundancy of propagation [32], for an excellent IM model, the seed nodes it selects often have higher D_{avg} values. D_{avg} is defined as

$$D_{\text{avg}} = \frac{1}{|S|(|S|-1)} \sum_{i \in S} \sum_{j \in S, j \neq i} d(i,j) \tag{7}$$

where $|S|$ is the number of seed nodes, and $d(i,j)$ is the distance between node i and node j.

4.4 Experimental Results and Analysis

In this subsection, we present the experimental results of our framework compared with other methods on four real-world social networks. The experiments demonstrate that our model can identify seed nodes with a wider range of influence more accurately.

We first examine the influence diffusion of each method under the IC diffusion model. As depicted in Fig. 2, across all datasets, APGD-IM consistently outperforms other algorithms in terms of the final influence diffusion scale $N(k)$. This can be attributed to the comprehensive consideration of network topology, global information, and importance features of nodes by APGD-IM, while other methods rely solely on network topology or individual node activities. Particularly, the diffusion results of S2V-DQN are generally superior to IMINFECTOR on SCHOLAT dataset in Fig. 2(d), unlike the results on other datasets. This can be attributed to the fact that S2V-DQN is designed for undirected graphs. Additionally, the lower diffusion results of the four methods on SCHOLAT dataset may be due to the presence of numerous isolated nodes in SCHOLAT. However, despite this, APGD-IM still outperforms other methods as shown in Fig. 2(d).

We then assume LT as the diffusion model to evaluate the final influence spread of each method. As shown in Fig. 3, our method consistently achieves larger-scale influence propagation across all datasets. Particularly, APGD-IM proves its effectiveness on the wiki-Vote dataset that can effectively infect 90% of nodes of the network with the seed set size of 50, yet other methods can only infect at most 50% of nodes. Surprisingly, APGD-IM can infect 88% of nodes of the network with just 20 seed nodes on the Email dataset, further demonstrating its superiority. Additionally, it can be observed that IMINFECTOR exhibits unstable performance across different datasets, which can be attributed to its lack of consideration for network topology, leading to inadequate adaptability to various scenarios. Furthermore, compared to the IC model, ToupleGDD fails to maintain high performance under the LT model, indicating its inadequate adaptability to different diffusion models.

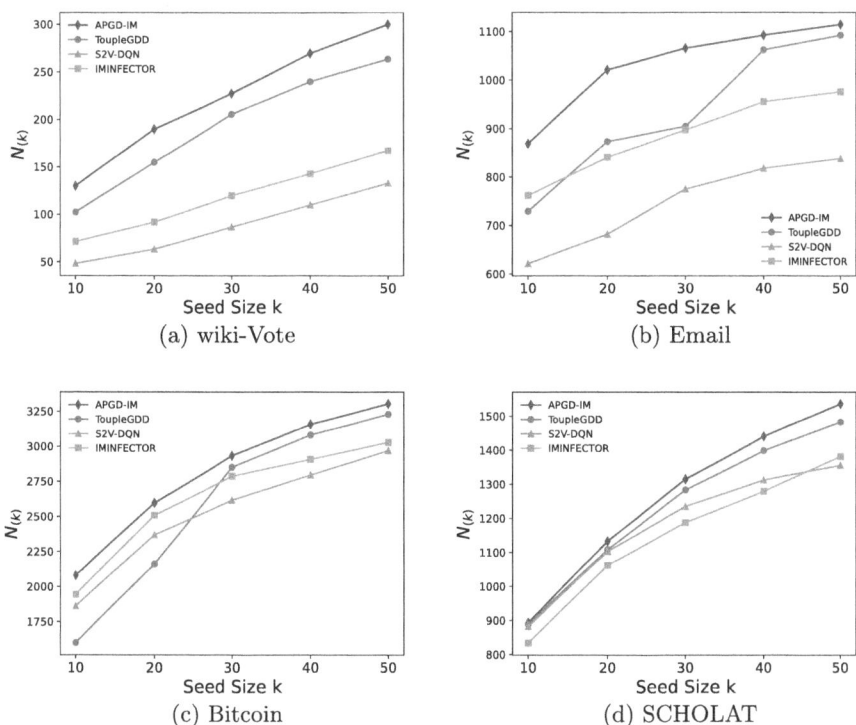

Fig. 2. Performance comparisons among different methods under IC diffusion pattern.

In conclusion, for each dataset, the influence diffusion results of APGD-IM consistently outperform the other three methods under both IC and LT models, which provides stronger evidence that our approach not only effectively improves the ability to solve the IM problem but also maintains stable performance advantages across diverse scenarios and diffusion models.

Additionally, we evaluate the average distance D_{avg} between selected seed nodes by different methods. As shown in Table 2, with the seed set size fixed at 10, the results demonstrate that compared to other methods, APGD-IM can select seed nodes with a wider distribution. This can be attributed to the comprehensive consideration of network topology and node importance information of our method, which helps to consider a wider range of network structures and features in seed node selection, increasing the likelihood of choosing more widely distributed seed nodes.

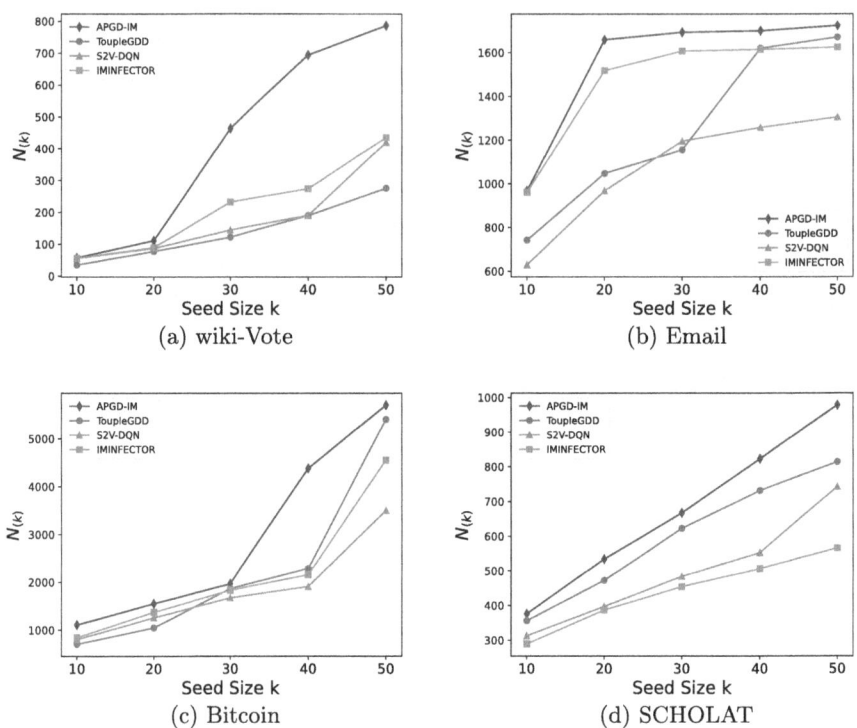

Fig. 3. Performance comparisons among different methods under LT diffusion pattern.

Table 2. Comparison of the average distance between seed nodes D_{avg} for different methods with a seed node quantity of 10.

Methods	wiki-Vote	Email	Bitcoin	SCHOLAT
S2V-DQN	1.42	1.18	1.24	1.00
IMINFECTOR	1.36	1.58	1.33	1.02
ToupleGDD	2.00	1.60	1.44	1.20
APGD-IM	**2.76**	**1.64**	**1.49**	**1.42**

4.5   Ablation Experiment

In this subsection, we conduct several ablation experiments to further demonstrate the validity of the various modules of our model APGD-IM. Since our model is primarily designed for directed graphs, we conduct ablation experiments on the Email and Bitcoin datasets to validate the effectiveness of our modules across different social networks. Four sets of experiments are included, and the specific variations are shown as follows:

- **APGD-IM$^{-\mathrm{DRA-PGNN}}$:** This variant employs a uniform random selection of neighboring nodes during the process of RWR, with each node adopting the same restart strategy. Additionally, the input information of GNNs only contains the initial node embeddings.

- **APGD-IM**$^{-PGNN}$: This variant utilizes DRA to obtain initial node embeddings, while the input of GNNs only includes the initial node embeddings.
- **APGD-IM**$^{-DRA}$: This variant utilizes PGNN to generate node embeddings. During the process of RWR, it employs a uniform random selection of neighboring nodes, with each node adopting the same restart strategy.

Table 3. Ablation experiment results on Email and Bitcoin datasets.

Methods	Email					Bitcoin				
	10	20	30	40	50	10	20	30	40	50
APGD-IM$^{-DRA-PGNN}$	728.79	873.07	904.47	1061.99	1092.05	1597.28	2160.68	2849.34	3079.88	3228.66
APGD-IM^{-PGNN}	860.53	1018.25	1058.01	1082.98	1108.32	1782.54	2589.40	2887.57	3099.29	3251.60
APGD-IM^{-DRA}	857.38	1016.03	1056.12	1086.00	1110.40	1933.51	2581.76	2896.98	3102.82	3249.25
APGD-IM	**868.54**	**1020.95**	**1065.58**	**1092.24**	**1114.37**	**2078.93**	**2595.29**	**2931.68**	**3156.34**	**3303.37**

As shown in Table 3, we examine the influence propagation scale $N(k)$ of each variant under the IC model. The results demonstrate the effectiveness of each module, and combining all the proposed modules results in better performance than any individual module alone. This further confirms the rationality of integrating these modules. The performance degradation of APGD-IM^{-DRA} suggests that guiding the walk based on the relative importance between nodes and dynamically adjusting the walking strategy according to node features can produce more comprehensive initial node embeddings, thereby enhancing overall model performance. Particularly, we observe that APGD-IM^{-PGNN} exhibits greater performance degradation in most cases, indicating the critical importance of comprehensively considering the network topology alongside the global information and importance features of nodes when addressing the IM problem.

5 Conclusion

Existing learning-based methods for solving the IM problem typically rely solely on the network topology or individual node activities, lacking comprehensive consideration of both network topology and important information of nodes, resulting in poor model performance. To address this issue, we propose a DRL model APGD-IM based on an adaptive DeepWalk method and a prior-enhanced GNN, which integrates network topology with global information and importance features of nodes. Specifically, we propose an adaptive DeepWalk method DRA, which enhances the effective capture of network structures by introducing the attention mechanism and dynamically adjusting the restart strategy of nodes. Additionally, we propose a prior-enhanced GNN module PGNN, to improve the quality of generated node embeddings by incorporating heuristic embeddings that contain global information and importance features of nodes into the input information of GNNs. Subsequently, we use double DQN for parameters learning.

Extensive experimental results demonstrate that our proposed model outperforms other learning-based baseline methods on four real-world social networks. Moreover, APGD-IM maintains stable performance advantages across different diffusion models, confirming the effectiveness and stability of APGD-IM. In the future, APGD-IM will be extended to handle more complex and diverse networks, enhancing its adaptability across different networks.

Acknowledgements. This work is supported in part by the Science and Technology Projects in Guangzhou (SL2022A04J00300).

References

1. Ahmad, I., Akhtar, M.U., Noor, S., Shahnaz, A.: Missing link prediction using common neighbor and centrality based parameterized algorithm. Sci. Rep. **10**(1), 364 (2020)
2. Berahmand, K., Bouyer, A., Samadi, N.: A new centrality measure based on the negative and positive effects of clustering coefficient for identifying influential spreaders in complex networks. Chaos Solitons & Fractals **110**, 41–54 (2018)
3. Bonacich, P.: Some unique properties of eigenvector centrality. Soc. Netw. **29**(4), 555–564 (2007)
4. Chen, T., Yan, S., Guo, J., Wu, W.: TupleGDD: a fine-designed solution of influence maximization by deep reinforcement learning. IEEE Trans. Comput. Soc. Syst. (2023)
5. Chen, W., Wang, Y., Yang, S.: Efficient influence maximization in social networks. In: Proceedings of the 15th ACM SIGKDD International Conference on Knowledge Discovery and Data Mining, pp. 199–208 (2009)
6. Csató, L.: Measuring centrality by a generalization of degree. CEJOR **25**, 771–790 (2017)
7. Estevez, P.A., Vera, P., Saito, K.: Selecting the most influential nodes in social networks. In: 2007 International Joint Conference on Neural Networks, pp. 2397–2402. IEEE (2007)
8. Feng, S., Cong, G., Khan, A., Li, X., Liu, Y., Chee, Y.M.: Inf2vec: latent representation model for social influence embedding. In: 2018 IEEE 34th International Conference on Data Engineering (ICDE), pp. 941–952. IEEE (2018)
9. Goyal, A., Lu, W., Lakshmanan, L.V.: SIMPATH: an efficient algorithm for influence maximization under the linear threshold model. In: 2011 IEEE 11th International Conference on Data Mining, pp. 211–220. IEEE (2011)
10. Han, L., Zhou, Q., Tang, J., Yang, X., Huang, H.: Identifying top-k influential nodes based on discrete particle swarm optimization with local neighborhood degree centrality. IEEE Access **9**, 21345–21356 (2021)
11. Jiang, Q., Song, G., Gao, C., Wang, Y., Si, W., Xie, K.: Simulated annealing based influence maximization in social networks. In: Proceedings of the AAAI Conference on Artificial Intelligence, vol. 25, pp. 127–132 (2011)
12. Kamarthi, H., Vijayan, P., Wilder, B., Ravindran, B., Tambe, M.: Influence maximization in unknown social networks: learning policies for effective graph sampling. In: Proceedings of the 19th International Conference on Autonomous Agents and Multiagent Systems, AAMAS 2020, Auckland, New Zealand, 9–13 May 2020, pp. 575–583. International Foundation for Autonomous Agents and Multiagent Systems (2020)

13. Kempe, D., Kleinberg, J., Tardos, É.: Maximizing the spread of influence through a social network. In: Proceedings of the Ninth ACM SIGKDD International Conference on Knowledge Discovery and Data Mining, pp. 137–146 (2003)
14. Khalil, E., Dai, H., Zhang, Y., Dilkina, B., Song, L.: Learning combinatorial optimization algorithms over graphs. In: Advances in Neural Information Processing Systems, vol. 30 (2017)
15. Kumar, S., Mallik, A., Khetarpal, A., Panda, B.S.: Influence maximization in social networks using graph embedding and graph neural network. Inf. Sci. **607**, 1617–1636 (2022)
16. Kumar, S., Hooi, B., Makhija, D., Kumar, M., Faloutsos, C., Subrahmanian, V.: REV2: fraudulent user prediction in rating platforms. In: Proceedings of the Eleventh ACM International Conference on Web Search and Data Mining, pp. 333–341. ACM (2018)
17. Kumar, S., Spezzano, F., Subrahmanian, V., Faloutsos, C.: Edge weight prediction in weighted signed networks. In: 2016 IEEE 16th International Conference on Data Mining (ICDM), pp. 221–230. IEEE (2016)
18. Leskovec, J., Krause, A., Guestrin, C., Faloutsos, C., VanBriesen, J., Glance, N.: Cost-effective outbreak detection in networks. In: Proceedings of the 13th ACM SIGKDD International Conference on Knowledge Discovery and Data Mining, pp. 420–429 (2007)
19. Li, H., Xu, M., Bhowmick, S.S., Rayhan, J.S., Sun, C., Cui, J.: PIANO: influence maximization meets deep reinforcement learning. IEEE Trans. Comput. Soc. Syst. (2022)
20. Ling, C., et al.: Deep graph representation learning and optimization for influence maximization. In: International Conference on Machine Learning, pp. 21350–21361. PMLR (2023)
21. Maas, A.L., Hannun, A.Y., Ng, A.Y., et al.: Rectifier nonlinearities improve neural network acoustic models. In: Proceedings ICML, Atlanta, GA, vol. 30, p. 3 (2013)
22. Maurya, S.K., Liu, X., Murata, T.: Fast approximations of betweenness centrality with graph neural networks. In: Proceedings of the 28th ACM International Conference on Information and Knowledge Management, pp. 2149–2152 (2019)
23. Mnih, V., et al.: Human-level control through deep reinforcement learning. Nature **518**(7540), 529–533 (2015)
24. Panagopoulos, G., Malliaros, F.D., Vazirgiannis, M.: Multi-task learning for influence estimation and maximization. IEEE Trans. Knowl. Data Eng. **34**(9), 4398–4409 (2022)
25. Riedmiller, M.: Neural fitted Q iteration–first experiences with a data efficient neural reinforcement learning method. In: Gama, J., Camacho, R., Brazdil, P.B., Jorge, A.M., Torgo, L. (eds.) ECML 2005. LNCS, vol. 3720, pp. 317–328. Springer, Heidelberg (2005). https://doi.org/10.1007/11564096_32
26. Rossi, R.A., Ahmed, N.K.: The network data repository with interactive graph analytics and visualization. In: AAAI (2015)
27. Sutton, R.S., Barto, A.G.: Reinforcement learning: an introduction. Robotica **17**(2), 229–235 (1999)
28. Tang, J., Tang, X., Xiao, X., Yuan, J.: Online processing algorithms for influence maximization. In: Proceedings of the 2018 International Conference on Management of Data, pp. 991–1005 (2018)
29. Tang, Y., Shi, Y., Xiao, X.: Influence maximization in near-linear time: a martingale approach. In: Proceedings of the 2015 ACM SIGMOD International Conference on Management of Data, pp. 1539–1554 (2015)

30. Tang, Y., Xiao, X., Shi, Y.: Influence maximization: near-optimal time complexity meets practical efficiency. In: Proceedings of the 2014 ACM SIGMOD International Conference on Management of Data, pp. 75–86 (2014)
31. Van Hasselt, H., Guez, A., Silver, D.: Deep reinforcement learning with double Q-learning. In: Proceedings of the AAAI Conference on Artificial Intelligence, vol. 30 (2016)
32. Wang, J., Ma, X.J., Xiang, B.B., Bao, Z.K., Zhang, H.F.: Maximizing influence in social networks by distinguishing the roles of seeds. Phys. A **604**, 127881 (2022)
33. Xu, Q., Qiu, L., Lin, R., Tang, Y., He, C., Yuan, C.: An improved community detection algorithm via fusing topology and attribute information. In: 2021 IEEE 24th International Conference on Computer Supported Cooperative Work in Design (CSCWD), pp. 1069–1074 (2021)
34. Yu, E.Y., Wang, Y.P., Fu, Y., Chen, D.B., Xie, M.: Identifying critical nodes in complex networks via graph convolutional networks. Knowl.-Based Syst. **198**, 105893 (2020)
35. Zhang, J., Luo, Y.: Degree centrality, betweenness centrality, and closeness centrality in social network. In: 2017 2nd International Conference on Modelling, Simulation and Applied Mathematics (MSAM2017), pp. 300–303. Atlantis Press (2017)
36. Zhang, Y., Shen, J., Zhang, R., Zhao, Z.: Network representation learning via improved random walk with restart. Knowl.-Based Syst. **263**, 110255 (2023)

Community-Aware Heterogeneous Graph Contrastive Learning

Xinying Li[1,2,3], Ling Wu[1,2,3], and Kun Guo[1,2,3(✉)]

[1] College of Computer and Data Science, Fuzhou University, Fuzhou 350108, China
gukn@fzu.edu.cn
[2] Engineering Research Center of Big Data Intelligence, Ministry of Education,
Fuzhou 350108, China
[3] Fujian Key Laboratory of Network Computing and Intelligent Information
Processing, Fuzhou University, Fuzhou 350108, China

Abstract. Recently, heterogeneous graph contrastive learning, which can mine supervision signals from the data, has attracted widespread attention. However, most existing methods employ random data augmentation strategies to construct contrastive views, which may destroy the semantic information in heterogeneous graphs. Moreover, they often select positive and negative samples based solely on node-level proximity and overlook hard samples that are difficult to distinguish from anchors. To solve the above problems, we propose a Community-Aware Heterogeneous Graph Contrastive Learning model called CAHGCL. In particular, we design an adaptive data augmentation strategy to construct views, including feature augmentation and topology augmentation. To improve the quality of samples, we propose a dynamic sample weighting strategy based on node similarity and community information, capable of identifying both hard positive samples and hard negative samples. Finally, we introduce community-level contrast to improve community cohesion. Extensive experiments and analyses demonstrate that CAHGCL consistently outperforms state-of-the-art baselines on three datasets.

Keywords: Heterogeneous Graph · Contrastive Learning · Community Aware · Hard Samples

1 Introduction

In the real world, complex connections among entities can be abstracted as heterogeneous graphs (HGs), which contain different types of nodes and edges. Typical heterogeneous networks include citation networks, social networks, and transportation networks. To take full advantage of the rich structural and semantic information in HGs, heterogeneous graph neural network (HGNN) [10] models learn meaningful node representations by aggregating and transforming their original or metapath-based neighbors to facilitate the performance of downstream tasks such as node classification, link prediction, and node clustering.

H. Sun et al. (Eds.): ChineseCSCW 2024, CCIS 2343, pp. 251–265, 2025.
https://doi.org/10.1007/978-981-96-2373-0_18

However, the ground-truth labels of nodes are often limited and difficult to obtain [12], limiting the application of supervised and semi-supervised HGNN models. Self-supervised learning [15] has received widespread attention for its ability to mine supervision signals from the data. Among them, graph contrastive learning generates multiple views through data augmentation, which can learn discriminative representations that contain deep information about the network.

Although some efforts [8,12,19] have extended the concept of graph contrastive learning to HGs, three fundamental issues still need to be addressed. The first problem is how to construct rich contrastive views to include information from different dimensions. The data augmentation strategy [2] of randomly adding or deleting edges, which is commonly used in homogeneous graphs, may destroy the connection relationships between different types of nodes in HGs, leading to changes in semantic information. The second problem is how to select high-quality positive and negative samples to mitigate sampling bias [7,16]. The existing methods [13] mainly rely on node-level proximity selecting samples without considering community structure information, and nodes from the same community may be sampled as negative pairs. Moreover, the current method [18] only focuses on hard negative samples and ignores hard positive samples. The last problem is how to design appropriate contrastive objectives to consider information at various levels. Previous studies [19] have not fully considered community-level information, but nodes within the same community are semantically similar.

In this paper, we propose a Community-Aware Heterogeneous Graph Contrastive Learning (CAHGCL) model to address the issues above. First, we adopt an adaptive data augmentation strategy to preserve important semantic and structural information in heterogeneous graphs. Then, we improve the quality of positive and negative samples through a dynamic sample weighting strategy that can identify hard samples. Finally, we employ node-level contrast and community-level contrast to learn node embeddings. The contributions of this paper are as follows:

1. We propose an adaptive data augmentation strategy that purposefully removes low-importance edges between nodes and adds edges to nodes at community boundaries. It is effective in preserving important structural and semantic information in heterogeneous graphs.
2. We propose a dynamic sample weighting strategy considering community information and node similarity. This strategy increases the weight of hard samples while decreasing the weight of simple samples to improve the model's discriminative ability against hard samples.
3. A joint contrastive objective function, including node-level contrast and community-level contrast, enhances the clarity of community boundaries and improves cohesion within the community.

2   Related Work

2.1   Heterogeneous Graph Neural Network

Heterogeneous graph neural network models have received significant attention in recent years. HAN [11] employs node-level and semantic-level attention mechanisms to learn the importance of nodes and metapaths. The ie-HGCN [17] model consists of type-level aggregation and object-level aggregation. This model solves the problem that GCN methods for heterogeneous graphs cannot explore all possible metapaths and can extract the most valuable metapaths for target objects.

2.2   Graph Contrastive Learning

Graph contrastive learning, a self-supervised learning method that maximizes the similarity between positive pairs and minimizes the similarity between negative pairs, enabling the model to generate more discriminative node representations, has shown great potential in graph representation learning. MVGRL [5] proves that adding more than two contrastive views does not improve the model's performance. The best performance is achieved by contrasting the first-order neighbor view with the view generated by the graph diffusion kernel. GRACE [20] proposes randomly removing edges and mask node features to generate two related views. Then, it uses contrastive loss to maximize the consistency between the node embeddings of two views. GCA [21] believes that uniform data augmentation strategies such as random edge dropout or feature shuffling will lead to suboptimal models, and proposes an adaptive data augmentation strategy that can preserve important structures and attributes in the graph.

2.3   Heterogeneous Graph Contrastive Learning

Some current works extend the concept of graph contrastive learning to heterogeneous graphs. HeCo [12] proposes a cross-view contrastive learning mechanism, which learns local structures through network schema view and higher-order structures through metapath view. STENCIL [19] advocates explicitly using structural information to sort negative samples, selecting the top-k negative samples as a candidate set and synthesizing multiple hard negative samples for each node by creating convex linear combinations of them. HeGCL [8] encodes the global and semantic representations of nodes based on the outline view and metapath view. MEOW [18] uses metapaths and metapath context information to construct views. The model performs multiple clustering and uses the number of times two nodes appear in the same cluster as the weight of negative samples. In order to mitigate sampling bias, HGCML [13] designs a positive sampling strategy that considers both topological information and semantic information, and selects the most similar k nodes for each node as positive samples.

However, these methods ignore the influence of community structure when constructing contrastive views, selecting positive and negative samples and designing contrastive objectives. In fact, nodes in the same community are semantically similar.

3   Preliminaries

In this section, we introduce the basic concepts of heterogeneous graph, metapath, and Metapath-based Subgraph.

Definition 1. *Heterogeneous Graph.* *Heterogeneous graph is composed of different types of nodes and edges, typically represented as $G = (V, E, T, R)$, V, E, T, and R denote the node set, edge set, node type set, and edge type set respectively, associated with a node mapping function $\Phi : V \to T$ and an edge mapping function $\varphi : E \to R$. Heterogeneous graph requires the sum of node types and edge types to be greater than 2, i.e. $|T| + |R| > 2$.*

Definition 2. *Metapath.* *Metapath is a specific sequence of nodes used to describe the relationship between different types of nodes in a heterogeneous graph. It is denoted in the form of $T_1 \xrightarrow{R_1} T_2 \xrightarrow{R_2} \dots \xrightarrow{R_l} T_{l+1}$, and abbreviated as $T_1 T_2 \dots T_{l+1}$. The metapath describes the composite relation $R = R_1 \circ R_2 \circ \dots \circ R_l$ between node type T_1 and T_{l+1}, where $\circ$ denotes the composition operator on relations.*

Definition 3. *Metapath-Based Subgraph.* *Metapath-based subgraph is a subgraph composed of relevant nodes and edges selected from the original heterogeneous graph based on a specific metapath. It is capable of capturing higher-order structural and semantic information.*

4   The Proposed Algorithm

In this section, we introduce the proposed CAHGCL and the overall framework is shown in Fig. 1. Firstly, we utilize metapaths to generate metapath-based subgraphs. Secondly, we generate the outline view by fusing metapath-based subgraphs and semantic view by feature augmentation and topology augmentation. Thirdly, we obtain a pseudo-label set through coarse clustering, combine community information and node similarity to identify hard samples and calculate dynamic sample weights. We use nodes from the outline view as anchors and select positive and negative samples from both views. Finally, we adopt node-level contrast and community-level contrast to learn node embeddings. Next, we describe each component of the model in detail.

4.1   Data Augmentation

Data augmentation can improve the generalization ability of the model while reducing noise. We design an adaptive data augmentation strategy to remove low-importance edges between nodes based on similarity and add edges to nodes at community boundaries based on the local clustering coefficient.

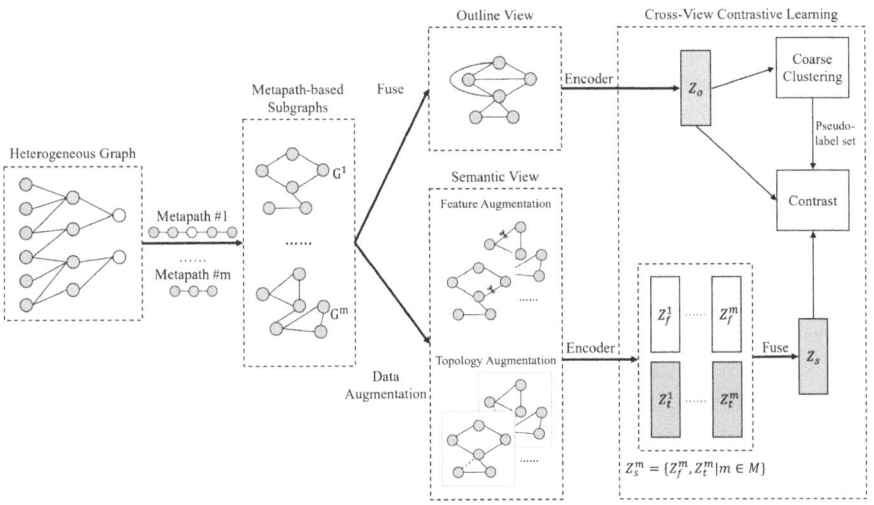

Fig. 1. The overall framework of the CAHGCL model.

Outline View. The noise information in the original heterogeneous graph is filtered out by fusing metapath-based subgraphs to generate an outline view. Given a metapath set M, $|M|$ is the number of metapaths, and the node embeddings of outline view are the weighted value [11] of the subgraph node embeddings.

$$Z^m = Encoder(\mathbf{A}^m, \mathbf{X}) \tag{1}$$

$$Encoder(\mathbf{A}^m, \mathbf{X}) = \sigma\left(\mathbf{D}^{-\frac{1}{2}} \mathbf{A}^m \mathbf{D}^{-\frac{1}{2}} \mathbf{X} \mathbf{W}_g\right) \tag{2}$$

where $\mathbf{A}^m$ is the adjacency matrix of the metapath-based subgraph, $\mathbf{X}$ is the attribute matrix, and Z^m is the embedding of the metapath-based subgraph. $Encoder(\cdot)$ represents a one-layer GCN [6] encoder, $\mathbf{D}$ is a diagonal matrix with $\mathbf{D}_{ii} = \sum_{j=1}^{|V|} \mathbf{A}_{ij}^m$, $\mathbf{W}_g$ is a trainable weight matrix, and $\sigma(\cdot)$ denotes an activation function.

$$w_m = \frac{1}{|V|} \sum_{i \in V} a^T \cdot \tanh(\mathbf{W}_{att} \cdot Z_i^m + b) \tag{3}$$

$$\alpha_m = \frac{\exp(w_m)}{\sum_{m=1}^{|M|} \exp(w_m)} \tag{4}$$

$$Z_o = \sum_{m=1}^{|M|} \alpha_m \cdot Z^m \tag{5}$$

Equation 5 indicates that Z_o is the weighted value of subgraph embeddings, where Z_o is the embedding of the outline view. Here, $\mathbf{W}_{att}$ is the weight matrix of the attention mechanism, b is the bias vector, a is the trainable attention vector, and w_m denotes the normalized weight.

Semantic View. Random data augmentation strategies such as node dropping and edge removing are commonly used in homogeneous graphs. However, due to the complex structural and semantic characteristics of heterogeneous graphs, randomly dropping nodes or edges will destroy the graph's semantics. Metapaths can preserve high-order information in the graph, and different metapaths can capture semantic information from different dimensions. Therefore, we adopt metapaths to construct metapath-based subgraphs and perform data augmentation on them, removing low-importance edges between nodes and adding edges for nodes at community boundaries.

Feature Augmentation. A metapath-based subgraph is represented as $G^m = (\mathbf{A}^m, \mathbf{X})$. For each metapath-based subgraph, calculate the similarity between nodes according to Eq. 6 to obtain the similarity matrix $\mathbf{S}^m$. If $\mathbf{S}^m_{ij} \geq f$, retain the edge between node i and j; Otherwise, remove the edge between node i and j, and f is a trainable similarity constraint.

$$cosine\_similarity(\mathbf{x}_i, \mathbf{x}_j) = \frac{\mathbf{x}_i \cdot \mathbf{x}_j}{||\mathbf{x}_i|| \cdot ||\mathbf{x}_j||} \tag{6}$$

where $\mathbf{x}_i$ and $\mathbf{x}_j$ denote feature vectors, and $\mathbf{x}_i \cdot \mathbf{x}_j$ denotes the inner product of two vectors. The more similar the two vectors are, the greater the cosine similarity value.

Topology Augmentation. The local clustering coefficient [14] measures the tightness of connections between neighbors of a node. If the local clustering coefficient of a node is low, it indicates a lack of close connections around the node, and the node may be at the community boundary. We need to add edges to enhance the local structure of such nodes. Specifically, if $lcc(i) < t$, connect the node to its second-order neighbors, where t is a learnable constraint. In addition, to avoid introducing noise information, cosine similarity between the newly connected node and node i must also be greater than f.

$$lcc(i) = \frac{2\sum_{u,v \in N(i)} \delta(u,v)}{n(n-1)} \tag{7}$$

$$\delta(u,v) = \begin{cases} 1, (u,v) \in E \\ 0, (u,v) \notin E \end{cases} \tag{8}$$

where u and v are first-order neighbors of node i, $n = |N(i)|$ is the number of first-order neighbors of node i. $(u,v) \in E$ denotes that the edge between nodes u and v exists, and $(u,v) \notin E$ denotes that the edge between nodes u and v does not exist.

The adjacency matrices after feature augmentation and topology augmentation are denoted as $\mathbf{A}^m_f$ and $\mathbf{A}^m_t$ respectively. To improve the generalization ability of CAHGCL, we randomly mask node attributes, and the new attribute matrix is denoted as $\widetilde{\mathbf{X}} = \mathbf{B} \odot \mathbf{X}$, where $\mathbf{B}$ is the masking matrix and $\odot$ is the Hadamard product. For each subgraph G^m, the enhanced adjacency matrix and attribute matrix are input into a one-layer GCN encoder to obtain embeddings. In this way, we can obtain embeddings $Z_s^m = \{Z_f^m, Z_t^m | m \in M\}$. These embeddings are fused through an attention mechanism to generate the final embedding Z_s of the semantic view.

$$
\begin{aligned}
Z_f^m &= Encoder(\mathbf{A}_f^m, \widetilde{\mathbf{X}}) \\
Z_t^m &= Encoder(\mathbf{A}_t^m, \widetilde{\mathbf{X}})
\end{aligned}
\tag{9}
$$

4.2 Sampling Strategy

The quality of positive and negative samples largely determines the model's performance. Existing works select samples based only on node-level proximity and fail to identify both hard positive and hard negative samples. Therefore, we propose a hard sample-aware sampling strategy to improve the quality of the samples and the model's discriminative ability.

First, we perform coarse clustering on the embeddings of the outline view to obtain a pseudo-label set and calculate the minimum distance between each node and the cluster center. Then, we take the first μ samples with the smallest distance as the high-confidence node set and the remaining as hard samples. Finally, we calculate the weight of each sample pair according to Eq. 10. Weight function $r(i,j)$ can identify simple, hard positive, and hard negative samples, increasing the weight of hard samples while decreasing the weight of simple samples.

$$
r(i,j) = \begin{cases} 1, & i \notin H \text{ or } j \notin H \\ 1 - S(z_i, z_j), & i,j \in H \text{ and } P_i = P_j \\ S(z_i, z_j), & i,j \in H \text{ and } P_i \neq P_j \end{cases}
\tag{10}
$$

where H is the high-confidence node set and P is the pseudo-label set. i is a node in the outline view, and j is any node except i.

We give higher weights to low-confidence samples and hard samples. The function $r(i,j)$ is analyzed as follows: $i \notin H \text{ or } j \notin H$ means that at least one node does not belong to the high-confidence node set H, where the weight of the sample pair is the highest; $i,j \in H \text{ and } P_i = P_j$ means that both nodes belong to H and belong to the same community. Samples in the same cluster but with low similarity are hard positive samples. The lower the similarity, the higher the weight; $i,j \in H \text{ and } P_i \neq P_j$ means that both nodes belong to H but do not belong to the same community. Samples in different clusters but with high similarity are hard negative samples. The higher the similarity, the higher the weight.

4.3 Contrastive Objective

After generating the outline view and semantic view, we utilize the objective function to learn the node embedding. We use a dynamic sample weighting function in node-level contrast to improve the model's ability to identify hard samples. In this way, we can learn discriminative node embeddings that promote the performance of downstream tasks. In community-level contrast, we shorten the distance between nodes and cluster centers and use the RBF weight function to make the model focus more on similar community pairs to improve the clarity of community boundaries and community cohesion.

Node-Level Contrast. The node-level loss function is an improved InfoNCE that maximizes the similarity between positive samples, minimizes the similarity between negative samples, and uses a dynamic sample weighting function to improve the model's discriminative ability against hard samples. We use nodes in the outline view as anchors and select positive and negative samples from both views.

$$L_i^{node} = -\log \frac{\Sigma_{j \in U_i} r(i,j) \cdot \theta(z_i, z_j)}{\sum_{j=1}^{2|V|} r(i,q) \cdot \theta(z_i, z_q)} \tag{11}$$

$$\theta(z_i, z_j) = \exp(S(z_i, z_j)/\tau) \tag{12}$$

where U_i denotes the set of nodes with similarity to node i greater than f and in the same cluster, and τ is the temperature parameter.

Community-Level Contrast. Node-level contrast only focuses on individual nodes and their local neighborhoods, and we add community-level contrast to enhance the model's understanding of the global structure. The community-level loss function is based on the clustering results of Sect. 4.3, which maximizes the similarity between nodes and cluster centers. In particular, we introduce the RBF weight function in L_i^{com}, which also employs the idea of hard samples. The more similar a node is to the center of another cluster, the greater the weight.

$$L_i^{com} = -\log \frac{\theta(z_i, c_r)}{\theta(z_i, c_r) + \sum_{k \neq r} \rho(i,k) \cdot \theta(z_i, c_k)} \tag{13}$$

$$\rho(i,k) = \exp(-\frac{\|z_i - c_k\|^2}{2\sigma^2}) \tag{14}$$

where c_r is the cluster center corresponding to node i, and $\rho(i,k)$ is the RBF weight function [1].

Overall Objective. We combine node-level contrast and community-level contrast through parameter λ. The two contrasts work synergistically to promote model performance.

$$L_i = L_i^{node} + \lambda L_i^{com} \tag{15}$$

5   Experiments

In this section, we first introduce three real-world datasets, eight widely recognized baselines, and experimental settings. Then, we perform node classification, node clustering, ablation experiments, and parameter experiments, followed by a detailed analysis of the experimental results.

5.1   Datasets

To evaluate the performance of CAHGCL, we use three widely recognized heterogeneous datasets: ACM [11], IMDB [4], and DBLP [4], where ACM and DBLP are academic networks, and IMDB is a movie network. The statistics of the three datasets are shown in Table 1.

Table 1. Statistics of the public datasets.

Datasets	Nodes	Metapaths	Descriptions
ACM	P(paper, 4025) A(author, 7167) S(subject, 60)	PAP PSP	Target node: P Number of classes: 3
IMDB	M(movie, 4278) A(actor, 5257) D(director, 2081)	MDM MAM	Target node:M Number of classes: 3
DBLP	A(author, 4057) P(paper, 14328) C(conference, 20) T(term, 7723)	APA APTPA APCPA	Target node:A Number of classes: 4

5.2   Baselines

Methods Designed for Homogeneous Graphs. GCN [6] obtains node representations by performing graph convolution operations on the adjacency matrix and degree matrix. GAT [9] utilizes an attention mechanism to learn the importance of neighbors and employs a multi-head attention mechanism to obtain more comprehensive information.

Unsupervised and Supervised Methods Designed for Heterogeneous Graphs. Metapath2Vec [3] combines the metapath-based random walk strategy with the skip-gram model. HAN [11] adopts node-level attention and semantic-level attention to learn the importance of nodes and metapaths, respectively.

Self-supervised Methods Designed for Heterogeneous Graphs. HeCo [12] introduces a cross-view contrastive mechanism, utilizing network schema and metapath views to capture local and higher-order structures. STEN-CIL [19] constructs hard negative samples for each node by creating convex linear combinations of negative samples. MEOW and HGCML are state-of-the-art contrastive learning methods for heterogeneous graphs. MEOW [18] utilizes metapaths and metapath context information to construct views and employs weighted negative samples to distinguish hard negatives from false negatives. HGCML [13] adopts intra-metapath and inter-metapath contrastive learning to acquire node embeddings, and introduces a positive sample construction strategy based on PPR similarity and L2 distance.

5.3   Experimental Settings

The model uses Adam as the optimizer and Xavier to initialize parameters. The embedding dimension is 64, the patience for early stopping is 20, and evaluation is performed every ten epochs. The cosine similarity constraint f and the local clustering coefficient constraint t range from 0.1 to 0.9. The value of the confidence ratio μ ranges from 0.5 to 0.9. We use Kmeans as the clustering algorithm in Sect. 4.3, with the cluster number k set to 30. The community-level loss weight λ ranges from 0.1 to 1. We choose Macro-F1 and Micro-F1 as evaluation metrics for the node classification task, and NMI and ARI as evaluation metrics for the node clustering task. Each experiment is performed ten times, and the average results are reported.

5.4   Node Classification

We compare the proposed CAHGCL with eight widely recognized models, among which GCN, GAT, and HAN are supervised algorithms, Mp2vec is an unsupervised algorithm, and the rest are self-supervised algorithms. We randomly select 20% of labeled nodes as the training set for node classification, and the evaluation metrics are Macro-F1 and Micro-F1. The experimental results are shown in Table 2, with the best results in bold. According to the results, we have the following analysis: The performance of CAHGCL is better than baselines on all three datasets, proving the effectiveness of our model. Specifically, CAHGCL achieves the best performance on IMDB, and compared with the state-of-the-art heterogeneous graph contrastive algorithms MEOW and HGCML, CAHGCL improves Macro-F1 by an average of 0.0313 and Micro-F1 by an average of 0.0266.

Table 2. Results of the node classification experiment.

Datasets	ACM		IMDB		DBLP	
Metrics	Macro-F1	Micro-F1	Macro-F1	Micro-F1	Macro-F1	Micro-F1
GCN	0.8756	0.8773	0.5808	0.5992	0.9165	0.9212
GAT	0.8822	0.8843	0.5714	0.5739	0.9183	0.9227
HAN	0.8983	0.8917	0.5198	0.5536	0.9186	0.9258
Mp2vec	0.7821	0.7943	0.4932	0.5091	0.8661	0.8730
HeCo	0.8893	0.8853	0.5169	0.5075	0.9105	0.9175
STENCIL	0.9054	0.9061	0.5244	0.5713	0.9152	0.9206
MEOW	0.9153	0.9141	0.6065	0.6138	0.9263	0.9315
HGCML	0.9120	0.9109	0.6083	0.6149	0.9250	0.9299
CAHGCL	**0.9164**	**0.9154**	**0.6387**	**0.6410**	**0.9271**	**0.9319**

5.5   Node Clustering

We use Kmeans to evaluate the performance of the node clustering task, where k is the number of classes of the target node type. We adopt NMI and ARI as evaluation metrics, and the results are reported in Table 3. The experimental results show that our proposed CAHGCL consistently achieves the best performance on node clustering. Specifically, CAHGCL achieves significant advantages on IMDB, raising both NMI and ARI to over 0.15. Compared with the state-of-the-art heterogeneous graph contrastive learning algorithms MEOW and HGCML, CAHGCL improves the NMI of ACM by an average of 0.0382, IMDB by an average of 0.0492, and DBLP by an average of 0.0288. Additionally, we observe that self-supervised algorithms generally outperform traditional algorithms on node clustering. Moreover, CAHGCL is superior to other heterogeneous graph contrast learning algorithms, which proves the effectiveness of considering community information in data augmentation, selecting positive and negative samples, and designing the objective function.

Table 3. Results of the node clustering experiment.

Datasets	ACM		IMDB		DBLP	
Metrics	NMI	ARI	NMI	ARI	NMI	ARI
GCN	0.5514	0.5805	0.0756	0.0655	0.7511	0.8021
GAT	0.6024	0.6338	0.0802	0.0705	0.7206	0.7774
HAN	0.6098	0.6396	0.0885	0.0846	0.7789	0.8215
Mp2vec	0.3649	0.3632	0.0253	0.0298	0.7375	0.7773
HeCo	0.6043	0.6312	0.0811	0.0974	0.7099	0.7667
STENCIL	0.6118	0.6591	0.1247	0.1335	0.7244	0.7836
MEOW	0.6621	0.7117	0.0960	0.1047	0.7546	0.8119
HGCML	0.6767	0.7208	0.1071	0.1087	0.7609	0.8166
CAHGCL	**0.7076**	**0.7477**	**0.1508**	**0.1639**	**0.7866**	**0.8402**

5.6   Ablation Experiment

In this section, we conduct ablation experiments to verify the effectiveness of each component of CAHGCL, as shown in Fig. 2. Specifically, we designed three variants of CAHGCL: CAHGCL-w/o-aug represents using random edge dropping instead of adaptive data augmentation strategy, CAHGCL-w/o-hard represents removing dynamic sample weighting strategy, and CAHGCL-w/o-com represents removing community-level contrast. From the figure, we can see that all three variants perform worse than the original CAHGCL, proving the effectiveness of each model component. Among them, CAHGCL-w/o-aug has the lowest NMI and ARI, which is attributed to the fact that after removing the dynamic sample weighting strategy, the model cannot identify hard samples in the network, resulting in a decrease in the accuracy of community detection.

5.7   Parameter Experiment

In this section, we analyze the hyperparameter sensitivity in data augmentation and coarse clustering on ACM and IMDB.

Analysis of the feature similarity constraint f: In feature augmentation, we utilize f to remove edges with low importance, while in topology augmentation, f is employed to avoid introducing noisy information. According to Fig. 3, it can be seen that the best performance is achieved at $f = 0.3$ for ACM and $f = 0.4$ for IMDB. In more detail, since the cosine similarity of nodes in IMDB is very low, the feature augmentation process on IMDB is insensitive to f. However, f is required to filter second-order neighbors in topology augmentation so that the experimental results will vary within a small range.

Analysis of the local clustering coefficient constraint t: In topology augmentation, we add edges to nodes whose local clustering coefficient is less than t. According to Fig. 4, it can be seen that the best performance is achieved at $t = 0.1$ for ACM and $t = 0.4$ for IMDB. On ACM, as t increases, NMI and ARI first

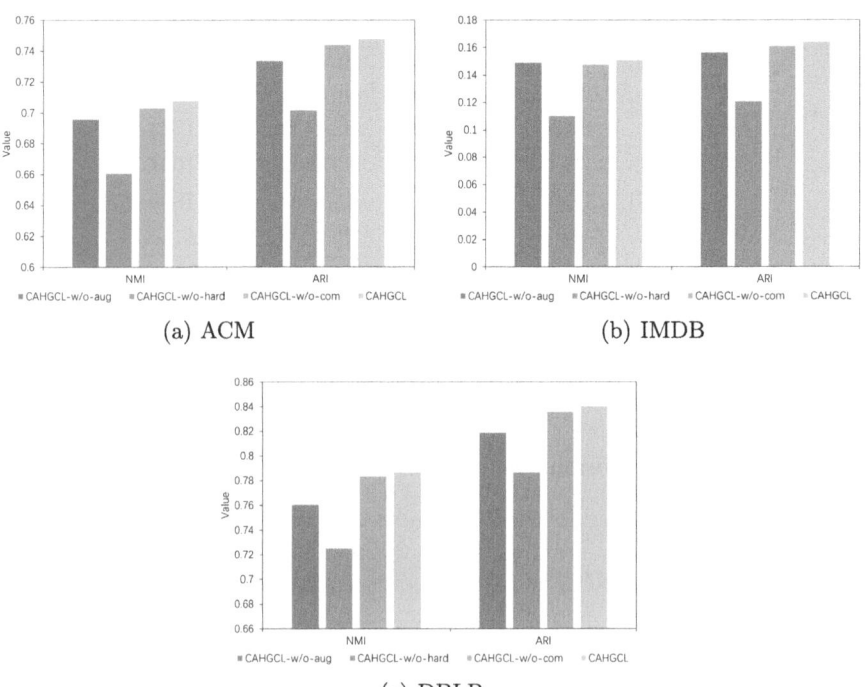

(a) ACM   (b) IMDB

(c) DBLP

Fig. 2. Ablation experiment of the proposed CAHGCL on node clustering.

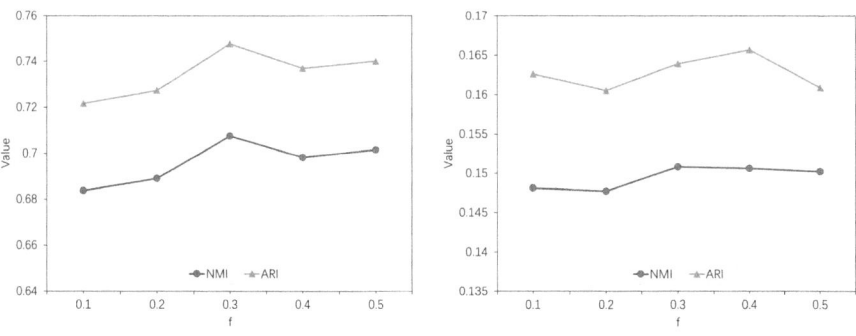

(a) Parameter experiment of f on ACM   (b) Parameter experiment of f on IMDB

Fig. 3. Hyperparameter sensitivity of f on node clustering.

remain stable and then gradually decrease. On IMDB, when t increases to 0.3 or 0.4, the evaluation metrics notably improve, which proves the effectiveness of adding edges to nodes at community boundaries.

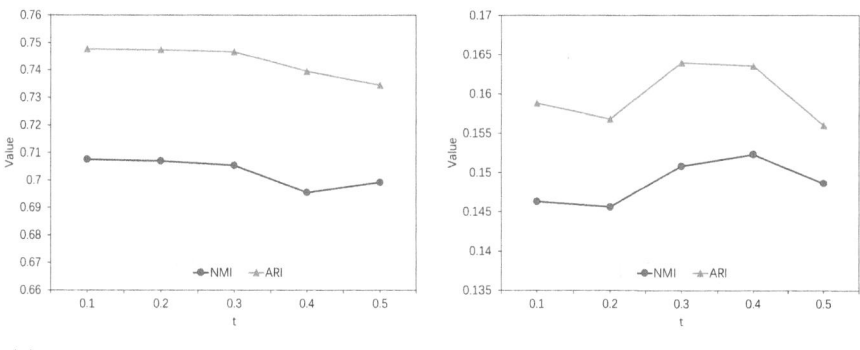

(a) Parameter experiment of t on ACM   (b) Parameter experiment of t on IMDB

Fig. 4. Hyperparameter sensitivity of t on node clustering.

The effect of confidence rate μ on model performance: Before calculating dynamic sample weights, we utilize μ to determine the number of high-confidence samples. According to Fig. 5, the best performance is achieved at $\mu = 0.8$ for ACM and $\mu = 0.7$ for IMDB. We observe that μ greatly impacts the experimental results, proving that the dynamic sample weighting strategy can effectively identify hard samples and improve the accuracy of community detection.

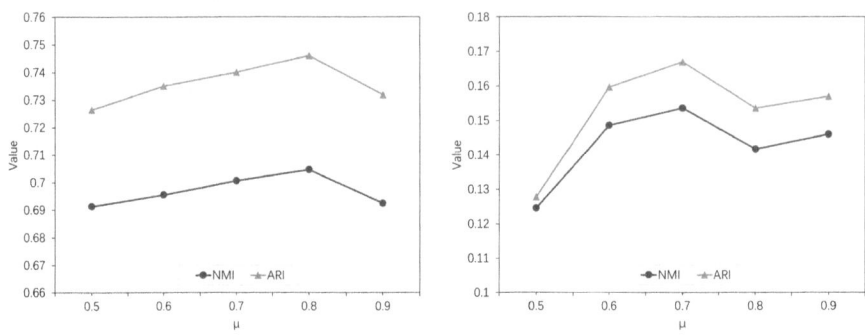

(a) Parameter experiment of μ on ACM   (b) Parameter experiment of μ on IMDB

Fig. 5. Hyperparameter sensitivity of μ on node clustering.

6   Conclusions

In this paper, we outline the research status of heterogeneous graph contrastive learning and three unresolved issues. We propose a Community-Aware Heterogeneous Graph Contrastive Learning model called CAHGCL. Specifically, we design an adaptive data augmentation strategy to construct the outline view and semantic view, introduce a dynamic sample weighting strategy to identify hard samples in the network and incorporate community-level contrast to improve community cohesion. Finally, we compare the proposed CAHGCL with eight widely recognized models on three datasets, and the experimental results validate the effectiveness of our model.

Acknowledgements. This work was supported by the National Natural Science Foundation of China under Grant No. 62002063 and No. U21A20472, the National Key Research and Development Plan of China under Grant No.2021YF-B3600503, the Natural Science Foundation of Fujian Province under Grant No. 2022J01118 and No. 2023J011062, the Major Science and Technology Project of Fujian Province under Grant No.2021HZ022007, Haixi Government Big Data Application Cooperative Innovation Center and the Hong Kong RGC TRS T41-603/20R.

References

1. Bhagat, S., Cormode, G., Muthukrishnan, S.: Node classification in social networks. In: Aggarwal, C. (ed.) Social Network Data Analytics, pp. 115–148. Springer, Boston (2011). https://doi.org/10.1007/978-1-4419-8462-3_5
2. Ding, K., Xu, Z., Tong, H., Liu, H.: Data augmentation for deep graph learning: a survey. ACM SIGKDD Explor. Newsl. **24**(2), 61–77 (2022)
3. Dong, Y., Chawla, N.V., Swami, A.: metapath2vec: scalable representation learning for heterogeneous networks. In: Proceedings of the 23rd ACM SIGKDD International Conference on Knowledge Discovery and Data Mining, pp. 135–144 (2017)

4. Fu, X., Zhang, J., Meng, Z., King, I.: MAGNN: metapath aggregated graph neural network for heterogeneous graph embedding. In: Proceedings of the Web Conference 2020, pp. 2331–2341 (2020)

5. Hassani, K., Khasahmadi, A.H.: Contrastive multi-view representation learning on graphs. In: International Conference on Machine Learning, pp. 4116–4126. PMLR (2020)

6. Kipf, T.N., Welling, M.: Semi-supervised classification with graph convolutional networks. arXiv preprint arXiv:1609.02907 (2016)

7. Liu, Y., et al.: Hard sample aware network for contrastive deep graph clustering. In: Proceedings of the AAAI Conference on Artificial Intelligence, pp. 8914–8922 (2023)

8. Shi, G., Zhu, Y., Liu, J.K., Li, X.: HeGCL: advance self-supervised learning in heterogeneous graph-level representation. IEEE Trans. Neural Netw. Learn. Syst. (2023)

9. Veličković, P., Cucurull, G., Casanova, A., Romero, A., Lio, P., Bengio, Y.: Graph attention networks. arXiv preprint arXiv:1710.10903 (2017)

10. Wang, X., Bo, D., Shi, C., Fan, S., Ye, Y., Philip, S.Y.: A survey on heterogeneous graph embedding: methods, techniques, applications and sources. IEEE Trans. Big Data 9(2), 415–436 (2022)

11. Wang, X., et al.: Heterogeneous graph attention network. In: The World Wide Web Conference, pp. 2022–2032 (2019)

12. Wang, X., Liu, N., Han, H., Shi, C.: Self-supervised heterogeneous graph neural network with co-contrastive learning. In: Proceedings of the 27th ACM SIGKDD Conference on Knowledge Discovery & Data Mining, pp. 1726–1736 (2021)

13. Wang, Z., Li, Q., Yu, D., Han, X., Gao, X.Z., Shen, S.: Heterogeneous graph contrastive multi-view learning. In: Proceedings of the 2023 SIAM International Conference on Data Mining (SDM), pp. 136–144. SIAM (2023)

14. Watts, D.J., Strogatz, S.H.: Collective dynamics of 'small-world' networks. Nature 393(6684), 440–442 (1998)

15. Wu, L., Lin, H., Tan, C., Gao, Z., Li, S.Z.: Self-supervised learning on graphs: contrastive, generative, or predictive. IEEE Trans. Knowl. Data Eng. 35(4), 4216–4235 (2021)

16. Xia, J., Wu, L., Wang, G., Chen, J., Li, S.Z.: ProGCL: rethinking hard negative mining in graph contrastive learning. arXiv preprint arXiv:2110.02027 (2021)

17. Yang, Y., Guan, Z., Li, J., Zhao, W., Cui, J., Wang, Q.: Interpretable and efficient heterogeneous graph convolutional network. IEEE Trans. Knowl. Data Eng. 35(2), 1637–1650 (2021)

18. Yu, J., Li, X.: Heterogeneous graph contrastive learning with meta-path contexts and weighted negative samples. In: Proceedings of the 2023 SIAM International Conference on Data Mining (SDM), pp. 37–45. SIAM (2023)

19. Zhu, Y., Xu, Y., Cui, H., Yang, C., Liu, Q., Wu, S.: Structure-enhanced heterogeneous graph contrastive learning. In: Proceedings of the 2022 SIAM International Conference on Data Mining (SDM), pp. 82–90. SIAM (2022)

20. Zhu, Y., Xu, Y., Yu, F., Liu, Q., Wu, S., Wang, L.: Deep graph contrastive representation learning. arXiv preprint arXiv:2006.04131 (2020)

21. Zhu, Y., Xu, Y., Yu, F., Liu, Q., Wu, S., Wang, L.: Graph contrastive learning with adaptive augmentation. In: Proceedings of the Web Conference 2021, pp. 2069–2080 (2021)

UGCM-LU: A Unified Stream and Batch Graph Computing Model with Local Update for Community Detection

Hong Li[1,2,3], Ling Wu[1,2,3], and Kun Guo[1,2,3(✉)]

[1] College of Computer and Data Science, Fuzhou University, Fuzhou 350108, China
gukn@fzu.edu.cn
[2] Engineering Research Center of Big Data Intelligence, Ministry of Education, Fuzhou 350108, China
[3] Fujian Key Laboratory of Network Computing and Intelligent Information Processing, Fuzhou University, Fuzhou 350108, China

Abstract. Unified stream and batch computing (USBC) aims to incorporate stream and batch computation into a unified framework, thereby enabling the development of a one-stop solution for stream and batch data processing and enhancing the generalization of the framework. However, research on unified graph computing models (UGCMs) faces several challenges. First, existing UGCMs need to consider all graph information in the cache during the incremental update phase, thus leading to decreased execution efficiency. Second, existing UGCMs use fixed bytes to store nodes without considering the actual space occupied by nodes resulting in wasted memory when dealing with large graphs. This paper proposes a UGCM with Local Updates for community detection (UGCM-LU). We first implement a local update strategy to consider partial information of the graph to achieve incremental updates. Secondly, we also designed a byte-compression-based module to store graph data according to the space occupied by nodes. The experimental results show the effectiveness and efficiency of the model in real-world and artificial networks.

Keywords: Unified stream and batch · Graph computing · Incremental algorithm · Community detection

1 Introduction

With the progress of science and technology, the scale of graph data is growing fast. The analysis of large-scale graph data can effectively extract valuable information from graph data. Real-world data such as social networks, transportation networks financial data, etc. can be represented by graph data. Graph data analytics is beneficial for discovering the community structure in social networks, avoiding financial risks, and formula traffic flow. To cope with different scenarios, these systems are usually classified into two categories: batch and stream processing. Batch systems tend to have higher accuracy, and streaming systems, while less accurate than batch systems, have greater real-time performance. For combining the strengths of both and avoid maintaining two systems at the same time. Unified stream and batch computing has become a better choice. Currently, the primary graph computation frameworks are in batch form, such as GraphX [21] and Gelly [2], and there are few models for USBC, only the USBGM [10] proposed by Dai et al., which implemented unified stream and batch graph computing. Applying USBC to the field of graph computing can mine graph information more effectively, achieve real-time response while ensuring accuracy, and only require the maintenance of one set of programs.

Several challenges remain in the research of UGCM. First, existing UGCMs use adjacency lists and adjacency matrices to store the graph data, without considering the size of the actual storage space occupied by node. In the case where a large number of nodes have common neighbors, it is necessary to store the same neighbor nodes repeatedly. Second, existing UGCMs need the entire information of the cached graph in the incremental update phase, which significantly increases the computational and communication overhead as the graph scale grows. Currently, a few USBC models have been proposed [3,10,16,17], however, the support for most community detection algorithms in the field of UGCM is inadequate.

In this paper, we propose a novel UGCM for community detection (UGCM-LU), which contains preprocessing and stream processing modules. The preprocessing stage is responsible for the initialization of computation and the incremental computation of the algorithm will be executed in the stream processing stage. In addition, we learn from Roaring Bitmap [8] and design a byte-compression-based module for graph storage to solve the high space overhead of traditional storage structures. The main contributions of this paper are as follows:

(1) The BCBM module proposed by UGCM-LU stores nodes according to the number of bytes they occupy and uses an additional list of nodes to index high-degree nodes by byte. Compared to the traditional graph storage structure, it can effectively reduce the memory overhead.
(2) The local update strategy proposed by UGCM-LU utilizes local information of the cache graph to achieve the state update in the incremental update phase, which avoids the computational overhead of the model on large-scale graphs and improves the efficiency of the model execution compared to the existing work.
(3) Experiments on real and artificial networks validate the effectiveness and efficiency of the proposed model applied to community detection.

2   Related Work

In this section, we describe the work related to this study of unified stream and batch computing, graph computation model, and streaming community detection.

2.1   Unified Stream and Batch Computing

Existing unified stream and batch computing can be categorized into hybrid-based and stream-based computing. For hybrid-based USBC, Nathan [15] proposed the lambda architecture to solve the problem in real-time data processing, which consists of a batch and stream processing layer and a service layer for responding to queries. Although the lambda architecture unified stream and batch components into a computing system, it still needs to maintain two sets of programs. Boykin et al. developed Summingbird [5] based on the lambda architecture, which provides a unified interface for real-time and batch processing improves efficiency by reducing conversions of data, and introduces a concept of time window. Montie [16] et al. proposed a unified framework for fast and slow stream learning and applied it to machine learning classification. The model designs interaction mechanisms between two modes to accommodate complex data scenarios. Pishgoo [17] et al. proposed a stream-batch unified anomaly detection method GHDBS based on lambda architecture, which consists of stream processing, batch processing, and a unified unit, and it uses a unified unit instead of a service layer to achieve USBC. For stream-based USBC, jay [12] proposed the kappa architecture, which is optimized based on lambda architecture by removing the batch processing layer and using only the high-speed processing layer for unified data processing, which reduces the waste of computational resources due to it. Akidau [1] et al. proposed the Dataflow model. Dataflow combines stream and batch data processing to form a unified programming paradigm. Flink [6] and Beam [4], a streaming and batch unified framework is based on the idea of Dataflow. Flink also simplifies the system architecture improves the flexibility of development, and provides fault-tolerant mechanisms.

2.2   Graph Computation Model

Existing graph computation models can be categorized into stream and batch. PowerGraph [11] and PowerLyra [9] are two classical models of batch graph computation that enable distributed graph computation by dividing large-scale graphs into multiple partitions. PowerLyra also introduces vertex partitioning to improve data processing efficiency further. Gonzalez et al. proposed Spark GraphX [21], which is a component of Spark, that provides excellent fault tolerance and rich conversion operations for batch graph processing. Spark Streaming [24] is widely used in graph processing thanks to the Spark framework. Tang et al. [19] proposed the IncGraph model based on GraphX to support incremental iterative computation on dynamic graphs, focusing on the part of the graph data that changes.

2.3   Streaming Community Detection

Streaming community detection handles the arrival of new data by automatically forming new communities or updating identified ones. Yun et al. [23] proposed an algorithm in which the space used grows linearly with the network to reduce memory consumption during computation. Liakos et al. [14] proposed a streaming community detection algorithm based on seed set expansion, which can determine the community size automatically and maintain the node information of the graph through an efficient structure that optimizes the space occupation. Yang [20] proposed an overlapping community detection algorithm based on streaming analysis. It divides the nodes based on the information such as degree, which has advantages over traditional methods in terms of execution time.

3   The Proposed Model

In this section, we first introduce the UGCM-LU model. The model consists of a preprocessing and an incremental update phase. The preprocessing phase includes the initialization of the model and the byte-compression-based module (BCBM) and the incremental update phase, which contains a local update strategy timed global update.

3.1   The Framework of UGCM-LU

We proposed a novel UGCM that can receive edge steam from multiple data sources to realize stream and batch computation. The model is shown in Fig. 1.

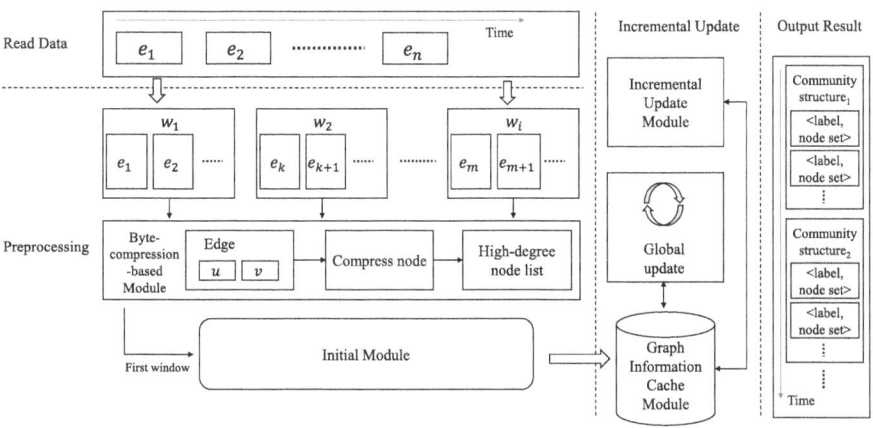

Fig. 1. The framework of UGCM-LU

Stage 1: Read Data. The model can fetch data from a variety of data sources, such as static datasets of files or message queues, which are presented by edge streams. As shown in Fig. 1, e represents an edge, and data will continue to arrive over time.

Stage 2: Preprocessing. In stream processing mode, the arriving edges data will be divided by time windows. As shown in Fig. 1, w represents the window for dividing data, and each window contains edge data of a certain time interval. The BCBM will compress the vertices and edges obtained. Then, compressed data will be initialized in the first window and results obtained are stored by the Graph Information Cache Module. In batch Processing mode the first time window will contain all the data and output the results directly after initialization.

Stage 3: Incremental Update. In stream processing mode, the data from the non-first window updates the graph cache model according to an established local update strategy. After the execution of each window is completed, the results are output to the downstream operators. Meanwhile, the Global Update Module conducts full information updates after a certain time interval to ensure the accuracy of the results.

Stage 4: Output Results. This phase outputs the result, which is the community structure after execution of each window, in the Graph Information Cache Module based on the updates of each time window and output.

3.2   Byte-Compression-Based Graph Store Module

The BCBM can be divided into two parts, the first part is used to store the neighbor structure of the node. We use the list index to represent the node. The neighbor structure of the node is shown in Fig. 2.

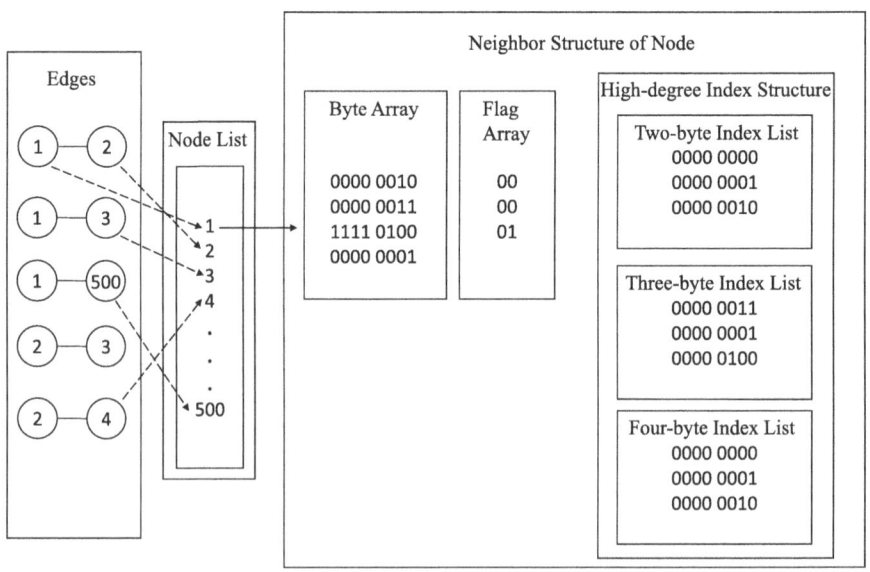

Fig. 2. Neighbor structure of node (Part one of BCBM)

It consists of a byte array, a flag array, and three high-degree index structures. We will describe the high-degree index structure in detail later. Every neighbor node is stored in a byte array according to the number of bytes it occupies. To be able to decode the neighbor nodes correctly, each byte array is associated with a flag array that stores the byte number of each neighbor node. We use 00, 01, 10, and 11 to denote byte numbers from 1 to 4.

The second part is the high-degree node structure shown in Fig. 3. In this part, three lists are used to store high-degree nodes of different byte numbers. Since the nodes stored in each list are of the same byte, all high-degree nodes can be queried using byte number as an interval. For example, in a two-byte node list, every two bytes represent a complete node. The high-degree index structure mentioned in the first part contains three lists corresponding to the three lists of High-degree Node Structure. For example, in the two-byte index list, each single byte can index a two-byte high-degree node. As shown in Fig. 3, in the two-byte node list, every two bytes constitute a complete node. 0000 1101 means the twelfth node in the two-byte node list. Therefore, the node consisting of the 24th and 25th bytes in the two-byte node list is the node to be searched. Each list in the high-degree index structure stores a limited number index of nodes due to byte limitations. For a two-byte index list, at most 2^8 ones are stored. Three-byte index list and four-byte index list also search for nodes in this way. The pseudocode for encoding node is shown in Algorithm 1.

Algorithm 1: EncodeNode

Input : Node id x
Output: Compressed data c, length flag l

1 $c \leftarrow \{\}; l \leftarrow \{\}$ // Initialize a bytes list c and a flag list l.
   // Store nodes according to the number of bytes they occupy.
2 **if** $x \in [2, 2^8 - 1]$ **then**
3   c.add(x AND 0xFF);
4   l.add(00);
5 **else if** $x \in [2^8, 2^{16} - 1]$ **then**
6   c.add(x AND 0xFF);
7   c.add(($x \gg 8$) AND 0xFF);
8   l.add(01);
9 **else if** $x \in [2^{16}, 2^{24} - 1]$ **then**
10   c.add(x AND 0xFF);
11   c.add(($x \gg 8$) AND 0xFF);
12   c.add(($x \gg 16$) AND 0xFF);
13   l.add(10);
14 **else**
15   c.add(x AND 0xFF);
16   c.add(($x \gg 8$) AND 0xFF);
17   c.add(($x \gg 16$) AND 0xFF);
18   c.add($x \gg 24$ AND 0xFF);
19   l.add(11);
20 **return** c, l;

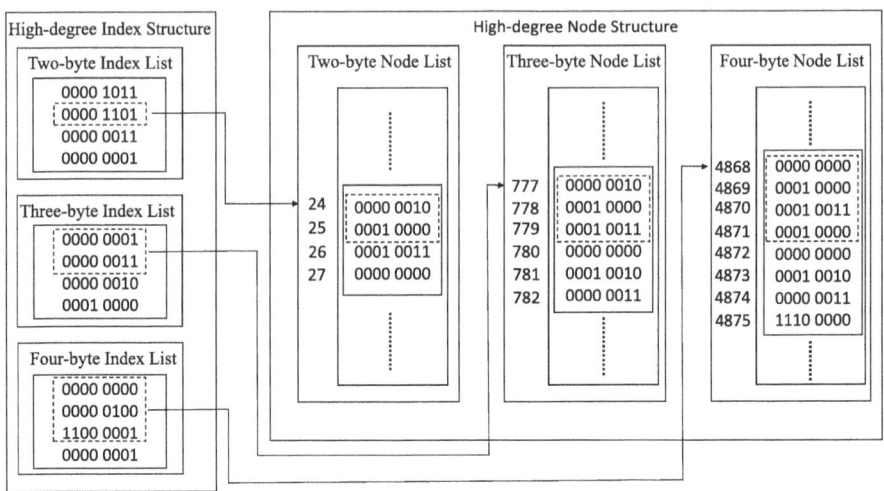

Fig. 3. The structure of high-degree node list(Part two of BCBM)

Calculation of Memory Saved by BCBM. We will analyze how much memory BCBM can save theoretically. Let the average degree of high-degree nodes in the graph be d_{max}. According to BCBM, the memory of two-byte, three-byte, and four-byte high-degree nodes calculation is shown by Eq. (1):

$$\begin{cases} M_{two} = 2^8 \times 1 \times d_{max} + 2 \\ M_{three} = 2^{16} \times 2 \times d_{max} + 3 \\ M_{four} = 2^{24} \times 3 \times d_{max} + 4 \end{cases} \tag{1}$$

When using traditional storage, the size of memory occupied by high-degree nodes is shown by Eq. (2):

$$M_t = 2^8 d_{max}(2 + 2^8(3 + 2^8 \times 4)) \tag{2}$$

The size of memory saved compared to traditional storage calculation is shown by Eq. (3):

$$M_{save} = 2^8 d_{max}(1 + 2^8(1 + 2^8)) + 9 \tag{3}$$

3.3   Local Update Strategy

The local update strategy works in the incremental update phase. An edge (u, v) arriving in this phase updates the graph cache using different methods according to their different types. The types of edges are shown in Fig. 4, Fig. 5 and Fig. 6:

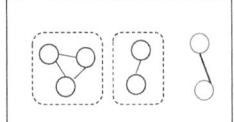 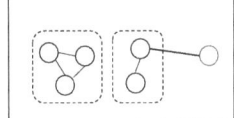 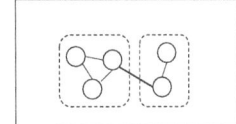

Fig. 4. Edge with two new nodes

Fig. 5. Edge with one new nodes

Fig. 6. Edge with no new nodes

Edge with Two New Nodes. For this type of edge, since it has no connection to the current graph cache model, a uniform new label is assigned to the two new nodes, forming a separate community.

Edge with One New Node. For this type of edge, it is assumed that node u has an identified label in the graph cache model. Borrowing from the label propagation algorithm [18], the new node v is given to the one, which is the highest number of neighbor nodes of u. The implementation pseudocode is shown in Algorithm 3 (lines 19 to 26), and we assume that node v is the new node.

Edge with No New Nodes. For this type of edge, two cases exist. In the first case, this edge connects two nodes of the same community. Adding such an edge usually increases the cohesiveness of the community, so no treatment is given for such an edge. In the second case, this edge connects two nodes belonging to different communities. When adding this type of edge, both communities need to be re-updated. We use the metric permanence [7] to determine if a node needs to be moved. The metric permanence is shown by Eq. (4).

$$P(v) = [\frac{I(v)}{E_{max}(v)} \times \frac{1}{d(v)}] - [1 - C_{in}(v)] \tag{4}$$

In Eq. (4), $I(v)$ is the number of neighbor nodes of v in the same community, $E_{max}(v)$ is the maximum number of connections of node v to other communities, $d(v)$ is the degree of node v. The calculation of C_{in} is shown by Eq. (5).

$$C_{in} = \frac{E_{neigh(v)}}{\binom{I(v)}{2}} \tag{5}$$

In Eq. (5), $E_{neigh(v)}$ is the number of connections between neighbor nodes in the community of node v. $\binom{I(v)}{2}$ is the number of connections for neighbor nodes of v in the community. The movement of a node is considered to be reasonable when the permanence of the node becomes larger after the node is moved. The algorithm of node movement is shown in Algorithm 2.

In Algorithm 2, it is assumed that the node to be moved is u. Firstly, the function declares a queue to store the nodes to be moved and obtains two communities connected by the edge e (lines 1 to 4). The queue stores all one-hop neighbors of node u, which are most probably affected by the addition of edge

e (lines 7 to 8). When the queue is not empty, the node is continuously moved to another community. If the permanence value of node n is improved compared to the original, the current node movement result is retained, otherwise, the original community structure is restored (lines 9 to 17). At last, we update the community structure and return it (line 18).

3.4   Community Detection Algorithm Based on UGCM-LU

We implemented unified stream and batch community detection algorithm UGCM-LU-COPRA based on UGCM-LU and ran it under stream processing (UGCM-LU-COPRA(Stream)) and batch processing modes (UGCM-LU-COPRA(Batch)) respectively. The pseudocode of UGCM-LU-COPRA algorithm is shown in Algorithm 3. The input data will be divided according to the time window W_i and sent to BCBM for compressing. Afterward, the initial community will be formed in the first window, and the community C_t will be updated in subsequent windows according to the local update strategy.

Algorithm 3: UGCM-LU-COPRA

Input   : BCBM B, Time Windows W_i, Initial Module $Init$, Local
              Update Module LUM
Output: Community Structure C_i

1 **for** $i = 0$ *to* t **do**
2 $\quad$ $d = B(W_i)$; // Store compressed graph data.
3 $\quad$ **if** $i = 0$ **then**
4 $\quad\quad$ | $\quad C_i \leftarrow Init(d)$;
5 $\quad$ **else**
6 $\quad\quad$ | $\quad C_{i+1} \leftarrow C_i \cup LUM(d)$;
7 **return** C_{t+1};

---

4   Experiments

4.1   Datasets

We use five data sets to verify the accuracy of the COPRA algorithm implemented based on UGCM-LU (UGCM-LU-COPRA) in both stream and batch processing modes. The five datasets include three real-world networks and two artificial networks. The parameter information of each real-world and artificial network is shown in Table 1, where k denotes the average degree.

4.2   Baselines Algorithm

We compared UGCM-LU-COPRA (Batch) with the COPRA algorithm implemented based on GraphX and UGCM-LU-COPRA (Stream) with the COPRA algorithm implemented based on Spark Streaming to evaluate the effectiveness of the batch and streaming modes, respectively. We have conducted experiments in three aspects including accuracy, running time, and memory overhead.

Algorithm 2: LocalUpdate

Input   : Edge $e(u, v)$, neighbor list of node u l, Old community structure
$C_t, list\ of\ all\ node\ l_g$
Output: New community structure C_{t+1}, $label\ of\ v\ C_v$

1 **if** $u \in l_g$ **and** $v \in l_g$ **then**
2 $\quad$ $q \leftarrow \{\}$ // Initialize a queue to store nodes that may be moved.
3 $\quad$ $q.add(u)$; // Add first node to be moved.
4 $\quad$ $C_v \leftarrow getCommunity(v)$;
5 $\quad$ $C_u \leftarrow getCommunity(u)$;
6 $\quad$ $C_t \leftarrow C_t - C_v - C_u$;
7 $\quad$ **for** $node \in l$ **do**
8 $\quad\quad$ $q.append(node)$;
9 $\quad$ **while** q $is\ not\ empty$ **do**
10 $\quad\quad$ $n \leftarrow q.pop()$;
11 $\quad\quad$ $perm_{old} \leftarrow calcPerm(n)$;
12 $\quad\quad$ C_u remove n;
13 $\quad\quad$ C_v add u;
14 $\quad\quad$ $perm_{new} \leftarrow calcPerm(n)$;
15 $\quad\quad$ **if** $perm_{new} \leq perm_{old}$ **then**
16 $\quad\quad\quad$ C_u add n;
17 $\quad\quad\quad$ C_v remove n;
18 $\quad$ $C_{t+1} \leftarrow C_t \cup C_u \cup C_v$;
19 **else if** $u \in l_g$ **or** $v \in l_g$ **then**
20 $\quad$ $D = \{\}$; // Initialize a dictionary to store labels of neighbor
$\quad\quad$ nodes.
21 $\quad$ $C_v = 0$; // Initialize variable to store the maximum value.
22 $\quad$ **for** $node \in l$ **do**
23 $\quad\quad$ $D \leftarrow D \cup \{C_{node} : 1\}$;
24 $\quad\quad$ **if** $D[C_{node}] > C_v$ **then**
25 $\quad\quad\quad$ $C_v \leftarrow C_{node}$;
26 $\quad$ $C_{t+1} \leftarrow C_t \cup \{C_v : v\}$;
27 **else**
28 $\quad$ $C_{t+1} \leftarrow C_t \cup \{C_u : u\} \cup \{C_u : v\}$; // Use node id of u as the label.
29 **return** C_{t+1};

4.3   Evaluation Metrics

We adopted two widely recognized community detection evaluation metrics for
our experiments. ONMI (Overlapping Normalized Mutual Information) [13] is
used to measure the similarity between the community structure obtained by the
algorithm execution and the ground-truth community structure. The equation
of ONMI is shown in Eq. (6).

$$ONMI = 1 - \frac{1}{2}[H(X|Y) + H(Y|X)] \tag{6}$$

Table 1. Real-world Networks

Networks	#Nodes	#Edges	#Communities	k
Amazon	334863	925872	75149	-
DBLP	317080	1049866	13477	-
YouTube	1134890	2987624	8385	-
D1	300000	3048184	3608	10
D2	500000	5761472	5356	12

In Eq. (6), X and Y represent the community sets obtained by algorithm execution and the ground-truth community sets respectively. $H(X|Y)$ is the conditional entropy of X with respect to Y.

Average F1-Score [22] matches each community C'_j obtained by algorithm execution with its most similar ground-truth one C_i, and calculates an average score of the matches. The equation of average F1-Score is shown in Eq. (7)

$$F1 = \frac{1}{2}\left(\frac{1}{|C^*|}\sum_{C_i \in C^*} f(C_i, C'_{g(i)}) + \frac{1}{|C'|}\sum_{C'_i \in C'} f(C_{g'(i)}, C'_i)\right) \tag{7}$$

In Eq. (7), C' and C^* are the community sets obtained and ground-truth community sets, respectively. $g(i)$ and $g'(i)$ are the best matches defined as follows:

$$\begin{aligned} g(i) &= argmax_j f(C_i, C'_j) \\ g'(i) &= argmax_j f(C_j, C'_i) \end{aligned} \tag{8}$$

where $f(C_i, C'_j)$ calculates the harmonic mean of precision and recall.

4.4 Accuracy Experiment

The accuracy of the algorithms on real-world and artificial networks are shown in Table 2 and Table 3.

Table 2 shows the F1-Score results of the UGCM-LU and comparison algorithms on all networks. From the table, we can see that the results obtained by UGCM-LU in stream processing mode are generally better than Spark Streaming. UGCM-LU does not have very obvious advantages on real-world networks. But on artificial networks, UGCM-LU can achieve better results than Spark Streaming. Observing the results of UGCM-LU on artificial networks alone, we can find that when the network scale becomes larger, the accuracy of the model decreases slightly. In batch mode, it can be seen that UGCM-LU is slightly improved compared to GraphX but not much different. This is because of the stability of the batch processing. Table 3 shows the ONMI results of the UGCM-LU and comparison algorithms on all networks. As can be seen from the table, whether in batch or stream processing, UGCM-LU has better results compared with the comparison algorithms.

Overall, UGCM-LU can achieve an improvement of up to 0.2 on artificial networks, which benefits from the Initial Module of UGCM-LU, which forms the initial community that provides the basis for subsequent updates and improves accuracy and global updates at regular intervals. It also reflects the rationality of the local update strategy, which can implement more efficient incremental updates without sacrificing accuracy.

Table 2. Accuracy of COPRA(F1-Score)

Networks	Stream Mode		Batch Mode	
	UGCM-LU(Stream)	Spark Streaming	UGCM-LU(Batch)	GraphX
YouTube	**0.0432**	0.0212	0.1578	**0.1584**
Amazon	**0.4211**	0.4054	**0.4647**	0.4634
DBLP	**0.2357**	0.1986	**0.3086**	0.3081
D1	**0.6365**	0.4349	**0.8652**	0.859
D2	**0.6347**	0.4278	**0.8643**	0.861

Table 3. Accuracy of COPRA(ONMI)

Networks	Stream Mode		Batch Mode	
	UGCM-LU(Stream)	Spark Streaming	UGCM-LU(Batch)	GraphX
YouTube	**0.0127**	0.0113	**0.0241**	0.0235
Amazon	**0.1709**	0.1705	**0.1825**	0.1822
DBLP	**0.0948**	0.0765	**0.1243**	0.124
D1	**0.5644**	0.4276	**0.8123**	0.8091
D2	**0.5578**	0.4101	**0.8116**	0.8092

4.5 Runtime Experiment

The running time experiments on real-world and artificial networks are shown in Fig. 7 and Fig. 8. From the figures, we can see that in streaming mode, the running time of UGCM-LU can be improved by about 10% compared with Spark Streaming. From the artificial network experiment, we can see that when the network scale becomes larger, the running time is shortened more significantly. This is because we adopt a local update strategy in streaming processing to avoid considering all graph cache information. When the scale of graph data increases, local updates require less graph information, so the execution efficiency is higher. In batch processing, when the network scale is large, the running time is slightly longer than GraphX. This is because our initialization module needs to perform more complex operations on the network, and the parallelization optimization is not enough.

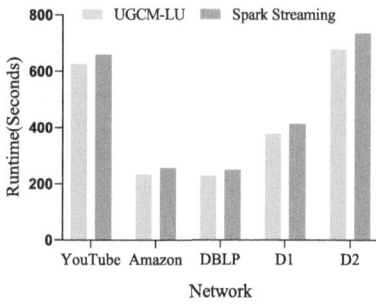

Fig. 7. Runtime on Real-world Networks

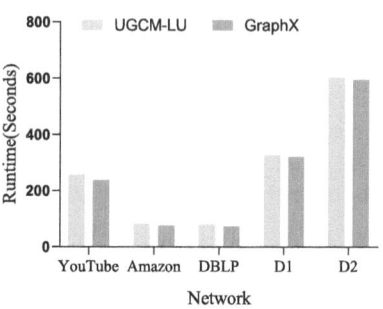

Fig. 8. Runtime on Artificial Networks

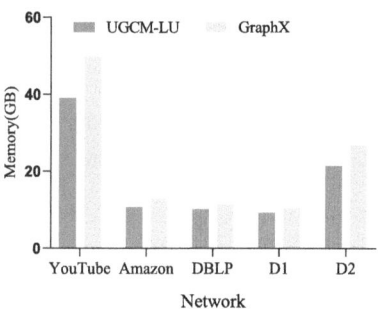

Fig. 9. Memory Overhead (Stream)

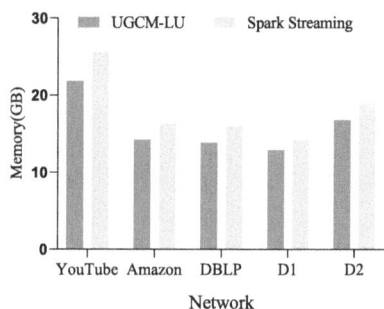

Fig. 10. Memory Overhead (Batch)

4.6   Memory Experiment

Figure 9 and Fig. 10 show the memory overhead results of COPRA on different networks in stream processing and batch processing mode respectively. We can see from the figure, that the total memory of our model at runtime is less than Spark Streaming, which can be reduced by up to 15%. This is because byte compression is used for storage, which consumes less memory during message delivery. In batch processing mode, our model has smaller memory consumption than GraphX. This is because GraphX uses an RDD structure when storing graphs, which requires additional space to store attributes and other information. In addition, when the network scale becomes larger, UGCM can save more memory.

5   Conclusion

In this paper, we propose a novel unified stream and batch graph computing model UGCM-LU. First, we designed a Byte-compression-based Module(BCBM) in the model to reduce the storage space of the adjacency matrix and nodes by compressing the input data, effectively reducing the runtime memory overhead. In addition, the local update strategy can update the graph cache by considering partial information about the graph during the incremental update phase, thereby eliminating the need to consider the entire graph cache information. When the scale of graph data is large, it can reduce the computational cost of program execution and improve program efficiency. In the future, we plan to implement more graph algorithms on UGCM-LU.

Acknowledgements. This work was supported by the National Natural Science Foundation of China under Grant No. 62002063 and No. U21A20472, the National Key Research and Development Plan of China under Grant No. 2021YFB3600503, the Natural Science Foundation of Fujian Province under Grant No. 2022J01118 and No. 2023J011062, the Major Science and Technology Project of Fujian Province under Grant No. 2021HZ022007, Haixi Government Big Data Application Cooperative Innovation Center and the Hong Kong RGC TRS T41-603/20R.

References

1. Akidau, T., et al.: The dataflow model: a practical approach to balancing correctness, latency, and cost in massive-scale, unbounded, out-of-order data processing. Proc. VLDB Endowment **8**(12), 1792–1803 (2015)
2. Bali, J.D.: Streaming graph analytics framework design (2015)
3. Bartoszkiewicz, M., et al.: Pathway: a fast and flexible unified stream data processing framework for analytical and machine learning applications. arXiv preprint arXiv:2307.13116 (2023)
4. Beam, A.: Apache beam: an advanced unified programming model. Apache beam: an advanced unified programming model (2017)
5. Boykin, O., Ritchie, S., O'Connell, I., Lin, J.: Summingbird: a framework for integrating batch and online mapreduce computations. Proc. VLDB Endowment **7**(13), 1441–1451 (2014)
6. Carbone, P., Katsifodimos, A., Ewen, S., Markl, V., Haridi, S., Tzoumas, K.: Apache Flink: stream and batch processing in a single engine. Bull. Tech. Committee Data Eng. **38**(4) (2015)
7. Chakraborty, T., Srinivasan, S., Ganguly, N., Mukherjee, A., Bhowmick, S.: On the permanence of vertices in network communities. In: Proceedings of the 20th ACM SIGKDD International Conference on Knowledge Discovery and Data Mining, pp. 1396–1405 (2014)
8. Chambi, S., Lemire, D., Kaser, O., Godin, R.: Better bitmap performance with roaring bitmaps. Softw. Pract. Experience **46**(5), 709–719 (2016)
9. Chen, R., Shi, J., Chen, Y., Zang, B., Guan, H., Chen, H.: PowerLyra: differentiated graph computation and partitioning on skewed graphs. ACM Trans. Parallel Comput. (TOPC) **5**(3), 1–39 (2019)
10. Dai, J., Wu, L., Guo, K.: A unified stream and batch graph computing model for community detection. In: Sun, Y., et al. (eds.) ChineseCSCW 2022. CCIS, vol. 1681, pp. 110–124. Springer, Singapore (2023). https://doi.org/10.1007/978-981-99-2356-4_9
11. Gonzalez, J.E., Low, Y., Gu, H., Bickson, D., Guestrin, C.: PowerGraph: distributed Graph-Parallel computation on natural graphs. In: 10th USENIX Symposium on Operating Systems Design and Implementation (OSDI 12), pp. 17–30 (2012)
12. Kreps, J.: Questioning the lambda architecture. Online article **205**, 18–34 (2014)

13. Lancichinetti, A., Fortunato, S., Kertész, J.: Detecting the overlapping and hierarchical community structure in complex networks. New J. Phys. **11**(3), 033015 (2009)

14. Liakos, P., Papakonstantinopoulou, K., Ntoulas, A., Delis, A.: Rapid detection of local communities in graph streams. IEEE Trans. Knowl. Data Eng. **34**(5), 2375–2386 (2020)

15. Marz, N.: How to beat the cap theorem. Thoughts from the Red Planet (2011)

16. Montiel, J., Bifet, A., Losing, V., Read, J., Abdessalem, T.: Learning fast and slow: a unified batch/stream framework. In: 2018 IEEE International Conference on Big Data (Big Data), pp. 1065–1072. IEEE (2018)

17. Pishgoo, B., Azirani, A.A., Raahemi, B.: A hybrid distributed batch-stream processing approach for anomaly detection. Inf. Sci. **543**, 309–327 (2021)

18. Raghavan, U.N., Albert, R., Kumara, S.: Near linear time algorithm to detect community structures in large-scale networks. Phys. Rev. E **76**(3), 036106 (2007)

19. Tang, Z., He, M., Fu, Z., Yang, L.: IncGraph: an improved distributed incremental graph computing model and framework based on spark GraphX. IEEE Trans. Knowl. Data Eng. **34**(6), 2783–2797 (2020)

20. Wang, M., Yang, Y., Bindel, D., He, K.: Streaming local community detection through approximate conductance. IEEE Trans. Big Data (2023)

21. Xin, R.S., Gonzalez, J.E., Franklin, M.J., Stoica, I.: GraphX: a resilient distributed graph system on spark. In: First International Workshop on Graph Data Management Experiences and Systems, pp. 1–6 (2013)

22. Yang, J., Leskovec, J.: Overlapping community detection at scale: a nonnegative matrix factorization approach. In: Proceedings of the Sixth ACM International Conference on Web Search and Data Mining, pp. 587–596 (2013)

23. Yun, S.Y., Proutiere, A., et al.: Streaming, memory limited algorithms for community detection. In: Advances in Neural Information Processing Systems, vol. 27 (2014)

24. Zaharia, M., et al.: Apache spark: a unified engine for big data processing. Commun. ACM **59**(11), 56–65 (2016)

D-FGNAE: Decentralized Federated Graph Normalized AutoEncoder

Yuting Liang[1,2,3], Weixin Cai[1,2,3], and Kun Guo[1,2,3(✉)]

[1] College of Computer and Data Science, Fuzhou University, Fuzhou 350108, China
gukn@fzu.edu.cn
[2] Engineering Research Center of Big Data Intelligence, Ministry of Education,
Fuzhou 350108, China
[3] Fujian Key Laboratory of Network Computing and Intelligent Information
Processing, Fuzhou University, Fuzhou 350108, China

Abstract. Graphs widely exist in real-world, and Graph Neural Networks (GNNs) have exhibited exceptional efficacy in graph learning in diverse fields. With the strengthening of data privacy protection worldwide in recent years, Federated graph neural networks (FedGNNs) have gained increasing attention in academia and industry owing to their ability to train the model in a collaborative manner while complying with the privacy protection regulations. However, in federated learning, the non-independent and identically distributed (non-IID) problem of local data possessed by multiple participants can significantly undermine model accuracy. We propose a new Decentralized Federated Graph Normalized AutoEncoder (D-FGNAE). First, the model is designed as a decentralized federated learning framework with dynamically assigned tripartite roles. This design eliminates the fixed server role found in traditional federated learning, enhances system fault tolerance, avoids single points of failure, and protects model privacy. Second, the splitting and correcting of calculation by layer in the model, along with the special design of the normalization layer, effectively tackle the non-IID problem in both the structural and attribute aspects. Experimental results on real-world networks demonstrate the effectiveness of D-FGNAE, which can achieve nearly the same accuracy as the centralized model.

Keywords: Decentralized Federated Learning · Graph AutoEncoder · Normalization layer · Non-IID problem · Data Privacy

1 Introduction

GNNs are a powerful tool extensively utilized for graph learning. Traditional centralized learning training a model using all available data, offering simplicity of operation and excellent model performance [28]. However, the requirement to centrally store all data for training is often impractical in real-world. First, data is typically naturally distributed across various holders, imposing significant costs on storage and computational resources. Second, the enactment of data security and privacy protection regulations [4] restricting the transfer of private data. Therefore, the development of distributed GNNs that protect data privacy is of paramount importance. FedGNNs [19] emerged as a promising solution to address the aforementioned challenges. It enables multiple participants to collaboratively train a shared global model in a distributed system without sharing their local raw data, thus completing cooperative training under privacy constraints. Yet, whether in distributed systems like federated learning (FL) [21] settings or in the real world, data is typically distributed across different participants, leading to a critical issue in FL known as the non-IID problem.

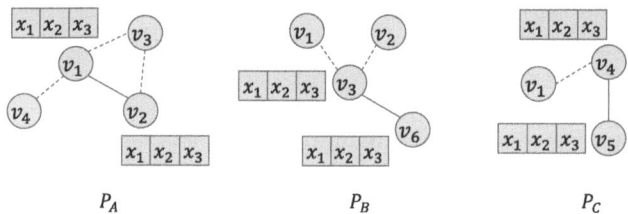

Fig. 1. A real-world scenario: custom networks among different banks.

Consider a typical real-world scenario as shown in Fig. 1: multiple banks(participants P_A, P_B, P_C) collaborate to rain a model based on their customer networks. Blue nodes represent customers registered with this bank(internal nodes), while yellow nodes represent customers from other banks(external nodes). The edge between them represents the existence of a transaction between the two customers. Since differences in geographic location and service orientation among banks will lead to large disparities in age, income, etc. of their customers, i.e., the nodes' attributes($[x_1, x_2, x_3]$) are non-identically distributed among different participants. Besides that, participant lacks complete neighbors about its external nodes. For instance, node v_3 exists in both the local networks of P_A and P_B, but P_A only has edge(v_3, v_1), while the complete edges about v_3 only available to P_B. It is obvious that an external node of a participant certainly exist as an internal node in another participant, and the edge between external and internal nodes will also appear again in another participant. This results in overlapping of nodes and edges, leading to mutual influence and dependence of structures between participants, i.e., local graphs' topology is non-independent among different participants.

The non-IID problem in scenarios like the one described above will lead to degraded model performance [29]. Existing works addressing this challenge can be broadly classified into three categories: optimization based on the single global model, personalized federated learning(PFL), and federated split learning. Whether aggregating local models to obtain a global model or training multiple personalized models, the simultaneous existence of multiple complete models makes these two approaches inevitably face performance declines caused by non-IID data. The combination of FL and split learning (SL) [10] is a novel exploration, by introducing SL to train one unique global model, which ensures the privacy and can achieve nearly the same accuracy as the centralized model.

However, there are still some problems with these methods. First, their consideration about the complexity of the graphs non-IID problem in real scenarios are not comprehensive enough, there is no research about the problem of topological non-independent and attributes non-identical distribution as shown in Fig. 1, which can cause a certain degree of accuracy loss. Second, these methods are based on the traditional "coordinator-participant" fixed two-role FL system, where the participant sends part of the data to central coordinator, which may increase the risk of privacy leakage; and the system relies on a single coordinator, which is weak against network failures or attacks, and prone to single point of failure problem.

In this paper, we propose a Decentralized Federated Graph Normalized AutoEncoder (D-FGNAE) to comprehensively address the non-IID problem from both topological and attribute perspectives. First, we introduce the concept of SL to split the networks and computation processes, designing a layered collaborative tripartite framework: "participant-coordinator-aggregator." We create a decentralized system with dynamically assigned the three roles, randomly selecting participants not only execute their local tasks but also temporarily take on the roles of aggregator or coordinator each epoch, instead of using a fixed server as in traditional FL. Second, we comprehensively address the non-IID problem in graphs in terms of topology and attributes. This is achieved by splitting and correcting the computation of embedding vectors in forward propagation and gradient matrices in backward propagation to handle topological non-independence caused by overlapping nodes and edges. Besides, we solve the attribute non-IID problem through special design in the normalization layer, using standard deviation as a weight and $L2$ norm as the scaling factor.

(1) We design a decentralized FL framework with dynamically assigned tripartite roles. The decentralized design eliminates the need for a fixed coordinator, enhancing system fault tolerance and avoiding single points of failure. Collaboration among roles involves splitting and correcting computation, addressing the non-IID problem caused by overlapping nodes and edges.
(2) We design a normalization layer for graphs, using standard deviation as the displacement weight and the $L2$ norm as the scaling factor, to normalize embeddings and address the non-IID problem caused by attribute distribution.
(3) We conducted extensive experiments with baselines on five real-world networks, demonstrating that D-FGNAE achieves accuracy nearly identical to centralized models, proving its effectiveness.

2   Related Work

2.1   Federated Graph Learning on Non-IID Graphs

Researches about the non-IID problem can be broadly categorized into three types: optimization based on the single global model, PFL, and the combination of FL with SL. Optimization based on a single global model tries to improve the effectiveness of the model in terms of local model training or global model aggregation. FedSage [32] and Fedni [23] train neighbor predictors for nodes or edges to complete missing local network information. FedStar [26] enhances model performance by extracting and aggregating shared common graph structure knowledge across graphs. FedCog [16] decouples local graphs into internal and external graphs and splits the training process into internal and external propagation. Lumos [22] employs a Monte Carlo Markov Chain-based algorithm to enhance the representation capability of limited local structural information. FedClust [13] uses the correlation between local model weights and client data distribution to dynamically group clients for local model training in real-time.

PFL trains a personalized model for each participant instead of a global model to sidesteps the non-IID problem. SFL [8] uses graph models to capture the heterogeneity among different clients, evaluate their similarity, and perform PFL. SpreadGNN [11] applies multi-task learning to capture the complex relationships between models of different participants for model personalization. FED-PUB [3] computes the similarity between local GNN model embeddings of different participants to collaboratively improve local models within the same community. FedSG [27] separates and combines topological and attribute information of local graphs to learn a personalized model for each client.

Federated Split Learning trains a special global model rather than multiple models, though it currently has limited research focused on the non-IID problem in graph learning and still faces issues that require more in-depth studies. SAPGNN [24] addresses the non-IID problem of local graphs in supervised federated graph learning scenarios through the introduction of SL. GCFGAE [9] focuses on unsupervised scenarios, proposing a model that can achieve accuracy lossless results on non-IID datasets with overlapping nodes. However, these works overlook the simultaneous overlapping of nodes and edges in local subgraphs and fail to consider the non-IID distribution of node attributes. As a result, they cannot achieve the accuracy of models trained under centralized training in real-world scenarios with multiple aspects of the non-IID problem.

2.2 Normalization Layer

The normalization layer standardize the distribution of the input data or hidden layer outputs in a neural network by shifting and scaling them so that the mean is zero and the variance is in units. This process improves model performance and speeds up training, making the normalization layer an integral part of neural networks. We will respectively summarize and present the existing work in terms of the design of normalization in graph learning and the application of normalization to address the non-IID problem in FL.

VGNAE [2] applies $L2$ normalization to node embeddings to prevent the Euclidean norm of isolated nodes from approaching zero. GraphNorm [5], in supervised edge prediction scenarios, proposes a normalization technique that subtracts part of the mean to enhance model accuracy. FairNorm [15] improves the accuracy and fairness of node classification tasks through a combination of normalization layers and loss function regularization. Tackling also adopts the idea of subtracting part of the mean, designing a new normalization layer, ResNorm [18], to improve model performance under long-tail node degree distributions.

Normalization techniques standardize the distribution of input data or hidden layer representations, and have been used to solve the non-IID problem in unstructured data. FedBN [17] incorporates BN layers into FedAvg [21] to tackle attribute non-IID problem in FL for images, improving model accuracy and convergence speed. FedGN [12], on the other hand, replaces BN with GN to address accuracy drops due to label non-IID, achieving more stable results than BN. Experiments on image datasets with attribute and label non-IID show that GN and LN outperform BN in terms of performance and stability [6]. The questions of how normalization layers can be designed to solve the non-IID graphs, and what effects this would have remain to be explored.

3 Preliminaries

3.1 Centralized GAE

In this paper, we take the standard GAE [14] as the centralized GAE in this paper, and adapt it in our D-FGNAE. The encoder consists of L layers of GCNs represented as Eq. (1):

$$\mathbf{H}^{(L)} = \tilde{\mathbf{A}}\sigma\left(\tilde{\mathbf{A}}\mathbf{X}\mathbf{W}^{(1)}\right)\ldots\mathbf{W}^{(L)} \tag{1}$$

where $\mathbf{A} \in \mathcal{R}^{n \times n}$ is the adjacency matrix of a graph G with n nodes and $\mathbf{D}$ is the degree matrix of G. $\tilde{\mathbf{A}} = \mathbf{D}^{-\frac{1}{2}}\mathbf{A}\mathbf{D}^{-\frac{1}{2}}$ is the normalized Laplacian matrix. $\mathbf{X}$ is the attribute matrix of nodes, $\sigma()$ is the activation function. $\mathbf{W}^{(1)}\ldots\mathbf{W}^{(L)}$ are the weight matrices of the first to the Lth layers. $\mathbf{H}^{(L)}$ is the node embedding matrix of the Lth layer. The decoder used to predict the reconstructed adjacency matrix $\hat{\mathbf{A}}$ is the inner product of $\mathbf{H}^{(L)}$ with itself, as Eq. (2):

$$\hat{\mathbf{A}} = \sigma\left(\mathbf{H}^{(L)}(\mathbf{H}^{(L)})^{\mathrm{T}}\right) \tag{2}$$

The loss function of GAE is the cross-entropy of $\hat{\mathbf{A}}$ with the original adjacency matrix $\mathbf{A}$, as shown in Eq. (3):

$$\mathcal{L} = -\frac{1}{n^2}\sum_{v_i,v_j}\mathbf{A}_{i,j}\log\hat{\mathbf{A}}_{i,j} + (1 - \mathbf{A}_{i,j})\log(1 - \hat{\mathbf{A}}_{i,j}) \tag{3}$$

3.2 Problem Definition

The problem addressed in this paper is the complex real-world scenario (as shown in Fig. 1), where the non-IID problem exists in both topological and attribute aspects. We first abstractly define the real-world scenario as follows: each participant P_k (where K is the number of participants and $k \in (0, K)$) possesses complete information about their local subgraph, including nodes, edges, adjacency matrix, and node attributes, denoted as $G_k = (V_k, E_k, \mathbf{A}_k, \mathbf{X}_k)$. Here, $V_k = V_{k,I} \cup V_{k,E}$, meaning P_k's node set V_k consists of an internal node set $V_{k,I}$ and an external node set $V_{k,E}$. Similarly, P_k's edge set $E_k = E_{k,I} \cup E_{k,E}$, indicating that the edge set comprises internal edges (edges between internal nodes) and external edges (edges between internal and external nodes). If an edge $(v_i, v_j) \in E_k$, then $A_{k,ij} = 1$; otherwise, $A_{k,ij} = 0$. $\mathbf{X}_k = \mathbf{X}_{k,I} \cup \mathbf{0}$, meaning each participant only has attribute information for internal nodes, with external nodes' attributes set to zero. Regarding node and edge overlap, $V_{k,O} = V_{k,IO} \cup V_{k,E}$ implies that the local overlapping node set is the union of the internal nodes overlapping with other participants ($V_{k,IO}$) and the entire external node set (since external nodes must appear as internal nodes in another participant). Since the edge between an internal node and an external node will reappear in reverse form in another participant, $E_{k,O} = E_{k,E}$.

We sets the learning scenario within the common semi-honest model [31]. As suggested in [20] that the structural information of graphs (including the edges and node degrees) and the attribute information of nodes or edges are critical privacy data that should be protected during the training process to resist semi-honest model.

4   The Proposed Model

4.1   Framework

The model we designed is a GAE consisting of L layers of GCNs and a normalization layer. We developed a decentralized system with dynamically assigned tripartite roles: "Participant-Coordinator-Aggregator" as shown in Fig. 2. First, we introduced the concept of SL to split the embedding computation in forward propagation and the gradient computation in backward propagation, as well as split the entire GAE model by layer.

Specifically, D-FGNAE deploys the $L - 1$ layers GCNs at all participants P_k, and deploys the Lth to $L + 1$th layers of GCN and normalization layer at the temporary coordinator(P_C). The number of layers can be flexibly split according to the experimental results in specific scenarios. During training, two parties are randomly selected from all participants to take on the temporary role of temporary aggregator(P_A) and coordinator(P_C) of this epoch, in addition to their regular local training tasks. Compared to the traditional FL with fixed coordinator and participant roles, dynamically and randomly assigning roles to participants ensures that no single participant holds the global data for an extended period, enhancing data privacy protection. It also makes it difficult for attackers to predict and target specific nodes, improving the system's defense against malicious attacks. Besides, when a participant fails, other participants can quickly take over its role, ensuring the system continues to operate smoothly and avoiding single points of failure. All participants have an equal chance of being selected, preventing resources from being monopolized by a few fixed roles and improving system fairness.

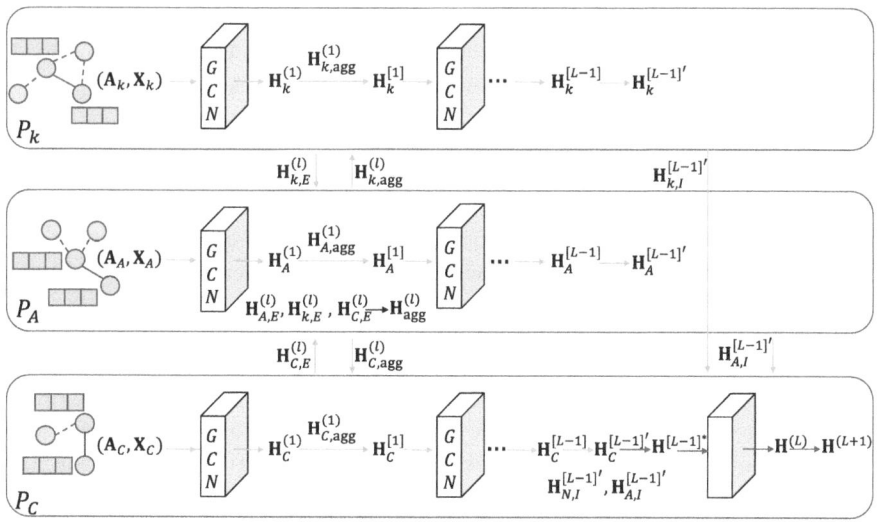

Fig. 2. Framework of D-FGNAE.

The splitting of model can ensure model privacy protection, as no single participant in the system can obtain the complete GAE model parameters, making it suitable for scenarios with higher privacy requirements. The splitting and correcting of computation can address non-IID problem caused by overlapping nodes and edges, which will be detailed in Sect. 4.3. The design of the graph normalization layer can adjust the node embedding obtained in each learning round to address the non-IID problem of node attributes, which will be detailed in Sect. 4.2.

In the 1 to $L-1$ layers of the model, the aggregator collaborates with the participants to complete the split computation for both forward and backward propagation, achieving nearly lossless accuracy compared to centralized models. In the L to $L+1$ layers of the model, the coordinator completes the training of the neural network and normalization layer deployed on it to obtain the final embedding. By collaborating on the computation between the aggregator and the participants, the errors caused by overlapping nodes and edges can be corrected to solve the non-IID problem at the topology level and achieve consistency with the centralized one. The coordination side completes the neural network and the normalization layer deployed on it, which can adjust the distribution of node embeddings, solve the non-IID problem at the attribute level, further improve the model accuracy and protect the model privacy.

4.2 Normalization Layer

Inspired by the design of many different normalization layers on graph-structured data, after conducted a lot of experimental attempts and analysis, we propose a new normalization layer to solve the problem of attribute non-IID in federated graph learning for the first time. It is incorporated into GAE to get the GNAE model in this paper. The normalization layer is designed as Eq. (4):

$$f([h_i, i \in \{1, 2, ..., n\}]^T) = [\frac{h_i - (1 - \frac{\sigma_i}{\sigma_{max}})\mu_i}{||h_i - (1 - \frac{\sigma_i}{\sigma_{max}})\mu_i||_2}, i \in \{1, 2, ..., n\}]^T \quad (4)$$

where $f(\cdot)$ represents the normalization function. The node embedding matrix $H = [h_i, i \in \{1, 2, ..., n\}] \in \mathcal{R}^{n \times m}$, where n is the number of nodes and m is the dimension of the node embedding vector. μ_i denotes the mean of all components within the embedding vector h_i, σ_i represents the standard deviation, and $\sigma_{max} = \max(\sigma_i, i \in \{1, 2, ..., n\})$, $|| \cdot ||_2$ denotes the $L2$ norm.

Due to the message-passing mechanism of GCNs, the computed node embedding aggregate information from their neighbors. Directly applying general normalization methods for shifting and scaling will lose structural information and reduce accuracy. Therefore, we propose a shifting weight $(1 - \frac{\sigma_i}{\sigma_{max}})$, replacing the standard deviation-based scaling with scaling based on the $L2$ norm of the shifted embedding vectors.

The motivation for this design stems from the correlation between the standard deviation of node embedding vectors and the node degree [18]. By introducing σ as a displacement weight, we incorporate the influence of graph structure information into the normalization process. Non-identically distributed attributes lead to node embeddings in the global embedding space exhibiting imbalances in their $L2$ norms. Using $L2$ norm can address the instability in update directions caused by norm imbalances [30].

4.3   Splitted Propagation

In this subsection, we will step-by-step detail how the correcting of the embedding matrix as well as the gradient matrix is accomplished by splitting the computation in both forward propagation and backward propagation. By splitting and collaborative correcting the computation between participants, we can solve the structural non-IID caused by overlapping nodes and edges.

Forward Propagation. Steps 2–4 show the splitting and correcting of the embedding vector computation implemented collaboratively by P_A and P_k. Steps 5–6 show the splitting of the model as implemented P_A and P_k.

Step 1: All participants share same initial weight matrices $\mathbf{W}^{(1)}$ to $\mathbf{W}^{(L-1)}$. Only the coordinator initializes $\mathbf{W}^{(L)}$ of the Lth layer. Randomly select two from all participants to serve as the temporary aggregator(P_A) and the temporary coordinator(P_C) for the current epoch.

Step 2: Participant P_k(including P_A and P_C) computes the embedding matrix $\mathbf{H}_{k,E}^{(l)}$ according to Eq. (1) for the lth layer, and selects the embedding vectors corresponding to external nodes as $\mathbf{H}_{k,E}^{(l)}$, sends it to P_A. Then P_k sets the embeddings of external nodes as $\mathbf{0}$.

Step 3: P_A aggregates each $\mathbf{h}_{k,E}^{(l)}$ corresponding to node v_i as $\mathbf{h}_{agg,i}^{(l)} = \sum \mathbf{h}_{k,i,E}^{(l)}$, and sends the aggregated results to the participant with v_i as an internal node for embedding correction.

Step 4: P_k corrects the embedding vector of the overlapping internal node $v_i \in V_{k,IO}$ as Eq. (5):

$$\mathbf{h}_{k,i}^{[l]} = \mathbf{D}_{k,i}^{-\frac{1}{2}} \mathbf{h}_{agg,i}^{(l)} + \mathbf{h}_{k,i}^{(l)} \tag{5}$$

P_k corrects the embedding vectors of all overlapping internal nodes and update them in $\mathbf{H}_k^{(l)}$ to get the correct embedding matrix for the lth layer $\mathbf{H}_k^{[l]}$.

Step 5: P_k computes $\mathbf{H}_k^{[L-1]'} = \widetilde{\mathbf{A}}_k \mathbf{H}_k^{[L-1]}$ which is an intermediate matrix during the computation of $\mathbf{H}_k^{(L)}$ because the weight matrix $\mathbf{W}^{(L)}$ of the Lth layer is possessed by the coordinator, then P_k sends it to P_C

Step 6: First, P_C aggregates the embedding, and use the aggregation results to correct and update embedding matrix to get $\mathbf{H}^{[L-1]^*}$. Second, P_C computes the embedding matrix for the Lth layer $\mathbf{H}^{(L)} = \sigma\left(\mathbf{H}^{[L-1]^*} \mathbf{W}^{(L)}\right)$, then computes the embedding matrix for the $L+1$th normalization layer to get final embedding matrix $\mathbf{H}^{(L+1)} = f(\mathbf{H}^{(L)})$. Third, P_C reconstructs the global adjacency matrix $\hat{\mathbf{A}}$ according to the Eq. (2).

Backward Propagation. Steps 1–3 show the splitting and correcting of the computation of the gradient matrix implemented collaboratively by P_C and P_k to update the weight matrix of the Lth layer. Steps 4–13 show the splitting and correcting of the computation implemented collaboratively by P_A and P_k to update the weight matrix of the remaining layers.

Step 1: First, P_C computes the gradient matrix set using the chain rule $\frac{\partial \hat{\mathbf{A}}}{\partial \mathbf{H}^{(L)}} = \frac{\partial \hat{\mathbf{A}}}{\partial \mathbf{H}^{(L+1)}} \frac{\partial \mathbf{H}^{(L+1)}}{\partial \mathbf{H}^{(L)}}$. Second, P_C selects the gradient matrix set $(\frac{\partial \hat{\mathbf{A}}}{\partial \mathbf{H}^{(L)}})_{k,I}$ related to participant P_k's internal nodes and extracts the matrix $\hat{\mathbf{A}}_{k,I}$ corresponding to participant P_k's internal nodes from $\hat{\mathbf{A}}$, then sends them to P_k.

Step 2: First, P_k computes the gradient matrix $\frac{\partial \mathcal{L}_k}{\partial \hat{\mathbf{A}}_{k,I}}$, where $\mathcal{L}_k$ is local loss. Second, P_k computes the local gradient matrix $\frac{\partial \mathcal{L}_k}{\partial \mathbf{H}^{(L)}}$ using the chain rule, then P_k adopts secret sharing [1] to transform $\frac{\partial \mathcal{L}_k}{\partial \mathbf{H}^{(L)}}$ into a secret $\langle \frac{\partial \mathcal{L}_k}{\partial \mathbf{H}^{(L)}} \rangle$, where $\langle \cdot \rangle$ denotes the additive secret sharing and sends this secret to P_C.

Step 3: First, P_C aggregates all received $\langle \frac{\partial \mathcal{L}_k}{\partial \mathbf{H}^{(L)}} \rangle$s to obtain $\frac{\partial \mathcal{L}}{\partial \mathbf{H}^{(L)}} = \sum_k \langle \frac{\partial \mathcal{L}_k}{\partial \mathbf{H}^{(L)}} \rangle$. Second, P_C computes the gradient matrix $\frac{\partial \mathcal{L}}{\partial \mathbf{W}^{(L)}} = \frac{\partial \mathcal{L}}{\partial \mathbf{H}^{(L)}} \frac{\partial \mathbf{H}^{(L)}}{\partial \mathbf{W}^{(L)}}$ and updates $\mathbf{W}^{(L)}$ based on $\frac{\partial \mathcal{L}}{\partial \mathbf{W}^{(L)}}$ via stochastic gradient descent (SGD) [25]. Third, P_C computes the gradient matrix $\frac{\partial \mathcal{L}}{\partial \mathbf{H}^{(L-1)}} = \frac{\partial \mathcal{L}}{\partial \mathbf{H}^{(L)}} \frac{\partial \mathbf{H}^{(L)}}{\partial \mathbf{H}^{(L-1)^*}}$, then he selects the gradient matrix $(\frac{\partial \mathcal{L}}{\partial \mathbf{H}^{(L-1)^*}})_{k,I}$ corresponding to P_k's internal nodes and sends it to P_k.

Step 4: P_k computes the local gradient matrix $(\frac{\partial \mathcal{L}_k}{\partial \mathbf{H}^{(L-1)}})$, selects the gradient matrix corresponding to the overlapping nodes from $(\frac{\partial \mathcal{L}_k}{\partial \mathbf{H}^{(L-1)}})$ to obtain $(\frac{\partial \mathcal{L}_k}{\partial \mathbf{H}^{(L-1)}})_O$ and transforms it into a secret $\langle (\frac{\partial \mathcal{L}_k}{\partial \mathbf{H}^{(L-1)}})_O \rangle$, then sends it to the P_A.

Step 5: P_A aggregates all received $\langle\left(\frac{\partial \mathcal{L}_k}{\partial \mathbf{H}^{(L-1)}}\right)_O\rangle$s to obtain $\left(\frac{\partial \mathcal{L}}{\partial \mathbf{H}^{(L-1)}}\right)_{agg,O} = \sum_k \langle\left(\frac{\partial \mathcal{L}_k}{\partial \mathbf{H}^{(L-1)}}\right)_O\rangle$ and sends it to all participants.

Step 6: P_k computes $\left(\frac{\partial \mathcal{L}}{\partial \mathbf{H}^{(L-1)}}\right)'_{k,IO}$ according to Eq. (6), $v_i \in V_{k,IO}$. The subtraction operation is used to deduct the $\left(\frac{\partial \mathcal{L}_k}{\partial \mathbf{H}^{(L-1)}}\right)_{i,IO}$ already containing $\mathbf{D}_{k,i}^{-1/2}$ from the $\left(\frac{\partial \mathcal{L}}{\partial \mathbf{H}^{(L-1)}}\right)_{agg,i,O}$ before multiplying $\mathbf{D}_{k,i}^{-1/2}$. The addition operation is used to recover $\left(\frac{\partial \mathcal{L}_k}{\partial \mathbf{H}^{(L-1)}}\right)_{i,IO}$. Second, P_k update $\left(\frac{\partial \mathcal{L}}{\partial \mathbf{H}^{(L-1)}}\right)'_{k,IO}$ in $\left(\frac{\partial \mathcal{L}_k}{\partial \mathbf{H}^{(L-1)}}\right)_k$ to obtain P_k's correct gradient matrix $\left(\frac{\partial \mathcal{L}}{\partial \mathbf{H}^{(L-1)}}\right)_k$.

$$\left(\frac{\partial \mathcal{L}}{\partial \mathbf{H}^{(L-1)}}\right)'_{k,IO} = \left[\mathbf{D}_{k,i}^{-1/2}\left(\left(\frac{\partial \mathcal{L}}{\partial \mathbf{H}^{(L-1)}}\right)_{agg,IO} - \left(\frac{\partial \mathcal{L}_k}{\partial \mathbf{H}^{(L-1)}}\right)_{i,IO}\right) + \left(\frac{\partial \mathcal{L}_k}{\partial \mathbf{H}^{(L-1)}}\right)_{i,IO}\right] \quad (6)$$

Step 7: First, P_k computes the gradient matrix $\frac{\partial \mathbf{H}_k^{(L-1)}}{\partial \mathbf{W}^{(L-1)}}$. Second, repeat steps 4–6 to correct $\left(\frac{\partial \mathbf{H}_k^{(L-1)}}{\partial \mathbf{W}^{(L-1)}}\right)_{k,I}$, then P_k computes local gradient matrix $\left(\frac{\partial \mathcal{L}}{\partial \mathbf{W}^{(L-1)}}\right)_k$ using the chain rule, transforms it into a secret $\langle\left(\frac{\partial \mathcal{L}}{\partial \mathbf{W}^{(L-1)}}\right)_k\rangle$, and sends to P_A.

Step 8: P_A aggregates the received $\langle\left(\frac{\partial \mathcal{L}}{\partial \mathbf{W}^{(L-1)}}\right)_k\rangle$s into $\frac{\partial \mathcal{L}}{\partial \mathbf{W}^{(L-1)}}$

Step 9: P_k first computes the gradient matrix set $\frac{\partial \mathbf{H}_k^{(L-1)}}{\partial \mathbf{H}_k^{(L-2)}}$, and selects the gradient matrices corresponding to overlapping nodes from it to obtain $\left(\frac{\partial \mathbf{H}_k^{(L-1)}}{\partial \mathbf{H}_k^{(L-2)}}\right)_O$ and transforms it into a secret and sends the secret to P_A.

Step 10: P_A aggregates the received $\langle\left(\frac{\partial \mathbf{H}_k^{(L-1)}}{\partial \mathbf{H}_k^{(L-2)}}\right)_O\rangle$ into $\left(\frac{\partial \mathbf{H}^{(L-1)}}{\partial \mathbf{H}^{(L-2)}}\right)_{agg}$ and extracts $\left(\frac{\partial \mathbf{H}^{(L-1)}}{\partial \mathbf{H}^{(L-2)}}\right)_{k,agg}$ corresponding to P_k, then sends it to P_k

Step 11: First, P_k computes the gradient matrices set $\left(\frac{\partial \mathbf{H}_k^{(L-1)}}{\partial \mathbf{H}^{(L-2)}}\right)_{k,I}$ corresponding to overlapping internal nodes according to Eq. (7), where $v_i, v_j \in V_{IO}$. Second, P_k computes the gradient matrix $\frac{\partial \mathcal{L}_k}{\partial \mathbf{H}^{(L-2)}}$ according to Eq. (8). Third, P_k extract $\left(\frac{\partial \mathcal{L}_k}{\partial \mathbf{H}^{(L-2)}}\right)_O$ corresponding to overlapping nodes, then transforms it into a secret and sends to P_A.

$$\left(\frac{\partial \mathbf{H}^{(L-1)}}{\partial \mathbf{H}^{(L-2)}}\right)_{k,IO} = \left\{\left[\mathbf{D}_{k,i}^{-1/2}\left(\frac{\partial \mathbf{H}_{i,j}^{(L-1)}}{\partial \mathbf{H}^{(L-2)}}\right)_{k,agg,E} \| \left(\frac{\partial \mathbf{H}_{k,i,j}^{(L-1)}}{\partial \mathbf{H}_k^{(L-2)}}\right)_I\right]\right\} \quad (7)$$

$$\frac{\partial \mathcal{L}_k}{\partial \mathbf{H}^{(L-2)}} = \sum_{i,j}\left(\left(\frac{\partial \mathcal{L}}{\partial \mathbf{H}^{(L-1)}}\right)_{k,I,i,j}\left(\frac{\partial \mathbf{H}_{i,j}^{(L-1)}}{\partial \mathbf{H}^{(L-2)}}\right)_{k,I}\right) \quad (8)$$

Step 12: P_A aggregates the received $\langle\left(\frac{\partial \mathcal{L}_k}{\partial \mathbf{H}^{(L-2)}}\right)_O\rangle$ according to equation to obtain $\left(\frac{\partial \mathcal{L}}{\partial \mathbf{H}^{(L-2)}}\right)_{agg,O}$, then sends it to all participants.

Step 13: P_k updates $\left(\frac{\partial \mathcal{L}_k}{\partial \mathbf{H}^{(L-2)}}\right)_O$ with $\left(\frac{\partial \mathcal{L}}{\partial \mathbf{H}^{(L-2)}}\right)_{agg,O}$ to obtain $\left(\frac{\partial \mathcal{L}}{\partial \mathbf{H}^{(L-2)}}\right)_k$.

Repeat steps 7 to 8 to obtain the gradient matrix $\frac{\partial \mathcal{L}}{\partial \mathbf{W}^{(L-2)}}$, then update the weight matrix. Repeat from Step 9 to update the weight matrices for layers $L-3$ to 1.

5 Experiment

5.1 Datasets and Metrics

The experiments utilized five real-world networks: Cora, Citeseer, DBLP, Amazon, and Lastfm. Cora and Citeseer were sourced from LINQS[1], while DBLP, Amazon, and Lastfm were obtained from SNAP[2]. Each network was divided into 2 to 10 sub-networks with overlapping nodes and edges to simulate participants' local graphs, as illustrated in Fig. 1. As the number of participants increases, the number of overlapping nodes and edges, the differences of attribute distributions between local graphs also increase, leading to a higher degree of non-IID. Therefore, we varied the number of participants to simulate different non-IID degrees.

We use normalized mutual information (NMI) [7] to evaluate the accuracy of all models. Higher NMI values indicate greater accuracy.

5.2 Baselines

We conducted three sets of comparisons to evaluate D-FGNAE. First, we compared D-FGNAE with the centralized GAE to verify the consistency of their outputs. Second, we compared D-FGNAE with GCFGAE, FedCog, SAPGNN, FedAvg, and SDGAE to assess their accuracy under varying degrees of non-IID graphs and to evaluate the impact of our design on both attribute and topological aspects. SDGAE runs the centralized GAE on each participant's data, identifying local communities and merging them to form the final global community. Third, we conducted experiments on the normalization by replacing our designed normalization layer in D-FGNAE. D-FGNAE(ResNorm) is the model in which D-FGNAE's normalization layer is replaced with ResNorm [18], an effective normalization layer for improving model accuracy on graphs. D-FGNAE(no norm) is D-FGNAE without the normalization layer. For these experiments, we used three-layer GCNs as the encoder and Eq. (2) as the decoder for all models.

5.3 Consistency Experiment

Figure 3 shows the results of the consistency experiment. The number in model's name represents the number of participants. It is evident that the accuracy of the D-FGNAE model is nearly identical to that of the centralized GAE, regardless of the number of participants involved. This indicates that D-FGNAE experiences

---

[1] https://linqs.soe.ucsc.edu/data.
[2] http://snap.stanford.edu/data.

minimal accuracy loss. We analyze that the extremely small difference in accuracy between D-FGNAE and centralized models might be due to floating-point calculation errors during backward propagation. The splitting and correcting of computations considering overlapping nodes and edges, and the normalization design significantly contributes to the superiority of D-FGNAE.

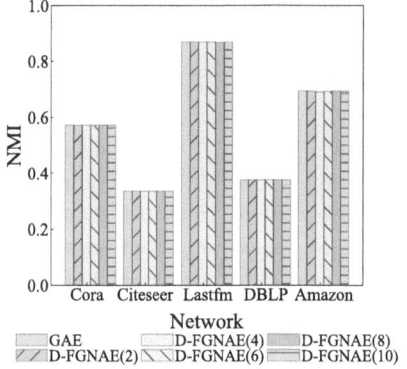

Fig. 3. Results of the consistency experiment

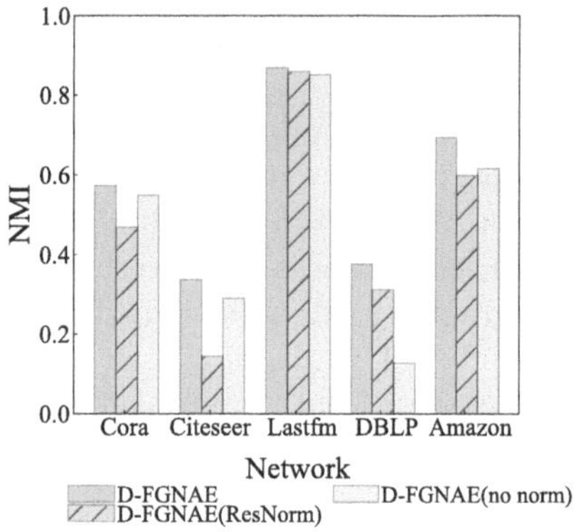

Fig. 4. Results of the normalization experiment

5.4   Normalization Experiment

The experimental results as shown in Fig. 4, the normalization layer of D-FGNAE improves accuracy by an average of 9.3% and 8.3% compared to the other two models. D-FGNAE outperforms and is more stable than ResNorm, which also uses a displacement weight factor for normalization. This is because we not only propose the displacement weight but also use the $L2$ norm instead of the conventional standard deviation as the scaling factor. Using the $L2$ norm addresses the imbalance in node embedding in the global embedding space caused by attribute non-IID, helping to correct the model's update direction. We can observe that in some cases, the experimental results of ResNorm are worse than those of no normalization setting, indicating that using the traditional standard deviation as the scaling factor for normalizing node embedding can potentially harm the model's training performance.

5.5   Accuracy Experiment

Figure 5 shows the results of the accuracy experiment for D-FGNAE and the baseline models. Figure 5(a) and (b) reveal that the accuracy of D-FGNAE surpasses nearly all baselines by at most 38.4%, reflecting the effectiveness of integrating FL with SL and the normalization design. SAPGNN performs inferior

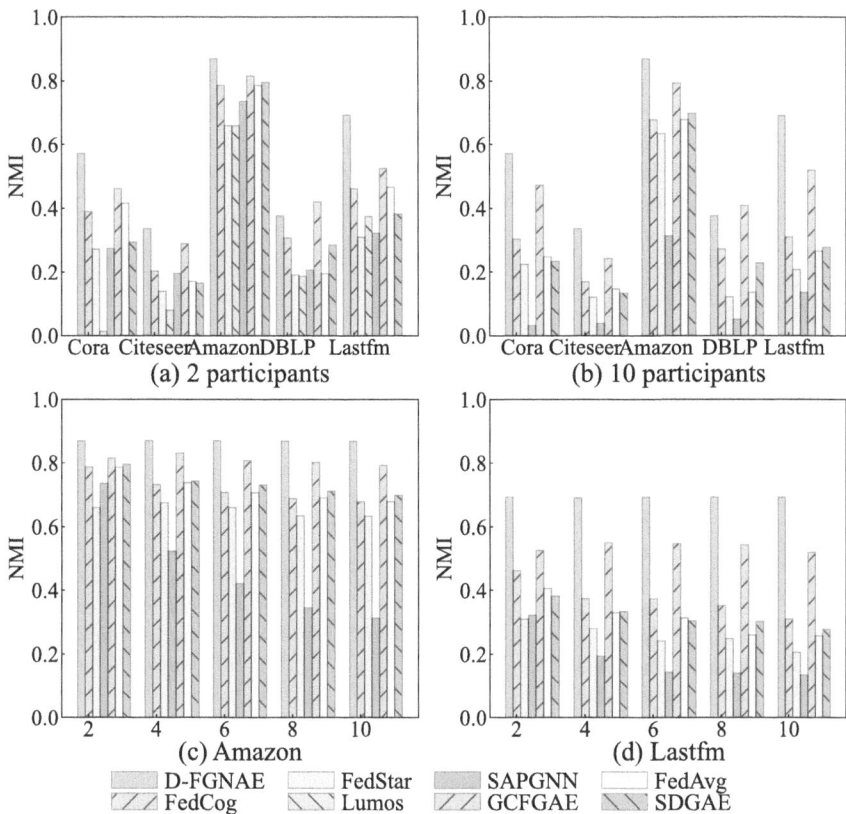

Fig. 5. Results of the accuracy experiment

to FedCog and FedAvg because it ignores the relationship between overlapping nodes. Figure 5 (c) and (d) show that the non-IID degree of local graphs does not affect the accuracy of D-FGNAE but has a substantial influence on the accuracy of baselines, proving the robustness of D-FGNAE.

6   Conclusion

In this paper, we propose the Decentralized Federated Graph Normalized AutoEncoder (D-FGNAE) to address the non-IID problem in FL from both topological and attribute perspectives. The model employs a decentralized tripartite framework, dynamically assigning roles to participants to enhance privacy, security, and system robustness while avoiding single points of failure. By splitting and correcting computation, D-FGNAE effectively addresses topological and attribute non-IID. Extensive experiments on real-world networks demonstrate the superior accuracy of D-FGNAE, maintaining performance nearly identical to centralized models.

Acknowledgements. This work was supported by the National Natural Science Foundation of China under Grant No. 62002063 and No. U21A20472, the National Key Research and Development Plan of China under Grant No. 2021YFB3 600503, the Natural Science Foundation of Fujian Province under Grant No. 2022J01118 and No. 2023J011062, the Major Science and Technology Project of Fujian Province under Grant No. 2021HZ022007, Haixi Government Big Data Application Cooperative Innovation Center and the Hong Kong RGC TRS T41-603/20R.

References

1. Adi, S.: How to share a secret. Commun. ACM **22**, 612–613 (1979)
2. Ahn, S.J., Kim, M.: Variational graph normalized autoencoders. In: Proceedings of the 30th ACM International Conference on Information and Knowledge Management, pp. 2827–2831 (2021)
3. Baek, J., Jeong, W., Jin, J., Yoon, J., Hwang, S.J.: Personalized subgraph federated learning. In: International Conference on Machine Learning, pp. 1396–1415. PMLR (2023)
4. Baik, J.S.: Data privacy against innovation or against discrimination?: The case of the California consumer privacy act (CCPA). Telem. Inform. **52**, 1–34 (2020)
5. Cai, T., Luo, S., Xu, K., He, D., Liu, T., Wang, L.: Graphnorm: a principled approach to accelerating graph neural network training. In: International Conference on Machine Learning, pp. 1204–1215. PMLR (2021)
6. Casella, B., Esposito, R., Sciarappa, A., Cavazzoni, C., Aldinucci, M.: Experimenting with normalization layers in federated learning on non-IID scenarios. IEEE Access (2024)
7. Chakraborty, T., Dalmia, A., Mukherjee, A., Ganguly, N.: Metrics for community analysis: a survey. ACM Comput. Surv. (CSUR) **50**(4), 1–37 (2017)
8. Chen, F., Long, G., Wu, Z., Zhou, T., Jiang, J.: Personalized federated learning with graph. arXiv preprint arXiv:2203.00829 (2022)
9. Guo, K., et al.: Globally consistent federated graph autoencoder for non-iid graphs. In: Proceedings of the Thirty-Second International Joint Conference on Artificial Intelligence, pp. 3768–3776 (2023)
10. Gupta, O., Raskar, R.: Distributed learning of deep neural network over multiple agents. J. Netw. Comput. Appl. **116**, 1–8 (2018)
11. He, C., Ceyani, E., Balasubramanian, K., Annavaram, M., Avestimehr, S.: SpreadGNN: decentralized multi-task federated learning for graph neural networks on molecular data. In: Proceedings of the AAAI Conference on Artificial Intelligence, vol. 36, pp. 6865–6873 (2022)
12. Hsieh, K., Phanishayee, A., Mutlu, O., Gibbons, P.: The non-IID data quagmire of decentralized machine learning. In: International Conference on Machine Learning, pp. 4387–4398. PMLR (2020)
13. Islam, M.S., Javaherian, S., Xu, F., Yuan, X., Chen, L., Tzeng, N.F.: Fedclust: optimizing federated learning on non-IID data through weight-driven client clustering. arXiv preprint arXiv:2403.04144 (2024)
14. Kipf, T.N., Welling, M.: Variational graph auto-encoders. arXiv preprint arXiv:1611.07308 (2016)
15. Kose, O.D., Shen, Y.: Fairnorm: Fair and fast graph neural network training. arXiv preprint arXiv:2205.09977 (2022)

16. Lei, R., et al.: Federated learning over coupled graphs. IEEE Trans. Parallel Distrib. Syst. **34**(4), 1159–1172 (2023)
17. Li, X., Jiang, M., Zhang, X., Kamp, M., Dou, Q.: FedBN: federated learning on non-IID features via local batch normalization. arXiv preprint arXiv:2102.07623 (2021)
18. Liang, L., Xu, Z., Song, Z., King, I., Ye, J.: Resnorm: tackling long-tailed degree distribution issue in graph neural networks via normalization. arXiv preprint arXiv:2206.08181 (2022)
19. Liu, R., Xing, P., Deng, Z., Li, A., Guan, C., Yu, H.: Federated graph neural networks: overview, techniques, and challenges. IEEE Transactions on Neural Networks and Learning Systems (2024)
20. Majeed, A., Lee, S.: Anonymization techniques for privacy preserving data publishing: a comprehensive survey. IEEE Access **9**, 8512–8545 (2020)
21. McMahan, B., Moore, E., Ramage, D., Hampson, S., y Arcas, B.A.: Communication-efficient learning of deep networks from decentralized data. In: Artificial Intelligence and Statistics, pp. 1273–1282. PMLR (2017)
22. Pan, Q., Zhu, Y., Chu, L.: Lumos: heterogeneity-aware federated graph learning over decentralized devices. In: 2023 IEEE 39th International Conference on Data Engineering (ICDE), pp. 1914–1926. IEEE (2023)
23. Peng, L., Wang, N., Dvornek, N., Zhu, X., Li, X.: FedNI: federated graph learning with network inpainting for population-based disease prediction. IEEE Trans. Med. Imaging **42**, 2032–2043 (2022)
24. Shan, C., Jiao, H., Fu, J.: Towards representation identical privacy-preserving graph neural network via split learning. arXiv preprint arXiv:2107.05917 (2021)
25. Shi, H., Fan, H., Kwok, J.T.: Effective decoding in graph auto-encoder using triadic closure. In: Proceedings of the AAAI Conference on Artificial Intelligence, vol. 34, pp. 906–913 (2020)
26. Tan, Y., Liu, Y., Long, G., Jiang, J., Lu, Q., Zhang, C.: Federated learning on non-IID graphs via structural knowledge sharing. In: Proceedings of the AAAI Conference on Artificial Intelligence, vol. 37, pp. 9953–9961 (2023)
27. Wang, Y., Guo, S., Qiao, D., Liu, G., Li, M.: FedSG: a personalized subgraph federated learning framework on multiple non-IID graphs. IEEE Trans. Emerg. Topics Comput. Intell. **8**, 3678–3690 (2024)
28. Wu, Z., Pan, S., Chen, F., Long, G., Zhang, C., Philip, S.Y.: A comprehensive survey on graph neural networks. IEEE Trans. Neural Netw. Learn. Syst. **32**(1), 4–24 (2020)
29. Xie, H., Ma, J., Xiong, L., Yang, C.: Federated graph classification over non-IID graphs. Adv. Neural. Inf. Process. Syst. **34**, 18839–18852 (2021)
30. Zhang, D., Li, Y., Zhang, Z.: Deep metric learning with spherical embedding. Adv. Neural. Inf. Process. Syst. **33**, 18772–18783 (2020)

31. Zhang, K., Cai, Z., Seo, D., et al.: Privacy-preserving federated graph neural network learning on non-IID graph data. Wirel. Commun. Mobile Comput. **2023**, 8585101 (2023)
32. Zhang, K., Yang, C., Li, X., Sun, L., Yiu, S.M.: Subgraph federated learning with missing neighbor generation. Adv. Neural. Inf. Process. Syst. **34**, 6671–6682 (2021)

Community Evolution Tracking Based on High-Order Neighbor Consideration and Node Change Identification

Yunan Zhang[1,2,3], Chaohui Wang[1,2,3], Ling Wu[1,2,3], and Kun Guo[1,2,3(✉)]

[1] College of Computer and Data Science, Fuzhou University, Fuzhou 350108, China
`gukn@fzu.edu.cn`
[2] Engineering Research Center of Big Data Intelligence, Ministry of Education,
Fuzhou 350108, China
[3] Fujian Key Laboratory of Network Computing and Intelligent Information
Processing, Fuzhou University, Fuzhou 350108, China

Abstract. Community evolution tracking is widely used in complex network analysis, which analyzes and identifies how communities evolve over time based on dynamic community detection. However, the current incremental dynamic community detection method has the phenomenon of 'concept drift', which leads to inaccurate tracking of community evolution. Although some studies on dynamic community detection have proposed to perform global community detection on the network by timing or when the error information accumulates to a certain extent, this method will lead to a sudden change in community division, which will interrupt the evolution sequence of some communities and bring great difficulties to the continuous tracking of community evolution. In addition, the current community evolution tracking methods match the communities of two adjacent snapshots, and it is difficult to capture the fine-grained evolution process within the community. This paper proposes a community evolution tracking algorithm based on high-order neighbor consideration and node change identification. Firstly, based on an incremental update strategy that considers high-order neighbors, we adaptively expand the scope of incremental updates to reduce the accumulation of error information. Secondly, through the node change identification strategy to mine fine-grained community evolution events. Experiments show that our method can effectively track the evolution of communities in dynamic networks.

Keywords: Complex network · Dynamic network · Community evolution · Evolution tracking

1 Introduction

There are a variety of complex networks in our lives to represent various interactions between different entities. Such as the social network composed of the user's friends in the instant messaging software, the citation network composed of the mutual citation of academic articles, etc. Most of the nodes in the complex network are clustered, that is, some nodes are closely related to each other, and the connection with other nodes is sparse. This closely related part is called community structure, which is one of the important characteristics of complex networks [8]. Dynamic complex networks undergo continuous evolution, leading to ongoing changes in the community membership of nodes. Detecting dynamic communities aims to mine the community structure of dynamic networks at each moment. Community evolution tracking involves analyzing the changes in community structure over time using dynamic community detection. This allows for the identification of various evolutionary events inside the community, such as birth, death, merging, split, expansion, and contraction [1]. It is common practice to monitor the development of social networks, biological communities, and other types of group structures via community evolution tracking.

Community evolution tracking is based on dynamic community detection to analyze and identify the evolution of communities over time. Incremental dynamic community detection is currently the most commonly used dynamic community detection method due to its computational efficiency advantage [11]. However, there is a 'concept drift' phenomenon in incremental community detection, where the local update strategy of the incremental method is prone to errors in community detection results. These errors often accumulate as the network evolves, and the accuracy of community detection gradually decreases, leading to inaccurate tracking of community evolution. Although the existing research [15] have proposed to perform global community detection on the network when the error information accumulates to a certain extent, this method does not fundamentally reduce the possibility of error information accumulation, but also leads to a sudden change in community division, which interrupts the evolution sequence of some communities and brings great difficulties to the continuous tracking of community evolution. In addition, the current community evolution tracking methods can be divided into two categories: similarity-based methods and core-node-based methods. But these two methods are essentially matching two adjacent snapshot communities, making it difficult to capture the fine-grained evolution process within the community.

In order to address these issues, we propose a community evolution tracking algorithm based on high-order neighbor consideration and node change identification. The algorithm includes an incremental update strategy considering high-order neighbors and a node change identification strategy. A concise overview of the paper's contributions is as follows:

1. Through the incremental update strategy considering high-order neighbors, our algorithm can adaptively expand the scope of incremental update to the high-order neighbors of the change nodes according to the degree of network change and the influence of the change nodes, so as to reduce the accumulation of error information in the process of incremental update.
2. Based on the node change identification strategy, our algorithm can process the change nodes and the affected nodes in a streaming manner while

incrementally updating, and mine the fine-grained evolution events that occur in the community by identifying changes in the community labels of nodes.
3. Experiments demonstrate that our method is capable of precisely and efficiently tracking the evolution of communities.

2   Related Work

2.1   Dynamic Community Detection

The existing dynamic community detection algorithms are mainly divided into three categories: snapshot-based methods, evolutionary clustering methods, and incremental methods.

In order to acquire the community structure, the snapshot-based method splits the dynamic network into numerous snapshots and applies the static community detection algorithm to each snapshot. In 2007, Palla et al. [9] used the CPM method to analyze the dynamic network. They ran the CPM technique separately to identify communities inside each snapshot of the network. In 2010, Doyle et al. [2] chose the non-overlapping community detection algorithm Louvain as the community detection method for each snapshot network.

The evolutionary clustering method considers the influence of clustering quality and time smoothness on the results, and makes the clustering results closer to the real community structure while ensuring the clustering quality. For the purpose of identifying communities that are changing over time in dynamic networks, Ma et al. [6] presented a technique for factorization called Cr-ENMF in 2020. In 2021, Yin et al. [18] presented a multi-objective evolutionary clustering algorithm for large-scale dynamic community detection, which integrates particle swarm optimization with evolutionary clustering.

The incremental method takes the community structure found by the previous snapshot as the basis, and updates the community structure by calculating the current changed part, which can greatly reduce the meaningless repeated calculation. In 2019, Zhuang et al. [20] introduced DynaMo, a modular-based algorithm designed to detect communities in dynamic networks. In 2020, Xu et al. [15] introduced an Error Accumulation Sensitive (EAS) incremental community detection method tailored for dynamic social networks. In 2023, Long et al. [5] devised an Incremental Algorithm, BBTA, to track changes in community backbone or bridge edges leading to backbone rupture or connection.

2.2   Community Evolution Tracking

At present, community evolution tracking algorithms can be divided into two categories5555: similarity-based methods and core-node-based methods.

The similarity-based community evolution tracking algorithm identifies the evolution events of the community by comparing the similarity between the communities in the two snapshots. The community similarity is usually measured by the Jaccard coefficient or the improved Jaccard coefficient. To describe and identify community development in social networks, Takaffoli et al. [12] presented a framework where each community is characterized by a sequence of key events. In 2017, Yu et al. [19] utilized the Jaccard coefficient to compute the similarity between nodes of two communities for community matching. They further defined community activity and community influence, based on these three parameters, different rules were established to identify community evolutionary events. An approach for measuring community evolution in dynamic social networks based on gravitational relationships and community structure was suggested by Liu et al. [4] in 2018. In 2020, Mohammadmosaferi et al. [7] proposed a method ICEM to identify community evolution through mapping. In 2021, Qiao et al. [10] proposed a community evolution tracking framework WECEM based on strong events and weak events.

Different from the similarity-based community evolution tracking algorithm, the core-node-based community evolution tracking algorithm selects some nodes to represent the community on the basis of network topology information, which is usually called core nodes, and tracks the evolution process of the community through the change of core nodes. In 2017, Yin et al. [17] introduced an approach for analyzing the development of core nodes by using gravitational connection reconstruction. In 2018, Wang et al. [14] conducted a study where they monitored the development of communities by analyzing the changes in core nodes inside the topological potential field. A superspreader and superblocker node-based community evolution tracking approach was presented by Xu et al. [15] in 2020.

3   Preliminaries

In this section, we will discuss dynamic network and community evolution events, which are the foundation of our work.

Definition 1 (Dynamic network). A dynamic network G is defined as a series of snapshot graphs, i.e. $G = \{G_0, G_1, \cdots, G_{t-1}, G_t\}$, where $G_t = (V_t, E_t)$ represents the snapshot graph at time t, V represents the node set, E represents the edge set, and t is the number of snapshots in the dynamic network. C_t^i represents the i-th community at time t.

Definition 2 (Community evolution events). It has been widely acknowledged in previous studies on dynamic network evolution analysis (e.g., [2,9]) that there are six events that can occur in a community's evolution: $BIRTH$, $DEATH$, $EXPAND$, $CONTRACT$, $MERGE$, and $SPLIT$. In the pseudodocode formulation of the algorithm in this study, we employ uppercase forms exclusively to highlight their status as constants. $BIRTH$ denotes the emergence of a new community composed of an arbitrary number of nodes. $DEATH$ denotes all member nodes leaving the community or disappearing from the network. $EXPAND$ denotes the increase in the size of the community due to the addition of new member nodes. $CONTRACT$ denotes several member nodes leaving the community or disappearing from the network. $MERGE$ denotes two or more communities merging into one. $SPLIT$ denotes a community splitting into two or more smaller communities. We use NEV_t^i to represent the node-level evolutionary events of the i-th community tracked by our algorithm at time t, and SEV_t^i to represent the snapshot-level evolutionary events of the i-th community tracked by our algorithm at time t.

4   Proposed Algorithm

This paper proposes a community evolution tracking algorithm based on high-order neighbor consideration and node change identification (CETHN). The framework of CETHN is shown in Fig. 1.

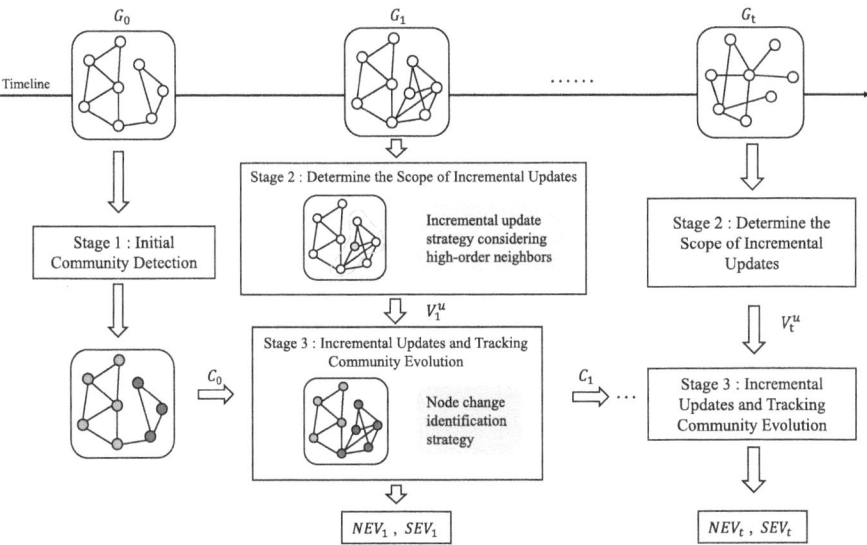

Fig. 1. Framework of CETHN.

Stage 1: We run the static community detection algorithm on the initial snapshot of the dynamic network to obtain the initial community structure.

Stage 2: In the subsequent snapshots, we calculate the network change rate and the local influence of the change nodes, and determine the incremental update scope based on this.

Stage 3: We use the prior snapshot as a basis to update the community structure of the current snapshot, and identify community evolution events based on node change recognition strategy.

4.1   Initial Community Detection

We use the well researched static community detection algorithm Leiden [13] to calculate network G_0 and generate a relatively accurate community structure C_0, which is concise as follows:

$$C_0 \leftarrow Leiden(G_0) \tag{1}$$

The Leiden algorithm necessitates three sequential steps. Initially, the algorithm relocates nodes between communities with the goal of optimizing the partition. Additionally, the algorithm improves upon an existing partition by dividing a community into multiple communities when they become poorly connected due to node movements. Ultimately, the algorithm carries out the process of combining the network elements together, using the newly defined partition. The process is iterated until no additional enhancements can be achieved.

4.2   Determine the Scope of Incremental Updates

In the subsequent snapshots, for the network G_t, we calculate the network change rate and the local influence of the change nodes. Taking into account both global and local factors, we add the change nodes and their high-order neighbors to the affected node set V_t^u. We consider set V_t^u as the scope of incremental updates.

We measure the network change rate of the current time based on the increase or decrease of nodes and edges compared to the previous time. For the NCR (Network Change Rate) at time t, we define it as follows:

$$NRC_t = \frac{|E_t^a| + |E_t^d| + |V_t^a| + |V_t^d|}{\min(|E_{t-1}|, |E_t|) + \min(|V_{t-1}|, |V_t|)} \tag{2}$$

where E_t^a, E_t^d respectively represent the set of edges that appear and the set of edges that disappear in the network at time t, while V_t^a, V_t^d respectively represent the sets of nodes that appear and disappear in the network at time t.

Currently, numerous researches [3,16] have been conducted on influence maximization. Inspired by these works, we measure the local influence of a node by calculating the strength of the connection relationships between the node and its neighbors, as well as between higher-order neighbors.

We use RSI (Relationship Strength Index) to measure the strength of the connection relationship between nodes within a local scope. The specific representation of RSI is as follows:

$$RSI(v_i, v_j) = RSI_1(v_i, v_j) + RSI_2(v_i, v_j) + RSI_3(v_i, v_j) \tag{3}$$

$$RSI_1(v_i, v_j) = \frac{a_{ij}}{d(v_i) + d(v_j)} \tag{4}$$

$$RSI_2(v_i, v_j) = \sum_{v_z \in \Gamma_1(v_i) \cap \Gamma_1(v_j)} \frac{1}{[d(v_i) + d(v_j)] \times d(v_z)} \tag{5}$$

$$RSI_3(v_i, v_j) = \sum_{v_x \in \Gamma_1(v_i), v_y \in \Gamma_1(v_j)} \frac{a_{xy}}{[d(v_i) + d(v_j)] \times d(v_x) \times d(v_y)} \tag{6}$$

where RSI_1, RSI_2, and RSI_3 represent the strength of the relationship when the path lengths between v_i and v_j are 1, 2, and 3, respectively. $\Gamma_1(v_i)$ represents the first-order neighbor set of v_i, a_{ij} represents the adjacency relationship between v_i and v_j, and $d(v_i)$ represents the degree of v_i.

For the LI (Local Influence) of v_i at time t, we obtain it by summing up the relationship strength index between v_i and its neighboring nodes within its third-order scope, represented as follows:

$$LI_t(v_i) = \sum_{v_j \in \Gamma_1(v_i) \cup \Gamma_2(v_i) \cup \Gamma_3(v_i)} RSI(v_i, v_j) \tag{7}$$

where $\Gamma_1(v_i)$, $\Gamma_2(v_i)$, $\Gamma_3(v_i)$ represents the first-order neighbor set, second-order neighbor set, and third-order neighbor set of v_i, respectively.

When the network experiences significant changes and the local influence of the change node is substantial, the neighboring nodes of the change node are also more likely to undergo changes in community membership. For the nodes with changes in the network at time t, we consider adding high-order neighbors of change nodes to the affected node set V_t^u based on the following rules:

(1) When $NRC_t \times LI_t(v_i) \leq \frac{d(v_i)}{d(v_i)+1}$, the change node and its first-order neighbors are added to the affected node set V_t^u.
(2) When $\frac{d(v_i)}{d(v_i)+1} < NRC_t \times LI_t(v_i) \leq \frac{d(v_i)+k}{d(v_i)}$, add the change node and its first and second order neighbors to the affected node set V_t^u.
(3) When $NRC_t \times LI_t(v_i) > \frac{d(v_i)+k}{d(v_i)}$, the change node and its first, second, and third order neighbors are added to the affected node set V_t^u. Among them, $d(v_i)$ represents the degree of v_i, and k represents the average degree.

Finally, we treat the set of affected nodes V_t^u as the scope for our algorithm's incremental updates. In contrast to other incremental methods, which focus solely on the nodes that have changed and their first-order neighbors, our algorithm considers the extent of network alterations and the impact of changing nodes on higher-order nodes around them during incremental updates. By adaptively broadening the incremental update scope to encompass the high-order nodes of the changed nodes, we can more precisely identify shifts in a node's community membership, laying the foundation for subsequent community evolution tracking (Table 1).

Table 1. Notations and Explanations

Notations	Explanations
V_t^a, V_t^d	The sets of nodes that appear and disappear in G_t
E_t^a, E_t^d	The sets of edges that appear and disappear in G_t
a_{ij}	The adjacency relationship between v_i and v_j
k	Average degree
$d(v_i)$	The degree of v_i
$\Gamma_i(v_j)$	The i-th order neighbor set of v_j

Algorithm 1: Determine the scope of incremental updates

Input: $G_t(V_t, E_t), G_{t-1}(V_{t-1}, E_{t-1})$
Output: V_t^u.

1 **begin**
2 $\quad$ $V_t^a \leftarrow V_t - V_{t-1}, E_t^a \leftarrow E_t - E_{t-1}$
3 $\quad$ $V_t^d \leftarrow V_{t-1} - V_t, E_t^d \leftarrow E_{t-1} - E_t$
4 $\quad$ $V_t^u \leftarrow V_t^a \cup V_t^d$
5 $\quad$ $NRC_t = \frac{|E_t^a| + |E_t^d| + |V_t^a| + |V_t^d|}{\min(|E_{t-1}|, |E_t|) + \min(|V_{t-1}|, |V_t|)}$
6 $\quad$ **for** $u \in V_t^u$ **do**
7 $\quad\quad$ $LI_t(u) = \sum_{w \in \Gamma_1(u) \cup \Gamma_2(u) \cup \Gamma_3(u)} RSI(u, w)$
8 $\quad\quad$ **if** $NRC_t \times LI_t(u) \leq \frac{d(u)}{d(u)+1}$ **then**
9 $\quad\quad\quad$ $V_t^u \leftarrow V_t^u \cup \Gamma_1(u)$
10 $\quad\quad$ **else if** $\frac{d(u)}{d(u)+1} < NRC_t \times LI_t(u) \leq \frac{d(u)+k}{d(u)}$ **then**
11 $\quad\quad\quad$ $V_t^u \leftarrow V_t^u \cup \Gamma_1(u) \cup \Gamma_2(u)$
12 $\quad\quad$ **else if** $NRC_t \times LI_t(u) > \frac{d(u)+k}{d(u)}$ **then**
13 $\quad\quad\quad$ $V_t^u \leftarrow V_t^u \cup \Gamma_1(u) \cup \Gamma_2(u) \cup \Gamma_3(u)$
14 **return** V_t^u.

4.3 Incremental Updates and Tracking Community Evolution

After determining the scope of incremental updates, we began updating the community structure based on the previous snapshot. Select a node with the highest degree from the affected node set V_t^u. If its neighbor with the highest relationship strength index has not yet been assigned to any community, create a new community for the affected node with the highest degree and its neighbor with the highest relationship strength index. On the contrary, if the neighbor with the highest relationship strength index is assigned to a community, the node is inserted into that community. This process repeats continuously until each affected node in the network is assigned to a corresponding community.

Meanwhile, during the incremental update process, when the affected nodes are assigned to a community that is different from before, we identify the node-level evolution events that occur in the community based on the following six definitions:

1. Community Birth at Node-level: At time t, for the newly added node v_i in community C_t^x, if node v_i does not exist at time $t-1$ and is assigned to community C_t^x at time t, and community C_t^x does not exist at time $t-1$, then we define that a node-level birth event occurred in community C_t^x at time t.

2. Community Death at Node-level: At time t, for the disappearing node v_i of community C_t^x, if node v_i belongs to community C_t^x at time $t-1$ and community C_t^x does not exist at time t, then we define that a node-level death event occurred in community C_t^x at time t.

3. Community Expansion at Node-level: At time t, for a newly added node v_i to community C_t^x, we define a node-level expansion event of community C_t^x if either of the following conditions holds: (1) Node v_i did not exist at time $t-1$ and is assigned to community C_t^x at time t, while community C_{t-1}^x exists at time $t-1$; (2) Node v_i belonged to community C_{t-1}^y at time $t-1$ and is assigned to community C_t^x at time t, where both community C_{t-1}^x and C_t^y exist at time $t-1$ and time t respectively.

4. Community Contraction at Node-level : At time t, for a disappearing node v_i from community C_t^x, we define a node-level contraction event of community C_t^x at time t if either of the following conditions holds: (1) Node v_i belonged to community C_{t-1}^x at time $t-1$ and does not exist at time t; (2) Node v_i belonged to community C_{t-1}^x at time $t-1$ and is assigned to community C_t^y at time t, where community C_{t-1}^y exists at time $t-1$.

5. Community Merging at Node-level: At time t, for a newly added node v_i to community C_t^x, if node v_i belonged to community C_{t-1}^y at time $t-1$ and is assigned to community C_t^x at time t, while community C_t^y does not exist at time t, we define a node-level merging event of communities C_{t-1}^x and C_{t-1}^y into C_t^x at time t.

6. Community Splitting at Node-level: At time t, for a node v_i in community C_t^x, if node v_i belonged to community C_{t-1}^y at time $t-1$ and is assigned to community C_t^x at time t, while community C_{t-1}^x does not exist at time $t-1$ and community C_t^y still exists at time t, we define a node-level splitting event of community C_{t-1}^y into communities C_t^y and C_t^x at time t.

Upon obtaining the collection of node-level evolutionary events for all communities at time t, we can infer the evolutionary events of communities at the snapshot level based on the node-level events that each community undergoes. We prioritize the handling of node-level evolutionary events according to the following order: birth, death, merging, splitting, expansion, and contraction.

Firstly, since each community can only experience one birth or death event in a snapshot, when a community undergoes a node-level birth or death event, we consider that the community experiences a birth or death event at the snapshot level.

Secondly, if a community does not experience node-level birth or death events but undergoes one or more merging or splitting events, we consider that the community experiences merging or splitting events at the snapshot level.

Lastly, if a community does not experience node-level birth, death, merging, or splitting events but undergoes multiple expansion or contraction events, we

---

Algorithm 2: Incremental updates and tracking community evolution

---

    Input: G_t, C_{t-1}, V_t^u

    Output: C_t, NEV_t, SEV_t.

1 **begin**

2     $C_t \leftarrow C_{t-1}, NEV_t \leftarrow \emptyset, SEV_t \leftarrow \emptyset$

3   **for** $u \in V_t^u \cap G_t$ **do**

4         $v \leftarrow argmax_u\{G^t.degree(u)|u \in V_t^u\}$

5         $w \leftarrow argmax_u\{RSI(v,u)|u \in \Gamma(v)\}$

6   **if** $w \notin C_t$ **then**

7             $k \leftarrow |C_{t-1}|, \quad C_t^{k+1} \leftarrow \{v,w\}$

8             $C_t \leftarrow C_t \cup C_t^{k+1}$

9             $V_t^u \leftarrow V_t^u - \{v,w\}$

10            $NEV_t^{k+1} \leftarrow \{BIRTH\}$

11   **else if** $w \in C_t^i$ **then**

12             $C_t^i \leftarrow C_t^i \cup \{v\}$

13             $V_t^u \leftarrow V_t^u - \{v\}$

14   **if** $v \notin C_{t-1}$ and $v \in C_t^x$ and $C_{t-1}^x \in C_{t-1}$ **then**

15                $NEV_t^x \leftarrow NEV_t^x \cup \{EXPAND\}$

16   **else if** $v \in C_{t-1}^y$ and $v \in C_t^x$ and $C_{t-1}^x \in C_{t-1}$ and $C_t^y \in C_t$ **then**

17                $NEV_t^x \leftarrow NEV_t^x \cup \{EXPAND\}$

                $NEV_t^y \leftarrow NEV_t^y \cup \{CONTRACT\}$

18   **else if** $v \in C_{t-1}^y$ and $v \in C_t^x$ and $C_{t-1}^x \in C_{t-1}$ and $C_t^y \notin C_t$ **then**

19                $NEV_t^x \leftarrow NEV_t^x \cup \{MERGE\}$

20   **else if** $v \in C_{t-1}^y$ and $v \in C_t^x$ and $C_{t-1}^x \notin C_{t-1}$ and $C_t^y \in C_t$ **then**

21                $NEV_t^x \leftarrow NEV_t^x \cup \{SPLIT\}$

22   **for** $v \in V_t^u - V_t^u \cap G_t$ **do**

23   **if** $v \in C_{t-1}^x$ and $C_t^x \notin C_t$ **then**

24             $NEV_t^x \leftarrow NEV_t^x \cup \{DEATH\}$

25   **else if** $v \in C_{t-1}^x$ and $C_t^x \in C_t$ **then**

26             $NEV_t^x \leftarrow NEV_t^x \cup \{CONTRACT\}$

27   **for** $NEV_t^i \in NEV_t$ **do**

28   **if** $NEV_t^i \cap \{BIRTH\} \neq \emptyset$ or $NEV_t^i \cap \{DEATH\} \neq \emptyset$ **then**

29             $SEV_t^i \leftarrow (NEV_t^i \cap \{BIRTH\}) \cup (NEV_t^i \cap \{DEATH\})$

30   **else if** $NEV_t^i \cap \{MERGE\} \neq \emptyset$ or $NEV_t^i \cap \{SPLIT\} \neq \emptyset$ **then**

31             $SEV_t^i \leftarrow (NEV_t^i \cap \{MERGE\}) \cup (NEV_t^i \cap \{SPLIT\})$

32   **else if** $NEV_t^i \cap \{EXPAND\} \neq \emptyset$ or $NEV_t^i \cap \{CONTRACT\} \neq \emptyset$ **then**

33             $M = \{m \mid m \text{ in } NEV_t^i \text{ and } m = EXPAND\}$

            $N = \{n \mid n \text{ in } NEV_t^i \text{ and } n = CONTRACT\}$

34   **if** $|M| > |N|$ **then**

35                $SEV_t^i \leftarrow \{EXPAND\}$

36   **else if** $|M| < |N|$ **then**

37                $SEV_t^i \leftarrow \{CONTRACT\}$

38 **return** C_t, NEV_t, SEV_t.

---

need to determine based on the number of node-level expansion and contraction events that the community experiences. If the number of expansion events exceeds that of contraction events, we consider that the community experiences an expansion event at the snapshot level; conversely, if the number of contraction events exceeds that of expansion events, we consider that the community experiences a contraction event at the snapshot level.

5   Experiments

5.1   Datasets

At now, there is a lack of available real-world network datasets that include labels for community evolution events. We utilize the LFR benchmark generator [2] to produce synthetic dynamic network datasets. The LFR benchmark generator is capable of producing a dynamic network that exhibits a fundamental community structure and undergoes community evolution events, including birth, death, expansion, contraction, merge, and split. The parameters of the LFR benchmark generator are shown in Table 2. The specific situation of the synthetic dynamic network generated by us is shown in Table 3.

Table 2. The parameters of the LFR benchmark generator

Parameter	Representation
N	nodes in total number
s	time step count
k	average degree
$maxk$	maximum degree
$minc$	lower limit for the size of the community
$maxc$	upper limit for the size of the community
$birth$	count of birth events at each time step
$death$	count of death events at each time step
$expand$	count of expand events at each time step
$contract$	count of contract events at each time step
$merge$	count of merge events at each time step
$split$	count of split events at each time step

Table 3. Synthetic networks

Dataset	N	s	k	$maxk$	$minc$	$maxc$	$birth$	$death$	$expand$	$contract$	$merge$	$split$
D1	10000	5	5	20	5	100	50	50	/	/	/	/
D2	10000	5	5	20	5	100	/	/	50	50	/	/
D3	10000	5	5	20	5	100	/	/	/	/	50	50

5.2   Evaluation Metrics

We use EMA [10](Event Mining Accuracy) and IEMA [21](Improved Event Mining Accuracy) as evaluation metrics for the experiment.

EMA(Event Mining Accuracy) measures the precision of event detection. It is determined by dividing the number of successfully detected communities by the total number of communities that really have events. The description of EMA is as follows:

$$\text{EMA}(p) = \frac{\sum_{t \in T} \left\{ \left| C_t^p \cap C_t^{p'} \right| \right\}}{\sum_{t \in T} \max \left\{ |C_t^p|, \left| C_t^{p'} \right| \right\}} \tag{8}$$

where $\text{EMA}(p)$ represents the EMA of a specific event p, T represents the total number of snapshots, C_t^p represents the set of communities detected by the algorithm where event p occurred at time t, and $C_t^{p'}$ represents the set of real communities where event p occurred at time t.

IEMA(Improved Event Mining Accuracy) overcomes the issue where EMA metrics may be disrupted when algorithms detect too many community evolution events. It is the harmonic mean of ER(Event Recall) and EP(Event Precision). The description of IEMA is as follows:

$$\text{IEMA}(p) = \frac{2 \times \text{ER}(p) \times \text{EP}(p)}{\text{ER}(p) + \text{EP}(p)} \tag{9}$$

ER(Event Recall) represents the proportion of accurately identified communities where event p occurred relative to the number of communities where event p actually occurred. The description of ER is as follows:

$$\text{ER}(p) = \frac{\sum_{t \in T} \{ |C_t^p \cap C_t^{p'}| \}}{\sum_{t \in T} |C_t^{p'}|} \tag{10}$$

EP (Event Precision) represents the proportion of the accurately identified number of communities where event p occurred relative to the total number of communities identified by the algorithm where event p occurred. The description of EP is as follows:

$$\text{EP}(p) = \frac{\sum_{t \in T} \{ |C_t^p \cap C_t^{p'}| \}}{\sum_{t \in T} |C_t^p|} \tag{11}$$

5.3   Baseline Algorithms

We compared the algorithm we proposed with four other community evolution tracking algorithms. The following provides a concise overview of these baseline algorithms.

Takaffoli [12]: Takaffoli et al. proposed a community evolution tracking framework that tracks community lifecycle related events. The framework matches each community based on common nodes and obtains community evolution relationships.

DOCET [14]: DOCET ascertains the initial community structure through the examination of node positions within the peak-valley structure of the topological potential field. Subsequently, DOCET identifies occurrences of community evolution through alterations within the topological potential field.

CETCE [21]: CETCE divides nodes into three categories based on their topological potential and uses a core node expansion strategy to get the community structure. Then, CETCE updates the community structure and tracks community evolution based on an edge variation discerning strategy.

5.4   Accuracy Experiment

Results of the EMA and IEMA on the synthetic dataset shown in Fig. 2. It can be seen that our algorithm has certain advantages in results compared to other baseline algorithms. Due to the same core expansion strategy used by DOCET and CETCE to detect communities, they achieved the same results on the D1 dataset. Takaffoli did not define the expansion and contraction events of the community, so the results on the D2 dataset were all zero. Takafoli detects communities through snapshot-based methods, with small fluctuations in the results at each time step. However, DOCET and CETCE are based on incremental methods to detect communities, and the accuracy will decrease at each time step. CETHN is also based on the incremental method for detecting communities, but it can be seen from the figure that the accuracy of CETHN has a relatively gentle downward trend. This is due to the incremental update strategy that considers high-order neighbors in CETHN, which reduces error accumulation. Furthermore, CETHN has significantly better accuracy in tracking community expansion, contraction, merging, and splitting events than other baseline algorithms. This is because it adopts a node change recognition strategy, which can more finely capture community changes and more accurately track community evolution.

310   Y. Zhang et al.

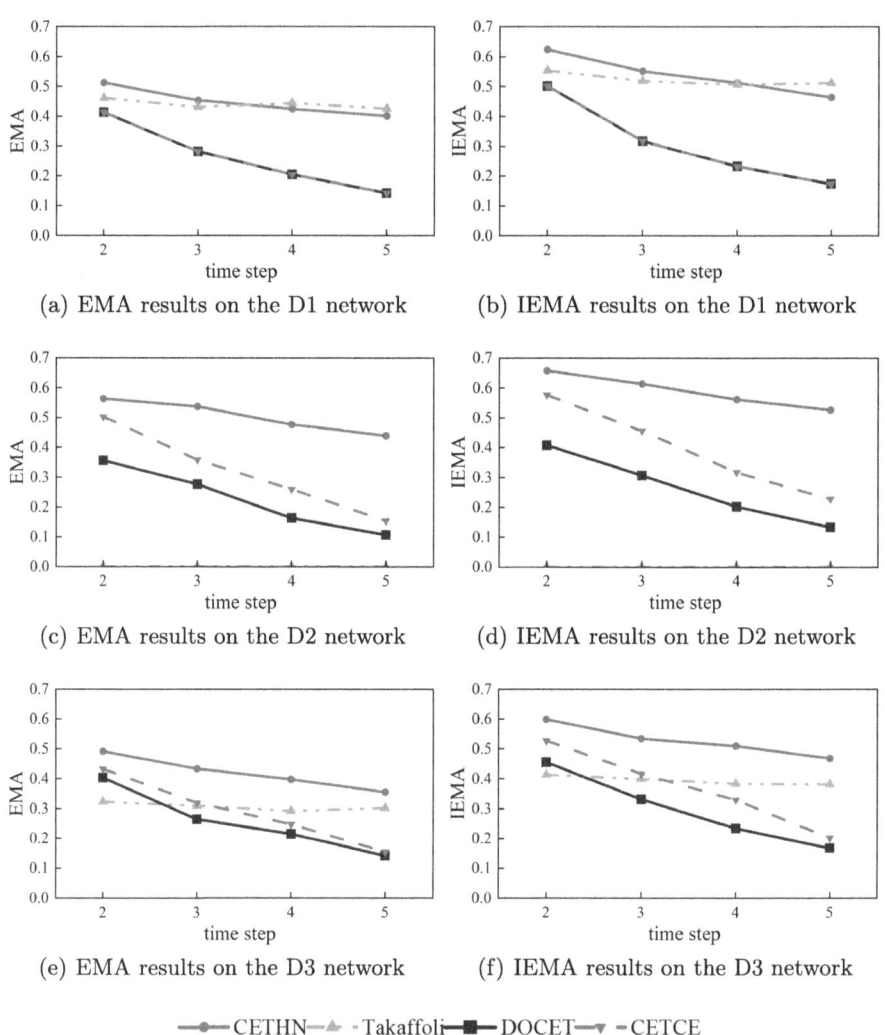

Fig. 2. Results of the EMA and IEMA on the synthetic dataset.

6 Conclusion

We propose a community evolution tracking algorithm based on high-order neighbor consideration and node change identification. Firstly, based on an incremental update strategy that considers high-order neighbors, our algorithm can adaptively expand the scope of incremental update to the high-order neighbors of the change nodes according to the degree of network change and the influence of the change nodes, so as to reduce the accumulation of error information in the incremental update process. Homogeneous, based on the node change identification strategy, our algorithm can process the change nodes and the affected nodes in a streaming manner while incrementally updating, and mine the fine-grained evolution events that occur in the community identifying changes in the community labels of nodes. Experiments demonstrate that our method is capable of precisely and efficiently tracking the evolution of communities. Our next focus will be on the application of the suggested algorithm to dynamic attribute networks.

Acknowledgements. This work was supported by the National Natural Science Foundation of China under Grant No. 62002063 and No. U21A20472, the National Key Research and Development Plan of China under Grant No.2021YFB3600503, the Natural Science Foundation of Fujian Province under Grant No. 2022J01118 and No. 2023J011062, the Major Science and Technology Project of Fujian Province under Grant No.2021HZ022007, Haixi Government Big Data Application Cooperative Innovation Center and the Hong Kong RGC TRS T41-603/20R.

References

1. Dakiche, N., Tayeb, F.B.S., Slimani, Y., Benatchba, K.: Tracking community evolution in social networks: a survey. Inf. Process. Manage. **56**(3), 1084–1102 (2019)
2. Greene, D., Doyle, D., Cunningham, P.: Tracking the evolution of communities in dynamic social networks. In: 2010 International Conference on Advances in Social Networks Analysis and Mining, pp. 176–183. IEEE (2010)
3. Huang, X., Chen, D., Wang, D., Ren, T.: Identifying influencers in social networks. Entropy **22**(4), 450 (2020)
4. Liu, J., Du, Y.J., Li, Q., Fu, C.L.: Social community evolution by combining gravitational relationship with community structure. Intell. Data Anal. **22**(5), 1143–1161 (2018)
5. Long, H., Li, X., Liu, X., Wang, W.: BBTA: detecting communities incrementally from dynamic networks based on tracking of backbones and bridges. Appl. Intell. **53**(1), 1084–1100 (2023)
6. Ma, X., Zhang, B., Ma, C., Ma, Z.: Co-regularized nonnegative matrix factorization for evolving community detection in dynamic networks. Inf. Sci. **528**, 265–279 (2020)
7. Mohammadmosaferi, K.K., Naderi, H.: Evolution of communities in dynamic social networks: an efficient map-based approach. Expert Syst. Appl. **147**, 113221 (2020)
8. Newman, M.E.: Detecting community structure in networks. Eur. Phys. J. B **38**, 321–330 (2004)
9. Palla, G., Barabási, A.L., Vicsek, T.: Quantifying social group evolution. Nature **446**(7136), 664–667 (2007)
10. Qiao, S., et al.: Dynamic community evolution analysis framework for large-scale complex networks based on strong and weak events. IEEE Trans. Syst. Man Cybern. Syst. **51**(10), 6229–6243 (2020)
11. Rossetti, G., Cazabet, R.: Community discovery in dynamic networks: a survey. ACM Comput. Surv. (CSUR) **51**(2), 1–37 (2018)
12. Takaffoli, M., Sangi, F., Fagnan, J., Zäıane, O.R.: Community evolution mining in dynamic social networks. Procedia. Soc. Behav. Sci. **22**, 49–58 (2011)

13. Traag, V.A., Waltman, L., Van Eck, N.J.: From Louvain to Leiden: guaranteeing well-connected communities. Sci. Rep. **9**(1), 5233 (2019)
14. Wang, Z., Li, Z., Yuan, G., Sun, Y., Rui, X., Xiang, X.: Tracking the evolution of overlapping communities in dynamic social networks. Knowl. Based Syst. **157**, 81–97 (2018)
15. Xu, Z., Rui, X., He, J., Wang, Z., Hadzibeganovic, T.: Superspreaders and superblockers based community evolution tracking in dynamic social networks. Knowl. Based Syst. **192**, 105377 (2020)
16. Yang, P., Zhao, L., Lu, Z., Zhou, L., Meng, F., Qian, Y.: A new community-based algorithm based on a "peak-slope-valley" structure for influence maximization on social networks. Chaos, Solitons Fractals **173**, 113720 (2023)
17. Yin, G., Chi, K., Dong, Y., Dong, H.: An approach of community evolution based on gravitational relationship refactoring in dynamic networks. Phys. Lett. A **381**(16), 1349–1355 (2017)
18. Yin, Y., Zhao, Y., Li, H., Dong, X.: Multi-objective evolutionary clustering for large-scale dynamic community detection. Inf. Sci. **549**, 269–287 (2021)
19. Yu, H., Jin, L., Zhou, B., Xiao, B., Zeng, X.: An event-based approach to overlapping community evolution by three-way decisions. In: 2017 IEEE 2nd International Conference on Big Data Analysis (ICBDA), pp. 772–778. IEEE (2017)
20. Zhuang, D., Chang, J.M., Li, M.: Dynamo: dynamic community detection by incrementally maximizing modularity. IEEE Trans. Knowl. Data Eng. **33**(5), 1934–1945 (2019)
21. Zhuang, Q., Yu, Z., Guo, K.: Community evolution tracking based on core node extension and edge variation discerning. In: Sun, Y., et al. (eds.) ChineseCSCW 2022. CCIS, vol. 1681, pp. 147–161. Springer, Singapore (2023). https://doi.org/10.1007/978-981-99-2356-4_12

NOBGP: A Novel Optimized Balanced Graph Partitioning Algorithm

Jiebin Chen[1,2,3], Ziqiang Hu[1,2,3], Renjie Ye[1,2,3], Qishan Zhang[4], and Kun Guo[1,2,3(✉)]

[1] College of Computer and Data Science, Fuzhou University, Fuzhou 350108, China
gukn@fzu.edu.cn
[2] Engineering Research Center of Big Data Intelligence, Ministry of Education, Fuzhou 350108, China
[3] Fujian Key Laboratory of Network Computing and Intelligent Information Processing, Fuzhou University, Fuzhou 350108, China
[4] Xianda College of Economics and Humanities Shanghai International Studies University, Shanghai, China

Abstract. Large-scale graphs have become prevalent with the advent of the big data era. Distributed graph computing systems are commonly used for processing and analyzing large-scale graphs, with graph partitioning being a key prerequisite for their efficient computation. Graph partitioning aims to balance the load across partitions while minimizing the number of cut-edges. Moreover, it should achieve high efficiency and scalability. However, the existing popular graph partitioning algorithms do not fully take into account the internal topology of real-world graphs, which affects the final partition quality and convergence. Meanwhile, they easily fall into the local optimum due to partition load constraints. This paper introduces a Novel Optimized Balanced Graph Partitioning algorithm (NOBGP). First, we propose an initialization strategy based on label propagation of core vertices to achieve initial partitions with good locality and accelerate convergence. Second, we optimize the label propagation process to ensure balanced partitions and propose a probability-based disruption strategy to avoid the local optimum. We implement NOBGP on the distributed graph computing framework GraphX. Extensive experimental results on real-world graphs show that the proposed algorithm is scalable and performs better than the existing algorithms. We also run PageRank and Louvain applications using the graph partitioning results to demonstrate the efficiency of our algorithm.

Keywords: Graph partitioning · Distributed graph computing · Label propagation · GraphX

1 Introduction

Graph-structured computation has become increasingly popular due to its applications in diverse fields, such as social networks, communication networks, natural language processing, and recommendation systems. Graph computation on a

H. Sun et al. (Eds.): ChineseCSCW 2024, CCIS 2343, pp. 313–328, 2025.
https://doi.org/10.1007/978-981-96-2373-0_22

single machine has been widely studied, with many systems (like GraphChi [13], GridGraph [28], and GGraph [24]) achieving high computational performance. However, the rapid increase in the size and complexity of graph datasets has posed significant challenges to single-machine graph computing systems, driving the rapid development of distributed graph computation frameworks such as Pregel [14], Giraph [2], GraphX [8], etc. They usually follow the vertex-centric programming model called Think-Like-A-Vertex (TLAV) [16].

Graph Partitioning (GP), also known as k-way graph partitioning, is crucial for optimizing performance in distributed graph computing systems. It is defined as splitting a graph into k disjoint partitions (or subgraphs), where each partition corresponds to a machine. The GP aims to minimize the number of edges across partitions (called cut-edges), which is equivalent to minimizing communication overhead. Meanwhile, the GP also requires that the number of edges allocated to each partition be roughly equal to maintain load balance across different partitions for maximum performance.

The GP problem has been proven to be NP-hard, and there is no approximation algorithm with a constant factor for general graphs [5]. As a result, many heuristic algorithms have been developed in recent decades to try to give acceptable solutions. Many previous algorithms are based on a local search approach like the Kernighan-Lin (KL) [12]. These algorithms require a large amount of computation to achieve the optimal cut-edges as the number of partitions and vertices grows, making them suitable only for smaller graphs. To reduce the computational cost, some studies have employed multilevel graph partitioning algorithms [11,19] to reduce the graph size through a coarsening process, followed by applying some heuristic algorithms, such as the KL algorithm, to the smaller graph. Although these methods can produce high-quality partitions, they are very memory-intensive, which means they cannot scale with large-scale graphs.

Recent works [15,21,26] have applied the label propagation (LP) approach [20] to graph partitioning, owing to its high computational efficiency and lightweight mechanism. The partition migration of this approach is represented by the change of vertex labels. Generally, this approach can obtain good results and is easy to parallelize. Existing popular algorithms have the following defects. (1) The graph theory suggests that most real-world graphs usually follow a power-law distribution and tend to show certain community structures with a high density of edges within groups of vertices and a lower density of edges between groups [17]. However, these features are not considered enough, affecting final partition quality and convergence. (2) Due to the limitation of partition capacity, algorithms easily fall into the local optimum, which affects the further improvement of partition quality. To address these issues, we propose a Novel Optimized Balanced Graph Partitioning algorithm (NOBGP) based on LP to produce high-quality graph partitions. The main contributions of this paper are as follows:

(1) We propose an efficient initialization strategy based on label propagation of core vertices, which speeds up convergence and improves partition quality by identifying core vertices in a large-scale graph and then utilizing the

influence of core vertices on their neighbors for accurate label propagation to form initial partitions with good locality.

(2) We optimize the label propagation process by introducing a penalty term related to partition load to ensure balanced partitions and propose a probability-based disruption strategy to escape the local optimum.

(3) We comprehensively evaluate the proposed graph partitioning algorithm on various large-scale real-world graph datasets. The experimental results demonstrate both the efficiency and effectiveness of our algorithm.

2   Related Work

The existing graph partitioning algorithms are mainly divided into three categories: local search approach, multilevel partitioning approach, and label propagation partitioning approach.

Local Search Approach. Many graph partitioning algorithms based on local search are derived from the KL algorithm [11]. It randomly assigns vertices to one of the partitions and then evaluates whether swapping vertices can increase the local score. Swapping vertices is performed if the local score is improved. This process continues until it is impossible to improve partition locality by swapping vertices. The FM algorithm [7] improves the search efficiency of the KL algorithm by moving vertices. It first calculates the gain score for each vertex, where gain refers to the number of cut-edges that can be reduced by moving the vertex to the other partition. Then, choose the vertex with the highest gain score for relocation and update the scores of its neighboring vertices appropriately.

Multilevel Partitioning Approach. Multilevel partitioning is a common partitioning strategy. The key idea is to reduce computational complexity by reducing the graph's size. It mainly consists of three phases: coarsening, initial partitioning, and refinement. During the coarsening phase, the size of the original graph is reduced by recursively using matching algorithms to collapse vertices and edges until the graph is small enough. Then, the graph resulting from the coarsening phase is partitioned into k partitions in the initial partitioning phase. The partitioning results are projected onto the original graph during the refinement phase. Metis [11] is one of the widely used algorithms of this approach. It employs a heavy edge matching algorithm to collapse vertices and edges during the coarsening phase and then uses the KL algorithm [11] in the initial partitioning phase. Finally, the partitions resulting from the initial partitioning phase are projected back to the original graph. Inspired by Metis, Scotch [19], Mt-KaHIP [1], and KaHyPar [23] proposed new strategies for different phases (coarsening, refinement, etc.) of the multilevel graph partitioning approach to improve partitioning quality further.

Label Propagation Partitioning Approach. The label propagation algorithm is mainly used for community detection in social networks. Recently, it has been employed in GP due to its high computational efficiency and lightweight mechanism. Compared with the multilevel partitioning approach, it has lower computational complexity and does not require storing a large number of intermediate results. Furthermore, the LP method is semantic-aware; given the existence of local closely connected substructures, a label tends to propagate within such structures [6]. Spinner [15] is the representative algorithm for this approach, which is based on the LP approach and implemented on Giraph for parallel execution. It divides vertices into k partitions while trying to keep a roughly equal number of edges in each partition. The authors of [6] defined a new initialization procedure by considering vertices having a high outgoing degree and proposed two partitioning objective functions: one for edge balance and another for vertex balance. The authors of [21] introduced OLPGP, a method that considers the difference of vertices in the process of partition selection and employs degree-weighted label propagation to optimize the initial partition. In [25], the authors proposed PuLP, a multiple objective and constraint partitioning algorithm. It presents a three-phase partitioning algorithm based on LP, where each phase's result becomes the foundation for initiating the partitioning in the following phase. In [26], the authors parallelize and extend PuLP to handle large-scale graphs.

3   Preliminaries

3.1   Basic Concepts and Definitions

Given a graph $G = (V, E)$ with the vertices set V and the edges set E. An edge $e \in E$ is represented as a pair of vertices (u, v) with u and v in V. The neighborhood of vertex v is denoted by $N(v)$, and the degree of v is given by $deg(v)$. Let $L = \{l_1, l_2, ..., l_k\}$ as a set of partition labels for the k partitions. The labeling function $\phi : V \to L$, where $\phi(v) = l_i (i \in [1, k])$, indicates that vertex v is assigned to the partition labeled l_i.

Definition 1 (K-way Graph Partitioning). *If a graph G is split into k mutually disjoint partitions $P_1 = (V_1, E_1)$, $P_2 = (V_2, E_2)$, ..., and $P_k = (V_k, E_k)$ with satisfied $V_1 \cup V_2 \cup \cdots \cup V_k = V$ and $V_i \cap V_j = \emptyset$ for all $i \neq j$, it is defined as a k-way graph partitioning and denoted as $P = \{P_1, P_2, ..., P_k\}$.*

Definition 2 (The Jaccard Index). *In graph G, the similarity between two vertices v and u denotes their proximity. The Jaccard index [9] is a simple and efficient measure for calculating the local similarity between two vertices. It is defined as follows:*

$$J_{sim}(u, v) = \frac{|N(u) \cap N(v)|}{|N(u) \cup N(v)|} \tag{1}$$

Definition 3 (The Boundary Vertex). *If a vertex v of V_i has neighbor vertex u in $V_j (i \neq j)$, we define that v as a boundary vertex of partition P_i and u as a boundary vertex of partition P_j.*

Definition 4 (The Weight Function). *To consider the number of directed edges between vertices u and v in the original directed graph G, we define the following weight function:*

$$w(u,v) = \begin{cases} 1, & e(u,v) \in E \oplus e(v,u) \in E \\ 2, & e(u,v) \in E \cup e(v,u) \in E \end{cases} \tag{2}$$

Definition 5 (The Core Vertices). *In a graph, core vertices are a small group of vertices (according to the power-law) with greater importance than other vertices. They are mostly in dense parts of the graph, which can be imagined as central points of communities and usually have high degrees and more connections with other vertices [22]. According to this, we use the following formula to measure the importance of vertices. If the importance score of a vertex is greater than or equal to the average importance score, the vertex is called a core vertex.*

$$IM(v) = deg^2(v) \times \sum_{u \in N(v)} w(u,v) J_{sim}(u,v) \tag{3}$$

where $deg(v)$ is the degree of vertex v, which shows the ability to connect with its direct neighbors; $\sum_{u \in N(v)} J_{sim}(u,v)$ is the sum of similarity, which shows the relations with neighbors of its neighbors.

Definition 6 (The Cut-Edge). *An edge $e(u,v) \in E$ is defined as a cut-edge between partitions P_i and P_j, if and only if $u \in V_i$ and $v \in V_j$ where $i \neq j$. The total cut-edge value $T_{ce}(P)$ for a graph partitioning P is given by Eq. (4).*

$$T_{ce}(P) = |e(u,v)| u \neq v, u \in V_i, v \in V_j, i \neq j, i,j \in [1,k]| \tag{4}$$

Definition 7 (The Partition Load). *The load of each partition P_i is defined as the total sum of the degrees of all vertices within that partition, as given by Eq. (5).*

$$load(P_i) = \sum_{v \in V_i} deg(v), i \in [1,k] \tag{5}$$

3.2   Label Propagation Algorithm (LPA)

LPA is a classical method for community detection [20]. It begins by randomly assigning an initial label l_i to each vertex in graph G, where $i \in [1,k]$ and then propagates these labels to neighboring vertices. Each vertex chooses the most frequent label among its neighbors during the iterative process. Specifically, each vertex v calculates a score for a specific label l based on the number of neighboring vertices that carry that label. The score is as shown in Eq. (6).

$$score(v,l) = \sum \delta(\phi(u), l), u \in N(v) \tag{6}$$

where δ is the Kronecher delta, which is equal 1 if $\phi(u) = l$, and 0 otherwise. The vertex label is updated to l_v using the following update function:

$$l_v = argmax \, score(v,l) \tag{7}$$

If multiple labels with the maximum score exist, one is randomly selected. LPA stops when no vertex changes its label.

3.3   Problem Statement

Balanced k-way graph partitioning P is to split all the vertices in a graph G into k mutually disjoint partitions, aiming to minimize the number of cut-edges between partitions while ensuring load balance across partitions. Thus, graph partitioning can be formulated as the following optimization problem:

$$\begin{cases} \text{minimize } T_{ce}(P) \\ \text{minimize } \max\{load(P_i)\} \\ \text{s.t. } load(P_i) \leq M, M = \varepsilon \cdot 2|E|/k \end{cases} \tag{8}$$

where M is a constant and represents the maximum load capacity of each partition. $\varepsilon \geq 1$ is a constant coefficient that defines the acceptable level of imbalance.

4   The Proposed Algorithm

4.1   The Framework of NOBGP

Figure 1 illustrates the framework of the NOBGP algorithm, which mainly consists of two stages:

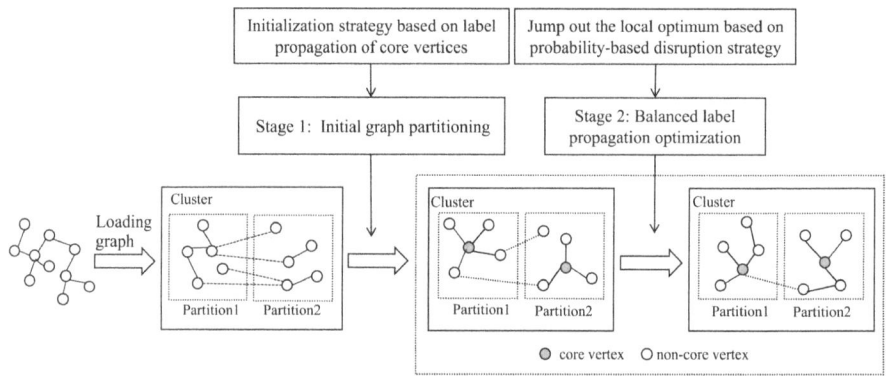

Fig. 1. The framework of NOBGP

   Stage 1: Initial Graph Partitioning. In this stage, the initial graph partitioning with good locality is obtained.
   Stage 2: Balanced Label Propagation Optimization. In this stage, we balance the partition load and further improve the partition quality.

4.2   Initial Graph Partitioning

The pseudocode for the initial partitioning algorithm is provided in Algorithm 1. Firstly, we use Eq. (3) to compute the importance score of each vertex (lines 3 to 6). Subsequently, the vertices whose importance scores are greater than or equal to the mean are defined as core vertices and their status is updated to true (lines 8 to 11). Each core vertex compares its importance score $(IM(v))$ with its most important neighbor core vertex, and if its importance score is less than the neighbor, it adopts the label of its most important neighboring core vertex for propagation and uses the dictionary D_v to store information for all core vertices (lines 12 to 19). In this way, the core vertices in the same community are clustered in the same partition as much as possible. Then, based on the theory of triadic closure [3], which indicates that they have strong connections if triangles are formed between vertices, we can confidently propagate the label of core vertices to their common non-core neighbor vertices. For a non-core vertex, the labels and ids of its neighbor core vertices are collected using the vertex label set S_{vl} and the vertex id set S_{vid}, respectively. If the intersection of the two sets is non-empty, it means that the non-core vertex is the common neighbor of the neighbor core vertex or the neighbor core vertex has the highest importance among its neighbors (lines 22 to 27). The dictionary D_v is used to find the most influential vertex in the intersection, and the label $v.nl$ of the non-core vertex is changed to the label nl of the core vertex in the dictionary D_v (lines 28 to 33). Finally, the hashing function $Hash$ is used to map each vertex label to its corresponding initial partition.

4.3   Balanced Label Propagation Optimization

The partition result with good locality can be obtained after the initial partitioning algorithm. However, it does not constrain partition size during the initial partitioning process, which can result in an unbalanced initial partitioning. Meanwhile, the naive LP algorithm does not care about the partition load balance during the vertex migration process. Therefore, further investigation and optimization are necessary to meet our objectives. as indicated in Eq. (8). A penalty term is added to penalize overloaded partitions, and the label score in Eq. (6) is rewritten as follows.

$$score_{balance}(v, l) = \frac{\sum_{u \in N(v)} w(u, v)\delta(\phi(u), l)}{\sum_{u \in N(v)} w(u, v)} - \frac{load(P_l)}{M} \tag{9}$$

where $\sum_{u \in N(v)} w(u, v)$ is the normalization factor of Eq. (9), and the notations δ and M have the same meanings as above. The term $-load(P_l)/M$ represents the penalty, indicating that as the ratio of a partition's load to its maximum capacity M increases, the penalty for migrating a vertex to that partition becomes higher. The parameter ε in M (see Eq. (8)) is used to control the trade-off between convergence speed and partition imbalance. A larger value of ε allows more vertices to migrate in each partition at each iteration, potentially accelerating

---

Algorithm 1: InitialPartitioning

Input: The graph $G(V, E)$, the number of partitions k
Output: The initial partitioning result G

1 $s_{vim} \leftarrow 0$;
2 **for** $v \in V$ **do**
   // Initialize current label, new label, importance, state, and
     the sum of similarity of vertex
3     $v.cl \leftarrow v.id,\ v.nl \leftarrow -1,\ v.im \leftarrow 0,\ v.us \leftarrow false,\ s_{sim} \leftarrow 0$;
4   **for** $u \in N(v)$ **do**
5        $\mid\ s_{sim} \leftarrow s_{sim} + w(v, u) \times J_{sim}(v, u)$;
6     $v.im \leftarrow s_{sim} \times deg^2(v)$;
7     $s_{vim} \leftarrow s_{vim} + v.im$;
8 **for** $v \in V$ **do**
9   **if** $v.im \geq s_{vim}/|V|$ **then**
10       $v.us \leftarrow true$;
11       $v.nl \leftarrow v.cl$;
12 $D_v \leftarrow \{\}$; // Initialize a dictionary $\{vid : \{im, nl\}\}$
13 **for** $v \in V$ **do**
14   **if** $v.us$ **then**
15       $temp \leftarrow v.im$;
16   **for** $u \in N(v)$ **do**
17   **if** $u.us$ and $u.im > temp$ **then**
18             $v.nl \leftarrow u.cl$;
19             $temp \leftarrow u.im$;
20       $D_v \leftarrow D_v \cup \{v.id : \{v.im, v.nl\}\}$
21 **for** $v \in V$ **do**
22   **if** $!v.us$ **then**
   // Initialize the set of vertex ids and labels to empty set
23       $S_{vid} \leftarrow \emptyset,\ S_{vl} \leftarrow \emptyset$;
24   **for** $u \in N(v)$ **do**
25   **if** $u.us$ **then**
26             $S_{vid} \leftarrow S_{vid} \cup u.id$;
27             $S_{vl} \leftarrow S_{vl} \cup u.nl$;
28       $S_{com} \leftarrow S_{vid} \cap S_{vl}$;
29   **if** $S_{com} \neq \emptyset$ **then**
30          $temp \leftarrow v.im$;
31   **for** $uid \in S_{com}$ **do**
32   **if** $D_v[D_v[uid].nl].im > temp$ **then**
33                $v.nl \leftarrow D_v[uid].nl$;
34                $temp \leftarrow D_v[D_v[uid].nl].im$;
35 **for** $v \in V$ **do**
36   **if** $v.nl \neq -1$ **then**
37       $v.cl \leftarrow v.nl$;
38       $v.nl \leftarrow -1$;
39    $v.cl \leftarrow Hash(v.cl, k)$;
40 **return** G;

---

the partitioning convergence. However, this also increases imbalance, allowing more vertices to be assigned to each partition than the ideal load value $2|E|/k$. After each vertex calculates the score of labels collected from its neighbors, select the label according to Eq. (7).

After the above steps, each vertex obtains the label that should be changed, which we refer to as the candidate vertex of the partition corresponding to the label. In the synchronous parallel model [27], each vertex changes its label independently, which can lead to a situation where a partition with a lower load will attract more vertices to migrate simultaneously because the penalty term is beneficial for the partition. This situation is likely to cause the partition to exceed its maximum load. A probabilistic approach is used to avoid it and adapt to the synchronous parallel model. The probability that a vertex will adopt its candidate label depends on the number of vertices vying for that specific label and the remaining capacity of the corresponding partition. Specifically, at iteration t, suppose the remaining capacity of partition l is $r_t(l)$, which is the difference between the maximum partition capacity M and the partition capacity $load(P_l)$, and the set of candidate vertices aiming to migrate to partition l is denoted as $C_m^t(l)$. If each candidate vertex for partition l migrates to that partition, the additional load will be $\sum_{v \in C_m^t(l)} deg(v)$, which may be higher than the remaining capacity $r_t(l)$. Therefore, each candidate vertex will decide whether to migrate to partition l according to the following probability $P_{migration}(l)$.

$$P_{migration}(l) = \begin{cases} \frac{r_t(l)}{\sum_{v \in C_m^t(l)} deg(v)} & r_t(l) > 0 \\ 0 & r_t(l) \leq 0 \end{cases} \quad (10)$$

In addition, the graph partitioning algorithm may converge at a local optimum because it only considers the most profitable moves for each vertex. However, there are still many potentially profitable moves. An example is shown in Fig. 2, where vertex v_1 and vertex v_2 are boundary vertices. It would actually make sense to swap v_1 and v_2, where moving v_2 from P_j to P_i reduces two cut-edges, and moving v_1 from P_i to P_j increases one cut-edge, which leads to a better allocation. However, the capacity constraints do not allow P_i and P_j to grow in size, and the graph partitioning will be stuck in the current configuration.

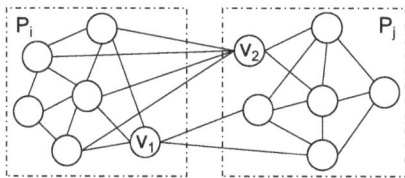

Fig. 2. An example of being trapped in the local optimum

To escape the local optimum, we propose a probability-based disruption strategy. The main idea of this strategy is to shake up the assignment of the current partition by migrating vertices with low locality out of the partitions to make space so that other more suitable vertices can move in. Specifically, we first select the boundary vertices from each partition with the following probability P_{dis}, where the boundary vertex with the worse locality is more likely to be selected. Then, each selected vertex will be randomly assigned to a partition to change the remaining capacity of the partition where the current vertex is located so that suitable vertices can be moved to that partition. Afterward, the balanced label propagation is continued to keep the partition load balanced and further reduce the cut-edges. Since we accurately identify the vertices that need to be migrated, it only takes a few iterations to reach convergence again.

$$P_{dis}(v,l) = \lambda \cdot \frac{load(P_l)}{M} \times \frac{e^{(1-loc(v,l))^{\alpha}} - 1}{e - 1} \tag{11}$$

where λ and α are constant, which determines the magnitude of the disruption and $loc(v,l) = \frac{\sum_{u \in N(v)} w(u,v)\delta(\phi(u),l)}{\sum_{u \in N(v)} w(u,v)}$ represents the locality value of vertex v in its partition l. The lower the value of $loc(v,l)$, the more likely the vertex v will be migrated out of the current partition and the more significant potential gain obtained by migrating vertex v. After extensive experimentation, we recommend setting λ to 0.8 and α to 3.

4.4 Convergence and Halting

Since graph partitioning needs to optimize cut-edges and partition balance, it is a natural approach to assess convergence based on the cut-edge and partition balance ratios. Specifically, the algorithm is considered to converge when it simultaneously satisfies the following two conditions at iteration t. 1) The increment of the cut-edge ratio is below a specific threshold as shown in Eq. (12). 2) The maximum load balance ratio does not exceed the partition capacity parameter ε shown in Eq. (13).

$$\Delta\mu(t) = \left|\frac{\mu(t-1) - \mu(t)}{\mu(t-1)}\right| \leq \sigma \tag{12}$$

$$\rho = \frac{\max\{load(P_1), load(P_2), \cdots, load(P_k)\}}{\sum_{i \in [1,k]} load(P_i)/k} \leq \varepsilon \tag{13}$$

where $\mu(t)$ denotes the cut-edge ratio of iteration t, and a large number of experimental results indicate that parameters σ and ε are suitably set to 0.005 and 1.05, respectively. Note that the algorithm really stops only after the execution of the probability-based disruption strategy.

4.5 Time Complexity Analysis

Let n be the number of vertices and k the average degree of the graph. In the initial graph partitioning phase, calculating the importance score for each vertex has a time complexity of $O(k^2 n)$. Then, for selected c core vertices, propagating labels to their neighbors requires time complexity equal to $O(ck_c)$, where

k_c is the average degree of the core vertices. In the balanced label propagation optimization phase, a balanced label propagation includes computing the candidate labels of vertices and updating the labels, with a time complexity of $O(kn + n)$. Therefore, the total time complexity for balanced label propagation is $O(t(kn + n))$, where t is the total number of iterations. Moreover, the time complexity for jumping out of the local optimum is $O(kn)$. In summary, the overall time complexity is $O(k^2n + ck_c + t(kn + n) + kn)$. Given that $k \ll n$ in the large-scale graphs, the total time complexity of NOBGP can be simplified to $O(n)$.

5   Experiments

In this section, extensive experiments are conducted on various real-world datasets to evaluate the performance and effectiveness of our algorithm compared to state-of-the-art algorithms, including Spinner [15], BGRAP [6] and OLPGP [21]. We execute several representative graph computing applications, including PageRank [18] and Louvain [4], across all experiments for comparison. All experiments are performed on a cluster consisting of one master node and four worker nodes. Each computing node has two Intel E5-2650 v4 12-core CPUs at 2.20GHz and is installed with GraphX 3.2.1 and Spark 3.1.3.

5.1   Real-World Datasets

The experiment uses four real-world graph datasets from Stanford University [10], which include both directed and undirected graphs, as detailed in Table 1.

Table 1. Experimental datasets.

Dataset	|V|	|E|	Directed
Youtube	1,134,890	2,987,624	No
WikiTalk	2,394,385	5,021,410	Yes
Patents	3,774,768	16,518,948	Yes
LiveJournal	3,997,962	34,681,189	No

5.2   Evaluation Metrics

The evaluation metrics for the experiment include the load balance ratio ρ shown in Eq. (13), the cut-edge ratio μ and the cut-edge gain ratio of the algorithm using the probability-based disruption $\Delta\mu$ shown in Eq. (14), and the running time of the algorithm. The smaller the load balance ratio, cut-edge ratio and running time, the better.

$$\mu = \frac{T_{ce}(P)}{|E|}, \Delta\mu = \frac{\mu_{nd} - \mu}{\mu_{nd}} \tag{14}$$

where μ_{nd} represents the cut-edge ratio without using the probability-based disruption strategy.

5.3 Experimental Results and Analysis

Table 2 presents the partitioning quality of graph partitioning algorithms across different real-world graph datasets, with the number of partitions k varying from 4 to 64. It can be observed that NOBGP achieves the best cut-edge ratio across all datasets and the best balance ratio in most cases, which proves the effectiveness of the initialization strategy and balanced label propagation optimization. Although our algorithm does not achieve the best balance ratio in a few cases, its cut-edge ratio is far lower than the baseline because that baseline achieves a better balance ratio at the expense of the cut-edge ratio. Furthermore, our algorithm is not affected by k and the scale of graphs, which indicates it is scalable. Table 3 shows that the probability-based disruption strategy can help our algorithm jump out of the local optimum and bring over 2% cut-edge ratio gain.

Table 2. Partitioning quality on different real-world datasets.

Graph	Algorithm	k = 4		k = 8		k = 16		k = 32		k = 64	
		μ	ρ	μ	ρ	μ	ρ	μ	ρ	μ	ρ
Youtube	Spinner	0.256	1.038	0.356	1.047	0.472	1.040	0.534	1.053	0.554	1.072
	BGRAP	0.248	1.038	0.351	1.044	0.455	1.038	0.524	1.056	0.548	1.093
	OLPGP	0.259	1.028	0.343	1.033	0.443	**1.036**	0.518	**1.039**	0.527	1.048
	NOBGP	**0.241**	**1.027**	**0.293**	**1.032**	**0.394**	1.036	**0.451**	1.048	**0.495**	**1.045**
WikiTalk	Spinner	0.361	1.046	0.445	1.055	0.496	1.042	0.533	1.049	0.558	1.081
	BGRPA	0.353	**1.036**	0.437	1.058	0.476	1.042	0.513	1.075	0.534	1.105
	OLPGP	0.349	1.038	0.426	1.045	0.458	1.041	0.494	1.047	0.493	1.050
	NOBGP	**0.332**	1.041	**0.413**	**1.044**	**0.449**	1.040	**0.479**	1.045	**0.485**	**1.046**
Patents	Spinner	0.250	1.028	0.322	1.035	0.372	1.034	0.403	1.040	0.430	1.033
	BGRAP	0.255	1.024	0.345	1.045	0.351	1.035	0.392	1.045	0.427	1.034
	OLPGP	0.267	1.019	0.369	1.041	0.339	**1.033**	0.394	1.034	0.421	**1.031**
	NOBGP	**0.225**	**1.018**	**0.275**	**1.031**	**0.308**	1.033	**0.333**	1.032	**0.344**	1.038
LiveJournal	Spinner	0.248	1.035	0.323	1.047	0.410	1.045	0.433	1.040	0.451	1.049
	BGRAP	0.245	1.038	0.319	1.046	0.416	1.038	0.435	**1.039**	0.463	1.046
	OLPGP	0.237	1.039	0.304	1.049	0.361	1.043	0.424	1.042	0.448	1.039
	NOBGP	**0.193**	**1.030**	**0.274**	1.043	**0.328**	**1.034**	**0.395**	1.039	**0.413**	**1.038**

In Fig. 3, we show the cut-edge ratio of initial partitioning. Due to space constraints, we only present the results for the LiveJournal dataset, with similar results observed for the other datasets. It is evident that NOBGP achieves

Table 3. The cut-edge gain ratio of NOBGP on different datasets when k = 64.

	Youtube	WikiTalk	Patents	LiveJournal
μ_{nd}	0.508	0.497	0.355	0.425
μ	0.495	0.485	0.344	0.413
$\Delta\mu$	2.56%	2.41%	3.10%	2.82%

the optimal initial partitioning cut-edge ratio, which benefits from our initialization strategy, which considers more features of the real-world graph. Figure 4 shows the normalized speedup of various graph partition algorithms, where the running times of algorithms are normalized to Spinner. From this figure, we can see that the processing speed of NOBGP outperforms that of baseline algorithms on all datasets when $k = 64$. This is because our algorithm has a better initial partitioning locality, which helps to reduce the number of iterations. Figure 5 shows the running time of PageRank and Louvain applications, where the Louvain application is run on YouTube and LiveJournal datasets since it works for undirected graphs [4]. We can observe that the running times of the

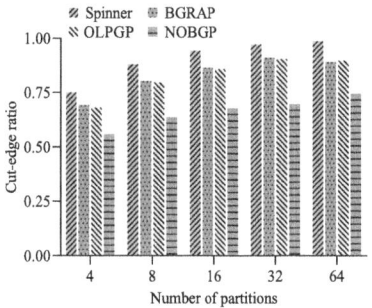

Fig. 3. Cut-edge ratio of initial partition on LiveJournal dataset.

Fig. 4. Normalized speedup on different real-world datasets.

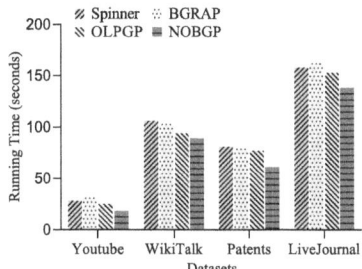
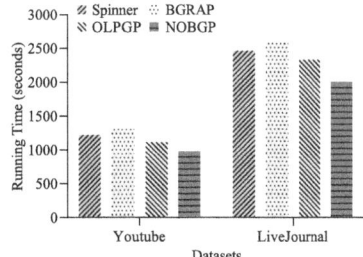

(a) Running time of PageRank application. (b) Running time of Louvain application.

Fig. 5. Running times of applications.

applications using the partitioning result of NOBGP are the shortest, demonstrating our algorithm's efficiency.

6   Conclusions

In this paper, we introduce a novel optimized balanced graph partitioning algorithm (NOBGP). First, we propose an initialization strategy based on label propagation of core vertices to initialize the partitions, which provides good locality and accelerates convergence. Second, optimize the label propagation process by introducing the penalty term related to partition load to ensure balanced partitions. Additionally, we propose a probability-based disruption strategy to avoid the local optimum. The experimental results with large-scale real-world graph datasets demonstrate that NOBGP achieves better performance than state-of-the-art algorithms. In the future, we aim to investigate additional optimization strategies to reduce cut-edges and partition imbalance further. We also plan to improve our algorithm to accommodate changes in dynamic graphs better.

Acknowledgements. This work was supported by the National Natural Science Foundation of China under Grant No.62002063 and No.U21A20472, the National Key Research and Development Plan of China under Grant No.2021YFB3600503, the Natural Science Foundation of Fujian Province under Grant No.2022J01118 and No.2023J011062, the Major Science and Technology Project of Fujian Province under Grant No.2021HZ022007, Haixi Government Big Data Application Cooperative Innovation Center and the Hong Kong RGC TRS T41-603/20R.

References

1. Akhremtsev, Y., Sanders, P., Schulz, C.: High-quality shared-memory graph partitioning. IEEE Trans. Parallel Distrib. Syst. **31**(11), 2710–2722 (2020)
2. Avery, C.: Giraph: Large-scale graph processing infrastructure on Hadoop. Proc. Hadoop Summit. **11**(3), 5–9 (2011)
3. Bianconi, G., Darst, R.K., Iacovacci, J., Fortunato, S.: Triadic closure as a basic generating mechanism of communities in complex networks. Phys. Rev. E **90**(4), 042806 (2014)
4. Blondel, V.D., Guillaume, J.L., Lambiotte, R., Lefebvre, E.: Fast unfolding of communities in large networks. J. Stat. Mech: Theory Exp. **2008**(10), P10008 (2008)
5. Bui, T.N., Jones, C.: Finding good approximate vertex and edge partitions is np-hard. Inf. Process. Lett. **42**(3), 153–159 (1992)
6. El Moussawi, A., Seghouani, N.B., Bugiotti, F.: BGRAP: balanced graph partitioning algorithm for large graphs. J. Data Intell. **2**(2), 116–135 (2021)
7. Fiduccia, C.M., Mattheyses, R.M.: A linear-time heuristic for improving network partitions. In: Papers on Twenty-Five Years of Electronic Design Automation, pp. 241–247 (1988)

8. Gonzalez, J.E., Xin, R.S., Dave, A., Crankshaw, D., Franklin, M.J., Stoica, I.: {GraphX}: graph processing in a distributed dataflow framework. In: 11th USENIX Symposium on Operating Systems Design and Implementation (OSDI 14), pp. 599–613 (2014)

9. Jaccard, P.: Étude comparative de la distribution florale dans une portion des alpes et des jura. Bull. Soc. Vaudoise Sci. Nat. **37**, 547–579 (1901)

10. Jure, L.: Snap datasets: Stanford large network dataset collection. http://snap.stanford.edu/data (2014). Accessed Dec 2021

11. Karypis, G., Kumar, V.: A fast and high quality multilevel scheme for partitioning irregular graphs. SIAM J. Sci. Comput. **20**(1), 359–392 (1998)

12. Kernighan, B.W., Lin, S.: An efficient heuristic procedure for partitioning graphs. The Bell Syst. Techn. J. **49**(2), 291–307 (1970)

13. Kyrola, A., Blelloch, G., Guestrin, C.: {GraphChi}:{Large-Scale} graph computation on just a {PC}. In: 10th USENIX Symposium on Operating Systems Design and Implementation (OSDI 2012), pp. 31–46 (2012)

14. Malewicz, G., et al.: Pregel: a system for large-scale graph processing. In: Proceedings of the 2010 ACM SIGMOD International Conference on Management of Data, pp. 135–146 (2010)

15. Martella, C., Logothetis, D., Loukas, A., Siganos, G.: Spinner: scalable graph partitioning in the cloud. In: 2017 IEEE 33rd International Conference on Data Engineering (ICDE), pp. 1083–1094. IEEE (2017)

16. McCune, R.R., Weninger, T., Madey, G.: Thinking like a vertex: a survey of vertex-centric frameworks for large-scale distributed graph processing. ACM Comput. Surv. (CSUR) **48**(2), 1–39 (2015)

17. Newman, M.E.: The structure and function of complex networks. SIAM Rev. **45**(2), 167–256 (2003)

18. Page, L., Brin, S., Motwani, R., Winograd, T., et al.: The pagerank citation ranking: Bringing order to the web (1999)

19. Pellegrini, F., Roman, J.: Scotch: a software package for static mapping by dual recursive bipartitioning of process and architecture graphs. In: Liddell, H., Colbrook, A., Hertzberger, B., Sloot, P. (eds.) HPCN-Europe 1996. LNCS, vol. 1067, pp. 493–498. Springer, Heidelberg (1996). https://doi.org/10.1007/3-540-61142-8_588

20. Raghavan, U.N., Albert, R., Kumara, S.: Near linear time algorithm to detect community structures in large-scale networks. Phys. Rev. E **76**(3), 036106 (2007)

21. Ren, H., Wu, B.: OLPGP: an optimized label propagation-based distributed graph partitioning algorithm. In: Tan, Y., Shi, Y. (eds.) Data Mining and Big Data. DMBD 2022. Communications in Computer and Information Science, vol. 1744, pp. pp. 120–133. Springer, Singapore (2022). https://doi.org/10.1007/978-981-19-9297-1_10

22. Roghani, H., Bouyer, A., Nourani, E.: PLDLS: a novel parallel label diffusion and label selection-based community detection algorithm based on spark in social networks. Expert Syst. Appl. **183**, 115377 (2021)

23. Schlag, S., Henne, V., Heuer, T., Meyerhenke, H., Sanders, P., Schulz, C.: K-way hypergraph partitioning via n-level recursive bisection. In: 2016 Proceedings of the Eighteenth Workshop on Algorithm Engineering and Experiments (ALENEX), pp. 53–67. SIAM (2016)

24. Si, B., et al.: GGraph: an efficient structure-aware approach for iterative graph processing. IEEE Trans. Big Data **8**(5), 1182–1194 (2020)

25. Slota, G.M., Madduri, K., Rajamanickam, S.: Pulp: Scalable multi-objective multi-constraint partitioning for small-world networks. In: 2014 IEEE International Conference on Big Data (Big Data), pp. 481–490. IEEE (2014)
26. Slota, G.M., Rajamanickam, S., Devine, K., Madduri, K.: Partitioning trillion-edge graphs in minutes. In: 2017 IEEE International Parallel and Distributed Processing Symposium (IPDPS), pp. 646–655. IEEE (2017)
27. Valiant, L.G.: A bridging model for parallel computation. Commun. ACM **33**(8), 103–111 (1990)
28. Zhu, X., Han, W., Chen, W.: {GridGraph}:{Large-Scale} graph processing on a single machine using 2-level hierarchical partitioning. In: 2015 USENIX Annual Technical Conference (USENIX ATC 2015), pp. 375–386 (2015)

Secure and Efficient Federated Multi-label Propagation via Secret Sharing

Chen Guo[1,2,3], Wenbin Hu[1,2,3], Zhishang Xiang[1,2,3], Shiyu Dong[1,2,3], Qishan Zhang[4], and Kun Guo[1,2,3(✉)]

[1] College of Computer and Data Science, Fuzhou University, Fuzhou 350108, China
[2] Engineering Research Center of Big Data Intelligence, Ministry of Education, Fuzhou 350108, China
[3] Fujian Key Laboratory of Network Computing and Intelligent Information Processing (Fuzhou University), Fuzhou 350108, China
`gukn@fzu.edu.cn`
[4] Xianda College of Economics & Humanities Shanghai International Studies University, Shanghai, China

Abstract. The Multi-Label Propagation Algorithm (MLPA) identifies and reveals community structure by passing labels between network nodes, and is also suitable for dealing with complex networks with overlapping communities. Due to its flexibility and effectiveness, the algorithm has been successfully applied in a number of fields, including image segmentation, text classification, and bioinformatics. In today's society where personal privacy protection is increasingly important, how to detect communities without revealing sensitive information has become a hot issue in the field of network analysis. Existing privacy-preserving multi-label propagation algorithms primarily rely on anonymization and homomorphic encryption techniques. While homomorphic encryption can protect privacy, the complex encryption and decryption processes incur significant computational costs, making it challenging to achieve efficient computation while ensuring accuracy and privacy. In this paper, we propose a Secure and Efficient Federated Multi-Label Propagation Algorithm (SEFMLPA) that combines an anonymization strategy with a secret sharing strategy, considering the attribute similarities between nodes to ensure privacy, accuracy, and efficiency. The experimental results indicate that SEFMLPA achieves an accuracy comparable to the latest algorithms and reduces runtime by 80%. These significant improvements validate the effectiveness and superiority of our approach.

Keywords: Multi-label propagation · Privacy-preserving · Secure and efficient · Federal learning

1 Introduction

Label Propagation Algorithms (LPAs) [1] hold a prominent position in network analysis owing to several advantages. Firstly, LPAs exhibit high computational efficiency, with a time complexity nearly linearly related to the size of the network, making them particularly effective in handling large-scale networks. Secondly, the core mechanism of the algorithm involves iterative label propagation among nodes, facilitating the clustering of nodes with the same label into communities without the need to pre-specify the number of communities. Researchers have developed Multi-Label Propagation Algorithms (MLPAs) to enable LPAs to adapt to complex networks where nodes may belong to multiple communities. These algorithms allow individual nodes to possess multiple labels, simultaneously affiliated with numerous communities.

In today's society, with an increasing emphasis on personal privacy protection, detecting communities without revealing sensitive information has become a hot topic in network analysis. To address this issue, privacy-preserving label propagation algorithms have emerged to effectively detect network communities without compromising privacy. Existing privacy-preserving label propagation algorithms rely on anonymization techniques and homomorphic encryption to achieve this goal. While cryptography-based homomorphic encryption techniques excel in protecting data privacy, they often come with significant computational overhead. Furthermore, as the number of participants and data volume increase, the upward trend in computational costs becomes more pronounced.

In this paper, we proposes a secure and efficient federated multi-label propagation algorithm, which combines anonymization strategy with secure sharing strategy while considering the attribute similarities between nodes and their neighboring nodes. This algorithm is designed to address community detection problems in distributed network environments. Considering the complexity of nodes that may span multiple communities, the algorithm ensures accuracy, maintains privacy, and achieves efficient computation. Through experiments conducted on real and synthetic networks, our algorithm achieves detection results comparable to Federated Multi-label Propagation Algorithm (FMLPA) [2] and reduces runtime by over 80%, demonstrating the effectiveness and superiority of the algorithm. The main contributions of this study are as follows:

1. Design the MP Sharing strategy to perturb local data with parameters, preventing local information leakage, and enhancing algorithm efficiency. This approach overcomes the high computational costs associated with using complex encryption algorithms.
2. Propose k-zero anonymization strategy to achieve k-degree anonymity for nodes, while maintaining accuracy. This strategy overcomes the issues of anonymization methods [3,4] that interfere with community detection.
3. Combining the anonymization strategy with the MP Sharing strategy and additive secret sharing technique enhances the efficiency of the label propagation algorithm and ensures privacy protection. This approach overcomes the limitations of privacy-preserving label propagation algorithms, which struggle to simultaneously achieve high computational efficiency and security.

2   Related Work

2.1   Multi-label Propagation Algorithm

In 2007, Raghavan et al. introduced the Label Propagation Algorithm (LPA) for non-overlapping community detection [1]. Subsequently, in 2010, Gregory et al. pioneered the COPRA algorithm [6] based on the LPA, allowing nodes to have multiple labels and extending each node to potentially belong to multiple communities, thus suitable for detecting overlapping communities. The introduction of MLPA marked an innovative milestone in community detection. El Kouni et al. proposed a Node Influence-based Label Propagation Algorithm (NI-LPA) [7], where the importance of nodes serves as a key parameter for prioritizing label propagation during the labeling phase. Zhang et al. introduced the Node Ability-based Label Propagation Algorithm (NALPA) [8], which innovatively integrates the network position of nodes and the mutual influence of their label distributions to enhance the stability of the MLPA algorithm.

2.2   Privacy-Preserving Label Propagation

Currently, algorithms in the field of privacy-preserving label propagation primarily rely on anonymization techniques and homomorphic encryption techniques to protect the nodes, weights, and link information in networks. Guo et al. introduced a perturbation strategy for node labels and combined homomorphic encryption techniques to enhance the protectiveness of FMLPA, aiming to safeguard the privacy of different participants [2]. Cryptographic techniques can provide privacy protection for graph data queries and mining [9] [10]. Anonymization-based methods can achieve faster processing speeds but still have a chance of privacy being compromised by attackers. Cryptographic methods such as homomorphic encryption and secret sharing ensure losslessness, but the encryption and decryption processes of homomorphic encryption incur significant computational overhead.

3   Preliminaries

3.1   Network Privacy

This study assumes that our algorithm operates under the scenario of semi-honest attackers, where participants do not intentionally disclose personal information and strictly adhere to the algorithm's procedures. Within this framework, privacy-preserving algorithms aim to defend against two main risks of information leakage in graphs:

1. *Network structural*, which includes node identifiers, node degrees, and edges. The degrees of most nodes in the network are unique. If attackers obtain node degree information, they can use it to infer node location information. Additionally, even when node IDs are unknown, attackers can infer node connectivity information by observing the relationships between nodes.

2. *Node and edge attribute information.* In label propagation algorithms, node attributes typically refer to the nodes' labels or initial marks, while edge attributes usually refer to edge weights or edge feature information. In large complex networks, nodes and edges with the same attributes are often very rare. Therefore, once sensitive node or edge attribute information is exposed, attackers may accurately identify these specific nodes or edges.

3.2 k-Degree Anoymity

k-degree anonymity is a common privacy protection method where k denotes the level of anonymity, ensuring that any given node shares the same degree with at least k-1 other nodes. Consequently, attackers can only identify nodes with a probability of up to $\frac{1}{k}$ [11].

3.3 Additive Secure Sharing

Additive Secret Sharing is a classic secret sharing scheme [12], commonly used for sharing secret information, where the secret is divided into multiple shares allocated to different participants who possess data. When it is necessary to reconstruct the original secret, participants can simply perform an addition operation on their shares to recover the secret, ensuring both simplicity and efficiency.

4 SEFMLPA Algorithm

4.1 Implementation of SEFMLPA Algorithm

We utilize Attributed COPRA(ACOPRA) [2] as a reference template for designing SEFMLPA. ACOPRA is an extension based on COPRA that incorporates the influence of vertex attribute similarity in the community detection process. SEFMLPA is intended to operate efficiently in a distributed environment while ensuring the privacy of the data of all participating parties. Algorithm 1 outlines the pseudocode of SEFMLPA, which is divided into five key steps:

Step 1: Overlapping id matching. The participants use the PSI protocol [13] to obtain the set of overlapping nodes X_h with other participants.

Step 2: Parameter Sharing. To prevent the label raw weight from leaking, we propose the MP Sharing strategy, where all participants share multiplication parameters through Secure Socket Layer (SSL) [5] and ensure that all participants agree on σ. All participants use MP Sharing strategy to jointly negotiate the multiplication parameter σ.

Step 3: Label initialization. Before the label propagation phase, each participant initialized the labels of each vertex, setting the initial label set of each vertex to its unique identifier (ID).

Step 4: label update. The label updating phase is one of the core processes of the algorithm, consisting primarily of six key substeps:

Substep 1: Each participant uses label information of shared vertices and their neighboring nodes in the local network to generate $Y_{h,i} = \{v_i : \{(l_j :$

$w_j)\}\}$, where l_j represents a label of vertex v_i, and w_j represents the weight corresponding to that label. $\{(l_j : w_j)\}$ represents the pairs of label weights associated with the shared vertex v_i.

Substep 2: Suppose participants directly share $Y_{h,i}$, it is possible to infer the degrees of other participants' nodes from the received $< \sigma[Y_{o,i}] >'$. To prevent leakage of node degree information, we propose the k-zero anonymization strategy. Specifically, participants added $|L_i| * K$ virtual labels with zero weight to the label set L_i of vertex v_i. Here, $|L_i|$ denotes the number of labels in the current L_i, and K is a parameter in the SEFMLPA algorithm used to control the number of virtual labels. By increasing the value of K, we can increase the number of virtual labels, thereby providing stronger protection for the node degrees. Furthermore, we analysis that k-zero anonymization strategy satisfies the k-degree anonymity criterion [11].

Substep 3: Each participant share the secret share of participant $Y_{h,i}$ with other participants P_o. By using additive secret sharing with parameter σ, each participant generate secret shares $< \sigma[Y_{h,i}] >_1$, $< \sigma[Y_{h,i}] >_2$, where$< \sigma[Y_{h,i}] >_1= \{H(v_i) : \{(H(l_j) : \sigma w_j - \lambda)\}, < \sigma[Y_{h,i}] >_2= \{H(v_i) : \{(H(l_j) : \lambda)\}$. Here, λ is a random number and $\lambda < 0$, and $H(\cdot)$ is a hash function, such as SHA-256 [14], used to encrypt the identifier (ID) of vertex v_i. Through the one-way and confusion properties of the hash function, it can conceal the true ID of the vertex, protecting the privacy of participant data.

Substep 4: Each participant sends one secret share to the corresponding participant and receives $< \sigma[Y_{o,i}] >'$, aggregating local node secret shares to obtain a new node secret share $< \sigma[Y_{h,i}] >_2 \cup < \sigma[Y_{o,i}] >'$. If the node labels are the same, the corresponding weights are added together. Following this, participants send their secret shares of all nodes $< Y_h >$ to the coordinator.

Substep 5: The coordinator receives secret shares $< Y_h >$ from all participants and performs an aggregation process using formula (1),(2) to recover the complete label sets for each overlapping node, resulting in Y_h. Here, $< Y_h >= \{H(v_i) : \{H(l_j) :< \sigma w_j >\}\}$, $Y_h = \{H(v_i) : \{H(l_j) : \sigma \widetilde{w_j}\}\}$. These labels are shuffled, each associated with a weight perturbed by a parameter. Subsequently, the coordinating end compares the weights after perturbation and selects the label with the highest weight. Virtual labels with zero weight are not considered during the label selection process. Meanwhile, we set the threshold α to 0.5. The label will be removed if a label's weight is below $\alpha \times \sum \sigma \widetilde{w_j}$. We will retain the label with the highest weight if all node labels have weights below $\alpha \times \sum \sigma \widetilde{w_j}$.

$$Y_h.keys =< Y_1 > .keys \cup ... < Y_h > .keys \tag{1}$$

$$\sigma \widetilde{w_j} = \sum_{\substack{H(l_j) \in L_i.keys \cap H(l_p)=H(l_j)}}^{n} < \sigma w_p > \tag{2}$$

Substep 6: After updating the labels of overlapping nodes at the coordinator side, the coordinator sends only the new overlapping node label corresponding to each participant to ensure privacy protection. After the participant receives the new label, the weights of the local vertices of the label are updated according to formula (3). Here N_i represents the neighbor set of v_i.

$$w_j = \sum_{l_p \in L_m.keys \cap l_p = l_j, v_m \in N_i}^{n} w_p \qquad (3)$$

Step 5: Community generation. After T rounds of label propagation, nodes with the same label are grouped into the same community. If a node has multiple labels, it belongs to multiple communities. Finally, each participant outputs their local communities.

4.2   Time Complexity Analysis

The time complexity analysis of different steps is as follows. The time complexity of step 1 is $O(n \times n_p^2)$. Here, n represents the maximum number of network nodes, while n_p denotes the number of participating parties. The time complexity of step 2 is $O(n_p^2)$. The time complexity of step 3 is $O(n \times n_p)$. The time complexity of computing $Y_{h,i}$ for all nodes in step 4 is $O(d \times n \times n_p)$. Here, d represents the maximum degree of network nodes. The worst time complexity of computing $< Y_h >$ for all nodes in step 4 is $O(n_p \times n_X)$. Here, n_X represents the maximum number of X_h. The worst time complexity of aggregating the label weights of all participant nodes in step 4 is $O(d \times n \times n_p^2)$. In step 4, the time complexity of sending new labels of overlapping nodes to the participants from the coordinating end is $O(n \times n_p)$. The time complexity for a participant to perform a label update in step 4 is $O(n \times n_V)$. Thus the time complexity of step 4 is $O(d \times n \times n_p^2)$. The time complexity of generating communities at step 5 is $O(n \times_h)$. Thus, the total time complexity of SEFMLPA is $O(d \times n \times n_p^2)$, which is close to linear with the network size.

4.3   Correctness Analysis

The correctness that k-zero anonymization strategy satisfies k-degree anonymity is as follows. An attacker can only infer the degree of a vertex v_i based on the labels obtained from its neighbors. After adding $|L_i| \times K$ virtual labels to the label set of each v_i's neighbor v_m, the adversary can infer an upper bound on the degree of vi to be $|N_i| + |L_i| \times K$ when each L_m has no intersection with the other L_m. When we want to ensure that the probability of the attacker guessing the correct degree L_i is reduced to $1/k$, then the value of k should satisfy $1/(|N_i| + |L_i| \times K) <= 1/k$, Thus, we have $K >= (k - |N_i|)/|L_i|$. If each vertex has a unique degree, then knowing the degree of a vertex is equivalent to determining its location. Therefore, the probability that the attacker locates v_i is no higher than $1/k$, which corresponds to the inability to distinguish v_i from at least $k - 1$ other vertices with the same degree. If there are multiple vertices with the same degree, the probability that the attacker locates v_i will be lower than $1/k$, which corresponds to the inability of the attacker to distinguish v_i from more than $k-1$ other vertices with the same degree.

Algorithm 1: SEFMLPA

Input: participans set P, network $G_h(V, E, R, A)$ of each participant P_h, vertices set V, edges set E, attributes set R, attribute matrix A, maximum number of iterations T, threshold of label weight α, virtual label parameter K

Output: communities set C_h for each participant P_h

    // STEP 1: OVERLAPPING ID MATCHING

1 All participants execute the PSI protocol to obtain each P_h's overlapping vertices X_h

    // STEP 2: PARAMETER SHARING

2 All participants communicate to share the parameter σ, where $\sigma > 0$

    // STEP 3: LABEL INITIALIZATION

3 **for** $v_i \in V$ **do**

4     $L_i \leftarrow \{v_i\}$

    // STEP 4: LABEL UPDATE

5 **for** $t = 1, ..., T$ **do**

6   **ParticiPant** P_h: **for** $v_i \in X_h$ **do**

7   Compute $Y_{h,i}$ for all $v_i \in N_i$ /* SUBSTEP 1 */

8       $Y_{h,i} \leftarrow Y_{h,i} \cup \{l_1 : 0, ..., l_{|L_i| * K} : 0\}$ /* SUBSTEP 2 */

9   **for** $P_o \in P$ **and** $P_o \neq P_h$ **do**

10   **for** $v_i \in X_h \cap v_i \in P_o.V$ **do**

11   Calculate $< \sigma[Y_{h,i}] >_1, < \sigma[Y_{h,i}] >_2$ /* SUBSTEP 3 */

12   Send $< \sigma[Y_{h,i}] >_1$ to P_o

13   Receive $< \sigma[Y_{o,i}] >'$ from P_o

14         $< Y_h > \leftarrow (< \sigma[Y_{h,i}] >_2 \cup < \sigma[Y_{o,i}] >')$

15   Send $< Y_h >$ to Coordinator   /* SUBSTEP 4 */

16   Receive $Y'_{h,r}$ from Coordinator

17   **for** $v_i \in X_h$ **do**

18      $L_i \leftarrow Y'_{h,r}(H(v_i))$

                                     /* SUBSTEP 6 */

19   **for** $v_i \in P_h.V \cap v_i \notin X_h$ **do**

20   Update the label set of v_i in the same manner as in the SUBSTEP 5

21   **Coordinator** :

22    $Y'_h = \emptyset$

23    $Y_h = \cup < Y_h >$

                                       /* SUBSTEP 5 */

24   **for** $H(v_i) \in Y_h.keys$ **do**

25      $S \leftarrow \cup\{H(l_j) : \sigma\widetilde{w_j}\}$

26   Remove $(H(l_j) : \sigma\widetilde{w_j})$ from S if $\sigma\widetilde{w_j} < \alpha \times (\sum \sigma\widetilde{w_j})$

27      $S \leftarrow (l_z, w^*)|w^* = max(\widetilde{w_j})$ if $S = \emptyset$

28   Add $(H(v_i) : S)$ to Y'_h

                                     /* SUBSTEP 6 */

29   Send $Y'_{h,r} \subset Y'_h$ to each P_h, where $Y'_{h,r}.keys = < Y_h >.keys$

    // STEP 5: COMMUNITY GENERATION

30 Each P_h merge nodes with identical labels into a single community and output its communities set C_h

---

4.4   Privacy Analysis

We analyse the possibility of an SEFMLPA privacy breach at each step of the process to ensure its security.

In the step 1, the PSI protocol enables the retrieval of overlapping vertices between each pair of participants while ensuring privacy protection [13].

In the step 2, semi-honest participants negotiate the parameter through the MP Sharing strategy without compromising local privacy.

In the step 3, all participants perform node initialisation locally without exposing local privacy.

In the step 4, the label update process comprises six substeps. In substep 1, the participants locally compute $Y_{h,i}$ without compromising privacy. In substep 2, the participants locally implement the k-zero anonymization strategy without compromising privacy. In substep 3, the participants locally utilize a hash function to blur the node ID and labels, combined with parameter σ to perturb the original weights, preventing leakage of node and label information. Secret shares are generated through additive secret sharing, where one share is positive and the other is negative, and shared with other participants. In substep 4, the participants send $< Y_h >$ to the coordinator. Due to the adoption of the k-zero anonymization and the concealment of the true node weights through parameter perturbation and secret sharing, the coordinator cannot infer the true node degrees and label weights from $< Y_h >$. In substep 5, the coordinator aggregates and recovers all label weights through additive operations. However, as the label weights have been perturbed, the coordinator cannot determine the true aggregated weights. In substep 6, the coordinator only transmits the new labels corresponding to overlapping nodes from the participants, without disclosing information about other overlapping nodes. Additionally, all label update-related operations are performed locally, ensuring privacy preservation. Consequently, step 4 also guarantees privacy.

In the step 5, each participant generates their community locally, ensuring privacy is not compromised.

In summary, in the case of a semi-honest adversary, SEFMLPA does not compromise participants' local network privacy.

5   Experiments

Firstly, we compared the accuracy of SEFMLPA and ACOPRA through a consistency experiment. Secondly, we examined the effectiveness of our strategy in SEFMLPA by comparing it with a distributed MLPA without a federated learning mechanism. Thirdly, through an accuracy experiment, we compared the network attribute-aware ACOPRA with FMLPA, which utilizes homomorphic encryption and anonymization strategy, to SEFMLPA, studying the correctness of SEFMLPA. Finally, we compared the efficiency of SEFMLPA and FMLPA through a runtime experiment.

5.1 Datasets

In this experiment, we utilized two real-world networks and four overlapping artificial networks with different parameter values. The real-world networks are Ego-twitter networks obtained from the work of Leskovec et al. [15]. The dataset comprises a total of 973 complex networks, covering 200 distinct attributes. The overall dataset structure consists of 81,306 vertices and 1,768,149 links. During the experimental process, we selected two networks for in-depth analysis, namely: twitter-1, twitter-2. Table 1 lists the parameters of the data set.

Table 1. Real-world Networks.

Networks	n	n_e	n_a
twitter-1	214	3430	973
twitter-2	220	4032	1413

The n_e parameter represents the number of edges and n_a represents the number of attributes of the node.

To construct artificial networks, we employed the LFR (Lancichinetti-Fortunato-Radicchi) benchmark method [16] to generate four composite networks. The parameters utilized are detailed in Table 2.

Table 2. Artificial Networks.

Networks	n	k	max_k	min_c	max_c	mu	om	on
mu networks	5000	10	25	10	50	$0.1 \sim 0.5$	2	20
n networks	$1000 \sim 5000$	10	25	10	50	0.2	2	20
om networks	5000	10	25	10	50	0.2	$1 \sim 5$	20
on networks	5000	10	25	10	50	0.2	2	$100 \sim 500$

The parameter mu regulates the degree of mixing in the community structure, influencing the cohesion among members within communities. The parameter om defines the maximum number of communities a vertex can belong to, directly impacting the granularity of community partitioning. Parameter on controls the number of communities sharing vertices in the network, reflecting the distribution of vertices among different communities. As the values of mu, om, and on increase, the complexity of the community structure also increases, making the accurate identification of true communities in the network more challenging.

5.2   Evaluation Metrics

In order to accurately assess the community discovery accuracy of the algorithm, this paper adopts the Overlap Normalised Mutual Information (ONMI) and Extended Modularity (EQ) metrics [17]. Among them, the ONMI metric is used to quantify the degree of overlap between the predicted community structure and the actual community structure, and its mathematical expression is as follows:

$$ONMI = 1 - \frac{1}{2}[H(X|Y)] + H(Y|X)] \tag{4}$$

where X and Y refer to: the ground-truth community matrix, and the community matrix detected by the algorithm, respectively. $H(X/Y)$ denotes the conditional entropy of X given Y. Higher values of ONMI indicate higher accuracy of the algorithm in identifying the community members and structures, thus reflecting superior performance of the algorithm. The mathematical expression for EQ is as follows:

$$EQ = \frac{1}{2\,m} \sum_{i,j} \frac{1}{O_i O_j} \left[A_{ij} - \frac{k_i k_j}{2\,m} \right] \tag{5}$$

EQ measures community cohesion by comparing the proportion of links within a community to the proportion of random links in the network to the total number of links in the network, which are $(\frac{A_{ij}}{2m})$ and $(\frac{k_i k_j}{4m^2})$, respectively. O_i and O_j represent the number of communities to which vertices i and j belong, respectively. A higher EQ value, closer to 1, indicates a higher level of cohesion within the generated communities.

5.3   Experimental Setup

We used ACOPRA [2] and FMLPA [2] as the benchmark algorithms for experiments. ACOPRA, an extension of COPRA to attributed networks, considers the influence of neighboring nodes' attribute similarity on label weights. FMLPA is a federated multi-label propagation algorithm that combines anonymization with homomorphic encryption techniques.

First, we compared the accuracy of SEFMLPA and ACOPRA through a consistency experiment with different data sets and the number of participants.

Secondly, we investigate the effectiveness of our strategy and federated learning in SEFMLPA through an ablation study. In the ablation study, we conducted a comparative analysis using a simplified Distributed Multi-Label Propagation Algorithm (SDMLPA). SDMLPA does not consider federated learning mechanisms; that is, each participant executes SEFMLPA on their local network to obtain local communities. Subsequently, the ONMI results were integrated, and the algorithm's accuracy was evaluated by computing the average value. Meanwhile, SE-S denotes SEFMLPA algorithm that employs only MP sharing, while SE-K represents SEFMLPA algorithm that utilizes only k-zero anonymization.

Thirdly, we study the correctness of SEFMLPA through an accuracy experiment in different *mu*, *n*, *om*, *on* values.

Finally, To investigate the performance of SEFMLPA across different datasets and parameters, we conducted runtime experiments on real-world networks and synthetic networks, comparing the FMLPA algorithm.

5.4 Consistency Experiment

As shown in Fig. 1, the ONMI and EQ values of SEFMLPA exhibit no difference across different datasets and parameters. Moreover, for varying numbers of participants, the accuracy of SEFMLPA matches that of the centralized ACOPRA. The experimental results demonstrate that the communities generated by SEFMLPA are entirely consistent with those obtained by the ACOPRA, while maintaining community detection accuracy intact.

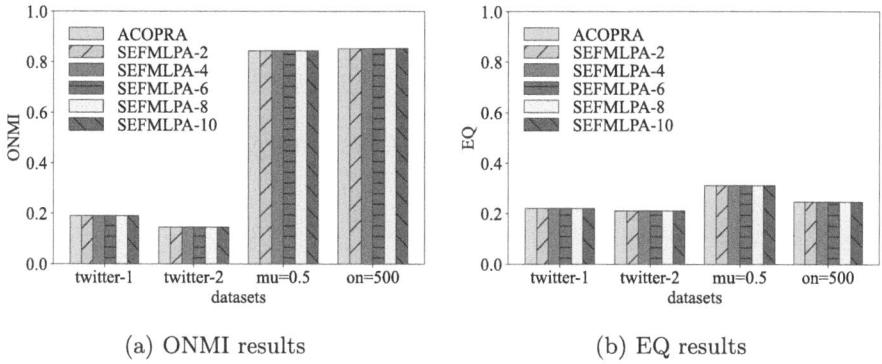

(a) ONMI results   (b) EQ results

Fig. 1. Results of the consistency experiment

5.5 Ablation Experiment

As illustrated in Fig. 2, on the "twitter-1" network, the precision of SEFMLPA exceeded that of SDMLPA by over 200%. Similarly, on a artificial network with the parameter mu set to 0.5, SEFMLPA's accuracy approached twice that of SDMLPA. Moreover, the ONMI values obtained by SE-S and SE-K are consistent with SEFMLPA, demonstrating that our strategy ensures the accuracy of label propagation. Due to SDMLPA's insufficientconsideration of the influence of shared vertices among participants, its performance exhibits a decreasing trend with an increasing number of participants. SEFMLPA, by incorporating the impact of data from different participants through federated learning, maintained good precision performance as the number of participants increased.

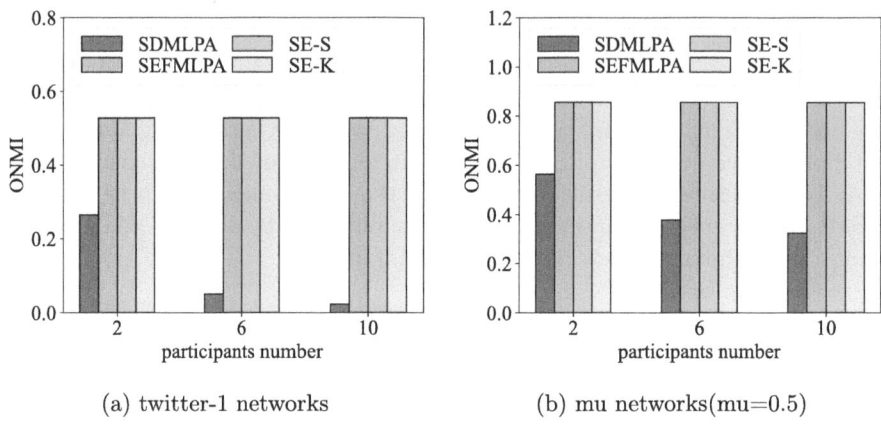

(a) twitter-1 networks   (b) mu networks(mu=0.5)

Fig. 2. Results of the ablation experiment

5.6 Accuracy Experiment

As depicted in Fig. 1 and 3, whether in real-world or artificial networks, and across various parameter settings, SEFMLPA achieves a level of accuracy comparable to ACOPRA and FMLPA. The experimental findings suggest that a solution combining secret sharing and anonymization can achieve results equivalent to those obtained by combining homomorphic encryption and anonymization, effectively ensuring algorithm accuracy and achieving precision without loss.

5.7 Runtime Experiment

As shown in Figs. 4a and 4b, the runtime of SEFMLPA exhibits a nearly linear proportional relationship with the network size growth. With the increase in network size, SEFMLPA maintains acceptable growth in its runtime efficiency, and in the worst-case scenario, SEFMLPA's runtime is at least 60% less than that of FMLPA.

(a) mu networks

(b) n networks

(c) om networks

(d) on networks

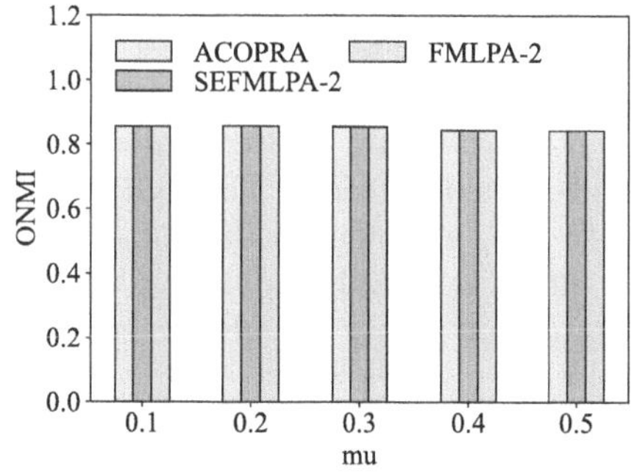

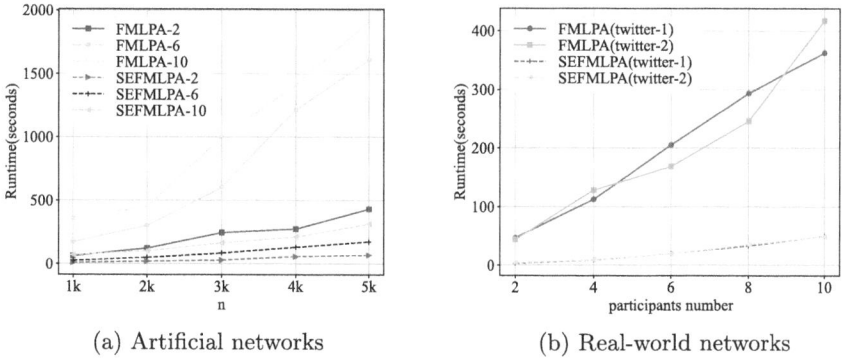

Fig. 3. Results of the accuracy experiment

(a) Artificial networks

(b) Real-world networks

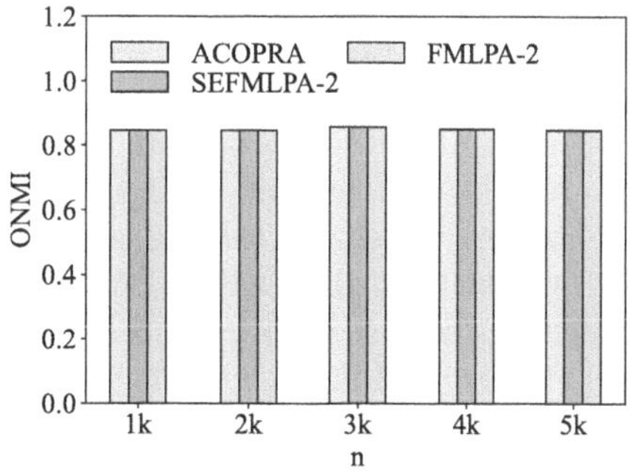

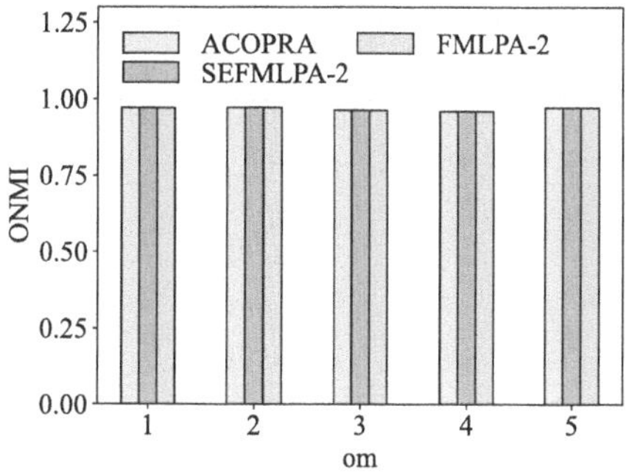

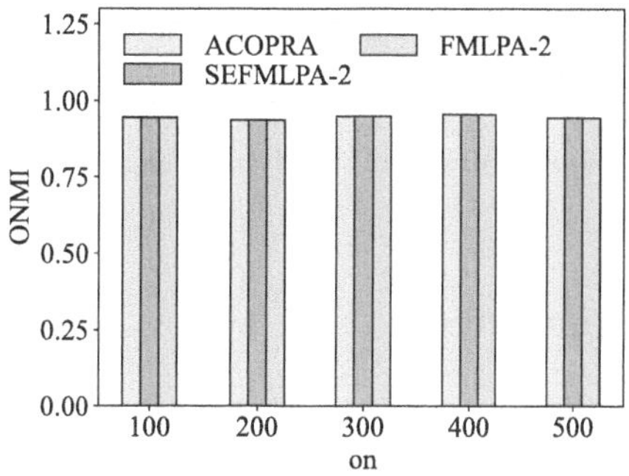

Fig. 4. Results of the runtime experiment

6   Conclusion

In this paper, we propose a secure and efficient federated multi-label propagation algorithm, SEFMLPA. The k-zero anonymization strategy and the MP Sharing strategy were proposed, privacy for each participant is safeguarded while ensuring lossless accuracy and achieving efficient computation. Through experiments conducted on real and synthetic networks, we validate the correctness and efficiency of the SEFMLPA algorithm. Looking ahead, we aim to explore algorithms for decentralized scenarios and investigate ways to enhance security and efficiency while maintaining high precision.

Acknowledgements. This work was supported by the National Natural Science Foundation of China under Grant No. 62002063 and No. U21A20472, the National Key Research and Development Plan of China under Grant No. 2021YFB3600503, the Natural Science Foundation of Fujian Province under Grant No. 2022J01118 and No. 2023J011062, the Major Science and Technology Project of Fujian Province under Grant No. 2021HZ022007, Haixi Government Big Data Application Cooperative Innovation Center and the Hong Kong RGC TRS T41-603/20R.

References

1. Raghavan, U.N., Albert, R., Kumara, S.: Near linear time algorithm to detect community structures in large-scale networks. Phys. Rev. E **76**(3), 036106 (2007)
2. Guo, K., et al.: Privacy-preserving multi-label propagation based on federated learning. IEEE Trans. Netw. Sci. Eng. **11**, 886–899 (2023)
3. Campan, A., Alufaisan, Y., Truta, T.M., Richardson, T.: Preserving communities in anonymized social networks. Trans. Data Priv. **8**(1), 55–87 (2015)
4. Kumar, S., Kumar, P., Bhasker, B.: Privacy preserving graph publishing using fuzzy set. In: 2016 12th International Conference on Natural Computation, Fuzzy Systems and Knowledge Discovery (ICNC-FSKD), pp. 1233–1238. IEEE (2016)
5. Wagner, D., Schneier, B., et al.: Analysis of the SSL 3.0 protocol. In: The Second USENIX Workshop on Electronic Commerce Proceedings, vol. 1, pp. 29–40 (1996)
6. Gregory, S.: Finding overlapping communities in networks by label propagation. New J. Phys. **12**(10), 103018 (2010)
7. El Kouni, I.B., Karoui, W., Romdhane, L.B.: Node importance based label propagation algorithm for overlapping community detection in networks. Expert Syst. Appl. **162**, 113020 (2020)
8. Zhang, Y., Liu, Y., Zhu, J., Yang, C., Yang, W., Zhai, S.: NALPA: a node ability based label propagation algorithm for community detection. IEEE Access **8**, 46642–46664 (2020)
9. Zhang, C., Zhu, L., Xu, C., Sharif, K., Zhang, C., Liu, X.: PGAS: privacy-preserving graph encryption for accurate constrained shortest distance queries. Inf. Sci. **506**, 325–345 (2020)
10. Sharma, S., Powers, J., Chen, K.: Privategraph: privacy-preserving spectral analysis of encrypted graphs in the cloud. IEEE Trans. Knowl. Data Eng. **31**(5), 981–995 (2018)

11. Zhou, B., Pei, J., Luk, W.: A brief survey on anonymization techniques for privacy preserving publishing of social network data. ACM SIGKDD Explor. Newsl. **10**(2), 12–22 (2008)
12. Shamir, A.: How to share a secret. Commun. ACM **22**(11), 612–613 (1979)
13. De Cristofaro, E., Tsudik, G.: Practical private set intersection protocols with linear complexity. In: Sion, R. (ed.) FC 2010. LNCS, vol. 6052, pp. 143–159. Springer, Heidelberg (2010). https://doi.org/10.1007/978-3-642-14577-3_13
14. Sotirov, A., et al.: Md5 considered harmful today, creating a rogue ca certificate. In: 25th Annual Chaos Communication Congress (2008)
15. Leskovec, J., Mcauley, J.: Learning to discover social circles in ego networks. In: Advances in Neural Information Processing Systems, vol. **25** (2012)
16. Lancichinetti, A., Fortunato, S., Radicchi, F.: Benchmark graphs for testing community detection algorithms. Phys. Rev. E **78**(4), 046110 (2008)
17. Chakraborty, T., Dalmia, A., Mukherjee, A., Ganguly, N.: Metrics for community analysis: a survey. ACM Comput. Surv. (CSUR) **50**(4), 1–37 (2017)

Multi-UAVs Reconnaissance Task Assignment Based on GLS-IGA

Tong Wang, Zhiwei Yu, Lu Wang$^{(\boxtimes)}$, Shan Gao, Min Quyang, and Chunhui Zhao

Shandong University, Jinan, China
Wanglu2019@hrbeu.edu.cn

Abstract. The task assignment problem for multiple UAVs is highly nonlinear and confrontational, with significant practical applications in multi-agent systems. In this paper, we study the task assignment problem involving isomorphic multiple UAVs and multiple stationary targets. Building on the Multiple Traveling Salesperson Problem (MTSP) model, we enhance the traditional genetic algorithm. Initially, we adopt a bidirectional coding method using distribution vectors and breakpoint vectors to simplify the routine coding process. Subsequently, a group selection strategy is introduced to select individuals, and a class 3-opt local search strategy is employed to find the optimal solution vector, which improves the convergence speed and global search capability of the algorithm. We propose an improved genetic algorithm based on the Group Local Search strategy (GLS-IGA). Experimental results demonstrate that the proposed GLS-IGA performs better in the multi-UAV reconnaissance task assignment problem.

Keywords: Multi-UAVs · genetic algorithm · group selection strategy · class 3-opt local search strategy · reconnaissance task assignment

1 Introduction

With the advancement of science and technology, UAV technology has found increasingly widespread applications. Due to their strong mobility, easy control, and ability to operate without risking human casualties, UAVs can serve various roles across different scenarios [1]. For example, in battlefield intelligence and surveillance, UAVs can conduct both day and night reconnaissance over enemy targets and timely transmit images and data to the command center, thereby securing a strategic advantage [1, 2]. However, due to the limited capabilities of a single UAV, completing large-scale combat tasks can be challenging. This highlights the advantages of deploying multiple UAVs, particularly in reconnaissance operations. Multi-UAV systems exhibit strong fault tolerance and adaptability, enabling them to function effectively in complex environments. When a multi-UAV system undertakes reconnaissance tasks, the assignment of tasks to each UAV—referred to as multi-UAV reconnaissance task assignment—is crucial. Currently, this topic is a major focus of research worldwide due to its complexity and significance.

Reconnaissance task assignment is one of the core problems in the application field of multi-UAVs. An efficient and reasonable assignment strategy can make a mission plan for multi-UAVs on the premise of meeting mission requirements. In recent years, optimization methods such as Exhaustive Search [4], Integer Programming [5], and Graph Theory [6], along with Meta-Heuristic Algorithms such as Clustering [7], Ant Colony Algorithm [8], Particle Swarm Algorithm [9], Simulated Annealing Algorithm [10], and Genetic Algorithm [11] have been widely applied to solve task assignment problems. Since the task assignment problem of multiple UAVs is an NP problem [12], traditional deterministic search algorithms are only suitable for small-scale and low-dimension problems. For example, Integer Programming requires detailed enumerations when solving problems, making it unsuitable for task assignment problems with high computational complexity [13]. When the complexity of the scene increases and the scale of the problem grows, it is necessary to find feasible solutions through intelligent operations and heuristic algorithms.

In literature [7], close-distance targets are grouped into target groups by optimizing the K-means clustering algorithm, which effectively improves the problem of targets being easy to repeat reconnaissance and enhances the efficiency of reconnaissance task allocation. In literature [2], a UAV cooperative combat and heterogeneous ground target reconnaissance task model with a time window is established, and an improved Multi-Target Symbiotic Search algorithm (MOOS) is proposed. The dual coding of MOOS not only meets the constraints of the reconnaissance task assignment model but also reduces the dimensions of decision variables. Although the traditional Particle Swarm Optimization algorithm is generally applicable to continuous space optimization problems, its fitness is low, and it cannot obtain the global optimal solution. Meanwhile, the traditional Particle Swarm Optimization algorithm is quantified in [14], where the Schrodinger equation is used to establish the quantized motion law, and the Monte Carlo method is used to establish the update mechanism of the quantized particle position. Unfortunately, this kind of Particle Search Optimization algorithm may produce a large number of infeasible individuals in the population iteration process, resulting in low search performance and algorithm efficiency. In literature [15], a Task Assignment Particle Swarm (TAPSO) algorithm is proposed, which avoids infeasible assignment schemes and improves the search efficiency of the algorithm. For the UAV cooperative reconnaissance task assignment under heterogeneous targets, literature aims to obtain the reconnaissance task scheme with the lowest global total cost, but this scheme does not take into account the dynamic threat of the target and the asymmetric assignment between the UAV and the target. In literature [16], a Swap and Judgment Simulated Annealing algorithm (SJSA) is proposed to solve the efficiency problem of generating feasible solutions, but the results show that the population-based algorithm may not be suitable for solving discrete combinatorial optimization problems. The Ant Colony Algorithm is used in [18] to solve the task assignment problem and provide the shortest distance for task execution. Although its superiority and convergence efficiency for the algorithm remain to be investigated, it performs well in discrete optimization problems [18]. In literature [8], a new UAV reconnaissance task model is established, which divides targets into points, lines, and faces according to their set characteristics. The Grouped Ant Colony (GACO) algorithm is proposed to improve the optimality and convergence efficiency of the algorithm by introducing a negative feedback mechanism. In literature [19], an improved Ant Colony algorithm is proposed to solve the task assignment and path planning problems of multiple UAVs. In literature [20], a fusion genetic algorithm based on improved simulated annealing (ISAFGA) is proposed, to improve the diversity of the population, but ISAFGA ignored the consideration of the stability of the operation results during the solution process and did not consider the task assignment method in a dynamic environment.

Among intelligent algorithms, the Genetic Algorithm is widely used. On the one hand, this algorithm offers fast convergence, high optimization accuracy, strong global search capability, and versatile solution representation, making it suitable for large-scale, complex problems. On the other hand, the Genetic Algorithm can easily be integrated with other algorithms and strategies for enhancement, and a balance between global and local search can be achieved through appropriate genetic operators. Therefore, the Genetic Algorithm is well-suited for solving problems related to multi-UAV reconnaissance task assignment. Considering scenarios that align more closely with practical applications, literature [21] addressed the problem of multi-type target reconnaissance in a complex, multi-base scenario, taking into account multiple constraints and utilizing the Genetic Algorithm to solve the model. The resulting reconnaissance scheme significantly reduced the UAVs' residence time within radar detection areas. Considering the heterogeneous types and task coupling constraints of UAVs, an Adaptive Genetic Algorithm (AGA) with a multi-type gene chromosome coding strategy was proposed in literature [22]. AGA demonstrates superior optimal solution search capability and convergence compared to the genetic algorithm, ant colony optimization algorithm, and particle search algorithm. To address the assignment model for a specific moment in air combat, literature [23] introduces a new UAV target assignment method—HGA, based on the Hungarian fusion algorithm. However, the limitation of this study is that it is only effective when the number of UAVs on both sides is the same. Additionally, the flight speed and altitude of UAVs must also be considered. A genetic algorithm with a new crossover operator scheme was proposed in literature [24], which has shown good performance in practical applications.

In this paper, based on the MTSP problem, combined with the characteristics of the reconnaissance task assignment scenario, considering the expected survival probability of the UAV after completing the task, a multi-UAVs reconnaissance task assignment model is constructed. In addition, in order to solve the above problems, this paper proposes a GLS-IGA algorithm combining group selection strategy and class 3-opt strategy. The main innovations of this algorithm are as follows:

1) The bidirectional coding method combining distribution vector and breakpoint vector is adopted to avoid the traditional crossover and mutation operations, and to avoid the failure to include all targets in the distribution vector after many iterations.

2) Based on the characteristics of bidirectional coding and MTSP, a class of 3-opt local search strategy is proposed for a given sequence vector. After adopting this strategy, 6 different distribution sequences are obtained, and the corresponding objective function values of each sequence are calculated by using the initial breakpoint vector. The task assignment sequence with the smallest objective function value is selected as the final task assignment sequence.

3) The genetic algorithm proposed in this paper no longer considers the hybridization between two individuals, but designs the variation as its own two-point crossover variation, so that even after multiple rounds of iteration, the distribution vector still contains all the targets, and no invalid distribution vector will be generated, simplifying the difficulty of constraint processing.

2 Multi-UAVs Reconnaissance Task Assignment Model

In the execution of reconnaissance tasks, a UAV can usually scout multiple targets successively. This means that the number of task performers will be significantly fewer than the number of tasks. In this case, the travel agent and its extended model are very suitable for solving the problem of task assignment for multiple UAVs in reconnaissance missions. It is assumed that when multiple UAVs perform a comprehensive task, they need to first detect N suspected targets in the task area, so that the set of targets to be detected is denoted as $T=\{T_1, T_2, \cdots, T_N\}$. Our M UAVs start reconnaissance from the same or different starting points, forming a collection of UAVs denoted as $U=\{U_1, U_2, \cdots, U_M\}$. Each drone can scout multiple targets; after the reconnaissance is completed, the drone either returns to the starting point or waits near the last reconnaissance target for the next mission.

After the characteristics of the reconnaissance task assignment are clear, the objective function of the assignment needs to be defined. There is no doubt that since the endurance of UAVs is always limited, and the longer the flight time, the longer the UAVs will be threatened by enemies. Therefore, to reduce the risk of carrying out reconnaissance missions, the overall range of the UAV should be as short as possible. For a given task assignment scheme, the formula for calculating the total range of the UAV is:

$$D = \sum_{i=1}^{M} L(i) \tag{1}$$

Where $L(i)$ is the total range of the UAV_i, including the UAV_i from the starting point to the first reconnaissance target, in the course of reconnaissance, from the last reconnaissance target to return to the starting point of three parts. The calculation formula is:

$$L(i) = L_{start}(i) + L_{mid}(i) + L_{back}(i) \tag{2}$$

If the drone does not need to return to its starting point after recon the last target, the formula for its calculation becomes:

$$L(i) = L_{start}(i) + L_{mid}(i) \tag{3}$$

Due to the performance limitation of the minimum turning radius of the UAV, the distance of the departure stage cannot be calculated by the Euclidean distance, so this paper uses the distance calculation formula based on the Dubins curve:

$$L_{start}(i) = Dubins(1, x_i(1)) \tag{4}$$

Due to the impact of emergencies, the heading angle of the UAV in the reconnaissance and the return process can not be determined, without the relevant information of the heading angle, it is impossible to calculate the corresponding Dubins distance. So the distance of these two parts is still calculated by Euclidean distance. Assuming that the reconnaissance task sequence of UAV_i is $x_i = [x_i(1), \cdots, x_i(|x_i|)]$, then the voyage of UAV_i during the reconnaissance process is:

$$L_{mid}(i) = \sum_{j=1}^{|x_i|-1} d(x_i(j), x_i(j+1)) \qquad (5)$$

The range of Drone i on return is:

$$L_{end}(i) = d(x_i(|x_i|), 1) \qquad (6)$$

In addition, there is a certain probability that the target to be reconnaissance will find our drones and attack it, so it is assumed that the survival probability of the drone will decrease with each reconnaissance target passed by the drone when it is reconnaissance. For a given task assignment scheme, the expected survival rate of UAV_i after completing its reconnaissance mission is:

$$Q_i = \prod_{j=1}^{|x_i|} q \qquad (7)$$

If you want the drone to have a survival probability of not less than 60% after executing its reconnaissance mission sequence, you can get:

$$\forall i, Q_i \geq 0.6$$
$$\Rightarrow q^{|x_i|} \geq 0.6$$
$$\Rightarrow |x_i| \leq \log_q 0.6 = 4.85 \qquad (8)$$

That is when the number of reconnaissance tasks performed by each UAV does not exceed 4.85, the UAV can have a survival probability of more than 60% after the execution of its reconnaissance task sequence. In the real scenario, the maximum number of reconnaissance tasks for each drone is no more than 4. It can be seen from the above that the constraints of expected survival probability can be transformed into the constraints on the number of reconnaissance tasks of UAV, and the restrictions on the maximum or minimum number of reconnaissance tasks of UAV can avoid the extreme situation of unbalanced task distribution.

Through the above analysis, in the reconnaissance task assignment model without returning to the starting point, the objective function is the minimization of the total range of the UAV:

$$\min D \qquad (9)$$

The constraints that the multi-UAV reconnaissance task assignment model should meet include:

1) Each target to be scouted needs to be scouted once:

$$\sum_{i=1}^{M} |x_i| = N$$

$$\forall i \neq m, j \neq n, x_i(j) \neq x_m(n) \tag{10}$$

2) Scout at least k targets per drone:

$$\forall i, |x_i| \geq k, k \geq 1 \tag{11}$$

Where k is determined by the expected survival probability of the drone.

3) The range of each drone does not exceed the upper limit:

$$L(i) \leq L_{\max} \tag{12}$$

3 GLS-IGA Design

The Genetic Algorithm (GA) [25] is a type of random search algorithm originally proposed by Professor Holland of the University of Michigan and later refined by researchers such as Dejong and Goldberg. Its scientific basis lies in the natural selection law of 'natural selection, survival of the fittest' observed in nature. In the problem-solving space, a certain number of solutions are generated to form the initial population. This population undergoes selection and evolution until an optimal solution is found or the cycle termination condition is met [26].

Through the analysis and research of the Genetic Algorithm and the UAV task assignment problem, the aspects of the Genetic Algorithm that can be improved to enhance its efficiency in solving task assignment are summarized as follows:

1) Tailoring the selection, crossover, and mutation mechanisms of the Genetic Algorithm to the specific problems being solved. For example, when addressing the traveling salesman problem, the mutation is adjusted to a unique crossover variation, eliminating the possibility of generating invalid task assignment sequences.
2) Adding local search operators to enhance the local search capabilities of the GA;
3) Enhancing the diversity of the algorithm's selection operations, increasing the differentiation between chromosomes in the later stages of the algorithm to expand the search scope, providing a variety of task assignment orders, and avoiding premature convergence of the algorithm.

3.1 Group Selection Strategy

In classical Genetic Algorithms, individuals are often selected using the roulette selection method. In this method, the probability of an individual being selected is positively correlated with the fitness value of the individual; the higher the fitness value, the greater the probability of selection. While the principle of the roulette selection method is simple and generally effective, it requires the fitness values of all individuals in the current population to be recalculated each time it is used. Consequently, the computational load increases sharply with the growth of the population and the number of iterations, making this method inefficient.

To enhance the performance and efficiency of the algorithm, this paper introduces a group selection strategy. This strategy divides the population into M+1 groups based on the number of operation types (assuming M), selecting the individual with the highest fitness value from each group as the selection result for that group. The coding employs a bidirectional quantity coding method combining a distribution vector and a breakpoint vector. Based on the three operations of cross mutation, slip, and region flipping, seven operation modes can be designed. These include the cross mutation, slip, and region flipping of the distribution vector, the random generation of the breakpoint vector, and the combination operation of the three operations of the distribution vector with the random generation of the breakpoint vector. After these seven operation modes are executed, seven new individuals are created. Together with the initial individuals, these new individuals form a group in the new population. The strategy is depicted in the diagram below (Fig. 1):

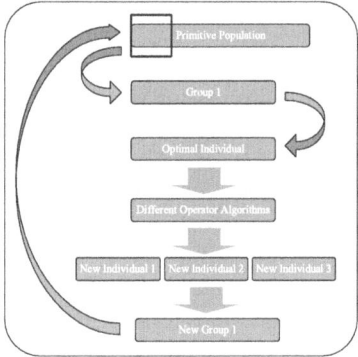

Fig. 1. Schematic diagram of the group selection strategy.

Since targets in the distribution vector should not have the same number, it is challenging to ensure that the distribution vector includes all targets after multiple iterations if conventional crossover and mutation operations are used. Therefore, the Genetic Algorithm proposed in this paper eliminates crossover between two individuals. Instead, it transforms the variation into a two-point crossover variation specific to a single individual. This approach ensures that even after multiple iterations, all targets remain included in the distribution vector, and no invalid distribution vectors are generated (Fig. 2).

1) Single-point sliding operator: This operator randomly selects a weapon point in the assignment sequence and inserts its target before another randomly selected weapon point.
2) Region flipping operator: This operator randomly selects a certain length of weapon point interval in the assignment sequence and reallocates the interval $[x_i, x_{i+1}, \cdots, x_{i+s}]$ to $[x_{i+s}, x_{i+s-1}, \cdots, x_i]$.
3) Cross mutation operator: Traditional mutation is uncertain, and the new solution may be invalid. Therefore, the cross mutation operator is adopted in this paper to ensure

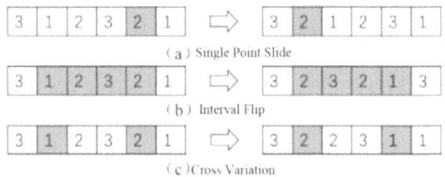

Fig. 2. Schematic diagram of the three operators.

that the new solution is still valid. The operator randomly selects two weapon points and then exchanges their targets.

3.2 Class 3-opt Local Search Strategy

The 3-opt algorithm is a classic local search algorithm for solving the Traveling Salesman Problem (TSP). In the TSP loop, the algorithm randomly selects three edges, deletes them, then tries seven different reconnection modes in sequence, calculating the path length for each. It adopts the reconnection mode with the shortest path length to generate a new individual. This process is repeated for the other three connections in the path until no better connections can be found for any set of three edges.

This paper addresses the reconnaissance task assignment problem, which is analogous to the Multiple Traveling Salesman Problem (MTSP). Theoretically, if the task returns to the starting point upon completion, the assignment result should include multiple loops. Applying the 3-opt operation to each loop requires substantial computing resources, significantly reducing the algorithm's solving efficiency, which is clearly not an optimal approach. To enhance the performance of the Genetic Algorithm (GA) in solving such problems, this paper proposes a class 3-opt strategy that acts on a specific allocation sequence vector. This strategy utilizes bidirectional quantity coding and incorporates features of the MTSP: first, three points in the distribution sequence vector are randomly selected and deleted. Then, five other permutations of these three points are tried sequentially. Finally, the objective function values for each distribution sequence are calculated based on the initial breakpoint vector. The distribution sequence with the smallest distance cost among the six permutations is selected as the new distribution sequence, while the corresponding breakpoint sequence remains unchanged. The schematic diagram of the strategy is as follows:

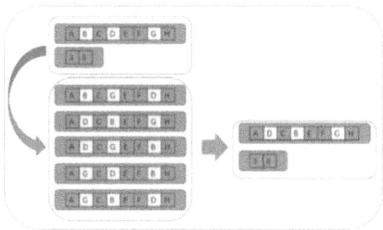

Fig. 3. Schematic diagram of the Class 3-OPT local search strategy.

As shown in Fig. 3, after selecting three points B, G, and H in the task assignment sequence, the order of the three tasks B-D-G is adjusted to B-G-D, D-B-G, D-G-B, G-B-D, and G-D-B respectively. This adjustment results in six different task assignment sequences. Then, the initial breakpoint vector is used to calculate the corresponding objective function value for each sequence. The task assignment sequence with the smallest objective function value is selected as the final task assignment sequence, while the breakpoint vector remains unchanged.

3.3   Algorithm Flow

The overall process of GLS-IGA is as follows:

1) Load the relevant information of the UAV and the target of the strike mission, and calculate necessary details such as the distance matrix.
2) Initialize the population and calculate the fitness value of each individual.
3) Divide the population into 10 groups, each consisting of 8 individuals. Select the optimal individual from each group for the class 3-opt operation, and replace all individuals in the corresponding group with the newly found local individuals, resulting in 8 identical individuals in each group.
4) For each group, perform the seven operation modes mentioned in Sect. 4.2.2 on seven individuals, respectively. The last individual in each group remains unmodified to form a new group, and all new groups together constitute a new population.
5) Update the relevant information for the optimal individual and check whether the iteration limit has been reached. If it has, output the task assignment result; otherwise, return to step (3).

4   Simulation Experiment and Analysis

4.1   Coding Method

In the Traveling Salesman Problem (TSP), the conventional matrix coding method is complex to handle. Therefore, this paper adopts a bidirectional coding method using a breakpoint vector and a distribution sequence. Suppose we have M UAVs and N targets to be detected. Then, the distribution sequence vector consists of numbers 1 through N arranged randomly, and the breakpoint vector contains M-1 numbers, each between 1 and N-1. This indicates that the distribution sequence vector is divided into M parts, corresponding to the execution sequence of reconnaissance tasks by the M UAVs in turn. To illustrate, consider an example where the number of targets is 8 and the number of UAVs is 3. The schematic diagram is as follows (Fig. 4):

As can be seen from the figure above, the elements in the breakpoint vector represent the positions where the task assignment sequence is divided. If the first element in the breakpoint vector is 3, then the first breakpoint occurs after the third position in the task assignment sequence. The tasks corresponding to the first three numbers form the task execution sequence for UAV 1. This coding method not only avoids the constraint that all tasks must be executed by a UAV but also increases the constraint on the minimum number of tasks a UAV must execute by controlling the generation conditions of the breakpoint vector.

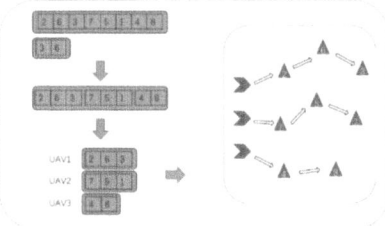

Fig. 4. Schematic diagram of bidirectional quantity coding scheme.

4.2 Evaluation Index

The results obtained by multiple operations of the heuristic algorithm are not exactly the same, and an approximate optimal solution is obtained each time. Therefore, it is obviously unscientific to judge the advantages and disadvantages of various algorithms based on the results of a single experiment. In this paper, each algorithm is repeated 30 times under the same conditions during the experiment. The average value, minimum value, and variance of the algorithm's running results are then compared. The average value reflects the overall performance of the algorithm; the smaller the average value, the stronger the overall performance. The minimum value reflects the limit performance of the algorithm; the smaller the minimum value, the stronger the limit performance. The variance reflects the stability of the algorithm; the smaller the variance, the more consistent the results obtained by multiple runs of the algorithm.

4.3 Simulation Experiment and Analysis

This paper verifies the effectiveness of GLS-IGA by using 3 UAVs and 20 targets for reconnaissance missions as the research background. Firstly, GLS-IGA is compared with LS-IGA, which is improved only by using the Class 3-opt strategy, and G-IGA, which is improved only by using the group selection strategy, as well as the classical GA algorithm in the three indicators mentioned in Sect. 3.2. Then, it is compared with another swarm intelligence algorithm—the Artificial Bee Colony Algorithm (ABC)—for variance, minimum value, and average value, respectively. The UAV does not return to the starting point after completing the reconnaissance mission to the last target but waits for the next action instruction near the last reconnaissance target. The relevant information of the 3 UAVs and 20 reconnaissance mission targets is shown in Tables 1 and 2, respectively.

The average value and minimum value of the objective function obtained by the simulation of the four algorithms are drawn into a bar chart, and Figs. 5 and 6 are obtained.

It can be seen from Figs. 5 and 6 that the average value and minimum value of GA's objective function are the worst among the four algorithms. The average and minimum results of LS-IGA and G-IGA are better than those of GA, indicating that the Class 3-opt local search strategy and group selection strategy can improve the search performance of GA. The average and minimum results of LS-IGA are slightly worse than those of G-IGA, indicating that the group selection strategy can improve the performance of GA

Table 1. Information of UAVs

Drone	x	y	θ
UAV1	0	5	0
UAV2	0	5	45
UAV3	0	5	−45

Table 2. Target information

Objectives	T1	T2	T3	T4	T5	T6	T7	T8	T9	T10	T11	T12	T13	T14	T15	T16	T17	T18	T19	T20
x	6.9	6.7	0.3	1.1	3.1	4.8	4.6	2.3	6.4	3.1	4.1	2	3.9	4.7	1.3	1.4	3.9	0.6	7.5	0.7
y	7.9	2.3	7.5	3.8	5.2	5.6	9.2	3.1	3.6	9.1	4	1.5	6.1	2.1	5.6	7.9	1.2	9.3	6.4	2.4

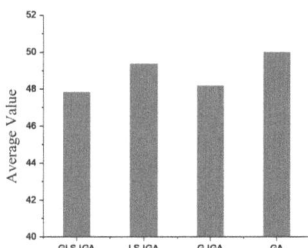

Fig. 5. Average experimental results.

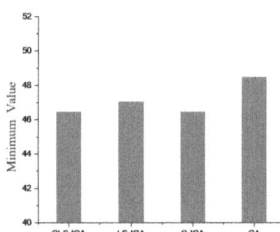

Fig. 6. Diagram of minimum experimental results.

better than the Class 3-opt local search strategy. The average value of GLS-IGA is better than those of the other three algorithms, and the minimum result is the same as G-IGA. Since LS-IGA and GA are combined, this indicates that the combination of the group selection strategy and the Class 3-opt local search strategy can further improve the search performance of GA.

In order to compare the stability of the four algorithms, the variance of the objective function value obtained from 30 experiments of each algorithm is plotted as shown in Fig. 7 below:

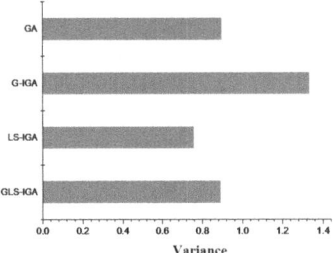

Fig. 7. Experimental results of variance.

As can be seen from Fig. 7, G-IGA has the largest variance, which indicates that the group selection strategy increases the uncertainty of the algorithm's search results to a certain extent. The variance of LS-IGA is the smallest, indicating that the Class 3-opt local search strategy can improve the stability of the algorithm's running results. The variance of GLS-IGA is almost the same as that of GA, indicating that the combination of the group selection strategy and the Class 3-opt local search strategy can ensure the relative stability of the algorithm's running results.

It can be seen from Fig. 6 that the minimum value of GLS-IGA is the same as that of G-IGA, so it can be inferred that this minimum value is the global optimal value. It is not difficult to conclude that the optimal solution is indeed the minimum value through deterministic branch-and-bound algorithms. To compare several algorithms more comprehensively, the convergence curve of each algorithm corresponding to the minimum value in 30 experiments is plotted in Fig. 8.

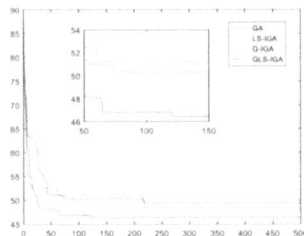

Fig. 8. Comparison diagram of convergence curves.

It is not difficult to see from the convergence diagram in Fig. 8 that the minimum values found by GLS-IGA and G-IGA are the same, but GLS-IGA reached the minimum value around the 120th generation, while G-IGA reached the minimum value around the 145th generation. In other words, GLS-IGA has a faster convergence speed and can converge to the minimum point earlier. This is due to the Class 3-opt local search strategy, which is also evidenced by the fast convergence of LS-IGA.

Table 3 summarizes the distribution vector and breakpoint vector when the minimum objective function value is obtained in the experiment with the four algorithms, as well as the corresponding multi-UAV distribution scheme. Here, U1, U2, and U3 represent UAV_1, UAV_2 and UAV_3 specific details to be filled, respectively.

Table 3. Distribution details

Algorithm	Allocation sequence	Breakpoint vector	Distribution scheme
GLS-IGA	[5,9,12,7,14,6,4,19,17,16, 11,8,2,20,10,3,15,18,13,21]	[6, 10]	U1:5-9-12-7-14-6 U2:4-19-17–16 U3:11-8-2-20-10-3-15-18-13-21
G-IGA	[4,19,17,16,5,9,12,7,14,6, 11,8,2,20,10,3,15,18,13,21]	[4, 10]	U1:4-19-17–16 U2:5-9-12-7-14-6 U3:11-8-2-20-10-3-15-18-13-21
LS-IGA	[5,9,12,6,16,21,13,18,15,3, 10,20,2,7,14,17,8,11,19,4]	[5, 15]	U1:5-9-12–6-16 U2:21-13-18-15-3-10-20-2-7-14 U3:17-8-11-19-4
GA	[12,15,3,10,20,2,7,14,6,16, 5,9,18,13,21,4,19,11,8,17]	[10, 15]	U1:12-15-3-10-20-2-7-14-6-16 U2:5-9-18-13-21 U3:4-19-11-8-17

As can be seen from Table 3, the distribution scheme obtained by the four algorithms meets the constraint that the minimum number of reconnaissance tasks is 4. Additionally, the experimental data show that the minimum objective function values obtained by GLS-IGA and G-IGA are the same. Although the corresponding distribution vectors and breakpoint vectors of the two algorithms are different, the distribution sequences of each UAV show that GLS-IGA and G-IGA divide the reconnaissance tasks into the same three parts: the task sequence assigned to UAV1 by GLS-IGA is the same as that assigned to UAV2 by G-IGA; the task sequence assigned to UAV2 by GLS-IGA is the same as that assigned to UAV1 by G-IGA; and the task sequence assigned to UAV3 by both algorithms is the same. The corresponding allocation schemes of each algorithm are illustrated in a two-dimensional planar graph, as shown in Fig. 9.

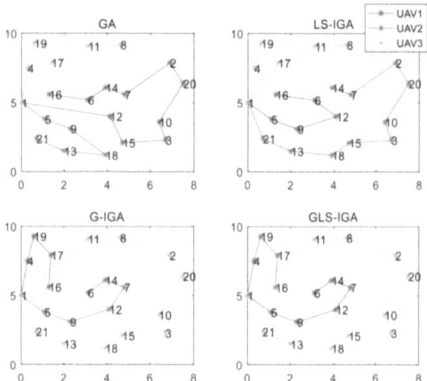

Fig. 9. Schematic diagram of distribution results.

Then, GLS-IGA and ABC were repeated 30 times under the same conditions to compare the variance, minimum value, and average value in order to evaluate the performance of GLS-IGA. The calculation results are shown in Fig. 10.

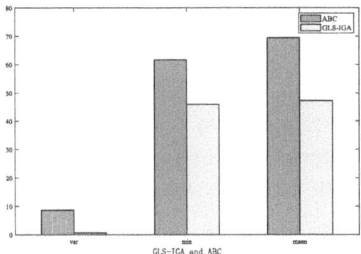

Fig. 10. Comparison of multiple categories of indicators.

In summary, it can be seen that the group selection strategy improves the performance of GA optimization more than the Class 3-opt strategy. However, the group selection strategy increases the instability of the algorithm, while the Class 3-opt strategy reduces it. The GLS-IGA, which combines the two strategies, can converge to the global optimal point at a faster rate while ensuring the stability of the algorithm. Compared with the swarm intelligence algorithm ABC, GLS-IGA demonstrates better optimization ability and stability in the process of finding the optimal solution. In other words, GLS-IGA can solve the reconnaissance task assignment problem stably and efficiently.

5   Conclusions

Based on the extended MTSP problem of the TSP problem and the characteristics of the multi-UAV reconnaissance task assignment scenario, this paper constructs a multi-UAV reconnaissance task assignment model, which not only considers the mobility limitation of the UAVs but also takes into account the balance of the task assignment. To simplify the difficulty of constraint processing, this paper adopts the bidirectional quantity coding method, combining breakpoint vectors and distribution vectors. To effectively solve the problem of reconnaissance assignment, this paper proposes a GLS-IGA algorithm based on group local search, incorporating the Class 3-opt local search strategy to improve the convergence speed and local search ability of the algorithm, given the characteristics of bidirectional quantity coding. Finally, by comparing GLS-IGA with LS-IGA, G-IGA, GA, and ABC algorithms, it is demonstrated that the GLS-IGA algorithm can effectively solve the problem of multi-UAV reconnaissance task assignment.

References

1. Deng, Q., Yu, J., Wang, N.: Cooperative task assignment of multiple heterogeneous unmanned aerial vehicles using a modified genetic algorithm with multi-type genes. Chin. J. Aeronaut. **26**(5), 1238–1250 (2013)

2. Chen, H., Nan, Y., Yang, Y.: Multi-UAV reconnaissance task assignment for heterogeneous targets based on modified symbiotic organisms search algorithm. Sensors **19**(3) (2019)
3. Xie, W., Tao, H., Gong, J., Luo, W., Yin, F., Liang, X.: Research advances in the development status and key technology of unmanned marine vehicle swarm operation. Chin. J. Ship Res. **16**(1), 7–17 (2021)
4. Rasmussen, S., Shima, T., Mitchell, J., Sparks, A., Chandler, P.: State-space search for improved autonomous UAVs assignment algorithm. In: IEEE Conference on Decision and Control, pp. 2911–2916 (2004)
5. Babel, L.: Coordinated target assignment and UAV path planning with timing constraints. J. Intell. Rob. Syst. **94**(3–4), 857–869 (2019)
6. Edison, E., Shima, T.: Integrated task assignment and path optimization for cooperating uninhabited aerial vehicles using genetic algorithms. Comput. Oper. Res. **38**(1), 340–356 (2011)
7. Pang, Q., Huang, Y.L.W.: Multi-UAV multi-target collaborative reconnaissance track planning algorithm. Chin. J. Inertial Technol. **3**, 340–348 (2019)
8. Gao, S., Wu, J., Ai, J.: Multi-UAV reconnaissance task allocation for heterogeneous targets using grouping ant colony optimization algorithm. Soft. Comput. **25**(10), 7155–7167 (2021)
9. De, A., Kumar, S., Gunasekaran, A., Tiwari, M.: Sustainable maritime inventory routing problem with time window constraints. Eng. Appl. Artif. Intell. **61**, 77–95 (2017)
10. Atencia, C., Ser, J., Camacho, D.: Weighted strategies to guide a multi-objective evolutionary algorithm for multi-UAV mission planning. Swarm Evol. Comput. **44**, 480–495 (2019)
11. Saeedvand, S., Aghdasi, H., Baltes, J.: Robust multi-objective multihumanoid robots task allocation based on novel hybrid metaheuristic algorithm. Appl. Intell. **49**(12), 4097–4127 (2019)
12. Whitbrook, A., Meng, Q., Chung, P.: Addressing robustness in time-critical, distributed, task allocation algorithms. Appl. Intell. **49**(1), 1–15 (2019)
13. Darrah, M., Niland, W., Stolarik, B.: Multiple UAV dynamic task allocation using mixed integer linear programming in a SEAD mission. In: Infotech Aerospace: Arlington, pp. 2655–2720. VA, USA (2005)
14. Geng, R., Ji, R., Zi, S.: Research on task allocation of UAV cluster based on particle swarm quantization algorithm. Math. Biosci. Eng. **20**(1), 18–33 (2023)
15. Chen, Z., Nguyen, Q., Gong, D.: Particle swarm optimization algorithm for the optimization of rescue task allocation with uncertain time constraints. Complex Intell. Syst. **7**(2), 873–890 (2021)
16. Huo, L., Zhu, J., Wu, G., Li, Z.: A novel simulated annealing based strategy for balanced UAV task assignment and path planning. Sensors (Switzerland) **20**(17), 1–21 (2020)
17. Zannou, A., Boulaaam, A., Nfaoui, E.: A task allocation In IoT using ant colony optimization. In: ISACS (2019)
18. Pendharkar, P.: An ant colony optimization heuristic for constrained task allocation problem. J. Comput. Sci. **7**, 27–47 (2015)
19. Zaza, T., Richards, A.: ant colony optimization for routing and tasking problems for teams of UAVs. In: 2014 UKACC International Conference on Control, pp. 652–655. Loughborough, UK (2014)
20. Wu, X., Yin, Y., Xu, L.: MULTI-UAV task allocation based on improved genetic algorithm. IEEE Access **9**, 100369–100379 (2021)
21. Cao, Y., Wei, W., Bai, Y., Qiao, H.: Multi-base multi-UAV cooperative reconnaissance path planning with genetic algorithm. Clust. Comput. **22**, 5175–5184 (2019)
22. Ye, F., Chen, J., Tian, Y., Jiang, T.: Cooperative task assignment of a heterogeneous multi-UAV system using an adaptive genetic algorithm, vol. 9(4), p. 9 (2020)
23. Yan, J., Wang, D., Bai, T., Yan, Z.: Multi-UAV objective assignment using hungarian fusion genetic algorithm. IEEE Access **10**, 43013–43021 (2022)

24. Qiu, Y., Jiang, H., Li, Q., Dong, X., Ren, Z.: Application of an adapted genetic algorithm on task allocation problem of multiple UAVs. In: Navigation and Control Conference. Xiamen, China (2018)
25. Fu, X., Sun, Y., Wang, H., Li, H.: Task scheduling of cloud computing based on hybrid particle swarm algorithm and genetic algorithm. Cluster Comput. 1–10 (2021)
26. Deng, Q., Yu, J., Wang, N.: Cooperative task assignment of multiple heterogeneous unmanned aerial vehicles using a modifed genetic algorithm with multitype genes. Chin. J. Aeronaut. **26**(05), 1238–2125 (2013)

MEH-GNN: Meta-path Enhanced Heterogeneous Graph Neural Network for Dual-Target Cross-domain Recommendation

Chao Yang$^{(\boxtimes)}$, Linli Peng , Bin Jiang , Chenglong Lei ,
and Mengchao Liu

Hunan University, Changsha 410082, China
`{yangchaoedu,linlipeng,jiangbin,lcl0136,mc_liu}@hnu.edu.cn`

Abstract. Dual-target cross-domain recommendation tasks aim to transfer knowledge between the source and target domains to help the mutual recommendation results in both domains. However, learning the user and the item features with a unique feature extraction and aggregation scheme always causes suboptimal results due to their significantly different knowledge transfer patterns. Meanwhile, many existing methods are "black-box", which cannot provide insightful interpretations for users. To this end, we propose a **M**eta-path **E**nhanced **H**eterogeneous **G**raph **N**eural **N**etwork (MEH-GNN) for dual-target cross-domain recommendation. First, we conduct a node-specific embedding paradigm to mitigate the knowledge conflicts from different domains, and introduce a new shared Bridge-BiLSTM aggregator to gather information from neighbor nodes. Besides, a hierarchical attention network is performed to improve the bi-directional knowledge transfer by adjusting the weights of instance-level, path-level and domain-level attentions adaptively to learn enhanced representations of the users and items. MEH-GNN considers both domain-specific and domain-shared features when fusing features and relies on the hierarchical attention mechanism to balance between them. Finally, our intra- and inter-domain meta-paths sampled in the cross-domain heterogeneous graph provide path-based interpretability. Extensive experimental results demonstrate that MEH-GNN outperforms existing state-of-the-art methods in recommendation accuracy and can achieve path-based interpretability.

Keywords: Recommender system · dual-target cross-domain recommendation · meta-path · graph neural network · interpretability

1 Introduction

Personalized recommendation systems can alleviate the problem of information overload, but in the real world, there is often a problem of data sparsity, and user behavior is mostly across different domains.To solve the data sparsity problem, the cross-domain recommendation has been proposed. Given the user-item interactions and auxiliary information in two or more domains, the goal of the cross-domain recommendation task is to aggregate or transfer these information from the source domains to the target domain to obtain more accurate recommendations in the target domain. Through collaborative filtering and transfer learning, many previous works can transfer user preferences uni-directionally to achieve cross-domain recommendation [16].

Recently, researchers find that it is possible to improve the recommendation accuracy of both source and target domains by aggregating or transferring the knowledge between the two domains. Early works, such as DDTCDR [8], uses mapping matrix to achieve bi-directional transfer learning, which does not fully consider the structured information between users and items. Lately, various graph-based methods have been proposed, which can effectively leverage the structured information in user-item interaction graphs to improve the performance of dual-target cross-domain recommendation, such as BiTGCF [11]. However, these works still suffer from three key challenges: (**1**) they treat overlapping and non-overlapping information between domains equally. While in real practice, the transferable information for the users and items are different. Simply leveraging existing node embedding techniques may not learn optimal node representations in dual-target cross-domain recommendation; (**2**) most existing works focus on transferring domain-shared features but ignore domain-specific features, which may lead to the "negative transfer phenomenon", i.e., the knowledge transferred from data-sparse domain to data-dense domain may be noisy and reduce the recommendation accuracy of the data-dense domain; and (**3**) most current methods train "black-box" models for dual-target cross-domain recommendation, which cannot provide insightful interpretations for users.

To address the above challenges, we propose a new deep learning method named Meta-path Enhanced Heterogeneous Graph Neural Network (MEH-GNN) for dual-target cross-domain recommendation. To address (**1**), we use different node representation learning schemes and node feature aggregation methods for users and items according to their different characteristics. With such design, items can obtain richer information from distant neighbors through the meta-paths and users can alleviate the noisy information by only considering local information. To address (**2**), we design a hierarchical attention mechanism to learn user preferences at different levels, i.e., instance-level, path-level and domain-level information at different scales. Besides, MEH-GNN can achieve adaptive fusion of domain-specific and domain-shared features through this hierarchical attention mechanism to ensure that knowledge can be correctly transferred bi-directionally, which can help to improve the recommendation accuracy of both source and target domains. Finally, to address (**3**), we construct a cross-domain heterogeneous graph and use Node2Vec [4] to initialize the representations of all the users and items. On this basis, the similarity between nodes is calculated to sample intra-domain and inter-domain meta-paths. Meanwhile, the novel node-specific embedding approach, mitigates the knowledge conflicts from different domains on the inter-domain meta-paths, providing more intuitive and

reasonable path-based interpretations for dual-target cross-domain recommendation.

In summary, the main contributions of this paper are summarized as follows:

– We introduce meta-paths into dual-target cross-domain recommendation task
  and design novel node embedding and aggregation methods for heterogeneous
  graph learning, especially proposing a node-specific embedding paradigm
  and a new shared Bridge-BiLSTM aggregator to enhance the representations
  of heterogeneous nodes and realize interactive modeling between users and
  items.
– We propose a hierarchical attention network composed of instance-level,
  path-level, and domain-level attention to integrate the domain-specific and
  domain-shared features, selecting the most critical knowledge adaptively for
  bi-directional cross-domain transfer and fusion.
– We propose a new meta-path enhanced heterogeneous graph neural network
  for dual-target cross-domain recommendation method, named MEH-GNN,
  which augments the representations of nodes and achieves the bi-directional
  cross-domain transfer of knowledge. Moreover, it can achieve interpretability
  and boost accuracy for dual-target cross-domain recommendation.
– Finally, extensive experiments on three datasets demonstrate that the accuracy of MEH-GNN has surpassed the existing baselines. Rigorous ablation
  studies also confirm the validity of each design in MEH-GNN.

The rest of the paper is organized as follows. Section 2 presents the related
work. Then we describe the details of our proposed method in Sect. 3. Section 4
presents the experiments. Finally, Sect. 5 concludes this paper.

2   Related Work

2.1   Heterogeneous Graph Learning-Based Recommendation

The works of graph learning in recommender systems are mainly based on the
heterogeneous graph, which has more than one type of nodes (user, item, etc.)
or edges. Early studies capture complex high-order relationships between users
and items through random walks, but these methods are based on heuristic
algorithms with suboptimal recommendation performance and low efficiency.
Some methods use matrix factorization to learn heterogeneous user and item
embeddings, considering the context of different types of nodes and realizing
recommendation. However, the above methods fail to learn the nonlinear interaction between users and items. With the rapid development of Graph Neural
Network(GNN), using GNN to learn user and item representations has proven
to be effective [2,5,7]. MCRec [7] designs a co-attention mechanism based on
the meta-path context, enhancing the node representation learning for the recommendation. This work introduces the attention mechanism into the meta-
path of the recommender system, inspiring numerous subsequent studies. To
avoid knowledge conflict between meta-paths from the source domain to the

target domain, HecRec [15] uses an Overpass Bridge to integrate node embedding obtained through different meta-paths for the recommendation. However, these heterogeneous graph embedding approaches have a common shortcoming of ignoring node content features, discarding all intermediate (content feature) nodes along the meta-path, or utilizing only a single meta-path. To solve these problems, I^2RCDR [13] designs a relation-aware graph convolutional network and introduces a gate mechanism to fuse domain-shared and domain-specific features, achieving dual-target recommendation by investigating multi-hop heterogeneous connections of intra- and inter-domain graphs. Heterogeneous graph learning can use the semantic information in the heterogeneous graph structure to mine richer relationships between users and items, which can help to improve the performance of cross-domain recommendation.

2.2 Cross-Domain Recommendation

Most existing works focus on single-target cross-domain recommendation, which aims to improve the recommendation accuracy in only the target domain. Depending on the different transferring strategies, existing approaches can be divided into three categories: content-based [12], embedding-based [14] and rating pattern-based [16] approaches. Such uni-directional cross-domain recommendation can only improve the accuracy in the data-sparse domain by transferring information from the data-dense domain. However, the data-sparse domain may also contain useful information of a particular type. Single-target cross-domain recommendation cannot make good use of it to improve the accuracy on both domains simultaneously. Dual-target cross-domain recommendation attempts to exploit information from both domains and improve recommendation accuracy for all domains simultaneously. Existing approaches [8] simply use a mapping matrix to transform existing uni-directional transfer learning into bi-directional transfer learning. These methods improve the accuracy of cross-domain recommendation but do not take structured information between users and items into consideration.

Recently, various graph-based methods for bi-directional cross-domain information representation and transferring have emerged [11]. They effectively take into account the structured information and make the result of dual-target cross-domain recommendation more accurate. For example, BiTGCF [11] uses Light-GCN [6] to design a bi-directional feature propagation layer, which improves the GCN more rationally on cross-domain recommendation tasks. PGACKG [9] proposes a graph attention network framework based on the knowledge graph to realize dual-target cross-domain recommendation. But these works usually treat overlapping and non-overlapping information in cross-domain recommendation equally, resulting in a poor quality of representations of users and items, therefore limiting model accuracy. In addition, other latest works use disentanglement techniques [17] or equivalent transformation learner [1] to obtain domain-shared and domain-specific features for dual-target cross-domain recommendations. However, these methods have poor ability to process heterogeneous information in cross-domain recommender systems and do not distinguish the influence of auxiliary information. Meanwhile, the interpretability of cross-domain recommendation is rarely studied so far.

3   Methods

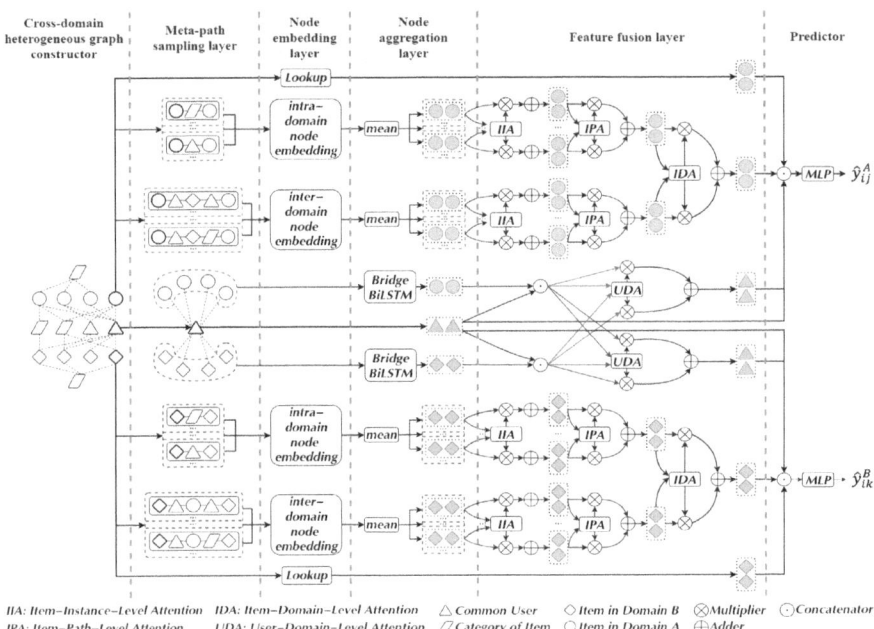

Fig. 1. The architecture of the proposed MEH-GNN method.

3.1   Overview of MEH-GNN

The overall framework of MEH-GNN is illustrated in Fig. 1, which consists of six key components: (1) cross-domain heterogeneous graph constructor, (2) meta-path sampling layer, (3) node embedding layer, (4) node aggregation layer, (5) feature fusion layer, and (6) predictor. We will elaborate the details below.

3.2   Cross-Domain Heterogeneous Graph Constructor

Given two domains A and B, the set of users in the two domains is denoted as U, the set of items for each domain is denoted as I^A and I^B, respectively, and the set of attribute information for the items is denoted as C (containing both domain-specific and domain-shared attributes). For user $u_i \in U$, the sequences of historical interactions for u_i in the two domains are $u_i^A = \{i_1^A, i_2^A, ..., i_m^A | i_p^A \in I_A, p \in [1, m]\}$ and $u_i^B = \{i_1^B, i_2^B, ..., i_n^B | i_q^B \in I_B, q \in [1, n]\}$, respectively. Then, we construct a user-item-attribute heterogeneous graph for two domains A and B, which contains four types of nodes: item nodes in domain A, item nodes in domain B, item attribute nodes and common user nodes in both domains. Concretely, we use the item category to represent the item attribute nodes. All users have historical interactions on both domains, i.e., $U^A = U^B = U$. There is no overlap of items in the two domains, i.e., $I^A \cap I^B = \emptyset$; Item category nodes include both domain-specific and domain-shared nodes, i.e., $C^A \cap C^B \neq \emptyset$ and $C^A \neq C^B$. The common nodes can bridge information from both domains.

3.3 Meta-path Sampling Layer

Following the work in [4], we use Node2vec to initialize the node representations in the graph. Inspired by the work [7], we calculate the similarities of adjacent nodes as the priority scores to sample from the current node to the next node, sampling paths with higher relevance and stronger semantic correlations. In this paper, we design two different types of meta-paths, i.e., intra-domain meta-path and inter-domain meta-path, and obtain the semantic features of nodes by sampling from them. The former contains only nodes of their own domain, representing the intra-domain-specific semantics, such as AUA and ACA. The latter contains not only nodes of their own domain but also nodes of another domain, expressing the inter-domain-shared semantics, such as $AUBUA$ and $ACBCA$. We consider both intra-domain-specific and inter-domain-shared semantics, which will facilitate the corresponding treatments according to their different characteristics.

3.4 Node Embedding Layer

In heterogeneous graphs, we first use one-hot encoding to encode different types of nodes. Since the computations using one-hot encoding are inefficient, we construct an intra-domain node embedding mapping layer to map the one-hot encoding of different node types into a uniform feature space. Meanwhile, we propose to add a domain transformation operation for the cross-domain nodes to alleviate their cross-domain peculiarity. We can finally combine these two through maximum pooling to obtain the representation $h_{v^{B \rightarrow A}}$ and $h_{v^{A \rightarrow B}}$ of the item nodes in both domains as follows:

$$h_{v^{B \rightarrow A}} = maxpooling(h_{v^B}, h'_{v^{B \rightarrow A}}), h_{v^{A \rightarrow B}} = maxpooling(h_{v^A}, h'_{v^{A \rightarrow B}}). \quad (1)$$

where h_v^B and h_v^A represent the obtained representation of node in domain B and A, respectively.

3.5 Node Aggregation Layer

For each item node, we need to aggregate its higher-order neighbors guided by the meta-path to get the final item representation. For each meta-path instance, we aggregate all the nodes in the meta-path instance to get its representation. Since the nodes in the item meta-path instances are unordered, we can aggregate them well by using only the mean operation with few parameters as an aggregator:

$$h_{p(v_j^*, v_t^*)} = Mean(h_v, \forall v \in p(v_j^*, v_t^*)) \tag{2}$$

where $p(v_j^*, v_t^*)$ is the meta-path instance starting from v_j^* and ending at v_t^*.

We obtain the initial preference of each user over the two domains by aggregating its first-order neighbors, i.e., the items with which the user has interacted in both domains. Since there is timestamp information for each interaction, we use the BiLSTM to model the user's first-order neighbors dynamically as follows:

$$h_{u_i^*} = \overrightarrow{LSTM}(h_t) \parallel \overleftarrow{LSTM}(h_t), t \in p(v_j^*, v_t^*) \tag{3}$$

where h_t is the hidden state of the t-th node, i.e., short-term memory, and $h_{u_i^*}$ is the user representation aggregated by BiLSTM. Note that the user interaction features $h_{u_i^A}$ and $h_{u_i^B}$ obtained by the BiLSTM aggregator on both domains will be shared in the user feature fusion process later. Here BiLSTM acts as a bridge between the two domains, so we call it Bridge-BiLSTM. This new Bridge-BiLSTM-based encoding architecture has two main advantages: (1) it can bridge the parameters of two domain networks so that these two networks use the same set of parameters training, resulting in a lower computational complexity and (2) it can well capture time series information and content information to get a more accurate feature representation.

3.6   Feature Fusion Layer

We use a hierarchical attention mechanism to fuse the features of both domains. The optimal retention ratio of user and item features on each domain is dynamically and adaptively controlled for the final recommendation.

Item-Instance-Level Attention (IIA). We use the multi-head self-attention to implement an instance-level attention layer to learn the representation of each meta-path. More specifically, for item node v, we have:

$$Attention(Q_\rho, K_\rho, V_\rho) = \frac{Q_\rho \cdot K_\rho^T}{\sqrt{d_k}} \cdot V_\rho, h_v^\rho = (head_1 \parallel ...... \parallel head_m) \cdot W_M, \tag{4}$$

where query Q, key K and value V are the self-attentive variables, d_k is the dimension, $head_i$ is the attention $(W_{Q_i} Q_\rho, W_{K_i} K_\rho, W_{V_i} V_\rho)$, W is the weight, and $\parallel$ is the concatenation operation.

Item-Path-Level Attention (IPA). In real cases, the contributions of different meta-paths are not consistent in the heterogeneous graph, so we use an attention mechanism to get different weights adaptively. For item node v, we have $|\mathcal{V}|$ latent vectors $h_v^{\rho_1}, h_v^{\rho_2}, ..., h_v^{\rho_l}$, where l is the number of meta-paths. First, we apply a nonlinear transformation and averaging operation to obtain a specific vector for each meta-path as follows:

$$m_{\rho_i} = \frac{1}{|\mathcal{V}|} \sum_{v \in \mathcal{V}} tanh(O \cdot h_v^{\rho_i} + b), \tag{5}$$

where O and b are learnable parameters. Then, we fuse each meta-path-specific vector of the target item node v as follows:

$$\beta_{\rho_i} = \frac{exp(R \cdot m_{\rho_i})}{\sum_{\rho \in \mathcal{P}_\alpha} exp(R \cdot m_{\rho_i})}, \tag{6}$$

where R is the parameterized attention vector and β_{ρ_i} is the importance of the meta-path ρ_i to the item nodes. We then use weighted sum over all meta-path latent vectors of v to obtain the intra- and inter-domain item meta-path representations, respectively, as follows:

$$h_v^{\mathcal{P}_j} = \sum_{\rho_i \in \mathcal{P}_j} \beta_\rho \cdot h_v^{\rho_i}, \mathcal{P}_j \in \{\mathcal{P}_{intra}, \mathcal{P}_{inter}\}. \tag{7}$$

Item/User-Domain-Level Attention (IDA/UDA). We consider both domain-shared and domain-specific features, and the importance of these features is controlled by attention weight. As shown in Eq. (8), when calculating the importance of the intra- and inter-domain meta-paths for the item nodes, we concatenate the item node representation h_v and the two meta-path representations $h_v^{\mathcal{P}_j}$. Though simple, this operation is proved to be effective in obtaining the importance that better matches each node. More details are described as follows:

$$e_v^{\mathcal{P}_j} = LeakyReLU(\gamma_{\mathcal{P}_j}^T \cdot [h_v \parallel h_v^{\mathcal{P}_j}]), \mathcal{P}_j \in \{\mathcal{P}_{intra}, \mathcal{P}_{inter}\},$$

$$\mu_v^{\mathcal{P}_j} = \frac{exp(e_v^{\mathcal{P}_j})}{\sum_{\mathcal{P}_j \in \{\mathcal{P}_{intra}, \mathcal{P}_{inter}\}} exp(e_v^{\mathcal{P}_j})}, h_v^{\mathcal{P}} = \sigma(\sum_{\mathcal{P}_j \in \{\mathcal{P}_{intra}, \mathcal{P}_{inter}\}} \mu_v^{\mathcal{P}_j} \cdot h_v^{\mathcal{P}_j}), \tag{8}$$

where $\gamma_{\mathcal{P}}$ is the attention vector corresponding to the intra- or inter-domain meta-paths, $e_v^{\mathcal{P}}$ denotes the importance of meta-paths to node v. Then the *softmax* function is used to normalize $e_v^{\mathcal{P}}$. Finally, we compute the meta-path representations of node v by the activation function $\sigma(\cdot)$.

Similarly, for user-domain-level attention, the user representation h_u and the user preferences $h_{u_i^A}$ and $h_{u_i^B}$ are fused in the same way as Eq. (8). We then obtain the final user feature representations $h_{u_i}^A$ and $h_{u_i}^B$, as Eq. (9),

$$e_u^* = LeakyReLU(\gamma_*^T \cdot [h_u \parallel h_u^*]), * \in \{A, B\},$$

$$\mu_u^* = \frac{exp(e_u^*)}{\sum_{* \in \{A, B\}} exp(e_u^*)}, h_u^* = \sigma(\sum_{* \in \{A, B\}} \mu_u^* \cdot h_u^*). \tag{9}$$

3.7   Predictor

Finally, we optimize the result of the dual-target cross-domain recommendation through concatenating the implicit feature calculated by the steps above and the explicit features of the users and items are as follows:

$$h_{ij}^A = h_{u_i} \parallel h_{u_i}^A \parallel h_{v_j}^{\mathcal{P}} \parallel h_{v_j}, h_{ik}^B = h_{u_i} \parallel h_{u_i}^A \parallel h_{v_k}^{\mathcal{P}} \parallel h_{v_k}, \tag{10}$$

where h_{ij}^A and h_{ik}^B represent the final interaction vectors of user and item respectively. The user-item recommendation scores are then obtained by two multilayer perceptrons (MLP) as follows:

$$\hat{y}_{ij}^A = MLP(h_{ij}^A), \hat{y}_{ik}^B = MLP(h_{ik}^B). \tag{11}$$

According to the work in [7], we adopt the classic tower structure for the MLP architecture with the hidden layer dimension halved layer by layer, and use $ReLU$ as the activation function and the $sigmoid$ as the output function.

3.8   Loss Function

To optimize the parameters of the model, we use the cross-entropy loss function with positive and negative samples for the whole model as follows:

$$L^A = -\log \hat{y}_{ij}^A - \sum_{n \in V_{neg}^A} \log(1 - \hat{y}_{in}^A), L^B = -\log \hat{y}_{ik}^B - \sum_{n \in V_{neg}^B} \log(1 - \hat{y}_{in}^B), \tag{12}$$

where V_{neg} is the negative sample set.

4   Experiments

4.1   Experimental Settings

Datasets. We conduct experiments on three widely used public datasets provided by the Amazon platform[1], including the Book (Book), Music (CDs_and _Vinyl), and Movie (Movies_and_TV) datasets. We pair these three datasets to form three new dual-target cross-domain recommendation datasets: Books-Music, Movies-Music and Movies-Books. More statistical details of the processed datasets are shown in Table 1, where I^O denotes the items in different domain compared to the items in I.

---

[1] https://jmcauley.ucsd.edu/data/amazon/.

Table 1. Statistical information of datasets.

Datasets	#Users	#Items	#Categories	#Interactions	Density	Intra-Domain Meta-paths	Inter-Domain Meta-paths
Book	3430	38387	565	68747	0.0522%	IUI, ICI	$IUI^OUI, IUI^OCI,$ ICI^OUI, ICI^OCI
Music	3430	11945	317	45601	0.1113%		
Movie	4137	17692	375	73453	0.1004%	IUI, ICI	$IUI^OUI, IUI^OCI,$ ICI^OUI, ICI^OCI
Music	4137	11916	307	57244	0.1161%		
Movie	4645	15555	330	96792	0.1340%	IUI, ICI	IUI^OUI, IUI^OCI
Book	4645	45794	541	111231	0.0523%		

Evaluation Metrics. We adopt two commonly used evaluation metrics for top-K recommendation: Hit Rate (HR@K) and Normalized Discounted Cumulative Gain (NDCG@K). HR@K measures whether the ground truth item appears in the top-K list, assigned 1 if it appears and otherwise 0.NDCG@K considers the relevance of each item and its position in the recommendation list to assess recommendation quality, and higher ranking of the ground truth item yields greater NDCG score. We choose k with 5 and 10 for experiment.

Baselines. In this paper, we compare MEH-GNN with the single domain methods as MAGNN$_{rec}$ [3], LightGCN [6], NCL [10], and cross domain methods as HecRec [15],DDTCDR [8] and BiTGCF [11], to demonstrate the effectiveness of our proposed MEH-GNN.

Implementation Details. We use Pytorch to implement MEH-GNN. The learning rate is 1e-3, the regularization parameter is 1e-6, the dropout parameter is 0.4, the batch size is 256, and the embedding dimension is 64. In meta-path sampling, we use the node representation obtained by Node2vec to calculate the

Table 2. Recommendation accuracy comparison on the Book-Music dataset.

Datasets	Book				Music			
Metrics	HR@5	NDCG@5	HR@10	NDCG@10	HR@5	NDCG@5	HR@10	NDCG@10
MAGNN$_{rec}$	0.2793	0.2240	0.3560	0.2501	0.2796	0.2275	0.3679	0.2567
LightGCN	0.1706	0.1303	0.2230	0.1473	0.3875	0.2844	0.4822	0.3149
TMER	0.8673	0.4407	0.9108	0.4867	0.5756	0.3105	0.7048	0.3317
NCL	0.1642	0.1262	0.2077	0.1382	0.3647	0.2603	0.4787	0.2971
HecRec	0.2656	0.2431	0.3419	0.2548	0.2257	0.1919	0.3077	0.2362
DDTCDR	0.3047	0.2612	0.4028	0.2985	0.2992	0.2158	0.3748	0.2641
BiTGCF	0.4985	0.3196	0.6924	0.3828	0.3501	0.2326	0.5248	0.2888
MEH-GNN	**0.9327**	**0.4801**	**0.9738**	**0.5351**	**0.6277**	**0.3315**	**0.7455**	**0.3516**

similarity. The sequence length of Bridge-BiLSTM is 10. In addition, we take advantage of the early stopping strategy: if HR@10 does not rise in 5 consecutive epochs, the training will be terminated early. We implement the baseline methods through the source code published by the authors and use the hyper-parameters offered by their papers with careful fine-tuning.

Table 3. Recommendation accuracy comparison on the Movie-Music dataset.

Datasets	Movie				Music			
Metrics	HR@5	NDCG@5	HR@10	NDCG@10	HR@5	NDCG@5	HR@10	NDCG@10
MAGNN_{rec}	0.2767	0.2253	0.3714	0.2553	0.2787	0.2263	0.3633	0.2526
LightGCN	0.3423	0.2537	0.4482	0.2880	0.4056	0.2954	0.5315	0.3360
TMER	0.5849	0.3156	0.7145	0.3287	**0.6349**	0.3214	0.6934	0.3405
NCL	0.3345	0.2435	0.4358	0.2764	0.3843	0.2759	0.5149	0.3181
HecRec	0.3036	0.2285	0.3971	0.2723	0.2478	0.2155	0.3354	0.2312
DDTCDR	0.3221	0.2371	0.4694	0.2758	0.2566	0.2312	0.3951	0.2766
BiTGCF	0.3783	0.2602	0.5277	0.3084	0.3732	0.2734	0.5354	0.3189
MEH-GNN	**0.6563**	**0.3377**	**0.7800**	**0.3421**	0.6000	**0.3452**	**0.7380**	**0.3685**

4.2   Overall Performance Comparisons

The results in Tables 2, 3, and 4 show that the recommendation accuracy of MEH-GNN is significantly better than the SOTA methods in terms of HR and NDCG metrics. In the Book-Music dataset, the results of MEH-GNN are 0.9738 and 0.5351 for HR@10 and NDCG@10 in the book domain (data-sparse domain), which are 6.9% and 9.9% higher than the best-performing baseline; and 0.7455 and 0.3516 for HR@10 and NDCG@10 in the music domain (data-dense domain), which are 5.8% and 6.0% higher than the best-performing baseline. MEH-GNN also shows similar accuracy improvements over the best-performing baseline in the other two datasets. These experimental results show that MEH-GNN can enhance the representation of nodes by means of meta-path and improve the accuracy of cross-domain recommendations effectively through the proposed node embedding and aggregation method and hierarchical attention mechanism. Besides, the results reveal that the accuracy is also improved in the data-dense domain, demonstrating MEH-GNN can effectively cope with the "negative transfer" problem.

Table 4. Recommendation accuracy comparison on the Movie-Book dataset.

Datasets	Movie				Book			
Metrics	HR@5	NDCG@5	HR@10	NDCG@10	HR@5	NDCG@5	HR@10	NDCG@10
MAGNN$_{rec}$	0.2770	0.2248	0.3612	0.2501	0.2746	0.2246	0.3641	0.2500
LightGCN	0.3643	0.2557	0.4915	0.2965	0.2553	0.1919	0.3384	0.2187
TMER	0.5737	0.3100	**0.7556**	0.3208	0.8413	0.3852	0.8884	0.4184
NCL	0.3718	0.2627	0.4947	0.3024	0.2357	0.1779	0.3100	0.2020
HecRec	0.2957	0.2455	0.4011	0.2523	0.2566	0.1745	0.3496	0.1996
DDTCDR	0.3125	0.2576	0.4298	0.2621	0.2543	0.2267	0.3729	0.2300
BiTGCF	0.3912	0.2700	0.5425	0.3185	0.4323	0.2871	0.6073	0.3424
MEH-GNN	**0.5959**	**0.3262**	0.7210	**0.3349**	**0.8713**	**0.4255**	**0.9414**	**0.4567**

4.3 Ablation Study

The Impact of the Node Embedding Method. MEH-GNN$_{fc1}$ uses only one fully connected layer for node embedding mapping. MEH-GNN$_{fc1+fc2}$ adds a fully connected layer on the basis of MEH-GNN$_{fc1}$ to realize domain transformation. Besides, all other experimental settings for these variants are the same as described in Subsect. 4.1. The results in Table 5 show that MEH-GNN$_{fc1+fc2}$ are better than MEH-GNN$_{fc1}$, which demonstrates the necessity of domain transformation operation for cross-domain nodes to integrate node features. After combining the results of embedding mapping and domain transformation by max-pooling, MEH-GNN obtains significant accuracy improvement, which illustrates the effectiveness of our node-specific embedding paradigm.

Table 5. Result of different node embedding methods on the Book-Music dataset.

Datasets	Book		Music	
Metrics	HR@10	NDCG@10	HR@10	NDCG@10
MEH-GNN$_{fc1}$	0.9521	0.5289	0.7082	0.3422
MEH-GNN$_{fc1+fc2}$	0.9645	0.5315	0.7238	0.3448
MEH-GNN	**0.9738**	**0.5351**	**0.7455**	**0.3516**

The Impact of the Node Aggregation Methods. MEH-GNN$_{Mean}$, MEH-GNN$_{LSTM}$, MEH-GNN$_{BiLSTM}$ and MEH-GNN represent *Mean*, *LSTM*, *BiL-STM*, and *Bridge-BiLSTM* as aggregators of user preferences, respectively. From the results shown in Table 6, we can see that the *Bridge-BiLSTM* aggregator achieves the best performance under both evaluation metrics. Compared with *BiLSTM*, *Bridge-BiLSTM* can bridge the network parameters in the two domain, gaining more accurate features. Feeding these more accurate features into the subsequent hierarchical attention module is conducive to obtain high-quality recommendations.

Table 6. Result of node aggregation methods on the Book-Music dataset.

Datasets	Book		Music	
Metrics	HR@10	NDCG@10	HR@10	NDCG@10
MEH-GNN$_{Mean}$	0.9275	0.5224	0.7014	0.3399
MEH-GNN$_{LSTM}$	0.9456	0.5286	0.7251	0.3420
MEH-GNN$_{BiLSTM}$	0.9619	0.5314	0.7398	0.3476
MEH-GNN	**0.9738**	**0.5351**	**0.7455**	**0.3516**

The Impact of the Hierarchical Attention. MEH-GNN$_{W/O\_UDA\_and\_All\_IA}$ denotes that user-domain-level, item-instance-level, item-path-level, and item-domain-level attention are removed from the MEH-GNN; MEH-GNN$_{W/O\_All\_IA}$ is that item-instance-level, item-path-level, and item-domain-level attention are removed from MEH-GNN; MEH-GNN$_{W/O\_IPA\_and\_IDA}$ denotes that item-path-level and item-domain-level attention are removed from MEH-GNN; MEH-GNN$_{W/O\_IDA}$ means that item-domain level attention is removed from MEH-GNN. Table 7 shows the results of this ablation experiments in Book-Music datasets. We can see from the results that the HR and NDCG metrics obtained by MEH-GNN outperform all its variants. It fully demonstrates the rationality and effectiveness of our attention design at each level. It can capture the domain-specific and domain-shared features, and integrate them dynamically and adaptively, so as to improve the quality of recommendation.

4.4   Case Study: Interpretability of Cross-Domain Recommendation

Fig. 2 shows examples of path-level and instance-level attention weights for analyzing why user *U560* reads book $I^A 9456$. From Fig. 2(a), we can see that the most important meta-paths for book $I^A 9456$ are $I^A U I^A$ and $I^A U I^B U I^A$. Therefore, we select some instances of these two meta-paths with high attention weights and conside the interaction history of user *U560* to demonstrate our interpretation of cross-domain recommendation. By analyzing, we find that the book $I^A 9456$ has six instances of these two meta-paths, whose end nodes are in the interaction history of user *U560*, as shown in Fig. 2(b). From Fig. 2(b), we can see that the most important instances are the 1st and 4th instances, so we can conclude that there are two main reasons why user *U560* reads book $I^A 9456$: (1) User *U560* and *U1087* have similar preferences in the book domain, and user *U1087* and *U3372* have similar preferences in the music domain, so the book $I^A 9456$ read by user *U3372* can be recommended to user *U560*; (2) User *U560* and *U379* have similar preferences in the book domain, so the book $I^A 9456$

that user *U379* has read can be recommended to user *U560*. It is proved that our model can determine the vital context for recommendation interpretation through the meta-path and hierarchical attention mechanism.

Table 7. Results of hierarchical attention on the Book-Music dataset.

Datasets	Book		Music	
Metrics	HR@10	NDCG@10	HR@10	NDCG@10
MEH-GNN$_{W/O\_UDA\_and\_All\_IA}$	0.8708	0.4023	0.5434	0.3155
MEH-GNN$_{W/O\_All\_IA}$	0.9415	0.4259	0.6149	0.3179
MEH-GNN$_{W/O\_IPA\_and\_IDA}$	0.9452	0.4598	0.7041	0.3469
MEH-GNN$_{W/O\_IDA}$	0.9668	0.4988	0.7009	0.3235
MEH-GNN	**0.9738**	**0.5351**	**0.7455**	**0.3516**

5   Conclusion and Future Work

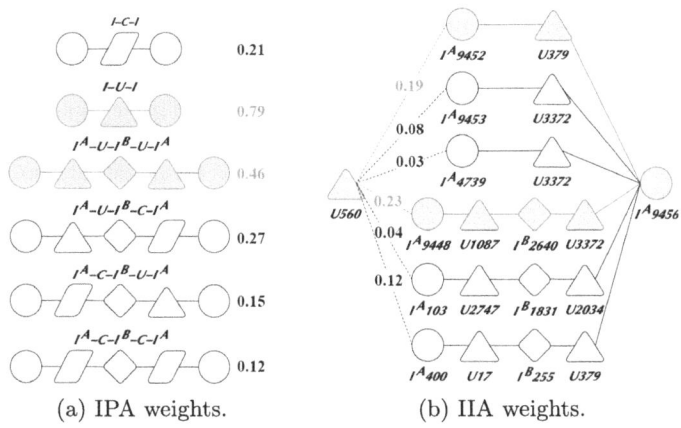

(a) IPA weights.   (b) IIA weights.

Fig. 2. The attention weights of IPA and IIA.

In this paper, we propose a meta-path enhanced heterogeneous graph neural network (MEH-GNN) for dual-target cross-domain recommendation. We construct a cross-domain heterogeneous graph, sample intra- and inter-domain meta-paths, and specifically design a node-specific embedding approach to alleviate knowledge conflict between domains. According to the different characteristics of users and items, we use different node aggregation methods for them respectively.

Finally, we design a hierarchical attention mechanism, consisting of instance-level, path-level and domain-level attentions to select the proportion of weights adaptively for bi-directional knowledge transfer, thus enhancing the representations of the recommended items. The attention mechanism in our method ensures the balance between the domain-specific and domain-shared features when fusing features. Our method can simultaneously improve the recommendation accuracy in both domains through bi-directional knowledge transfer. Meanwhile, the intra- and inter-domain meta-paths provide interpretability for the recommendations. Extensive experiments show that the accuracy of MEH-GNN can surpass the existing baselines.

Future work would conside the self-supervised graph learning-based cross-domain recommendation and interpretable cross-domain recommendation based on causal learning.

Acknowledgements. This work was supported in part by the National Natural Science Foundation of China under Grant 62172156, and the Natural Science Foundation of Hunan Province, China under Grant 2021JJ30152.

References

1. Chen, X., Zhang, Y., Tsang, I.W., Pan, Y., Su, J.: Toward equivalent transformation of user preferences in cross domain recommendation. ACM Trans. Inf. Syst. **41**(1), 1–32 (2023)
2. Fan, S., et al.: Metapath-guided heterogeneous graph neural network for intent recommendation. In: Proceedings of the 25th ACM SIGKDD International Conference on Knowledge Discovery & Data Mining, pp. 2478–2486. Association for Computing Machinery (2019). https://doi.org/10.1145/3292500.3330673
3. Fu, X., Zhang, J., Meng, Z., King, I.: MAGNN: metapath aggregated graph neural network for heterogeneous graph embedding. In: Proceedings of The Web Conference 2020, pp. 2331–2341. Association for Computing Machinery, New York, NY, USA (2020). https://doi.org/10.1145/3366423.3380297
4. Grover, A., Leskovec, J.: Node2vec: scalable feature learning for networks. In: Proceedings of the 22nd ACM SIGKDD International Conference on Knowledge Discovery and Data Mining, pp. 855–864. Association for Computing Machinery, New York, NY, USA (2016). https://doi.org/10.1145/2939672.2939754
5. Han, X., Shi, C., Wang, S., Yu, P.S., Song, L.: Aspect-level deep collaborative filtering via heterogeneous information networks. In: Proceedings of the Twenty-Seventh International Joint Conference on Artificial Intelligence, IJCAI-18, pp. 3393–3399. International Joint Conferences on Artificial Intelligence Organization, Melbourne, Australia (2018). https://doi.org/10.24963/ijcai.2018/471
6. He, X., Deng, K., Wang, X., Li, Y., Zhang, Y., Wang, M.: LightGCN: simplifying and powering graph convolution network for recommendation. In: Proceedings of the 43rd International ACM SIGIR Conference on Research and Development in Information Retrieval, pp. 639–648. Association for Computing Machinery (2020). https://doi.org/10.1145/3397271.3401063
7. Hu, B., Shi, C., Zhao, W.X., Yu, P.S.: Leveraging meta-path based context for top-n recommendation with a neural co-attention model. In: Proceedings of the

24th ACM SIGKDD International Conference on Knowledge Discovery & Data Mining, pp. 1531–1540. Association for Computing Machinery (2018). https://doi.org/10.1145/3219819.3219965

8. Li, P., Tuzhilin, A.: DDTCDR: deep dual transfer cross domain recommendation. In: Proceedings of the 13th International Conference on Web Search and Data Mining, pp. 331–339. Association for Computing Machinery, New York, NY, USA (2020). https://doi.org/10.1145/3336191.3371793

9. Li, Y., Hou, L., Li, J.: Preference-aware graph attention networks for cross-domain recommendations with collaborative knowledge graph. ACM Trans. Inf. Syst. **41**(3), 1–26 (2022)

10. Lin, Z., Tian, C., Hou, Y., Zhao, W.X.: Improving graph collaborative filtering with neighborhood-enriched contrastive learning. In: Proceedings of the ACM Web Conference 2022, pp. 2320–2329. Association for Computing Machinery (2022). https://doi.org/10.1145/3485447.3512104

11. Liu, M., Li, J., Li, G., Pan, P.: Cross domain recommendation via bi-directional transfer graph collaborative filtering networks. In: Proceedings of the 29th ACM International Conference on Information & Knowledge Management, pp. 885–894. Association for Computing Machinery, New York, NY, USA (2020). https://doi.org/10.1145/3340531.3412012

12. Wang, J., Lv, J.: Tag-informed collaborative topic modeling for cross domain recommendations. Knowl.-Based Syst. **203**, 106119 (2020)

13. Wang, K., Zhu, Y., Liu, H., Zang, T., Wang, C., Liu, K.: Inter- and intra-domain relation-aware heterogeneous graph convolutional networks for cross-domain recommendation. In: Database Systems for Advanced Applications, pp. 53–68. Springer, Cham (2022). https://doi.org/10.1007/978-3-031-00126-0_4

14. Xie, R., Liu, Q., Wang, L., Liu, S., Zhang, B., Lin, L.: Contrastive cross-domain recommendation in matching. In: Proceedings of the 28th ACM SIGKDD Conference on Knowledge Discovery and Data Mining, pp. 4226–4236. Association for Computing Machinery (2022). https://doi.org/10.1145/3534678.3539125

15. Yin, J., Guo, Y., Chen, Y.: Heterogenous information network embedding based cross-domain recommendation system. In: 2019 International Conference on Data Mining Workshops (ICDMW), pp. 36–369. IEEE, Beijing, China (2019). https://doi.org/10.1109/ICDMW.2019.00060

16. Yuan, F., Yao, L., Benatallah, B.: DARec: deep domain adaptation for cross-domain recommendation via transferring rating patterns. In: Proceedings of the Twenty-Eighth International Joint Conference on Artificial Intelligence, IJCAI-19, pp. 4227–4233. International Joint Conferences on Artificial Intelligence Organization, Macao, P.R. China (2019). https://doi.org/10.24963/ijcai.2019/587

17. Zhang, X., Li, J., Su, H., Zhu, L., Shen, H.T.: Multi-level attention-based domain disentanglement for bidirectional cross-domain recommendation. ACM Trans. Inf. Syst. **41**(4), 1–24 (2022)

Human-Machine-Things Fusion and Human-AI Collaborative Computing

Meta-instance Incorporated Chinese Composition Review Generation

Luyang Zheng[1], Hailan Jiang[2], and Yuqinq Sun[1(✉)]

[1] School of Software, Shandong University, Jinan, China
sun_yuqing@sdu.edu.cn
[2] Shandong Polytechnic, Jinan, China
1792@sdp.edu.cn

Abstract. In the open composition review scenario for primary and secondary school students, there are no clear criteria and less labeled data that correlates the reviews with the grade level and the type of composition. To help students understand the reviews for improving the quality of composition, it is necessary to show the relevance between the reviews and the compositions content. In this paper, we propose the meta-instance incorporated composition review generation method, which learns from the similar compositions for reviewing new compositions. We employ a composition segmentation method to construct a meta-instance dataset that contains composition fragments and their corresponding reviews. To eliminate the issue of hallucination caused by the meta-instance, the cross-content detection method and the masking mechanism are designed. We also design the retriever model to find the relevant meta-instances with a new composition, where the text semantic encoder is trained by contrastive learning. Then the review for a new composition is generated by combining the content of the new composition with the meta-instances' reviews. Experiments were conducted on a real-world composition review dataset, and the results demonstrated that our method outperformed the existing approaches. We also compare the diversity of reviews generated by different models.

Keywords: Composition review · Meta-instance · Text generation

1 Introduction

In the open composition review scenario for primary and secondary school students, there are no clear criteria and less labeled data that correlates the reviews with the grade level and the type of composition. It is necessary to introduce evaluation criteria that align the compositions with the generated reviews. For example, different types of compositions are often associated style-specific review requirements. Also, to help students understand the reviews for improving the quality of composition, it is necessary to show the relevance between the reviews and the compositions content.

© The Author(s), under exclusive license to Springer Nature Singapore Pte Ltd. 2025
H. Sun et al. (Eds.): ChineseCSCW 2024, CCIS 2343, pp. 379–389, 2025.
https://doi.org/10.1007/978-981-96-2373-0_26

Existing composition review generation methods typically design multiple modules to analyze the composition and generate reviews. These analysis results can be used as a basis for evaluation. Gong et al. [2] present a Chinese assessment system. They design multi-level analytical modules and combine the analysis results with pre-defined templates to generate reviews. To solve the problem of less flexibility of templates, Zhang et al. [16] proposed a planning-based model. It plans some keywords related to a specific writing skill, then predicts the review keywords based on the composition, and finally expands these keywords into a coherent review through a language model. However, these analysis results contain limited information and cannot reflect the differences between the evaluation criteria for different types of compositions. Also, the keywords constrained the content of the generated reviews to some extent, making the relationship between reviews and compositions unclear.

The controlled text generation methods are also relevant to our task. To enhance the controllability of the generated text, the existing methods introduce the neighbor information or prompts. Some researchers have improved the controllability by introducing nearest-neighbor information related to the attributes of composition, which is in the form of a graph or the keywords. Yuan et al. [14] proposed an knowledge-guided model for academic paper reviews, which incorporates the knowledge of citation graph and concept knowledge from the content. Whereas, on our task, there is no explicit relationship between the evaluation criteria, so the information in the form of the graph is not applicable. Also, keywords can be used as the neighbor information. Xie et al. [13] first generate a query based on user and product information and retrieve a set of related reviews. Next, a sequence of keywords is generated based on the query information and related reviews. Finally, a large language model(LLM) is used to generate reviews based on the keywords. But the keywords cannot reflect differences between the criteria for the different compositions types. Another approach is to guide the decoding process via prompts. Some researchers introduce the trainable prefix representations [9] or prompts in the form of natural language. For example, Li et al. [5] retrieve highly relevant prompts for new text, and then let the model learn how to generate reasonable text through contextual learning. However, these prompts are task-oriented and cannot be directly applied to our task.

To address the above problems, we propose the meta-instance incorporated composition review generation method. We constructed a meta-instance dataset as the fine-grained reference evaluation basis. Considering that the direct introduction of the review content of the meta-instances may lead to the problem of hallucination in the new composition reviews, we have designed the content masking mechanism. In the generation process, we first retrieve the relevant meta-instances based on the new composition content. To enhance the relevance of the retrieval results, we trained the composition encoder using contrastive learning. Since the retrieved results are closely related to the compositions and the meta-instances are introduced in the form of prompts, our method not only enhances the reliability of the reviews but also strengthens the relevance between the generated text and the compositions. Experiments were conducted on a real-world composition review dataset, and the results demonstrated that our proposed method outperformed baseline models. We also compare the diversity of reviews generated by different models.

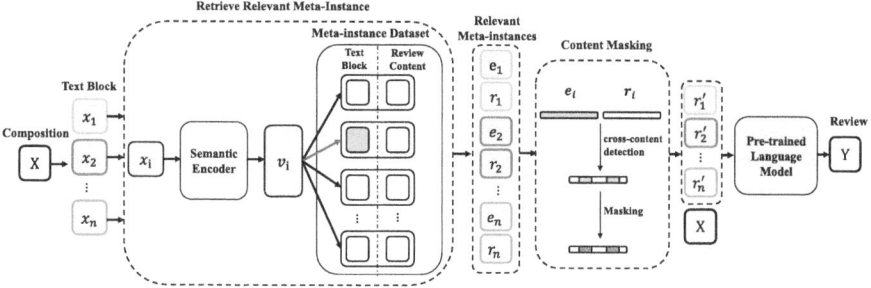

Fig. 1. Overview of our MIRG model.

2   Method

Inspired by the process of humans reviewing compositions, we propose the Meta-Instance incorporated composition Review Generation method(MIRG). To reflect the latent relationships between the reviews and compositions, we use the instances that are similar with a new compositions and their reviews as the references to generate the reviews. The overall framework is shown in Fig. 1.

2.1   Construction of Meta-instance Dataset

To construct the fine-grained reference dataset on reviews, each original composition is separated into several meta-instances. Each meta-instance consists of a text block of composition and the correlated review content. The construction process is as follows:

1)Composition semantic segmentation: Considering the paragraphs containing different semantics in a composition, such as texts that describe landscapes or express emotions, we perform semantic segmentation on each composition so as to reflect their expressive techniques. Each paragraph is treated as a text block. Since some paragraphs are too short, we set a minimum length of 300 characters for each block.

2)Annotation on the relationships between text blocks and review content: The core of constructing meta-instances is to identify the relationship between composition text blocks and review content. We manually annotated the review content that evaluates each text block.

2.2   Composition Semantic Encoder

The MIRG method first retrieves the relevant meta-instances for a new composition. Generally, different students may employ different expressive techniques
even on similar topics, which means that reviews on compositions with similar content may not necessarily be similar. Therefore, to improve the relevance
of the retrieval results, we use the pre-trained text encoder as the base model,
and train the Composition Semantic Encoder(SemEncoder) through contrastive
learning. The training strategy is as follows:

1) **Constructing positive and negative samples:** We use positive and negative samples to enable SemEncoder to learn the similarities and differences
   in expressive techniques between texts. Since each review content definitely
   belongs to a certain evaluation criteria, and the reviews belonging to the same
   criteria are similar in their assessment perspective, the expressive techniques
   used in the reviewed composition segments are also likely similar. Firstly,
   we categorize evaluation perspectives into 7 distinct categories, denoted by
   the set C. Then we label the review content for each meta-instance with the
   evaluation perspective. Each meta-instance is represented as a tuple (e_i, r_i),
   where e_i represents a text block and r_i represents its corresponding review
   content. We label r_i with an evaluation perspective label $l_i \in C$.
   Based on these annotations, the samples are classified into positive and negative ones according to whether they are with the same label. For each
   annotated meta-instance (e_i, r_i), the samples that belong to the same type
   and the same evaluation perspective l_i are regarded as the positive sample
   (e_i^+, r_i^+, l_i^+). The samples that have different composition type than e_i and the
   different evaluation perspective than l_i are regarded as the negative sample
   (e_i^-, r_i^-, l_i^-).

2) **Training the SemEncoder:** To make SemEncoder to learn expressive techniques within the text blocks from positive and negative samples, we design
   the contrastive loss function L_{sim}. For each (e_i, r_i, l_i), the SemEncoder is
   optimized by minimizing the L_{sim}. The L_{sim} is calculated as follows, where
   $d()$ denotes the function that measures the distance between two vectors. γ
   denotes the temperature parameter.

$$L_{sim} = -log\left(\frac{\frac{exp(d(e_i, e_i^+))}{\gamma}}{\frac{exp(d(e_i, e_i^+))}{\gamma} + \frac{exp(d(e_i, e_i^-))}{\gamma}}\right). \tag{1}$$

2.3   Meta-Instance Incorporated Composition Review Generation

The MIRG method involves the retrieval of the relevant meta-instances and the
review generation guided by the meta-instances.

   To obtain the evaluation criteria that matches the composition, we first use
SemEncoder to retrieve the relevant meta-instances of the new composition. The

retrieval process is as follows: 1)The composition X is segmented into a sequence of text blocks $\{x_1, x_2, ..., x_n\}$, where x_i denotes the ith text block, and n denotes the number of text blocks in the X. 2)For each x_i, it is input into SemEncoder to get the embedding v_i. We use the Euclidean distance to measure the similarity between v_i and the embedding of all the meta-instances' text blocks. Then we select the nearest meta-instance as the relevant meta-instance, which is denoted as (e_i, r_i), e_i denotes the text block, and r_i denotes the corresponding review content.

Although r_i can provide the effective information for the generation process, the direct introduction of r_i may bring about the hallucination problem. This is because each r_i may contain the original composition content from e_i, which is irrelevant to X. Therefore, we perform content masking on each r_i. Specifically, the r_i and its corresponding text block e_i is segmented into words. Then, we marked the positions of tokens that appear simultaneously in both r_i and e_i, except for stop words. All the marked tokens in r_i are replaced with the $[MASK]$ token.

We adopt a pre-trained language model(PLM) as the base model for composition review generation. Let $r_i^{'}$ denote the r_i after content masking. Firstly, we concatenate each $r_i^{'}$ of X to form the instance information $R = \{r_1^{'}; r_2^{'}; ...; r_n^{'}\}$. Secondly, to enable the encoder to better distinguish the semantics of the X and R, we use a prompt $\mathcal{I}$. The final input of the encoder is $\{\mathcal{I}; R; X\}$. Finally, through the cross-attention mechanism in the decoder, the X and R is dynamically integrated into the decoding process to generate the more realistic composition reviews. The review generation model of MIRG is optimized by minimizing the generation loss function $loss_g$, which is calculated as follows:

$$loss_g = \sum_{t=1}^{T} - \log P(Y_t | \mathcal{I}, R, X, Y_{<t}), \qquad (2)$$

where Y_t denotes the tth token in the real review, $Y_{<t}$ denotes the review generated in the first $t - 1$ steps, $P(Y_t | \mathcal{I}, R, X, Y_{<t})$ denotes the probability distribution of the decoder output at the tth time step, and T denotes the length of the generated review.

3   Experiments

3.1   Datasets and Baselines

Experiments are conducted on a Chinese **Composition Review(CR)** dataset.The statistical information of the CR dataset is shown in Table 1. In the first column of the Table 1, Total denotes the overall sample size. Con, Sum, and Rev denote the average number of tokens of the source text, the summary, and the review respectively. The **CR** dataset contains the compositions for students from grades 4 to 12. Each composition is labeled with the title, content, review, grade, type, and the score. Since some of the reviews were short and contained little valid information, we filtered the sample for reviews less than 50 tokens in length.

There were no duplicate samples between the CR dataset and the meta-instance dataset. To ensure a balanced number of meta-instances across types, we collected the same number of samples for each type. The meta-instance dataset used for our experiments contains a total of 927 samples, where the average length of all text blocks is 223 words, and the average length of the review content is 48 words.

Table 1. Statistics of the dataset.

	Train	Dev	Test
Total	11578	1450	1450
Con	752.7	755.4	750.4
Sum	422.4	422.6	422.4
Rev	92.7	92.1	93.4

For automatic evaluation, we used ROUGE [6] to analyze the overlap of n-grams between the generated reviews and real reviews. We used BARTScore [15] to assess the coherence of the generated reviews. Also, we designed a evaluation metric $Faith_w$ that assesses the relevance between the generated reviews and the compositions by the degree of lexical overlap, which is calculated as $Faith_w = \frac{1}{|D|} \sum_{i=1}^{|D|} m_w(X_i, Y_i)$, where $|D|$ is the number of samples, X_i is the composition content in the ith sample, Y_i is the review in the ith sample, and $m_w(X_i, Y_i)$ is the number of words appearing in the both X_i and Y_i. A larger value of $Faith_w$ indicates that the generated reviews are more relevant to the composition.

The baseline models we used are as follows: 1)**BPGN**: Based on the pointer generator model [12], we combined a pre-trained BERT model [1] and a layer of LSTM [3] as its new encoder; 2)**BART** [4]; 3)**T5** [10]; 4)**ChatGPT-3.5**; 5)**ERNIE Bot 3.5**; 6)**Chatglm3**; 7)**Tongyi Qianwen 2.1**.

3.2   Experimental Settings

Because some compositions are longer than the maximum input length that most PLM can handle, we extract the abstract A from the composition X by the unsupervised TextRank algorithm [8]. In our experiments, we concatenated the relevant meta-instances' review content, composition title and composition abstract as the encoder's input. The prompt $\mathcal{I}$ is divided into two parts, the prompt concatenated before the relevant meta-instances is "The prompted review:" and the prompt concatenated before the title is "Compositions content:".

We select the pre-trained Sentence-BERT [11] as the base model of the SemEncoder. In the training stage, the learning rate of the SemEncoder is set to 1e-5, the temperature parameter γ is set to 0.05. We use AdamW [7] as the optimizer. In the decoding stage, both MIRG and the baseline models use beam search and the beam size is set to 4. The learning rate of MIRG is set to 4E-5.

Due to the large number of parameters in the LLMs, the experiment use the API interface of the comparative LLMs, and input the prompt and composition content into the LLMs. The prompt is "Please make a reasonable evaluation of the following composition:".

Table 2. Model comparison results.

Data	Models	Rouge-1	Rouge-2	Rouge-L	BARTScore	Faith$_w$
CR	BPGN	25.90	7.00	23.46	4.86	−4.09
	T5	28.90	6.63	21.10	26.17	−4.23
	BART	36.79	11.83	32.35	24.25	−3.88
	MIRG	**42.37**	**14.66**	**37.25**	**48.91**	**−3.78**
$CR_{limited}$	ChatGPT−3.5	29.13	6.30	30.63	14.55	−4.07
	ERNIE Bot 3.5	30.98	6.93	29.37	13.13	−4.11
	Chatglm3	29.66	6.48	31.51	15.04	−4.07
	Tongyi Qianwen 2.1	36.74	7.89	34.02	22.19	−3.91
	MIRG	**41.49**	**13.17**	**37.24**	**50.04**	**−3.77**

3.3 Model Performance Comparison

We compare our method with the lightweight baseline models, and the LLMs separately.

The results between the lightweight baselines and the MIRG are shown in the upper part of Table 2. We find that the MIRG outperforms the baselines on all evaluation metrics, which shows the superior performance of our method. Compared with BART, ROUGE-1/2/L of MIRG are 5.58, 2.83, and 4.9 points higher respectively. It indicates that the relevant meta-instances retrieved by the MIRG are appropriate, thus effectively assisting the review generation process. Observing the $Faith_w$, the reviews generated by MIRG have the highest associations with the compositions. It indicates that the integration of meta-instances enables our model to learn the underlying relationships between compositions and reviews. Also, the results of the BARTScore demonstrate that the reviews generated by the MIRG are superior in terms of fluency and accuracy compared to other methods.

To compare the performance of the LLMs with the MIRG method, we randomly selected the 100 samples from the test set. The comparison results are shown in the lower part of Table 2, which indicate that the MIRG model outperforms the compared LLMs on all evaluation metrics. From the results of ROUGE and $Faith_w$, compared to the LLMs, the MIRG method improves the n-gram prediction accuracy and the association with the composition content.

It indicates that the meta-instances can effectively assist in generating reviews. Due to the similarity between the relevant meta-instances and the compositions, the meta-instances' reviews can help the model learn how to evaluate the compositions. The relatively poor performance of LLMs may be attributed to the difference between the style of their generated reviews and the real reviews. From the BARTScore results, we can see the reviews generated by the MIRG exhibit superior fluency and accuracy. Compared to Tongyi Qianwen 2.1, the MIRG method shows a 0.14 point improvement in the BARTScore.

3.4 Model Ablation Experiments

To show the validity of each part in MIRG, we conduct the ablation experiments. We remove the following parts respectively: 1)**w/o mask**: In the MIRG method, the unmasked meta-instances' review content is concatenated with the composition content and then used as the model input. 2)**w/o meta-instance**:In the review generation process, we only use the composition content as input. 3)**w/o contrastive learning**:In the retrieval process of the MIRG method, an untrained SemEncoder is used to retrieve the relevant meta-instances.

The results are shown in Table 3. We find that the performance of the MIRG model drops after removing the meta-instances, the content masking module, or the training of SemEncoder. According to the Table 3, it can be observed that after removing the meta-instances information(w/o meta-instance), the performance drops the most. It shows that the accurate meta-instances can help the model learn how to enrich the reviews and generate reasonable reviews. Also, removing the training of the SemEncoder leads to a decline in performance. This is because the untrained SemEncoder only retrieves based on semantic similarity, therefore provides limited valid information.

Table 3. Ablation experiments on MIRG.

Models	Rouge-1	Rouge-2	Rouge-L
MIRG	42.37	14.66	37.25
w/o mask	41.98	14.20	37.27
w/o contrastive learning	41.69	14.44	36.86
w/o meta-instance	37.37	12.41	32.92

3.5 Discussion of the Diversity of Reviews Generated by Different Models

We also verify the diversity of reviews generated by different models. On the test dataset, comparing with the real review, the average number of new n-grams appearing in the generated reviews is calculated. It measures the diversity of the review generated by different models. The results are shown in Fig. 2. The vertical axis represents the number of new n-grams, where higher values indicate greater diversity in the reviews.

From Fig. 2, it can be observed that the number of new n-grams in the reviews generated by the MIRG is the highest. This is due to the introduction of the reasonable and diverse meta-instances, which allow the model to not only rely on real reviews for training but also learn various evaluation. Also considering the Table 2, the MIRG method enhances the diversity of review while maintaining accurate evaluation. As illustrated in Fig. 2, the number of new n-grams in the reviews generated by the BPGN, BART, and T5 did not surpass that of the MIRG. This is likely because these models are trained on real reviews, which make them not learn the nuances between reviews of similar compositions, thus hinder the diversity. The BPGN has the poorest diversity, which might be due to its simpler structure, limiting its capacity to learn comprehensive review knowledge. Conversely, the BART and T5 demonstrate greater diversity than the BPGN model, attributed to their complex model structures and pre-training on extensive datasets.

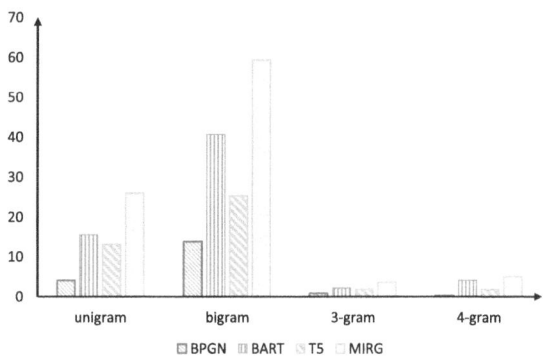

Fig. 2. Comparison results of the diversity of generated reviews.

4   Conclusion

To address the issues of unclear evaluation criteria and less relevance between reviews and compositions, we propose the meta-instance incorporated composition review generation method. We employ a composition segmentation method to construct a meta-instance dataset. To eliminate the issue of hallucination caused by the meta-instance, the content masking mechanism is designed. We also design the retriever model to find the relevant meta-instances with a new composition, where the text encoder is trained using contrastive learning. Then the reviews for the new composition are generated by combining the new composition with the meta-instances' reviews. Experiments were conducted on a real-world composition review dataset, and the results demonstrated that our method outperformed the existing approaches. We also compare the diversity of reviews generated by different models. In the future, we will focus on how to construct the more suitable instances, witch can assist LLMs in better understanding the requirements of various scenarios.

Acknowledgements. This work was supported by the National Natural Science Foundation of China (62376138) and the Innovative Development Joint Fund Key Projects of Shandong NSF (ZR2022LZH007).

References

1. Devlin, J., Chang, M., Lee, K., Toutanova, K.: BERT: pre-training of deep bidirectional transformers for language understanding. In: Proceedings of the 2019 Conference of the North American Chapter of the Association for Computational Linguistics, pp. 4171–4186 (2019)
2. Gong, J., et al.: IFlyEA: a Chinese essay assessment system with automated rating, review generation, and recommendation. In: Proceedings of the 59th Annual Meeting of the Association for Computational Linguistics, pp. 240–248 (2021)
3. Hochreiter, S., Schmidhuber, J.: Long short-term memory. Neural Comput. **9**(8), 1735–1780 (1997)
4. Lewis, M., et al.: BART: denoising sequence-to-sequence pre-training for natural language generation, translation, and comprehension. In: Proceedings of the 58th Annual Meeting of the Association for Computational Linguistics, pp. 7871–7880 (2020)
5. Li, X., et al.: Unified demonstration retriever for in-context learning. In: Proceedings of the 61st Annual Meeting of the Association for Computational Linguistics, pp. 4644–4668 (2023)
6. Lin, C.Y.: ROUGE: a package for automatic evaluation of summaries. In: Text Summarization Branches Out, pp. 74–81 (2004)
7. Loshchilov, I., Hutter, F.: Decoupled weight decay regularization. In: 7th International Conference on Learning Representations (2019)
8. Mihalcea, R., Tarau, P.: Textrank: Bringing order into text. In: Proceedings of the 2004 Conference on Empirical Methods in Natural Language Processing, pp. 404–411 (2004)
9. Qian, J., Dong, L., Shen, Y., et al.: Controllable natural language generation with contrastive prefixes. In: Findings of the Association for Computational Linguistics, pp. 2912–2924 (2022)
10. Raffel, C., Shazeer, N., Roberts, A., et al.: Exploring the limits of transfer learning with a unified text-to-text transformer. J. Mach. Learn. Res. **21**, 140:1–140:67 (2020)
11. Reimers, N., Gurevych, I.: Sentence-BERT: sentence embeddings using Siamese BERT-networks. In: Proceedings of the 2019 Conference on Empirical Methods in Natural Language Processing, pp. 3980–3990 (2019)
12. See, A., Liu, P.J., Manning, C.D.: Get to the point: summarization with pointer-generator networks. In: Proceedings of the 55th Annual Meeting of the Association for Computational Linguistics, pp. 1073–1083 (2017)

13. Xie, Z., Singh, S., McAuley, J.J., Majumder, B.P.: Factual and informative review generation for explainable recommendation. In: Thirty-Seventh AAAI Conference on Artificial Intelligence, pp. 13816–13824 (2023)

14. Yuan, W., Liu, P.: Kid-review: knowledge-guided scientific review generation with oracle pre-training. In: Thirty-Sixth AAAI Conference on Artificial Intelligence, pp. 11639–11647 (2022)

15. Yuan, W., Neubig, G., Liu, P.: BARTScore: evaluating generated text as text generation. In: Advances in Neural Information Processing Systems 34: Annual Conference on Neural Information Processing Systems 2021, pp. 27263–27277 (2021)

16. Zhang, Z., et al.: Automatic comment generation for Chinese student narrative essays. In: Proceedings of the The 2022 Conference on Empirical Methods in Natural Language Processing, pp. 214–223 (2022)

TEmory: A Temporal-Memory Approach to Weakly Supervised Colonic Polyp Frame Detection

Yufei Liu[1], Jianzhe Gao[1], Zhiming Luo[1,2(✉)], and Shaozi Li[1,2]

[1] Department of Artificial Intelligence, Xiamen University, Xiamen, Fujian, China
`zhiming.luo@xmu.edu.cn`
[2] Fujian Key Laboratory of Big Data Application and Intellectualization for Tea Industry, Wuyi University, Nanping, China

Abstract. In recent years, weakly supervised colonic polyp frame detection based on colonoscopy, widely recognized as the 'gold standard' for colorectal polyps screening, has attracted significant attention. However, in colonoscopy videos, a minority of normal frames exhibit a distribution that differs from the majority, potentially affecting the assessment of frame abnormality. To address these challenges, we propose TEmory, a model featuring a **T**emporal **E**ncoder and Me**mory** Unit, designed for weakly supervised colonic polyp frame detection with a comprehensive understanding of normal frame characteristics. Specifically, the Temporal Encoder leverages the contextual information of adjacent frames within video segments, enhancing the encoding's expressive power. Additionally, the Memory Unit adeptly captures and retains the essential traits of both normal tissues and polyps with heightened precision and exhaustiveness, fortifying the model's robustness against the nuances of minority normal structures. Experimental outcomes on one of the most extensive and challenging colonoscopy video datasets indicate TEmory's state-of-the-art performance, showcasing a 1.48% improvement in average precision (AP) over recent advanced techniques. The code of this project is at https://github.com/Liu-Yufei/TEMory.

Keywords: Polyp Detection · Weakly supervised video anomaly detection · Weakly supervised learning · Temporal encoder · Memory bank

1 Introduction

According to the World Health Organization (WHO), colorectal cancer is the second most frequent cause of cancer [16]. The primary cause of these fatalities is the malignant transformation of colorectal polyps [14]. It is early detection of these polyps that is crucial for enhancing patient prognoses. Colonoscopy, a gold standard in the diagnosis of polyps, is pivotal in detecting precancerosis [7,9].

H. Sun et al. (Eds.): ChineseCSCW 2024, CCIS 2343, pp. 390–401, 2025.
https://doi.org/10.1007/978-981-96-2373-0_27

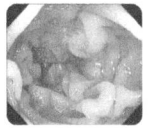 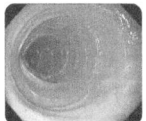 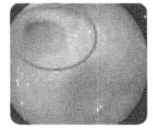 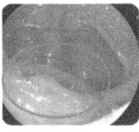 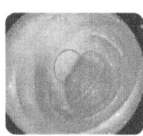

(a) Intestinal exsufflation (b) Intestinal insufflation (c) Appendiceal orifice (d) Ileocecal valve (e) Ileocecal orifice

Fig. 1. (a) A colonoscopic photo of exsufflation state. As a result of the reduced air pressure, the intestinal tract exhibits pronounced folds. **(b) Simultaneous insufflation state of the same intestinal segment of (a).** Most of colonoscopic video frames are as shown in (b). Differences between (a) and (b) may lead models to classify exsufflation state as abnormal and overlook polyps within exsufflation frames. **(c)-(e) Specialized structures in colonoscopy.** Appearances of specialized structures are considerably similar to polyps, presenting difficulty in distinguishing them from polyps.

Recent advancements in deep learning have precipitated an influx of artificial intelligence applications in the analysis of medical imagery. Subject to manual endoscopic screening' high misdiagnosis rate [1,5,13,17], weakly supervised colonic polyp frame detection has emerged as a focal point of interest and active research within the medical imaging and computer vision communities.

This task aims to enable the model to achieve frame-level detection outcomes through video-level training data. Before 2022, researchers typically applied anomaly detection techniques from natural videos [4,11,12,15,18,19] to colonoscopy videos. Tian et al. [13] reformulate the task of polyp frame detection in videos into a weakly supervised video anomaly frame detection problem by constructing the Contrastive Transformer-based Multiple Instance Learning (CTMIL) model. Gao et al. [5] propose the Temporal Prototype Network (TPNet), enhancing weakly supervised polyp frame detection with a temporal encoder and a prototype-based memory bank.

As illustrated in Fig. 1, despite the successes of these methodologies in abnormal frame detection in colonoscopic videos, they fall short in comprehending the intestinal constriction induced by air exsufflation performed by colonoscopy doctors and certain distinctive normal structures within the intestinal tract. Clinically, physicians assess the presence of polyps in the current exsufflation frame by referencing an insufflation one at the identical location in the frame sequence. These specialized structures may vary in different individuals, but their relative positioning remains consistent. In summary, both exsufflation state and specialized structures make the assessment of adjacent frames particularly important.

Improving polyp detection in colonoscopy videos requires two key strategies: exploiting the inter-frame relationships and temporal characteristics to facilitate the robust extraction of information and intensifying the focus on learning paradigms that pertain to the understanding of normal structures.

Drawing from the analysis, we propose TEmory, a novel weakly supervised polyp frame detection model. Specifically, the Temporal Encoder is designed based on Bidirectional Long Short Time Memory (Bi-LSTM) [10] and Global and Local Multi-Head Self-Attention (GL-MHSA) [20], exploiting temporal information and augmenting the descriptive power of embeddings, enabling the precise capture of information and delineation of associations between adjacent frames. Additionally, the Memory Unit, constituted by multiple parallel self-attention memory banks, not only elevates the dimensionality of the input feature space but also comprehensively stores a variety of features pertaining to specialized structures, thereby enhancing the capability for feature retrieval.

To summarize, the main contributions of this study are as follows:

- We propose TEmory, a novel weakly supervised colonic polyp frame detection model.
- We design a Temporal Encoder to fully leverage temporal information, thereby enhancing the expressiveness of feature encoding.
- We design multiple parallel self-attention memory modules to constitute the Memory Unit, enabling deeper interaction between input features and memory modules for enhanced feature retrieval and preservation.
- Extensive experiments demonstrate that our TEmory achieves new state-of-the-art performance on one of the largest and most challenging colonoscopy video datasets.

2   Method

As shown in Fig. 2, the video segment $v \in \mathbb{R}^{T \times H \times W}$ is fed into a pre-trained I3D model [3] to extract frame features. These features then pass through a Temporal Encoder and a Memory Unit, producing temporally and memory-enhanced features. The enhanced features are concatenated and processed by a linear layer to generate an anomaly score for each frame. During training, the top k anomaly scores are averaged and supervised using video-level ground truth labels. During testing, the anomaly scores for each frame are compared with a preset threshold to detect anomalies.

2.1   Overall Architecture

The model takes video segment $v \in \mathbb{R}^{T \times H \times W}$ as input, which is then fed into a pretrained I3D model. Where T is the number of video frames and $W \times H$ denotes the resolution of each frame.

$$X_{I3D} = \text{I3D}(v), \tag{1}$$

where $X_{I3D} \in \mathbb{R}^{T \times D_{I3D}}$ and D_{I3D} is the dimensional length. The extracted features are processed by the Temporal Encoder to obtain temporally-enhanced features $X_{TE} \in \mathbb{R}^{T \times D}$:

$$X_{TE} = \text{Temporal Encoder}(X_{I3D}), \tag{2}$$

utilized to capture the temporal and relational dependencies within video segments, obtaining high-quality embeddings.

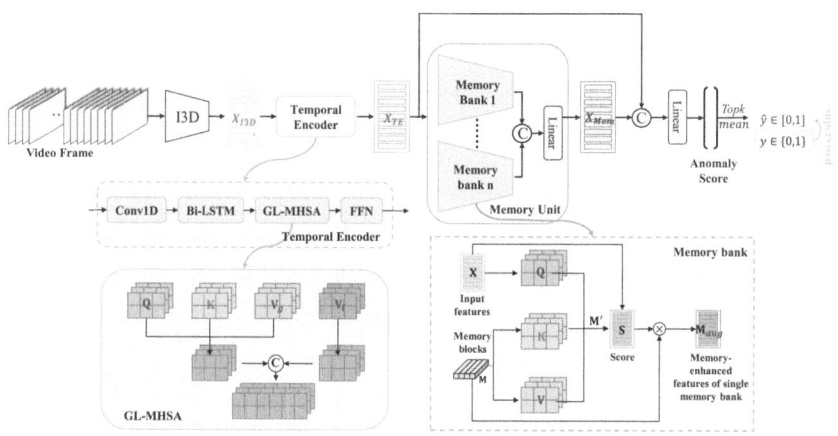

Fig. 2. The framework of our TEmemory model consists of two parts: Temporal Encoder and Memory Unit.

Then, X_{TE} is processed through multiple parallel memory banks within the Memory Unit, which use attention mechanisms to update and integrate individual features, forming memory-enhanced features $X_{Mem} \in \mathbb{R}^{T \times D}$:

$$X_{Mem} = \text{Memory Unit} \left(X_{TE} \right). \qquad (3)$$

The memory-enhanced features are concatenated with the temporally-enhanced features and mapped through a Linear layer to obtain the anomaly scores:

$$y_T = \text{Linear} \left(\text{Concat} \left(X_{TE}, X_{Mem} \right) \right), \qquad (4)$$

where $y_T \in \mathbb{R}^T$. Since the training utilizes video-level annotations, where $y \in \{0, 1\}$, to supervise the training with ground truth labels, we takes the mean of the top K largest anomaly scores as the output $\hat{y} \in [0, 1]$:

$$\hat{y} = \text{Mean} \left(\text{topK} \left(y_T \right) \right). \qquad (5)$$

2.2 Temporal Encoder

To leverage temporal information and enhance feature encoding for capturing inter-frame associations, this paper employs a Temporal Encoder for colonoscopy video segments. After preprocessing, extracted features are fed into the Temporal Encoder, then passed into a Bi-LSTM network to learn temporal information. Using a GL-MHA mechanism, we capture each frame's relative importance. Finally, a feedforward network layer derives the temporally enhanced features.

Specifically, the input features $X_{I3D} \in \mathbb{R}^{T \times D_{I3D}}$ are subjected to temporal modeling using a Bi-LSTM as follows:

$$X_{LSTM} = \text{Bi-LSTM} \left(\text{Conv1D} \left(X_{I3D} \right) \right), \qquad (6)$$

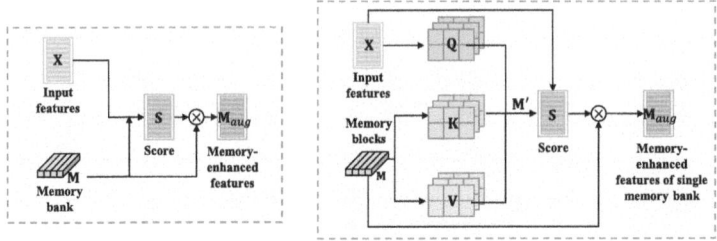

Fig. 3. Classical vs. multi-head attention updated memory bank.

where Conv1D denotes a one-dimensional convolutional layer designed to extract local features and capture spatial information within each video segment.

Then, a linear transformation is applied to X_{LSTM} to derive the matrices for queries (Q), keys (K), global values (V_g), and temporal mask values (V_l):

$$
\begin{aligned}
Q &= X_{LSTM} \times W^Q, \\
K &= X_{LSTM} \times W^K, \\
V_g &= X_{LSTM} \times W^{V_g}, \\
V_l &= X_{LSTM} \times W^{V_l}.
\end{aligned}
\tag{7}
$$

Global modeling is then conducted using self-attention:

$$
X_{att} = \text{Concat}\left(\text{Softmax}\left(\frac{QK^T}{\sqrt{d}}\right)V_g ; \text{Softmax}\left(T_m\right)V_l\right) + X_{LSTM}, \tag{8}
$$

where d represents the dimensionality of the vectors that make up Q and K, and T_m denotes the temporal mask, calculated as follows:

$$
T_m = -\frac{|i-j|}{e^\tau}, \tag{9}
$$

where τ is the sensitivity factor that balances the local distance. Finally, we further processes X_{att} using a FFN:

$$
X_{TE} = \text{FFN}\left(X_{att}\right) + X_{att}, \tag{10}
$$

where $X_{TE} \in \mathbb{R}^{T \times D}$, FFN denotes a linear layer following the Gaussian Error Linear Unit (GELU) [6] activation function.

2.3 Memory Unit

The exsufflation state and specialized structures exhibit varied manifestations. A single memory module cannot fully store the critical video features, as classical memory modules lack the dimensionality for deep interaction with input features, hindering effective retrieval. Therefore, we propose the Memory Unit, composed of multiple parallel memory modules updated via an attention mechanism. We have improved the original update mechanisms of each memory module by integrating a multi-head attention mechanism, as shown in Fig. 3. Specifically, after $X_{TE} \in \mathbb{R}^{T \times D}$ passes through multiple linear layers, it transforms into the tensor required for multi-head attention; the memory module weights $\mathbf{M}$ are processed similarly:

$$\begin{aligned} \mathbf{Q} &= X_{TE} \times W^Q, \\ \mathbf{K} &= \mathbf{M} \times W^K, \\ \mathbf{V} &= \mathbf{M} \times W^V. \end{aligned} \tag{11}$$

The computed $\mathbf{Q}$, $\mathbf{K}$, $\mathbf{V}$ are modeled using the multi-head attention mechanism to obtain $\mathbf{M}' \in \mathbb{R}^{T \times D}$:

$$\mathbf{M}' = \text{Multi} - \text{head attention} \left(\mathbf{Q}, \mathbf{K}, \mathbf{V} \right). \tag{12}$$

Subsequently, the transpose of the memory unit weights $\mathbf{M}'$ is multiplied, normalized, and passed through a Sigmoid activation to yield the query scores $\mathbf{S} \in \mathbb{R}^{T \times T}$:

$$\mathbf{S} = \text{Sigmoid} \left(\frac{\mathbf{X}_{TE}\mathbf{M}'^T}{\sqrt{D}} \right), \tag{13}$$

The query scores $\mathbf{S}$ are then multiplied by the memory module weights $\mathbf{M}$ to obtain the memory-enhanced features $\mathbf{M}_{aug} \in \mathbb{R}^{T \times D}$:

$$\mathbf{M}_{aug} = \mathbf{SM}, \tag{14}$$

where $\mathbf{M}_{aug} \in \mathbb{R}^{T \times D}$ is the output of the feature $\mathbf{X}_{TE}$ after entering a single memory unit.

In addition to the improvements mentioned above, as shown in Fig. 2, due to the potential limitation of a single memory module in storing features, a single memory module is expanded into multiple memory modules. Assuming the output of the i-th memory module is $\mathbf{M}_{aug_i} \in \mathbb{R}^{T \times D}$, $i \in \{1, 2, \ldots, n\}$, after all $\mathbf{M}_{aug_i}$ are computed in parallel, they are concatenated into $\mathbb{M}_{aug} \in \mathbb{R}^{T \times D \times N_{banks}}$. Finally, a linear layer with $W \in \mathbb{R}^{N_{banks} \times 1}$ (where N_{banks} is the number of memory modules) is applied to produce the final output $\mathbf{X}_{Mem} \in \mathbb{R}^{T \times D}$.

2.4 Loss Function

Given the final video scores $\hat{y} \in [0, 1]$, we employ a binary cross-entropy loss function for supervised training:

$$Loss = - \sum_{i=1}^{B} \left(y_i \log \left((\hat{y_i}) \right) + (1 - y_i) \log \left(1 - (\hat{y_i}) \right) \right), \tag{15}$$

where $y \in \{0, 1\}$ represents the labels, and B denotes the size of the batch.

Table 1. Compared with advanced methods

Method	Year	Feature	AP(%)↑	AUC(%)↑
DeelMIL [11]	2018	I3D(RGB)	68.53	89.41
GCN-Ano [19]	2019	I3D(RGB)	75.39	92.13
CLAWS [18]	2020	I3D(RGB)	80.42	95.62
AR-Net [15]	2020	I3D(RGB)	71.58	88.59
MIST [4]	2021	I3D(RGB)	72.85	94.53
RTFM [12]	2021	I3D(RGB)	77.96	96.30
CTMIL [13]	2022	I3D(RGB)	86.63	98.41
TPNet [5]	2023	I3D(RGB)	90.74	98.97
ours	**2024**	**I3D(RGB)**	**92.22**	**99.43**

3 Experiment

3.1 Experiment Settings

Dataset. We use a combined dataset of HyperKvasir [2] and LDPolypVideo [8], totaling over one million frames with varied polyps. In alignment with the methodology of [5] and [13], the training set includes 61 normal and 102 polyp videos, while the test set has 30 normal and 60 polyp videos. Training annotations are at the video-level frames; testing uses frame-level frames.

Evaluation Metrics. Consistent with the approach outlined in [5] and [13], this study employs the frame-level Area Under the Receiver Operating Characteristic curve (AUC) and AP as the metrics for evaluation.

Implement Details. To ensure the fairness of the experiments, this paper adheres to the experimental setup proposed by Gao *et al.* [5] and Tian *et al..* [13], conducting training on the PyTorch platform using an NVIDIA 2080 Ti GPU. Each video is segmented into 32 video clips, and a pre-trained I3D model [3] is utilized to extract 2048-dimensional features from the mixed5c layer. The Adam optimization algorithm is employed, with a training batch size set to 16, over 2500 epochs, and a learning rate of $1e-4$, without the application of any data augmentation techniques. Additionally, the number of memory blocks within each memory module of the Memory Unit is set to 256, and the dimensionality D in X_{TE} and X_{Mem} is configured to 512.

3.2 Comparison with Advanced Methods

Quantitive Evaluation. To provide a comprehensive evaluation of the performance of the model proposed in this paper, this chapter compares it with the most recent state-of-the-art weakly supervised video anomaly frame detection models [4, 11, 12, 15, 18, 19], as well as the latest techniques designed specifically

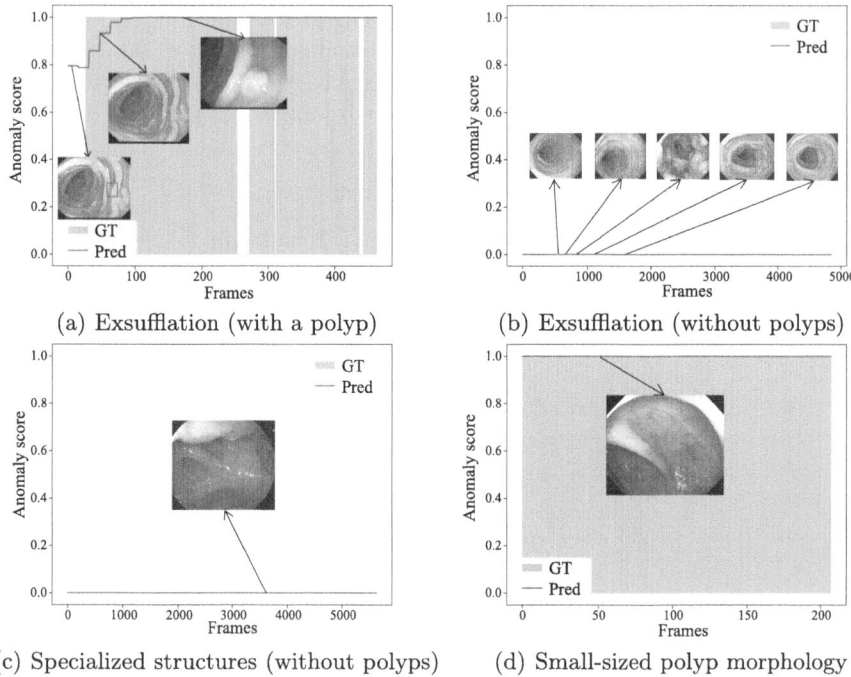

(a) Exsufflation (with a polyp)

(b) Exsufflation (without polyps)

(c) Specialized structures (without polyps)

(d) Small-sized polyp morphology

Fig. 4. Anomaly score visualization: 'GT' denotes ground truth, while 'Pred' signifies the prediction conclusion.

for polyp frame detection, CTMIL [13] and TPNet [5]. In this experiment, our model maintains consistent parameter settings with the aforementioned models and conducts a fair comparison using the same features extracted from a pre-trained I3D model. As depicted in Table 1, the AP of our model is 92.22%, which represents an improvement of approximately 1.5% over TPNet. The AUC is 99.43%, marking an enhancement of about 0.46% over TPNet and nearing the 100% threshold. Surpassing the state-of-the-art methods in both AP and AUC metrics, our model substantiates the effectiveness of integrating associations between different frames and mapping data into a higher-dimensional space for storage, retrieval, and updating.

Qualitative Evaluation. In Fig. 4(a) and 4(b), analyze the large intestine under exsufflation, with and without polyps, showing the model's ability to differentiate normal and abnormal frames without false positives or negatives. Figure 4(c) illustrating the model's ability to accurately differentiate between specialized structures and polyps. Figure 4(d) shows the model's response when polyps are of a smaller size, indicating that the proposed model has a strong capability to identify even minor polyps.

The experiments confirm the model's efficacy in distinguishing between normal and polyp structures and in reducing exsufflation-related interference in colonoscopies. The model adeptly learns specialized characteristics, enhancing its robustness in the exsufflated intestinal environment.

Table 2. Ablation experiment

Multiple memory banks	GL-MHSA	MHA-updated memory bank	Bi-LSTM	AP(%)↑	AUC(%)↑
				86.20	98.58
✓				90.29	98.88
✓	✓			91.77	99.31
✓	✓	✓		91.17	99.10
✓	✓		✓	91.60	99.22
✓	✓	✓	✓	**92.22**	**99.43**

3.3 Ablation Experiment

Ablation studies elucidate the contributions of various components in this chapter's methodology. Key insights from Table 2 include:

(1) Multiple memory modules significantly boost precision. This suggests that utilizing multiple memory modules allows for more effective storage and retrieval of information, thereby improving the model's ability to distinguish between colorectal polyps and normal tissue.

(2) GL-MHSA led to an improvement in performance, which proves the importance of acquiring and integrating global and local temporal information.

(3) Combining Bi-LSTM with multi-head attention outperforms their individual use, capturing and storing temporal patterns more effectively through enhanced guidance and broader retrieval.

(4) Compared to the baseline model, the inclusion of multiple memory modules, GL-MHSA, multi-head attention for updating memory modules, and Bi-LSTM are indispensable. This demonstrates that after the Temporal Encoder captures extensive information, the memory unit stores essential features and enables more precise and robust colorectal polyp frame detection.

3.4 Parameter Experiment

We investigate the impact of the number of memory modules in the Memory Unit on model performance. The number of memory blocks ranged from 1 to 8, and the results are summarized in Table 3. The data indicates that with two memory modules, both AP and AUC reach their highest performance levels.

Table 3. Parameter Experiment

Memory banks	AP(%)↑	AUC(%)↑
1	91.82	99.19
2	**92.22**	**99.43**
4	91.23	99.13
8	91.28	99.14

4   Conclusion

In this work, we introduce TEmory, a novel weakly supervised polyp frame detection method. Our approach employs a Temporal Encoder to capture global and interactive relationships within colonoscopy videos, thereby improving robustness by addressing inter-frame relationships and mitigating exsufflation event interference. Additionally, we propose a Memory Unit composed of multiple parallel memory modules, each updated via a multi-head attention mechanism. This Memory Unit effectively stores and retrieves salient information, enabling deeper interaction between memory modules and input features to select more representative features. This enhances the model's ability to distinguish polyps from normal structures. Extensive experiments demonstrate that our method achieves state-of-the-art performance in weakly supervised polyp frame detection.

Acknowledgements. This work is supported by the National Natural Science Foundation of China (No. 62276221, No. 62376232); the Open Project Program of Fujian Key Laboratory of Big Data Application and Intellectualization for Tea Industry, Wuyi University (No. FKLBDAITI202203).

References

1. Ahn, S.B., Han, D.S., Bae, J.H., Byun, T.J., Kim, J.P., Eun, C.S.: The miss rate for colorectal adenoma determined by quality-adjusted, back-to-back colonoscopies. Gut Liver **6**(1), 64 (2012)
2. Borgli, H., et al.: Hyperkvasir, a comprehensive multi-class image and video dataset for gastrointestinal endoscopy. Sci. Data **7**(1), 283 (2020)
3. Carreira, J., Zisserman, A.: Quo vadis, action recognition? A new model and the kinetics dataset. In: Proceedings of the IEEE Conference on Computer Vision and Pattern Recognition, pp. 6299–6308 (2017)
4. Feng, J.C., Hong, F.T., Zheng, W.S.: MIST: multiple instance self-training framework for video anomaly detection. In: Proceedings of the IEEE/CVF Conference on Computer Vision and Pattern Recognition, pp. 14009–14018 (2021)
5. Gao, J., Luo, Z., Tian, C., Li, S.: TPNet: enhancing weakly supervised polyp frame detection with temporal encoder and prototype-based memory bank. In: Chinese Conference on Pattern Recognition and Computer Vision (PRCV), pp. 470–481. Springer (2023)

6. Hendrycks, D., Gimpel, K.: Gaussian error linear units (GELUs). arXiv preprint arXiv:1606.08415 (2016)
7. Itoh, H., Misawa, M., Mori, Y., Kudo, S.E., Oda, M., Mori, K.: Positive-gradient-weighted object activation mapping: visual explanation of object detector towards precise colorectal-polyp localisation. Int. J. Comput. Assist. Radiol. Surg. **17**(11), 2051–2063 (2022)
8. Ma, Y., Chen, X., Cheng, K., Li, Y., Sun, B.: LDPolypVideo benchmark: a large-scale colonoscopy video dataset of diverse polyps. In: de Bruijne, M., et al. (eds.) MICCAI 2021. LNCS, vol. 12905, pp. 387–396. Springer, Cham (2021). https://doi.org/10.1007/978-3-030-87240-3_37
9. Macrae, F.A., Bendell, J., Tanabe, K., Savarese, D., Grover, S.: Clinical presentation, diagnosis, and staging of colorectal cancer. UpToDate. https://www.uptodate.com/contents/clinical-presentation-diagnosis-and-stagingof-colorectal-cancer. Accessed on Feb 2016
10. Shi, X., Chen, Z., Wang, H., Yeung, D.Y., Wong, W.K., Woo, W.C.: Convolutional LSTM network: a machine learning approach for precipitation nowcasting. Adv. Neural Inf. Process. Syst. **28** (2015)
11. Sultani, W., Chen, C., Shah, M.: Real-world anomaly detection in surveillance videos. In: Proceedings of the IEEE Conference on Computer Vision and Pattern Recognition, pp. 6479–6488 (2018)
12. Tian, Y., Pang, G., Chen, Y., Singh, R., Verjans, J.W., Carneiro, G.: Weakly-supervised video anomaly detection with robust temporal feature magnitude learning. In: Proceedings of the IEEE/CVF International Conference on Computer Vision, pp. 4975–4986 (2021)
13. Tian, Y., et al.: Contrastive transformer-based multiple instance learning for weakly supervised polyp frame detection. In: International Conference on Medical Image Computing and Computer-Assisted Intervention, pp. 88–98. Springer (2022)
14. Tresca, A.: The Stages of Colon and Rectal Cancer. The New York Times (2010)
15. Wan, B., Fang, Y., Xia, X., Mei, J.: Weakly supervised video anomaly detection via center-guided discriminative learning. In: 2020 IEEE International Conference on Multimedia and Expo (ICME), pp. 1–6. IEEE (2020)
16. World Health Organization: Colorectal cancer fact sheet. https://www.who.int/zh/news-room/fact-sheets/detail/colorectal-cancer. Accessed 11 July 2023
17. Xu, J., et al.: Real-time automatic polyp detection in colonoscopy using feature enhancement module and spatiotemporal similarity correlation unit. Biomed. Sig. Process. Control **66**, 102503 (2021)
18. Zaheer, M.Z., Mahmood, A., Astrid, M., Lee, S.-I.: CLAWS: clustering assisted weakly supervised learning with normalcy suppression for anomalous event detection. In: Vedaldi, A., Bischof, H., Brox, T., Frahm, J.-M. (eds.) ECCV 2020. LNCS, vol. 12367, pp. 358–376. Springer, Cham (2020). https://doi.org/10.1007/978-3-030-58542-6_22
19. Zhong, J.X., Li, N., Kong, W., Liu, S., Li, T.H., Li, G.: Graph convolutional label noise cleaner: train a plug-and-play action classifier for anomaly detection. In: Proceedings of the IEEE/CVF Conference on Computer Vision and Pattern Recognition, pp. 1237–1246 (2019)

20. Zhou, H., Yu, J., Yang, W.: Dual memory units with uncertainty regulation for weakly supervised video anomaly detection. In: Proceedings of the AAAI Conference on Artificial Intelligence, vol. 37, pp. 3769–3777 (2023)

RGB+Skeleton: Cross-Modal Fusion Training for Human Action Recognition

Ming-Xuan Lin[1], Wei-Huang Zhang[1], Hong-Ming Qiu[1], Hong-Bo Zhang[1(✉)], and Miao-Hui Zhang[2]

[1] Department of Computer Science and Technology, Huaqiao University, Xiamen, China
{lmx,21014083101,qiuhongming}@stu.hqu.edu.cn, zhanghongbo@hqu.edu.cn
[2] Institute of Energy Research, Jiangxi Academy of Sciences, Nanchang, China

Abstract. Single-modality Human Action Recognition (HAR) approaches often fall short in achieving satisfactory performance in recognizing specific actions, attributable to inherent data features. Therefore, we propose a multimodal fusion approach for HAR, rooted in the fusion of skeleton and RGB video. This framework entails training the model separately using both skeleton and RGB video to extract action features intrinsic to each modality. Subsequently, the fusion of skeleton and RGB video is pursued from two key perspectives: classification results and action features. In terms of classification results, we explore and discuss four methods: the confidence-based optimal selection method, the bimodal weighted sum method, and two variations of models reliant on the fusion of classification probability. Regarding action features, we propose a cross-modal fusion training based on action features, operating on both skeleton and RGB video models. This strategy utilizes features from one modality to augment the training of the other, facilitating multimodality fusion at the feature level. The proposed multimodal fusion strategy is compared to existing methods on two large datasets: NTU RGB+D and NTU RGB+D 120. Experimental results underscore the effectiveness of the propsoed approach.

Keywords: Human Action Recognition · Multi-modality Fusion · Classification Results · Action Features

1 Introduction

The purpose of Human Action Recognition (HAR) is to identify the intentions and purposes behind human actions through the analysis of body postures and movements. It has wide applications in human daily life. For example, recognizing and scoring the movements of athletes in sports such as figure skating, gymnastics, and diving [1]. Besides, it can also be applied in the fields of video surveillance [2] and human-computer interaction [3], etc. The challenge of the task is to model spatio-temporal information from preprocessed temporal sequences, analyze the motion cues inherent in the input data, and establish a mapping between input data and action categories [1].

H. Sun et al. (Eds.): ChineseCSCW 2024, CCIS 2343, pp. 402–413, 2025.
https://doi.org/10.1007/978-981-96-2373-0_28

Current methods mainly use two data modalities: skeleton and RGB video. Skeleton data provides skeleton joint coordinates and motion trajectory data of the human body. Previous work utilizing deep learning methods extracts spatio-temporal information from skeleton data, such as CNN [4,5], RNN [6,7], GCN [8–10], Transformers [11–13]. Some methods focus on using RGB videos as input and have achieved notable performance [14,15]. However, single-modal data have some limitations. skeleton data only captures human movement and deformation, lacking scene context. Many action recognition tasks require semantic understanding based on scene context and interaction goals, which cannot be fully captured by skeleton data alone. In contrast, the RGB video contains complete information about the scene. Therefore, it is necessary to fuse the RGB video and skeleton data to obtain richer human action information.

To address the limitations of single-modal data, we propose a cross-modal fusion method based on RGB and Skeleton data, as illustrated in Fig. 1. We investigate multimodal fusion methods from the perspectives of classification probabilities and action features. From the perspective of classification probabilities, we treat two single-modal feature extraction models as independent entities and discuss four different fusion methods using the classification probabilities outputted by these models. From the perspective of action features, we propose a feature cross-fusion training strategy that allows the data from the skeleton and RGB video to be mutually correlated during model training. To further validate the effectiveness of the proposed method, it is compared with the existing approaches on the NTU RGB+D [16], and NTU RGB+D 120 [17] dataset, and the results demonstrate that the proposed method outperforms similar methods.

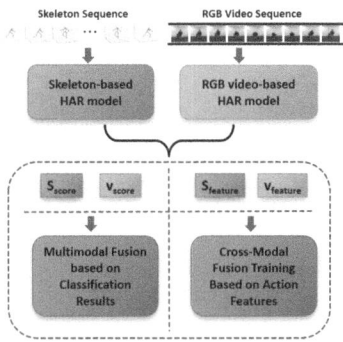

Fig. 1. Illustration of the proposed Cross-Modal fusion method based on Skeleton and RGB videos.

2   Methodology

In this section, we provide a concise overview of the overall architecture of the proposed method, followed by a detailed discussion on the selection of human action feature extraction models. Subsequently, we delve into the exploration of multimodal fusion methods from two key perspectives: classification probabilities and action features.

2.1   HAR Model on Single Modal

Skeleton-Based HAR Model. Due to the difficulty of effectively capturing spatial correlations between human joints using CNNs and RNNs, and the over-reliance on the natural topology of human skeletons in methods based on GCNs, which easily overlooks correlations between non-adjacent joints. To address the above problem, we integrate the advantages of GCNs and Transformers and propose a Skeleton-based Sub-action Partition-Aggregation Network (S-SPAN) for extracting skeleton features, as shown in Fig. 2. This method consists of two key components: the Sub-action Encoding (SaE) and Sub-action Attention-Aggregation (SaA-A). In SaE, we employ the raw skeleton data as input, which is used to partition sub-actions and capture the skeleton features of these sub-actions. To effectively focus on the inherent topology of human skeletons, we utilize GCN to process the skeleton features of the raw skeleton data. To model the temporal dependencies between sub-actions, in SaA-A, the attention weights within each sub-action are first computed. Subsequently, we employ Temporal Convolutional Network (TCN) [19] to process the sub-action sequences.

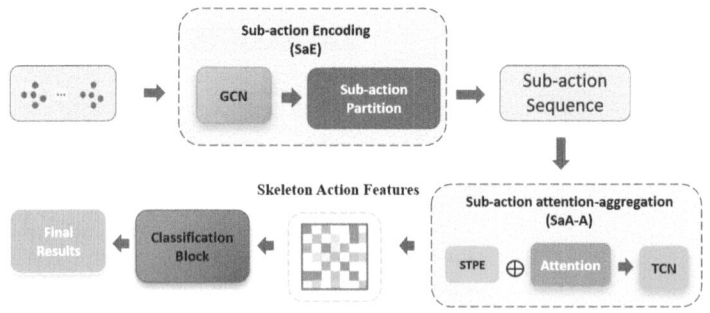

Fig. 2. Illustration of the proposed skeleton-based HAR model.

RGB Video-Based HAR Model. For RGB video-based HAR approach, we chose the Video Swin Transformer [15] as the baseline model. This model reduces the explosive growth in computational complexity caused by the transition from images to videos, limiting the computational load to a reasonable range while maintaining recognition accuracy.

This is a classic video processing model that effectively models the temporal and spatial information present in RGB video and extracts the action features of human actions from the video. The loss function for the RGB video-based HAR model is:

$$Loss_{cls} = -\sum_{i=1}^{c} \left(\widehat{Y}^i \times log \left(Y^i_{scores} \right) \right) \tag{1}$$

where C is the number of action categories, $\widehat{Y}^i$ represents the one-hot vector of the true human action label, and Y^i_{scores} represents the predicted results of the raw RGB video corresponding to the i-th human action category.

2.2   Multimodal Fusion Based on Classification Results

This method treats two basic HAR models as independent entities, taking the recognition results of two single-modal models as inputs. It integrates skeleton and RGB video based on classification results, as shown in Fig. 3. Specifically, we use four different fusion strategies to merge the two modalities.

Confidence-Based Optimal Selection Method. Due to the respective advantages and limitations of skeleton and RGB video, the results obtained by the model may vary significantly. In response to this phenomenon, we choose to use the best recognition result as the confidence measure for each modality data. Specifically, as shown in Fig. 3(a), we draw inspiration from Markov chains and histogram inspection kernel methods. We regard the process of solving the optimal classification score as the construction of a special optimal solution tree and use the skeleton classification scores and RGB video classification scores as the raw data to build the optimal solution tree. Finally, the predicted probability obtained after softmax is taken as the maximum value, which serves as the optimal classification score for that class. The formula is defined as:

$$Best\_score_i = \begin{cases} S_{score_i} \ if Softmax(S_{score_i}) > Softmax(V_{score_i}) \\ V_{score_i} \ if Softmax(S_{score_i}) < Softmax(V_{score_i}) \end{cases} \tag{2}$$

where S_{score_i} represents the raw classification score extracted by the skeleton-based HAR model. V_{score_i} represents the raw classification score extracted by the RGB video-based HAR model. $Best\_score_i$ is the optimal classification score for the i-th human action category.

Bimodal Weighted Sum Method. For a time series of human action, such as "jumping rope", regardless of how it is input as original data, it represents the action of "jumping rope" in terms of motion features, albeit with different emphases. Therefore, we propose the bimodal weighted sum method, as shown in Fig. 3(b). This method combines the classification scores of the two modalities through weighted fusion to obtain a more comprehensive representation of the classification scores. The formula is defined as:

$$Final\_score = W_S \times S_{score} + W_V \times V_{score} \tag{3}$$

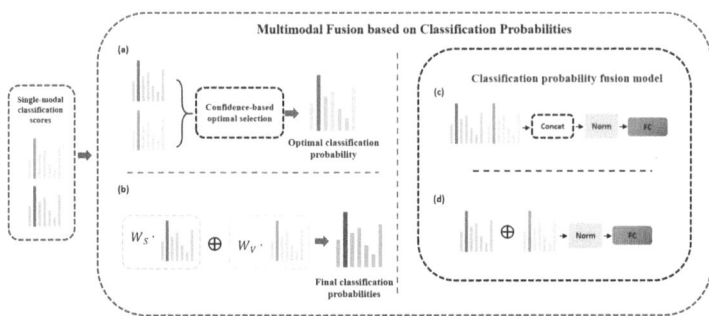

Fig. 3. The four methods used for multimodal fusion based on classification probabilities.

where $Final\_score$ is the weighted final classification score. W_S is the weight corresponding to the skeleton data and W_V is the weight corresponding to the RGB video.

Model for Fusion of Classification Probability Features. Both of the above methods involve direct computation on classification probabilities without model training. To enhance the fusion capability of classification probabilities without increasing time costs, we designed two variants of the classification probability feature fusion model.

Probability feature concatenation method. Regardless of the modality, for each data point, the channels represent spatial representations of its motion information. So, as shown in Fig. 3(c), we first normalize the features of different modalities. Then, we concatenate and fuse the feature channels of different modalities. Finally, we classify the action features after channel fusion through a fully connected layer.

Probability feature addition method. Both modalities of data, after model training and processing, are transformed into feature maps to represent action features. Based on this commonality, we add the feature maps representing different modality motion features at the "pixel" level for fusion processing, and finally classify them. The structure is shown in Fig. 3(d).

2.3   Cross-Modal Fusion Training Based on Action Features

To fuse different modality data at the level of action features, we propose a feature cross-fusion training strategy, where, in the feature extraction model, the action features of another modality are used to assist training. The action features $S_{feature}$ and $V_{feature}$ of skeleton data and RGB video can be obtained from the following equations:

$$S_{feature} = Skeleton\_Model(X_S) \qquad (4)$$

$$V_{feature} = Video\_Model(X_V) \qquad (5)$$

where $Skeleton\_Model(\cdot)$ is the skeleton-based HAR model. $Video\_Model(\cdot)$ is the RGB video-based HAR model. X_S and X_V represent the original skeleton and RGB video, respectively.

As shown in Fig. 4, during model training, the model not only receives the original modality data but also accepts the action features of another modality. For example, during training on the skeleton model, the original skeleton data X_S and the video action feature $V_{feature}$ are input together into the model for training. To prevent adverse effects on training due to the large difference in quantity between the auxiliary training features and the single-modal features, the auxiliary training features are normalized after being input into the model. Then, the auxiliary training features are concatenated with the features obtained by the single-modal model in each training iteration and normalized. The final formulas for this process can be written as follows:

$$S'_{feature} = Norm\_S(S_{feature}) \qquad (6)$$

$$V'_{feature} = Norm\_V(V_{feature}) \qquad (7)$$

$$S_{output} = FC(Norm(Concat(Skeleton\_Model(X_S), V'_{feature}))) \qquad (8)$$

$$V_{output} = FC(Norm(Concat(Video\_Model(X_V), S'_{feature}))) \qquad (9)$$

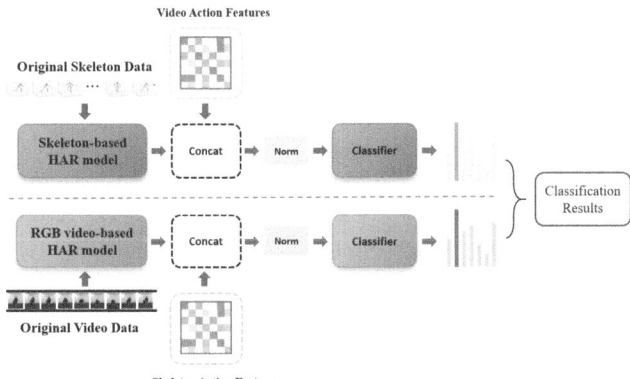

Fig. 4. Illustration of Architecture of Cross-Modal Fusion Training Based on Action Features.

3   Experiments

3.1   Dataset and Setup

Following previous work, we evaluate our method on two benchmark datasets: NTU RGB+D and NTU RGB+D 120. Both datasets contain skeleton data and video data. They are divided into training and testing sets according to different criteria: Cross-Subject (X-Sub) is divided by person ID, and Cross-View (X-View) is divided by camera ID. NTU RGB+D 120 is an extension of NTU RGB+D, adding 57,367 new data sequences, resulting in a total of 114,480 samples.

Implementation Details. We implemented the proposed framework using PyTorch. For the skeleton-based HAR model, we used SGD as the optimizer with a momentum value of 0.9 and weight decay set to 0.0004. The batch size was set to 64, and the number of training epochs was 90. The initial learning rate was set to 0.1, and the learning rate was decayed by a factor of 0.1 at the 60th and 80th epochs. Each input video consists of 120 frames.

For the RGB video-based HAR model, the batch size was set to 32. The number of training epochs was set to 40, and the initial learning rate was set to 0.01. The learning rate was decayed by a factor of 0.1 at the 20th and 30th epochs. Each input video consists of 24 frames, and if a video has fewer than 24 frames, it is padded with frames by cyclically repeating them to make up 24 frames. Other settings were the same as the skeleton-based HAR model. For the cross-modal fusion training based on action features, the initial learning rate was set to 0.001, and the other settings were the same as the RGB video-based HAR model.

Evaluation Metric. Following the experiments conducted on the NTU RGB+D [8,20,21] previously. We use top-1 accuracy as the evaluation metric.

3.2   Ablation Studies

In this section, we conduct ablation experiments to validate the effectiveness of each component. All experiments are conducted on the NTU RGB+D dataset. For the skeleton data, joint data streams are used in this section for experimentation.

Table 1 compares different fusion methods, all of which show significant improvements in accuracy compared to the single-modal baseline methods. Among them, the bimodal weighted sum method achieved the best performance. Based on these experimental results, subsequent comparisons will use the bimodal weighted sum method as the multimodal fusion method based on classification probabilities.

Compared with the method based on classification probabilities, the result show that regardless of the baseline model, using the cross-modal fusion training based on action features resulted in better performance. This is because the strategy incorporates features from different modalities into the training process of single-modal models, facilitating better feature representation by capturing features that cannot be adequately addressed using only single-modal data.

On another note, comparing the training strategies between the two models, the cross-modal fusion training based on action features is more effective in integrating skeleton and RGB video, particularly in enhancing the performance of the RGB video.

Table 1. Comparison of different multimodal fusion based on classification results in ablation experiments.

Method	X-Sub	X-Set
Single RGB Model	82.1%	88.0%
Single Skeleton Model	89.8%	94.8%
Confidence-based optimal selection method	90.4%	95.2%
Bimodal weighted sum method	**92.5%**	**97.2%**
Probability feature concatenation method	92.3%	95.0%
Probability feature addition method	92.0%	96.1%
Cross-modal fusion training (RGB model)	**92.0%**	**95.8%**
Cross-modal fusion training (Skeleton model)	89.9%	95.2%

Table 2. HAR results on NTU RGB+D comparing our methods with SoTA methods on top-1 accuracy.

Method	Type	Stream	X-Sub	X-View
I3D [18]	RGB	RGB	82.1%	88.0%
Our Skeleton Method	Skeleton	4S	92.5%	96.7%
SGM-Net [22]	RGB+Skeleton	4S	89.1%	95.9%
Separable STA [23]	RGB+Skeleton	4S	92.2%	94.6%
PoseMap [24]	RGB+Skeleton	4S	91.7%	95.2%
MMNet(MS-G3D) [27]	RGB+Skeleton	4S	92.7%	97.0%
Multimodal fusion based on classification results	RGB+Skeleton	4S	93.6%	**97.8%**
Cross-modal fusion training (RGB model)	RGB+Skeleton	joint	92.0%	95.8%
Cross-modal fusion training (Skeleton model)	RGB+Skeleton	4S	**93.8%**	97.4%

3.3   Compared with State-of-the-Art Methods

To evaluate the effectiveness of the proposed method, we compare it with state-of-the-art (SoTA) approaches on two datasets: NTU RGB+D and NTU RGB+D 120. For skeleton data, we fuse four streams(4S): joint, bone, joint motion, and bone motion, with RGB video to obtain the final results.

Table 2 and Table 3 compares our method with SOTA methods on NTU RGB+D and NTU RGB+D 120 datasets, respectively. This result indicates that by fusing the classification probabilities of single-modal models, the recognition accuracy of the model can be effectively improved. As for the cross-modal fusion training based on action features, it can effectively integrate the data from skeleton and video modalities at the feature level.

Table 3. HAR results on NTU RGB+D 120 comparing our methods with SoTA methods on top-1 accuracy.

Method	Type	Stream	X-Sub	X-Set
I3D [18]	RGB	RGB	74.4%	75.4%
Our Skeleton Method	Skeleton	4S	88.7%	90.1%
VPN [25]	RGB+Skeleton	4S	86.3%	87.8%
TSMF [26]	RGB+Skeleton	4S	87.0%	89.1%
Multimodal fusion based on classification results	RGB+Skeleton	4S	90.2%	91.5%
Cross-modal fusion training (RGB model)	RGB+Skeleton	4S	**90.5%**	**92.1%**

3.4   Model Results Visualization

To further validate the effectiveness of the proposed methods, we conducted a visual analysis of the results on the X-Sub subset of the NTU RGB+D dataset. As shown in Fig. 5, the confusion matrix depicts the predicted labels on the x-axis and the true labels on the y-axis. Gradient colors indicate the corresponding sample counts. Due to the features of skeleton and RGB video, there were significant differences in recognition accuracy for certain classes. For example, for the action "typing on a keyboard," the skeleton model baseline achieved an accuracy of only 74.6%, while the video model baseline achieved 80.7%. After fusion, the multimodal fusion based on classification results achieved an accuracy of 85.8%, while the cross-modal fusion training based on action features achieved 84.7%. Both fusion methods demonstrated substantial improvements in accuracy. These results validate the effectiveness of the proposed fusion methods.

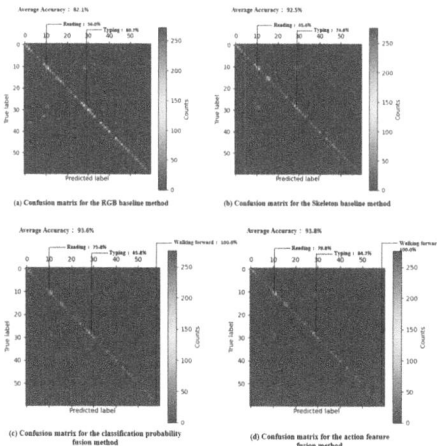

Fig. 5. Visualize the results of the single skeleton and RGB video baseline on X-Sub of the NTU RGB+D and compare them with multimodal fusion method based on classification probabilities and the cross-modal fusion training based on action features.

4   Conclusion and Future Work

We presents a cross-modal fusion method for HAR based on RGB and Skeleton integration. The model trains skeleton and RGB video-based HAR model separately using skeleton and RGB video, respectively, to obtain action features and classification scores for each modality. Subsequently, fusion of skeleton and video modalities is explored from the perspective of classification probabilities and action features. In future research, we plan to incorporate modules that specifically learn hand motion features to enhance the recognition of fine hand movements. Additionally, we aim to strengthen the recognition of similar actions by focusing on the interaction between individuals and the context of the actions.

References

1. Kong, Yu., Yun, F.: Human action recognition and prediction: a survey. Int. J. Comput. Vis. **130**(5), 1366–1401 (2022)
2. Liu, D., et al.: Towards unified surgical skill assessment. In: Proceedings of the IEEE/CVF Conference on Computer Vision and Pattern Recognition (2021)
3. Xu, Z., Wang, G., Guo, X.: Sensor-based activity recognition of solitary elderly via stigmergy and two-layer framework. Eng. Appl. Artif. Intell. **95**, 103859 (2020)
4. Wang, L., Qiao, Y., Tang, X.: Action recognition with trajectory-pooled deep-convolutional descriptors. In: Proceedings of the IEEE Conference on Computer Vision and Pattern Recognition, pp. 4305–4314 (2015)
5. Chéron, G., Laptev, I., Schmid, C.: P-CNN: pose-based CNN features for action recognition. In: Proceedings of the IEEE International Conference on Computer Vision, pp. 3218–3226 (2015)

6. Du, W., Wang, Y., Qiao, Y.: RPAN: an end-to-end recurrent pose-attention network for action recognition in videos. In: Proceedings of the IEEE International Conference on Computer Vision, pp. 3725–3734(2017)
7. Wu, Z., et al.: A coarse-to-fine framework for resource efficient video recognition. Int. J. Comput. Vis. **129**(11), 2965–2977 (2021)
8. Yan, S., Xiong, Y., Lin, D.: Spatial temporal graph convolutional networks for skeleton-based action recognition. In: Proceedings of the AAAI Conference on Artificial Intelligence (2018)
9. Liu, Z., Zhang, H., Chen, Z., et al.: Disentangling and unifying graph convolutions for skeleton-based action recognition. In: Proceedings of the IEEE/CVF Conference on Computer Vision and Pattern Recognition, pp. 143–152 (2020)
10. Niepert, M., Ahmed, M., Kutzkov, K.: Learning convolutional neural networks for graphs. In: International Conference on Machine Learning. PMLR, pp. 2014–2023 (2016)
11. Shi, L., Zhang, Y., Cheng, J., et al.: Decoupled spatial-temporal attention network for skeleton-based action-gesture recognition. In: Proceedings of the Asian Conference on Computer Vision (2020)
12. Plizzari, C., Cannici, M., Matteucci, M.: Spatial temporal transformer network for skeleton-based action recognition. In: Pattern Recognition. ICPR International Workshops and Challenges: Virtual Event, January 10-15, 2021, Proceedings, Part III. Springer, pp. 694–701 (2021)
13. Qiu, H., et al.: Spatio-temporal tuples transformer for skeleton-based action recognition. arXiv preprint arXiv:2201.02849 (2022)
14. Dosovitskiy, A., et al.: An image is worth 16x16 words: transformers for image recognition at scale. arXiv preprint arXiv:2010.11929 (2020)
15. Liu, Z., Ning, J., Cao, Y., et al.: Video swin transformer. In: Proceedings of the IEEE/CVF Conference on Computer Vision and Pattern Recognition, pp. 3202–3211 (2022)
16. Shahroudy, A., Liu, J., Ng, T.T., et al.: Ntu RGB+ D: a large scale dataset for 3D human activity analysis. In: Proceedings of the IEEE Conference on Computer Vision and Pattern Recognition, pp. 1010–1019(2016)
17. Liu, J., et al.: NTU RGB+ D 120: a large-scale benchmark for 3D human activity understanding. IEEE Trans. Pattern Anal. Mach. Intell. **42**(10), 2684–2701 (2019)
18. Carreira, J., Zisserman, A.: Quo vadis, action recognition? A new model and the kinetics dataset. In: Proceedings of the IEEE Conference on Computer Vision and Pattern Recognition, pp. 6299–6308 (2017)
19. Hewage, P., et al.: Temporal convolutional neural (TCN) network for an effective weather forecasting using time-series data from the local weather station. Soft Comput. **24**, 16453–16482 (2020)
20. Shi, L., Zhang, Y., Cheng, J., et al.: Two-stream adaptive graph convolutional networks for skeleton-based action recognition. In: Proceedings of the IEEE/CVF Conference on Computer Vision and Pattern Recognition, pp. 12026–12035 (2019)
21. Weinzaepfel, P., Rogez, G.: Mimetics: towards understanding human actions out of context. Int. J. Comput. Vis. **129**(5), 1675–1690 (2021)
22. Li, J., et al. SGM-Net: skeleton-guided multimodal network for action recognition. Pattern Recogn. **104**, 107356 (2020)
23. Das, S., Dai, R., Koperski, M., et al.: Toyota smarthome: real-world activities of daily living. In: Proceedings of the IEEE/CVF International Conference on Computer Vision, pp. 833–842 (2019)

24. Liu, M., Yuan, J.: Recognizing human actions as the evolution of pose estimation maps. In: Proceedings of the IEEE Conference on Computer Vision and Pattern Recognition (2018)
25. Das, S., et al.: VPN: learning video-pose embedding for activities of daily living. In: Computer Vision-ECCV 2020: 16th European Conference, Glasgow, UK, August 23-28, 2020, Proceedings, Part IX 16. Springer (2020)
26. Bruce, X.B., Liu, Y., Chan, K.C.C.: Multimodal fusion via teacher-student network for indoor action recognition. In: the AAAI Conference on Artificial Intelligence (2021)
27. Bruce, X.B., et al.: MMNet: a model-based multimodal network for human action recognition in RGB-D videos. IEEE Trans. Pattern Anal. Mach. Intell. **45**(3), 3522–3538 (2022)

A Domain-Adapted Brain-Computer Interface for Implicit Emotion Tagging of Multimedia Content

Yanmeng Cui, Wenbin Liang, Yikun Yang, Kechen Hou, Yuhan Shi, Qiqi Zhao, and Xiaowei Zhang

Lanzhou University, Lanzhou 730000, China
{220220941511,liangwb19,yangyk20,houkch22,220220943121,zhaoqq21,
zhangxw}@lzu.edu.cn

Abstract. Tagging multimedia content in terms of emotions can improve the efficiency of user recommendations. Using a Brain-Computer Interface of emotion based on Electroencephalogram (EEG) is a reliable method to annotate the emotions evoked by content. However, the subject-independent models' generalization and re-usability often degrade due to individual differences in EEG data. Hence, in this paper, we proposed a novel unsupervised domain adaptation method incorporating a variant of MMD (Maximum Mean Discrepancy) called Categorical MMD (CMMD) with a curriculum pseudo-labeling module to tackle the above mentioned issue. Unlike the original MMD, CMMD considers the relationship between data belonging to the same category from the source and target domain so that CMMD can align the distribution more than fine-grained. Besides, to mitigate the influence of false pseudo labels on CMMD and final classification, we proposed a curriculum pseudo labeling module that leverages reliable pseudo-target samples and labeled source samples to train the classifier. The experiment was conducted on the SEED dataset to verify our method. The experimental results showed that the proposed method achieves significant performance.

Keywords: Brain-Computer Interface · Emotion Tagging · Electroencephalogram · Domain Adaptation

1 Introduction

How to recommend the content that users crave has been the top priority of numerous multimedia platforms. Established content recommendation methods mainly rely on the content itself or the similarity of interests between users. However, emotion tags can provide additional information about users' preferences and achieve personalized recommendations.

Emotions can be described using the discrete emotion description approach [1] or the dimension approach [2]. For the discrete emotion description approach,

---

Y. Cui and W. Liang—These authors contributed equally to this work.

H. Sun et al. (Eds.): ChineseCSCW 2024, CCIS 2343, pp. 414–425, 2025.
https://doi.org/10.1007/978-981-96-2373-0_29

the emotions are represented by eight basic emotions, all emotions are considered to be a combination of the eight basic emotions. The dimension approach describes emotions in continuous form, in which the emotions are characterized by three dimensions [3] (valence, arousal,and dominance) or simply two dimensions (valence and arousal).

Current emotion tagging methods can be classified into explicit and implicit categories [4]. Explicit tagging methods rely on human tagging with expert system assistance, but they are laborious, expensive, and inefficient. Hence, implicit tagging methods have been proposed, and categorized into two groups. The first is based on non-physiologic signals, such as facial expression images [5], body gestures [6], and voice signals [7]. The second is based on the affective Brain-Computer Interface(BCI). Affective BCI is a technology that can detect, influence, and stimulate affective states, and can be used to adjust human-computer interaction [8]. Electroencephalography (EEG) is collected by several electrodes located on the surface of the human head, reflecting the neural activity directly. Compared with other behavioral signals, EEG signals reflect changes in the central nervous system in human emotional expression, which provides more reliable information for emotions [9]. Based on the aforementioned situation, using BCI-based methods to assign emotion tags to multimedia content is feasible [10]. However, these methods face challenges due to individual differences in EEG data, making it difficult to have a universal model for all participants. Based on this observation, we leveraged unsupervised domain adaptation (UDA) [11] to solve this problem. In this paper, we proposed a novel unsupervised domain adaptation method to assign emotion tags based on EEG signals. Unlike domain adaptation methods that only focus on adjusting global source and target distributions, our approach considers the correlation among data with the same emotion labels. We leverage Categorical Maximum Mean Discrepancy (CMMD) [12] to ensure proper alignment. To address the negative impact of misclassified target pseudo labels on CMMD, we introduced a curriculum pseudo labeling module [13]. Unlike previous UDA methods that only train the classifier on the source domain and assign pseudo labels to target data, our curriculum pseudo labeling module iteratively trains the classifier using both source data and selected reliable pseudo-labeled target data, thereby improving the classifier's performance on the target data.

To sum up, our contributions can be summarized by following three aspects: 1. We proposed a domain adaptation method for implicit emotion tagging based on EEG. 2. We incorporated CMMD with metric learning, thus not only aligning the distribution more fine-grained, but also improving tagging accuracy. 3. We designed a curriculum pseudo-labeling module, thus providing more reliable target labels.

2   Related Works

In recent years, extensive research has been applied to emotion recognition. Zhang et al. [14] proposed a group sparse canonical correlation analysis method for simultaneous EEG channel selection and emotion recognition. Zheng et al. [15] introduced deep belief networks (DBNs) to construct EEG-based emotion recognition models for three emotions. Song et al. [16] combined the graph theory with CNN and proposed a multichannel EEG emotion recognition method based on a dynamic graph convolutional neural network. These algorithms typically involve two main steps: 1. Extracting discriminative EEG features. 2. Inputting the features into a model for classification.

The latest deep learning domain adaptation methods can be divided into two categories. The first category includes adversarial-based methods, such as DANN [17], which encourage the feature extractors to generate non-discriminative features for different domain samples. The second category consists of statistic moment matching-based approaches, like MMD, which construct metrics to measure distribution divergence and employ them as loss functions to reduce domain shift [12,18,19]. Some domain adaptation methods have been applied to EEG-based applications. For instance, Li et al. [20] used a gradient reverse layer to make the source EEG features and target EEG features non-discriminative, thus improving the EEG emotion recognition across subjects and sessions. Zhao et al. [21] introduced a domain discriminator into their model to reduce the divergence. These methods aim to address domain shifts in deep learning and enhance model accuracy.

3   Method

In this section, we introduce our method. Firstly, we define the definition of the problem and introduce relevant concepts. Secondly, we provide a detailed explanation of our model architecture. Finally, we describe the optimization process for our model.

3.1   Problem Definition

In unsupervised domain adaptation, we give two domains: a labeled source domain D_s and an unlabeled target domain D_t. They are sampled from two related distributions p and q. Generally, we denote the labeled source domain $D_S = \{x_{s_i}, y_{s_i}\}_{i=1}^n$ with n labeled samples, and the target domain $D_t = \{x_{t_i}\}_{i=1}^n$ with n unlabeled samples. Our goal is to design a deep neural network $G(x)$ to extract meaningful representations for the input data, and a classifier $f(x)$ to classify target data. There are two challenges to tackle: the first one is how to reduce the divergence between two distributions, and the second is how to build a reliable classifier for target data. To address these challenges, we propose several modules to constitute our model.

We illustrate the overall idea through the model architecture in Fig. 1. The input is extracted from differential entropy features. During training, we feed the network with mini-batches, half of the batch is source data, and the other is target data. We extracted the shallow layer's output to feed into the categorical alignment module. The categorical alignment module utilizes a novel CMMD as the loss function to measure the divergence between conditional distributions. By optimizing CMMD, the source and target distributions are drawn closer, and their alignment by category improves the precision of domain adaptation [22]. CMMD requires both labeled source data and labeled target data for computation. However, in our case, we only have access to labeled source data and unlabeled target data. One common approach in unsupervised domain adaptation (UDA) is to train a classifier using the source data and assign pseudo-labels to the target data. However, this approach has a drawback as it introduces noise from the pseudo-labels. Since our method relies on accurate labels to compute divergence by category, inaccurate labels can negatively impact the performance. Therefore, we designed a curriculum pseudo-labeling module, trying to decrease the influence of noisy pseudo-labels. The working mechanism is shown on the right side of Fig. 1. We borrow the idea of progressive training from curriculum learning [23]. Our proposed module initially uses reliable pseudo-labeled target samples along with labeled source samples to train the classifier. As the training progresses, the number of reliable pseudo-labels increases, and a greater proportion of target domain samples are utilized to train the classifier. After the iteration, the reliable target samples are fed into the model to improve its performance. During the test phase, we input the target domain samples into the frozen Feature Extractor. Then the extracted features are fed into the classifier to obtain the emotion label for the target sample. Finally, we assign the emotion label to the corresponding multimedia content.

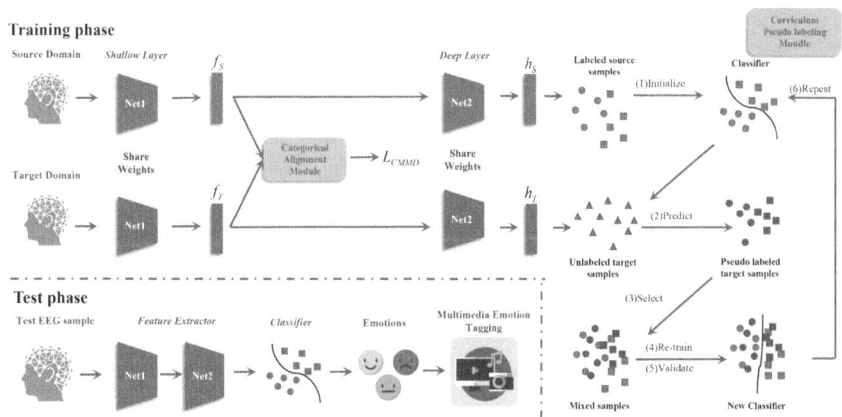

Fig. 1. The flowchart of our method.

3.2   Proposed Method

Our proposed model consists of two main modules: the categorical alignment module and the curriculum pseudo-labeling module. In this section, we provide a detailed introduction to these modules.

Categorical Alignment Module. We implemented this module with a variant of MMD called Categorical Maximum Mean Discrepancy (CMMD). MMD is a kernel two-sample test used to accept or reject the null hypothesis p = q based on observed samples. As a non-parametric distance estimate method, the output of MMD means the divergence between two distributions. The definition of MMD is as follows:

$$d_{\mathcal{H}}(p,q) \triangleq |E_p[\phi(x^s)] - E_q[\phi(x^t)]|^2. \tag{1}$$

where $\mathcal{H}$ represents the reproducing kernel Hilbert space (RKHS) which is specified by a hyperparameter kernel k. In equation (1), $\phi(\cdot)$ denotes the mapping function which can map the original samples to RKHS. The kernel k means $k(x^s, x^t) = \langle \phi(x^s), \phi(x^t) \rangle$, where $\langle \cdot, \cdot \rangle$ means the inner product of two vectors.

Due to its property, MMD is widely used as a loss function in domain adaptation to minimize the divergence between source and target distribution. But as equation (1) implied, the original MMD focuses on reducing marginal distribution between two domains, overlooking the inner relationship of data. Consequently, this approach may lead to misalignment between different types of samples, potentially reducing the robustness of our model. Hence, in domain adaptation, it is crucial to prioritize minimizing the divergence of conditional distributions. Instead of solely reducing the difference between $P_s(x_s)$ and $P_t(x_t)$, the focus shifts to minimize the difference between $P_s(y_s|x_s)$ and $Q_t(y_t|x_t)$. Since there are no labeled samples in the target domain, we can not compute the $Q_t(y_t|x_t)$ directly. Under the assumption of domain adaptation, it is considered that after the completion of domain adaptation, the data from the source and target domains can be regarded as independent and identically distributed (i.i.d). As a result, we can train a classifier on the source domain to provide reliable pseudo-labels for the target data. The categorical maximum mean discrepancy (CMMD) is formulated as follows:

$$d_{\mathcal{H}}(p,q) = \frac{1}{C} \sum_{c=1}^{C} \left\| \sum_{x_i^{sc} \in \mathcal{D}_s} \phi\left(x_i^{sc}\right) - \sum_{x_j^{tc} \in \mathcal{D}_{tc}} \phi\left(x_j^{tc}\right) \right\|_{\mathcal{H}}^2. \tag{2}$$

where C represents the number of categories, and c means each category. Through it, we can compute the differences between different categories of the two distributions. By minimizing CMMD, we can achieve alignment of the conditional distributions.

Curriculum Pseudo Labeling Module. It is evident that CMMD relies on the quality of pseudo labels. Traditional unsupervised domain adaptation methods utilize labeled source samples to train a classifier, and then use the classifier to predict pseudo labels for the target sample. However, this approach is not always reliable. If incorrect pseudo labels are used in the model, the CMMD will align the distributions of different types in the source and target domain, resulting in adverse optimization.

We propose a curriculum pseudo-labeling method that extends the concept of curriculum learning, initially designed for semi-supervised settings, to unsupervised domain learning in our approach. It functions through the following procedures: Initially, the classifier f_θ^t is obtained by sole training on the labeled source samples. Then apply it to the unlabeled target samples to predict their pseudo labels. Each target sample has its labels with prediction scores. In our experiment, the predicted score is obtained by taking the output of SoftMax. The third procedure is selecting, we set a threshold *theres*. The sample with prediction scores bigger than *theres* can be involved in the following steps. We train a new classifier f_θ^{t+1} using the labeled source samples and the selected pseudo-labeled target samples. To ensure the reliability of the classifier, we validate its performance on labeled source samples. If the new classifier f_θ^{t+1} performs worse than the previous version, we retain the previous classifier f_θ^t. On the contrary, if the new classifier shows better performance, we update the classifier to f_θ^{t+1}. This process is repeated, ensuring continual improvement of the classifier through validation and potential roll-back operations.

3.3   Overall Optimization Objective

Based on previous analysis, we can derive the overall objective function as follows:

$$L = L_{classification} + \lambda * L_{alignment}. \tag{3}$$

The first item $L_{classification}$ aims to optimize the classifier on source data. In practice, cross-entropy is commonly used to optimize the classifier. We have:

$$L_{classification} = -\sum_{c=1}^{C} y_c log \hat{y}_c. \tag{4}$$

where y_c denotes the ground-truth labels and $\hat{y}_c$ denotes the predicted labels. c and C mean each category and the number of categories respectively. In this work, we utilized CMMD to compute $L_{alignment}$, the mathematical form is presented in equation(2). Moreover, there is one hyperparameter λ in equation(3). It is utilized to balance the emphasis on training between classification and alignment objectives.

4   Experiment

In this section, we conduct extensive experiments on the SEED (SJTU Emotion EEG Database) [24] dataset which is widely used in EEG signal analysis to evaluate the feasibility of our proposed methods. Initially, we present the experiment results of the tagging task on the SEED dataset. Subsequently, we conduct ablation experiments to demonstrate the superiority of the two-stage sampling triplet loss over the original loss.

4.1   Dataset

The SEED dataset contains EEG data of 15 subjects (7 males and 8 females, the mean age and standard deviation are 23.27 and 2.37). The EEG signals were recorded while the participants watched 15 emotional film clips representing three emotional states: positive, neutral, and negative. During the experiment, a 62-channel electrode cap was used to collect the EEG signals, and the ESI NeuroScan System was applied to record the data with the sample rate 1000 Hz. The film clips were played in random order, and there was a 10-second hint before each clip and a 20-second rest after each clip.

4.2   Preprocessing and Feature Extraction

To address the presence of noise and artifacts in the raw EEG data, several data preprocessing methods were applied. EEG data were downsampled with a sampling frequency of 200 Hz to improve computational efficiency. A bandpass frequency filter from 0 to 75 Hz was utilized to eliminate noise and artifacts. Each preprocessed EEG data was extracted with non-overlapping 1-second time windows. The total number of samples for each subject was 3394 with an equal number of samples for each of the three emotion states. In this study, we employed Differential Entropy (DE) as a feature. DE was computed for each segment in five critical frequency bands: Delta (1–3 Hz), Theta (4–7 Hz), Alpha (8–13 Hz), Beta (14–30 Hz), and Gamma (31–50 Hz). The feature dimension is 310.

4.3   Implementation Details

In our experiments, we utilized a three-layer fully-connected neural network as our feature extractor [25]. The neurons of each layer were 310, 128, and 3. The activation function used for all layers was ReLU [26]. We utilized the 128-dimension output for conditional distribution alignment and computed loss. The last layer of the network is a task-specific layer, and we utilize the 3-dimension output for classification. For optimizing the feature extractor, we utilized the Adam optimizer, which demonstrated superior performance compared to traditional SGD. The learning rate was 0.001. The parameter of Adam was set by default. The training batch size was 96. To avoid noisy activation during the initial stages of training, instead of fixing the trade-off parameter λ, we gradually change it from 0 to 1 by a progressive schedule: $\lambda = 2/(1 + e^{\frac{-10m}{M}}) - 1$, where m and M represent the current epoch and total epoch.

4.4   Experiment Setting

In this section, we introduce the unsupervised domain adaptation experiment setting for EEG-based tagging methods. We follow the experiment setting designed for EEG emotion recognition proposed in a previous work [27]. They conclude with two experiment paradigms: 1. one-to-one transfer (O → O). This setting is used to evaluate the performance of the proposed model under the cross-subject transfer scenario. In each session, the target domain consists of the EEG data from one subject while the data from the remaining subjects are utilized as the source domain. The model's performance on the target subject is evaluated by calculating the mean accuracy across all O → O experiments conducted on the target subject. 2. many-to-one transfer (M → O). In M → O experiment setting, we select one subject as the target domain and utilize the data from all the remaining subjects as the source domain. To validate the feasibility and effectiveness of our model, we compared our methods with other domain adaptation methods including DeepCoral, DAN, and DANN. DeepCoral [28] is an unsupervised domain adaptation method that aligns the second-order statistics of the source and target distributions with a linear transformation. DAN [18] embeds hidden representations of all task-specific layers in a reproducing kernel Hilbert space where the mean embeddings of different domain distributions can be explicitly matched. DANN [17] proposes a new gradient reversal layer to make the features indiscriminate concerning to the shift between the domains.

4.5 Results and Discussion

This section shows the experiment results and explains the improvement brought by our model through visualization.

Table 1. Mean (%) accuracy in One-to-One transfers.

Subject	DeepCoral	DAN	DANN	Our Method
1	68.77	**71.80**	63.95	71.42
2	**60.64**	60.58	53.92	59.31
3	58.95	58.54	**59.68**	59.40
4	**68.71**	66.14	61.48	65.24
5	63.51	63.27	61.18	**64.06**
6	64.59	67.15	62.17	**71.66**
7	65.82	62.14	58.57	**66.48**
8	65.22	67.09	69.27	**71.16**
9	70.00	69.68	64.01	**73.93**
10	**66.31**	65.42	58.20	62.47
11	**71.39**	69.20	62.47	69.19
12	59.47	61.72	59.70	**62.70**
13	67.22	64.98	58.90	**69.21**
14	65.72	66.32	62.01	**71.68**
15	64.69	72.79	63.01	**79.95**
average	65.40	65.78	61.23	**67.85**

One-To-One Transfer. Table 1 shows the performance of four different domain adaptive methods. The first 15 rows show the mean accuracy of all O → O experiments on each target subject, and the last row shows the average results. We can see that our methods perform better than other methods. For all subjects, our method achieves the best performance on 9 subjects. Although our method does not achieve the top performance on the remaining 6 subjects, it consistently achieves the second-best performance.

To verify the effectiveness of the added module, an ablation experiment was conducted by removing the curriculum pseudo-labeling module. The model without the curriculum pseudo-labeling module achieved an accuracy of 65.04, while the complete model achieved an accuracy of 67.85. This ablation experiment confirms the effectiveness of the curriculum pseudo-labeling module. Additionally, it can be observed that the algorithm using conditional distribution alignment outperformed DANN, which aligns only the marginal distributions (Fig. 2).

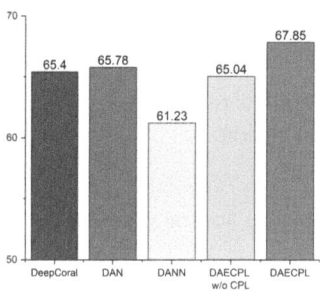

Fig. 2. Ablation experiments.

Multiple-to-One Transfer. Table 2 shows the performance of different methods on multiple-to-One transfer. Our method is far better than other methods, achieving an average accuracy of 82.25%. Compared with other methods, the accuracy of our method is increased by 9.76%-19.27%.

Visualization. T-distributed stochastic neighbor embedding (t-SNE) [29] is a dimensionality reduction technique commonly used for visualizing high-dimensional vectors. In our study, we utilized t-SNE to visualize the features extracted from the shallow layer. As an example, we utilized the data from subject 15, as depicted in Fig. 3. From Fig. 3.a, we can observe that data corresponding to different emotion labels are mixed. From Figs. 3.b–Fig. 3.d, the comparativemethods are more or less able to discriminate EEG data belonging

Table 2. Mean (%) accuracy in Multiple-to-One transfers.

Subject	DeepCoral	DAN	DANN	Our Method
1	76.61	72.39	66.38	**82.50**
2	72.48	67.74	75.60	**79.26**
3	65.23	63.26	74.16	**78.52**
4	76.52	80.02	63.79	**94.20**
5	70.57	68.06	67.00	**85.39**
6	76.99	74.10	66.00	**78.11**
7	71.60	64.41	66.18	**82.26**
8	**77.73**	67.83	69.42	74.31
9	76.93	65.32	78.37	**80.05**
10	82.09	69.42	73.57	**84.50**
11	82.41	72.89	67.65	**90.54**
12	70.71	62.64	66.44	**71.80**
13	76.08	70.48	70.57	**85.42**
14	74.07	67.53	67.00	**83.88**
15	73.95	68.24	67.00	**83.15**
average	74.93	68.96	69.20	**82.25**

to different emotion labels. However, in Fig. 3.e, which is the visualization of our method's t-SNE embedding, we can find that the data corresponding to different emotion labels are well separated.

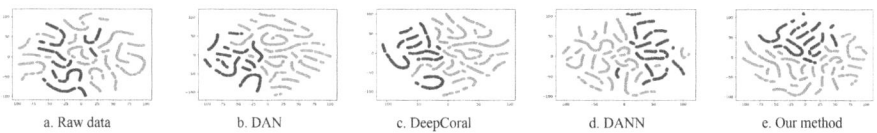

a. Raw data   b. DAN   c. DeepCoral   d. DANN   e. Our method

Fig. 3. Visualization of raw data and four methods' learning representations using t-SNE on One-to-One task for subject 15.

Discussion. Compared to other domain adaptation methods applied to EEG emotion recognition, our method has better performance in both one-to-one transfer and multiple-to-one transfer. Especially, our method has significant improvement over other methods on multiple-to-one transfer. Given the presence of individual differences among subjects, it is crucial to consider the inner variations when the source domain comprises multiple subjects. Merely aligning the marginal distribution between the source and target domains is likely to result in misalignment. Therefore, aligning the conditional distribution becomes necessary to account for these differences. The results verified our hypothesis, that our method has the best performance. The suboptimal method DeepCoral also takes label information into consideration. But it only minimizes the second moment (covariance) between domains, while CMMD can measure infinite moment's divergence between domains by using kernel tricks, so our method has better performance than theirs.

5   Conclusions

In this paper, we proposed a novel unsupervised domain adaptation method for tagging multi-media contents based on EEG signals, which performs better than other methods. Our method can align different distributions by category and embed similar samples closely. Moreover, to eliminate the influence of noisy pseudo-target labels, we introduce a curriculum pseudo-labeling module. The results show an improvement in terms of accuracy. Our method provides a new solution for EEG-based implicit tagging, which is promising for developing robust and reliable automatic emotion tagging applications.

Acknowledgment. This work was supported in part by the National Natural Science Foundation of China (Grant No.62072219), in part by the Natural Science Foundation of Gansu Province, China (Grant No. 22JR5RA401), and in part by the Fundamental Research Funds for the Central Universities (No. lzujbky-2022-ey13).

References

1. Plutchik, R.: The nature of emotions: human emotions have deep evolutionary roots, a fact that may explain their complexity and provide tools for clinical practice. American scientist, vol.89, JSTOR, pp. 344–350 (2001)
2. Mehrabian, A.: Framework for a comprehensive description and measurement of emotional states. In: Genetic, Social and General Psychology Monographs, vol.121, pp. 339–361. IEEE (1995)
3. Mehrabian, A.: Pleasure-arousal-dominance: a general framework for describing and measuring individual differences in Temperament. Current Psychol. **14**, 261–292 (1996)
4. Soleymani, M., Lichtenauer, J.: A multimodal database for affect recognition and implicit tagging. IEEE Trans. Affect. Comput. **3**, 42–55 (2011)
5. Truong, K.P., Van Leeuwen, D.A.: Automatic discrimination between laughter and speech. Speech Commun. **49**, 144–158 (2007)
6. Tong, Y., Liao, W., Ji, Q.: Facial action unit recognition by exploiting their dynamic and semantic relationships. IEEE Trans. Pattern Anal. Mach. Intell. **29**, 683–1699 (2007)
7. Lee, C.M., Narayanan, S.S.: Toward detecting emotions in spoken dialogs. IEEE Trans. Speech Audio Process. **13**, 292–303 (2005)
8. Steinert, S., Friedrich, O.: Wired emotions ethical issues of affective brain-computer interfaces. Sci. Eng. Ethics **26**(1), 351–367 (2020). https://doi.org/10.1007/s11948-019-00087-2

9. Zhang, X., Liu, J., et al.: Emotion recognition from multimodal physiological signals using a regularized deep fusion of Kernel machine. IEEE Trans. Cybern. **51**, 4386–4399 (2021)
10. Li, R., Ren, C., et al.: MTLFuseNet: a novel emotion recognition model based on deep latent feature fusion of EEG signals and multi-task learning. Knowl. Based Syst. **276**, 110756 (2023)
11. Wilson, G., et al.: A survey of unsupervised deep domain adaptation. ACM Transactions on Intelligent Systems and Technology (TIST), vol.11, pp. 1–46. ACM, New York, NY, USA (2020)
12. Long, M., et al.: Transfer feature learning with joint distribution adaptation. In: Proceedings of the IEEE International Conference on Computer Vision (ICCV), pp. 2200–2207 (2013)
13. Cascante-Bonilla et al.: Curriculum labeling: revisiting pseudo-labeling for semi-supervised learning. arXiv preprint arXiv:2001.06001, vol. Proceedings of the AAAI Conference on Artificial Intelligence, pp. 6912–6920 (2021)
14. Zheng, W.: Multichannel EEG-based emotion recognition via group sparse canonical correlation analysis. IEEE Trans. Cogn. Dev. Syst. **9**, 281–290 (2016)
15. Zheng, W.-L., Lu, B.-L.: Investigating critical frequency bands and channels for EEG-based emotion recognition with deep neural networks. IEEE Trans. Autonom. Mental Dev. **7**, 162–175 (2015)
16. Song, T., et al.: EEG emotion recognition using dynamical graph convolutional neural networks. IEEE Trans. Affect. Comput. **11**, 532–541 (2020)
17. Ganin, Y., et al.: Deep coral: domain-adversarial training of neural networks. J. Mach. Learn. Res. **17**, 2030–2096 (2016)
18. Long, M., et al.: Learning transferable features with deep adaptation networks. Int. Conf. Mach. Learn. **37**, 97–105 (2015)
19. Long, M., Zhu, H., et al.: Deep transfer learning with joint adaptation networks. Int. Conf. Mach. Learn. **70**, 2208–2217 (2017)
20. Li, J., et al.: Domain adaptation for EEG emotion recognition based on latent representation similarity. IEEE Trans. Cogn. Dev. Syst. **12**, 344–353 (2019)
21. Zhao, H., et al.: Deep representation-based domain adaptation for nonstationary EEG classification. IEEE Trans. Neural Netw. Learn. Syst. **32**, 535–545 (2020)
22. Chai, Z., et al.: Dual-stream transformer with distribution alignment for visible-infrared person re-identification. IEEE Trans. Circuits. Syst. Video Technol. **33**, 6764–6776 (2023)
23. Bengio, Y., et al.: Deep coral: Curriculum learning. In: Proceedings of the 26th Annual International Conference on Machine Learning, pp. 41–48 (2009)
24. Zheng, W.-L., et al.: Identifying stable patterns over time for emotion recognition from EEG. IEEE Trans. Affect. Comput. **10**, 417–429 (2017)
25. Paszke, A.: Gross, S.: Pytorch: an imperative style, high-performance deep learning library. In: Advances in Neural Information Processing Systems, vol. 32 (2019)
26. Glorot, X., Bordes, A.: Deep sparse rectifier neural networks. In: Proceedings of the Fourteenth International Conference on Artificial Intelligence and Statistics, vol.15, pp. 315–323. JMLR Workshop and Conference Proceedings (2011)
27. Li, J., et al.: Multisource transfer learning for cross-subject EEG emotion recognition. IEEE Trans. Cybern. **50**, 3281–3293 (2020)
28. Sun, B., Saenko, K.: Deep CORAL: correlation alignment for deep domain adaptation. In: Hua, G., Jégou, H. (eds.) ECCV 2016. LNCS, vol. 9915, pp. 443–450. Springer, Cham (2016). https://doi.org/10.1007/978-3-319-49409-8_35
29. der Maaten, Van, et al.: Visualizing data using t-SNE. J. Mach. Learn. Res. **9**, 2579–2605 (2008)

FuNEUA: An Intelligent Edge User Allocation Approach Based on Fuzzy Neural Networks

Shangzhen Zeng[1] and Ningjiang Chen[2,3,4(✉)]

[1] School of Computer and Electronic Information, Guangxi University, Nanning 530004, China
[2] Graduate School, Guangxi University, Nanning 530004, China
chnj@gxu.edu.cn
[3] Key Laboratory of Parallel, Distributed and Intelligent Computing (Guangxi University), Education Department of Guangxi Zhuang Autonomous Region, Nanning 530004, China
[4] The Guangxi Center of Technology Innovation for Intelligent Digital Services, Nanning 530004, China

Abstract. Efficiently allocating users to edge servers in dynamic Mobile Edge Computing (MEC) environments is challenged by fluctuating demands and diverse user preferences. The paper presents FuNEUA (Fuzzy Neural Network based Edge User Allocation), merging fuzzy logic decision-making with neural networks' learning capabilities. By incorporating self-attention mechanism, FuNEUA captures and integrates contextual relationships between users and edge servers, enhancing context-awareness in allocation. Based on fuzzy logic, FuNEUA facilitates localized load balancing optimization among edge servers situated near users. Experiments on real-world datasets demonstrate that FuNEUA outperforms baseline methods across multiple performance metrics.

Keywords: Edge User Allocation · Self-Attention Mechanism · Fuzzy Logic

1 Introduction

The surge in mobile and IoT devices demands high-performance applications, constrained by device resources and battery life. Mobile Edge Computing (MEC) addresses this by deploying edge servers near base stations for immediate services [1]. The Edge User Allocation (EUA) problem, an NP-hard [2] challenge, aims to optimize user assignment to edge servers for swift response times, efficient resource utilization, and reduced service costs, crucial for mobile and IoT providers.

In recent years, numerous methods have emerged to tackle the user allocation challenge in edge computing environments. Traditional approaches include Integer Linear Programming (ILP) [3, 4], game theory [5–8], and Genetic Algorithms (GA) [9], which have been widely used to optimize user allocation on edge servers. Some methods focus on Quality of Service (QoS) requirements [3–6], spatiotemporal proximity [10], historical information [11], and system efficiency [12]. Additionally, techniques based on swarm intelligence [13] and the Lyapunov optimization framework [14] have been explored. Recent advances in deep learning and reinforcement learning have driven the development of edge user allocation algorithms. Methods utilizing Deep Reinforcement Learning (DRL) [15, 16] have significantly enhanced the performance of edge user allocation algorithms. Furthermore, emerging research directions focus on factors such as individual criticality [17], user roles [18], and inter-group latency differences [19], emphasizing the importance of addressing specific demands and environmental constraints in edge computing scenarios. Despite advancements, challenges persist in optimizing allocation rates and maximizing resource utilization efficiency, addressing these conflicting objectives. The paper introduces FuNEUA (Fuzzy Neural Network based Edge User Allocation), combining fuzzy logic flexibility with neural network learning capabilities to enhance edge user allocation amidst complex computing dynamics and uncertainties. FuNEUA integrates a self-attention mechanism to separately encode user and edge server features, integrating critical information from related users and relevant edge servers. Furthermore, FuNEUA employs fuzzy logic for optimizing local load balancing among edge servers, which more accurately reflects current resource usage of edge servers available to users compared to traditional global strategies. The main contributions of our work are summarized as follows:

(1) A novel edge user allocation algorithm, FuNEUA, is proposed, integrating a multi-head attention mechanism for encoding user and edge server features, enhancing contextual awareness, and employing fuzzy logic for intelligent user-to-edge server assignment.
(2) Proposes a local load balancing strategy using fuzzy logic to optimize resource distribution among nearby edge servers in the vicinity of users, mitigating the complexities of global load balancing.

The paper is structured as follows: Sect. 2 presents a case study on edge user allocation (EUA). Section 3 formulates the EUA problem, followed by Sect. 4's introduction of the approach. Section 5 details the experimental evaluation, and Sect. 6 concludes.

2 Motivating Scenario

Efficient localized data processing in agriculture requires innovative resource allocation and service quality solutions. The Edge User Allocation (EUA) problem in smart agriculture involves connecting the sensors deployed in farmlands to their nearby edge servers for efficient data processing. However, limited resources of each edge server necessitate consideration of one sensor's connection impacting others. Service providers aim to minimize server rental costs while maximizing sensor connectivity. The following example illustrates this scenario.

In Fig. 1, if user u_1 is allocated to edge server s_2, the remaining resources in s_2 may not suffice to meet the demands of users u_2 and u_4. This could necessitate either user u_2 or user u_4 connecting to a remote cloud server, thereby increasing latency. However, allocating users u_1 and u_3 to edge server s_1, and users u_2 and u_4 to edge server s_2, ensures that all users can be efficiently served by the edge servers. In practical applications, the EUA problem, encompassing numerous users and edge servers, complicates the quest for an optimal allocation strategy.

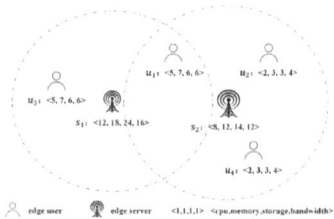

Fig. 1. Example of edge user allocation scenario

3   Problem Formulation

In Mobile Edge Computing (MEC), edge servers are constrained by limited resources and specific service regions. The goal is to devise a strategy that maximizes the number of users served while minimizing active edge servers.

A total of m edge servers are deployed within a geographical area. Let $S = \{S_1, S_2, ..., S_m\}$ represent each edge server, with $slas_{S_i}$ and $slos_{S_i}$ denoting the latitude and longitude of edge server S_i. The signal coverage radius of edge server S_i is denoted by $d(S_i)$, and $a_{S_i}^t$ indicates whether edge server S_i is active at time step t. The remaining resource capacity of edge server S_i at time step t, represented by $C_{t,i} = \langle s_{t,i}^C, s_{t,i}^M, s_{t,i}^B, s_{t,i}^S \rangle$, encompasses CPU, memory, storage, and bandwidth. The set $U = \{U_1, U_2, ..., U_n\}$ represents edge users, where ula_{U_j} and ulo_{U_j} denote the latitude and longitude of user U_j, respectively. $N_{U_j} = \langle n_{U_j}^C, n_{U_j}^M, n_{U_j}^B, n_{U_j}^S \rangle$ represents the resource demand of user U_j across CPU, memory, storage, and bandwidth.

The EUA problem's distance constraint requires user allocation within an edge server's coverage area, which is assessed by projecting coordinates $(slas_{S_i}, slos_{S_i})$ and (ula_{U_j}, ulo_{U_j}) onto a flat plane using the Miller method. The Euclidean distance $distance_{ij}$ between these points determines if a user is within the server's coverage.

$$distance_{ij} \leq d(S_i), \forall S_i \in S; \forall U_j \in U \tag{1}$$

At each time step, the resource constraint ensures that the remaining capacity of each resource type on the edge server accommodates the demands of connected users.

$$S_{t,i}^\sigma \geq n_{U_j}^\sigma, \forall \sigma \in \{C, M, B, S\} \tag{2}$$

4   The Approach

The FuNEUA approach utilizes a multi-head attention (MHA) mechanism to process the input of all user's resource demands $N = [N_{U_1}, ...N_{U_n}]$ and server resource capacity $C = [C_{0,1}, ...C_{0,m}]$. Equation (3) linearly transforms these inputs into a high-dimensional space to improve feature representation.

$$X = W_{proj}x + b_{proj}, \forall x \in \{C, N\} \tag{3}$$

Where W_{proj} and b_{proj} represent the weight matrix and bias vector for the linear mapping. After obtaining the mapped features X, the next step involves projecting the input query, key, and value vectors into different subspaces, as shown in Eq. (4).

$$Q_{h_k} = W_{h_k}^Q X, K_{h_k} = W_{h_k}^K X, V_{h_k} = W_{h_k}^V X \tag{4}$$

Where $W_{h_k}^Q$, $W_{h_k}^K$ and $W_{h_k}^V$ are the weight matrices for the query, key, and value of the k-th head, independent attention calculations are conducted in each subspace.

For each head h_k, the algorithm computes the dot product between each pair (Q_{h_k}, K_{h_k}), then scale it by the scaling factor $\sqrt{d_k}$ to prevent the gradients from becoming very small after the softmax operation. Next, apply softmax operation to the scaled dot products to obtain attention scores. The attention scores are then used to weight the corresponding value vectors V_{h_k} and compute the weighted sum, resulting in the self-attention output for each head, as shown in Eq. (5). For each head h_k, the calculation of self-attention can be represented as Eq. (6).

$$Attention(Q, K, V) = softmax(\frac{QK^T}{\sqrt{d_k}})V \tag{5}$$

$$head_k = Attention(Q_{h_k}, K_{h_k}, V_{h_k}) \tag{6}$$

Next, attention outputs from all heads are concatenated and passed through a linear layer, integrating information into a unified output. The result is added to the original input X for skip connection, followed by layer normalization, as shown in Eq. (7).

$$X\prime = LayerNorm(X + Concat(head_1, head_2, ..., head_k)W^O) \tag{7}$$

Where W^O is the weight matrix for the linear transformation. Subsequently, a two-layer feedforward neural network is utilized to process $X\prime$, as illustrated in Eq. (8).

$$FFN(X\prime) = max(0, X\prime W_1 + b_1)W_2 + b_2 \tag{8}$$

Finally, the output of the feedforward neural network is optimized using skip connections and layer normalization, as depicted in Eq. (9).

$$y = LayerNorm(X\prime + FFN(X\prime)) \tag{9}$$

Having elaborated on the application of self-attention mechanisms, we now delve into the specifics of fuzzy logic. In the FuNEUA framework, the fuzzification layer is employed to transform the residual resource capacity of local edge servers into fuzzy sets using triangular membership functions trim(c, low, mid, high), as depicted in Eqs. (10) to (13).

$$cpu\_fuzzy = trimf(s_{t,i}^C, 0, 0.4 \cdot s_{0,i}^C, 0.8 \cdot s_{0,i}^C) \tag{10}$$

$$mem\_fuzzy = trimf(s_{t,i}^C, 0, 0.5 \cdot s_{0,i}^M, 0.8 \cdot s_{0,i}^M) \tag{11}$$

$$bw\_fuzzy = trimf(s_{t,i}^C, 0, 0.3 \cdot s_{0,i}^B, 0.7 \cdot s_{0,i}^B) \tag{12}$$

$$storage\_fuzzy = trimf\,(s_{t,i}^C, 0, 0.5 \cdot s_{0,i}^S, 0.8 \cdot s_{0,i}^S) \tag{13}$$

Where $S_{t,i}^C$, $S_{t,i}^M$, $S_{t,i}^B$, $S_{t,i}^S$ denote the residual capacity of CPU, memory, storage, and bandwidth of edge server S_i at time step t, and $S_{0,i}^C$, $S_{0,i}^M$, $S_{0,i}^B$, $S_{0,i}^S$ denote their initial capacities. Subsequently, the inference layer computes the mean and standard deviation of the fuzzification layer outputs for each resource type of the local edge server, yielding a fuzzy weight for each resource. This weight ω is then utilized to compute a comprehensive weight W, as specified in Eq. (14).

$$W = \omega^C + \omega^M + \omega^B + \omega^S \tag{14}$$

Where ω^C, ω^M, ω^B, ω^S denote the fuzzy weights for CPU, memory, bandwidth, and storage, respectively. The resulting W is employed in the subsequent output layer to compute the score of the edge server relative to the current user, which integrates the normalized residual resource capacity rcr_{S_i} of the current edge server, self-attention score att_{S_i} and activation status $a_{S_i}^t$, as depicted in Eq. (15).

$$score_{S_i} = (W * rcr_{S_i} + (1 - W) * a_{S_i}^t + att_{S_i}) \tag{15}$$

Finally, the edge server with the highest score is selected for allocation. The model's loss function harmonizes user allocation rates and edge server utilization, delineating into two components: user allocation loss L_{user} and edge server activation loss L_{server}, both evaluated using Binary Cross Entropy Loss, as depicted in Eq. (16).

$$L = -\left[ylog\hat{y} + (1 - y)log(1 - \hat{y}) \right] \tag{16}$$

Where y denotes the target label, and $\hat{y}$ denotes the model's predicted probability. For L_{user}, $y = 1$, while for L_{server}, $y = 0$. The total loss $L_{total} = L_{user} + L_{server}$. Finally, the weighted total loss $L_{weighted}$ is calculated, as depicted in Eq. (17).

$$L_{weighted} = \sum_{i=1}^{n} p_i \cdot L_{total} \tag{17}$$

Where p_i is the normalized value of the i-th element of the mutil-head attention mechanism context vectors, and n is the dimensionality of the context vector.

This section outlines the FuNEUA approach, encompassing multi-head attention, and the fuzzification and inference processes. Further sections detail experimental evaluation, showcasing FuNEUA's efficacy over baseline methods.

5   Experiments and Evaluation

5.1   Experiment Setup

The experiment utilized the EUA dataset [1] [2] from Melbourne's CBD, Australia, widely used in this research field.

---

[1] www.github.com/swinedge/eua-datase

Edge Server Dataset: A network of 125 edge servers was configured with randomly varying coverage radii (100–150 m) to mimic non-uniform deployment. Initial server resource capacities were randomly drawn from a normal distribution.

Edge User Dataset: To simulate real-world edge computing environments, user nodes were randomly positioned within the coverage areas of edge servers, with random resource demands allocated. Based on reference [5], resource demand patterns were randomly selected from { $< 1,2,1,2>$, $<2,3,3,4>$, $<5,7,6,6>$ }.

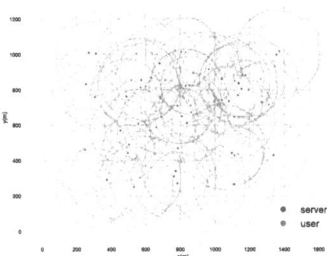

Fig. 2. Example Distribution of Edge Servers and Users.

Data Settings: Experimental setups and parameters are detailed in Table 1. Experiments covered dynamic user counts, edge server numbers, and server capacity means. Each group included 100 independent test datasets. Figure 2 depicts the spatial layout of 500 users and 65 edge servers in one dataset. The FuNEUA model used 100,000 additional datasets for training. Model parameters included an embedding dimension of 128, 8 attention heads, and a hidden layer dimension of 512. Training optimization spanned 100 epochs with an initial learning rate set to le^{-3}.

All the experiments were conducted on a system with an Intel Core i7-12700 processor (20 CPUs, 2.10GHz) and 32GB RAM.

Table 1. Experiment Dataset Settings

	Number of users	Number of servers	Mean server resource capacity (μ)
Set #1	100, 200, …, 1000	50%	40
Set #2	500	10%, 20%,…, 100%	40
Set #3	500	50%	20, 30, …, 80

The proposed method was benchmarked against four representative approaches. Details of the baseline methods are as follows:

- Random: Users are randomly allocated to edge servers based on geographic coverage and adequate hardware resources to meet their demands.

- Greedy: Users are assigned to edge servers with the highest resource capacity, disregarding the current activation status of these servers.
- MCF [5]: Users are sorted by ascending resource needs and allocated in a manner akin to a greedy algorithm, prioritizing already activated edge servers.
- DRoEUA [12]: A fuzzy control mechanism is used for real-time user allocation to edge servers, relying only on local information for quick responses.

5.2   Results and Analysis

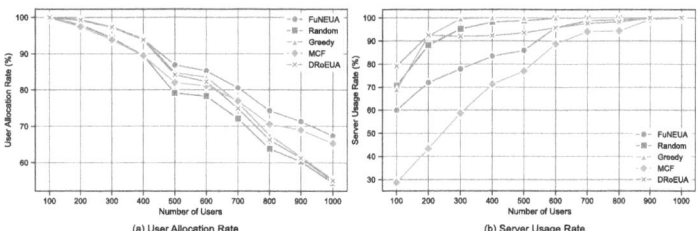

Fig. 3. Performance metrics for user number variation

In Experiment Set #1, as the number of edge users increased from 100 to 1000 in increments of 100, Fig. 3a illustrates that FuNEUA surpasses other methods by approximately 3% in allocation rates when user numbers exceed 400, attributed to its adept integration of user and server features in the deep learning phase. Figure 3b indicates that FuNEUA and MFC both excel in server activation rates; MFC enhances performance by prioritizing inactive servers during allocation, while FuNEUA uses fuzzy logic control for local load balancing among active servers, optimizing their workload. Overall, FuNEUA adapts effectively to increasing user counts while maintaining lower server activation rates.

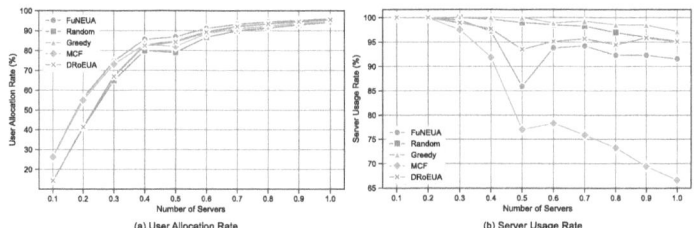

Fig. 4. Performance metrics for edge server number variation

In Experiment Set #2, edge servers spanned from 10% to 100% of the total 125 servers in 10% increments. Figure 4a indicates that FuNEUA consistently leads in allocation rates, outperforming other methods by about 2% when server availability exceeds 20%. Figure 4b shows that both FuNEUA and MCF exhibit a rapid decline in activation rates

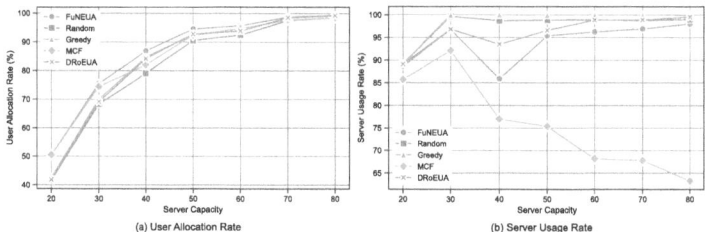

Fig. 5. Performance metrics for mean edge server resource capacity variation

as more servers become available. Overall, FuNEUA adapts effectively to fluctuating server numbers while ensuring efficient resource utilization.

In Experiment Set #3, edge server mean capacity ranged from 20 to 80 in 10-unit increments. Figure 5a illustrates that FuNEUA consistently maintains the highest user allocation rate. In Fig. 5b, FuNEUA's activation rate remains lower than Random, Greedy, and DRoEUA with increasing capacity. Overall, FuNEUA adeptly adapts to increasing resource capacities while optimizing server activation rates.

Experiments highlight FuNEUA's enhanced performance in user allocation and resource management over baseline methods. It enables effectively adapting to diverse user counts, server numbers, and resource capacities in edge computing.

5.3 Ablation Experiments

The ablation experiments evaluate the effectiveness of the self-attention mechanism and fuzzy logic, respectively, using the best-performing Experiment Set #1.

NAT-EUA omitting fuzzy logic selects edge servers based on attention scores.

Fu-EUA excluding self-attention follows the MFC baseline to prioritize user needs and select edge servers.

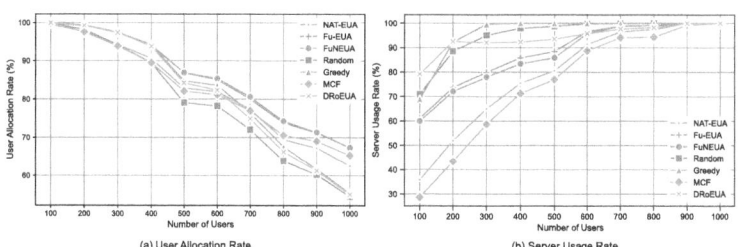

Fig. 6. Performance metrics for ablation experiments

Figure 6 shows that both NAT-EUA and Fu-EUA methods fall short in user allocation and server activation rates compared to the proposed FuNEUA method. This confirms that the integration of self-attention and fuzzy logic in FuNEUA can enhance user allocation and reduce server activation rates.

6 Conclusions

In this study, we introduce FuNEUA, an edge user allocation method that combines neural networks and fuzzy logic. By utilizing a multi-head attention mechanism, FuNEUA effectively encodes user and edge server features, thereby enhancing contextual awareness in allocation decisions. Furthermore, it incorporates a fuzzy logic-based local load balancing strategy to optimize resource utilization among adjacent edge servers, circumventing the need for complex global load balancing. Through a well-trained model, FuNEUA achieves real-time high-quality solutions. Evaluations on a real dataset demonstrate that FuNEUA not only improves edge user allocation rates but also maintains relatively low edge server activation rates.

Acknowledgments. This work is supported by the National Natural Science Foundation of China (No. 62162003) and the Central Guiding Local Technology Development Fund (No. GuikeZY24212059).

References

1. Hu, Y.C., Patel, M., Sabella, D., Sprecher, N., Young, V.: Mobile edge computing—a key technology towards 5G. ETSI White Paper, Sophia Antipolis, France (2015)
2. Lai, P., et al." Optimal edge user allocation in edge computing with variable sized vector bin packing. In: Proceedings of the 16th International Conference Service-Oriented Computing (ICSOC) , pp. 230–245. Hangzhou, China (2018)
3. Lai, P., et al.: QoE-aware user allocation in edge computing systems with dynamic QoS. Future Gener. Comput. Syst. **112**, 684–694 (2020)
4. Lai, P., et al.: Edge user allocation with dynamic quality of service. In: Proceedings of the 17th International Conference Service-Oriented Computing (ICSOC), pp. 86–101. Toulouse, France (2019)
5. Kumar, S., et al.: A cost-effective and QoS-aware user allocation approach for edge computing enabled IoT. IEEE Internet Things J. **10**(2), 1696–1710 (2022)
6. Lai, P., et al.: Quality of experience-aware user allocation in edge computing systems: a potential game. In: Proceedings of the 40th International Conference Distributed Computing Systems (ICDCS), pp. 223–233 (20200
7. Cui, G., et al.: Interference-aware SaaS user allocation game for edge computing. IEEE Trans. Cloud Comput. **10**(3), 1888–1899 (2020)
8. He, Q., et al.: A game-theoretical approach for user allocation in edge computing environment. IEEE Trans. Parallel Distrib. Syst. **31**(3), 515–529 (2019)
9. Zou, G., et al.: ST-EUA: Spatio-temporal edge user allocation with task decomposition. IEEE Trans. Serv. Comput. **16**(1), 628–641 (2022)
10. Zou, G., et al.: Spatial-temporal edge user allocation: an expectation confirmation perspective approach. IEEE Trans. Network Serv. Manage. **19**(4), 4918–4931 (2022)
11. He, X., et al.: History-assisted online user allocation in mobile edge computing. In: Proceedings of the IEEE International Conference Web Serv. (ICWS), pp. 140–149 (2022)
12. Wu, C., et al.: Online user allocation in mobile edge computing environments: a decentralized reactive approach. J. Syst. Archit. **113**, 101904 (2021)
13. Li, T., Niu, W., Ji, C.: Edge user allocation by FOA in edge computing environment. J. Comput. Sci. **53**, 101390 (2021)

14. Lai, P., et al.: Dynamic user allocation in stochastic mobile edge computing systems. IEEE Trans. Serv. Comput. **15**(5), 2699–2712 (2021)
15. Panda, S.P., Banerjee, A., Bhattacharya, A.: User allocation in mobile edge computing: A deep reinforcement learning approach. In: Proceedings IEEE International Conference Web Services (ICWS), pp. 447–458 (2021)
16. Chang, J., et al.: Attention-based deep reinforcement learning for edge user allocation. IEEE Trans. Network Serv. Manage. 590–604 (2023)
17. Liu, E., et al.: Criticality-awareness edge user allocation for public safety. IEEE Trans. Serv. Comput. **16**(1), 221–234 (2021)
18. Liu, E., et al.: Role-based user allocation driven by criticality in edge computing. IEEE Trans. Serv. Comput. 3636–3650 (2023)
19. Dang, Y., et al.: Research on fairness algorithm of user allocation problem in MOBA edge gaming. In: Proceedings of the IEEE 96th Vehicular Technology Conference (VTC2022-Fall), pp. 1–5 (2022)

A Class Incremental Network Based on Conditional Strategy for Personalized Feature Combination

Quanyi Ma[1], Haiyan Zhao[1(✉)], Jian cao[2], and Qingkui Chen[1]

[1] University of Shanghai for Science and Technology, Shanghai 200093, China
zhaohaiyan1992@foxmail.com
[2] Shanghai Jiaotong University, Shanghai 200030, China

Abstract. Class-Incremental Learning (CIL) aims to develop a classification model where the number of classes increases gradually over time. CIL needs to address the stability-plasticity dilemma between learning new and existing classes: high plasticity can lead to catastrophic forgetting of old classes, while high stability can impair the model's ability to learn new classes. To alleviate this issue, unlike previous research that starts with a small number of classes, this paper explores a more realistic CIL scenario, beginning class-incremental learning with a model pre-trained on a large set of base classes. For this scenario, this paper proposes a Personalized Feature Combination Network (PFCN), which incorporates a three-stage training strategy. The first stage is feature expansion, where parts of the branches are cloned and expanded, and the network is fine-tuned to learn new data. The second stage is feature separation, where features are separated into global and personalized features using a conditional strategy. The final stage is knowledge fusion, where a unified probability distribution is generated through feature combination. Extensive experiments were conducted on image classification datasets, comparing the proposed model with current state-of-the-art CIL benchmark models. The results show that the proposed model achieves superior performance.

Keywords: Deep Learning · Increment Learning · Catastrophic forgetting · Image Classification

1 Introduction

Current incremental learning methods [1–3] typically begin training with a small number of base classes and gradually add only a few new classes at a time. However, this setup does not align with the requirements of many real-world scenarios. In practical applications, it is often necessary to commence with a pre-trained model containing a large number of categories, which can then be iteratively updated to incorporate new categories and data as needed. Therefore, a practical scenario is to start incremental training with a large number of base classes, and then gradually add a small number of new categories. Part of the technical gap between a small number of classes and a large

H. Sun et al. (Eds.): ChineseCSCW 2024, CCIS 2343, pp. 436–446, 2025.
https://doi.org/10.1007/978-981-96-2373-0_31

number of classes depends on whether pre-training with a large number of classes may be helpful for subsequent new classes, while a small number of classes may lack certain generalization due to the small number of classes. The technical challenge is how to migrate the pre-trained features.

To address this issue, this paper proposes a Personalized Feature Combination Network (PFCN) based on conditional strategies in the context of class-incremental learning. Model training is divided into three stages. The first stage is feature expansion. A branch of the old network is cloned and expanded. The second stage is feature separation, which separates the personalized features that adapt to the new category data and the global features that retain the ability to recognize the old category data in an end-to-end learnable manner, and uses the maximum mean difference (MMD) loss function [4] to form a similar probability distribution. The third stage is knowledge fusion. The global features and personalized features obtained in each incremental stage are fused to generate a unified probability distribution.

The work of this paper makes three contributions:

- A more realistic CIL scenario was studied, which is to use a large number of base classes (for example, 800) to pre-train a model, and then add a small number of new classes in the incremental phase.
- Proposed a three-stage CIL training strategy, including feature expansion, feature separation and knowledge fusion.
- Introduce conditional calculations into CIL, and use conditional policy networks to effectively separate features into personalized features and global features in an end-to-end learnable manner.

2 Related Work

Current techniques utilized in incremental learning can be broadly categorized into three main classes: network regularization, memory or data replay, and dynamic architectures. Network regularization [6, 7] involves introducing additional penalty terms in the loss function or optimizing parameter gradients to constrain the network's parameter updates. Memory or data replay [2] allows the model to access a limited-capacity memory buffer or generate synthetic data for replay [8, 9]. Dynamic architectures typically involve expanding the network architecture or dynamically routing and selecting sub-networks to allocate different parameters for each incremental task, thereby enhancing the model's adaptability.

FedCP [5] applies this concept in federated learning by designing the CPN module to separate and extract global and personalized features on the client side, while integrating features on the server side. Inspired by this, we can also apply it to incremental learning. FA [10] proposed a two-stage training strategy, In contrast, our proposed model delineates three stages, introducing a conditional computation strategy in the feature separation stage to further separate features into global and personalized features. Additionally, we have further refined the score fusion algorithm to adapt to the modified strategy.

3 Algorithm

This chapter introduces the Personalized Feature Combination Network (PFCN) model. The overall architecture of the model is illustrated in Fig. 1. Structurally, the training of PFCN is divided into three phases: the feature expansion stage, the feature separation stage, and the knowledge fusion stage.

3.1 Feature Expansion Stage

In the initial training phase, a pre-trained feature extractor is developed, which is divided into two distinct subnetworks, as illustrated in Fig. 2. The parameters of these subnetworks are denoted as Φ_s and Φ_b, respectively. Here, Φ_s represents the shared parameters within the neural network of the pre-trained model. These parameters will be frozen during the subsequent incremental learning phases and will no longer be updated. On the other hand, Φ_b signifies the task-specific parameters of the neural network, dedicated to training on specific tasks.

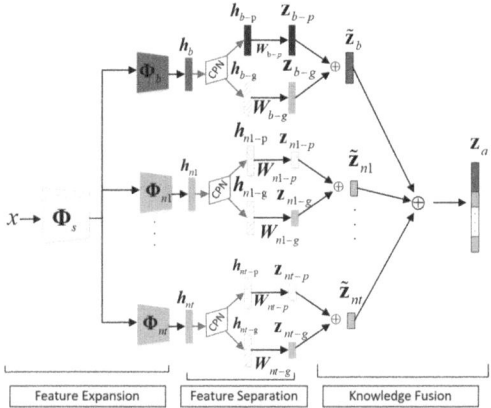

Fig. 1. Overall architecture of PFCN algorithm model. The training of PFCN is divided into three phases: the feature expansion stage, the feature separation stage, and the knowledge fusion stage.

Upon transitioning to the incremental training phase, Φ_b is replicated to create a new subnetwork, denoted as Φ_{nt}, which represents the parameters of the t-th incremental phase. Concurrently, Φ_{nt} is integrated with the subnetwork composed of Φ_s, horizontally expanding the overall network structure. After training during the base phase, Φ_s as the shared parameters remains unchanged and is not updated in subsequent incremental phases. This approach ensures that the feature information embedded in Φ_s is preserved, providing a stable foundation for the recognition of previously learned categories. Simultaneously, by fine-tuning Φ_{nt} and training the weights of the new linear classifier, the model acquires the capability to learn features of new categories.

In order to study the impact of choosing different training layers. The experiment uses Resnet10 [16] as the base network for feature extraction. Based on the number of trainable layers, four experimental groups are divided, the results are summarized (Introduced below) in Table 1.

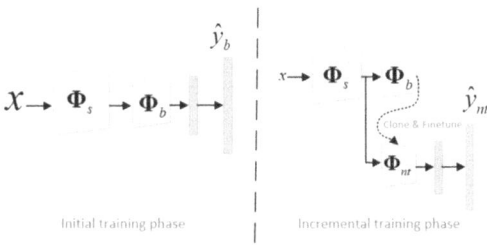

Fig. 2. Schematic diagram of feature expansion. The left side represents the initialization phase, and the right side represents the incremental phase.

Table 1. Effects of Different Training Layers on ImageNet-1K Selection

Dataset	Training	A_{all}	A_{base}	A_{novel}	A_{bal}
ImageNet-1K	1–4 layers	52.34	51.45	75.32	63.38
	2–4 layers	57.15	**55.73**	77.37	66.55
	3–4 layers	57.08	55.50	80.37	67.93
	4 layers	**57.12**	55.27	**83.10**	**69.18**

3.2 Feature Separation Stage

In the feature expansion phase, the feature vector extracted can be denoted as $h_i = f(x_i; \Phi_i)$, where Φ_i represents the weight parameters of the feature layer in the i-th phase, with $i \in \{b, n1, \ldots, nt\}$, and $(x_i, y_i) \in \mathcal{D}_i$ corresponds to its specific dataset. This feature vector (h_i) typically contains both global and personalized feature information. To effectively distinguish and leverage these two types of information, the algorithm introduces the Conditional Policy Network (CPN) [5].

Specifically, the CPN is a compact computational network comprising fully connected layers, normalization layers [11], and ReLU [12] activation functions, parameterized by Θ_i. In the i-th incremental phase, the conditional generation policy can be represented as $\{r_i, s_i\} := \text{CPN}(C_i; \Theta_i)$, where the input $C_i \in R^K$ is specific information introduced to effectively distinguish different features, and the output $\{r_i, s_i\}$ represents the effective parameters for feature separation (as illustrated in Fig. 3). The process of feature separation is accomplished by element-wise multiplying the policy $\{r_i, s_i\}$ with the feature vector h_i, resulting in the global feature $h_{i-g} = r_i \odot h_i$ and the personalized feature $h_{i-p} = s_i \odot h_i$. Given that there may be correlations among features, the degree of this correlation can be quantified by real numbers $r_i^k \in (0,1)$ and $s_i^k \in (0,1)$, where $r_i^k + s_i^k = 1$ for all $\forall k \in [K]$, with K denoting the dimension of the feature space. Inspired by the Gumbel-Max strategy generation trick [11], r_i^k and s_i^k can be generated through the following two steps. First, the CPN generates a pair of constant intermediate values $a_i^k \doteq \{a_{i,1}^k, a_{i,2}^k\}$, and then the softmax function is introduced to calculate the values of r_i^k and s_i^k, ensuring that the sum of r_i^k and s_i^k is always 1, and their values are between $(0, 1)$, as shown in Eq. (1):

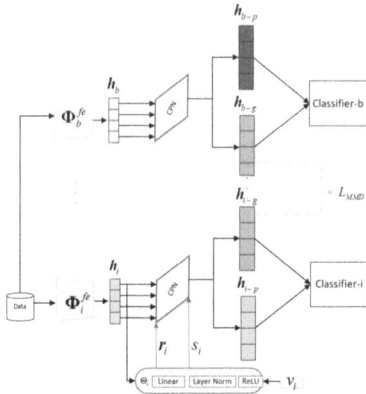

Fig. 3. Schematic diagram of feature separation. Use CPN network to divide features into personalized features and global features.

$$r_i^k = \frac{\exp\left(a_{i,1}^k\right)}{\sum_{j \in \{1,2\}} \exp\left(a_{i,j}^k\right)}, s_i^k = \frac{\exp\left(a_{i,2}^k\right)}{\sum_{j \in \{1,2\}} \exp\left(a_{i,j}^k\right)}. \tag{1}$$

In normal circumstances, the weights of a classifier can be represented as a matrix $W_i^{cls} \in \mathrm{R}^{C \times K}$, where K and C represent the dimensions of the feature space and label space. By selecting specific rows of the matrix, a new vector $v_i = \sum_{c=1}^{C} w_c^T \in \mathrm{R}^K$ is obtained, where each row corresponds to a specific feature in the original matrix. Regarding the acquisition of the specific information input C_i is obtained by element-wise multiplying the personalized features with the vector v_i, v_i is normalized by dividing by its own L2 norm. Each column of this new vector can be matched with the corresponding feature in the separated personalized feature h_{i-p}. Next, by calculating $C_i = (v_i/\|v_i\|_2) \odot h_{i-p}$, where $\odot$ denotes the Hadamard product. v_i is recalculated before each iteration to ensure that it accurately reflects the current state of the model.

In the method, to ensure that the global features $h_{i-g} (i \in \{n1, \ldots, nt\})$ in the incremental stages match the global features h_{b-g} in the basic stage, the MMD [4] loss is introduced to align the output features of these two stages. The core idea of the Maximum Mean Discrepancy loss is to compare the means of two distributions in the Reproducing Kernel Hilbert Space (RKHS) [18], which can effectively calculate the difference between distributions in high-dimensional space. The Eq. (2) is as follows:

$$L_{MMD} = \|E_{(x_i,y_i) \sim \mathcal{D}_i} \Phi\left(h_{i-g}\right) - E_{(x_b,y_b) \sim \mathcal{D}_b} \Phi\left(h_{b-g}\right)\|_{\mathrm{H}}^2, \tag{2}$$

where H is a Reproducing Kernel Hilbert Space (RKHS), and Φ is a specific kernel function (e.g., RBF).

3.3 Knowledge Fusion Stage

The knowledge fusion stage introduces a strategy (as shown in Fig. 1), which integrates the knowledge from all branches to produce a comprehensive output. Mainly includes knowledge transfer and balance optimization methods.

Knowledge Transfer. Each phase's expert model $\{\Phi_i, W_i\}(i \in \{b, n1, \ldots, nt\})$ calculates the probability of individual classifiers. This probability is obtained by applying the softmax function to the logit score $z_i = W_i^T h_i (W_i \in R^{k \times |Y_i|})$. Since the features have been separated, the weights in individual classifiers can be further refined into global weights W_{i-g} and personalized weights W_{i-p}. Therefore, the logit score z_i can also be subdivided into global scores $z_{i-g} = W_{i-g}^T h_{i-g}$ and personalized scores $z_{i-p} = W_{i-p}^T h_{i-p}$. To fuse personalized knowledge and global knowledge, these two scores are added together to get $\tilde{z}_i = z_{i-g} + z_{i-p}$. In a new incremental training phase, the strategy of freezing previously trained feature layer parameters Φ_i, global weights W_{i-g}, and personalized weights W_{i-p} is frozen. Finally, to obtain a unified classifier containing all categories, a concatenation approach is used to combine the logit scores from different branches, forming $z_a = \tilde{z}_b \oplus \tilde{z}_{n1} \oplus \cdots \oplus \tilde{z}_{nt}$, where $\tilde{z}_i \in R^{|Y_i|}, i \in \{b, n1, \ldots, nt\}$.

Balanced Optimization. The training data at each stage can be represented as $x_i \in \mathcal{E} \cup \mathcal{D}_{nt}(i \in \{n1, \ldots, nt\})$, where $\mathcal{E}$ represents a portion of the replayed data from old classes. We uniformly sample a subset $\mathcal{B} \subset \mathcal{E} \cup \mathcal{D}_{nt}$ over all classes, With this class-balanced sampling, the classification loss can be represented as Eq. (3):

$$L_{cls} = \frac{1}{|\mathcal{B}|} \sum -log \hat{p}^{(y_i)}(x_i), \hat{p}(x) = \sigma(z_a). \tag{3}$$

To maintain a balance between the base classes and new classes, an additional regularization mechanism is introduced. First, we design an auxiliary routing classifier aimed at balancing the maximum base class logit score $\tilde{z}_b$ and the maximum new class logit score $\tilde{z}_{nt}$. This routing classifier is defined as Eq. (4):

$$\hat{r}(x) = \sigma\left(W_{r,aux}^T\left(\max_l \tilde{z}_b^{(l)} \oplus \max_l \tilde{z}_{n1}^{(l)} \oplus \cdots \oplus \max_l \tilde{z}_{nt}^{(l)}\right)\right), \#(4) \tag{4}$$

The weight matrix $W_{r,aux} \in R^{(t+1) \times (t+1)}$ is a linear weight, and $\oplus$ denotes vector concatenation. To further achieve the re-balancing of class losses, a re-weighting strategy is adopted, as represented in Eq. (5):

$$L_{rt-bal} = \frac{1}{2|\mathcal{E}|x_i \in \mathcal{E}} \sum_{rt} l_{rt}(x_i, r_i) + \frac{1}{2|\mathcal{D}_n|x_i \in \mathcal{D}_n} \sum_{rt} l_{rt}(x_i, r_i). \tag{5}$$

Finally, a comprehensive loss function considering multiple factors is obtained, as shown in Eq. (6):

$$L_{total} = (1 - \alpha) \cdot L_{cls} + \alpha \cdot L_{rt-bal} + \beta L_{MMD} \tag{6}$$

In this function, α and β are hyperparameters that control the weight of the routing loss and the weight of the global feature probability distribution similarity. The impact of these two hyperparameters on the experimental results is thoroughly investigated through experiments based on the ResNet10 model on the ImageNet-1K dataset. The experimental results using A_{bal} (in %, Introduced below) as the evaluation metric are shown in Table 2. The results show that as α increases, the performance of new classes significantly improves, while the performance of base classes decreases slightly. The results also show that as β increases, the overall performance of new classes exhibits a trend of first increasing and then decreasing. When selecting the best hyperparameters, it

Table 2. The impact of choosing different α and β on the results

	$\beta = 0$	$\beta = 1$	$\beta = 5$	$\beta = 10$	$\beta = 20$
$\alpha = 0.0$	38.93	45.67	53.57	**56.41**	53.25
$\alpha = 0.4$	51.94	67.37	**71.14**	63.21	48.24
$\alpha = 0.6$	54.77	68.64	**70.94**	58.83	52.92
$\alpha = 1.0$	37.45	53.43	53.56	**57.97**	45.44

is necessary to comprehensively consider different design choices and expected measurement methods. If A_{bal} is used as the evaluation metric to select the best hyperparameters, it can be denoted as $A_{bal-best}$.

4 Experiments

4.1 Dataset and Implementation Details

Dataset. ImageNet-1K [13] uses 800 base classes to train the initial model, adding 40 new classes at a time. CIFAR-100 [14] selects 80 classes as base classes and adds 5 new classes at a time.Cars-196 [15] selects 146 classes as base classes for initial model training, adding 10 new classes at a time.

Metrics. Define an evaluation metric $A(S) \in [0,1]$, which measures the overall classification performance of the model on the dataset S at the current stage. Traditional evaluation methods $A_{all} = A(\mathcal{D}_{test})$ focus on the overall accuracy of all classes, Average Incremental Accuracy (A_{avg}) calculates the average accuracy of each incremental stage, as shown in Eq. (7):

$$A_{avg} = \frac{\sum_{d \in \{b, n1, ..., nt\}} A_d}{t+1},$$ (7)

where b represents the base stage, and nt represents the t-th incremental stage. Additionally, The accuracy of base classes (A_{base}) [10] reflects the model's recognition ability for base classes at the end of the current stage, while the accuracy of incremental classes (A_{novel}) [10] measures the model's recognition effect on newly added classes. The specific formulas 8 and 9 are as follows:

$$A_{base} = A(\{(x, y) : (x, y) \in \mathcal{D}_{test}, y \in Y_b\}),$$ (8)

$$A_{novel} = A(\{(x, y) : (x, y) \in \mathcal{D}_{test}, y \in Y_n\}),$$ (9)

The balanced accuracy (A_{bal}) combines the performance of base classes and incremental classes, as shown in Eq. (10):

$$A_{bal} = \frac{(A_{novel} + A_{base})}{2} . \#(11)$$ (10)

4.2 Comparative Experiments

This section experimentally compares the proposed algorithm with benchmark methods such as LwF [6], iCaRL [2], BiC [3], and DER [17]. LwF uses knowledge distillation loss to balance the performance of old tasks and achieves incremental training without accessing any old task data. iCaRL uses a fixed-size memory to store the most representative old task samples and uses the nearest neighbor classifier to expand the classifier. BiC samples a part of the old data for incremental learning and introduces a bias correction layer after the fully connected layer to offset the bias as much as possible. DER decouples feature learning from classifier learning and uses differentiable channel-level masks for dynamic pruning. The overall results are shown in Tables 3 and 4.

The results show that FPCN has a significant advantage over other methods in A_all and A_{bal}. Although LwF [6] surpasses the proposed method in A_{novel}, it also shows that it is biased towards new classes and forgets old classes.

Table 3. Comparative experimental results of different methods (ImageNet-1K)

Model	ResNet10				ResNet18			
	A_{all}	A_{base}	A_{novel}	A_{bal}	A_{all}	A_{base}	A_{novel}	A_{bal}
LwF [6]	9.5	5.54	**88.53**	47.04	9.50	5.46	**90.30**	47.88
iCaRL [2]	16.26	13.91	63.40	38.66	10.65	8.15	60.80	34.78
BiC [3]	30.3	27.55	85.20	56.38	31.50	28.75	86.60	57.68
DER [17]	52.31	52.43	50.10	51.27	54.97	54.19	50.24	52.22
FA [10]	58.90	57.73	82.40	63.06	65.83	64.85	82.50	73.17
ours-$A_{all-best}$	**63.52**	**63.57**	51.67	57.71	**68.83**	**70.01**	58.45	64.23
ours-$A_{bal-best}$	62.15	61.50	75.23	**68.37**	67.14	66.32	82.37	**74.34**

4.3 Ablation Experiments

Ablation Settings. Ablation experiments were conducted on ImageNet-1K with ResNet10 as the base network, and the model was measured using $A_{bal-best}$. First, only the parameters of the classifier were trained without introducing additional model parameters (as shown in Fig. 4a), which was named "only-FC". Second, the performance of the model was studied when CPN was used (as shown in Fig. 4b). This variant was labeled "w/o CPN". In addition, the case of using CPN but not using MMD loss was considered, which was called "w/o MMD". In order to independently study the effect of knowledge transfer, personalized features were tried to be attached to the global logit values of other stages. This variant was called "extra transfer", as shown in Fig. 4c. In addition, we explored the performance of the model without adding the balanced optimization loss parameter to evaluate the impact of balanced optimization on model performance, which was recorded as "w/o balanced". The experimental results are summarized in Table 5.

Table 4. Comparative experimental results of different methods (CIFAR-100)

Model	ResNet10				ResNet18			
	A_{all}	A_{base}	A_{novel}	A_{bal}	A_{all}	A_{base}	A_{novel}	A_{bal}
LwF [6]	13.54	7.89	**77.54**	42.71	14.54	8.58	86.30	47.44
iCaRL [2]	19.53	14.98	75.34	45.16	23.55	23.44	**86.45**	54.95
BiC [3]	35.64	28.76	78.34	53.55	36.25	35.38	82.36	58.87
DER [17]	54.60	50.68	59.43	55.05	61.56	54.19	81.54	67.87
FA [10]	60.34	58.87	74.79	62.32	62.14	59.57	78.42	64.41
ours-$A_{all-best}$	**64.32**	**61.57**	65.67	63.62	**66.54**	**62.42**	67.54	64.98
ours-$A_{bal-best}$	59.67	58.50	74.35	**66.43**	61.55	60.45	79.54	**69.99**

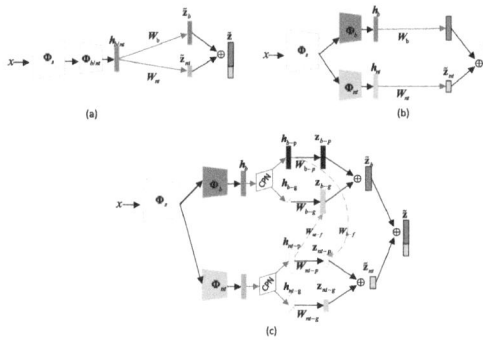

Fig. 4. Schematic diagram of ablation experiment variants. Various ablation experiment variations of the model are included.

Ablation Results. The experiment shows that the classifier of the only-FC model shows excessive bias towards new categories. With the introduction of feature expansion (No. 1 and No. 2), the performance of the model is improved by up to 37.89%. When the CPN network is introduced for feature separation (No. 2 and No. 3), the performance is improved. However, when the MMD loss (No. 3 and No. 6) is removed, the performance of the model decreases. Although additional knowledge transfer is attempted in sequence 4, this strategy does not bring performance improvement compared with sequence 6.

Table 5. Results of ablation experiment (ImageNet-1K)

number	methods	A_{all}	A_{base}	A_{novel}	A_{bal}
1	only-FC	10.42	14.70	79.43	47.06
2	w/o CPN	48.31	45.08	56.27	50.68
3	w/o MMD	56.32	55.56	65.30	60.43
4	extra-transfer	58.50	58.34	66.57	62.46
5	w/o balance	59.69	59.48	71.50	65.49
6	all	62.15	61.50	75.23	68.37

5   Conclusions

This paper proposes a personalized feature combination network (PFCN) based on conditional strategy, divides the model into three stages: feature expansion stage, feature separation stage, and knowledge fusion stage, compares it with the mainstream incremental learning algorithm, and proves its effectiveness through ablation experiments.

Acknowledgments. This work is supported by the Program of Technology Innovation of the Science and Technology Commission of Shanghai Municipality (Granted No. 21511104700).

References

1. Zhao, B., Xiao, X., Gan, G., Zhang, B., Xia, S.-T.: Maintaining discrimination and fairness in class incremental learning. In: Proceedings of the 2020 IEEE/CVF Conference on Computer Vision and Pattern Recognition, pp. 13205–13214. IEEE, Seattle, USA (2020)
2. Rebuffi, S.-A., Kolesnikov, A., Sperl, G., Lampert, C.H.: ICARL: Incremental classifier and representation learning. In: Proceedings of the 2017 IEEE/CVF Conference on Computer Vision and Pattern Recognition, pp. 3366–3375. IEEE, Piscataway, USA (2017)
3. Wu, Y., et al.: Large scale incremental learning. In: Proceedings of the 2019 IEEE/CVF Conference on Computer Vision and Pattern Recognition, pp. 374–382. IEEE, Long Beach, USA (2019)
4. Gretton, A., Borgwardt, K.M., Rasch, M.J., Schlkopf, B., Smola, A.J.: A kernel method for the two-sample-problem. In: Proceedings of the 19th International Conference on Neural Information Processing Systems, pp. 513–520. ACM, Vancouver, Canada (2007)
5. Zhang, J., et al.: FedCP: separating feature information for personalized federated learning via conditional policy. In: Proceedings of the 29th ACM SIGKDD Conference on Knowledge Discovery and Data Mining, pp. 3249–3261. ACM, Long Beach ,USA (2023)
6. Li, Z., Hoiem, D.: Learning without forgetting. IEEE Trans. Pattern Anal. Mach. Intell. **40**(12), 2935–2947 (2017)
7. Kirkpatrick, J., et al.: Overcoming catastrophic forgetting in neural networks. Proc. Natl. Acad. Sci. **114**(13), 3521–3526 (2017)
8. Liu, X., et al: Generative feature replay for class-incremental learning. In: Proceedings of the 2020 IEEE/CVF Conference on Computer Vision and Pattern Recognition Workshops, pp. 226–227. IEEE, Seattle, USA (2020)

9. Shin, H., Lee, J.K., Kim, J., Kim, J.: Continual learning with deep generative replay. In: Proceedings of the 31st International Conference on Neural Information Processing Systems, pp. 2994–3003. ACM, Long Beach, USA (2017)

10. Wu, T.-Y., et al.: Class-incremental learning with strong pre-trained models. In: Proceedings of the 2022 IEEE Conference on Computer Vision and Pattern Recognition, pp. 9601–9610. IEEE, New Orleans, USA (2022)

11. Ioffe, S., Szegedy, C.: Batch normalization: accelerating deep network training by reducing internal covariate shift. In: Proceedings of the 37th International Conference on Machine Learning, pp. 448–456. PMLR, Lille, France (2015)

12. Glorot, X., Bordes, A., Bengio, Y.: Deep sparse rectifier neural networks. In: Proceedings of the Fourteenth International Conference on Artificial Intelligence and Statistics, pp. 315–323. JMLR, Lauderdale, USA (2011)

13. Deng, J., Dong, W., Socher, R., Li, L.-J., Li, K., Fei-Fei, L.: Imagenet: a large-scale hierarchical image database. In: Proceedings of the 2009 IEEE/CVF Conference on Computer Vision and Pattern Recognition, pp. 248–255. IEEE, Miami, USA (2009)

14. Krizhevsky, A., Hinton, G. Learning multiple layers of features from tiny images. Handbook of Systemic Autoimmune Diseases, vol. 1(4), pp. 1–60 (2009)

15. Krause, J., Stark, M., Deng, J., Fei-Fei, L.: 3d object representations for fine-grained categorization. In: Proceedings of the 2013 IEEE International Conference on Computer Vision Workshops, pp. 554–56. ACM, Washington, USA (2013)

16. He, K., Zhang, X., Ren, S., Sun, J.: Deep residual learning for image recognition. In: Proceedings of the 2016 IEEE Conference on Computer Vision and Pattern Recognition, pp. 770–778. IEEE, Las Vegas, USA (2016)

17. Yan, S., Xie, J., He, X.: Der: Dynamically expandable representation for class incremental learning. In: Proceedings of the 2021 IEEE/CVF Conference on Computer Vision and Pattern Recognition, pp. 3014–3023. IEEE, Nashville, USA (2021)

DeepSORT for Human and Cage Vehicle Tracking in Tobacco Logistics

Yucai Shen[1], Xun Zhang[2], Lingfeng Xu[2], Miaowen Guo[2], Jiahong Su[2], and Pengyang Lai[2(✉)]

[1] Fujian Tobacco Company Zhangzhou City, Zhangzhou, China
[2] Xiamen University, Xiamen, China
19105952126@163.com

Abstract. In light of the burgeoning advancements in deep learning, object detection and tracking technologies leveraging surveillance camera infrastructure have emerged as a paramount research focus within computer vision. While multi-object tracking algorithms have long been instrumental in security surveillance applications for monitoring and analyzing human behavior, similar requirements have surfaced in tobacco logistics. Concerning target detection, the erstwhile reliance on sliding window methodologies, plagued by prolonged processing times and elevated false positive rates when scanning entire scenes, has given way to deep learning solutions, which offer enhanced efficiency. This study, therefore, specifically addresses the exigency of detecting illicit activities involving tobacco cage trucks during transportation, presenting a novel DeepSORT-based algorithm for concurrent human and cage truck detection and tracking. The proposed framework is designed to proficiently monitor the movement of individuals and vehicles involved, and automatically identify and report any human violations, thereby facilitating the automation and liberation of human labor in this domain. The main research of this paper is as follows, Harnessing the cutting-edge YOLOv7 algorithm for the detection and classification of humans and cage trucks, thereby significantly enhancing the speed and precision of the detection process. Implementing the DeepSORT algorithm to track and annotate humans and cage trucks, generating valuable time-series data that inform subsequent violation detection procedures. Within the context of the violation detection module, the cost matrix is constructed by calculating the Euclidean distance between the detection frames corresponding to the human and the cage-caged vehicle. The LAPJV algorithm is then employed to establish associations between individuals and their respective cage trucks, followed by the detection and recording of any rule infractions committed by individuals whose actions surpass pre-established violation thresholds.

Keywords: Object detection · Multi-object tracking · Cage Vehicle · DeepSORT

1 Introduction

The rapid advancement of automation technology has increased the demand for intelligent systems in tobacco logistics and transportation, where multi-target tracking and anomaly detection play crucial roles in enhancing efficiency and safety. This paper explores the application of target tracking algorithms in detecting violations within the tobacco logistics sector.

Most visual multi-target tracking research relies on the Tracking by Detection (TBD) paradigm, which includes a target detector and a tracker. Efficient target detection algorithms are critical for accurate tracking. Traditional methods are often time-consuming and less accurate compared to deep learning-based approaches, which can automatically extract features, improving both accuracy and speed. Deep learning-based target detection algorithms can be categorized into one-stage and two-stage methods. Given the need for real-time detection, this paper focuses on the single-stage YOLO algorithm, known for its speed and efficiency. To detect and localize illegal activities, multi-target tracking algorithms are necessary to correlate targets and their trajectories. This paper adopts DeepSORT, which combines deep learning-based target detection with multi-object tracking, balancing real-time processing and accuracy.

In tobacco logistics, real-time surveillance and autonomous detection of infractions are essential. An integrated approach using an allocation algorithm and a logical judgment algorithm helps identify deviations in behavior and take appropriate actions, mitigating the risk of cargo loss and ensuring product integrity and security.

2   Related Work

2.1   Object Detection

Object detection has perennially constituted a thriving research subject within the realm of computer vision. Recently, the confluence of neural network technology advancements and computational power enhancements has catalyzed the ascendancy of deep learning-based object detection methods. As a critical challenge confronting computer vision, the YOLO (You Only Look Once) series of algorithms have found extensive applications in the domain of object recognition. YOLOv1 introduced a straightforward, expedient solution, yet its limitations in detection accuracy restricted its applicability across diverse scenarios. With the maturation of computer vision techniques, the SSD (Single Shot MultiBox Detector) model embraced the Anchor mechanism [1], enabling direct regression of target coordinates and categorical predictions, thereby efficiently accommodating objects of varying scales and achieving heightened detection accuracy compared to YOLOv1. Consequently, SSD gained widespread adoption in object detection tasks.

In pursuit of enhanced accuracy without sacrificing detection speed, YOLOv2 underwent enhancements. Despite these improvements, its detection accuracy remained inferior to that of two-stage models, thus limiting its widespread utilization. To rectify the foreground-background class imbalance issue, the RetinaNet [2] model was proposed, elevating the performance of single-stage detectors, particularly in low-light and intricate backgrounds. Technological progression led YOLOv3 to adopt the Anchor concept, employing various Anchor size configurations and quantities to facilitate the detection of differently sized targets, thereby excelling in complex environments. YOLOv4 further augmented model accuracy through data augmentation techniques and training strategies, pushing detection accuracy to unprecedented levels. Data augmentation-wise, YOLOv4 incorporated a diverse array of methods such as random cropping, rotation, and flipping, bolstering model generalization. Training-wise, it embraced an adaptive learning rate adjustment technique, expediting model convergence during the training phase.

Although YOLOv5 has not published a paper, it builds upon YOLOv4, further refining accuracy while maintaining exceptional speed and enabling swift detection of vast image datasets. Most recently, YOLOv7 has emerged, outperforming extant detectors in both speed and accuracy within the 5 fps to 160 fps range [3]. The advent of YOLOv7 elevates the practical performance of object detection technology, furnishing a more convenient and efficient solution for myriad application contexts.

2.2 Target Tracking

Multi-target tracking revolves around the detection and assignment of distinct identifiers to numerous targets, such as pedestrians, vehicles, and animals, within videos where the quantity and nature of targets remain unknown. This process enables subsequent trajectory forecasting and accurate target retrieval. Fundamentally, it tackles the data association dilemma in target tracking, leveraging cues like motion and appearance features to facilitate this association.

The current visual multi-target tracking research mainly uses the detection tracking (TBD) model, which combines object detection and tracking functions. In practical implementations, detection-driven multi-target tracking necessitates the deployment of both detection and tracking models. Recently, a substantial portion of advancements in TBD methodologies have emerged through enhancements and investigations of algorithms akin to SORT [4] and DeepSORT [5], collectively referred to as Sort-like algorithms. Among the classics are SORT, DeepSORT, ByteTrack, and OC-SORT [6].

The SORT algorithm employs a Kalman filter for predicting target motion states. It then utilizes the Intersection over Union (IOU) values between the predicted bounding boxes and those output by the detection network as correlation costs, harnessing the Hungarian algorithm for data association and effective target tracking. DeepSORT improves upon SORT by incorporating deep learning networks for extracting target features as a matching criterion and implementing cascaded matching to mitigate ID switches amidst target overlaps, occlusions, or abrupt motions. By employing the Mahalanobis distance between prediction and detection frames to encapsulate target motion characteristics, it assigns new labels to outliers, thereby diminishing ID switches during target proximity. ByteTrack [7] further refines this methodology via a dual-matching strategy. Leveraging the affinity between detection frames and tracking trajectories, it filters out low-confidence background detections while preserving high-confidence ones, unearthing true objects amidst challenging scenarios such as occlusions and blur, thus minimizing detection leakage and bolstering trajectory consistency. Many of the subsequent algorithms also refer to all three ideas.

3   Application of YOLOv7

Considering the stringent demands for precision and real-time performance in tobacco logistics modeling, this study eschews conventional object detection approaches in favor of the YOLO end-to-end framework for the object detection phase. Within the lineage of

YOLO algorithms, YOLOv7 stands out for its superior detection accuracy and processing velocity, its capability to accommodate higher resolution imagery, and its efficacy in detecting multi-scale targets, thereby furnishing dependable data inputs for succeeding tracking algorithms. The principal architecture of the YOLOv7 object detection model (see Fig. 1).

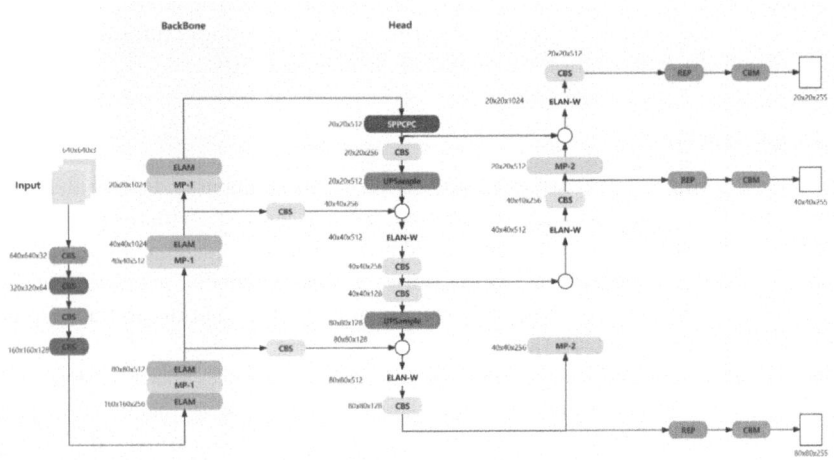

Fig. 1. YOLOv7 network structure.

3.1 Input Section

The input component entails resizing the input image to a consistent dimension, conforming to the backbone's specified input requirements. YOLOv7's input module mirrors the preprocessing methodology and pertinent source code employed in YOLOv5. A distinguishing factor lies in YOLOv7's primary training and evaluation on relatively larger images, such as 640*640 and 1280*1280, consequently necessitating more substantial memory provisions compared to YOLOv5. Adopted techniques encompass mosaic data augmentation, adaptive anchor box calculation, and adaptive image scaling for optimized performance.

Adaptive Anchor Box Calculation. Within the YOLO framework, datasets vary in their initial provision of anchor boxes with specific dimensions. Network training involves refining these anchors through iterative comparisons with ground-truth bounding boxes. YOLOv3 and YOLOv4 required an external process to compute anchor values for different datasets. From YOLOv5 onwards, this functionality is integrated, dynamically calculating optimal anchor dimensions for each training dataset. YOLOv7 further integrates adaptive anchoring into the stochastic gradient descent process. The decision to use adaptive anchors depends on the dataset and requires empirical evaluation. While theoretically advantageous, practitioners must rigorously validate its effectiveness through model evaluations and hyperparameter tuning.

Adaptive Image Scaling. In object detection, input images are typically preprocessed to a standardized dimension before model inference to ensure accuracy and efficiency. However, this can lead to issues with datasets having diverse aspect ratios, causing varying black border dimensions after scaling and padding. Recent YOLO versions (e.g., YOLOv5 and YOLOv7) address this by dynamically appending minimal black borders. This reduces information redundancy and accelerates inference. For example, resizing an image from 1920*1080 to 1280*1280 involves calculating the scaling factors $Kw = 1280/1920$ and $Kh = 1280/1080$, choosing the smaller one, and applying it to both dimensions. The required padding is then calculated to reach the target dimensions. YOLOv7 uses conventional direct resizing during training but employs this adaptive scaling technique during inference.

Considering YOLOv7 undergoes five stages of down-sampling, to optimally exploit the information characteristics inherent in the network's receptive field, residuals are contemplated 2^5, ultimately necessitating the addition of a 3-pixel black border on both image edges. Practically, however, YOLOv7 confines the utilization of conventional direct resizing to the model training phase; it is exclusively during model inference that this particular approach is employed by YOLOv7.

3.2 Backbone Structure

Backbone architecture encompasses CBS convolutional layers, ELAN convolutional layers, and MPConv convolutional layers. It is embodied in the lower blue part of the structure picture (see Fig. 1) and is mainly used to extract salient image features. Regarding the CBS module [9] (see Fig. 2), it is comprised of a Conv layer (a standard convolutional layer), a BN layer (implementing Batch Normalization), and a Silu layer (an activation function). Depending upon the kernel size and stride, the CBS module manifests three distinct functionalities. The least computationally intensive variant in the illustration features a 1×1 convolution kernel with a stride of 1, chiefly utilized for altering channel dimensions. Meanwhile, a marginally more complex instance within the figure employs a 3×3 convolution kernel, also with a stride of 1.

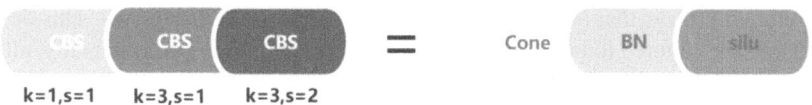

Fig. 2. Schematic diagram of CBS structure

The CBS convolutional layer essentially embodies a composition of Convolution, Batch Normalization, and SiLU activation, with its primary function dedicated to feature extraction. The E-ELAN, a high-efficiency layer aggregation network, enhances the network's learning capacity without disrupting the inherent gradient pathways, thereby facilitating the acquisition of a broader spectrum of features through the guidance of computational blocks across diverse feature sets. Furthermore, the MPConv convolutional layer introduces a MaxPooling layer atop the CBS layer, establishing dual pathways— upper and lower branches [10]. The features procured from these bifurcated routes are subsequently integrated via Concatenation, augmenting the network's proficiency in feature extraction.

The MP module comprises dual branches, primarily serving the purpose of down-sampling. In the first branch, the data traverses a max pooling operation—illustrated as MaxPool in the subsequent figure—whose effect is to reduce spatial dimensions. Subsequently, it undergoes a CBS module to modulate channel depth. Conversely, the second branch initially encounters a 1x1 convolution within the CBS module, effectuating channel alteration before being subjected to a down-sampling convolution module. The concatenation of these two branches achieves an augmented down-sampling effect. Notably, the MP module within the Backbone layer exhibits a channel configuration designated MP-1, as depicted in the figure, whereas the MP module nestled in the Head layer (see Fig. 3) assumes a configuration labeled MP-2. The distinction resides in their dissimilar methodologies for modifying channel counts.

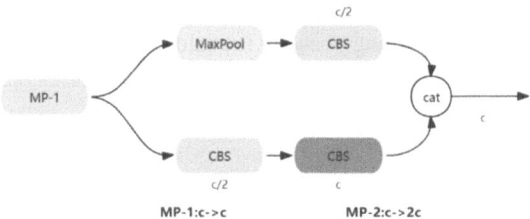

Fig. 3. Schematic diagram of MP-1 structure

Through meticulous regulation of the shortest and longest gradient paths, profound neural networks can effectively facilitate learning and expedite convergence. The ELAN architecture, as proposed by YOLOv7, also integrates a series of varied convolutional concatenations, specifically, multiple instances of CBSs (see Fig. 4). ELAN maintains parity between the dimensions of its input and output features, with the initial two CBSs witnessing variable channel counts [11]. Subsequently, the input channels of the proceeding stages align with the output channels, until the final stage where the channel configuration mirrors that of the initial two CBSs, albeit with adjustments. This design is meticulously tailored to bolster the network's learning prowess incrementally, all the while preserving the integrity of the original gradient path.

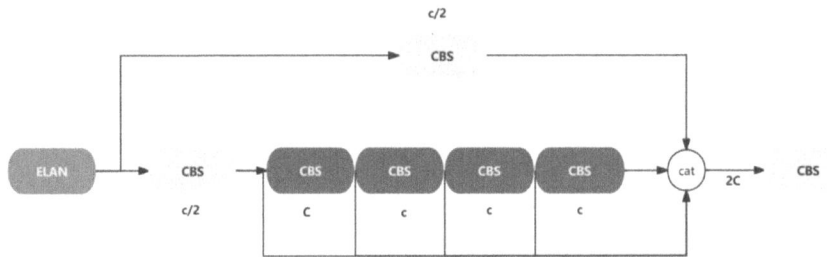

Fig. 4. ELAN structure schematic

3.3 Head Structure

The head network of YOLOv7, situated at the base of the orange section in the illustrated schematic (see Fig. 1), follows a design akin to its predecessors YOLOv4 and YOLOv5. It initiates with the adoption of the Spatial Pyramid Pooling (SPP) structure, enabling the accommodation of multi-sized inputs. Following this, an aggregated feature pyramid network (AFPN) configuration is employed to convey information from lower to higher tiers along an ascending bottom-up trajectory, thereby achieving the integration of multi-level features.

The SPP pyramid structure plays a pivotal role in expanding the receptive field, thereby enhancing the algorithm's adaptability to images of diverse resolutions [12]. By leveraging varied scales of max pooling, the SPP enriches the receptive field, allowing the algorithm to handle objects of different scales effectively. Specifically, as depicted in the subsequent figure, the first branch bifurcates into four sub-branches through distinct scale MaxPools (5 * 5, 9 * 9, 13 * 13, and 1 * 1), each representing a unique receptive field tailored to discern objects of varying sizes. This versatility is crucial for distinguishing between large and small objects within datasets, such as humans and enclosed vehicles, which exhibit notable scale disparities.

This module partition features into dual pathways: one undergoing standard processing and the other processing through the SPP pyramid structure, with subsequent merging of these pathways. This approach halves computational demand, thereby accelerating processing speed while concurrently boosting accuracy (see Fig. 5).

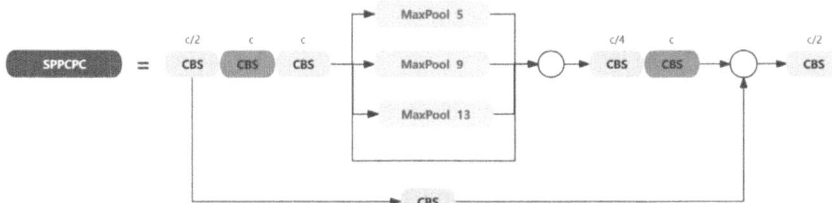

Fig. 5. Schematic diagram of the Head

The header network incorporates a UPSample module, which serves as an up-sampling component utilizing nearest neighbor interpolation methodology. Concomitantly, the ELAN-W module embedded within the header network, as its nomenclature implies, bears a striking resemblance to the fundamental ELAN module (see Fig. 6). The distinguishing characteristic lies in the selection of output quantities within the secondary branch: while the ELAN module consolidates three output features, the ELAN-W module escalates this by integrating five output features for fusion.

At the end of the network, the number of channels is adjusted for different scales of features through the REP module. YOLOv7 uses a different REP module for training than for inference. As shown in the figure below, the training REP module has three branches, the top branch is a 3x3 convolution for feature extraction, the middle branch is a 1x1 convolution for feature smoothing, and the last branch is an IDentity without

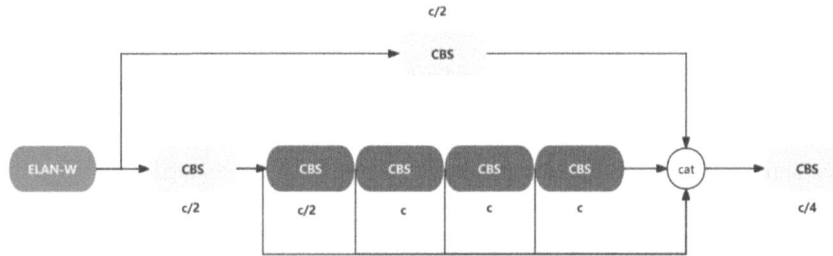

Fig. 6. ELAN-W structure schematic

convolution, and the three branches are merged at the end. module eliminates the residuals in ResNet and splicing in DenseNet, providing more gradient diversity for different feature mappings; the REP module (see Fig. 7) for inference requires the structural reparametrization of the three branches from training, and using matrix addition, to sum up their weights to obtain a 3×3 convolution.

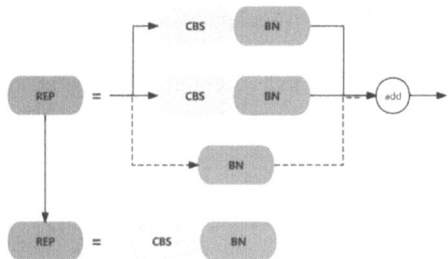

Fig. 7. Schematic diagram of REP structure

The last module to go through is the CBM module, which is roughly the same structure as the CBS module, and also has a convolutional layer, a BN layer, and a layer of sigmoID - an activation function. The convolution kernel is 1x1 with a step size of 1.

4 DeepSORT Target Tracking Algorithm

The TBD model is the paradigm for many current multi-target tracking methods, with recent research predominantly focusing on Sort algorithm derivatives, colloquially referred to as Sort-like algorithms. These frameworks typically encompass two primary components: the first is the "motion branch," which engages in motion modeling and state estimation to forecast trajectories in subsequent frames; the second associates newly detected targets with the current trajectory set.

Within the motion branch, target tracking algorithms conventionally employ a constant velocity model via a discrete Kalman Filter to model planar image object motion [13]. By leveraging the present motion parameters, predictions for the immediate future are made, constituting what is termed a "Track." This Track necessitates correlation with the upcoming frame's detection outcomes in the succeeding stage, known as data association. There are two main approaches: computation of predicted intersections (IoU) between trajectory targets and detected targets based on localization, and computation of associations via appearance features of the ReID model.

The Sort algorithm confines itself to calculating IoU distances between the current frame's detections and the Kalman-filter-predicted Tracks from the preceding frame. These IoU distances serve as metrics for constructing a cost matrix, which is then inputted into the Hungarian algorithm to yield linear assignments. Nonetheless, in scenarios involving abrupt target movements, such as a person forcefully pushing a cart, substantial discrepancies may arise between the consecutive frames' prediction and detection outcomes for the cart. Relying solely on IoU as a metric, Sort algorithms are prone to ID switches, misidentifying carts involved in such actions. To solve this problem, we used the DeepSORT algorithm in our research, which follows the procedural framework of Sort, but modifies the second stage of data association. Unlike Sort, which promptly discards unmatched Tracks, DeepSORT categorizes prediction results into confirmed and unconfirmed states. Freshly minted Tracks are unconfirmed by default, requiring consistent matching with detector outputs over a set number of frames to attain confirmed status. Conversely, confirmed Tracks require a series of mismatches before deletion. Moreover, to mitigate frequent ID switching inherent in IoU-based Sort algorithms, cascaded matching and ReID features are incorporated for enhanced discrimination.

The DeepSORT algorithm employs two methods of correlating motion and appearance information [14]. The correlation method of motion information is to use the squared Mahalanobis distance between the predicted Kalman filtered state and the object detection result to merge the motion information, and the squared Mahalanobis distance is a good correlation metric when the target motion state is in uncertainty.

$$d^{(1)}(i,j) = (d_j - y_i)^T S_i^{-1} (d_j - y_i) \qquad (1)$$

where $d^{(1)}(i,j)$ denotes the Mahalanobis distance between the ith prediction frame and the jth detection frame, d_j is the state of the jth prediction frame, y_i is the state of the ith detection frame, and S_i denotes the covariance matrix of the observation space at the current moment obtained by the Kalman filter prediction.

In the scenario of this paper, when a violation occurs, the speed of the target will undergo a dramatic increase, and this situation will be manifested as a large change in the position between frames, which may be somewhat different from that predicted by Kalman filtering. At this time, if only position information such as IoU is still used for matching, ID switching will easily occur, and it will not be possible to track the same target stably and continuously, which seriously affects the subsequent violation detection algorithms. Therefore, it is necessary to use other related indexes to improve the accuracy, i.e., the ReID feature introduced in the DeepSORT algorithm. When such appearance features are added, even if the target undergoes a large change in position, the target can still be tracked stably based on the appearance information, which greatly improves the tracking stability. The extraction of the appearance features utilizes a deep appearance descriptor, which is instantiated by a primary Convolutional Neural Network (CNN) and pre-trained on the recognition dataset MARS. This helps to extract appearance features from the detection and tracking frames.

DeepSORT employs a dedicated re-identification network for each object detection frame to obtain appearance features and subsequently generates normalized feature vectors representing these appearance features. The prediction frames generated by the tracker go through a similar process of appearance feature extraction. These features constitute a library of 100 frame features that are successfully associated with their respective targets. The cosine distance between the predicted and detected frames is then calculated.

$$d^{(2)}(i,j) = min\{1 - r_j^T r_k^{(i)} | r_k^{(i)} \in R_i\} \qquad (2)$$

The final composite match is obtained by weighting the motion information with the appearance information.

$$c_{i,j} = \lambda d^{(1)}(i,j) + (1 - \lambda)d^{(2)}(i,j) \qquad (3)$$

Parameter *lambdaconstitutes* a hyperparameter, tunable in magnitude, governing the impact of the integrated matching correlation. When configured minimally, it mitigates the effects of sudden high-speed cage car movements, thereby emphasizing reliance on appearance information as the metric. Hence, for disparate tracking objectives, the parameter's scale can be adaptively adjusted by real-time operational contexts to optimally gauge the relevancy of data cues.

As elucidated previously, DeepSORT segregates matching outcomes into definitive and indeterminate states, cascading matches exclusively to targets in definitive states. Initially, tracking frames in a definitive state undergo appearance feature extraction in conjunction with the detected detection frames. Subsequently, a sequential matching process ensues, commencing with the longest uninterrupted trajectories and concluding with the most protracted lost trajectories. Specifically, for a duration of 30 frames from the apex of the uninterrupted timeline to the onset of loss, trajectories are matched to detected counterparts individually for each correspondence established. This prioritization ensures that persistently tracked trajectories are matched beforehand, while the longest-lost trajectories are relegated to the final stages. This strategic sequencing prolongs the lifespan of each trajectory, averting premature termination due to mismatches and thereby diminishes the likelihood of track swapping amidst violation incidents.

5   Violation Detection Algorithms

During the transportation of tobacco products, occurrences of individuals forcefully kicking or pushing cage carts away from themselves, enabling the carts to move autonomously, constitute a violation. This algorithm effectively detects and reports such violations through the combined efforts of target tracking and logical reasoning applied to both persons and cage carts.

The tracking algorithm here first identifies all the targets within a particular frame and then feeds these targets into the violation detection mechanism. Firstly, the targets are classified by type and then the Euclidean center distance between the person and the caged vehicle is calculated. These distances are normalized to construct a cost matrix, and the cage car is assigned a value of 1 for distances exceeding a predetermined multiple of the width of the detection frame for a particular person class - effectively shielding the cage car outside a certain radius. This measure prevents possible distortions from the image viewpoint and ensures the robustness of the analysis. The cost matrix is calculated as Eq. (4).

$$C_{i,j}^{\text{ecu}} = \begin{cases} d_{i,j}^{ecu}, (d_{i,j}^{ecu} < \lambda \times width_i) \\ 1, otherwise \end{cases} \tag{4}$$

The cost matrix undergoes optimization via the LAPJV algorithm, an extension of the classic Hungarian method, rooted in graph theory and operational research, tailored for resolving assignment problems [15]. Central to such problems is pairing entities across two distinct sets, aiming to minimize a predefined cost function. In our context, this cost function embodies the Euclidean centroid distance between monitored individuals and tracked cage carts. In this paper, a cost matrix is set up by mapping the rows of the matrix to the personnel being tracked and the columns to the caged vehicles being tracked, where each entry denotes a 'cost' determined through a Euclidean-centred metric. The Hungarian algorithm, leveraging graph-theoretic and linear programming methodologies, identifies the least costly pairing arrangement. Notably, its application necessitates equal set sizes, a limitation circumvented by LAPJV, which caters to disparate cardinalities—a feature pertinent to our scenario where human and cage cart counts often diverge. The enhancement involves augmenting the original cost matrix with surrogate rows or columns, thereby facilitating the resolution of the primary assignment issue within this expanded framework.

In the protocol for infraction detection, decisions on violation presence transcend singular frame distance breaches, incorporating a temporal constraint mechanism. Concretely, upon acquiring a matched cage cart and registering its identifier, the pair's status remains initialized as FALSE, transitioning to TRUE only upon persistence over a defined frame sequence. Conversely, alterations in matched cage carts, sustained over a similar duration, prompt a switch, safeguarding against spurious associations from momentary proximities.

Actual monitoring for transgressions initiates post-confirmation of a TRUE pairing state. Upon forcible ejection of a cage cart by a person, the rapid deviation in their relative positioning triggers the algorithm. Upon detecting a TRUE tracking target combination, the system scrutinizes the alignment, initiating a violation tally should the inter-centroid distance exceed a threshold—positively correlated with the target's detection frame width. Persistent violation beyond a set frame count prompts a violation report, thereby mitigating sporadic misalignments that might engender false positives. This dual-threshold strategy ensures a vigilant response to actual violations while mitigating false alarm probabilities due to incidental factors. Targets flagged for violations are annotated, and visually indicated, and corresponding violation snapshots are retained, fortifying the system's diagnostic accuracy and evidentiary capabilities. In this algorithm, the judgment is based on whether the center relative distance suddenly becomes larger in a very short number of frames, i.e. in a short period the person and the caged vehicle undergo a large relative motion, so when the person leaves the caged vehicle normally, the center relative distance directly between them does not undergo a sudden increase, avoiding the misjudgment that a person is considered to violate the law due to the increase in the center relative distance when he or she leaves the caged vehicle on his or her initiative.

6 Experiments

6.1 Training

Dataset. We conducted an exhaustive annotation exercise on a total of 1,430 Sample tobacco images, categorizing them into two primary segments: 1,100 images designated for training, aimed at facilitating the algorithm's learning and feature refinement, and a 330-image test subset to gauge the model's generalization capacity and performance. In adherence to the rigorous requisites of lightweight and real-time application scenarios, YOLOv7-tiny was selected as the foundational framework for pre-training the model, primarily due to its substantial reduction in computational complexity and memory consumption while still upholding high detection accuracies.

Throughout the training phase, meticulous parameter tuning was executed to optimize model performance: the number of epochs was set to 300 to ensure ample learning opportunities from the dataset; a batch_size of 16 was adopted to strike a balance between learning efficiency and memory utilization; and the input image dimension (img_size) was adjusted to 1280 pixels, a compromise that allowed capturing finer details without compromising training efficiency. Of utmost significance, the model's performance was meticulously documented at every epoch, culminating in the preservation of the model weights that demonstrated the pinnacle of performance on the validation set. These optimal weights were then employed in the subsequent testing phase, thereby ensuring the reliability of evaluation outcomes and the overall optimality of the model.

Evaluation Metric. In the implementation of the methodology in this paper, we adopt a series of classic and comprehensive evaluation metrics, namely Precision (P), Recall (R), and Mean Average Precision (mAP), to systematically measure and monitor the training effectiveness. As the number of iterations increases, the model's precision and recall increase significantly, which not only highlights the effectiveness of the algorithm optimization but also further confirms the efficiency and success of the training strategy adopted (see Fig. 7). In summary, the training session of this study demonstrated a high degree of effectiveness, laying a solid foundation for subsequent experimental analyses and practical applications.

This study meticulously integrates and assesses a diverse array of multiple object tracking (MOT) algorithms (see Table 1), with the paramount objective of meticulously dissecting the performance disparities amongst these algorithms through a rigorous battery of comparative experiments. Adhering scrupulously to the canonical MOT evaluation framework, three pivotal metrics are employed: MOTA (Multiple Object Tracking Accuracy), MOTP (Multiple Object Tracking Precision), and IDF1 (Identity F1 Score), each of which contributes uniquely to appraising the algorithmic performance under multifaceted dynamic conditions. Complementarily, the algorithms' computational efficiency is quantified via the Frames Per Second (FPS) metric.

MOTA is the core metric of this analysis, providing a comprehensive assessment of tracking accuracy and error rates. It combines the assessment of false detections,

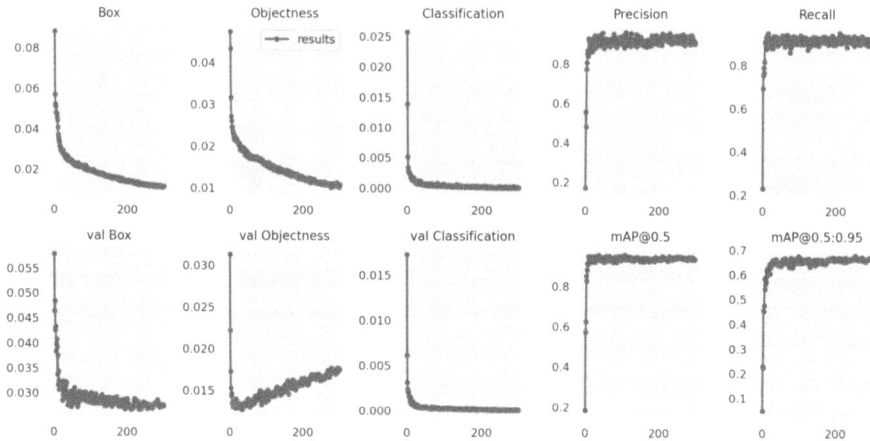

Fig. 8. Model training evaluation metrics

false alarms, and identity conversions to visualize the overall accuracy of monitoring numerous targets. In contrast, MOTP focuses on the localization accuracy of individual targets, emphasizing tracking fidelity through the average difference between predicted and actual bounding boxes. Finally, IDF1 is a metric that combines recognition and recall capabilities and is particularly suitable for measuring the robustness of an algorithm when targets overlap, occlude, or have problematic morphology. As such, it ensures consistent discrimination and uninterrupted tracking of discrete entities even in highly dynamic environments.

Table 1. Targeted tracking evaluation indicators.

Target tracking algorithms	IDF1	MOTA	MOTP	Fps
Sort	70.0%	40.9%	0.059	26
DeepSORT	80.6%	60.3%	0.038	31
Bytetrack	82.0%	56.7%	0.041	50
deepmot	69.1%	44.5%	0.068	32

Presentation of Results. Under standard conditions, the algorithm assigns distinct colors to separate trajectories, and cage-cars inherit the color of their paired person's detection box. This color-coding aids in visualizing the correlation between entities and analyzing behavioral patterns. Potential violations are highlighted with a red detection frame to draw immediate attention to anomalies (see Fig. 8) (Fig. 9) .

Fig. 9. Algorithm results are shown. The figure shows the combined human and caged vehicle, the human-vehicle pairing that did not exceed the threshold, and the caged-vehicle pairing that exceeded the threshold, respectively.

References

1. Liu, W., et al.: SSD: single shot multibox detector. In: Leibe, B., Matas, J., Sebe, N., Welling, M. (eds.) Computer Vision – ECCV 2016. ECCV 2016. LNCS, vol. 9905. Springer, Cham (2016). https://doi.org/10.1007/978-3-319-46448-0_2
2. Lin, T.Y., Goyal, P., Girshick, R., He, K., Dollár, P.: Focal loss for dense object detection. In: Proceedings of the IEEE International Conference on Computer Vision (pp. 2980–2988) (2017)
3. Wang, C.Y., Bochkovskiy, A., Liao, H.Y.M.: YOLOv7: trainable bag-of-freebies sets new state-of-the-art for real-time object detectors. In: Proceedings of the IEEE/CVF Conference on Computer Vision and Pattern Recognition, pp. 7464–7475 (2023)
4. Bewley, A., Ge, Z., Ott, L., Ramos, F., Upcroft, B.: Simple online and realtime tracking. In 2016 IEEE International Conference on Image Processing (ICIP), pp. 3464–3468. IEEE (2016)
5. Wojke, N., Bewley, A., Paulus, D.: Simple online and realtime tracking with a deep association metric. In: 2017 IEEE International Conference on Image Processing (ICIP), pp. 3645–3649. IEEE (2017)
6. Cao, J., Pang, J., Weng, X., Khirodkar, R., Kitani, K.: Observation-centric sort: Rethinking sort for robust multi-object tracking. In: Proceedings of the IEEE/CVF Conference on Computer Vision and pattern Recognition, pp. 9686–9696 (2023)
7. Zhang, Y., et al.: Bytetrack: Multi-object tracking by associating every detection box. In: Avidan, S., Brostow, G., Cissé, M., Farinella, G.M., Hassner, T. (eds.) Computer Vision – ECCV 2022. ECCV 2022. LNCS, vol. 13682. Springer, Cham (2022). https://doi.org/10.1007/978-3-031-20047-2_1
8. Chen, X., Yuan, M., Yang, Q., Yao, H., Wang, H.: Underwater-ycc: underwater target detection optimization algorithm based on YOLOv7. J. Marine Sci. Eng. **11**(5), 995 (2023)
9. Arifando, R., Eto, S., Wada, C.: Improved YOLOv5-based lightweight object detection algorithm for people with visual impairment to detect buses. Appl. Sci. **13**(9), 5802 (2023)
10. Yasir, M., et al.: Instance segmentation ship detection based on improved YOLOv7 using complex background SAR images. Front. Mar. Sci. **10**, 1113669 (2023)
11. Wang, X., Li, H., Yue, X., Meng, L.: A comprehensive survey on object detection YOLO. Proceedings http://ceur-ws.org ISSN, 1613, 0073 (2023)
12. He, K., Zhang, X., Ren, S., Sun, J.: Spatial pyramid pooling in deep convolutional networks for visual recognition. IEEE Trans. Pattern Anal. Mach. Intell. **37**(9), 1904–1916 (2015)
13. Yoon, J.H., Yang, M.H., Lim, J., Yoon, K.J.: Bayesian multi-object tracking using motion context from multiple objects. In: 2015 IEEE Winter Conference on Applications of Computer Vision, pp. 33–40. IEEE (2015)

14. Kapania, S., Saini, D., Goyal, S., Thakur, N., Jain, R., Nagrath, P.: Multi object tracking with UAVs using deep SORT and YOLOv3 RetinaNet detection framework. In: Proceedings of the 1st ACM Workshop on Autonomous and Intelligent Mobile Systems, pp. 1–6 (2020)
15. Dell'Amico, M., Toth, P.: Algorithms and codes for dense assignment problems: the state of the art. Discrete Appl. Math. **100**(1–2), 17–48 (2000). Author, F., Author, S.: Title of a proceedings paper. In: Editor, F., Editor, S. (eds.) CONFERENCE 2016, LNCS, vol. 9999, pp. 1–13. Springer, Heidelberg (2016)

MindMemory:Augmented LLM With Long-Term Memory And Mental Personality

Qinyao Zhang, Bin Guo$^{(\boxtimes)}$, Yao Jing, Yan Liu, and Zhiwen Yu

School of Computer Science, Northwestern Polytechnical University,
Xi'an 710072, China
qinyao_z@mail.nwpu.edu.cn, {guob,liu.yan,zhiwenyu}@nwpu.edu.cn

Abstract. In recent years, the rapid development of large language models have revolutionized human-machine interactions. These models have showcased remarkable potential in various tasks, such as open-domain conversations and language generation. However, due to the lack of long-term memory mechanisms, large language models struggle to effectively recall past conversations or remember user personality traits and roles, thus posing a significant challenge in models that require long-term interactions with the users. To address this issue, we propose a novel human-like memory mechanism named MindMemory. Inspired by human long-term memory cognition mechanisms, MindMemory dynamically recalls and updates memories to enhance user interaction. Drawing inspiration from the intricacies of human memory, it divides stored memories into four distinct categories: episodic, semantic, abstract and working. This allows for a more nuanced retrieval process, mimicking the way our minds sift through past experiences. Moreover, MindMemory actively adapts to changes in the user's personality traits and character information through the lens of mind-based theory, which constructs a more comprehensive portrait of the user during prolonged engagements. By constantly refreshing its memory library, it ensures that interactions remain relevant and personalized over time, enhancing the user's engagement. The experiment validates that large language models incorporating MindMemory mechanisms perform well in retrieving relevant memories from the past in long-term interaction scenarios. By understanding user roles and personalities, these models can generate higher quality dialogues, enhancing consistency in interactions and user engagement in dialogues.

Keywords: Large Language Model · Long-term Memory · Response Generation · Long-term Persona Ability

1 Introduction

The outstanding performance of large language models (LLMs) on various tasks highlights the development potential of dialogue agents, such as ChatGPT [1]

H. Sun et al. (Eds.): ChineseCSCW 2024, CCIS 2343, pp. 462–476, 2025.
https://doi.org/10.1007/978-981-96-2373-0_33

and GPT-4 [2], with applications in fields including health care [3] and emotional support [4,5], etc. These advanced LLMs demonstrate significant capabilities in problem understanding and response generation. With tens of billions of parameters, these LLMs have huge knowledge storage capacity, and can achieve the human-like response level. Although LLMs have shown excellent performance in many domains, their lack of long-term memory remains a critical flaw that must be addressed in order to achieve truly human-like response. In human-computer interaction, memory is crucial for maintaining user role information, personality characteristics and prior conversations, effectively serving as "prior knowledge" [6]. This is especially important in scenarios requiring long-term involvement, such as companionship, psychological counseling and medical advice, etc. For example, AI partners need to grow together with users, remembering key information, interests, special memories, to provide better companionship. Therefore, LLMs without long-term memory can seriously hinder their performance and user experience.

In general, studies aimed at improving the ability of LLMs to handle long-term inputs can be divided into two main categories: (1) Special position coding: These approaches involve using special position coding to learn relative positions of longer input text. For example, Phang et al. [7] found that a staggered, block-local Transformer with global encoder tokens achieves a good balance of performance and efficiency. (2) Methods based on an external memory repository: They leverage physical space as a cache to store long-term memory. Through this way, the LLMs are able to retrieve the associated historical information from the external memory banks. However, some token-based caching mechanisms often need to change the model structure of LLMs which makes it difficult to adapt to various LLMs. Moreover, adjusting the model structure without fine-tuning or incorporating cross attention to encode the context and fuse it with the decoder (Fusion-in-Decoder) [8] still remains computationally expensive. Therefore, in this paper, we focus on designing an independent external memory storage mechanism that is not tied to the LLM itself, to enhance the long-term memory capacity of the LLMs and reduce the expense.

In long-term human-computer interaction, the user's role information is crucial. The ability of the large language model to remember and actively use the user's role information is called the long-term role capabilities, which is the key to establishing long-term connections between LLMs and users. Recent studies in open-domain dialogue (Wu et al. [6]; Xu et al. [9]) have proposed methods for memorizing and using historical conversations to obtain user role information (Zhang et al. [10]). These studies abstractly summarize the user's role information and uses it as a condition for subsequent conversations to generate responses. Experimental results demonstrate that this approach can enhance the consistency of chat-bot systems and improve user engagement. However, existing research falls short in detailing user personality traits and character information, limiting the ability to combine user role information with past interactions to generate human-like responses. Additional, in real life, user role information is constantly changing and updated, while previous researches only accumulate and maintain stored memories and information in memory without updating them to reflect these changes.

To tackle these problems, we propose MindMemory, a novel method inspired by the theory of mind and human memory mechanism. It aims to equip LLMs with long-term memory, while also leveraging the theory of mental portrait to continuously adapt to the user's personality characteristics and role information during extended interactions. By facilitating the recall of past memories, MindMemory can effectively improve performance and the user's engagement in long-term interaction scenarios. MindMemory is a general method. It modularizes memory storage/retrieval and mind-engraving functions, and relies only on the dialogue generation ability of LLMs, which makes MindMemory applicable to a wide range of LLMs, such as ChatGPT, ChatGLM, Claude etc.

Our contributions are summarized as follows:

- **We propose a novel MindMemory** based on human long-term memory mechanism, which enables storage, recall, and continuous updating of memory through episodic memory, semantic memory, working memory and high-level abstract memory coordination in long-term memory.
- We employ the theory of mind to capture the user's character information and personality characteristics. This empowers LLMs to retain user personality details, thereby enhancing the generation of personalized responses.
- Through experiments, we demonstrate that MindMemory is effective in improving the coherence and consistency of long-term conversations, as well as increasing user engagement and providing a personalized interaction experience

2 Related Work

2.1 Large Language Model

In recent years, LLMs have demonstrated excellent performance on a wide range of natural language processing tasks, such as open-domain conversations [9], sentiment support [4] etc. These models such as the top closed-source model PaLM [11], ChatGPT [1], GPT-4 [2], the open source model LLaMa [12],ChatGLM [13]. have been widely used for various types of task weights, and researchers have also appropriately adapted LLMs for different downstream tasks, e.g., a number of strategies are proposed to fine-tune the pretrained models for a particular task to further improve the performance of the LLM performance in specific domains. In addition, the research on large language modeling also covers architectural innovations [13], efficient tuning of parameters [14], context length improvement [15], multimodal LLMs and completely new datasets [16]. All of these approaches aim to improve LLM's ability to understand the real world in order to generate conversational responses that meet people's expectations. However, there are still some drawbacks of these powerful large language models, and one of the notable shortcomings is the inability of LLMs to store long-term memories, which hampers the ability of LLMs to process context and retrieve relevant historical information in long-term interaction scenarios.

2.2   Long-Term Memory

The modeling and utilization of long-term memory has become a hot topic direction that has attracted much attention. Researchers have explored various new approaches to enhance the long-term memory capacity of LLMs at multiple levels. An important research thread is to explicitly model long-term memory by combining attention mechanisms with external memory modules. Weston et al. [17] proposed a memory network that demonstrated good memory capacity by reading, writing and addressing long-term memories, using specialized memory modules and attention mechanisms. The study of dialogue models with external memory has also experienced a long period of development, from rule-based dialogue system to external memory cache designed with memory model. Zhong et al. [18] quantitatively represented the Ebbinghaus Memory Forgetting Curve, and proposed a MemoryBank mechanism which is capable of storing, recalling relevant memories, and forgetting memories that have not been brought up for a long period of time. Liu et al. [19] proposed a Tim framework that allows LLMs to maintain an evolving memory that stores historical thoughts in the conversational stream. However, the above approaches have their own respective problems and challenges, and it is difficult to achieve a LLM with a reliable and continuously updated long-term memory mechanism. Specifically, these approaches are simplistic in their incorporation of memory mechanisms, considering only the storage of raw conversational text or highly abstracted and summarized memories. In reality, human beings do not only rely on abstract and condensed memories to recall the past and carry out conversations, but rather, a variety of memories coordinate with each other to construct memories suitable for current conversational scenarios.

2.3   Personalized Dialogue System

Personalized dialogue system aims to provide a more humanized and individualized dialogue experience by tailoring the dialogue content and interaction mode according to the user's personal characteristics and role information, and is one of the new research topics in the field of natural language processing, aiming to build human-like chat-bots. Roller et al. [20] and Thoppilan et al. [21] have developed chat-bots that are more humane and can ensure that the dialogue meets human values. Open-domain chatbots are also increasingly being used for a wide range of applications, including role assignment(Bae et al. [22]) and personalized conversations (Zhang et al. [10]). It is worth noting that user role information is crucial for establishing the connection between the personalized dialogue system and the user. Huang et al. [23] proposed that the existing work on role dialogue is mainly divided into implicit and explicit role models. In the implicit model, the user's role information is represented in the form of a semantic role vectors, but since the role information is combined with the dialog system as an implicit way, it is harder to interpret and control in the target generation response. In explicit models, personalized dialogue systems usually use predetermined role models and user role profiles or extract user roles from dialogue history (Xu et al. [6]). Due to the rapid development of LLMs, explicit models are more suitable for the current research work, but these studies have not been careful enough to portray the role information and there are still challenges on how to manage the extracted role information.

2.4   Theory of Mind

Theory of mind (ToM) refers to the ability of humans to understand, represent, and reason about the mental states(e.g., beliefs, intentions, emotions, etc.) of others, which is a key component of human social cognition. The term "theory of mind" was first proposed by David Premack et al. [24] in 1978. Later, ToM was introduced into the field of artificial intelligence, aiming to give intelligent systems similar psychological reasoning ability, so as to realize more natural and humanized human-computer interaction and reasoning. Wu et al. [25] proposed the first cognitive knowledge graph of machine mind theory, COKE +, which constructed multiple artificially verified cognitive chains that characterize human cognitive mental activities and behaviors. Yan et al. [26] constructs an open-world game and designs a complex cognitive architecture based on cognitive psychology, which enables multi-intelligent agents under the framework to interact with and make decisions about the player, the environment, and the world through the construction of their own cognitive mind.

3   MindMemory

In this paper, we propose a human-like memory mechanism based on the theory of mind, which is an external memory repository we built specifically for LLM. In this section we will introduce MindMemory in detail. As shown in Fig. 1, MindMemory is a unified mechanism consisting of three modules: (1) Mind Module (4.1) as a discriminant module for fine-grained portrayal of user's personality traits and role information; (2) Memory Storage Module (4.2) as a repository of long-term memory storage; (3) LLM module (4.3) generates personalized responses with the powerful dialog response capabilities of LLM.

Each conversation of the user will be input into the MindMemory. ① Calculates the corresponding desire type through the mind module. ② Stores the desire type as part of the memory storage module, specifically in the semantic memory area, and each conversation sentence with time stamps will be stored in the episodic memory area for subsequent retrieval. ③ For the user's current input, it will retrieve the associated semantic memory and episodic memory from the memory module and form the working memory input generator for this interaction to generate a response.

4   Methodology

4.1   Mind Module

We depict user portraits based on the theory of mind and Freud's desire theory. Freud's desire theory holds that desire is an individual's strong desire to satisfy

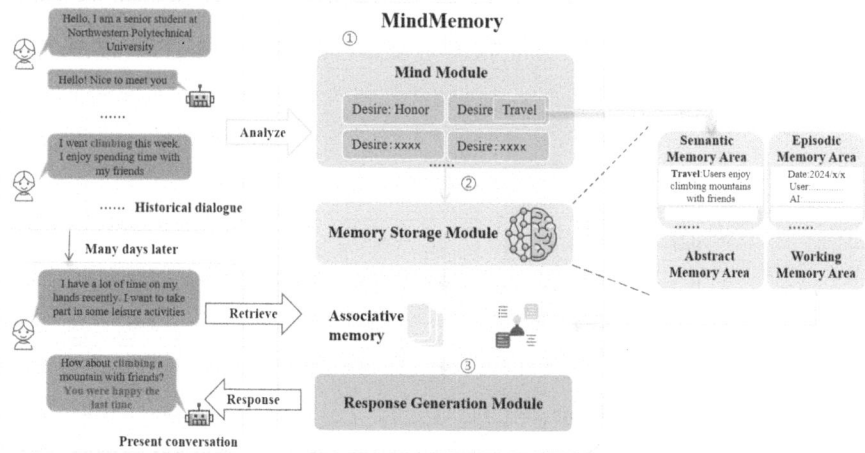

Fig. 1. Overall MindMemory framework

physiological and psychological needs, and is the driving force for individuals to pursue pleasure, satisfy physical and mental needs on the basis of self preservation and survival. Desire can be divided into physiological desire and spiritual desire. Physiological desires are the most fundamental human desires, originating from individual biological instincts and physiological needs, such as eating, drinking, housing, and transportation. Spiritual desires are related to an individual's cognition and understanding of themselves, others, and the world, such as the desire for achievement, love and being loved desire, self actualization desire. Specifically, we collected 2k chat sentences containing multiple topics from online forums and manually labeled the type of desires corresponding to each sentence for fine-tuning the ChatGLM, so that the ChatGLM can more accurately identify the desire information contained in the user input. The final LLM inference returns the ['Desire'] corresponding to the input. The desire category will be used as part of the user roles and personality traits in the subsequent memory module, with user roles of the same desire type being more similar.

4.2 Memory Storage Module

The memory storage module is the most important module of MindMemory, which stores the historical memory, the user's personality characteristics and the role information. It not only stores the daily conversation records, but also highly summarizes past events to build a continuously updated memory bank with a multi-level memory structure. The memory storage module is divided into four parts: episodic memory area, semantic memory area, abstract memory area and working memory area. The specific implementation of each memory area will be introduced in detail next. In the field of cognitive science, long-term memory (LTM) is composed of two types of memory: declarative memory and procedural memory, and declarative memory can be further divided into episodic memory and semantic memory [27]. This study mainly constructs memory storage modules according to the composition of declarative memory (Fig. 2).

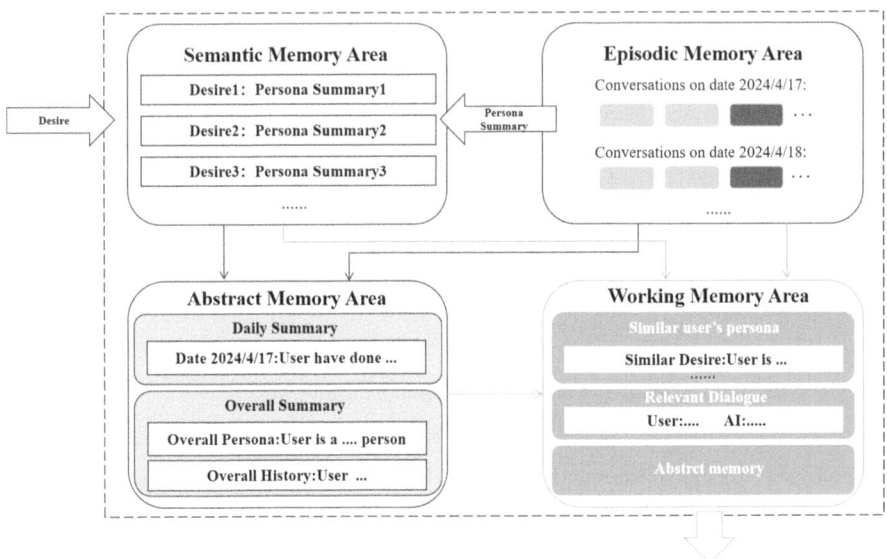

Fig. 2. Memory storage framework of human-like memory mechanism

Episodic Memory Area. Episodic memory refers to the memory of events (scenes) experienced personally and occurring at a certain time and place. These are dialogue historical events that the Agent needs to memorize during the conversation with the user. Episodic memory is the highest human memory system that allows us to recall the source of a particular memory. At the same time, episodic memory can be further developed into semantic memory, which means that semantic memory is summarized by the partial abstraction of situational memory. In the episodic memory area of our memory storage system, we use a vector database to store and retrieve these memories. Moreover, episodic memory records multiple rounds of conversations between the user and Agent through detailed chronological order, with each dialogue time-stamped. This storage facilitates subsequent memory updates and detailed retrieval of the conversation history. Vector databases represents data as numerical vectors, and compared with general databases, vector databases have greater advantages in terms of computational cost and retrieval efficiency. At the same time, the unique characteristics of vectorized data can better focus on the associated data at the semantic level, which is very favorable for obtaining the historical memory associated with the current input from the situational memory area.

Semantic Memory Area. Semantic memory refers to the memory of general knowledge acquired through knowledge about the concepts and facts of the world, which is an understanding of the facts and concepts of general knowledge. Semantic memory is usually developed through episodic memory, and it is a kind of objective knowledge. In the context of the long-term interactive dialogue with the user, the semantic memory stores the user role information summarized from the dialogue (episodic memory) as the factual knowledge of the subsequent Agent dialogue with the user. User roles and personality characteristics are stored in ['Desire: Persona Summary']. The storage format of desire with user summary can depict the role and personality characteristics of users more carefully from the perspective of the bottom level of human cognition.

Semantic memory area is implemented using a hash-based storage. Our goal is to keep the inferred user role information and personality characteristics in the semantic memory area according to certain rules, that is, the similar and related personality characteristics should be stored in the similar retrieval area to improve efficiency. Therefore, we use the hash table as the infrastructure for the semantic memory area storage, and the similar personality characteristics and character information inferred by the mind module are assigned the same hash index. Given a user personality trait inferred from a conversation, we propose to quickly search for the most similar personality traits and character information in a high-dimensional embedding space. This is achieved through a hash-based position-sensitive hash algorithm (LSH). LSH gives a hash-embedding $F(x)$ to each n-dimensional embedding vector of x Rn, where the nearby vector gets the same hash-index with higher probability.

Another key to the semantic memory area is to ensure that the user's personality traits and role information are constantly updated. For this reason, we define two operations of the semantic memory area: storage and override. We first initialize a transformer model E to process the input user character and character information ρ_i, encoding it as a sentence vector representing $E_\rho(\rho_i)$. For user characteristics summarized from episodic memory, needs to eliminate duplication before writing. Specifically, it is necessary to calculate the cosine similarity between ρ_i and similar role information ρ_j in the semantic memory region. When the similarity of ρ_i and ρ_j exceeds a given threshold $S_d = 0.9$, it is necessary to cover the ρ_i in the original semantic memory area with ρ_j to ensure that very similar features will not appear in the semantic memory. Otherwise, deposit the ρ_i directly into the semantic memory area. Measure distance using cosine similarity:

$$sim(\rho_i, \rho_j) = \cos(E_\rho(\rho_i), E_\rho(\rho_j)) \tag{1}$$

Abstract Memory Area. The abstract memory area is an important part of high-dimensional, multilevel memory. When processing cognitive tasks, humans first start from an abstract general memory and then recall the source and specific content of particular events. Therefore, the abstract memory area stores memories that are highly abstracted from the semantic and episodic memory areas, reflecting the complexity of human memory. The abstract memory area processes and distills the user's daily conversations with the Agent into highly summarized daily events $E_{summary} = \{E_{date_1}, E_{date_2}, ..., E_{date_n}\}$. At the same time, the daily event summary set $E_{summary}$ will be further summarized as a global abstract memory. This process constitutes a hierarchical memory structure, which can effectively improve the reliability of LLMs recall. The concrete implementation is to use daily dialogue E_{date} and event summary set $E_{summary}$ as input to LLMs, and require LLMs to summarize these in a highly refined manner.

Working Memory Area. Working memory refers to the individual's ability to temporarily store and operate information while performing cognitive tasks. The working memory area mainly preserves the information needed for reasoning and interactive tasks and the long-term memory retrieved [28]. In our memory storage system structure, working memory is used as the area of memory cache placed into the context of cue words for performing each response generation task. The specific extraction process of the working memory area is to input query: (1) Extract k-round related dialogue history and specific memories from the episodic memory area; (2) Extract k associated user character information and personality characteristics from the semantic memory area; and (3) Extract high-level abstract summary memory from the abstract memory area. After each round of response generation, the working memory area will be emptied. Wait for the next round of input, and so on.

4.3 LLM Module

We integrated ChatGLM [13], an open source bilingual language model which has 6.2 billion or more parameters, to demonstrate the effectiveness of the Mind-Memory mechanism. The model without external memory repository in the very beginning lack long-term memory of the dialogue in the long-term interaction scenario.

As we have mentioned before, the MindMemory is a modular design, which means that the dialogue model used can be dynamically adjusted according to the actual needs. During retrieval, a series of partitioned memories are integrated into conversation prompts, including associated memories, user roles and personality traits, and high-level summary summaries. So MindMemory can provide personalized interaction based on the user's past memory and the user's personal portrait.

To sum up, we studied the long-term memory module can give big language model long-term memory ability, make a basic AI dialogue model into a long-term memory AI memory auxiliary dialogue agent, can constantly update and stored from the past interaction memory, bring personalized and closer dialogue experience.

5   Experiment

The main goal of our experiments is to evaluate whether MindMemory is effective in enhancing the long-term memory capacity of LLM. In particular, we focus on whether the embedded memory module can enhance the accuracy of the

LLM's retrospective memory, its understanding of the user's role information and personality traits. In addition, we aimed to test LLM for a more personalized response with memory and familiarity with the user's personality. MindMemory Is a multi-modular design, so we performed separate validation evaluations of each module in the experimental section to demonstrate the role of each module in the whole mechanism. Here are the specific methods of our experiments.

5.1   Evaluation Protocol

For Mind Module We collected 2k chat sentences from online forums on a variety of topics including weather, food, and emotions. These 2k sentences are manually marked according to the Freud's desire theory subdivided in the Theory of Mind (4.1), and the labels are the desire types corresponding to the sentences. 0.4k sentences to verify whether the adjusted LLM can correctly classify the types of desires contained in the sentences. We used "Accuracy" to evaluate the inference accuracy of desire categories.

For Memory Module For the memory module, we set questions related to the dialogue history to retrieve whether the memory could be correctly recalled. These questions are designed to prompt the memory modules to retrieve specific memory details from the chat history. To more intuitively represent the role of our memory module, we used the same dialogue and retrieval questions to ask ChatGPT and SiliconFriend. We used the following two indicators to evaluate the results:

– Retrieval Accuracy: Assessment of whether the relevant memory is successfully recalled (label: 0: none; 1: successful recall)
– Response Correctness: Assessment whether the prompt question was answered correctly (label: 0: no; 0.5: part; 1: correct)

For Overall System For the whole dialogue system, we take the Self-chat approach to conduct the experiment. Self-chat has been widely used for the evaluation of conversational systems [20,29]. The model plays the role of both sides in the dialogue. ChatGLM as the user, our dialog system (ChatGLM with MindMemory) and two other baseline chat-bots, each chatting with the user simulator for 10 days, containing 5 rounds of conversations per day on different topics, and three of them come from the LLMs, the other two come from manually set retrieval questions. Finally, we asked the manual force to evaluate the dialogue effect, using the following three discourse-level indicators:

– **Coherence**: An utterance-level metric, measuring whether the response is relevant and consistent with the context.
– **Consistency**: An utterance-level metric, evaluating whether the response is consistent with the persona in the dialogue history.
– **Engagingness**: An utterance-level metric, assessing whether the annotator would like to talk with the speaker for each response in the long-term conversation.

The three human volunteers need to start from these three indicators and score each round of dialogue. The score range is [0,1]. The higher the score, the better the effect. For the accuracy of the experiment, volunteers did not know which model each round of conversation was generated.

The baseline models use ChatGPT [1] and SiliconFriend [18]. At the same time, we also used the dialogue system without the mind module to perform ablation study for comparison.

5.2 Experiment Results

For the mind module, the experimental results are shown in Table 1. It can be seen that in the test set, 349 out of 400 sentences could be correctly categorized and the accuracy of the classification of the mind module is 0.873, which shows that the mind module can infer the desire corresponding to the sentences by following the Freud's desire classification.

Table 1. Results of Mind Module

Module	Correct Sentences/Test	Accuracy
Mind Module	349/400	0.873

For the memory module, the experimental results are shown in Table 2. As can be seen, in terms of the retrieval accuracy of related questions, the Chat-GPT score without any long-term memory module is only 0.482. One of the most likely reasons is that ChatGPT may give an made-up answer or answer "I don't remember" (this type of reply was treated as "retrieval failure" in the experiment). In contrast, our memory module can achieve a score of 0.859 in retrieval accuracy, which is higher than ChatGPT, indicating that our long-term memory module can be effectively retrieved for response generation.

For the whole dialogue system, the results compared with the two baseline models are shown in Table 3. ChatGPT, without an external memory repository, obviously has problems with fictitious memories, hypothetical non-existing user roles and personality traits. For example, the user's personality is "hate spicy food". However, after several rounds of dialogue, ChatGPT thinks that users love spicy food and recommends the hot pot. This also leads to a significantly lower

Table 2. Results of memory module comparison

Model	Retrieval Acc.	Response Correctness
MindMemory	0.849	0.573
SiliconFriend(ChatGLM)	0.83	0.52
ChatGPT	0.482	0.47

score of ChatGPT in the consistency than our model and SiliconFriend. And SiliconFriend performs well in terms of consistency, consistency, and engagement. Our model scored slightly higher than SiliconFriend in consistency and engagement, which indicates that our model can further improve the understanding and application of user roles and personality characteristics. In common terms, our model can better utilize the inferred user roles and characteristics to conduct dialogue and generate personalized responses. Our model performs less than SiliconFriend in coherence, possibly because the SiliconFriend collected psychological domain-related multi-rounds fine-tuning the LLMs, making SiliconFriend responses more empathy and more smooth in dialogue coherence. The dialogue system without the mind module has a poor score on consistency, and the scores of other indicators are less different from the whole system, which indicates that the mental module is effective in characterizing the user's character.

Table 3. Results of overall system comparison

Model	Coherence	Consistency	Engagingness
SiliconFriend(ChatGPT)	0.675	0.71	0.756
SiliconFriend(ChatGLM)	0.562	0.68	0.732
MindMemory(ChatGLM)	0.56	0.74	0.81
MindMemory(Without Mind)	0.55	0.70	0.78
ChatGPT	0.53	0.472	0.58

6   Conclusion

In this work, we propose a new human-like memory mechanism MindMemory. This mechanism can solve that LLMs do not have the ability of long-term memory. Meanwhile the multi-level desire classification based on the theory of mind describes the user's role and personality characteristics in more detail. MindMemory empowers LLMs to retrieve associated memories from long-term conversation history, retain contextual information, and understand and remember users' roles and personalities. This mechanism is based on the inspiration of human long-term memory mechanism: episodic memory and semantic memory are stored separately, long-term memory and working memory are coordinated with each other, and relevant memory and abstract memory work together. MindMemory is able to build a separate external memory repository for each user, and is able to memorize each profile of them. This design enables LLMs to enhance user dialogue engagement in long-term interaction scenarios, and to give personalized responses according to the user's characteristics. Overall, the design of the MindMemory improves the quality of conversations for long-term human-AI interactions (Fig. 3).

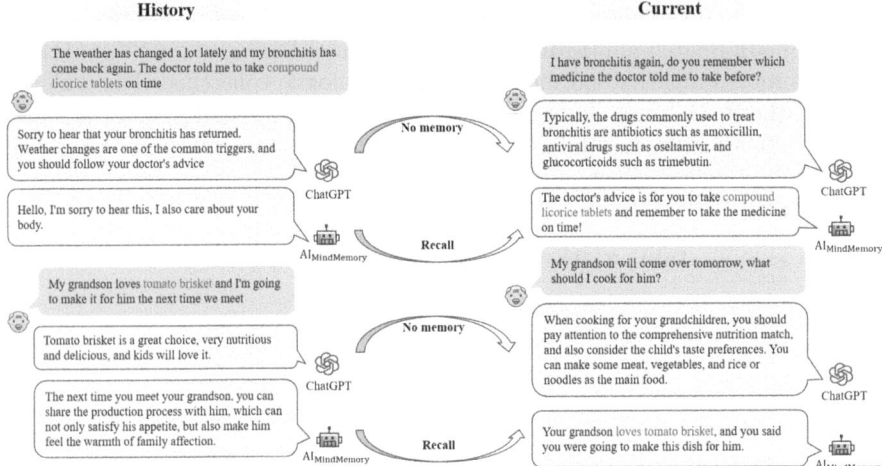

Fig. 3. Example responses from MindMemory and ChatGPT in memory recall.

References

1. OpenAI. Chatgpt (2022)
2. OpenAI OpenAI. Gpt-4 Technical report, March 2023
3. Zhang, H., et al.: Huatuogpt, towards taming language model to be a doctor. arXiv preprint arXiv:2305.15075 (2023)
4. Sabour, S., Zheng, C., Huang, M.: Cem: commonsense-aware empathetic response generation. In: Proceedings of the AAAI Conference on Artificial Intelligence, pp. 11229–11237, July 2022
5. He, J., Zhou, C., Ma, X., Berg-Kirkpatrick, T., Neubig, G.: Towards a unified view of parameter-efficient transfer learning. Cornell University - arXiv, Cornell University - arXiv (2021)
6. Xu, X., et al.: Long time no see! open-domain conversation with long-term persona memory (2020)

7. Phang, J., Zhao, Y., Liu, P.J.: Investigating efficiently extending transformers for long input summarization, August 2022
8. Hofstätter, S., Chen, J., Raman, K., Zamani, H.: Fid-light: efficient and effective retrieval-augmented text generation. In: Proceedings of the 46th International ACM SIGIR Conference on Research and Development in Information Retrieval, pp. 1437–1447 (2023)
9. Xu, J., Szlam, A., Weston, J.: Beyond goldfish memory: long-term open-domain conversation. In: Proceedings of the 60th Annual Meeting of the Association for Computational Linguistics (Volume 1: Long Papers), January 2022
10. Zhang, S., Dinan,E., Urbanek, J., Szlam, A., Kiela, D., Weston, J.: Personalizing dialogue agents: i have a dog, do you have pets too? In: Proceedings of the 56th Annual Meeting of the Association for Computational Linguistics (Volume 1: Long Papers), January 2018
11. Chowdhery, A., et al.: Palm: Scaling language modeling with pathways (2023)
12. Touvron, H., et al.: Llama: Open and efficient foundation language models (2023)
13. Zeng, A., et al. GLM-130b: an open bilingual pre-trained model. arXiv preprint arXiv:2210.02414 (2022)
14. He, J., Zhou, C., Ma, X., Berg-Kirkpatrick, T., Neubig, G.: Towards a unified view of parameter-efficient transfer learning. arXiv preprint arXiv:2110.04366 (2021)
15. Pal, A., Karkhanis, D., Roberts, M., Dooley, S., Sundararajan, A., Naidu, S.: Giraffe: adventures in expanding context lengths in LLMS. arXiv preprint arXiv:2308.10882 (2023)
16. Bae, S., et al.: Keep me updated! memory management in long-term conversations, October 2022
17. Becattini, F., Uricchio, T.: Memory networks. In: Proceedings of the 30th ACM International Conference on Multimedia, October 2022
18. Zhong, W., Guo, L., Gao, Q., Wang, Y.: Enhancing large language models with long-term memory, Memorybank (2023)
19. Shen, Y.: Think-in-memory: Recalling and post-thinking enable LLMS with long-term memory (2013)
20. Roller, S., et al.: Recipes for building an open-domain chatbot. In: Proceedings of the 16th Conference of the European Chapter of the Association for Computational Linguistics: Main Volume, January 2021
21. Thoppilan, R., et al.: Lamda: Language models for dialog applications (2022)
22. Bae, S., et al.: Building a role specified open-domain dialogue system leveraging large-scale language models, April 2022
23. Huang, M., Zhu, X., Gao, J.: Challenges in building intelligent open-domain dialog systems. ACM Trans. Inf. Syst. **38**, 1–32 (2020)
24. Premack, D., Woodruff, G.: Does the chimpanzee have a theory of mind? Behav. Brain Sci. **1**, 515–526 (1978)
25. Jincenzi, W., Chen, Z., Deng, J., Sabour, S., Huang, M.: A cognitive knowledge graph for machine theory of mind, Coke (2023)
26. Yan, M., Li, R., Zhang, H., Wang, H., Yang, Z., Yan, J.: Language-agent role play for open-world games, Larp (2023)

27. Dudas, R.B., Clague, F., Thompson, S.A., Graham, K.S., Hodges, J.R.: Episodic and semantic memory in mild cognitive impairment. Neuropsychologia **43**, 1266–1276 (2005)
28. Baddeley, A.: Working memory: looking back and looking forward. Nat. Rev. Neurosci. **4**, 829–839 (2003)
29. Bao, S., et al.: Plato-2: towards building an open-domain chatbot via curriculum learning. In: Findings of the Association for Computational Linguistics: ACL-IJCNLP 2021, January 2021

FPSFT: Frame-Patch-Select Fusion Transformer for Action Recognition

Yilong Xiao[1], Xin Jing[1], Shiyu Yu[2], Jingyu Liu[2], Keming Mao[1(✉)], Xiaochun Yang[1], and Bin Zhang[1]

[1] Software College, Northeastern University, Shenyang, China
`maokm@mail.neu.edu.cn`
[2] China Mobile Group Liaoning Company Limited, Shenyang, China

Abstract. Video action recognition plays a crucial role in numerous applications. However, current research encounters significant challenges, such as the difficulty in extracting features that maintain long-term connections within the video feature space and the inefficiency of attention computation. Therefore, we propose an innovative feature fusion method based on attention mechanism. This method employs the Transformer to create a Key Frame and Key Patch Selection module alongside a Small-Big Patch Transformer module. These components efficiently establish relationships between features with long-term connections in video data. By integrating these modules within the Transformer and combining them with Convolutional Neural Networks, our approach leverages the strengths of different frameworks. This integration significantly enhances the computational efficiency and accuracy. The experiments conducted on the generic video datasets demonstrate that our model surpasses the performance of most previous efforts at the same input scale.

Keywords: Action recognition · Key patch&frame selection · Feature fusion

1 Introduction

Action recognition is one of the principal research areas in the fields of computer vision and artificial intelligence [1, 2, 13, 16, 33]. Action recognition technology has matured and is applied in various aspects of everyday life such as violence detection, intelligent surveillance [4, 8, 20], autonomous driving, and human-computer interaction [10, 12]. However, due to the limitations of hardware equipment in real-world scenarios and the complexity of scenes and actions in videos, there is still significant room for improvement in action recognition algorithms.

In recent years, action recognition based on CNNs (Convolutional Neural Networks) and transformers has made significant advancements. Generally, the input video is split into a sequence of frames at equal time intervals. Subsequently, a series of preprocessing operations such as rotation and cropping are applied. Finally, classification and prediction are performed based on the trained

H. Sun et al. (Eds.): ChineseCSCW 2024, CCIS 2343, pp. 477–491, 2025.
https://doi.org/10.1007/978-981-96-2373-0_34

deep network. The success of the Vision Transformer (ViT) has validated the potential of applying Transformers to the field of computer vision. However, there are still some areas need to be improved. As previously mentioned, videos contain a large number of ineffective regional features, and the ViT involves substantial spatial redundancy in computation. This is due to the need to process every patch in the global context, where the computational load increases exponentially with additional patch input. Consequently, these features can interfere with the model's learning of key features and result in significant computational overhead. Furthermore, a characteristic of the ViT is its computation of the relationships between patches globally. This operation inherently weakens the natural connections that exist between closely situated patches, especially those local features in videos that maintain relative positional consistency. The division into separate patches disrupts the connections between them.

The above serves as the motivation for this paper. We believe that the frame sequence sampled at intervals contains a significant spatial redundancy. Therefore, we also pre-filter the patches input into the Transformer Encoder, selecting key patches for subsequent self-attention operations. Subsequently, we analyze and hypothesize about the issue of Transformers not being sufficiently friendly to local features. We construct a hybrid architecture combining CNNs and Transformers to accomplish the task of action recognition. Additionally, the division of patches during the splitting process disrupts the original spatial structure. To address the fragmentation of spatial features caused by spatial splitting, we propose a Small-Big Patch Video Transformer model. This model introduces a global feature map, the size of which matches the divided patches in the input sequence. This allows the Transformer to better learn the relationships between local and global spatial features. Our contributions are as follows:

(1) We devise a module integrating keyframe selection and key patch filtering. This significantly reduces the computational overhead associated with applying Transformer models to video tasks.
(2) Introducing a Small-Big Patch Transformer module specifically tailored for action recognition, we address spatial feature fragmentation caused by patch division. This enables local attention computations within each region, thereby improving the model's capability for accurate action recognition.
(3) We achieve state-of-the-art performance on two prominent public datasets, UCF101 and SSv2. Our hybrid model, amalgamating convolutional neural networks and the Transformer framework, showcased superior results in video-based action recognition tasks compared to existing approaches.

2   Related Works

2.1   CNN for Action Recognition

As a breakthrough method, CNNs resolves the issues of manually determining features and the severe disjunction between feature representation and classification methods [6,18,21,26,28,31]. Two-dimensional convolutional structures extract appearance information from images and have been used as the backbone for image recognition. However, they are incapable of capturing temporal relationships between frames, which leads to poor performance when applied to video understanding. To address this issue, two-stream CNNs for video action recognition were proposed [15, 22]. It used two separate branches to extract spatial and temporal features, respectively, enabling capture different modals. In [29], an improved two-stream Temporal Segment Network (TSN) that use sparse interval sampling of video frames was designed. TSM method was introduced in [19], which achieved temporal information extraction for action recognition through a time-shifting operation, at a minimal cost, using a two-dimensional CNNs.

Three-dimensional CNNs(3D-CNNs) incorporate a time convolution as the third dimension, enabling the joint learning of spatio-temporal feature. The first 3D-CNNs method was proposed in [14]. Essentially, it adds an extra dimension to the traditional 2D-CNNs kernels, allowing them to perform convolution across multiple frame feature maps. C3D was introduced in [25] by expanding the network structure. Compared to 2D-CNNs, 3D-CNNs have a significantly larger number of parameters. To address this issue, I3D was designed [7].

2.2 Transformer for Action Recognition

For video understanding, extracting temporal, motion, and spatial features play a significant impact on model performance. Consequently, for better connections between key features, module-level attention mechanisms such as Non-local [30] and SmallBig Unit [17]were proposed. The Transformer [27] framework was first proposed as an attention-based framework to solve problems in natural language processing. Due to its unique attention mechanism that enables the model to obtain information about key features within the global perceptual field. Vision Transformer was one of the first attempts to apply the Transformer framework to computer vision [9]. Subsequently, TimeSformer [5] and ViViT [3] applied the Transformer to action recognition. They used a temporal attention module with the existing Vision Transformer to better understand temporal dynamics.

This paper proposes a Small-Big Patch Video Transformer model, where we pre-filter the patches, select key patches for subsequent self-attention operations. Additionally, to address the issue of fragmentation of spatial features caused by spatial splitting, this model introduces a global feature map of the same size as the patches into the input sequence. Each local area entering the Encoder not only computes with the surrounding areas but also concurrently processes with all regions of the entire image. This enables the Transformer to better learn the relationship between local and global spatial features.

3 Method

In this section, We describe keyframe and key patch selection modules, along with a feature fusion module called Small-Big Patch Transformer. The overall framework is illustrated in Fig. 1.

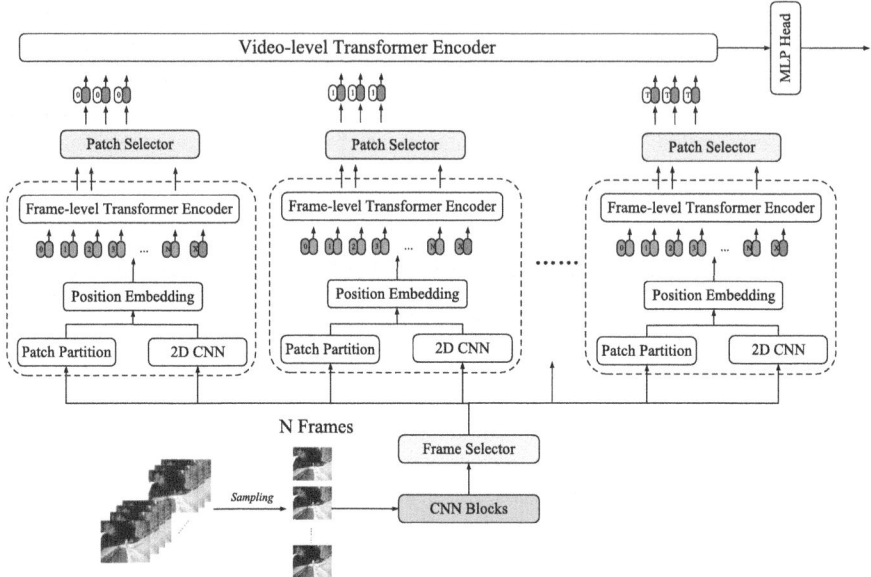

Fig. 1. Overview of the overall framework.

We first extract the low-level semantic information such as texture of each frame by 2D CNNs after cropping and enhancement. We then use Transformer architecture for global comparison and extract primary semantic information. In order to reduce the computational pressure on the Transformer framework and to minimize the spatial redundancy computation, we designed a keyframe filtering module to generate a sequence of keyframe feature maps after comparing and learning the feature maps of each input frame. In the design of the transformer framework, we adopt a hierarchical architecture, i.e., we distinguish the attention computation framework into intra-frame level Attention computation and video level Attention computation. For intra-frame operations, we design a Small-Big Patch Transformer Encoder module to perform intra-frame attention computation between patches for each frame in the video keyframe sequence. Before we perform Attention computation on the input Transformer Encoder at the video level, we first perform a filtering operation on the patches in each of the input frames. The key patches from each frame are then fed into the multilayer video-level Transformer Encoder for Attention computation, and finally the results are mapped and categorized by the MLP Head to get the final result.

3.1   Key Frame Selection Module

We first sample the video after cropping and data enhancement of the X_{input} so that it passes through a convolutional layer with a step size of 2 in $1 \times 7 \times 7$ and a maximum pooling layer with a step size of 3 in $1 \times 3 \times 3$, which is subsequently input into our model. In the shallow part of the model we use a conventional 2D-CNNs with to extract low-level semantic information such as texture contours for each frame. The specific operational formula is as follows:

$$X'_{input} = MaxPool\left(Conv\left(X_{input}\right)\right).$$ (1)

The process of key frame selection module utilizes the attention mechanism of Transformer Encoder to compute the attention between frames, and according to the results of the computation, the feature map of each frame is scored and sorted. The frame with the highest score is taken as the key frame. The result obtained by the shallow CNNs is set as $X'_{input} \in \mathbb{R}^{N \times C \times T \times H \times W}$, where N is the batch size, C is the number of channels, and T, H, and W are the number, height and width of the frames, respectively. Average pooling and convolution kernel with a step size of 2 are used to reduce the spatial size and the number of channels, and deform the result to $X''_{input} \in \mathbb{R}^{N \times T \times d}$, that is, the channel dimension and spatial dimension of the result are compressed into the same dimension. The specific operation formula is as follows:

$$X''_{input} = Conv\left(AvgPool\left(X'_{input}\right)\right).$$ (2)

The operation of attention computation for frame-to-frame interrelationships can then be described as the following equation:

$$X_{att} = Linear\left(LN\left(MSA\left(X''_{input} + e^{pos}\right)\right)\right).$$ (3)

where e^{pos} is a randomly generated number of N×T×d. It is used to distinguish the position of the frame in Encoder. The result is learned by Multihead Self-Attention (MSA) mechanism. We obtain the features of each frame by multilayer perceptron learning. For the obtained feature results we map them to the original input tensor and pick the feature maps of the key n frames. The picking operation in this can be described as the following equation:

$$Selection\left(X_{input}, X_{att}\right) = Index\left(Rank\left(mean\left(MLP\left(X_{att}\right)\right)\right), X_{input}\right).$$ (4)

The specific approach of the selection is that we feed the obtained X_{att} into a multilayer perceptron for learning and dimensional contraction, and average the obtained results over the feature dimensions, and subsequently sort the frames according to the average of each frame and select the indexes of the n frames with the highest scores, and obtain the sequence of feature maps for these n frames according to the indexes. Thus we get the filtered video key frame sequence feature map. The internal structure of the module is shown in Fig. 2.

3.2   Action Recognition Module of the Small-Big Patch Transformer

The role of Small-Big Patch Transformer module is to learn the interrelationships between patches at the frame level. In order to reduce the overall computation

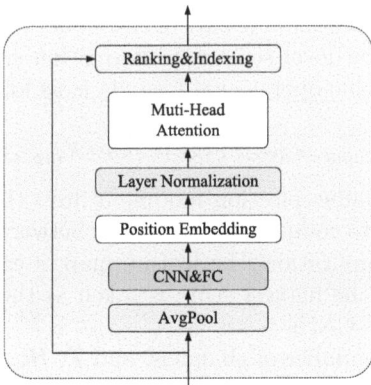

Fig. 2. Overview of Key-frames selection module.

of the model, we adopt a hierarchical architecture, i.e., after the shallow CNNs, we build a Transformer Encoder, which is also known as Frame-level Transformer, that only compute attention on all the patches in the frame, and after attention enhancement within the frame, we do video-level, i.e., global attention computation on all the picked key patches to do video-level, i.e., global, attention computation. In order to perform better frame-level attention computation, we mix different scales of patches in the input patch sequence to make the model have better spatial understanding. By using different scale patches, the Transformer gets both local field of view patches and larger field of view patches as inputs, which allows the model to repair the local spatial structure damage caused by slicing, and allows the sliced local features to be quickly localized in the frame.

Before calculating the interrelationships of intra-frame features, we adopt different processing methods for the input frame sequence as shown Fig. 3. We divide the feature map of the frame sequence into two equal parts as $X_{in} \in \mathbb{R}^{N \times C \times T' \times H \times W}$, where N is the size of the Batch Size, C is the number of channels, T' is the number of frames filtered by keyframes, and H and W are the height and width of the feature map. The result is set as $X'_{in} \in \mathbb{R}^{N \times P \times D}$, where P represents the number of patches after cutting, set $P = n_h \times n_w$ n_w and n_h are the number of horizontal and vertical rows of the patches, and D represents the spatial size of each patch and the number of dimensions of the channels after compressing them into the same dimension. Let $D = p_1 \times p_2 \times C$, where p_1, p_2 are the height and width of the sliced Patch, and C is the number of channels, $p_1 = H/n_w$, $p_2 = H/n_h$. Since the dimension of the compressed D is too high, its dimension is compressed using a linear transformation and it is processed with Layer Normalization to enable it to accelerate convergence in training. As for the processing of the other part, since we set the number of patches as 16, we use a maximum pooling operation with a step size of 2 and 3×3, and a convolution operation with a step size of 2 and a convolution kernel size of 3×3 to get the scaled result $X''_{in} \in \mathbb{R}^{N \times P \times D}$, which reduces the original spatial size to $1/4$, and the scaled-down spatial size is $1/16$ of the original size. This operation reduces the original space size to $1/4$, and then the reduced space size is $1/16$ of the original one, so that the size of the original frame feature map after scaling is comparable with the size of the sliced Patch. Figure 3 gives the structure of the Small-Big Patch Transformer module and an abstract representation of the slicing and scaling.

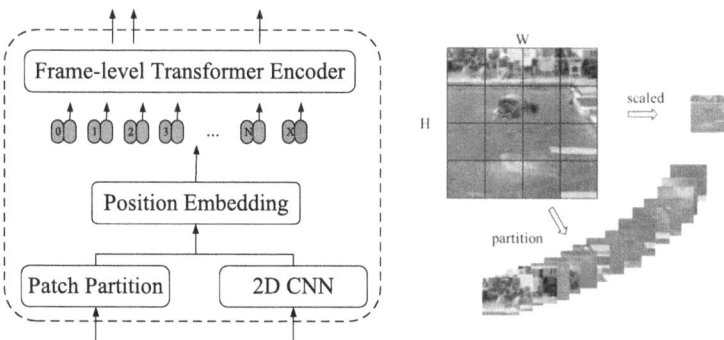

Fig. 3. Small Big Patch Transformer Module & Small Big Partition and Scaling Diagram. We scale the original frame feature map to match the size of the segmented patch.

We concatenate the obtained two processed Patch in P dimension. and add it with the randomly generated position embedding. The specific concatenation operation formula is as follows:

$$X_{out} = Concat\left(LN\left(Patch\left(X_{in}\right)\right), Conv\left(MaxPool\left(X_{in}\right)\right)\right). \tag{5}$$

3.3 Key Patch Selection Module

Regarding the key Patch selection module, we take similar operations as in the key frame selection module, and Fig. 4 shows the internal structure of the key patch selection module. Before doing the attention computation between the Patches of each frame, we first perform the enhancement process on all the Patches. We take the input feature map $X_i \in \mathbb{R}^{N \times P \times d}$, where $X_i \in X$, $X \in \mathbb{R}^{N \times T \times P \times d}$ is the feature of the ith frame, where P is the number of patches and d is the dimension. We map X_i to higher dimensions by MLP, and subsequently decompose the obtained result in the last dimension into three dimensions n_h, n_w, and c, where n_h and n_w are the height and width of the Patch, and c is the channel. Afterwards, the patch is reduced to the dimension $N \times C \times H \times W$, and then a maximum pooling operation is performed. After that, the enhanced result is reduced to the dimension of the input and multi-attention is computed on it, we average the obtained result X_p and sort it to select the most critical n patches in this frame. The operation formulas are as follow:

$$X_p = MSA\left(MaxPool\left(MLP\left(X_i\right)\right)\right) \tag{6}$$

$$Selection\left(X_i, X_p\right) = Index\left(Rank\left(mean\left(X_p\right)\right), X_i\right). \tag{7}$$

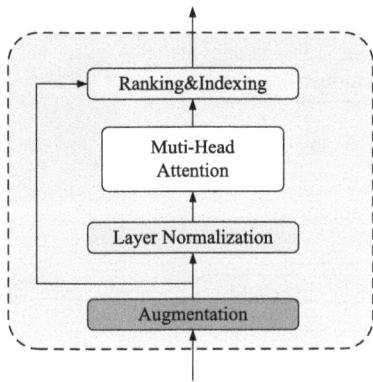

Fig. 4. Overview of Key-patch selection module.

3.4 Video Transformer Module

Video Transformer module is the final module where we perform action recognition. The purpose is to take the previously extracted features for further learning to accomplish the final classification task. We input the feature vector X_{vin} into the Transformer Encoder at the multilayer video level with the input feature vector X_{vin} as:

$$X_{vin} = [X_1, X_2, \ldots, X_N]. \tag{8}$$

where $X_1, X_2, \ldots, X_N$ are the key Patch features in each frame. X_{vin} is computed in Transformer Encoder with multi-head self-attention, and finally mapped and categorized by MLP Head to get the final result y. The specific operation formula is:

$$y = MLP\left(MSA\left(LN\left(X_{vin}\right)\right)\right). \tag{9}$$

4   Experiments

In this section, we first introduce the dataset. Subsequently, we compare FPSFT with some state-of-the-art approaches. Finally, ablation studies are given to demonstrate the efficacy of our method.

4.1   Dataset

Two widely-used video recognition datasets UCF-101 [23] and Something-Something v2 [11] are utilized.

(1) Something-Something dataset. The Something-Something dataset comes in two versions: Something-Something V1 and Something-Something V2. It includes 174 categories of human-object interactions, providing a higher granularity of action description compared to other datasets like Kinetics and UCF-101. The categories in the Something-Something dataset primarily encompass actions such as 'opening something', 'turning something upside down', 'stacking something', among others.
(2) UCF-101 dataset. UCF-101 is a traditional video classification dataset sourced from YouTube, comprising 13,320 videos across 101 action categories. This dataset is particularly rich in variations such as camera angles, object poses, changes in object size, backgrounds, and lighting conditions. Additionally, the action categories in UCF-101 are diverse, broadly categorized into five types: human-object interaction, human-human interaction, individual body movements, musical instrument performance, and sports.

4.2   Comparison with Related Works

We set up two sets of comparative experiments. The first set is conducted on the UCF-101 dataset, which is scene-oriented with lower granularity of action segmentation. The second set of experiments utilize the Something-Something V2 dataset, which is more sensitive to temporal sequencing and features higher granularity in action segmentation. In the first set of experiments, we primarily examine how our model, utilizing a fusion framework, compares in accuracy with methods based on 2D-CNNs and 3D-CNNs. For the accuracy metrics, we use the Top-1 accuracy rate. We also list the pre-training datasets and the backbone networks of the models. In the second set of experiments, we compare our model's performance on the Something-Something V2 dataset against other state-of-the-art methods in terms of computational efficiency and accuracy. We display the Top-1 and Top-5 accuracy rates for each method, and provide their computational complexities measured in TFLOPs. To offer a more comprehensive presentation of the results, details such as the frame rate of the model inputs, the pre-training approach, and the backbone networks of the models are also included.

Comparison on UCF-101. The results of the first set of experiments are shown in Table.1. We compare our method with 2D-CNNs approaches such as TSN [29] and TSM [19], and 3D-CNNs methods like C3D [25] and I3D [7] on the UCF-101 dataset. It outperforms the 2D-CNNs methods and C3D, with a difference in Top-1 accuracy of 12.3% ($\Delta_{\text{prec@1}} = 12.3\%$). However, it is slightly less effective than the I3D method, with a difference of 0.5% ($\nabla_{\text{prec@1}} = 0.5\%$). The experimental results demonstrate that our fusion-architecture-based model achieves excellent outcomes on datasets oriented towards spatial scenes, proving that the model possesses strong spatial modeling capabilities and can effectively perform classification tasks.

Table 1. Comparison experiment result on UCF-101 dataset.

Method		Top-1(%)	Backbone	Pre-train
2D CNNs	TSN [29]	80.1	Resnet-50	ImageNet
	TSM [19]	94.5	Resnet-50	ImageNet + Kinetics
3D CNNs	C3D [25]	82.3	3D VGG-11	Sports-1M
	I3D [7]	95.1	Inception-V1	ImageNet + Kinetics
Our Method		94.6	-	ImageNet

Table 2. Comparison experiment result on Something-Something V2 dataset.

Method	Backbone	Frames	TFLOPs	Pre-Train	Top-1(%)	Top-5(%)
TSN [29]	ResNet-50	8	N/A	Kinetics	32.3	59.6
TRN Multi-Scale [32]	BNInception	8	N/A	ImageNet	48.8	77.6
TRN Two-stream [32]	BNInception	8+8	N/A	ImageNet	55.5	83.1
GSN [24]	BNInception	8	N/A	ImageNet	56.1	82.2
TSM [19]	ResNet-50	8	N/A	ImageNet + Kinetics	59.1	85.6
TimeSformer [5]	-	8	0.59	ImageNet	59.5	-
Our Method	-	8	0.25	ImageNet	62.1	85.4

Comparison on Something-Something V2. In the second set of experiments, with the same number of input frames, we compare some CNNs based methods and some Transformer based method on the Something-Something V2 dataset. The results are displayed in Table.2. Our method achieves a Top-1 Accuracy of 62.1%, which is higher than the CNNs-based method TSN by 29.8%, and higher than the Transformer-based method TimeSformer by 2.6%. In terms of computational efficiency, our model operates at 0.25 TFLOPs, with lower computational complexity than these methods, enabling higher real-time performance. Based on these results, we analyze that our method can achieve superior outcomes with less computational cost, reflecting the model's advancement.

4.3   Ablation Study

To verify the effectiveness of the model's keyframe selection mechanism, we set up three groups of ablation experiments. The first one assesses the impact of the model's keyframe selection module and key patch selection module on computational accuracy and efficiency. The second one is to validate the effectiveness of the Small-Big Patch Transformer. We compare models with and without the Small-Big View mechanism in terms of accuracy changes on two datasets. The last one, we compare and analyze the impact of different architectures on model accuracy.

Keyframe and Key Patch Selection Modules. We verify the functionality of the model's keyframe selection module and key patch selection module. Four control models are set to compare the effectiveness of these modules. The first model eliminates the keyframe selection and key patch modules. For this model, the inputs to the frame-level Transformer model are the raw inputs obtained directly from the previous convolutional neural network steps, and the entire patch sequence is used to the video-level Transformer model. The second model utilized the keyframe selection module, which selects keyframes after primary semantic features are extracted by the convolutional neural network. This is followed by frame-level attention computation, and the resulting outputs are then directly fed into the video-level Transformer without selecting patches. The third experiment eliminates the keyframe selection module but includes the key patch selection module. The fourth experiment involved complete model, which employs both the keyframe selection module and the key patch selection module. The experimental results are shown in Table.3. For the models that utilize the keyframe selection module and the key patch selection module, the floating-point operations per second (GFLOPs) are 48. This computation efficiency is significantly higher than the other three models, and the experimental accuracy is comparable to the other models. It can be inferred that the use of the keyframe selection module and the key patch selection module make the model substantially reduce computational complexity while maintaining computational accuracy.

Table 3. Effectiveness of frames selection and patches selection operation.

Module	UCF-101			Something-Something V2			
	Top-1(%)	Top-5(%)	Loss	Top-1(%)	Top-5(%)	Loss	GFLOPs
None	94.102	99.567	0.18339	63.157	86.273	1.40586	102
Frame Selection	93.966	99.528	0.20293	61.345	84.769	1.48803	72
Patch Selection	94.724	99.702	0.15685	62.207	85.921	1.43817	74
Both	94.562	99.648	0.16794	62.108	85.352	1.44403	48

Small-Big View Mechanism. The second set of experiments validate the impact of the Small-Big View mechanism on the model. Two models are set up: one without the Small-Big View mechanism and another as our method's complete model. To maintain consistency in input and output across submodules in the comparative model, we add an average patch to the input of the

Small-Big Patch Transformer. Subsequently, we train and test both models on two video datasets. As shown in Table.4, our model achieves an accuracy of 94.562% on UCF-101, which is 2.76% higher than the comparative model without the Small-Big View mechanism. On the Something-Something V2 dataset, our method achieves a Top-1 accuracy of 62.108%, which is 0.828% higher than the comparative model. Therefore, it can be inferred that using the Small-Big View mechanism at the frame-level can enhance the model's recognition accuracy.

Table 4. Effectiveness of small-big patch on accuracy.

Patch Mechanism	UCF-101	Something-Something V2
Ordinary Patch	91.802	61.28
Small-Big Patch	94.562	62.108

Baseline Architecture. For the third group of experiments, as shown in Table.5, we compare the accuracy of three different architectures on the Something-Something V2 dataset. The first architecture is a pure 2D-CNNs, for which ResNet is used as the base backbone. The second architecture is Factorised encoder from the ViViT method. The third architecture is our method's fusion architecture model. To control variables, all models are given the same input size ($16 \times 3 \times 8 \times 224 \times 224$) and are trained over 50 epoch. According to the experimental results, our model achieves a Top-1 accuracy of 62.1% on the Something-Something V2 test set, which is significantly higher than the methods based on CNNs, and 0.9% higher than the action recognition methods based on Transformer. Therefore, It can be concluded that the fusion architecture method outperforms both the CNNs-based methods and the Transformer-based methods under these experimental conditions.

Table 5. Influence of different Baseline framework(Accuracy on the Something-Something V2 dataset).

Baseline	Top-1(%)	Top-5(%)
CNNs	32.3	59.6
Transformer	61.2	85.3
Our Method	62.1	85.4

5   Conclusion

In this paper, we propose an end-to-end motion recognition model based on a fused architecture of CNNs and Transformers. We analyze the characteristics of some mainstream algorithms based on these two model types, propose a series of improvements, and ultimately construct a keyframe selection module, a key patch selection module, and a Small-Big Patch Transformer module for intra-frame attention computation. These modules are integrated into a tiered Transformer architecture, enabling highly efficient video classification tasks.

This paper validates the effectiveness of the model. In comparative experiments, the model's advancements are confirmed by comparing it with other mainstream algorithms. Additionally, in ablation experiments, the proposed model can significantly reduce computational complexity while maintaining high accuracy.

Acknowledgements. This work was supported by the Natural Science Foundation (No. 2022-MS-112) of Liaoning Province, China.

References

1. Mao, K., Jin, P., Ping, Y., Tang, B.: Modeling multi-scale sub-group context for group activity recognition. Appl. Intell. **53**(1), 1149–1161 (2023)
2. Wang, B.-H., Jie, Yu., Wang, K., Bao, X.-Y., Mao, K.: Fall detection based on dual-channel feature integration. IEEE Access **8**, 103443–103453 (2020)
3. Arnab, A., Dehghani, M., Heigold, G., Sun, C., Lučić, M., Schmid, C.: VIVIT: a video vision transformer. In: Proceedings of the IEEE/CVF International Conference on Computer Vision, pp. 6836–6846 (2021)
4. Bai, S.Z., Yi, Y.: Study on the information sharing incentive and supervisory mechanism in supply chain. In: 2008 4th International Conference on Wireless Communications, Networking and Mobile Computing, pp. 1–4. IEEE (2008)
5. Bertasius, G., Wang, H., Torresani, L.: Is space-time attention all you need for video understanding? In: ICML, vol. 2, p. 4 (2021)
6. Bilen, H., Fernando, B., Gavves, E., Vedaldi, A.: Action recognition with dynamic image networks. IEEE Trans. Pattern Anal. Mach. Intell. **40**(12), 2799–2813 (2017)
7. Carreira, J., Zisserman, A.: Quo vadis, action recognition? A new model and the kinetics dataset. In: proceedings of the IEEE Conference on Computer Vision and Pattern Recognition, pp. 6299–6308 (2017)
8. Da costa, C., Mendes, C., Osaki, R.: Modelagem de um sistema supervisório para aquisição de dados de uma célula de manufatura1
9. Dosovitskiy, A., et al.: An image is worth 16 ×16 words: transformers for image recognition at scale. arXiv preprint arXiv:2010.11929 (2020)
10. Gabeur, V., Sun, C., Alahari, K., Schmid, C.: Multi-modal transformer for video retrieval. In: Vedaldi, A., Bischof, H., Brox, T., Frahm, J.-M. (eds.) ECCV 2020. LNCS, vol. 12349, pp. 214–229. Springer, Cham (2020). https://doi.org/10.1007/978-3-030-58548-8_13
11. Goyal, R., et al.: The "something something" video database for learning and evaluating visual common sense. In: Proceedings of the IEEE International Conference on Computer Vision, pp. 5842–5850 (2017)
12. Han, Y., Zhang, P., Zhuo, T., Huang, W., Zhang, Y.: Going deeper with two-stream convnets for action recognition in video surveillance. Pattern Recogn. Lett. **107**, 83–90 (2018)

13. Hwang, J., Kim, S., Son, J., Han, B.: Weakly supervised instance segmentation by deep community learning. In: Proceedings of the IEEE/CVF Winter Conference on Applications of Computer Vision, pp. 1020–1029 (2021)
14. Ji, S., Xu, W., Yang, M., Yu, K.: 3d convolutional neural networks for human action recognition. IEEE Trans. Pattern Anal. Mach. Intell. **35**(1), 221–231 (2012)
15. Karpathy, A., Toderici, G., Shetty, S., Leung, T., Sukthankar, R., Fei-Fei, L.: Large-scale video classification with convolutional neural networks. In: Proceedings of the IEEE Conference on Computer Vision and Pattern Recognition, pp. 1725–1732 (2014)
16. Laskin, M., Lee, K., Stooke, A., Pinto, L., Abbeel, P., Srinivas, A.: Reinforcement learning with augmented data. Adv. Neural. Inf. Process. Syst. **33**, 19884–19895 (2020)
17. Li, X., Wang, Y., Zhou, Z., Qiao, Y.: Smallbignet: integrating core and contextual views for video classification. In: Proceedings of the IEEE/CVF Conference on Computer Vision and Pattern Recognition, pp. 1092–1101 (2020)
18. Li, Y., Song, S., Li, Y., Liu, J.: Temporal bilinear networks for video action recognition. In: Proceedings of the AAAI Conference on Artificial Intelligence, vol. 33, pp. 8674–8681 (2019)
19. Lin, J., Gan, C., Han, S.: TSM: temporal shift module for efficient video understanding. In: Proceedings of the IEEE/CVF International Conference on Computer Vision, pp. 7083–7093 (2019)
20. Neto, A.D., Melo, J.D., Duarte, M.M., Bezerra, V.M.: Desenvolvimento de supervisórios para monitoração de processos simulados (2016)
21. Ng, J.Y.H., Davis, L.S.: Temporal difference networks for video action recognition. In: 2018 IEEE Winter Conference on Applications of Computer Vision (WACV), pp. 1587–1596. IEEE (2018)
22. Simonyan, K., Zisserman, A.: Two-stream convolutional networks for action recognition in videos. In: Advances in Neural Information Processing Systems vol. 27 (2014)
23. Soomro, K., Zamir, A.R., Shah, M.: A dataset of 101 human action classes from videos in the wild. Center Res. Comput. Vision **2**(11), 1–7 (2012)
24. Sudhakaran, S., Escalera, S., Lanz, O.: Gate-shift networks for video action recognition. In: Proceedings of the IEEE/CVF Conference on Computer Vision and Pattern Recognition, pp. 1102–1111 (2020)
25. Tran, D., Bourdev, L., Fergus, R., Torresani, L., Paluri, M.: Learning spatiotemporal features with 3d convolutional networks. In: Proceedings of the IEEE International Conference on Computer Vision, pp. 4489–4497 (2015)
26. Varol, G., Laptev, I., Schmid, C.: Long-term temporal convolutions for action recognition. IEEE Trans. Pattern Anal. Mach. Intell. **40**(6), 1510–1517 (2017)
27. Vaswani, A., et al.: Attention is all you need. In: Neural Information Processing Systems (2017). https://api.semanticscholar.org/CorpusID:13756489
28. Wang, L., Li, W., Li, W., Van Gool, L.: Appearance-and-relation networks for video classification. In: Proceedings of the IEEE Conference on Computer Vision and Pattern Recognition, pp. 1430–1439 (2018)
29. Wang, L., et al.: Temporal segment networks: towards good practices for deep action recognition. In: Leibe, B., Matas, J., Sebe, N., Welling, M. (eds.) ECCV 2016. LNCS, vol. 9912, pp. 20–36. Springer, Cham (2016). https://doi.org/10.1007/978-3-319-46484-8_2
30. Wang, X., Girshick, R., Gupta, A., He, K.: Non-local neural networks. In: Proceedings of the IEEE Conference on Computer Vision and Pattern Recognition, pp. 7794–7803 (2018)

31. Zhao, Y., Xiong, Y., Lin, D.: Recognize actions by disentangling components of dynamics. In: Proceedings of the IEEE Conference on Computer Vision and Pattern Recognition, pp. 6566–6575 (2018)
32. Zhou, B., Andonian, A., Oliva, A., Torralba, A.: Temporal relational reasoning in videos. In: Ferrari, V., Hebert, M., Sminchisescu, C., Weiss, Y. (eds.) ECCV 2018. LNCS, vol. 11205, pp. 831–846. Springer, Cham (2018). https://doi.org/10.1007/978-3-030-01246-5_49
33. Zoph, B., Vasudevan, V., Shlens, J., Le, Q.V.: Learning transferable architectures for scalable image recognition. In: Proceedings of the IEEE Conference on Computer Vision and Pattern Recognition, pp. 8697–8710 (2018)

Author Index

The manufacturer's authorised representative in the EU is Springer
Nature Customer Service Centre GmbH, Europaplatz 3, 69115 Heidelberg,
Germany. If you have any concerns regarding our products, please
contact ProductSafety@springernature.com

Printed and bound by CPI Group (UK) Ltd, Croydon, CR0 4YY

27/04/2026

02097586-0018